A382

995299

World'

The Addison-Wesley Series in Economics

Abel/Bernanke
Macroeconomics

Bade/Parkin
Foundations of Economics

Bierman/Fernandez
*Game Theory with
Economic Applications*

Binger/Hoffman
Microeconomics with Calculus

Boyer
*Principles of
Transportation Economics*

Branson
Macroeconomic Theory and Policy

Bruce
*Public Finance and the
American Economy*

Byrns/Stone
Economics

Carlton/Perloff
Modern Industrial Organization

Caves/Frankel/Jones
*World Trade and Payments:
An Introduction*

Chapman
*Environmental Economics:
Theory, Application, and Policy*

Cooter/Ulen
Law and Economics

Downs
An Economic Theory of Democracy

Ehrenberg/Smith
Modern Labor Economics

Ekelund/Ressler/Tollison
Economics

Fusfeld
The Age of the Economist

Gerber
International Economics

Ghiara
Learning Economics

Gordon
Macroeconomics

Gregory
Essentials of Economics

Gregory/Stuart
*Russian and Soviet Economic
Performance and Structure*

Hartwick/Olewiler
*The Economics of Natural
Resource Use*

Hoffman/Averett
*Women and the Economy:
Family, Work, and Pay*

Holt
*Markets, Games, and
Strategic Behavior*

Hubbard
*Money, the Financial System,
and the Economy*

Hughes/Cain
American Economic History

Husted/Melvin
International Economics

Jehle/Reny
Advanced Microeconomic Theory

Johnson-Lans
A Health Economics Primer

Klein
*Mathematical Methods
for Economics*

Krugman/Obstfeld
International Economics

Laidler
The Demand for Money

Leeds/von Allmen
The Economics of Sports

Leeds/von Allmen/Schiming
Economics

Lipsey/Courant/Ragan
Economics

Melvin
*International Money
and Finance*

Miller
Economics Today

Miller
*Understanding Modern
Economics*

Miller/Benjamin
The Economics of Macro Issues

Miller/Benjamin/North
The Economics of Public Issues

Mills/Hamilton
Urban Economics

Mishkin
*The Economics of Money,
Banking, and Financial Markets*

Mishkin
*The Economics of Money,
Banking, and Financial Markets,
Alternate Edition*

Murray
*Econometrics: A Modern
Introduction*

Parkin
Economics

Perloff
Microeconomics

Perman/Common/McGilvray/Ma
*Natural Resources and
Environmental Economics*

Phelps
Health Economics

**Riddell/Shackelford/Stamos/
Schneider**
*Economics: A Tool for Critically
Understanding Society*

Ritter/Silber/Udell
*Principles of Money, Banking,
and Financial Markets*

Rohlf
*Introduction to Economic
Reasoning*

Ruffin/Gregory
Principles of Economics

Sargent
*Rational Expectations
and Inflation*

Scherer
*Industry Structure, Strategy,
and Public Policy*

Stock/Watson
Introduction to Econometrics

Studenmund
Using Econometrics

Tietenberg
*Environmental and Natural
Resource Economics*

Tietenberg
*Environmental Economics
and Policy*

Todaro/Smith
Economic Development

Waldman
Microeconomics

Waldman/Jensen
*Industrial Organization:
Theory and Practice*

Weil
Economic Growth

Williamson
Macroeconomics

WORLD TRADE AND PAYMENTS

AN INTRODUCTION

TENTH EDITION

RICHARD E. CAVES
HARVARD UNIVERSITY

JEFFREY A. FRANKEL
HARVARD UNIVERSITY

RONALD W. JONES
UNIVERSITY OF ROCHESTER

PEARSON

Addison
Wesley

Boston San Francisco New York
London Toronto Sydney Tokyo Singapore Madrid
Mexico City Munich Paris Cape Town Hong Kong Montreal

Publisher: Greg Tobin
Editor in Chief: Denise Clinton
Assistant Editor: Julia Boyles
Managing Editor: Nancy Fenton
Senior Production Supervisor: Kathryn Dinovo
Senior Design Manager: Chuck Spaulding
Supplements Supervisor: Heather McNally
Senior Marketing Manager: Roxanne Hoch
Marketing Assistant: Kate MacLean
Senior Manufacturing Buyer: Carol Melville
Cover Designer: Leslie Haimes
Text Design, Production Coordination, Composition, and Illustrations: Thompson Steele, Inc.
Cover Photo: ©Allan Baxter

ISBN: 0-321-24855-4

3 4 5 6 7 8 9 10—EB—10 09 08

Contents

Preface   xv

CHAPTER **1** **Introduction**   **1**
1.1   The Subject of International Economics   2
1.2   Patterns of International Trade   5
1.3   The Organization of This Book   8

PART I   **COMPARATIVE ADVANTAGE AND THE BASIC MODEL OF INTERNATIONAL TRADE**   **11**

CHAPTER **2** **The Gains from Trade**   **13**
2.1   Background Behavior: Demand   14
2.2   Background Behavior: Supply   17
2.3   Gains from Trade and Free-Trade Equilibrium   20
2.4   Winners and Losers: Autarky to Free Trade   27
2.5   Summary   29
       CHAPTER PROBLEMS   30
       APPENDIX A: The Box Diagram   31
       APPENDIX B: Substitution and Income Effects   32
       APPENDIX C: The Offer Curve Diagram   34

CHAPTER **3** **Applications of the Basic Model**   **37**
3.1   Disturbances from Abroad and the Terms of Trade   38
3.2   Protecting the Import-Competing Commodity   40
3.3   Growth and International Trade   42
3.4   The Transfer Problem   43
3.5   Wider Interpretations of the Basic Trade Model   47
3.6   Trade and Market Structure   51
3.7   Summary   51
       CHAPTER PROBLEMS   52
       SUGGESTIONS FOR FURTHER READING   53
       APPENDIX: The Stability Issue   53

PART II   GLOBALIZATION: TRADE PATTERNS
AND INCOME DISTRIBUTION   57

CHAPTER 4   Technology and International
Income Distribution: The Ricardian Model   59

4.1   The Ricardian Setting   60
4.2   Free-Trade Equilibrium   61
4.3   International Wage Comparisons and Productivities   64
4.4   A Many-Commodity and Many-Country World   68
4.5   Winners and Losers from Productivity Shocks   69
4.6   Nontraded Commodities   72
4.7   Summary   75
      CHAPTER PROBLEMS   76
      SUGGESTIONS FOR FURTHER READING   77
      APPENDIX: Transitional Unemployment   77

CHAPTER 5   Factor Endowments and
Trade I: The Specific Factors Model   79

5.1   Diminishing Returns and Factor Hires   79
5.2   Outputs and Income Distribution in the Closed Economy   80
5.3   Outputs and Income Distribution with Free Trade   82
5.4   Growth in Factor Endowments   84
5.5   Consequences for Political Economy   85
5.6   The Pattern of Trade   86
5.7   Alternative Interpretations: Specific Capital or Specific Labor   87
5.8   Dutch Disease   88
5.9   Summary   90
      CHAPTER PROBLEMS   92
      SUGGESTIONS FOR FURTHER READING   93
      APPENDIX: The Transformation Schedule   93

CHAPTER 6   Factor Endowments and
Trade II: The Heckscher-Ohlin Model   95

6.1   If Technology Is Rigid   96
6.2   Flexible Technology   99
6.3   Possible Trade Patterns and the Distribution of Income   102

6.4 International Trade with Many Commodities   106

6.5 How Concentrated Is Production?   108

6.6 Changing Comparative Advantage with Economic Growth   109

6.7 Heckscher-Ohlin Theory and Empirical Evidence   110

6.8 Summary   114

CHAPTER PROBLEMS   116

SUGGESTIONS FOR FURTHER READING   117

APPENDIX: The Production Box   118

CHAPTER 7 **Imperfect Competition, Increasing Returns, and Product Variety   121**

7.1 The Prevalence of Intra-Industry Trade   122

7.2 Consumer Behavior and the Demand for Product Variety   123

7.3 Increasing Returns in Production   125

7.4 Summary   131

CHAPTER PROBLEMS   132

SUGGESTIONS FOR FURTHER READING   132

CHAPTER 8 **Resource Trade, Outsourcing, and Product Fragmentation   133**

8.1 Given Resources and Footloose Production Processes   134

8.2 Footloose Inputs: The Joint Role of Comparative and Absolute Advantage   137

8.3 Outsourcing and the International Fragmentation of Production   141

8.4 Outsourcing and Advanced Country Wage Rates   144

8.5 Summary   147

CHAPTER PROBLEMS   148

SUGGESTIONS FOR FURTHER READING   148

CHAPTER 9 **International Factor Movements: Labor and Capital   151**

9.1 Factor Movements, Efficiency, and Welfare   151

9.2 International Capital Movements: Selected Issues   154

9.3 Multinationals and Foreign Direct Investment   158

9.4 Summary   164

CHAPTER PROBLEMS   165

SUGGESTIONS FOR FURTHER READING   166

PART III   THE THEORY AND PRACTICE OF COMMERCIAL POLICY   167

CHAPTER 10   Protection and the National Welfare   169

10.1   Protection by a Small Country   170
10.2   Protection by a Large Country   177
10.3   Taxing Trade: Domestic Welfare   178
10.4   Taxing Trade: World Welfare   179
10.5   Summary   181
CHAPTER PROBLEMS   181
SUGGESTIONS FOR FURTHER READING   182
APPENDIX: Tariffs and the Offer Curve   182

CHAPTER 11   The Political Economy of Protection   187

11.1   Protection as a Device for Raising Revenue   187
11.2   Commercial Policy as a Second-Best Device   189
11.3   Protection and Rent-Seeking Activities   192
11.4   Growth, Protection, and Welfare   197
11.5   Protection and Unemployment   200
11.6   Summary   200
CHAPTER PROBLEMS   201
SUGGESTIONS FOR FURTHER READING   201

CHAPTER 12   Trade Policy and Imperfect Competition   203

12.1   Monopoly and the Gains from Trade   203
12.2   Cartels and the Interests of Producing and Consuming Countries   207
12.3   Monopoly and Policies of Exporting and Importing Countries   209
12.4   Intellectual Property Rights   218
12.5   Summary   220
CHAPTER PROBLEMS   221
SUGGESTIONS FOR FURTHER READING   222
APPENDIX: International Duopoly and National Strategy   223

CHAPTER 13   Trade Controls in Practice   227

13.1   Tariffs: Levels and Trends   227
13.2   Multilateral Tariff Reduction   229
13.3   Devices for Special Protection   233

13.4   Special Protection in Action   236

13.5   Prospects for Special Protection   241

13.6   Summary   242

CHAPTER PROBLEMS   243

SUGGESTIONS FOR FURTHER READING   244

CHAPTER **14   Preferential Arrangements
and Regional Issues in Trade Policy   245**

14.1   Regional Preferences and Regional Trade   245

14.2   Welfare Effects of Trade Preferences   247

14.3   Preferential Arrangements in Practice   251

14.4   Trade Problems of the Economies in Transition   257

14.5   Trade and Growth: China and the Asian NICs   260

14.6   Preferential Arrangements: New Policy Issues   264

14.7   Summary   267

CHAPTER PROBLEMS   269

SUGGESTIONS FOR FURTHER READING   269

PART IV   **MONEY, INCOME, AND THE BALANCE OF PAYMENTS   271**

CHAPTER **15   The Balance of Payments Accounts   273**

15.1   Breakdown of the Accounts   275

15.2   How Individual Transactions Are Recorded   278

15.3   Double-Entry Bookkeeping   280

15.4   The Balances   282

15.5   Statistical Errors in the Payments Accounts   286

15.6   Summary   288

CHAPTER PROBLEMS   288

CHAPTER **16   The Foreign Exchange Market and Trade Elasticities   291**

16.1   The Flow of Supply and Demand for Foreign Exchange   291

16.2   Empirical Effects of Devaluation on the Trade Balance   297

16.3   Summary   300

CHAPTER PROBLEMS   301

SUGGESTIONS FOR FURTHER READING   303

APPENDIX: Stability of the Foreign Exchange Market   303

CHAPTER 17   National Income and the Trade Balance   307

17.1   The Small-Country Keynesian Model   307

17.2   The National Saving-Investment Identity   309

17.3   Multipliers   310

17.4   The Transfer Problem   314

17.5   For a Large Country: The Two-Country Keynesian Model   316

17.6   Summary   321

CHAPTER PROBLEMS   322

SUGGESTIONS FOR FURTHER READING   324

APPENDIX: The Two-Country Model in Graphical Form   324

CHAPTER 18   Spending and the Exchange Rate in the Keynesian Model   327

18.1   Transmission of Disturbances   327

18.2   Expenditure-Switching and Expenditure-Reducing Policies   330

18.3   Monetary Factors   337

18.4   Summary   343

CHAPTER PROBLEMS   344

SUGGESTIONS FOR FURTHER READING   346

APPENDIX A: The Laursen-Metzler-Harberger Effect   346

APPENDIX B: The Assignment Problem   350

CHAPTER 19   The Money Supply, the Price Level, and the Balance of Payments   353

19.1   The Nonsterilization Assumption   353

19.2   The Purchasing Power Parity Assumption   358

19.3   Purchasing Power Parity in a Hyperinflation   369

19.4   PPP in the Model of the Balance of Payments   372

19.5   Summary   374

CHAPTER PROBLEMS   375

SUGGESTIONS FOR FURTHER READING   377

APPENDIX A: The Gold Standard   378

APPENDIX B: Reserve Flows After Spending Increase and Devaluation   382

APPENDIX C: The Determination of the Balance of Payments in the Monetarist Model   384

CHAPTER **20** **Developing Countries and Other Small Open Economies with Nontraded Goods**   **391**

20.1   Nontraded Goods   392

20.2   Expenditure and the Relative Price of Nontraded Goods   395

20.3   The Monetary Approach with Nontraded Goods   401

20.4   Summary   407

CHAPTER PROBLEMS   407

SUGGESTIONS FOR FURTHER READING   408

PART V **INTERNATIONAL FINANCIAL MARKETS AND THEIR MACROECONOMIC IMPLICATIONS**   **409**

CHAPTER **21** **The Globalization of Financial Markets**   **411**

21.1   The Postwar Financial System (1944–1973)   412

21.2   The Foreign Exchange Market   414

21.3   Liberalization   419

21.4   Innovation   426

21.5   Advantages of Financial Integration   435

21.6   Summary   439

CHAPTER PROBLEMS   439

SUGGESTIONS FOR FURTHER READING   440

APPENDIX: The Effect of a Budget Deficit
            Under Intertemporal Optimization   441

CHAPTER **22** **The Mundell-Fleming Model with Partial International Capital Mobility**   **445**

22.1   The Model   447

22.2   Fiscal Policy and the Degree of
         Capital Mobility Under Fixed Rates   450

22.3   Monetary Policy and the Degree of
         Capital Mobility Under Fixed Rates   452

22.4   When Money Flows Are Not Sterilized   454

22.5   Other Automatic Mechanisms of Adjustment   456

22.6   The Pursuit of Internal and External Balance   457

22.7   Summary   460

CHAPTER PROBLEMS   461

SUGGESTIONS FOR FURTHER READING   461

APPENDIX: Zones of Internal and External Balance   461

CHAPTER 23   **Fiscal and Monetary Policy Under Modern Financial Market Conditions   467**

23.1   Fiscal Policy Under Floating:
An Effect Mitigated by Capital Mobility   468

23.2   Monetary Policy Under Floating:
An Effect Enhanced by Capital Mobility   474

23.3   Policy Under Perfect Capital Mobility   477

23.4   Summary   486

CHAPTER PROBLEMS   486

SUGGESTIONS FOR FURTHER READING   487

CHAPTER 24   **Crises in Emerging Markets   489**

24.1   Inflows to Emerging Markets   489

24.2   Managing Outflows   498

24.3   Speculative Attacks   499

24.4   Contagion   504

24.5   IMF Country Programs   506

24.6   Contractionary Effects of Devaluation   510

24.7   Capital Controls   515

24.8   Reform of International Financial Architecture   518

24.9   Summary   520

CHAPTER PROBLEMS   521

SUGGESTIONS FOR FURTHER READING   522

CHAPTER 25   **Interdependence and Policy Coordination   525**

25.1   International Transmission of Disturbances
Under Floating Exchange Rates   525

25.2   Econometric Models of the Interdependent World Economy   530

25.3   International Macroeconomic Policy Coordination   535

25.4   Summary   540

CHAPTER PROBLEMS   540

SUGGESTIONS FOR FURTHER READING   541

CHAPTER **26**   **Supply and Inflation**   **543**

26.1   The Aggregate Supply Relationship   543

26.2   Supply Relationship with Indexed Wages   551

26.3   Inflation   554

26.4   Alternative Anchors for a Country's Money   556

26.5   The Choice of Exchange Rate Regime   559

26.6   Summary   567

CHAPTER PROBLEMS   568

SUGGESTIONS FOR FURTHER READING   568

PART **VI**   **THE DETERMINATION OF EXCHANGE RATES IN INTERNATIONAL ASSET MARKETS**   **571**

CHAPTER **27**   **Expectations, Money, and the Determination of the Exchange Rate**   **573**

27.1   Interest Rate Parity Conditions   573

27.2   The Monetary Model of Exchange Rates with Flexible Prices   575

27.3   Two Examples of the Importance of Expectations   585

27.4   Overshooting and the Real Exchange Rate   588

27.5   Two More Examples of the Importance of Expectations   599

27.6   Summary   603

CHAPTER PROBLEMS   604

SUGGESTIONS FOR FURTHER READING   605

CHAPTER **28**   **Exchange Rate Forecasting and Risk**   **607**

28.1   Forecasting the Spot Exchange Rate   607

28.2   The Role of Exchange Risk   612

28.3   Portfolio Balance Effects on the Exchange Rate   616

28.4   Summary   620

CHAPTER PROBLEMS   621

SUGGESTIONS FOR FURTHER READING   622

PART **VII**   **SUPPLEMENTS FOR SELECTED CHAPTERS**   **S-1**

SUPPLEMENT TO CHAPTER 2: The Equations of Exchange Equilibrium   S-3

SUPPLEMENT TO CHAPTER 3: Stability and Comparative Statics in the Basic Trade Model   S-10

SUPPLEMENT TO CHAPTER 5: The Specific-Factors Model of Production   S-17

SUPPLEMENT TO CHAPTER 6: The Two-Sector Heckscher-Ohlin Model   S-22

SUPPLEMENT TO CHAPTER 10: Real Incomes, Prices, and the Tariff   S-27

SUPPLEMENT TO CHAPTER 11: Tariffs, Growth, and Welfare   S-33

SUPPLEMENT TO CHAPTER 12: Imperfect Competition,
Trade Restrictions, and Welfare   S-39

SUPPLEMENT TO CHAPTER 16: Import and Export Elasticities   S-43

SUPPLEMENT TO CHAPTER 19: The Monetarist Two-Country Model
of the Balance of Payments   S-44

SUPPLEMENT TO CHAPTER 24: Debt Dynamics   S-47

SUPPLEMENT TO CHAPTER 25: The Locomotive Theory   S-48

SUPPLEMENT TO CHAPTER 26: Real Wage Indexation   S-50

SUPPLEMENT TO CHAPTER 27: The Monetary Model of the Exchange Rate   S-51

SUPPLEMENT TO CHAPTER 28: The Optimally Diversified Portfolio   S-55

Index   I-1

Preface

The Tenth Edition of *World Trade and Payments* arrives at a time when major new issues confront the international economy. The economy of China has blossomed swiftly, its growth heavily dependent on large volumes of exports of simple manufactures. Competing firms in North America and Western Europe find their businesses unprofitable and reduce their outputs. But they do not go quietly, instead beseeching their governments to restrict imports from China. The United States frets over its huge excess of imports over exports. The trade deficit can persist only because the rest of the world is willing to hold huge volumes of U.S. debt. Yet the U.S. creditors become less complaisant as the dollars pile up. Across the Atlantic the European Union continues to reap the benefits of reduced trade barriers among its members. It is in the process of absorbing a large bloc of Eastern European nations. Their trade is being redirected from the former Soviet Union's bloc and toward the industrial nations of Western Europe.

Although it is easy to dramatize these fresh events, international economists know that they all have their historical antecedents. China enters onto a path of development previously traveled by Japan, then by the "Asian tigers": Taiwan, Korea, Hong Kong, and Singapore. The U.S. trade imbalance and the dollar glut also have their historical parallels—once upon a time, there was a dollar shortage. Fortunately, economic analysis shows clearly how to conceptualize these recurring issues. For example, the U.S. trade deficit bears a fundamental relationship to saving and investment decisions made by both American households (who save little) and governments (the U.S. government spends much more than its revenue—it dissaves). Other major issues of policy and behavior in the international economy also enjoy rigorous links to important components of theoretical international economics.

We cannot claim clairvoyance about how the current major issues of international economics will be resolved over time. We do believe that international economics provides the intellectual structure that the student needs to interpret the evolving events and issues that make up the current news about the international economy. We have tried to present a clear and rigorous framework for the student, along with applications to contemporary issues such as those just listed (plus the odd antique issue, or perspective).

International economics shares with other branches of economics a basic dedication to the objective of maximum economic welfare. That goal can be made conceptually rigorous, but it does prod us to recognize some complicating factors. Whose welfare? The United States, or the world? Are they in conflict and, if so, when? What about the distribution of income among individuals? Many international economic disturbances and policy changes that raise national (aggregate) welfare leave some folk worse off. In fact the real wages of unskilled labor have been declining, while suppliers of skilled labor and capital have gained. This pattern appears in the United States but also in other nations. Does this redistribution result from increased exports of simple manufactures from developing countries, produced by their abundant low-skill labor? Does it result from immigration to the industrial countries of workers with low skill levels? Or does it stem from causes independent of international trade? A prime suspect is changes in technology and demand that favor sophisticated goods (and services), shifting the demand for labor toward those workers with more education and higher skill levels. This issue of income distribution arises at several points in the book, because of the several explanations offered for it.

What's New in This Edition

Through this and previous editions of *World Trade and Payments* we have sought to combine clear exposition of the proven and long-lasting basic theories and analytical constructs of international trade and finance with applications that illustrate their uses. We have incorporated new theoretical developments as they have come on stream, adjusting the emphasis given to those—new or old—that seem particularly helpful to the student seeking to understand the currently high-profile issues. At the same time we have kept a place for analyses focused on issues currently shaded from popular attention, but likely to blossom in future public discourse.

   This general objective guides the changes that were made in this tenth edition. Parts I and II, dealing with the theory of international trade, have undergone a good deal of reorganization. Part I has been streamlined from three to two chapters, to use the "basic model" of trade to illustrate the gains from taking part in international trade, and some of the consequences of taking part in a globalized trading world when shocks occur within your own country or abroad. Part II turns to the important competitive trade models: Ricardo, Specific Factors, and Heckscher-Ohlin, followed by a new chapter integrating material on more recent models that emphasize increasing returns and imperfect competition. Emphasis is on both explaining trade patterns and showing how price and technology changes affect the distribution of real incomes among and within countries. A new chapter (Chapter 8) emphasizes the causes and consequences of "outsourcing" and fragmentation of production networks because of returns to scale and high technological improvements in service activities. Chapter 9 now deals with the effects of international factor movements, particularly the relatively empirical issues concerning international movements of capital.

   In Part III, dealing with issues of international trade policy, Chapters 12 through 14 have been extensively rewritten to reflect the turnover of public issues. In Chapter 12 we include a case study of international competition in commercial aircraft—Boeing versus Airbus. Their rivalry, not new, has recently rekindled the policy issues that they raise. Changes in Chapter 13 reflect governments' shifting away from traditional tariffs to controlling trade through anti-dumping regulations. Anti-dumping raises interesting issues of strategic interactions between international oligopolists. Chapter 14 on regional preferences contains much new material on the expansion of the European Union and the effects of the North American Free Trade Area. It also includes a study of trade's role in China's rapid development.

An important addition in the chapters on macroeconomics and financial markets is a section on the question whether China should abandon the effective pegging of its currency to the U.S. dollar. A new section deals with debt dynamics—the conditions under which a growing international debt (such as that of the United States) is sustainable over time. The innovative Chapter 24 on crises in emerging markets is significantly updated.

To accompany the text, an *Online Instructor's Manual* is available, providing instructors with chapter summaries, key concepts, suggested answers to end-of-chapter problems, and a variety of multiple-choice questions. PowerPoint® presentations include all figures and tables from the text for easy use in the classroom. On the Companion Website, students can extend their practice with the *Online Study Guide,* which includes chapter summaries, along with practice questions and quantitative problems, with suggested answers for all. Visit **www.aw-bc.com/caves** for further details. We owe a great deal of thanks to Bill Seyfried at Winthrop University for his phenomenal work on these supplements.

Adapting the Course

World Trade and Payments is adaptable to various tracking styles. Some chapters are followed by one or more appendixes that explain specialized points or analytical constructions that some instructors might favor but others prefer to avoid. Omitting any appendix will not lessen comprehension of the chapter. For instructors wanting a more advanced approach we have retained, at the back of the text, the mathematical supplements present in previous editions.

The book covers a conventional full line of topics and with some additional material can serve as the basis for a full-year course at the undergraduate level or for separate semester (quarter) courses on the real and financial aspects of international trade. We have paid special attention, however, to the needs of one-semester courses. The chapters in Part I and Chapters 16, 17, 23, and part of 19 provide the nucleus of a one-semester course that covers both the core of the real theory (with applications) and elements of open-economy macroeconomics and balance-of-payments adjustment. Many of the chapters outside this core are at least somewhat independent of one another so that instructors can round out the course with selections from them (examples are Chapters 9 and 14). A course in international macroeconomics might add Chapters 15, 19 (especially Section 19.2), 22, 23, 25, 26, and 27. It might then also employ Chapters 20 and 24 if the orientation is toward developing countries, or Chapters 21 and 28 if the orientation is toward finance.

Acknowledgments

As authors of a textbook in its Tenth Edition, we have acquired debts to colleagues, students, and various helpers that stretch the bounds of memory, let alone explicit acknowledgment. We confine ourselves to recognizing those who helped with the tenth edition. Thanks go to Stephen Golub, Swarthmore College; Gökçe Soydemir, University of Texas, Pan American; Kevin Zhang, Illinois State University; Frank Weiss, Johns Hopkins University; Rodney Swanson, University of California, Los Angeles; Carsten Kowalczyk, Tufts University; Maria Muniagurria, University of Wisconsin, Madison; Pershing J. Hill, University of Alaska, Anchorage; and Theo Eicher, University of Washington.

RICHARD E. CAVES
JEFFREY A. FRANKEL
RONALD W. JONES

CHAPTER 1

Introduction

U nique among the concerns of economics, international trade has always carried a note of romance—the lure of the exotic, the hint of danger. Traders' dreams of bartering for the riches of the Orient spurred the European voyages of discovery that began in the fifteenth century. Today, supertankers move hundreds of thousands of tons of crude oil at a time from producing to consuming lands at strikingly low cost—except when the breakup of a tanker at sea pollutes hundreds of miles of shoreline.

The romance of international commerce surges through its contact with public policy. British restrictions on colonial trade helped fuel the American Revolution. After World War II the nations of Western Europe, sickened by the recurrent wars spawned by modern nationalism, sought permanent reconciliation and peace through a trade treaty that removed barriers to commerce through the European Union.

This book promotes an understanding of the economic causes and consequences of international exchange. Any branch of economics rests on theoretical concepts and models. The scholar's job is to bring systematic observation and explanation to the chaotic diversity of the world. The Census Bureau records data on about 14,000 classifications of commodities entering into the foreign trade of the United States—4,000 for exports and 10,000 for imports. Are 14,000 explanations for these trade flows truly necessary? Could one explanation possibly cover every bundle of merchandise? Our quest is for the simplest model, or the smallest family of models, capable of answering the important questions about trade patterns and how public policy should deal with them.

The foreign commerce of nations, one of the oldest branches of economics, has drawn the attention of some of history's greatest economists. Indeed, many of the ideas in this book can boast of famous ancestors. Modern economics owes much of its understanding of money in international trade to the philosopher David Hume (Chapter 19). One principal model of international trade and production derives from David Ricardo (Chapter 4), an English stockbroker with a powerful, analytical mind. Still, much of present-day international economics is quite new. A fruitful model relating trade to factors of production comes from two twentieth-century Swedish economists, Eli F. Heckscher and Bertil Ohlin (Chapter 6). As well, our understanding of how trade relates to employment, and how policy can deal properly with both, is in part a late fallout of the Keynesian Revolution of the late 1930s (Chapter 17).

1.1   The Subject of International Economics

International economics is somewhat curiously related to the other conventional branches of economics. Public finance, money and banking, and labor economics select a neatly distinguished group of transactors or markets in the economy for special study. "But," you may ask, "doesn't international economics similarly deal with international markets?" It does, and these markets are capable of exact *legal* definition. Sovereign states are ubiquitous; therefore, we always can tell whether the two parties to a transaction are citizens of different countries.

Still, are international transactions economically unique and readily separated from transactions within nations? Do Kansas wheat farmers know or care whether the bushels of wheat they sell will be exported? When you buy a handkerchief, do you inspect it closely for a label indicating manufacture abroad? International transactions are indeed interrelated with domestic markets. Ultimately our explanation of international trade must be part of an explanation of each national market.

This intertwining of international and national markets runs throughout international economics. If India decides to train more physicians, the supply of physicians in Britain is apt to increase (through immigration). If the United States raises government spending to increase employment, employment in Canada is almost sure to increase. Clearly then, international economics can easily (and usefully) be viewed as "international aspects of supply and demand," "international aspects of money and finance," or "international aspects of taxation." Nonetheless, international trade and payments must be treated—for many good reasons—as a separate field of study. Following are two of the most important reasons for such treatment.

The Power of International Economic Theory

The most useful models for explaining international trade are those that are simple, strong, and general. They not only explain international trade patterns, they also tell much about patterns of production, income distribution, and so on, within countries.

What, indeed, is the simplest possible way to model the international economy? The central questions about international trade deal solely with *exchange* between traders in two national markets. This book argues that the sparest and clearest explanation of trade between nations, and of the gains nations derive from trade, requires only a description of the exchange of fixed endowments of goods. Such simplification, by concentrating first on exchange, stems from putting aside the details of how goods are produced. We then can explain, for example, what happened in 1973 when the exporting nations quadrupled the price of oil. Having set the essentials, the basic model of trade can be expanded to explore details of how bundles of goods are produced.

Why should economists employ separate models to explain international trade and domestic trade? The traditional answer holds that in the long run the factors of production—labor and capital—move freely within the national economy but are immobile between countries. Presumably labor and capital move freely between New York and California whenever workers or lenders feel that such a shift will improve their real incomes. Does California produce movies because of its abundance of movie stars? Did the movie stars arrive in response to the casting calls of the moviemakers? Or did moviemakers and stars simply converge because of California's abundant sunshine—a matter of economic geography? When labor and capital are largely immobile between nations, however, they become a "given" that can explain trade patterns—along with the gifts of nature.

Once the theory of international trade and production is constructed with capital and labor assumed immobile internationally, the immobility assumption can be peeled away to allow several perspectives on factor mobility. One approach tightens the mobility constraint by assuming that each sector employs a specialized factor of production not useful in other industries (shoemakers can only make shoes). Another loosens it by allowing factors to be mobile internationally.

Models of the macroeconomy enjoy the same flexibility to deal with capital flows along with international trade flows. Fifty years ago, macroeconomists mostly used (and taught) models of national income and employment that ignored international transactions. Events in the international economy then forced economists to change their tactics. For example, international capital flows play an important macroeconomic role by representing a difference between domestic saving and investment. Any major disturbance to domestic saving or investment decisions—for instance, when the government decides to run a large budget deficit—triggers a large change in international capital flows and other important macroeconomic variables.

The Importance of Nationhood for Policy

The other factor that distinguishes international economics is rooted in policy-making, especially in the context of policies toward international trade and payments. Trade occurs between sovereign nations, between us and them. Two governments, with potentially clashing objectives, can choose policies affecting the flow of trade between them so as to harm each other's interests. More profoundly, the fear and suspicion of outsiders felt by even the most saintly mortal repeatedly prompts debate over whether or not the nation benefits from trading with foreigners. No one doubts that Vermont gains from trading with New Hampshire, or Minneapolis with St. Paul. The proposition that the United States and France both gain from trading with each other might not, however, win a majority vote in either country. Rich countries fear they will suffer by importing the products of low-wage foreign labor; poor countries dread imports created by high-level foreign technology.

This universal xenophobia contributes to the often bitter and protracted nature of countries' international economic policy disputes. For example, a major issue in a 1988 Canadian election was approval of a free-trade agreement to end restrictions on trade flows between the United States and Canada. There was widespread consensus among economists suggesting that the arrangement would add at least several percentage points to Canada's national income. However, many Canadians considered the arrangement an invasion of their sovereignty and nationhood. This debate was dramatic but by no means unusual. Such disputes over international policy are often bitter, not only because some parties gain and some lose but also because dollars-and-cents issues become emotionally charged.

The last few years have seen an extraordinary disjoint between economic welfare and public attitudes over *globalization*. This ill-defined term generally refers to an increase in the share of the world's transactions that comprise exchanges between nations. That increase in turn flows from many supportive changes in public policy: reduced restrictions on international trade and investment, especially among the developing countries; the transformation to market economies of crumbling centrally planned regimes in Eastern Europe and China; and widespread privatization and deregulation in many domestic markets that tended to increase the economic efficiency of both domestic and international transactions. Economists regard these changes as a great boon to economic welfare. However, several high-profile meetings on international economic policy have been vigorously disrupted by protesters who see globalization as impoverishing unskilled labor, fostering sweatshop conditions in developing countries, and degrading the global environment. These views of burgeoning international commerce as boon and bane could hardly be farther apart. In the following chapters we flag the analyses that shed light on these deep misunderstandings.

How, then, does international economics pick its way through this minefield of nationalistic attitudes and controversies? A critical role for the theory of international trade is to identify the gains from trade and their indications for economic policy. Hence the spare, clear explanation of trade through a simple model of exchange is particularly useful for determining the gains from trade.

After the gains are determined, the next focus is the division of gains among the trading nations. International economics takes a flexible approach to this question. Following the tradition of general economics, international economics often concentrates on maximizing the welfare—the real income—of a single country's citizens. However, economic analysis also identifies policies that maximize global welfare, which in many situations can differ from policies serving a particular nation's interest. Certain policies that raise the welfare of one trading nation lower the global welfare and perforce the welfare levels of other trading nations. Identifying the clashes and harmonies between national and world welfare is an important task of this book. In addition, the welfare of groups of countries (such as the European Union) and of groups of income recipients within a country must be considered. Changes in the international economy or in trade policies almost always change the distribution as well as the level of a country's income. Only by understanding the relation between trade and income distribution can we discover why American labor has opposed foreign investment by U.S. companies or why the South once opposed, but now favors, high tariffs.

Issues of international conflict and harmony also arise over macroeconomic policies and their implications. For several years both the United States and China have followed economic policies that foster rapidly growing exports from China to the United States (and other countries) and a large excess of imports over exports for the United States. Chinese policy contributed to this outcome by keeping its currency tied to the U.S. dollar at a low rate (making Chinese goods cheap to Americans). U.S. policy contributed by running a very large excess of federal government spending over tax revenue, a government deficit that (we see later) almost necessarily is matched by a large excess of imports over exports of goods and services. These merchandise imports furnished stiffened competition for many American manufacturers, who then clamored for restrictions on imports from China. The countries' governments fell to blaming each other for a situation that was to a large extent their own doing. In 2005 China began small steps to adjust its exchange rate, but the U.S. government refused to stanch its government deficit.

In short, international economics seeks to cast light through the dark waters of contention over economic policy by (1) showing how international exchange and improvements in economic policies can result in gains; (2) identifying the bases for conflict over international economic policy, both within nations (between interest groups) and among them; and (3) pointing to ways in which conflicting groups or nations can resolve their differences for mutual benefit.

1.2 Patterns of International Trade

We all pick up some casual knowledge of patterns of international trade: The United States exports a lot of commercial aircraft, Japan a lot of automobiles, and Saudi Arabia a lot of petroleum. The following data aim to provide an impression of important patterns in international commerce and introduce a few puzzles to be dealt with in this book.

Although politicians fret that there may be too much international trade, since World War II underlying economic forces have been steadily nudging upward the proportion of market economies' transactions that involve international trade in goods and services. Between 1960 and 1995 real world output grew by 3.8 percent annually while real world trade grew by 6.1 percent, more than half again as fast. Among the many forces behind the growing importance of international transactions are the spectacular reductions that have occurred in the real costs of international shipping and international travel. Between 1920 and 1990 average ocean freight and port charges for U.S. import and export cargo fell almost 70 percent. Between 1930 and 1990 average air-transport fares per passenger mile fell by 84 percent, and the cost of a three-minute telephone call between New York and London plummeted 98.6 percent.[1]

Table 1.1 shows the pattern of trade of the United States, described in two ways. The first and third columns indicate how the value of total exports and imports is divided among various industries. For agricultural and forest products, food, chemicals, computers and electronic products, and several others, the share of exports exceeds that of imports, and the United States has in some sense an advantage against foreign competitors. It markedly lacks that advantage in minerals and petroleum (and petroleum and coal products), apparel, and leather. In sophisticated or so-called high-technology products, such as machinery and transportation equipment, we are heavy importers as well as heavy exporters: An explanation is forthcoming about why countries both export and import similar goods.

The second and fourth columns of Table 1.1 show the share of each sector's domestic production that is exported and the share of imports in domestic use (which

---

[1]U.S. Council of Economic Advisors, *Economic Report of the President, 1997,* p. 243.

TABLE 1.1

U.S. Merchandise Trade by Industry, 2001, Shares of Total Trade and Production or Use (percentages)

	Exports		Imports	
Industry	Share of Total Exports	Share of Production	Share of Total Imports	Share of Use
Agriculture and forest products	4.7	13.9	2.2	11.4
Minerals, petroleum	0.9	5.1	7.1	43.0
Food products	4.2	5.9	1.8	4.4
Beverages and tobacco products	0.7	3.7	0.8	7.1
Textiles and fabrics	1.1	15.5	0.6	14.1
Textile mill products	0.3	6.2	0.7	20.2
Apparel and accessories	1.0	11.8	5.8	56.5
Leather and allied products	0.4	25.9	2.0	77.0
Wood products	0.6	4.5	1.4	15.2
Paper products	2.2	9.0	1.7	11.4
Printing, publishing	0.8	4.8	0.4	4.1
Petroleum and coal products	1.3	3.7	3.3	14.3
Chemicals	12.2	17.5	7.5	18.2
Plastics and rubber products	2.5	9.2	1.6	9.8
Nonmetallic mineral products	1.2	7.8	1.3	13.4
Primary metal products	2.9	13.1	3.4	23.2
Fabricated metal products	3.1	7.7	2.6	10.8
Machinery, nonelectrical	12.1	28.7	6.7	27.5
Computers, electronic products	21.2	31.3	19.2	41.0
Electrical equipment	3.6	15.4	3.6	29.9
Transportation equipment	19.4	20.4	19.7	30.7
Furniture, fixtures	0.4	3.4	1.4	18.9
Miscellaneous manufactures	3.3	17.9	5.3	37.2

Source: Statistical Abstract of the United States, 2004–2005, Tables 799, 987, 1302.

equals production minus exports plus imports). The trade flow holds at least a 5 percent share in most cases. Although we depend heavily on imports for some consumption goods (apparel, leather), the machinery sectors are the ones with consistently heavy involvement in trade flows.

A central indicator of globalization is the rising ratio of countries' merchandise trade (average of goods exports and imports) to gross domestic product (GDP) or to domestic value-added in the goods sector. Eight of the eleven countries listed in Table 1.2 showed substantial rises in the former; all showed large increases in the latter. Why the difference? As incomes grow, people tend to spend proportionally more of their incomes on services and less on goods. Merchandise trade hence rises more relative to merchandise production than to total production, including services. Globalization has revealed itself in times past—ratios of trade to production were high between 1890 and 1913—but the recent trend has been long and strong. Why has it occurred? Lower transport costs and government restrictions such as tariffs are obvious reasons. Less obvious but important is increased vertical specialization: Finished goods available for export are often made of components themselves imported from abroad. This specialization increases merchandise trade without any clear effect on value-added.

TABLE 1.2

Merchandise Trade Relative to GDP and Merchandise Value-Added, 1960–1990 (percent)

Country	Merchandise Trade / GDP		Merchandise Trade / Merchandise Value-Added	
	1960	1990	1960	1990
Australia	13.0	13.4	24.4	38.7
Canada	14.5	22.0	37.6	69.8
Denmark	26.9	24.3	60.2	85.9
France	9.9	17.1	16.8	53.5
Germany	14.5	16.5	24.6	57.8
Italy	10.0	15.9	19.2	43.9
Japan	8.8	8.4	15.3	18.9
Norway	24.9	28.8	60.0	74.8
Sweden	18.8	23.5	39.7	73.1
United Kingdom	15.3	20.6	33.8	62.8
United States	3.4	8.0	9.6	35.8

Source: Robert C. Feenstra, "Integration of Trade and Disintegration of Production in the Global Economy," *Journal of Economic Perspectives,* 12 (Fall 1998): 31–50, Tables 1, 2.

We think of services such as haircuts and dry cleaning as locally produced and not entering into international trade. Tourism and many important business services, however, frequently cross national boundaries. Although the United States has a widely noted trade deficit (excess of merchandise imports over exports), the country is a net exporter of services. Services exports (relative to GDP) are growing even faster than goods exports. Services here include both the conventional services that we sell to foreigners (consulting and financial services and tourism) and the services of American factors of production working abroad (in particular, the foreign earnings of U.S. multinational companies). The growing importance of services in international trade is a worldwide phenomenon. While world exports of goods (nominal values) grew at a rate of 5.8 percent annually from 1980 to 1990, world exports of services grew 8.2 percent annually. Growth rates for the major classes of (nonfactor) services were:

Shipping	4.5%
Passenger services	10.4
Other transportation	3.8
Travel	9.8
Royalties and fees	10.8
Other private services	9.4

Data from United Nations, *World Economic Survey, 1993,* p. 74.

Table 1.3 shows a few broad facts about the distribution of merchandise trade among the industrial nations, the developing countries, and the former centrally planned economies that are now called "economies in transition." The developed countries, which in 1998 accounted for two thirds of world exports, trade extensively with each other. The developing countries ship the bulk of their exports to the developed

TABLE 1.3

Percentage Distribution of Exports by Major Trading Groups, 1985–1998

Exporter		Importer		
		Developed Countries	Economies in Transition	Developing Countries
Developed	1985	72.7	—	23.0
Countries	1998	71.8	4.4	22.8
Economies	1995	50.7	34.9	13.6
in Transition	1998	51.4	34.6	13.5
Developing	1985	64.0	—	30.6
Countries	1998	55.2	1.8	40.6

Source: United Nations, *World Economic and Social Survey,* 1999, Table A-14. Percentages add to less than 100 percent because of discrepancies in the underlying data, and usable data on the economies in transition are available only from 1995.

nations but sell a fast-growing share of these goods to each other. Before the economies in transition abandoned their regimes of central planning, they traded mostly with each other. By 1995, however, a majority of their exports went to the developed countries, mainly Western Europe. Table 1.3 fails to show the increasing divergence of trade patterns among the developing nations, with some remaining mired in underdevelopment, while others—newly industrialized countries, or NICs—have expanded their trade and income levels rapidly. Between 1970 and 1986 the developing countries' share of world exports of manufactures rose from 3.5 to 13.0 percent while their share of world exports of agricultural products fell from 29.3 to 25.4 percent.[2]

1.3 The Organization of This Book

International economics builds models to explain the links between national economies and to show how nations' policies can yield maximum welfare and stability. We begin with the simplest model of trade between nations, and that is the focus of Part I. Chapter 2 establishes the gains from international trade and relates them to the conditions of production and demand. In Chapter 3 the basic trade model is applied to the effects of various changes and disturbances—altered tastes of consumers, the size (growth) of the national economy, and the like.

Into the simple model of Part I, Part II builds various explanations of the nation's production apparatus. We first describe production processes in the fashion of David Ricardo, with a unit of each output requiring inputs of only a certain number of labor-hours (Chapter 4). Another scenario assumes that each output requires labor, plus units of a factor of production used only in that sector (Chapter 5). In a third scenario,

---

[2]The calculation excludes the developing countries that are petroleum exporters. See Anne O. Krueger, "Global Trade Prospects for the Developing Countries," *The World Economy,* 15 (July 1992): 457–474.

each output requires both capital and labor but in different proportions (Chapter 6). Chapter 7 introduces product differentiation and the market equilibrium associated with monopolistic competition, adding new consequences of international trade for welfare. Chapter 8 deals with goods that are inputs to the production of other goods; it details the consequences of stages of production being mobile from country to country. Chapter 9 addresses the international mobility of factors of production—labor migration and international capital transfers; it explains the role of multinational enterprises.

Part III considers tariffs and other controls on trade, identifying their effects and asking in what circumstances they might be desirable from the controlling nation's point of view. A major clash of interests exists in that the welfare of all countries together generally would be raised by removing all restrictions on international trade, but one country acting alone sometimes can improve its own welfare by maintaining or increasing restrictions. Chapters 10 and 11 present the theory of controls on trade, and Chapters 12, 13, and 14 apply this theory to present-day trade policies. Chapter 12 analyzes special problems posed by imperfectly competitive markets, in which nations attempt to exert monopoly power in international trade or to combat similar efforts by other countries. Chapter 13 examines types of trade restrictions in actual use and the industrial nations' efforts to reduce restrictions through international cooperation. Chapter 14 explores trade-policy issues in selected regions or groups of countries: preferential trading arrangements such as the European Union and the North American Free Trade Agreement; the former centrally planned economies in their transition to market organization; and the Asian nations that are enjoying rapid growth and expansion of their foreign trade.

Part IV presents models of short-run disequilibrium and adjustment in order to understand what happens when income and expenditure are not equal or when money prices are sticky. The analysis begins with simple models, then allows additional factors to vary. Chapter 15 explains the balance of payments accounts. Chapter 16 introduces the influence of the exchange rate on the balance of trade. Chapters 17 and 18 allow for variations in income (or employment) and the rate of interest. Chapter 19 discusses the influence of the money price level. Chapter 20 focuses on adjustment in a special, but important, case—the small, open economy that takes as a given the prices of all the goods it buys and sells on the world market but also contains a sector producing goods and services that are not traded internationally.

While Part IV addresses international movements of money and holdings of foreign currency reserves, Part V examines international capital movements. Chapter 21 provides background on the international financial markets—trends and major innovations, plus the liberalization and internationalization that has increasingly integrated national financial markets. Chapters 22 and 23 develop the implications of financial market integration for the domestic macroeconomy, in particular for the operation of fiscal and monetary policy. Chapter 24 on emerging markets and financial crises pursues the causes and consequences of the Asian financial crisis. Chapter 25 applies this analysis to the international interdependence of policies; Chapter 26 examines the role of inelastic supplies of output as an influence on price levels and inflation.

Part VI considers exchange rate determinants. Chapter 27 develops the role of expectations when determining the foreign exchange rate. Lastly, Chapter 28 discusses the problem of exchange rate forecasting and the role of risk in determining interna-tional asset portfolios and prices.

Following the final chapter is a group of supplements to the principal theoretical chapters of the book. We have added these supplements, which demand some mathe-matical sophistication, namely a basic knowledge of differential calculus, to satisfy readers who seek a more formal approach. The supplements are designed to be read with the text; the text is independent of the supplements. The text is completely free of any formal mathematics, other than a sprinkling of high school algebra, and draws instead upon simple diagrams and verbal reasoning.

PART I

Comparative Advantage
and the Basic Model
of International Trade

Chapter 2 ■ **The Gains from Trade**
PAGE 13

Chapter 3 ■ **Applications of the Basic Model**
PAGE 37

CHAPTER 2

The Gains from Trade

S ome trade patterns need little explanation. If you live in the United States and like coffee, you have your coffee imported from Brazil or some other coffee-growing country because it is not produced at home. If you live in Germany or Italy, you depend on foreign sources to supply fuel and lubricants for your sports car. If such imports were to be cut off, your level of well-being or "real income" would surely be reduced. If all trade were of this kind—with every country producing commodities desired by all countries but available only locally—there would be little need for the economist either to expound on the virtues of trade or to explain trade patterns. These would be almost self-evident. Billions of dollars in world trade are spent each year on coffee, chromium, copper, tea, oil, sugar, and other items that nature has placed in some areas but not in others.

Many items that are exchanged on world markets, however, could be produced in a number of locations. Cost comparisons dictate that some countries produce and export computers or steel or textiles to other countries that find it advantageous to concentrate on agricultural or mineral products. Countries differ from each other in their technologies, climates, and skill levels, as well as in their relative supplies of primary factors such as land and labor; these differences all bear upon production costs and trade patterns. Some productive activities require a large scale of output to bring costs down, so these occur in relatively large countries. Historical experience has conditioned labor forces in different countries to acquire different skills, thus imparting an advantage in the production of particular commodities and not in others.

How best to acquire an understanding of these various sources of gains from trade? Our strategy throughout this book is to start with the simple before moving to the complex. Therefore, in order to describe the fundamental forces that determine trade, this opening part of the book is ruthless in its simplifications. We consider a model in which two countries engage in trade and in which each country is capable of producing only two kinds of commodities (food and clothing).[1] Labor and any other inputs in the production process are assumed to be trapped within national boundaries, and international trade provides each country the opportunity to consume food and clothing in proportions different from those produced locally. If the basis for mutual

---

[1] These commodities do not sound as exotic as computer chips and potato chips or airplanes and widgets, but they have been chosen partly because their broad, bland nature is meant to be purely representational of what in the real world is a myriad of different, highly differentiated commodities that enter world trade.

gains from trade can be established in such a simple, stripped-down setting, there is even more reason to expect flourishing trade in a world of many countries and many commodities.

There is a result that is absolutely basic in the comparison of a country's well-being if it were cut off from all international trade with the country's real income if it is allowed to trade. In a setting of only two countries (as in this chapter). the result can be stated as follows:

> *If relative commodity prices differ between countries in the absence of trade, both countries can gain by exchanging commodities at any intermediate price ratio, with each country exporting the commodity that is relatively inexpensive in that country before trade.*

Such a powerful proposition requires a closer study of background behavior in the standard determinants of market prices, namely, demand and supply.

2.1   Background Behavior: Demand

We begin our discussion of demand by considering a single individual and then by making a heroic assumption that a country's demand behavior can be represented in similar fashion.

The Budget Constraint and Relative Prices

The concept of *relative* price arises naturally in this simplified two-commodity trading world. Clothing's relative price is the amount of food that must be surrendered in a market exchange for one unit of clothing. You are more used to prices being quoted in money terms—dollars in the United States, euros in France, and yen in Japan. If you know money prices, you can compute relative prices; if clothing costs $5 a yard and food $10 a bushel, the relative price of clothing is one half, measured in bushels (of food) per yard (of clothing). If food and clothing are traded on world markets, their relative price is known as the *terms of trade*.

The reason we wish to concentrate on relative prices instead of absolute (currency) prices is that we are making an extremely simple assumption about the link between expenditures and incomes represented by production (or ownership) of clothing and food: Individuals (and, therefore, nations as well) spend exactly the value of their incomes. In reality, an individual often manages a close balance between current spending and current income, with discrepancies met by net cash outflows or inflows or by changes in other assets and/or liabilities. Here we assume an exact balance.

Such an assumption, which we refer to as the *classical form of the budget constraint*, greatly eases our task in the first half of this book because it allows us to postpone issues dealing with exchange rate crises, the international monetary system, and a nation's balance-of-payments adjustment problems. Does this mean we are assuming a barter economy? No. Instead, we take for granted the advantages that a monetary system conveys in easing transactions. We require only that any market purchase of food

FIGURE 2.1

The Budget Constraint

The slope of the budget line *BEA* is *HJ/JE*. It shows the relative price of clothing. Its inverse, *JE/HJ,* is the relative price of food.

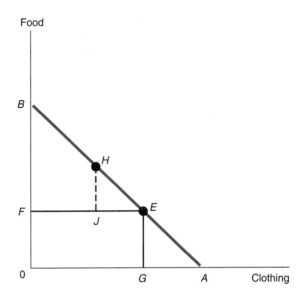

be matched exactly by a sale of clothing of equivalent value. Because of this restriction on spending behavior, it becomes important to pierce the monetary veil of currency prices to know how much clothing must be exchanged per unit of food or how much food must be surrendered to purchase one clothing unit.

　　Figure 2.1 illustrates the consumption choices available to an individual who possesses a fixed endowment bundle E ($0G$ units of clothing and $0F$ units of food) but who is allowed to trade food for clothing (or vice versa) at some specified market prices. Given these prices, the individual can compute all the combinations of food and clothing that have the same value as does endowment point, E. These combinations are shown in Figure 2.1 by a downward-sloping line through E, the *budget constraint line BEA*. For example, suppose the individual wishes to consume the commodity bundle shown by point H on this line. Let food and clothing prices be denoted by p_F and p_C, respectively. If H is to have the same value as endowment point E, the value of net purchases of food (p_F times amount HJ) must equal the value of clothing given up in exchange (p_C times amount JE). That is, clothing's relative price, p_C/p_F, is shown by the absolute value of the slope of the budget line, which is HJ/JE.

　　The slope of the budget line indicates how much of one commodity must be given up to obtain one unit of the other. If commodity prices change but the individual's endowment point (E in Figure 2.1) does not, the budget line changes slope but still must pass through the endowment point. Suppose that food's relative price increases. Would this be shown by rotating budget line BEA around point E in a clockwise or counterclockwise direction? This is a simple question, but experience reveals that it is well worth thinking through. A higher relative food price than is shown by line BEA in Figure 2.1 would be shown by a flatter line through E—more clothing would have to be given up in exchange for one unit of food.

The budget line through the endowment point shows only what food and clothing bundles *could* be purchased; it does not specify which point *would* be demanded. To determine consumption choices, we must have information about taste patterns or preferences, as well as about endowments and relative prices.

Preferences: Indifference Curves

Indifference curves, expressing our individual preferences or tastes concerning food and clothing, are illustrated in Figure 2.2. Start by considering the bundle of food and clothing shown by point E (quantity $0D$ of clothing and $0F$ of food). How do possible consumption points I and H compare with E? This is easy. H is preferred to E, and I, having less of both food and clothing, is inferior to E. The challenge is to ask how bundles with more of one commodity and less of the other compare with E. To take this step by step, suppose one unit of clothing is added to the consumption basket at E. This leads to the higher level of satisfaction that would be obtained from bundle J. Then ask how much food must be taken away from the individual so that welfare is restored exactly to what it was at E. Suppose this quantity is JB. If so, the individual is indifferent to the choice of consuming bundle E or bundle B. E and B lie on the same indifference curve, labeled y_0 in Figure 2.2. (Throughout the book the symbol y indicates real income, utility, or satisfaction.)

The preceding remarks establish that indifference curves are negatively sloped: A sacrifice in the quantity of one commodity consumed must be balanced by an appropriate increment in the quantity of the other commodity. The indifference curves in Figure 2.2 also are *bowed in* toward the origin, reflecting the common assumption

FIGURE 2.2

Indifference Curves

The bowed-in shape reflects diminishing marginal rates of substitution. All points on indifference curve y_1 are preferred to any point on indifference curve y_0.

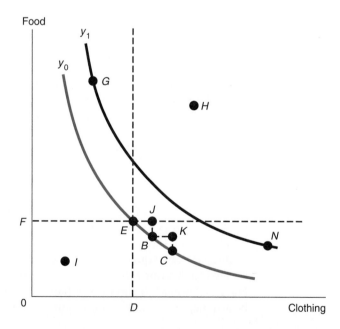

that the marginal rate at which individuals are willing to substitute more of one commodity for less of another changes along an indifference curve. In particular, the amount of food the individual is willing to sacrifice to obtain another unit of clothing diminishes as more clothing is consumed. (Ratio KC/BK is smaller than ratio JB/EJ). The *marginal rate of substitution* is indicated by the (absolute value of the) slope of the indifference curve. It diminishes along the curve y_0 as more clothing is substituted for food.

The indifference curve y_0 is one of many that could be drawn. Indeed, the "commodity space" is filled with these curves. Another is curve y_1, which is farther out from the origin and therefore indicates a higher level of real income than does curve y_0. For example, point G is preferred to point E. If the individual initially possessed the bundle of food and clothing indicated by point E and then was able to exchange some clothing for food to allow consumption at point G, the individual's well-being would clearly be improved. If, instead, the possibility of exchanging food for clothing were available at a substantially lower relative price for clothing, the individual might be able to consume at point N, by giving up some food for clothing, again representing a consumption bundle superior to endowment point E. As we illustrate later, it is precisely this kind of gain that can be achieved by international trade.

2.2 Background Behavior: Supply

The preceding account of how an individual's demand for commodities depends on relative prices assumes that the individual possesses a given endowment bundle of food and clothing. Consider now a more general accounting for a country as a whole. At any given time certain technological knowledge of how to transform inputs of labor, land, and various kinds of capital into commodities (food and clothing) is possessed by producers in this economy. Furthermore, the resource base available for production is assumed to be given and known. Together, technology and the resource base determine the maximal amounts of food and clothing that could be produced in the country. The locus of these quantities is called the *production-possibilities schedule* or the *transformation curve*.

The Transformation Curve

The transformation curve shows the maximum amount of one commodity that can be produced, given the quantities of all other commodities produced. A general illustration of such a schedule is the TT' curve in Figure 2.3, which depicts a simple economy capable of producing only two commodities, food and clothing. For example, if clothing output is distance $0G$, the maximum amount of food that can be produced is AG.

Several properties of production are illustrated by curve TT':

(i) Some points of production (e.g., D) are beyond the productive capacity of this community. If the resource base expands with time, or if better production techniques are developed, then point D eventually could be produced.

FIGURE 2.3

The Production-Possibilities Schedule

The bowed-out curve *TT'* shows the maximum amount of food that can be produced for each amount of clothing, subject to the constraints of technological knowledge and a fixed resource base. The slope shows the opportunity cost of producing clothing, which increases as more clothing is produced.

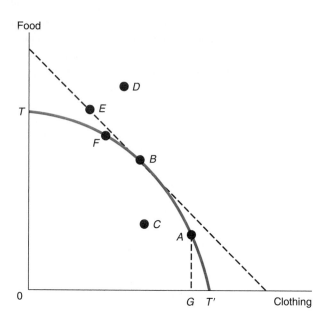

(ii) The *TT'* schedule is negatively sloped. To produce more food than indicated by point *A* on curve *TT'*, some current production of clothing must be sacrificed to release resources from clothing into the food industry.

(iii) A point such as *C* could be produced. For example, during the depression of the 1930s, most industrial countries faced severe unemployment of labor and capital equipment. Perhaps less obvious is the possibility that the combination of production shown by *C* can occur *even with* full employment of all resources. Point *C* might represent the outcome of an arbitrary across-the-board decision by a central planning authority to employ exactly 68 percent of every factor of production in the clothing industry, with the remaining 32 percent producing food. Such a decision would not take into account the fact that some resources are especially productive in one sector and not in the other, or more generally, the fact that techniques of producing clothing are qualitatively different from those of producing food. An economic answer lurks behind the question of how to allocate the community's resources most efficiently, and one of the strong arguments in favor of using the price system and competitive markets is that it causes society's production of commodities to be efficient, thus lying on the production-possibilities curve.

(iv) The *TT'* schedule bows out from the origin, reflecting the so-called *law of increasing costs*. That is, this shape embodies the assumption that the opportunity costs of obtaining an additional unit of a commodity increase as more of that commodity is produced.

What accounts for the general relationship whereby the opportunity cost of any commodity rises as its output increases? Some factors, such as highly skilled labor

especially trained to produce clothing, may be fully employed already in clothing production so that a further expansion in clothing production will rely on less-skilled labor
released from food production. Even if each factor has the same potential skills in one
occupation as in another, the fact that the two industries may require inputs such as
labor and capital in different proportions is sufficient to generate increasing costs.
(Chapters 5 and 6 explore these issues in more detail.)

Some productive processes may, at least for a range of outputs, exhibit what is
known as increasing returns to scale (see Chapter 7). That is, costs per unit produced
may fall as output expands. Here we emphasize that even if such economies of scale
prevail, they may not be sufficiently strong to overcome the tendency for *opportunity*
costs to increase as a result of industries requiring different factor proportions and/or
the variability of factors' aptitudes in different occupations. We continue to assume
that the transformation curve for the economy is in general bowed out.

Special Cases

Two special cases warrant separate diagrams. Figure 2.4(a) illustrates the case in which
resources find it impossible to be reallocated from sector to sector. Full employment is
found at point *E*, and even if prices change, outputs do not. That is, supply curves would
be vertical. This is like the situation portrayed in Figures 2.1 and 2.2 where point *E*
reflects fixed production. One reason this case is important is that we show that such
an economy gains in the move from autarky (no international trade) to free trade,
despite the fact that no consequent change takes place in the production of commodities. Indeed, in such a case it is impossible to identify the *costs* of production.

FIGURE 2.4

Transformation Schedules: Special Cases

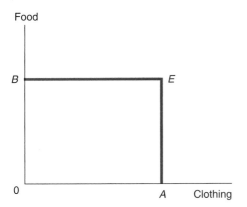

(a) Fixed Allocation of Resources

Any price changes leave production at
point *E*.

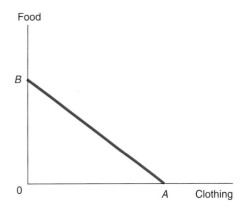

(b) Linear Schedule

If clothing's relative price is higher (lower) than
shown by the slope of line *BA*, representing the
economy's transformation schedule, production
takes place at point *A* (point *B*).

The second special case is illustrated in Figure 2.4(b). The transformation schedule is a downward-sloping straight line. That is, if clothing production increases, the opportunity cost reflected in foregone production of food remains constant. This case is associated with the name of David Ricardo and is pursued in detail in Chapter 4.

2.3   Gains from Trade and Free-Trade Equilibrium

We begin by showing how two countries can each gain from trade even in the case in which price changes cannot lead to any changes in production. For this setting a possible free-trade equilibrium is illustrated in Figures 2.5 and 2.6, where the indifference curves illustrated for each country are assumed to possess the same properties as those for an individual. (Later we discuss international trading possibilities for a country composed of individuals with dissimilar demand conditions). When no international trade is allowed, the slope of the home country's indifference curve at E (and the foreign country's at E^*) must reflect relative commodity prices in the no-trade state of autarky. In the home country's Figure 2.5, two budget lines are drawn through E: line CED and line AEB. They each represent a different set of relative prices, with food relatively cheaper (and thus clothing relatively more expensive) along CED than along AEB. For each relative price (and associated budget line) there is a most-preferred consumption point if the community can exchange commodities at those prices. For example, point F is the best consumption point along line CED; all other points would lie on lower indifference curves than curve y_1. Note that consumption could not reach point F if the community were not allowed to trade with other nations, for it would then be forced to consume food and clothing precisely in the amounts locally available (as shown by E). The slope of line AEB shows the relative price of clothing that must

FIGURE 2.5

The Trade Triangle
for the Home Country

The home country originally consumes its endowment bundle, E, at relative prices shown by line AB. If it could trade at prices shown by line CD, it could export GE units of clothing to obtain FG units of food, thus consuming the bundle shown by F and improving its real income to the level indicated by the y_1 indifference curve.

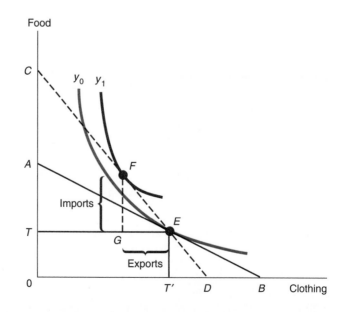

FIGURE 2.6

**The Trade Triangle
for the Foreign Country**

The foreign country consumes its endowment bundle, E^*, at relative prices shown by line A^*B^*. If it could trade at prices shown by line C^*D^*, it could export E^*G^* units of food to obtain G^*F^* units of clothing, thus consuming the bundle shown by F^* and improving its real income to the level shown by the y_1^* indifference curve.

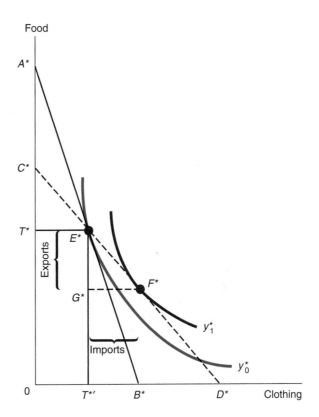

exist if trade is disallowed. At no other price would the community be content to consume food and clothing in the proportions indicated by point E.

Line CED in Figure 2.5 illustrates the possibilities open to this community to trade at relative prices different from those prevailing before trade. The community then could offer to export GE units of clothing, which have the same market value as FG units of food. Such trade would allow the community to consume the bundle F, on the indifference curve y_1. This indifference curve is higher than the original curve, y_0, passing through the endowment bundle. Thus:

> *the opportunity to trade at relative prices different from those in isolation at home must improve real incomes at home.*

Figure 2.6 illustrates the foreign country's behavior both in autarky and if trading opportunities along line $C^*E^*D^*$ are made available (it has the same slope as line CED in Figure 2.5 for the home country). Along budget line $C^*E^*D^*$ the foreign country's most desired consumption point is F^*. It would be willing to export E^*G^* of food (equal to FG in Figure 2.5). Thus these figures and the associated trade triangle illustrate that:

> *A divergence in the relative price of commodities in the two countries before trade indicates a mutual potential gain from trade for both countries at a common intermediate price ratio.*

Something for Nothing?

Does this discussion have a something-for-nothing flavor to it? Recall that as a consequence of our strict assumption that no interindustry resource transfers are allowed, letting countries trade with each other keeps world totals of each commodity unchanged. And yet both countries gain from trade. This is a powerful result, for it suggests that in talking of world trade we are *not* referring to a zero-sum situation, in which one country's gains are at the expense of another country's losses. Opening up markets to trade can increase consumer satisfaction every bit as much as producing more commodities. Trade need not involve one set of countries exploiting another.

Example: A POW Camp

Shortly after World War II, R. A. Radford, an Allied prisoner of war in Italian and German prison camps for several years, published an account of the manner in which markets developed among prisoners in order to exchange endowments that had originated primarily from fairly even allocations of Red Cross parcels.[2] Taste differences stimulated active trade flows within each camp. An item such as cigarettes, found regularly in the parcels, would be in heavy demand by some and would offer virtually zero value for others—except as a medium of exchange. Of special note for our purposes is Radford's observation that different national groups on average had different tastes. As a consequence they supported different relative prices. Any individual with access to more than one such group could make great gains by arbitraging among the price differences. (*Arbitrage* refers to the act of buying and selling in two markets in which prices differ, thus guaranteeing that gains can be made.) Radford describes a priest who started with a tin of cheese and five cigarettes and converted them into a sizable hoard by this activity. Coffee was relatively more expensive in French camps, tea in English and Canadian ones. If these camps were connected by a common price system, all would gain. If the camps were kept separate, some of the potential gains would accrue to arbitragers. As Radford emphasized, this was an economy in which production virtually did not exist. The gains from trade (that is, the gains to arbitrageurs) derived from differences in individual evaluations of initial endowments.

Gains from Trade with Resource Reallocation

Figures 2.7 and 2.8 repeat the argument for mutual gains from trade when transformation schedules are bowed out and international trading equilibrium is attained at a common terms of trade that coaxes each country to alter its production pattern by reallocating production toward greater output of the commodity that has become higher priced in trade. This commodity is clothing for the home country and food for the foreign country.

---

[2]R. A. Radford, "The Economic Organization of a P.O.W. Camp," *Economica,* 12 (November 1945): 189–201.

FIGURE 2.7

The Trade Triangle in the Home Country

With free-trade prices shown by the slope of line 2, production at home takes place at A and consumption at B. BDA is the trade triangle. The community exports DA units of clothing in exchange for imports of BD units of food. Autarky consumption and production are at point E, with autarky prices shown by line 1.

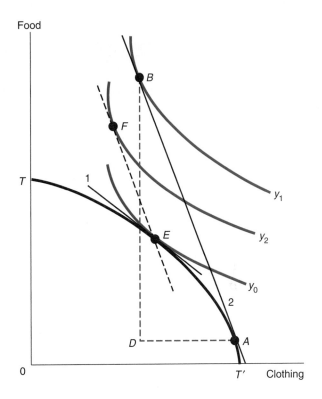

Figure 2.7 shows the consequence of trade for the home country. If the home country is not allowed to engage in international trade, its consumption possibilities are restricted to points on its transformation schedule, TT'; of these the best is shown by point E, where indifference curve y_0 is tangent to TT'. The pretrade relative price of clothing that clears the local market is shown by the slope of line 1. Suppose that with the opening of trade world prices are shown by the slope of line 2. Because clothing is relatively expensive abroad, free trade encourages resources to flow from food production into the clothing industry until local marginal costs equal world prices (at point A). Line 2 shows the new expanded locus of consumption possibilities, and the most desired consumption bundle along this line is point B. At these prices the community desires to export DA of its clothing output in exchange for BD imports of food. BDA represents the trade triangle.

The gains from trade are shown by the increase in real income, moving from curve y_0 to the higher curve, y_1. If resources were frozen into their occupations at point E, the country still would gain from trade with the consumption point moving from E on curve y_0 to F on curve y_2. The movement in consumption from F on y_2 to B on y_1 shows the *extra* gains provided by trade when production is allowed to change from E to A.

World prices are determined by supply and demand in both countries. In a free-trade equilibrium the home country's import demand for food must be matched by the foreign country's willingness to export the same quantity of food. If price line 2 in

FIGURE 2.8

The Trade Triangle
in the Foreign Country

The slope of line 2 is the same as
in Figure 2.7. Trade is balanced as
the foreign country's trade triangle,
$A*D*B*$, matches the home country's
BDA in Figure 2.7.

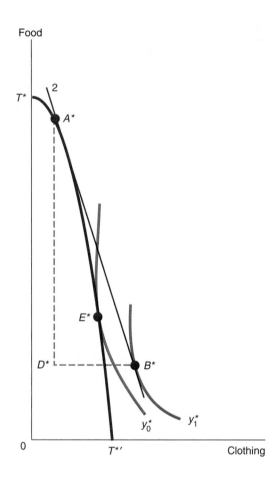

Figure 2.7 is to reflect an *equilibrium* price ratio, trade triangle BDA must find its mirror image in the foreign country. That is, production and consumption decisions abroad must show matching amounts, as in Figure 2.8. The foreign country also gains from trade, with the change in consumption from $E*$ to $B*$ entailing a rise in real incomes abroad from level y_0^* to y_1^*. Foreign exports of $A*D*$ of food match home imports of BD. The slope of $A*B*$ is, of course, the same as the slope of BA in Figure 2.7.

In comparing this illustration of mutual gains from trade with our earlier diagrammatic treatment (Figures 2.5 and 2.6), note not only that the gains from free trade are greater for each country if resources can be reallocated toward the better location suggested by trade, but that relative commodity prices now reflect both the trade-offs along indifference curves and also the opportunity costs measured by slopes of the transformation schedules. For example, in Figure 2.7 the autarky relative price at home is illustrated by the opportunity cost of producing another unit of clothing at point E, measured not in dollars or hours of labor but in terms of the quantity of food that would have to be reduced in order to release the resources sufficient to produce the extra unit of clothing. Once opening international markets makes trade-offs along price line 2 possible, the higher relative price for clothing encourages its greater production at point A.

Comparative Advantage and Comparative Costs

The illustration of mutual gains in Figures 2.5 and 2.6 suggests the technical term *comparative advantage*. A country has a comparative advantage in a commodity if, in autarky, that commodity is relatively less expensive than in the other country. Put this way, it is clear that as long as autarky relative prices are not identical between countries, each country must have a comparative advantage in some commodity, and trade patterns according to comparative advantage lead to mutual gains. What the illustrations in Figures 2.7 and 2.8 suggest is that these price ratios can often be linked to relative costs of production. This leads to a new technical term, *comparative costs*, and the famous *doctrine of comparative costs: A country gains from international trade by exporting the commodity in which its costs are comparatively lower than in the other country.*

If resources cannot be reallocated, as in Figures 2.5 and 2.6, countries still gain from trade that is aligned with positions of comparative advantage. Once comparative costs can be identified, a new issue arises. Must a country have superior productivity in producing the commodity in which its comparative costs are lower? Not necessarily. This was the great observation made by economist David Ricardo in the early nineteenth century, for it suggested that a general inferiority in productive skills did not mean a country could not find export markets for some of its products. A technically inferior labor force, for example, has lower wage rates than in a superior country, but if the extent of inferiority is relatively different from one commodity to another, trade according to comparative advantage does lead to mutual gains. Professor Paul Samuelson of the Massachusetts Institute of Technology, America's first Nobel laureate in economics, once remarked that in his youth when with the Society of Fellows at Harvard, he was challenged by the eminent mathematician, Stanislaw Ulam, to mention one proposition in the social sciences that was true but not trivial. It was only later that Samuelson realized that the doctrine of comparative advantage was the perfect response to this challenge. It is easy to find many people in academia (ideally not economists), business, the media, and politics, who refuse to believe a country that faces rivals with lower wage rates can benefit from international trade.[3] As well, there are those who do not understand that a country with lower productivity in producing food may nonetheless be able to gain by exporting food to a country whose productivity is higher.

Issues regarding productivity are explored in depth in Part II. Here it is important to recognize that comparative costs are measured by the amount of one commodity (say, food) that must be reduced in production in order to release resources to produce an extra unit of the other commodity (clothing). If resource use is frozen, such as depicted in Figures 2.5 and 2.6, such cost measures do not exist, but taste patterns suffice to reveal which country has a comparative advantage in clothing.

A glance at Figures 2.7 and 2.8 reveals the strong bias in the transformation schedules—the home country's curve has been drawn flatter than the foreign country's. This (arbitrary) assumption allows us to speak of a production bias toward the home country possessing a comparative advantage in producing clothing. Note the double comparison

---

[3]Paul Samuelson, "The Way of an Economist," original talk in 1968, reprinted in R. Merton (ed.), *The Collected Scientific Papers of Paul A. Samuelson*, vol. 3 (Cambridge, MA: MIT Press, 1972).

FIGURE 2.9

Comparative Advantage

The pair of relative supply curves illustrates the production bias in favor of the foreign country possessing a comparative advantage in producing food. If tastes are comparable, positions of comparative advantage and the trade pattern (foreign country exports food) are consistent with the production bias.

involved. It is the pretrade cost ratio (p_C/p_F) in one country as opposed to another that is the object of comparison in determining comparative advantage.

Figure 2.9 illustrates the production bias found in Figures 2.7 and 2.8. At this stage of the discussion, we deliberately ignore relative country size as a material consideration in affecting relative costs and concentrate on the composition of demand and production by showing how *ratios* of food to clothing respond to relative prices. Figure 2.9 shows that for any price ratio faced in common by both countries—for example, free-trade price ratio $0T$—the foreign country would, in a competitive market, produce relatively more food at G^* than the home country would at G. A vertical comparison of these supply curves shows that if both countries attempt to produce goods in the same proportion, the relative cost of producing food abroad, at A^*, would be lower than at home, at A. How about the *demand* side of the market? If taste patterns were identical and captured by a common downward sloping relative demand curve in Figure 2.9, the autarky price of food at home would have to be higher than that found abroad. However, it is possible to conceive of a situation in which demand patterns differ so much between countries that food is relatively inexpensive at home before trade. Both demand and supply conditions affect positions of comparative advantage, although we generally consider supply conditions to be more important.

What causes a production bias between countries? Part II develops the rationale along two different lines: The foreign country possesses relatively superior technical knowledge required to produce food, and/or the foreign country is relatively well endowed with those productive factors that are especially well suited to food production.

2.4   Winners and Losers: Autarky to Free Trade

If a country is made up of individuals with different incomes or tastes, opening up the country to international trade may hurt some people. Perhaps images come to mind of skilled American workers undercut by cheaper foreign labor or nineteenth-century British landlords seeing their rents suffer as low-cost sources of food are opened up abroad. Take a close look at what happens in most communities before they engage in trade with other countries: Individuals at home will be trading with each other, and some equilibrium price ratio will be established at which all the net sellers of clothing will find purchasers who are willing to give up an equivalent value of food in exchange. Now suppose the community has an opportunity to trade in food and clothing with the outside world, and suppose that food is relatively cheap abroad (and clothing relatively expensive). Not everyone at home need gain by this new trading opportunity. Indeed, the potential losers are easy to identify—all the individuals who were net sellers of food at home before world trade is opened up.

The situation of one of these individuals is shown in Figure 2.10. Owning the bundle of food and clothing shown by E, the individual "exports" EA units of food (to fellow citizens) in order to purchase AG units of clothing. International trade lowers the relative price of food; the individual's budget line rotates from line 1 to line 2 (around the endowment point E). Consumption is reduced from G to H, and the individual is unquestionably worse off.

If some individuals gain from opening up their country to international trade while others lose, what can be said about the community as a whole? This is an issue typically faced in the political realm, where decisions (in this case, trade policy) almost

FIGURE 2.10

International Trade Can Hurt

This individual is a net seller of food (amount *EA*) at home in autarky, with home prices shown by line 1. With food relatively cheaper on world markets (line 2), the individual's consumption is reduced from *G* to *H*. The individual is hurt by international trade.

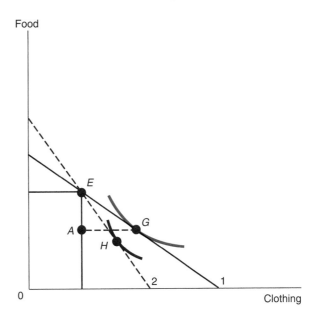

Food

Clothing

always entail some groups being hurt and others gaining. Although the typical result in such cases is that some groups *do* get hurt while others gain, the economist is tempted to ask about the *possibility* of compensation so that all parties can gain by the move.

A Compensation Scheme

This line of argument is worth pursuing because it *is* possible to design a scheme whereby all individuals who would lose by a move from no international trade to free international trade can be compensated by those individuals who stand to gain by such a move, with the original gainers still better off after paying the compensation. The redistribution scheme involves switching the original endowment point for each individual to the consumption point that would be chosen when internal trade (but not international trade) is allowed. Thus, in Figure 2.10 the individual is compensated by an addition of AG units of clothing while a sacrifice of AE units of food is made, thus switching the "endowment" point from E to G. Are there enough supplies of food and clothing to go around? Yes, because the local market was originally cleared. Now open the community to international trade. With prices different in the world market, every individual can gain by a move from that person's new, "compensated" endowment point. Free trade, with compensation, benefits everyone.[4]

   To summarize, everyone stands to gain from trade as such, even in this simple setting. The move from local trade to more extended international trade can be defended if one ignores the local redistribution of income or makes appropriate compensations. However, it is precisely this redistribution that often causes such controversy over new initiatives in the trade area. We seldom witness a country debating whether to engage at all in trade with other countries (nineteenth-century Japan aside), but we have witnessed Britain's original agony in deciding whether to enter the European Community (now the European Union) and special-interest groups lobbying the U.S. Congress for protection from imports. Even when sharp changes in international prices are described in crisis terms, they are not harmful to all. How should an American shareholder in a major oil company feel about the renewed energy crisis in the early years of this century? Would such views be shared by a nonstockholding neighbor? Countries in the European Union (EU) have high levels of protection for agricultural commodities. If you were not a farmer, would you be in favor of these?

Free Trade in North and Central America

The Canadian parliamentary election held in 1988 was one of the most animated and hard-fought in recent history. One issue—free trade—dominated, and it split the electorate. Explicitly, the question was this: Should Canada proceed to ratify an agreement

---

[4]For the individual in Figure 2.10, the budget line appropriate to world prices now passes through G, with the same slope as line 2. Trade now will clearly benefit such a person. Of course, those who were originally clothing exporters do not gain as much as they would have if there were no compensation, but they still gain to some extent.

with its large southern neighbor whereby remaining tariff barriers to goods traveling between the United States and Canada would be gradually abolished over the next ten years? The agreement, already passed through the U.S. Congress, awaited only Canadian approval. The anti-free-trade forces seemed to tap a raw nerve in the Canadian electorate when they predicted that such a move would endanger Canadian sovereignty and interfere with Canada's ability to follow its own social programs and maintain its own cultural identity. The election returns in Canada's three-party system provided a parliamentary majority for the Progressive Conservative party, which had negotiated the agreement, despite the fact that less than 50 percent of those voting seemed to favor the proposal. The issue of free trade proved enormously divisive.

The possibility of pursuing a North American Free Trade Area that included Mexico led to the 1993 agreement, but not before the issue of NAFTA was hotly debated in the U.S. Congress and in the media. Fears that U.S. jobs would be lost to lower-paid Mexican labor were captured by Ross Perot, the independent presidential candidate in the 1992 election, who referred to the "giant sucking sound" that would be heard. Others argued that such a sound was really that of Mexicans drinking Coca-Cola through straws—suggesting that U.S. exports to Mexico would be greatly stimulated by NAFTA, which is what happened. We have more to say about NAFTA as well as the 2005 agreement to form CAFTA, the Central America Free Trade Agreement, in Part III.

2.5 Summary

The advantage of allowing countries to engage in the free trade of commodities has been shown to hold even in the stripped-down setting of two countries and two commodities. The key to understanding the gains from trade is the situation of these countries before they engage in trade: The relative price of clothing in each country is determined by that country's own supply and demand patterns and is probably different between the two countries. If so, they each can gain by trading at a price ratio lying between the two autarky ratios.

Although we have argued that a country can gain from trade, not every individual or group within a country need share in these gains. Suppose the home country imports food as a consequence of its lower price once it engages in trade. Such a price drop would tend to hurt local suppliers of food. We have shown how compensation could be possible so that *every* individual gains from trade, but such compensation schemes are rarely undertaken. As a consequence, in almost every country there will be groups strongly opposed to any moves toward freer trade. Such opposition to free trade need not be seen as ignorance on the part of opponents. It may represent an awareness on the part of such groups that, at least in the short run, freer trade endangers their own real incomes. But of course almost any change in technology, tastes, or endowments creates losers as well as winners, and trade is no exception.

CHAPTER PROBLEMS

1. With reference to the home country's trade triangle illustrated in Figure 2.5, suppose the world relative price of clothing stays at the slope shown by line *CED*. How would the home country's volume of imports and exports be altered if (a) a fire destroyed 10 percent of its clothing endowment, or (b) a bumper harvest expanded its food production by 10 percent?

2. Referring to the previous exercise, if a fire destroys quantity *GE* of clothing in Figure 2.5, will the home country cease to trade if the world relative price of clothing is shown (again) by the slope of line *CED*?

3. In a pair of diagrams such as Figures 2.7 and 2.8, illustrate the mutual gains from trade if (a) tastes are similar between countries but transformation schedules differ, and (b) tastes are different but transformation curves are the same.

4. The home country in Figure 2.7 is shown to respond to the trading opportunities indicated by line 2 by increasing production of clothing (from *E* to *A*) and actually reducing the quantity of clothing consumed. Show why:
   a. For a country in which production cannot change (e.g., the home country in Figure 2.5), trade *must* result in a drop in consumption of the good exported.
   b. If production can respond to new world prices as in Figure 2.7, the quantity of clothing consumed at home could increase.
   c. In Figure 2.7 reduction in clothing consumption results in an increase in well-being, compared with taking advantage of trade to consume more of both commodities.

5. Some consumers have quite rigid taste patterns. Suppose the indifference curves for a community are strictly right-angled, and the corner of each ever-higher indifference curve lies on a ray from the origin. To be precise, suppose that whatever the prices prevailing in the market, two units of food are demanded for each unit of clothing demanded. Furthermore, suppose the transformation schedule shows considerable flexibility in production, so much so that it is a downward-sloping straight line such as in Figure 2.4(b), with a vertical food intercept of 20 units and a horizontal clothing intercept of 40 units.
   a. If the country cannot engage in trade, how much of each commodity does it consume and produce?
   b. In the no-trade (autarky) state, what is the relative price of food?
   c. Suppose world trade is now opened up and the relative price of clothing is double what it was in autarky. Describe what happens to consumption and production.
   d. Is the country better off with trade?

6. The individual whose tastes are shown by the indifference curves in Figure 2.10 is a net seller of food at autarky home prices, shown by line 1. This individual loses if trade with the rest of the world is allowed and food prices are lower there, shown by line 2. Show how this same individual might gain if the world price of food is even lower than that shown by line 2.

APPENDIX A

The Box Diagram

Economists devised the box diagram to illustrate welfare propositions in those cases in which the distribution between participants of fixed total bundles of commodities is at issue. These fixed total supplies provide the dimensions of the box.[5]

In Figure 2.A.1 any point within the box can represent a division of the fixed world totals between two nations, where these commodities are assumed to be identical between countries. For example, point $E(E^*)$ shows the original endowment allocation. Measure quantities belonging to the home country with respect to the southwest 0 origin, and those belonging to the foreign country with respect to the northeast 0^* origin. A pair of indifference curves is drawn through endowment point $E(E^*)$. The curve y_0 for the home country illustrates that a consumption bundle such as A would be valued exactly as highly by the home country as would endowment point E. The shape of the foreign indifference curve y_0^* through E^* is explained by the measurement of foreign clothing consumption leftward from 0^* and foreign food consumption downward from 0^*. Consumption at point A^* means as much to foreigners as does

FIGURE 2.A.1

The Box Diagram and the Contract Curve

The CC' curve is the contract curve, which is the locus of all points where an indifference curve of the home country is tangent to an indifference curve of the foreign country. Point Q represents free-trade equilibrium.

---

[5]One reason for studying a model of fixed production first is that it reveals the basic nature of the gains from trade, independent of any additional gains that can be obtained if trade causes resources to be reallocated to increase world outputs.

endowment point E^* because they both lie on curve y_0^*. Note that any redistribution of the world totals between countries that lies in the shaded area between curves y_0 and y_0^* represents an improvement in welfare for *both*. Free trade leads to one such point of mutual welfare gains.

The CC' curve is the locus of all distributions that equate marginal rates of substitution between countries. That is, move along any indifference curve for the home country (for example, y_0) until you find a point where a foreign indifference curve is tangent to it (point A has foreign curve y_2^* tangent to home curve y_0). This point is especially significant: It shows the redistribution that obtains the maximum welfare abroad that is possible without altering welfare at home. The contract curve CC' collects all points of mutual tangency. From any point off the contract curve (for example, E) it would be possible to redistribute commodities and to improve welfare in *both* countries. (Anywhere in the shaded area would do.) From any point on the contract curve it is still possible to make one country better off, but not without inflicting harm on the other. All points on the contract curve thus pass the efficiency test.

Free trade leads to a world consumption point at which marginal rates of substitution in each country are equated to a common price ratio, shown by the slope of line QE in Figure 2.A.1. The free-trade point is on the contract curve. Free trade raises the welfare of both participants and leaves the world at a point from which further mutual gains are not possible.

Granted that free trade leads to an efficient point on the contract curve, is it the best such point? Countries obviously will disagree over this issue because other points involve a gain for one country (but a loss to the other). A more pertinent question is whether either country might be tempted to try (and perhaps to succeed) to improve its level of well-being beyond that obtainable at free trade. Later discussions of the application of tariffs, quotas, and other instruments of commercial policy explore this issue. Even in the stripped-down illustration of free trade represented by point Q in Figure 2.A.1, however, two points can be made: (1) Any measures taken by one country that cause its welfare level to rise above the free-trade level must harm the other country. (2) Any such measure will prove inefficient from a world standpoint if it pushes the equilibrium point off the contract curve. This comment needs to be stressed because most devices employed by countries attempting to maneuver to a better position than that obtainable with free trade introduce price distortions that do push the trading point away from the contract curve.

APPENDIX B

Substitution and Income Effects

When a country is already engaged in international trade, any change in the terms of trade encourages resource reallocations and has an effect on consumer demand. The analysis of consumer response to price changes breaks behavior into two parts—substitution effects and income effects. For this review, assume production remains fixed.

There are two important aspects of the income effect on demand when price changes: (1) determining how real income is affected by the price change, and (2) determining what the impact of a given change in real income is on demand for importables. The latter reflects only the consumer preference pattern. Revert for the moment to the practice of quoting incomes and prices in dollar units. If income rises by $100 and spending on food (the good being imported) rises by $40, by definition, the *marginal propensity to import* (food) is 0.4. The answer to (1) depends greatly on the extent of trade. The greater the quantity of food currently imported, the more severely will real incomes be hit by a rise in food's relative price.

These points are illustrated in Figure 2.B.1. Suppose that production is fixed at point E and initially the home country imports food at the price ratio shown by line 1, consuming at A. Now let the terms of trade improve. The price reduction for imports is shown by the slope of a steeper line (2 or 3, which are parallel). With the budget line rotating around production point E, consumption of food rises from A to B. This demand change can be broken down into two parts: (1) The move from A to C is the *substitution effect;* that is, the change in demand if consumption is restricted to the same indifference curve, and (2) the move from C to B is the *income effect*. A fall in import prices raises real income (from curve y_1 to curve y_2). The income effect shows how such an increase in real income at constant prices spills into increased demand for both commodities.

Remember that the income effect is strongly influenced by the extent (and direction) of trade. To illustrate, consider the following exercise: In Figure 2.B.1 suppose that the production point is G instead of point E; that is, suppose imports of food initially are roughly twice the amount illustrated (distance AG is roughly twice the distance

FIGURE 2.B.1

Substitution and Income Effects

With point E the production point, consumption is initially at A at terms of trade shown by line 1. A fall in food's import price is shown by steeper lines 2 or 3. The substitution effect is the move from A to C along the initial indifference curve. The income effect is the move from C to B.

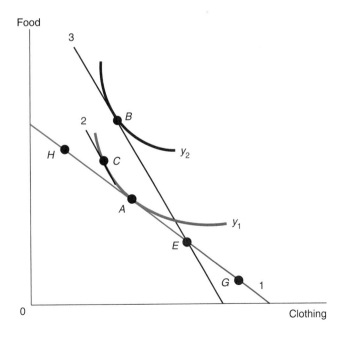

AE). Then show, by drawing the new budget line through G, that the drop in food prices raises real income by more than previously shown (indeed, by roughly twice as much).

This discussion illustrates an important general point: For a country engaged in trade, any price change of traded goods affects real income:

> *The extent of the impact of a change in the terms of trade on real income is proportional both to the extent of the price change and to the original volume of trade.*

These basic points find many applications throughout this book. Appendix C relates these changes to the elasticity of import demand as well as including production changes along the offer curve.

APPENDIX C

The Offer Curve Diagram

Many diagrams used to show free-trade equilibrium and the pattern of trade illustrate directly how quantities demanded and supplied respond to relative prices. An alternative diagrammatic apparatus contrasts directly the quantity of one commodity a country wishes to import against the quantity of the commodity offered in exchange as exports. Retaining the assumption that the home country is an exporter of clothing in a free-trade equilibrium, Figure 2.C.1 illustrates the *offer curves* for the two countries.

Because quantities are shown along the axes, relative prices are indicated in this diagram by the slopes of the rays from the origin. Consider the home country's response to the world relative price of clothing shown by the slope of ray $0A$. At this relative price the home country chooses to demand quantity AF of food over and above its local production. In order to obtain this by imports, it must be prepared to export $0F$ units of clothing, which have an equivalent value. Should the relative price of food fall to the level shown by ray $0B$, home demand for imports of food would rise. In this range, home import demand is elastic because the quantity of clothing exports it is willing to give up increases from A to B; a rise in total revenue spent on a product when its price falls indicates an elastic demand.[6] By contrast, a further reduction in food's relative price to the ray $0Q$ shows a reduction in clothing exports. More food imports are demanded at Q than at B, but the fall in food's price is relatively more severe than the increase in quantity demanded, so that total outlay (as measured by clothing exports) has fallen. This inelasticity in import demand reflects a behind-the-scenes conflict between greater production of clothing at Q than at B (because clothing's relative price has risen) coupled with lower local demand for clothing via the substitution effect, on the one hand, and a stimulus to local demand for clothing via the income effect on the other. (The rise in clothing's relative price from B to Q raises real

---

[6]The elasticity of demand for imports can be shown by the offer curve in the following manner: At point A draw the line tangent to the offer curve. It will intersect the horizontal axis at N. It can be shown (consider this a useful exercise) that the elasticity of import demand at A is the ratio $0F/0N$, which is greater than unity.

FIGURE 2.C.1

Offer Curves

Free-trade equilibrium is shown by point *Q*, with the equilibrium terms of trade equal to the slope of ray 0*Q*.

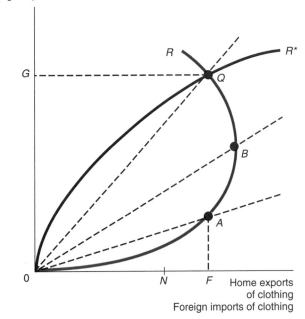

incomes for the home clothing-exporting country.) This conflict is won by the income effect in the move from *B* to *Q* and by the substitution effects in production and consumption in the move from *A* to *B*.

The foreign offer curve, 0*R**, has (arbitrarily) been drawn as elastic throughout. Decreases in the relative price of the commodity imported abroad (clothing) correspond to steadily rising import demand and export supply as clockwise-moving rays from the origin sweep the curve 0*R**. Equilibrium is attained at a price ratio (shown by ray 0*Q*) at which home demand for imports of food matches foreign supply. This equilibrium point, *Q*, also reveals that foreign demand for clothing imports matches home export supply.

CHAPTER 3

Applications of the Basic Model

I f Brazil has a bumper coffee crop, what happens to the world price of coffee? To real incomes in France? To welfare in Brazil? If oil supplies from the Middle East are restricted, how does the impact on Japan compare with that on the United States? If a country discovers new mineral deposits, how does this affect its current balance of trade? These are examples of questions that can be asked of the basic trade model outlined in the preceding chapter.

A strong result was obtained in Chapter 2's basic setting:

Any country that moves from autarky to free trade can experience gains in real income. Compensation schemes exist that guarantee all members of that country can gain from international trade.

In considering various simple applications of the basic trade model, we start not from autarky but rather from a setting in which two countries already find themselves engaged in a free-trade equilibrium. Now the question of gains and losses becomes different, because once countries are engaged in trade they find themselves in an "open" position in that any disturbance in the terms of trade (i.e., world prices) either helps them or harms them, depending on whether the relative price of their exportables has risen or fallen. Furthermore, the applications we discuss all have a common theme: An initial disturbance or shock has a direct effect on a nation's welfare. But the terms of trade must adjust to clear markets, and this price change induces a change in real income as well. Do the direct and indirect effects reinforce each other or pull in opposite directions? Suppose the latter. For example, might a country that is unambiguously sustaining growth (an outward shift in its transformation schedule) nonetheless find its real income lowered because of the nature of its links with the global economy?

We start by briefly exploring a more simple question: What are the effects on the home country of demand and supply changes originating in the rest of the world? Then we consider changes that directly alter production and/or consumption at home or in both countries simultaneously. The chapter concludes with a wider set of assumptions and interpretations of the basic trade model studied in this and the preceding chapter.

3.1   Disturbances from Abroad and the Terms of Trade

There are several ways of illustrating a free-trade equilibrium. In Chapter 2, Figures 2.5 and 2.6 showed matching-sized trade triangles for the case of fixed production, and Figures 2.7 and 2.8 did the same when production responds to the move to free trade. An alternative, not shown here, would add up world demand for one of the commodities, say clothing, for each relative price of clothing and thus portray a world demand curve. In addition, for each such relative clothing price, the quantity of clothing produced in each country is determined, and these could be added together to yield an upward sloping world supply curve.[1] Here we illustrate a world free-trade equilibrium in a slightly different fashion. Assuming the home country will be the exporter of clothing in the trade equilibrium, we draw a rising *net* export supply curve for clothing for the home country (say curve X_1 in Figure 3.1) intersecting a downward-sloping import demand curve for clothing from the foreign country (curve M^* in Figure 3.1).[2]

An Increase in Foreign Demand

From the initial equilibrium shown by point Q in Figure 3.1, suppose foreign tastes change so they demand more of our export commodity, clothing, at any relative price. This is shown by the shift of their demand curve to $M^{*\prime}$. The consequence: an increase

FIGURE 3.1

An Outward Shift in Foreign Demand

An outward shift in foreign demand for home exports of clothing raises clothing's price but may or may not increase home exports of clothing.

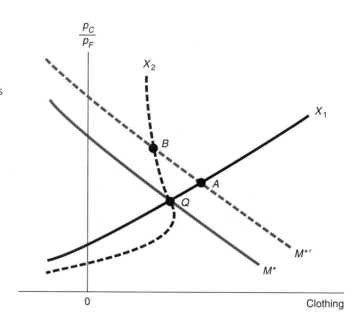

---

[1]In the special case shown in Figure 2.4(a), this supply curve would be a vertical line; and in Figure 2.4(b) it would be a "step" function such as we illustrate in Chapter 4.
[2]Autarky price ratios in each country correspond to positions along the vertical axis where the X_1 and M^* curves cut the axis.

in the relative price of our exports and, if our supply curve is X_1, a greater export quantity of clothing supplied to the foreign country, shown by point A.[3] Such an improvement in the home terms of trade raises real incomes at home. By how much? The relative improvement in home real incomes is proportional both to the relative improvement in the terms of trade and the fraction of the national income represented by the country's exports of that commodity. Formal details are provided in the supplement to this chapter.

Supply Shocks: Energy Prices

Changes in commodity supplies can dramatically affect world prices and incomes. The most severe fluctuations seem to characterize markets in natural resources. Few commodity markets have changed as much or have received as much attention as the markets in oil and natural gas. In the (so-called) first energy crisis, the rapid growth in world demand for energy in the late 1960s and early 1970s caused some tightening of oil prices even before the politically inspired decision of Arab oil producers to cut production and raise prices. The price rise was dramatic. For a complete decade (1960–1970) the posted price of Arabian light crude oil remained a constant $1.80 per barrel. (Actual prices differed a little from the posted price.) By October 1, 1973, this price had increased to $3.01, but a scarce three months later the posted price increased almost fourfold (to $11.65 per barrel). Although the nominal price of oil continued to rise in the succeeding four years, in real terms (i.e., relative to other prices) it fell slightly until the next round of sizable increases in 1979. By the mid-1990s oil prices were reaching low levels. At approximately $10 a barrel (nominal prices) concern was expressed that Russia and some other oil-exporting nations would be hard-pressed. By the end of the century, new heights of more than $35 a barrel had been reached, eclipsed, in nominal terms, by above $70-a-barrel prices by 2006. (In *real* terms the rise in price did not exceed earlier levels.)

Consider the terms-of-trade impact on real incomes of the first oil crisis in the early 1970s. U.S. imports of petroleum products rose from $7.6 billion in 1973 to a figure of $24.3 billion in 1974, the value more than tripling. Quantity figures remained roughly constant (imports of crude products were up slightly, refined products were down by approximately 10 percent); thus as a first approximation the rise in oil prices entailed a real income loss of roughly $16.7 billion (the increased cost of purchasing the same quantity of imports).

---

[3]Also illustrated in Figure 3.1 is an alternative shape for the home supply curve, X_2, resulting in a new equilibrium in which the increase in foreign demand leads as before to a higher relative clothing price but now to a reduced export supply. The backward-bending supply curve for exports reveals that although more clothing may be produced at higher prices, the home country's real income improves as a consequence of these rising clothing prices, and some of these gains spill over to greater home demand for clothing. If such an increase in home demand exceeds the greater quantity produced, a *lower* quantity is available for export. Probably the example of a backward-bending supply curve most familiar from earlier courses is that of labor supply as the wage rate rises and, with it, the demand for leisure. In Appendix C to Chapter 2, this phenomenon of a reduction in export supply as the price of exports increases is shown in the BQR segment of the home country's *offer curve*, which is the segment in which home import demand becomes inelastic (i.e., less revenue required to purchase greater imports of food as food's relative price falls).

Changes in export prices also can severely affect a nation's terms of trade. For example, Sweden is almost completely dependent on imports of oil. On the export side, though, wood, pulp, and paper are important, and these products were rising in price at the same time oil prices were rising. Sweden's terms of trade in 1971 and 1972, before the first oil crisis, were not much different from those in 1975 and 1976. Indeed, in spite of the second round of oil price rises in 1979, Sweden's terms of trade improved by approximately 35 percent from 1978 to 1982.[4]

3.2 Protecting the Import-Competing Commodity

We turn now to situations in which the shock to a preexisting equilibrium comes not from abroad but from changes taking place at home. First we consider an example in which the shock is a policy change administered by the home country—an interference with market prices and resource allocation.

The doctrine of comparative advantage reveals the gains a country can obtain if it allows resources to be reallocated toward their best use given world prices. Thus in Figure 3.2 the country can do no better than to produce at A if world relative prices are shown by the slope of line 1, allowing consumption at point E. At point A prices reflect marginal costs, a hallmark of competitive behavior. Is there any rationale for the government to step in and to interfere with resource allocation—in particular, to protect the import-competing food sector?

Such interference in market outcomes could well be promoted by special interests. For example, suppliers of agricultural equipment would gain if food output is raised from A to B. Special-interest groups frequently do lobby the government to interfere in free markets in order to further their own ends. Such interference not only opposes the national interest but the lobbying effort also wastes resources that might otherwise have been used to produce commodities.

Putting aside these pressures, is there an argument for government interference for the *national* benefit? Perhaps. The key is the possibility that government action can alter prevailing world prices.

A policy of restricting food imports by tariffs or quotas encourages local production, say to point B in Figure 3.2. For a country too small to affect world prices, such resource reallocation makes no sense because it places the country on a lower budget line, line 2. But a large country restricting imports could cause the world price of food importables to be lowered. One possible consequence is an improvement in the terms

---

[4]See the United Nations, *Yearbook of International Trade Statistics,* 1980, 1981 (New York: United Nations); and International Monetary Fund, *International Financial Statistics,* 36 (10) (October 1983). For an example of more violent ups and downs in the terms of trade, consider the case of Zambia. When oil prices rose from 1973 to 1974, the unit value of imports (price index) rose 30 percent, but the rise in world copper prices increased the unit value of exports by 20 percent. The following year (1975), import prices continued to rise, but copper prices crashed. With 1973 as a base year of 100, Zambia's terms of trade only deteriorated to 92 in 1974 but fell to 47 one year later. (These figures are computed from the International Monetary Fund, *International Financial Statistics.*)

FIGURE 3.2

Restriction on Exportables Production

If free-trade world prices are indicated by the slopes of lines 1 and 2, the home country might benefit by lowering clothing output from *A* to *B*, if such a policy could raise world clothing prices to those indicated by line 3.

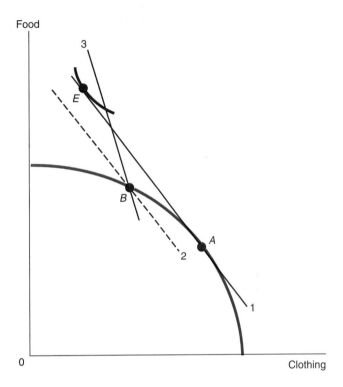

of trade such that the original consumption bundle (*E* in Figure 3.2) is dominated by some consumption points on the new budget line at world prices, that is, line 3.

This argument provides possible rationalizations for commercial policy that we explore in greater depth in Part III. Here our point is that a particular policy that creates losses at *initial* terms of trade may nonetheless prove to be welfare enhancing once the required terms-of-trade adjustments are taken into account. That is, the secondary price changes may have more of a welfare impact than the primary shock that caused the price changes. This reasoning should be familiar from your earlier studies of monopoly or monopsony behavior: Lowering quantities bought or sold can raise profits by causing prices to change.

Although Figure 3.2 illustrates a case suggesting possible gains from protection of the import-competing sector, several warnings should be posted. First, we have left unexplored just what the policy of protection does to *domestic* prices. For example, producers are content to move resources to point *B* only if the domestic price of food is raised to match the slope of the transformation schedule at *B*. But this distorts consumption choices as well, preventing the best point along line 3 from being chosen. Second, we have not explicitly investigated the world market for food, which reveals how much prices change when food production is protected, leading to an inward shift in the net home demand for imports of food. Finally, foreign countries may retaliate with restrictions of their own when the home country protects its food producers. Part III continues and extends the story.

3.3 Growth and International Trade

Does a country necessarily gain by producing more? The wary reader may wonder about the quality of life as it is affected by the extra production. Is growth beneficial if it leads to increased congestion, pollution, and crime in urban areas? In a different vein, is aggregate growth desirable if it reflects a population explosion that threatens to lower per capita income? These arguments against growth are both popular and easily understood, but there is a less obvious question: Can an outward shift of the production-possibility schedule in a country with a constant population—with food and clothing "goods" instead of "bads"—ever lead to a lowering of real incomes at home? If a country is engaged in foreign trade, the answer is perhaps.

The preceding discussion of the manner in which changing the composition of output can alter the terms of trade and real income serves as the key to the possibility that these terms-of-trade changes might even outweigh the directly beneficial effect of growth. Consider Brazil, heavily committed to an export crop, coffee, for which world demand is highly inelastic. Suppose it is a good season, or that for some other reason Brazil's transformation schedule shifts outward, primarily in the direction of coffee production. The world price of coffee might fall so much that Brazil loses real income as a consequence of the good crop. The argument also is valid for groups within a country. Agriculture provides the prime example. On behalf of their farmers, many nations attempt to encourage crop-restriction programs—the opposite of growth—to keep farm prices from falling in the face of inelasticity in demand.

We start our discussion by considering the case of *balanced* growth: Suppose the country's transformation curve expands outward by a uniform 20 percent and, as well, its demand for both food and clothing expand by 20 percent at initial world prices. What is the impact on world markets? The country's demand for imports has risen, and its supply of exports has expanded as well since its trade triangle has been enlarged (at initial prices). The result: *The sheer act of growing more than other countries induces a deterioration in the terms of trade that to some extent may erode the gains from growth.* But note the bright side: The country's growth causes real incomes to rise in other countries that are importers of the growing country's exports.

Turn now to a more paradoxical-sounding case, the extreme possibility that growth could *lower* real incomes by being concentrated in a nation's export sector and by significantly worsening the country's terms of trade. This is known as a case of *immiserizing growth* and is illustrated in Figure 3.3. Initially, the terms of trade are given by the slope of line 1, with the home country's production at A and consumption at B. Growth in some form that favors the nation's export industry, clothing, shifts the transformation schedule outward from TT to $T'T'$. As a consequence, it is assumed the relative price of clothing in world markets drops to the level shown by the slope of line 2. The home country adjusts its production to point C and, at the new terms of trade, maximizes its real income by consuming at point D. However, its real income after growth, as indicated by the y_1 indifference curve, is lower than the original real income shown by indifference curve y_0. Economic growth has hurt the country.

Two basic factors contribute to this result: (1) Growth primarily increases capacity and output in a nation's export industries, and (2) Demand elasticities throughout the world for the country's export commodity are quite low. The first factor ensures that

FIGURE 3.3

Immiserizing Growth

Growth biased toward the nation's export industry (clothing) can reduce real income by so worsening the terms of trade (from line 1 to line 2) that consumption (at D) ends up on a lower indifference curve than initially (at B).

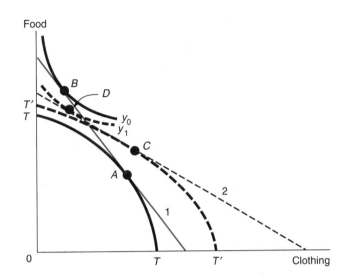

the major effect of growth in world markets is the increased supply of the nation's exports, whereas the second suggests that the terms of trade must deteriorate sharply to raise world demand for these exports enough to clear commodity markets.

The importance of the secondary effects of changes in the terms of trade is not limited to this case of immiserizing growth. If demand elasticities are low, outward shifts in the supply of a nation's exportable tend to worsen its terms of trade and thus serve at least to dampen any gains even if real incomes improve. In many countries farmers look askance at bumper crops that face inelastic demands.

International trade forges strong links among national real income levels. Suppose your country is growing *less* rapidly than others. Your country's terms of trade are apt to improve if net world supplies of your imports are thereby increased. Growth anywhere in the world benefits the trading community as a whole, but whether all participants share in the gains depends not only on the initial allocation of growth among nations, but also on trading patterns and the succeeding adjustments in world prices.

3.4 The Transfer Problem

Terms-of-trade changes serve to *transfer* real income between importing and exporting nations. Historically, more direct forms of transfer have been important as well, leading economists to analyze the resulting welfare consequences for open economies, once the secondary transfers, represented by price changes, are considered together with the initial direct transfer.

The Transfer Problem: Purchasing Power

Consider the following cases: The home country is obligated to make a gift or reparations payment to the foreign country. The home country could be France after the Franco-Prussian War in 1870–1871 or Germany after World War I. To broaden the possible categories, consider a different kind of gift, the Marshall Plan, whereby the United States sent aid to Europe after World War II. For analytic purposes international lending and borrowing will also be included, but the future problems of repaying loans (a reverse transfer) will be ignored. More recent examples emerge from conflicts in the Middle East: The rise in oil prices following the OPEC actions in the early 1970s or late 1990s involved a "recycling" of surpluses earned by oil-exporting countries into loans to Western Europe. And following the Gulf War in 1991, Japan, Germany, Kuwait, and Saudi Arabia made Desert Storm payments to the United States. In 1998 the International Monetary Fund arranged large transfers to countries in the Far East whose economies were severely affected by the financial crashes in 1997. All these cases have something in common: One or more countries transfer purchasing power to another.

The easiest way to prepare the basic trade model to handle this problem is to let the home country, assumed to be the transferor, cut the aggregate value of its spending below the current value of its produced income by precisely the same amount as the foreign country expands its spending above its current aggregate production level. (Only in this way can world expenditure balance world production.) This amount is called the *transfer*.

How does such a transfer affect the terms of trade? To answer this question, ask what the transfer does to world demand and supply for one of the traded commodities (e.g., food). A transfer only of purchasing power would leave the world supply schedule in place but might cause the world demand curve to shift. At any given price ratio, the home, or transferring, country can be expected to cut back its spending on all normal commodities such as food. Abroad, the receipts of the transfer are disbursed in general over all commodities, including food. Therefore, the home demand curve for food shifts leftward while the foreign curve shifts rightward; depending on the difference in the two countries' taste patterns, the world demand curve could shift in or out.

The first conclusion, then, is that transfer can move the terms of trade in either direction. To probe more formally, let m and m^* denote home and foreign *marginal propensities to import*. These propensities indicate, for each country, the fraction of a unit of extra total spending that would be allocated to the consumption of importables at initial prices. Thus, if T denotes the transfer, the home country, at initial prices, cuts its spending on food by mT. The foreign country imports clothing, so it allocates $(1 - m^*)$ times the transfer to extra food consumption. Thus the world demand curve for food shifts to the right if, and only if, $(1 - m^*)T$ exceeds the home cut, mT. That is, the terms of trade turn against the transferor (the relative price of food rises when the home country makes a transfer) if and only if the sum of the two countries' marginal propensities to import falls short of unity.

If the sum of the marginal propensities to import does fall short of unity, economists speak of the *secondary burden* of the transfer to acknowledge the fact that price changes create an international redistribution of income *additional* to the initial loan or grant. Between the two world wars, a number of eminent economists were concerned with the practical importance of this issue. John Maynard Keynes eloquently argued that the reparations payments imposed by the Allies on Germany after World War I underestimated the true payment that Germany would have to make.[5] According to Keynes, Germany's export prices would have to fall considerably, coupled perhaps with a rise in its import prices, in order for it to create the export surplus that would comprise the counterpart of the financial transfer. In reply to Keynes, Bertil Ohlin proposed that the transfer itself, by lowering spending in Germany and raising spending in the recipient country, could bring about the required export surplus without imposing a change in the terms of trade. Ohlin's reasoning is closer to the analysis here, which suggests that it is not necessary for the terms of trade to change one way or the other.[6] In any event, tracing the adjustments that the German reparations required is difficult, for this period was characterized by an additional reverse transfer in the form of private loans and capital movements from the United States to Europe.

Is It Better to Give or to Receive?

The transfer criterion tells us that the terms of trade move in favor of the country making the transfer if the sum of import propensities exceeds unity. How favorable can the terms of trade become? The discussion of the possibility of immiserizing growth in Section 3.3 makes clear the analogous possibility that the home country, by giving away purchasing power, might so improve its terms of trade that it ends up with improved welfare. This, however, cannot happen in this two-country setting, for "it is never better to give than to receive." Figure 3.4 helps explain the limits of any "secondary blessing" of the transfer.

The initial world equilibrium in the food market is shown by a relative price of food, $0A$, and quantities produced and consumed, $0F$. (Instead of illustrating equilibrium in the world food market by the balance between net import demand at home and net export supply abroad, we show total world demand and total world supply.) If the home country makes a transfer, its real income is reduced. Conversely, if its terms of trade improve (the price of food falls), this loss will not be so severe. Let price $0B$ represent exactly the improvement in the terms of trade (compared with $0A$) required fully to compensate the home country for the transfer. That is, if the price of food should fall to level $0B$, neither country's welfare would be altered from its pretransfer level. The question boils down to the following: Can the transfer shift world demand to the left sufficiently to reduce food's price to $0B$ or lower? No. After the transfer, if the price *were* $0B$, world demand for food would have to exceed its initial value, $0F$. The reason follows from looking at income and substitution effects. By assumption, net real income in both countries is unchanged if the price of food falls to $0B$; therefore, there is no income effect.[7] Substitution effects refer to changes in demand that would take

---

[5]John Maynard Keynes, *The Economic Consequences of the Peace* (New York: Harcourt, Brace and Howe, 1920).

[6]See the exchange between Keynes and Ohlin: Keynes, "The German Transfer Problem," *Economic Journal,* 39 (March 1929): 1–7, and B. Ohlin, "The Reparation Problem: A Discussion," *Economic Journal,* 39 (June 1929): 172–173. Both are reprinted in American Economic Association, *Readings in the Theory of International Trade.* A discussion of the effect of a transfer on the balance of payments appears in Chapter 17.

[7]Price $0B$ is the price that leaves the home transferor's real income unaltered, by assumption. But the transfer itself cannot create or destroy real income in the world, so at $0B$ foreign real income also is undisturbed. Warning: This conclusion needs some modification if more than two distinct countries are engaged in trade.

FIGURE 3.4

Transfer and the Terms of Trade

A transfer may improve the terms of trade of the transferor, as shown by the drop in food's relative price from 0A to 0G when the home country (the importer of food) makes a transfer. 0B represents such an improvement in the home country's terms of trade that real income would be unaffected by the payment. Therefore, at price 0B, world demand must exceed world supply because only substitution effects are involved in demand.

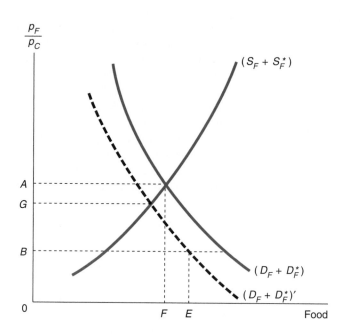

place along initial indifference curves. Because at price $0B$ real incomes are unchanged in both countries, food's lower relative price must call forth a substitution of food for clothing in demand patterns for both countries. Therefore, even if the transfer shifts the world demand schedule to the left, it must be to some position such as $(D_F + D_F^*)'$, with a new relative price for food $0G$ above $0B$.

Brazil might improve its position by burning part of a bumper coffee crop. It cannot improve its position by giving that coffee away. Growth (or the reverse) shifts the world supply curve; a transfer of purchasing power does not. Without a change in supply, price changes in this two-country world do not outweigh the direct effect of the transfer.

The Transfer Problem: Real Resources

A transfer in the form of a gift, a loan, or reparations often involves more than a redistribution of purchasing power. Real resources may be moved from one country to another. This movement may be direct, as in the stripping of German capital equipment at the end of World War II and its relocation in Eastern Europe and the old Soviet Union. The process may also be indirect: Canada, for example, may borrow funds in the New York market, causing a greater investment in new capital equipment in Canada and perhaps less new capital equipment in the United States.

A transfer of real resources may alter net world supplies at any given price. A scenario that reveals it *might* be possible for a country to gain by giving away resources can easily be suggested: Suppose that each country produces a different commodity, so if the home country transfers resources abroad, supplies of its own export good are cut and supplies of its import commodity are expanded. The result: Its terms of trade tend to improve, perhaps enough to make such a transfer justifiable even if no payment is made for it.

3.5 Wider Interpretations of the Basic Trade Model

The basic trade model is simple—a stripped-down version in which only two countries are engaged in trade, producing only two commodities, with the value of each country's imports exactly balanced each period by the value of its exports. The real world of international trade is much richer than this, and yet the key to understanding its complexities is indeed provided by the simple basic model. Here are some of the wider interpretations.

Many Final Traded Commodities

Trade usually takes places in a large set of completely different commodities, some of which may be good substitutes for each other in demand or production, and others not. Furthermore, such broad aggregates as food and clothing may really mask a variety of goods differing in characteristics to demanders but produced in similar fashion. Thus a country might export some varieties of clothing and import others. This kind of *intra-industry* trade is examined in Chapter 7.

The basic point is that trade allows the item-by-item balance between a nation's consumption and production, which holds in autarky, to be replaced by only an overall balance in the value of all exports on the one hand and all imports on the other. Furthermore, with many commodities produced and traded, it is easier to see that a nation may export a much reduced set of commodities than it imports. That is, international trade allows each country to concentrate its production to a small subset of goods in which it has the greatest comparative advantage and to rely on other countries for a wider set of the remaining traded goods. Such an asymmetry suggests even greater gains from international trade.

Many Countries

If the world consists of many countries, what happens to the requirement that the value of a nation's exports be equal to the value of its imports? Is this condition applicable to each pair of countries? No. Overall balance certainly does not imply bilateral balances. The United States can run a trade deficit with China and Japan along with trade surpluses with Australia, Latin America, and/or the European Union. What sense is then to be found, say, with requiring the United States to have balanced trade with China? In a free-trade world, it is normal to find bilateral surpluses or deficits between any pair of countries. It is only *overall* balance that counts, yet again allowing asymmetries that lead to even greater gains from trade.

In a two-country world, trade patterns are mirror images of each other. A many-country world is different. One country might expands its exports, causing a drop in the price of such exports, but all other countries do not thereby gain because some other countries may well be exporting the same commodity and thus lose.

Trade in Intermediate Goods and International Factor Mobility

Countries such as Japan and Canada often are portrayed as opposites in their trading patterns. Japan is starved for oil, coal, rubber, and many raw materials required for its manufacturing sector, whereas Canada possesses an abundance of many primary products and energy, which it can trade for automobiles, television sets, and computers. The sheer volume of world trade in nonconsumer goods is impressive—over three quarters of the world's exports are categorized as producer goods, raw materials, or intermediate goods, and this fraction is increasing as the world's production facilities become ever more integrated. Lower transport costs and technical advances that serve to reduce the costs of services that link various fragments of previously integrated production processes lead to *outsourcing* these fragments among several locations where costs of production are lower. As well, productive factors such as labor, capital, and management services may, to some extent, be capable of moving from country to country. Multinational enterprises often facilitate such factor mobility. Furthermore, any nation may find its level of technological knowledge enhanced by its trading contacts with other nations. (Chapters 8 and 9 pick up these themes.)

Nontradable Final Commodities

Just as some inputs and producer goods may be traded on world markets, some final consumer goods may have their markets restricted nationally or locally. High transport costs account for some of these, but currently governmental regulations are frequently more responsible. Obviously the use of the simple two-commodity basic trade model does not allow much scope for such nontradable final consumer goods. As Chapter 4 reveals, the two-commodity model can still portray the situation for a small open economy that is a price-taker for all traded goods and produces and consumes a nontradable. The secret lies in the strategy of aggregating all the tradable goods into a single composite commodity, with spending shares on individual traded goods serving as weights in a price index.

Intertemporal Trade

Not only might a nation not have a bilateral balance with any other particular country, it might not have an overall balance in any particular year. Such a situation does not necessarily reflect a crisis in desperate need of repair. Instead, it is quite normal for some countries to borrow and others to lend. The analogy: A young person may plan to spend now in excess of current earnings and to make it up later when earnings are expected to rise. In similar fashion, the aggregate of individual decisions within a country may call for a deficit or surplus in current spending plans, with borrowing or lending in world markets allowing intertemporal smoothing of consumption and production plans. Goods today and goods tomorrow are different. Comparative advantage, taste patterns, and productive potential can vary over time, just as they do over commodity types, and can suggest optimal patterns of net trade over time as well as net trade in autos or computers.

Consider a simple example. Suppose a nation, initially balanced in exporting a variety of commodities that matched in value its current imports, discovers new deposits of natural gas that will take time to develop. In future years it can confidently expect outputs to rise significantly over current levels. Assuming it does not expect prices to be much affected by these discoveries, how might its trading pattern be affected? Its current discounted level of wealth has increased because of expectations of greater production in the future. It probably would be best to spread the benefits of this wealth over time, and such consumption smoothing would entail running current deficits (an excess of imports over exports), to be made up later when production expands by planned trade surpluses (an excess of future exports over imports).

Such intertemporal trade requires using assets with internationally recognized value, just as exchanges of commodities within any time period are aided by using money to avoid the transaction costs required by barter. More is said later about such assets and the problems encountered when using different currencies because one obvious problem with intertemporal trade is the possibility of changes over time in the exchange rates that link currency values in various countries. The emphasis here is on a different set of prices: interest rates. Countries that tend to discount future consumption relatively heavily may be encouraged by the opportunity to borrow on world markets at interest rates that seem low by their national standards. The world pattern of interest rates, and of commodity prices, reflects the diversity among countries in tastes and production plans. Just as it is not necessary for a country's trade in any commodity category or with any group of countries to balance, so it is not necessary to balance overall payments within any given time period. This merely reflects the gains from trade over all commodities, present and future, when world markets supplement or replace the requirement for item-by-item balance found in autarky.

A simple illustration of intertemporal trade is provided in Figure 3.5. Suppose point E is the production point, reflecting a brighter future in which next year more of a composite good will be produced than is the case this year. Furthermore, suppose world interest rates are shown by the slope of line EA. More particularly, the slope of this line is $(1 + r)$, where r is the rate of interest. The trade triangle is EGA, where the country runs a deficit (excess of consumption this year over production this year) of GA, paid for by a promise to pay back EG next year. EG exceeds GA. (The ratio of EG to GA is 1 plus the interest rate, so that trade is balanced intertemporally.) The slope of the home indifference curve at E reflects the higher rate of time preference in autarky for the home country. As this example illustrates, intertemporal trade yields standard gains from trade if autarky prices differ from those on world markets.

A country such as the United States may run a current account deficit, as it has in recent years, but this may not necessarily represent a disequilibrium position in dire need of policy correctives. Although views regarding the urgency of the need to combat such deficits vary widely, the argument sketched here is that this deficit represents an imbalance in one time period that can be offset by opposite imbalances in the future. Intertemporal trade can yield gains to all participants.

FIGURE 3.5

Intertemporal Trade

The home country expects a larger endowment of goods next year than it has this year. It gains by giving up more next year (*EG*) than it borrows for extra consumption this year (*GA*).

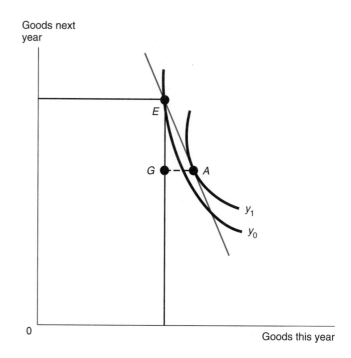

Trade in Assets

The portfolios held by individuals and firms in one country often contain assets representing claims on other countries. The reasons such diversification takes place are not hard to find and reflect the fact that countries differ from each other in various ways: the kinds of business firms that issue securities, the attitude of governments toward activities in the private sector, resource endowments, and climatic conditions. International trade itself encourages countries to concentrate productive activities according to comparative advantage, and trade in financial assets makes it possible for residents in one country to avoid the greater degree of risk such production concentration entails by obtaining income streams based on productive performance in other countries. Thus, even if a country has a balance between current exports and imports and does not, *on net*, engage in intertemporal trade, it may be exchanging assets with other countries.

Any changes in interest rates, exchange rates, or commodity prices could well lead to a reshuffling of these asset holdings as well as to introduce real gains or losses. For example, in 1994 Japanese investors took big losses when they sold off American real estate, hotels, and resorts (primarily in Hawaii and California) they had purchased at top prices a few years earlier before the U.S. recession and when the yen was weaker. In 1997 and 1998 much asset reshuffling took place as a consequence of severe turmoil in Asian financial markets. (More on this in Part V.)

The fundamental principle of trade underlying all these remarks is that international trade frees up the lockstep connection between patterns of consumption and production that characterizes a state of autarky. In general, severing the umbilical cord connecting local demand and supply allows a wider choice for consumers and encourages a concentration of resources in production. This is a fundamental lesson imparted by the basic model. In the next set of chapters we analyze in more depth the details of how technology, relative factor endowments, scale economies, and the possibility of trade in nonfinal commodities shape trading patterns and the distribution of income.

3.6 Trade and Market Structure

Discussions about international trade and the sources of gains from trade have traditionally assumed that commodity and factor markets are characterized by perfect competition: Both firms and consumers take market prices as given in making decisions about purchases and sales. Such an assumption implies that indifference curves are tangent to budget lines (which we assume throughout) and that, with marginal costs equal to prices, budget lines are also tangent to production possibilities curves. Such an assumption is usually rendered more realistic in a context of international trade because a greater degree of competition exists than would prevail in autarky. However, pure competition is not ubiquitous, and we have occasion in later chapters to pursue the consequences of departures from the competitive paradigm, especially in Chapter 7.

3.7 Summary

Part I of this book was devoted to developing what we call the basic trade model. Chapter 3 shows how that model can be applied to the following issues that characterize the world trading community:

1. Any disturbance abroad that causes world markets to settle at new prices affects the home country. A change in foreign tastes or in foreign supplies involves a terms-of-trade impact for the home country, which may be sizable, as our discussion of the oil crisis suggests.

2. A country with a volume of trade sufficient to influence world prices can, by interfering with its competitive production pattern, engineer an improvement in its terms of trade. This observation proves significant in understanding noncompetitive behavior in trade and its relevance to the analysis of commercial policy.

3. A growing community finds that repercussions of its growth are reflected in its terms of trade. We argued that in a two-country world, the benefits of growth in one country would spill over favorably to affect the other country by cheapening the growing country's exports. We even considered extreme cases in which growth might leave a country in a worse position. Agriculture supplies many examples in which crop restriction (the opposite of growth) might benefit farmers.

4. Some disturbances may affect both countries in opposite directions. The transfer process, wherein a gift or loan is made between countries, provides the classic

example. If only purchasing power is transferred, the crucial consideration involves how tastes differ between payer and receiver. Any required price adjustment involves a secondary transfer of real income. If productive resources are transferred, further price adjustments may be necessary.

5. The basic trade model is broadly applicable to settings in which many countries produce and exchange a wide range of goods and services. The requirements of overall balance do not necessarily imply a bilateral balance between any pair of countries. Furthermore, countries may exchange assets with each other and may take advantage of trading contacts to rearrange aggregate consumption and production over time. International net borrowing and lending may represent an equilibrium outcome by which interest rates help balance national dissimilarities in time preference and expected changes in resources and wealth.

"Every exit is an entrance to another stage." This survey of the basic trade model prepares the way for a more detailed investigation in Part II of what lies behind a nation's production possibilities. Although Part II focuses on different issues such as the effect of trade on the distribution of income and the influence of technology and factor endowments on the pattern of trade, the models developed there represent more detailed variations of the basic model discussed in Part I. Can expansion in an open economy's supply of capital bring about actual harm? Once we know how such growth affects the nation's output pattern, the material discussed in this chapter will help expose the elements that determine the fate of the nation's real income.

CHAPTER PROBLEMS

1. Figure 3.3 illustrates the phenomenon of immiserizing growth when the country's growth is strongly biased toward its export industry (clothing). Construct a diagram that illustrates the possibility that a country may suffer a welfare loss when growth (at initial terms of trade) results in a balanced (proportional) increase in food and clothing outputs. Can such immiserization accompany growth that is concentrated in food (the import-competing sector)?

2. If imports of food represent 20 percent of a country's national income and the relative price of food rises by 10 percent, by approximately how much is real national income reduced?

3. Suppose that home and foreign countries' taste patterns differ but that each is inflexible: The home country consumes food to clothing in proportions 2:1 (at any prices); the foreign food to clothing consumption ratio is always 1:1. The two countries have identical bowed-out transformation schedules. What happens to the home country's terms of trade if it makes a consumption loan to the foreign country? Is there a secondary burden of the loan?

4. Draw a diagram to illustrate the case of uniform growth—the transformation schedule shifts out radially from the origin by 30 percent. How might such growth affect the country's terms of trade? Now suppose a country receives as a transfer a quantity of

resources from its trading partner. Suppose also that this has the effect of causing its transformation schedule to shift outward by 10 percent and the giving country's schedule to shift uniformly inward by 10 percent. Would the giving country suffer a secondary burden or blessing? How is the growth case related to the transfer exercise?

5. Suppose that only two countries engage in trade and that initially trade is balanced in the current period. If the home country discovers a new process that will raise productivity in its export sector in the next period, how would the current balance of trade be affected? Would your answer be modified if both countries also expect that the discovery will worsen the home country's terms of trade during the following period? (*Hint:* Could the foreign country's real net wealth be increased by more than the home country's as a consequence of the expected terms-of-trade change?)

SUGGESTIONS FOR FURTHER READING

Bhagwati, Jagdish. "Immiserizing Growth: A Geometrical Note," *Review of Economic Studies,* 25(3) (June 1958): 201–205. A treatment of the possibility that growth can harm a country.

Jones, Ronald W. "The Transfer Problem Revisited," *Economica* (May 1970): 178–184. A simple analysis of the transfer problem making use of the box diagram analysis in Appendix A of Chapter 2.

APPENDIX

The Stability Issue

Chapter 3 illustrated world market equilibrium in Figures 3.1 and 3.4. Each of these figures shows a unique stable equilibrium in which stability is guaranteed by two features: (1) Supply and demand curves are drawn so that at prices above equilibrium world supply exceeds world demand while at prices below equilibrium world demand exceeds world supply. (2) It is assumed that price is driven up if, and only if, excess world market demand exists.

Competitive markets that are not so well behaved can be illustrated. For example, the counterpart to Figure 3.1's illustration of a stable free-trade equilibrium is Figure 3.A.1's depiction of *multiple* free-trade equilibria. Point *C* in Figure 3.A.1(a) shows world demand and supply for food in balance, but the equilibrium point is unstable. If the price of food were slightly higher, at 2, world demand for food would exceed world supply by distance *AB*. Such an excess demand would drive food's price upward, away from point *C*. (Similarly, for a price of food lower than 1, world excess supply would drive food's price lower, toward stable equilibrium point *E*.)

Figure 3.A.1(b) illustrates this instability in an offer curve diagram. At disequilibrium terms of trade 2, *TV* indicates the excess of the home country's import demand

FIGURE 3.A.1

Multiple Equilibria

There may be multiple free-trade equilibria. The middle equilibrium point [C in (a) or Q in (b)] is unstable but is flanked by a pair of stable equilibria.

(a)

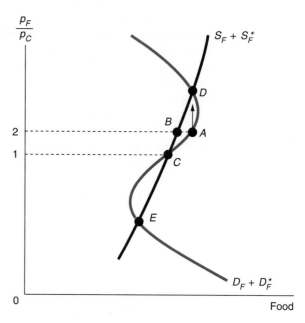

(b)   Home imports of food
       Foreign exports of food

for food (given by point W along home offer curve $0IWQHR$) over foreign export supplies (given by point V along foreign offer curve $0HQVIR^*$). Food's relative price will rise, rotating price line 2 clockwise toward stable intersection point I and away from unstable point Q. Point Q in 3.A.1(b) corresponds to point C in 3.A.1(a).

Each diagram helps reveal the ingredients that conspire to make an equilibrium unstable. As point Q in panel (b) indicates, instability requires a high degree of inelasticity in both countries' offer curves.[8] Panel (a) shows that for instability the aggregate world demand curve in the neighborhood of equilibrium must be positively sloped and even flatter than the world supply curve.

Can the world demand curve be positively sloped? Yes, if at least one country's demand curve has a positive slope in the neighborhood of a free-trade equilibrium. Consider first the importer of food, the home country. As food's price rises from (1), substitution effects suggest less food is demanded. Furthermore, real income falls; therefore, assuming that food is a normal commodity, both income and substitution effects conspire to reduce the home country's demand for food. Thus instability must stem from the demand behavior of the exporter. For foreign exporters of food, income and substitution effects run counter to each other. As the price of food rises, so does foreign real income, and this tends to make the foreign demand curve for food positively sloped. In order for the *world's* demand curve to be positively sloped, the exporter's income effect must outweigh the income effect of the importer, as well as both countries' substitution effects. In order for the market to be unstable, the exporter's income effect must in addition outweigh any positive production response of food producers at home and abroad.

Nothing automatically guarantees market stability in the relationship between income and substitution effects. Therefore, an additional assumption that the market is stable must be made. Little interest attaches to equilibria that are unstable because prices tend to run away from such equilibria. The applications of the basic trade model considered in Chapter 3 involve comparing one equilibrium with another, under the assumption that prices do approach the second equilibrium after the market is disturbed (by growth, taste changes, or transfers). Such a procedure makes sense only if the market is assumed stable. The supplement to Chapter 3 probes more deeply into the analytics of this issue.

---

[8]As the supplement to Chapter 3 proves, the criterion for stability is that the sum of the two countries' elasticities of demand for imports exceeds unity, the so-called *Marshall-Lerner condition*.

PART II

Globalization: Trade Patterns and Income Distribution

Chapter 4 ■ Technology and International Income
Distribution: The Ricardian Model
PAGE 59

Chapter 5 ■ Factor Endowments and Trade I:
The Specific Factors Model
PAGE 79

Chapter 6 ■ Factor Endowments and Trade II:
The Heckscher-Ohlin Model
PAGE 95

Chapter 7 ■ Imperfect Competition, Increasing Returns,
and Product Variety
PAGE 121

Chapter 8 ■ Resource Trade, Outsourcing,
and Product Fragmentation
PAGE 133

Chapter 9 ■ International Factor Movements:
Labor and Capital
PAGE 151

CHAPTER 4

Technology and International Income Distribution: The Ricardian Model

W hat characteristics of production help explain patterns of world trade? What are the repercussions of trade both on the international distribution of income among countries and the intranational distribution of income among workers, land, and capital? Do the forces promoting and reflecting greater globalization tend to help all trading countries? Is there a tendency for labor to be left behind as world income levels rise? Are less developed countries particularly at risk in the globalization process?

Countries, commodities, and productive factors each exhibit striking differences: Countries differ from each other in technology, climate, the skill levels of factors of production, the composition of the factor endowment base, and size. Commodities differ from each other, both in the techniques used to produce them and in their quality and appeal to consumers. Factors differ from each other in the ease with which they can leave one occupation and move to a more promising sector of the economy, or, indeed, can move from one country to another. Some countries are abundant in natural resources and land, whereas others possess relatively plentiful supplies of labor but are poorly endowed with accumulated capital. International trade can have a profound effect in realigning the functional distribution of income within as well as between countries. The models presented in Part II help reveal why various groups within a nation hold such strong views about trade policy.

The role of technology in explaining trade patterns and productivities is the focus of this chapter. Technology is constantly in the news these days, especially with concerns about wage rates for the unskilled. It is perhaps ironic that the earliest model of trade, that associated with the name of David Ricardo (1817), can be used to discuss technology as a source of trade.[1] Chapter 2 has already demonstrated the basic result concerning gains from trade: Countries can mutually benefit from trade if the relative prices of commodities differ between countries in the absence of trade. Ricardo is credited with establishing this result in a simple model in which a country's prices must reflect the relative ratio of labor costs of production. Thus, the trade pattern in a Ricardian world is determined by differences in labor productivity among countries.

---

[1] A recent edition is David Ricardo, *The Principles of Political Economy and Taxation* (Cambridge, UK: Cambridge University Press, 1981), Chapter 7.

4.1   The Ricardian Setting

The tradition in the theory of international trade of exploring issues by using models of the economy that are frugal in limiting complexity is exemplified in the Ricardian setting: Only a single productive factor (labor) is required to produce commodities, so we postpone questions of internal income distribution until the next pair of chapters. This serves as well to push to the forefront the issue of the productivity of labor and how differences among countries in *relative* productivities provide the key to explaining trade patterns. Changes in these productivities can affect relative and real wage rates for labor in different countries.

If a country is unable to trade in world markets, relative commodity prices in the Ricardian setting are described by the *labor theory of value*: Within the country, labor, the only scarce productive factor, is homogeneous and all occupations pay the same wage rate in a competitive setting in which prices are driven down to the level of costs. The relative price of clothing in a two-commodity setting is given by the ratio of the hours required to produce a unit of clothing (a_{LC}) to the hours required to produce a unit of food (a_{LF}). The reciprocals of these numbers are sometimes used instead (e.g., labor's productivity in producing food is given by $1/a_{LF}$).

These productivity figures incorporate information not only about technology but labor skills and perhaps climate as well. (For example, one of the commodities used by Ricardo was wine, and climatic differences between Portugal and England certainly would affect labor productivities in producing wine.) Higher education levels or more appropriate attitudes toward discipline in the workplace show up in higher output per unit of labor, just as would be the case with superior technology. Improvements in labor productivity are created in the classroom, in the research labs, and in attitudes of labor.

Suppose the home country's supply of labor available for employment (L) is fixed. A production-possibilities curve resembling Figure 2.4(b) can then be drawn, Figure 4.1, because it is assumed the labor input figures for each commodity are known constants—they do not change with levels of output although they would be reduced if there is technical progress. The slope of the schedule is thus the constant ratio, a_{LC}/a_{LF}. If full employment prevails, as we assume, the labor supply, L, is assigned partly to clothing—given by the product of the labor required per unit of clothing, a_{LC}, and the output of clothing, x_C, and partly to food, $a_{LF}x_F$. (Economists sometimes refer to the *extensive* margin (x_i) and the *intensive* margin (a_{Li}).) The full-employment condition is thus the equation of the transformation schedule, shown in Equation 4.1:

$$a_{LC}x_C + a_{LF}x_F = L \tag{4.1}$$

The endpoints of the transformation schedule show the maximum amount of each commodity that could be produced (by channeling all labor for that purpose), and the slope shows how much food must be sacrificed in order to release enough labor to produce another unit of clothing.

A closed economy must rely on its own production to satisfy its consumption needs. Therefore, relative prices in such an economy are shown by the constant slope of the transformation schedule. The pretrade consumption (and production) pattern would be illustrated in Figure 4.1 by point A, at which an indifference curve (y_0) is

FIGURE 4.1

The Ricardian Production
Possibilities Schedule

The opportunity cost of producing
clothing is shown by the slope of
the straight-line transformation
schedule, which is the ratio of
labor coefficients a_{LC}/a_{LF}. Before
international trade, the country
produces and consumes at A,
with welfare levels shown by the
indifference curve, y_0.

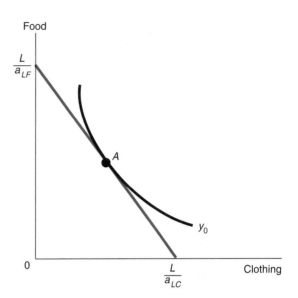

tangent to the straight-line transformation schedule. These remarks easily generalize to
a closed economy with any number of commodities. Relative prices are all technologically determined by the invariant labor productivities. As will soon become clear, this
view of the determinants of prices is no longer applicable once the economy is opened
to trade.

4.2   Free-Trade Equilibrium

The labor theory of value, identifying commodity price ratios with labor cost ratios,
must come to grief in a world of international trade. Why? Because cost ratios differ
between countries, whereas price ratios do not when commodities are freely traded.
The resolution? A country may be forced by international competition to abandon
some line of production. If so, it is precisely *because* the international price of that commodity falls short of the costs per unit required to produce it at home, so that no local
production can take place.

Figure 4.2 illustrates a free-trade equilibrium in which it has been assumed the
home country possesses a comparative advantage in the production of clothing, as
reflected in Inequality 4.2:

$$\frac{a_{LF}^*}{a_{LC}^*} < \frac{a_{LF}}{a_{LC}} \tag{4.2}$$

In this illustration it is assumed in free trade there are equilibrium terms of trade that
call for each country to be completely specialized in producing (and exporting) the
commodity in which it has a comparative advantage. The rationale for the gains from

FIGURE 4.2

Free-Trade Equilibrium

Pretrade equilibrium at home is shown by point A in the left-hand diagram, (a); abroad it is shown by A^* in the right-hand diagram, (b). Equilibrium terms of trade are illustrated by the slope of the dashed line for each country. With trade the home country produces at A and consumes at B; the foreign country produces at E^* and consumes at B^*. Each country gains from trade. The trade triangles match.

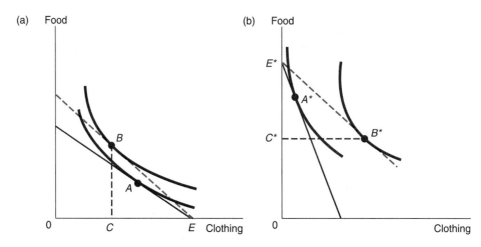

trade is similar to that described for the basic trade model in Part I. What is special about the Ricardian model is the potentially drastic consequence of trade for patterns of production. In each country not only are some resources attracted to the export sector, *all* resources flow there. Clearly this reflects the assumption of constant opportunity costs as opposed to increasing opportunity costs (along a bowed-out production-possibilities curve). Each country gains from trade, with free-trade consumption points, B and B^*, lying on higher indifference curves than do pretrade consumption bundles, A and A^*. Note that the absolute values of labor productivities have no role to play in determining the pattern of trade or the terms of trade. These depend on comparative cost *ratios*.

Country Size

Does the assumption of constant (labor) costs necessarily require each country to become completely specialized with trade? No. For example, if one country is much larger than the other, the world terms of trade could settle at the cost ratio of the large country. If the world were made up of the United States and Mexico, it would be impossible for Mexico, with a presumed comparative advantage in tomatoes, to supply the entire American market. In such a case, world prices would have to reflect American costs, so that some American tomato production also would take place.

FIGURE 4.3

The World Transformation Schedule

The locus *ABC* shows world output possibilities with free trade. Free trade generally enlarges world outputs over autarky (e.g., the move from *G* to *B*).

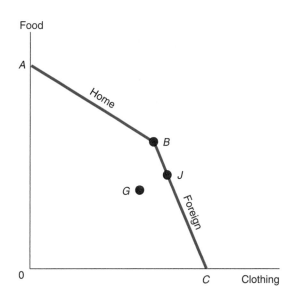

World Production Possibilities

If these two countries engage in free trade, it is possible to sketch out a *world production-possibilities schedule*. Figure 4.3 depicts such a locus, and two extreme points on it are easy to calculate: Point *A* adds up the maximum possible food output in the two countries and point *C* does the analogous job for clothing production. From point *A* the diagram shows that if the world wants to produce any clothing, the country with the comparative advantage in producing clothing (the home country) should be first off the mark. The foreign country will be drawn into clothing production only after the home country can no longer expand its production, and then only if "the price is right." The foreign country, with the comparative *dis*advantage in producing clothing, can be enticed to do so only if the world relative price of clothing reaches the height of its cost ratio, shown by the slope of its transformation schedule. Locus *ABJC* in Figure 4.3 represents the best attainable outputs for the world in a free-trade equilibrium.

The World Market for Food

The trade triangles in Figure 4.2 illustrate the free-trade equilibrium. The world transformation schedule in Figure 4.3 illustrates in a different way the world supply conditions, and world demand conditions could easily be illustrated by indifference curves if the two countries shared the same (homothetic) taste pattern. Suppose so, and imagine one such curve tangent to the world transformation schedule at point *J*. This would correspond to the foreign country producing both commodities and the home country specializing completely in clothing. The kind of equilibrium illustrated in Figure 4.2, with the world price ratio lying strictly between the cost ratios in each country, would

FIGURE 4.4

The World Market for Food

The world supply curve is composed of two horizontal steps, each at the price corresponding to a country's relative labor cost of food; the vertical sections are at outputs A and B.

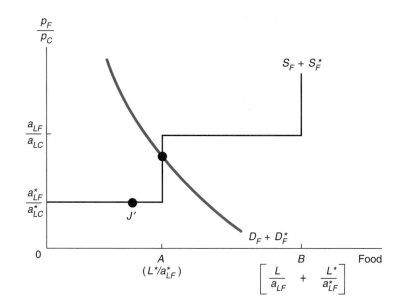

be shown in Figure 4.3 by a world indifference curve passing through the "kink" point, B, with slope equal to an intermediate price ratio.

A more traditional demand/supply diagram for the world market in one of the commodities (food) is drawn in Figure 4.4. The world supply curve is a step-function: Only if food's relative price rises to the foreign cost ratio, a^*_{LF}/a^*_{LC}, can any food be produced, and if p_F/p_C rises above the home cost ratio, a_{LF}/a_{LC}, both countries will devote their entire labor forces to producing food. Kink-point B in Figure 4.3 corresponds to the vertical riser for prices in between the two cost ratios. With the foreign country specialized in food there, world output equals L^*/a^*_{LF}. The world demand curve may cut in this section, as portrayed, or perhaps at a point such as J', corresponding to point J in Figure 4.3. Either of these diagrams confirms that any world equilibrium must require at least one country to be completely specialized, and perhaps both.

4.3 International Wage Comparisons and Productivities

The Ricardian setting is the first of several models displaying an economy with a given technology and resource base (not mobile internationally) in which a full equilibrium can be determined, either in autarky, with national demands balanced by national supplies, or in a free-trade equilibrium with a supply/demand balance at the world level. In either case equilibrium determines output levels, commodity prices, and factor prices. (This is not quite true because as we observed in Chapter 2, only price *ratios* can be determined in the absence of information on monetary aggregates.) Of particular interest here is the connection between wage rates and productivities, especially in the case of international trade when countries might specialize to different commodities.

In any economy, wage rates are closely linked to productivity. This relationship is exact in a model that assumes competition exists. Begin the argument by considering the general relationship between costs and prices in the home country. In a competitive *equilibrium* the unit costs of producing any commodity cannot fall short of that commodity's market price. The reason is simple: If unit costs in food production were less than the price of food, the consequent profits would signal new entrants into the food industry. Enlarging food output would drive down the price of food; increasing the demand for labor would cause the wage rate to be bid up. This process, whereby new firms are attracted to the food industry, would continue until unit costs were raised enough to equal price. Unit costs can, however, exceed price, even in a competitive equilibrium. You may wonder why an entrepreneur would continue producing food if it is priced lower than the labor costs of production. In this competitive model the answer is none would. Therefore, local food production would be zero.

The Competitive Profit Conditions

Although we have emphasized the importance of *relative* prices in determining trade patterns, it becomes convenient now to refer to absolute prices in terms of a common unit of account. For example, the wage rate at home will be referred to as w, meaning dollars per labor-hour. An expression such as w/p_F eliminates the nominal currency unit of account and denotes food units per hours of work. With this in mind, consider the *competitive profit conditions* shown in Inequalities 4.3 and 4.4:

$$a_{LC}w \geqq p_C \tag{4.3}$$

$$a_{LF}w \geqq p_F \tag{4.4}$$

These inequalities formally express the argument in the preceding paragraph. A competitive equilibrium must be characterized by an equality between unit cost and price if production is carried on in that equilibrium. Unit cost never can be less than price in a competitive equilibrium. Unit costs may exceed price, but only if all producers leave the industry. A similar set of conditions would, of course, apply to the foreign country, except that the wage rate abroad, denoted by w^*, need not be the same as at home, although with free trade the price of either commodity will be identical in the two countries.

Productivity and Wages

Labor's physical productivity is measured in each industry by the inverse of the labor coefficient. For example, $1/a_{LC}$ is the number of units of clothing that can be produced with an input of one hour of labor.[2] If this is multiplied by the price of clothing, to obtain $p_C \cdot (1/a_{LC})$, a measure is derived of the value of labor's productivity in clothing. Therefore, the competitive profit condition can be restated as:

   (i) *In any industry with positive output, the wage rate must equal the value of labor's (average or marginal) productivity.*

   (ii) *In any industry forced to shut down because of international competition, it is because the prevailing wage rate would exceed the value of labor's productivity.*

---

[2]Because the input coefficients, a_{LC} and a_{LF}, are assumed to be constant, $1/a_{LC}$ denotes both labor's average product and its marginal product.

International Wage Comparisons

In studying the link between productivities and wages for our two countries, it becomes convenient to embed them in a world of many countries producing just food and clothing. This allows us to consider not only the case in which our two countries have balanced trade with each other, with the home country exporting clothing and the foreign country food, but to consider, as well, world market outcomes in which our two countries share a common trade and production pattern. Indeed, we start with such a situation: Suppose the relative price of clothing in world markets is so low that even the home country, which possesses a comparative advantage in clothing, is driven to put all its labor into food. What will be the resulting wage comparison? At home,

$$a_{LF}w = p_F$$

whereas abroad,

$$a_{LF}^*w^* = p_F$$

Both countries face a common world food price, p_F. Dividing these two equalities reveals that:

$$\frac{w}{w^*} = \frac{1/a_{LF}}{1/a_{LF}^*} \tag{4.5}$$

Thus the concept of *absolute* advantage comes into its own: If the foreign country's labor force is twice as productive in producing food as the home country's, its workers will earn twice as much if world prices drive both of them to produce the same commodity, food. Similarly, a very high price of clothing in world markets would encourage both of our countries to specialize in clothing, and their relative wages would be a direct reflection of productivities in the clothing sector. These provide the limits for relative wages.

Now suppose the world's relative price of clothing lies between the cost ratios in the two countries (as in Figure 4.2), with home producers responding by producing just clothing. Thus:

$$a_{LC}w = p_C$$

while in the foreign country,

$$a_{LF}^*w^* = p_F$$

Dividing these two yields Equation 4.6:

$$\frac{w}{w^*} = \frac{1/a_{LC}}{1/a_{LF}^*} \cdot \frac{p_C}{p_F} \tag{4.6}$$

Therefore, if countries produce different commodities, a comparison of their wage rates reflects not only the productivities of their labor forces in the good produced in that country, but the terms of exchange between commodities as well. All of this is

FIGURE 4.5

Relative Wages and the Terms of Trade

If the terms of trade lie strictly between the cost ratios in the two countries, an improvement in the home terms of trade has a proportionally favorable effect on the home relative wage. If the terms of trade allow both countries to produce the same commodity, relative wages reflect labor's productivity in this commodity.

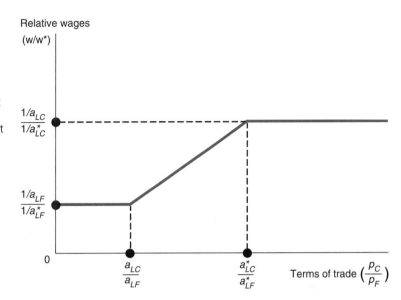

summarized in Figure 4.5, showing that if the terms of trade lie strictly between the cost ratios in the two countries, a 10 percent increase in clothing's relative price would raise home wages by 10 percent relative to foreign wages.

Suppose the home country is more efficient than the foreign country in *every* line, although relatively even more efficient in clothing than in food. With trade, the home country then imports food from abroad. Does this mean residents at home are purchasing food from a (foreign) source that is more expensive than food locally available? No. Despite the fact that a^*_{LF} is (by assumption) higher than a_{LF}, this is compensated for by the fact that foreign wages must be lower than those at home. This discussion of the limits to the wage rate comparison shows that if one country's labor has an absolute advantage in every occupation, it must receive a higher wage rate.

Viewed from the high-wage country, what can be made of the argument that cheap foreign labor threatens to undermine our competitive position in a wide array of industries? This is the so-called *pauper-labor argument* and is invalid because low foreign wage rates are solidly grounded in (and caused by) less efficient labor productivities.

Recent International Wage Disparities

The Bureau of Labor Statistics in the U.S. Department of Labor publishes hourly compensation costs (in U.S. $) for production workers in manufacturing. For 2003 these show (rounded-off) wage rates of $30 for Germany (West only), $20 for Japan, and $10 for South Korea. Where does the United States fit in? It comes in at $22.

Much has been made of low-wage rates in countries such as China and India, especially in comparison with those in the United States. Although wage rates are much lower, so is productivity. In 2002 Ceglowski and Golub calculate that on average the Chinese level of productivity was approximately 9% of the American figure. However, the wage rate was only 3% of that in the United States. Evidently an undervalued Chinese exchange rate is largely responsible for China's relative low unit labor costs.[3]

4.4 A Many-Commodity and Many-Country World

The real world is made up of many countries, producing and exchanging many commodities. A great advantage of the Ricardian model is its drastic simplicity in how goods are produced (only labor, with constant cost technology). As a consequence the model can yield insights into this complicated higher dimensional world. This is especially the case in understanding how a small country would react when exposed for the first time to free trade in a world of many countries and commodities. This small country has relied on its own technology, as summarized by a set of labor input coefficients for all the commodities it consumes. Following Ricardo's model, it is assumed the country's technology is determined by local conditions and need bear no resemblance to technology and labor skills found in other countries. It is also assumed the country is "small," so that once this nation is allowed to trade, preexisting world prices are not disturbed. The small country is a price-taker, much like an individual or firm in a competitive market.

What Gets Produced at Home?

What will this country produce and trade when contact is made with the world economy? Suppose the new trading country adopts the same currency as the rest of the world.[4] How do local costs of production compare with world prices? Given local technology, everything depends on the wage rate. If the wage rate is ridiculously low, the new country might find it could produce all, or almost all, commodities at a cost lower than the world price. This could not represent an equilibrium, for the wage rate would be bid up. Suppose the wage rate is so high that costs locally exceed world prices for all commodities. This clearly would not represent equilibrium either. Would it be correct to split the difference and argue that the wage rate probably will settle at a level allowing the country an edge in monetary costs in, for example, half the commodities, while for the other half world prices are below local costs? No. If local technology is really unrelated to that in the rest of the world, this small country likely will produce only *one* commodity, and its wage rate will be determined by labor productivity in the single commodity in which this country has the greatest comparative advantage.

---

[3]These figures are reported in Janet Ceglowski and Stephen Golub, "Just How Low Are China's Labor Costs?", unpublished manuscript, 2005.
[4]This is not the place to launch into a discussion of different currencies and the exchange rates that link them together (see Part IV). It will become clear, however, that a country can change its exchange rate as it pleases so long as the wage rate is changed proportionately.

So which commodity is best produced at home? Calculate for each commodity, i, the ratio between the world price p_i and the technical labor-hours required in this country to produce one unit of commodity i, a_{Li}. This ratio, p_i/a_{Li}, shows the quantity of dollars obtainable per labor-hour if labor is used to produce i and the output is sold at world prices. Clearly, the commodity with the highest p_i/a_{Li} ratio is the most attractive. The forces of competition ensure that this ratio is precisely the wage rate. If the wage were lower than this, entrepreneurs would rush to employ all the labor they could to produce i, which would yield a positive profit over and above payments to labor. Such competition would drive up the wage. Could the wage be higher than the highest p_i/a_{Li}? No, because then to produce any commodity would involve losses. If the wage exactly equals the highest p_i/a_{Li}, it would exceed (barring ties) such a ratio for any other commodity.

If such a small country would hear complaints from all the industries that trade has shut down that trade is unfair to workers in these industries, what can be made of this argument? The reason these industries are wiped out by trade is that the wage rate in the country is *too high*! If all labor is of the same homogeneous quality (as we have assumed), they all find work in the country's industry displaying labor's greatest comparative advantage and all laborers gain. Output and employment in that industry become much higher than in autarky because it now produces for the world market.

All this assumes the country is small. But suppose, instead, it is large enough that its entrance into the world's trading arena has an effect on world prices. Being relatively large, the country may well end up producing more than one tradable item, with world prices now adjusting to reflect the country's own technology for producing these goods. We now turn to a scenario in which the world comprises two large countries and in which new discoveries result in improved technology in one of them, with repercussions on prices, trading patterns, and relative wages.

4.5   Winners and Losers from Productivity Shocks

Meetings of international organizations such as the World Trade Organization (WTO), the World Bank, and the International Monetary Fund used to be considered rather dull affairs as far as the media were concerned. Riots in the streets of Seattle at the 1999 meetings of the WTO and subsequent disturbances in places like Cancún, Mexico, all served to highlight the public awareness that globalization and changes in world trade seem to create losers as well as winners. Unskilled labor in advanced countries seemed to be in danger of job losses to emerging production sites in China, India, and other developing countries. Environmentalists were also concerned that expanded trade would seriously contribute to global warming. Of course any shock to productivity and prices, such as new discoveries leading to so-called Dutch Disease problems (discussed in Chapter 5) can easily lead to unemployment, even if temporary. Changes in the patterns of world trade are no exception, but economists often try to look beyond the period of temporary disruptions and at the type of equilibria expected to emerge once resources are reallocated. Academic economists have had their voices heard as well, especially on the issue whether increased globalization is a boon to all countries.[5] The message we sounded in Part I about the mutual gains expected by all countries in the move from autarky to free trade is not the issue. Instead, once countries are engaged in trade, further changes represented by increased globalization may *not* be of benefit to all.

This chapter's Ricardian model is not general enough for the purposes of discussing whether globalization can create winners and losers *within* countries—the next few chapters address that issue. But the simple structure of the Ricardian model makes it ideal in investigating how growth, productivity changes, and changes in world prices directly affect the *international* distribution of income.

Consider the repercussions of an improvement in technology that is localized to one sector in one country. This clearly represents an improvement in overall world welfare. As for the repercussions of this productivity shock, three possibilities exist: (1) Both countries might gain, (2) the country that experiences the productivity improvement might lose, or (3) the other country might lose. That is, if greater globalization is brought about by such localized technological progress, both countries might share in the gains or one country might lose as the other gains. To link up with current policy debates, denote the two countries as the United States and China. Between them they produce many commodities. Let the United States have a *comparative* advantage in the lower numbered commodities with China possessing a comparative advantage in the higher numbered ones. In a free-trade equilibrium the two countries either produce one of the commodities in common (suppose this is commodity *15*) or are specialized to different commodity groups (the United States producing, say, the first fourteen commodities and China specialized to the rest).

We begin by assuming that both countries share in the production of commodity *15*. By the competitive profit conditions, their wage rates are connected by the relative productivities for the commodity produced in common. If the United States has an absolute advantage in the fifteenth commodity, the American wage rate will be higher than in China. Suppose, now, that China develops a superior technology for producing some commodity that it alone produces, say that of the twentieth, but that this does not alter the ranking of commodities by comparative advantage. This is a case in which both countries must gain. To see this, let (arbitrarily) the nominal price of the commonly produced fifteenth commodity be set at unity, which fixes the nominal wage rate in each country. The price of commodity *20* must therefore fall by an amount exactly equivalent to the extent of technical progress, with no other commodity price changes in either country. The consequence: The *real* wage rate in *each* country must increase. That is, the real income of workers (the only income recipients) in both countries goes up by an amount proportional both to the price fall and to their consumption levels of

[5]The *New York Times* posted a widely read article on September 9, 2004, entitled, "Elder Challenges Outsourcing's Orthodoxy," concerning Paul Samuelson's suggestion that some economists, such as Alan Greenspan, former chairman of the Federal Reserve, and Jagdish Bhagwati of Columbia University, had gone too far in celebrating the widespread gains from globalization. As Samuelson pointed out, some countries are adversely affected by changes in the terms of trade that are brought about, say, by growth of countries such as China and India. Samuelson's article, published in the *Journal of Economic Perspectives* (Summer 2004, pp. 135–146), uses the Ricardian model discussed in this chapter.

the commodity that has gone down in price. International trading links have ensured that the initial localized gain in world welfare gets spread to both trading nations.

Suppose, instead, that the United States produces the first fourteen commodities and China the remainder. With no commodity produced in common, the price level (and nominal wage rate) in one country is divorced from that in the other. Now let the Chinese again experience an improvement in their labor productivity in producing the twentieth commodity (without disturbing the ordering of commodities by comparative advantage). If commodity *15* is again selected to be the *numeraire*, so that its nominal price is fixed at unity, the nominal level of Chinese wages is also unaltered (because China produces this commodity) as are the prices of all other goods produced by China (except for the reduced price of commodity *20*). But what happens to the price level of all fourteen commodities produced in the United States? Their prices relative to each other all remain the same, so let us lump them all together and label this aggregate commodity *A*. If the price of this aggregate commodity remained the same (as in our earlier case when the two countries produced a commodity in common), clearly every worker in both countries would gain because of the reduced price of commodity *20*. But if no commodity is produced in common, the American price level could rise (in which case American workers would gain) or could fall, and if that fall were sufficiently large, American workers could lose.

To probe these possibilities consider Figure 4.6, showing initial world demand and supply for the American aggregate commodity *A*. With the American labor force assumed fixed and fully employed, the supply curve is drawn vertical and remains in position because the technical progress takes place in China. The world demand curve, $(D_A + D_A^*)$, however, may shift after technical progress, in either direction. Consider world demand at the initial price, p_A^0, after the technology shock. World real incomes (in both countries at the initial price) increase, and this by itself would tend to shift the

FIGURE 4.6

Technological Progress

Commodity *A* represents an aggregate of all commodities produced in America. Technological progress is assumed to take place in commodity *20*, produced only in China, and no commodity is produced in common by both countries. If prices in China for all commodities produced there (except commodity *20*) are kept constant, the price of America's aggregate, p_A, will increase if income effects are stronger than substitution effects, but will fall if substitution effects are stronger.

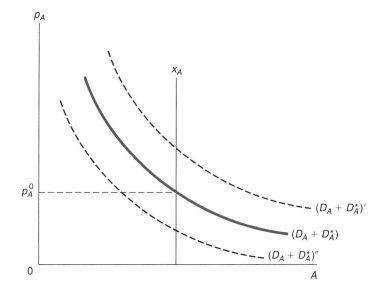

world demand curve to the right. However, even though America produces none of the commodity (*20*) that has gone down in price, this commodity might be a good substitute in taste patterns (in both countries) for some or all of the commodities in the American aggregate, and this force by itself would encourage a leftward shift in world demand.

If these two effects, the substitution and income effects, exactly balance, there would be no shift in demand.[6] Consider, now, the two alternative possibilities: (1) If income effects are relatively stronger than substitution effects, the demand curve shifts to the right, say to $(D_A + D_A^*)'$ in Figure 4.6. Furthermore, if the resulting rise in the relative price of all goods produced in America is sufficiently large, China will end up worse off than originally. This outcome follows from the strong deterioration in China's terms of trade and is an example of Chapter 3's discussion of immiserizing growth. (2) By contrast, if substitution effects are relatively strong, the world demand curve in Figure 4.6 would shift to the left, to $(D_A + D_A^*)''$, and if commodity *20* is an especially good substitute in consumer tastes with some or all of the goods comprising the American aggregate, *A*, the technology shock in China could so drain world demand away from *A* that American terms of trade deteriorate despite the fall in the import price for commodity *20*.

To conclude, a favorable improvement in Chinese productivity in producing some commodity not produced in the United States could benefit both countries, or might actually hurt China (if demand elasticities throughout the world are very low), or, by contrast, might hurt American real wages (if demand elasticities are high and biased toward reducing demand for American-produced commodities).[7]

4.6   Nontraded Commodities

Thus far the Ricardian model has neglected the costs involved in transporting commodities from one location to another, as well as artificial impediments (tariffs, quotas) to international trade. Realistically, no commodity can be freely shipped from one country to another. Theory abstracts from many aspects of reality, however, and trade theory often neglects the costs of transport and the discrepancies they create between prices of traded commodities in different locales. For some purposes, however, it is convenient to consider those commodities for which transport costs are so high that no international trade can take place. The Ricardian model's production structure is so simple that introducing commodities whose markets are purely local is a relatively easy task.

Recall the case of a country too small to be able to influence world prices. If these prices do not reflect the small country's own technology, that country picks the best of

---

[6]This case, in which substitution and income effects precisely balance, leads to constant expenditure shares on every commodity.

[7]As an exercise (see Problem 7) consider what would happen if both countries produce commodity *15* and China's technology for this commodity improves somewhat but not enough to wipe out American production in this sector.

the traded goods to produce, the one with the highest p_i/a_{Li} ratio. The wage rate equals this maximum figure for dollars per labor-hour in producing tradables. Suppose there is also some commodity (call it N) that cannot be obtained from the rest of the world (for example, personal services supplied by local labor—lawyers, physicians, etc.), but for which there is local demand. Let a_{LN} represent the (constant) labor cost of obtaining one unit of the nontraded commodity. Then N must be priced so that

$$p_N = a_{LN}w \tag{4.7}$$

That is, the price of the nontraded good is determined by local technology and prices of traded goods (that serve to determine the wage rate).

A Composite Traded Commodity

Suppose world prices for all the commodities that can enter trade are fixed. It is then possible to think of a *composite* traded commodity, an aggregate of all the individual traded commodities as was the aggregate, A, in Section 4.5. The demand for such a composite behaves in the same regular way as the demand for any single commodity. Because all tradables are assumed to have a fixed price relationship with each other, any arbitrary unit of output of the composite can be adopted. In particular, the dollar value can be considered a unit. Consider the transformation schedule FAJ in Figure 4.7. Distance $0F$ measures the maximum dollar value of tradables that can be produced if all labor is devoted to producing the tradable item, call it i, that maximizes the number of dollars that can be earned per hour's worth of labor. If, instead, the entire labor force produced the nontradable commodity, quantity $0J$ (in natural physical units) of

FIGURE 4.7

Nontradables and Tradables

A composite traded good can be formed if world prices of tradables are constant. Equilibrium production and consumption response for nontradables can be shown by the tangency of transformation schedules and indifference curves.

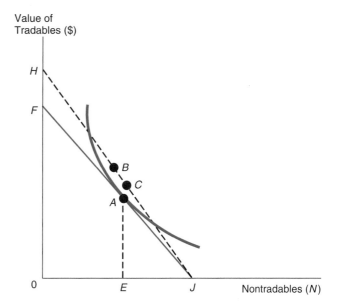

commodity N could be produced. With Ricardian technology, the transformation schedule must be a straight line whose slope is the dollar price of the nontradable. Figure 4.7 also shows an indifference curve tangent to FAJ at point A, the free-trade equilibrium for this small country.

A word of warning: Figure 4.7's depiction of an equilibrium where an indifference curve is tangent to the transformation curve may remind you of the way in which equilibrium for a *closed economy* is described. The reason for this is that the details of the composition of trade are suppressed in the diagram. Distance $0E$ represents the quantity of nontradables, N, that is produced. It also shows how much N is consumed in equilibrium. These must balance. Distance AE shows two things: It shows the dollar value of *production* of tradable commodity i, the good reflecting the optimal use of labor among the set of all tradables. It also shows the aggregate value of *consumption* of *all* tradables. Hidden from view is the allocation of this amount over all the commodities purchasable on world markets. Figure 4.7 does not deny trade; instead, point A shows a position of *balanced trade*. It shows that the aggregate value of consumption of all tradables (spread out over many commodities) equals the aggregate value of production of all tradables (concentrated on one product, commodity i).

Technological Change in a Single Tradable Commodity

Suppose, now, that conditions of production at home change, with no change in world prices. In particular, suppose that some new process is discovered whereby the quantity of labor required to produce a unit of commodity j is reduced, so much so that p_j/a_{Lj} now exceeds p_i/a_{Li}. With Ricardian-type technology, the impact on this economy is simple but drastic. It is drastic in the sense that local production of commodity i is wiped out. The new method of producing commodity j establishes it as the new best way of earning dollars on the world market, at the expense of the previous best-traded industry, i. However, an asymmetry now becomes apparent: The nontradable sector is not competed away in the manner in which commodity i is. In Figure 4.7 the change in technology leads to the new schedule $HBCJ$. If all labor were devoted to tradables, approximately 20 percent greater value could be produced by switching from i to j. The wage rate is driven up by this amount, as is the dollar price of nontradables. The N sector can pass on its higher costs to consumers; the ith sector, competing at given world prices for i, cannot.

The rise in p_N may cause consumption and production of nontradables to fall, as is shown in the move from A to B in Figure 4.7. Indeed, this would be the case if demand for tradables as a group were elastic. The new indifference curve, however, could be tangent at C; substitution effects might be weak and newly created incomes might spill over primarily in the direction of nontradables. That is, despite the wage-provoked increase in the price of nontradables, this sector of the economy actually may expand.

The kind of reaction described here, in which progress in one tradable sector spells trouble for another, may be caused by changes in world prices instead of technical progress. Chapter 5 returns to this kind of question in a model in which nonlabor resources also are required for production.

4.7 Summary

The Ricardian model is both the oldest and the simplest model of trade in which the details of production are fully incorporated. It is an especially useful model to examine an important general question: If one country in a trading equilibrium experiences a productivity improvement in some commodity that it produces, how are real incomes affected in other countries? And how do the repercussions of consequent price changes affect the real income of the originating country?

The simplifications embedded in the Ricardian model serve to highlight some basic truths about world trade, and these may require modification in the next several chapters. In particular:

1. The pattern of trade is dictated solely by the supply side. In particular, in the two-commodity case the home country must export clothing and import food if the invariant labor productivity in clothing in the home country is *relatively* higher than that abroad. This assumption was embodied in Inequality 4.2. In more general models, both supply and demand differences contribute to the relationship between pretrade commodity-price ratios in the two countries and therefore to the pattern of trade. (In an extended Ricardian model, with many countries and commodities, demand does play a role in determining trade patterns.)

2. If the world terms of trade lie strictly between the cost ratios in the two countries, each will specialize completely in the production of one commodity (clothing in the home country and food abroad). This severe shift of resources is not characteristic of the models of trade to be considered next, in which a country might engage in trade while supporting an import-competing industry.

3. The Ricardian model places extreme emphasis on differences in technology between countries, without explaining why methods of production should differ. Subsequent models incorporate the influence of nonlabor factors of production affecting labor productivities and allow a distinction between similarity in technical knowledge and similarity in techniques of production actually adopted. (Rice may be grown differently in Thailand and in Louisiana, even though no technological secrets may be guarded.)

4. The spillover effects of technological change in one country on real incomes at home and abroad are simple to analyze in a Ricardian model because technology firmly binds relative costs of goods produced within a country. Progress in one country may benefit all. Alternatively, the home country may lose (the case of immiserizing growth) or foreigners may lose (if the markets for their products are strongly disrupted by the reduction of costs at home).

5. Some commodities do not enter international trade because of high transport costs. In a world in which technology and/or prices for some traded commodities change, nontraded commodities are not subject to as intense competitive pressure as tradables. In the Ricardian model for a small country, progress in one tradable sector may completely wipe out another sector. These extremes are moderated in models that we examine in subsequent chapters.

CHAPTER PROBLEMS

1. Draw the array of world outputs that free trade allows, as is illustrated in Figure 4.3. What is the menu of the *worst* combinations of outputs? Show that it is made up of two linear segments if full employment is maintained in each country.

2. In the discussion of Section 4.5 suppose in a three-commodity setting that both the United States and China produce commodity *3*. What can be said about the distribution of income between these countries if American demand switches a small amount from commodity *2* to commodity *3*? If American technology for producing commodity *1* improves?

3. Suppose costs of production depend only on labor costs and to produce a unit of each commodity in each country takes the number of labor-hours shown.

	Commodity A	Commodity B	Commodity C
Home	10	10	10
Foreign	3	5	7

   a. In which commodity does the home country possess the greatest comparative advantage?
   b. If the foreign wage rate is $1 per labor-hour and a free-trade equilibrium is reached, what is the most that the home wage rate can be? Why?
   c. If the foreign wage rate is $1 per labor-hour, what would a possible home wage rate be so that the home country can produce only one commodity? Which commodity would it be?

4. In a Ricardian world, with labor the only factor of production being paid, the following table gives the constant labor costs per unit of producing different commodities for countries α and β.

	Wheat	Cars	Tankers	Atomic Reactors	Tractors
α	10	10	10	10	10
β	5	8	10	12	14

   a. In which goods does country α have an absolute advantage? Why?
   b. In which goods does country β have a comparative advantage? Why?
   c. Which country would export tankers? Explain.

5. Consider the world to consist of two countries (home and foreign) made up of individuals with identical (and "homothetic") taste patterns. Portray these by a set of smoothly bowed-in indifference curves (which are radial blowups of each other in the homothetic case). Suppose production in the home country requires two labor-hours per unit of food and only one labor-hour per unit of clothing, whereas the foreign country's figures for food and clothing are just the opposite. The foreign country's labor force consists of 1 million labor-hours.

   a. If the home country is small relative to the foreign country, one of the countries will produce both goods. Which country? What will be food's relative price?
   b. If the home country is large relative to the foreign country, one of the countries will produce both goods. Which country? What will be food's relative price?

   c. Construct world supply and demand schedules for food, with p_F/p_C on the vertical axis and world food output on the horizontal.

6. A small country has been in total isolation, with labor input coefficients (labor is the only factor of production) shown by $a_{L1} = 10; a_{L2} = 8; a_{L3} = 12;$ and $a_{L4} = 7$.

   a. In this autarky state how many units of the first commodity would be required to exchange for a single unit of the third commodity?

   b. This country is now open to free trade with the rest of the world. Dollar prices in the rest of the world are given by $p_1 = 1; p_2 = 8; p_3 = 10;$ and $p_4 = 2$. What is the pattern of production in this small country after trade is opened up?

   c. Show what happens to the real income of a worker in the small country who consumes only the fourth commodity before and after trade.

7. In Section 4.5 it was assumed that China gets better at producing a commodity not produced in America. But suppose both countries do produce commodity *15* in common, and that Chinese productivity in producing this commodity improves, but not to the extent that would wipe out American production. What happens to American real income? Would American real income be reduced if America *is* a net importer of commodity *15*?

SUGGESTIONS FOR FURTHER READING

Graham, Frank. *The Theory of International Values* (Princeton: Princeton University Press, 1948). Many numerical examples of the many-commodity Ricardian case.

Jones, Ronald W. "Technical Progress and Real Incomes in a Ricardian Trade Model," Chapter 17, in R. W. Jones, *International Trade: Essays in Theory* (Amsterdam: North-Holland, 1979). A more complete discussion of Section 4.5.

Krugman, Paul. *Pop Internationalism* (Cambridge: MIT Press, 1996). An easy but valuable read. See especially pp. 49–68.

Ricardo, David. *The Principles of Political Economy and Taxation* (New York: Penguin, 1971). Chapter 7 is the classic source, with the examples of England and Portugal producing wine and cloth cited in most textbooks.

Samuelson, Paul A. "Where Ricardo and Mill Rebut and Confirm Arguments of Mainstream Economists Supporting Globalization," *Journal of Economic Perspectives*, 18 (2004): 135–146. A critique of arguments for the benefits of greater globalization.

APPENDIX

Transitional Unemployment

Much of the current criticism of movements toward freer trade, especially in the United States, focuses on the possibility that labor in some sectors is thrown out of work. There is no doubt that changes in world prices or technological progress can affect some

FIGURE 4.A.1

Unemployment in Transition

Autarky equilibrium is at *A* and free-trade equilibrium production is at *C*. The transition from *A* to *C* may involve some temporary unemployment, as shown along path *AGC*, but the economy still gains. Even if production is at *E*, the economy is better off than consuming at *A* in autarky.

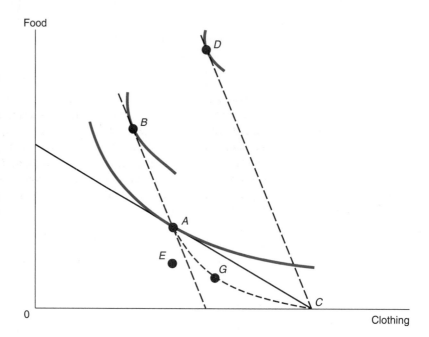

sectors adversely, and that during the transition phase to a new equilibrium there could easily be found certain factors of production that suffer a period of unemployment. But would the social arithmetic then conclude that such changes in world prices or technology are harmful? One defense would suggest that *after* the adjustments have taken place, the community will have benefited. Figure 4.A.1 illustrates how a movement from autarky to free trade when a country is presented with trading opportunities at different prices could result in gains even *during* the transition process when some labor becomes unemployed.

In autarky the community produces and consumes at point *A*. If it could trade at prices reflecting lower relative prices for food (and thus a higher relative price for clothing), the free-trade production point moves to *C*, with complete specialization in clothing, and consumption moves to point *D*, showing a substantial increase in real income. Note that in Chapter 2 we discussed the case in which resources are trapped in their separate occupations so that production remains at *A* even with trade. Consumers still gain by the movement from *A* to *B*. The dotted curve *AGC* in Figure 4.A.1 shows a possible transition path along which labor is increasingly hired in the clothing sector, but not at the same rate at which it is released from producing food. At point *G*, for example, some labor is unemployed, and such labor has lost out. But a budget line drawn through *G* with free-trade prices would reveal that the community is better off than in autarky, so that some unemployment may not imply overall losses. Indeed, consider point *E*: Here no extra labor has been hired by the clothing sector while some labor has been laid off in the food sector. And yet the community would still gain from trade with production at *E*. To convince yourself, draw a budget line through *E* at free-trade prices and compare the indifference curve that can be reached with the original curve tangent at *A*.

CHAPTER 5

Factor Endowments and Trade I: The Specific Factors Model

C ountries differ considerably in the range of productive factors located within their borders. Such asymmetries in factor endowments can be expected heavily to influence the pattern of production when international trade is allowed, in a manner not captured in the Ricardian labor-only scenario discussed in the preceding chapter. Links between factor endowments and the pattern of trade, as well as the consequences of international trade on the rewards earned by the various productive factors, are analyzed in this and the succeeding chapter.

In exploring these issues we take a two-step approach. In this chapter we add capital and land to the use of labor in rounding out the classical trinity of productive factors. However, whereas we retain the Ricardian assumption that labor is homogeneous in quality and freely mobile among productive sectors of the economy, we require that capital can only be employed in producing clothing and that land is *specific* in its use in producing food. Thus labor is the only mobile factor of production. An alternative interpretation of this specific-factors model is also considered, one in which the only input in addition to labor is capital, but in the short run the form in which capital is available in one sector (say tractors in the food sector) makes it useless in the other (say the clothing sector needs textile machinery). This opens up the possibility that with sufficient passage of time such factor specificity can be overcome, so one type of capital can be altered to another. This, indeed, is what is assumed in Chapter 6.

As in the Ricardian setting the issue of the effects of international trade on the distribution of income receives prime attention, but now a shift is made to the consequences of trade for the welfare of separate factors *within* a country, as revealed by the effect of international trade on local wage rates and returns to land and capital.

5.1 Diminishing Returns and Factor Hires

One of the earliest concepts encountered in the study of economics is that of *diminishing returns*. As more and more of a variable factor is added in the production process to given amounts of a specific factor, what happens to total output produced? It increases. But the incremental output is not maintained—it falls as more of the variable input is added to a fixed factor. This is a property of production that is perfectly consistent with our assumption that technology exhibits *constant returns to scale*: Increasing *all* inputs in proportion results in output going up by the same proportion. In the Ricardian model there is only one homogeneous factor of production, labor, so the concept of diminishing returns is not relevant.

Consider the food sector, now assumed to employ both labor and land. Suppose the quantity of land is fixed, and ask how total food output varies as more and more labor is employed in this sector. Food output rises at an ever-decreasing rate. The marginal product of labor in producing food is defined as the extra output of food obtainable if one more unit of labor is added to a fixed supply of land. The law of diminishing returns implies that this marginal product falls as output expands.

How much labor would be hired by a competitive food producer owning a given parcel of land and facing both a given market price for food and a given wage rate at which labor can be hired? The marginal (physical) product of labor depends on the quantity of labor hired in the market, and if this is multiplied by the price of food, the *value of the marginal product of labor* is determined. This is what needs to be compared with the prevailing wage rate. If it is higher than the wage rate, *w*, it pays the producer to hire more labor; if less, the producer can gain by cutting back on the amount of labor hired. Profits are maximized at the amount of labor hired that equates the value of the marginal product of labor to the wage rate. (The diagrammatic treatment is given in Figure 5.2.) How about the return to land? This is literally in the form of rent—the excess of revenue over the required payment to labor.

We assume here that technology exhibits constant returns to scale: Doubling both inputs serves to double output. This implies that if both the wage rate and rental on land should double, so would the unit cost of production and, in a competitive market, the market price of food. This implies an important relationship among prices:

> If factor prices change, the percentage change in the commodity price must lie between the percentage changes in factor returns.

The rationale is simple. Suppose the wage rate increases by 10 percent and the rental on land by 20 percent. Unit costs must rise by at least 10 percent, which would be the exact outcome if the rental had risen by 10 percent instead of 20 percent, but cannot rise by more than 20 percent, which would be the exact result if wages had risen by 20 percent. In competitive markets, prices reflect unit costs, so that the percentage price change must be trapped between the percentage changes in wages and rents.

Similar remarks can be made for the clothing sector, except we now assume that the fixed factor is capital. All revenue earned in the clothing sector will, in competitive markets, either be represented in the wage bill or will be captured as rents to owners of capital equipment.

5.2 Outputs and Income Distribution in the Closed Economy

Figure 5.1 illustrates that the economy's production-possibilities schedule no longer has the straight-line shape of the Ricardian model. The reason? Diminishing returns. Consider the movement from point N to N'. The only way in which clothing output can be expanded is by releasing labor from the food sector and putting it to work with cap-

FIGURE 5.1

Production Possibilities with Increasing Opportunity Costs

The closed economy equilibrium is at N. The transformation curve is bowed out, reflecting the law of diminishing returns.

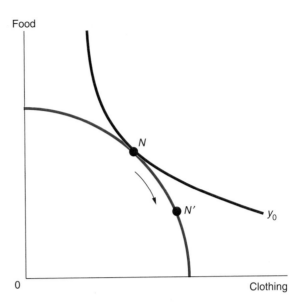

ital to produce clothing. But such a transfer alters the marginal productivity of labor in both sectors—in opposite directions. Adding more labor to a fixed quantity of capital in the clothing sector does cause output to increase, but at a diminishing rate. The marginal product of labor in clothing at point N' is smaller than it is at point N. In the food sector the departure of labor serves to *increase* labor's marginal product in producing food because there is now more land used per unit of labor at N' than at N.

The slope of the bowed-out transformation schedule in Figure 5.1 is equal to (minus) the ratio of labor's marginal product in the two sectors. The reasoning is simple: The drop in food output in going from N to N' is (roughly) equal to labor's marginal product in producing food times the quantity of labor lost to the clothing sector. The increase in clothing output is equal to labor's marginal product in producing clothing times the extra labor hired. Because the amount of labor leaving the food sector equals the amount added to clothing production, our assertion is proved:

> *The slope of the transformation schedule equals (minus) labor's marginal product in food divided by its marginal product in producing clothing.*

And such a ratio increases as more clothing is produced. The closed-economy equilibrium point (N) is located at the point where indifference curve, y_0, is tangent to the transformation schedule. The common slope at N reflects the relative price of clothing.

The next diagram we consider, Figure 5.2, is extremely useful in examining how price changes and/or alterations in factor endowments bring about a change in the internal distribution of incomes. This diagram focuses on the equilibrium in the country's labor market, a state of affairs in which the value of labor's marginal product in both sectors is equal to the prevailing wage rate and all labor is fully employed. Suppose both commodity prices are given initially. The value of the marginal product of labor in food schedule (the VMP_L^F curve) is declining with increases in the quantity of labor (L_F) used to produce food. In this "back-to-back" diagram, the schedule for

FIGURE 5.2

Wage Rate Determination

Equilibrium wages (at *A*) equate the values of the marginal product of labor in the two sectors by labor allocation at *G*. If free trade raises clothing's price, labor shifts out of food into clothing (from *G* to *G'*). The wage rate rises but not as much as clothing's price.

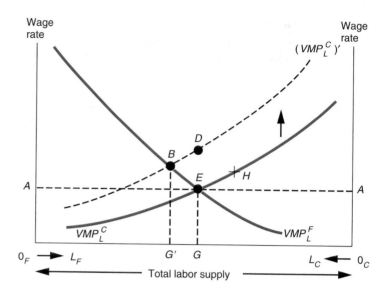

the value of the marginal product of labor in producing clothing (the VMP_L^C curve) is drawn from right to left, with L_C measured leftward from the "labor in clothing" origin, 0_C. The base of the diagram reflects the total labor supply, so any point on the horizontal axis reveals the allocation of labor between sectors. For example, the initial equilibrium assigns $0_F G$ units of labor to food production and the remainder to clothing because such an allocation serves to equate the value of labor's marginal product in the two sectors, and thus to determine the equilibrium wage rate $(0_F A)$. Each of the specific factors, land and capital, receives the amount by which total revenue exceeds wage payments in the sector employing that factor.

5.3   Outputs and Income Distribution with Free Trade

When this economy is opened up to trade, which factors of production benefit? Could all benefit? If not, which lose? Is it possible to identify each group unambiguously? We make use of Figures 5.1 and 5.2 in tracing, step by step, the impact on an economy initially in autarky. Suppose clothing is relatively expensive on world markets, so that output responds as shown by the movement from *N* to *N'* in Figure 5.1—clothing output expands. (As shown in Chapter 2, a new budget line is tangent at point *N'*, allowing an indifference curve higher than the y_0 curve in Figure 5.1 to be reached with trade.) In Figure 5.2 we have illustrated this country's emergence into the world market by (arbitrarily) keeping the price of food (and thus the VMP_L^F schedule) unchanged and raising the price of clothing. If clothing's price is, say, 40 percent higher in world markets, the VMP_L^C schedule shifts upward by exactly 40 percent. The reason: Any given labor input into clothing (e.g., at an initial level of $0_C G$) and the fixed background quantity of capital yield the same marginal *physical* product of labor, but a price increase of 40 percent implies a 40 percent higher *value* of the marginal product of labor.

If, in response to the price changes brought about by free trade, labor could *not* be reallocated between sectors, a 40 percent wage gap (*DE*) would be created in Figure 5.2. But such a gap serves as a signal to attract labor to clothing and out of the food sector. This process of reallocation alters marginal productivities in each sector, until allocation point *G'* is reached with the new wage rate *G'B*, representing an increase in nominal wages.

How do landlords, capitalists, and laborers react to the move to free trade?

1. Owners of capital are delighted by the new higher clothing price. As workers move into the clothing sector, the marginal physical product of capital increases. Add to this the price rise for clothing (40 percent) and the return to capital is twice blessed—it goes up by more than 40 percent.

2. Landlords are at the other end of scale. Stuck in the food sector, whose relative price is now lower, they are also forced by the market to pay more for labor as workers decamp for the clothing sector. Thus less labor is available per unit of land and the marginal physical product of land falls. The consequence: Land rentals fall relative to the price of food and even more so compared with the higher price of clothing. Landlords unambiguously lose. Their self-interest would be served by opposing free trade. Not all factors can gain by the move to free trade.

3. The fate of laborers is less extreme. As just seen, the land/labor ratio used to produce food increases as labor leaves the agricultural sector, so that wages rise in terms of food. But the price of clothing has increased more than the wage rate. In Figure 5.2 the price of clothing has risen by 40 percent, the ratio *DE/EG*. Wages have increased in the move from *E* to *B*, but by less than 40 percent. This confirms point 1, that the return to capitalists increases by more than 40 percent, and point 2, that landlords' returns fall, relative to the given price of food, because nominal wages have gone up. In each industry the price (and unit cost) change must be flanked by the relative changes in factor rewards for inputs used in that sector.

The preceding arguments show that changes in relative commodity prices have uneven impacts on the incomes of various categories of productive factors. The factor of production (labor in this setting) that has opportunities for employment in all sectors of the economy and is highly mobile may find its real position not significantly altered by changes in the terms of trade. However, specific factors (land and capital) are severely affected. A specific factor used only in the industry suffering from a fall in relative price has no other outlet for employment. Its low mobility ensures that its real return falls. By contrast, the specific factor in the favored industry (an owner of capital in the clothing sector) finds its return unambiguously increased. It is sheltered from increased competition because no similar factor exists in the other industry (no textile machines are available in the food industry) and benefits from the arrival of the newly attracted other factor (labor) that serves to raise capital's productivity.

Any government policy (for example, a tariff change) that serves to affect relative commodity prices will be viewed differently by various factor groups. Factors used only in the favored sector would strongly support the proposed measure. Factors used only in the rest of the economy would unambiguously lose. In the model there is a third category—a factor (such as labor) that is not affected much one way or the other by such a policy. This is why political scientists find such a model useful in explaining why some sectors of the population do not bother voting on certain issues whereas others care deeply. Very few policies that have an impact primarily on relative commodity prices can be expected to gain widespread approval.

5.4   Growth in Factor Endowments

A nation's resource base need not remain static. Over time, one can expect the capital stock to rise, and perhaps more (or less) land to be brought into productive use. Population might grow, but this could be offset by shortening the work week or, in the opposite direction, by increased participation of both spouses in the marketplace or by an increase in the retirement age. As well, foreign investment could encourage capital accumulation or immigration might expand supplies of labor. How do such changes alter production choices and factor returns in an economy too small to have these supply changes affect world prices?

First, let us suppose that growth is confined to one of the specific factors. To be precise, consider for this small trading community the consequence of a 50 percent increase in the quantity of land available. The primary impact of such a change is to increase labor's productivity in producing food. At constant commodity prices this will entail a reallocation of labor resources and will bring in its wake a change in all factor returns and an outward shift in the community's production possibilities curve.

Figure 5.3 reproduces the initial equilibrium at E shown in Figure 5.2. Whereas the commodity price rise shown in Figure 5.2 depicts the value of labor's marginal product curve shifting *upward* by a given percentage amount, a rise of 50 percent in the quantity of land available would be illustrated in Figure 5.3 by a *rightward* shift of 50 percent in the schedule showing the value of labor's marginal product in producing food. The reasoning behind this shift is based on the assumption that returns to scale are constant and that commodity prices are being kept fixed. Therefore, if the quantity of labor used in the food sector were to be raised by 50 percent when the land supply is raised 50 percent, the marginal product (and value of the marginal product) of labor would remain unchanged; a 50 percent increase in both labor and land raises output by exactly 50 percent but leaves marginal physical products the same. Such a shift encourages labor to move out of clothing into food, and the equilibrium value of the wage rate is pushed upward to point B in Figure 5.3.

How is this change reflected in the country's transformation schedule? Suppose the economy in initial trade is at point N' in Figure 5.1, and suppose that the relative commodity price there remains constant when its endowment of land increases by 50 percent. The transformation schedule shifts outward but in a biased direction. With prices remaining constant, output of food expands and of clothing shrinks as this sector loses labor. Therefore in Figure 5.1 the new transformation curve (not drawn) would have the same slope as at N' at a point northwest of N'—with more food and less clothing.

Comparable changes occur if the capital supply should grow by 50 percent, with total land and labor supplies constant. The production-possibilities schedule shifts out

FIGURE 5.3

An Increase in Land

An increase of 50% in land shifts the VMP_L^F schedule rightward by 50% to $(VMP_L^F)'$, and increases the wage rate.

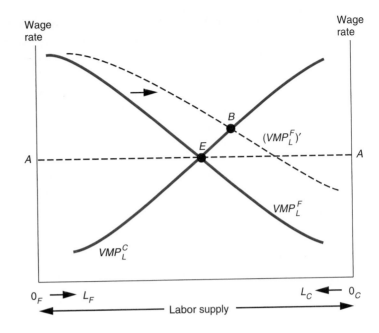

such that at constant commodity prices (and thus at a given slope for the transformation schedule) larger quantities of clothing are produced, with a smaller output in the food sector.

Labor growth at constant commodity prices leads to a more balanced expansion of both outputs. The base in Figure 5.3 would have to be enlarged. Keep the VMP_L^F schedule anchored to the 0_F origin, and the VMP_L^C schedule anchored to the 0_C origin. Thus an increase in the labor force would slide these schedules farther apart, serving to decrease the equilibrium wage rate. Each sector would respond by hiring more labor at the lower wage; outputs in both sectors would increase.

The effect of a change in factor endowments on factor prices as of a given set of commodity prices is both clear and not surprising: Any increase in land or capital serves to increase the wage rate and thus to drive down the returns to *both* specific factors. By contrast, an increase only in the economy's labor force serves to lower the wage rate and drive up the returns to both land and capital.

5.5 Consequences for Political Economy

These remarks on the effects of price changes and endowment changes lead to a strong set of results for the effects of trade on the distribution of income, results that have significant consequences for questions of political economy:

1. If factor endowments change (say via immigration) but world commodity prices remain constant, the fortunes of the specific factors (land and capital) rise or fall together and are opposed to those of the mobile factor (labor).

2. By contrast, if commodity price ratios in world markets change (and endowments remain constant), the returns to the specific factors are driven widely apart, whereas the return to mobile labor is relatively unaffected. If the relative price of clothing increases, capitalists unambiguously gain and landlords lose.

The first generality suggests a natural political alliance between landlords and capitalists in small, but growing, communities immersed in a trading world. One would expect a mutual interest of landlords and capitalists in legislation designed to encourage immigration of labor, whereas workers already in the country might oppose immigration. In the 1920s the United States imposed tight immigration restrictions, largely because of pressure from labor unions. In Australia, more liberal immigration policy is supported both by capitalists and by landholders, although trade unions find it in their interests to control such inflows. As Europe boomed in the decades after World War II, the American labor movement was often outspoken in its criticism of U.S. capital flows lured by burgeoning European markets.

The second generality suggests that if the legislation under consideration concerns relative commodity prices, landlords and capitalists would be diametrically opposed. A classic historical example concerns the Corn Laws in nineteenth-century Britain. Parliamentary overrepresentation of the landed gentry allowed laws that prevented the importation of cheap grains. After 1832 and the Reform Bill, parliamentary representation of industrialists (and labor) expanded. By 1846 the movement to freer trade was in full swing. The interests of capitalists were clear. Lower food prices would drive workers off the land and serve to lower the industrial wage, thus leading to greater profits.[1] A current analogy is found in present-day Japan, which has been highly restrictive in its tolerance of agricultural imports. (Japanese rice is over four times as expensive as that found in the world market.) The United States, ever anxious to improve its bilateral trade balance with Japan, has loudly denounced these agricultural trade restrictions. But, perhaps, American manufacturers who compete with Japanese exporters would not be pleased if restrictions were loosened, and thus allowed workers in Japan to receive nominal pay cuts while enjoying higher real wages as food prices fall. Larger agricultural imports into Japan could also lead to greater Japanese exports of manufactures. Japanese landlords and industrialists are at odds over these trade restrictions, and, as in the case of nineteenth-century Britain, major changes may require political reforms to dilute the power of rural areas.

5.6   The Pattern of Trade

In some respects, the pattern of trade in this setting should be easy to predict. Countries with relatively large amounts of land will export food; countries with relatively large amounts of capital will export clothing. The close identification of these two factors, land and capital, with unique outputs, food and clothing, makes obvious the logic

---

[1] The wage would not fall as much as the price of food.

whereby production patterns are linked to the underlying factor endowment comparison between countries. The setting we examine in Chapter 6 is less obvious because there each factor is utilized at least to some extent in both industries. Nonetheless, the bias imparted to production patterns emanating from inter-country differences in supplies of productive factors will still prevail. However, other features of demand and supply also have a bearing on the equilibrium pattern of trade:

1. *Tastes.* Even if the home country has a relatively large supply of capital and thus a bias to produce relatively large quantities of clothing if home and foreign countries face a common set of commodity prices with free trade, differences in tastes could affect the trade pattern. For example, a strong taste bias for clothing at home could result in the home country being a relatively expensive source of clothing, so that with trade it imports this item.

2. *Technology.* The Ricardian model of Chapter 4 emphasized the role of differences in technology in dictating patterns of trade. The concepts of relative demand and relative supply, as illustrated in Figure 2.9, are appropriate in showing how differences in endowments or technology play a role in determining trade patterns. In that situation, the foreign relative supply curve for food, which lies to the right of the home relative supply curve, could reflect an underlying, higher relative endowment of land compared with capital in the foreign country. Or, it might be the case that foreign food technology is relatively superior; points A and $A*$ illustrate that for comparable relative output proportions the relative cost of producing food is lower abroad. Endowment differences and technology differences may reinforce each other. Alternatively, they could push costs in opposite directions.

Finally, we have yet to comment on the consequences of one country having a relatively large labor force. Does this bias the likely pattern of trade? The answer to this question is more subtle. We have already shown that an expansion of the labor force shifts the production possibilities schedule outward, such that at the same terms of trade, more of both commodities will be produced. Whether the ratio of their production is altered, however, depends on the manner in which food and clothing technologies differ, both in the intensity with which they require labor and the elasticity of their demand for labor. Details are banished to the supplement to this chapter.

5.7 Alternative Interpretations: Specific Capital or Specific Labor

So far our discussion has portrayed labor as completely mobile between sectors, with capital only used to produce clothing and land an input only in the food sector. But we can depart from this classical trilogy of land, labor, and capital, and suppose that land is an insignificant input into production. This frees us up to consider two alternative interpretations of this simple model.

In the first interpretation, suppose that two different types of capital are used in production—say textile capital in clothing and tractors in production of food, with labor still mobile between these two sectors. In considering the effect of world price changes on income distribution and outputs for a small open economy, contrast the results now with those we discussed in Chapter 4's Ricardian model. If the relative price of clothing increases in world markets, labor is drawn to this sector from the food industry. The wage rate rises in terms of food, but falls in terms of clothing—the kind of intermediate result we found for mobile labor in Figure 5.2. The return to each kind of capital is much different in the two sectors: The rental on textile machinery rises by more than any price, and the return to tractors used to produce food falls. These *rents* on capital serve as shock absorbers, as seen by the comparison with a Ricardian labor-only model. In the latter case, suppose initially the economy produces both goods before the price of clothing increases. After the price rise the food sector would be completely wiped out, unable to compete at the new world price. In the present case, changes in rents on specific capitals absorb the price shocks so that some food production can still take place. This comment proves relevant to the next section's discussion of the so-called Dutch Disease.

Trade and Unskilled Wage Rates

Consider, now, an alternative scenario—one in which all capital is completely mobile between sectors (e.g., computers), but labor is no longer homogeneous. Suppose some part of the labor force has "skills" while the remainder is unskilled. To nail things down, suppose skilled labor is used to produce clothing and unskilled labor to produce food—with homogeneous and mobile capital used in both sectors. Furthermore, suppose clothing is this country's export industry and that changes in world prices take place such that the price of clothing increases and food's price remains constant. What is the consequence for local income distribution? The real return to capital does not change very much, but the fates of skilled and unskilled labor are vastly different. The real wage for skilled workers goes up, while that for the unskilled falls. This scenario, whereby changing prices on world markets cause grief for a country's unskilled labor force but not for skilled workers, is often invoked in describing the fate of labor in the United States in the past three decades. Of course, other factors may play a key role, such as changes in technology that favor the use of skilled workers relative to the unskilled.

In both of these alternatives there is a time dimension suggested, since specific capital does wear out and new capital can take different forms. That is, specificity may be a short-run state of affairs, whereas in the long run capital is in effect mobile between sectors. As well, with time unskilled labor may be able to acquire skills through education or experience, so that specificity here is also a short-run phenomenon. Chapter 6 builds on this theme.

5.8   Dutch Disease

The several energy crises of the past few decades, along with the associated increases in the prices of some world-traded products and resources, have led to radical internal stresses in the economic sectors producing commodities whose world prices have not changed much. In Europe this kind of phenomenon came to be called the Dutch Disease. The name referred specifically to the rapid development in the Netherlands of the sector producing natural gas and the resulting squeeze put on other traditional export sectors of the Dutch economy. Similarly, in Norway and Great Britain, rapid exploitation of North Sea oil deposits created severe hardships for manufacturing sectors that competed in world markets. Much less disruption was brought about in the sectors servicing purely local markets—the nontraded sector.[2]

The simple model developed in this chapter can be utilized to reveal strategic features of this phenomenon. Suppose a number of industries are producing for the world market. In each one of these, labor is drawn from a common pool (labor is the mobile factor) and combined with another factor specific to that sector and in fixed supply. Let each sector have its own supply of capital equipment (and managerial expertise) that is uniquely designed for use in that sector. Suppose the world price of the output in one of these sectors increases. As already outlined, the main features of the food-clothing model generalize readily to this multisector case.[3] In particular, returns to factors specifically used in the favored (booming) traded sector increase by more than price. More crucially, the nominal wage rate is bid up, and this increase in wages squeezes all the other traded sectors that have not benefited by a price increase. In Chapter 4's Ricardian model with fixed labor coefficients, a wage rise would cause the complete collapse of any traded sector facing fixed world prices. Here the industry may survive, but only as long as lower returns are accepted by specific factors. Higher wage rates triggered by the rise in price in the booming sector put the squeeze on profits (or returns to specific capital and management) in any other traded sector.

Figure 5.4 illustrates the case of the Dutch Disease. A typical, traditional export sector facing a constant price, $\bar{P}$ on world markets has an upward-sloping supply curve,

FIGURE 5.4

The "Dutch Disease"

A boom in a new export sector raises wages, which shifts costs upward for a traditional export sector. Returns to capital are squeezed and output falls.

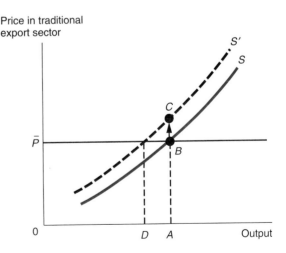

[2]An analytic treatment of some aspects of this issue is found in W. M. Corden and J. Peter Neary, "Booming Sector and De-Industrialization in a Small Open Economy," *Economic Journal* (December 1982): 825–848.
[3]Formal extensions are found in R. W. Jones, "Income Distribution and Effective Protection in a Multi-Commodity Trade Model," *Journal of Economic Theory* (August 1975): 1–15.

S, as increases in output are achieved by combining more labor with a fixed quantity of capital. The presumed boom in another export sector pushes up the wage rate and, through this connection, affects costs throughout the rest of the economy. For this traditional export sector, the supply curve shifts up to S', the returns to the specific factor are squeezed, and output is lowered from $0A$ to $0D$ if the sector does not benefit from a rise in price.

The Fate of the Nontraded Sector

The discussion of the Ricardian model concluded with the introduction of the concept of a nontraded sector, an industry producing a commodity that can be neither exported nor imported because of high costs of transport. Suppose such a sector is added here. When one export sector expands, pushing up wage rates, the nontraded sector also experiences a cost increase. However, for nontraded goods the price to consumers can be raised. If there were no shift in demand, these cost increases could be partially passed on to consumers, with output reduced. The situation is further alleviated for nontradables because the demand curve shifts to the right. Why? With an export boom caused by a price rise, the community's real income expands with the favorable movement in the terms of trade. This will partly spill over to increased demand in the nontradable sector. In addition, local demand might increase as a consequence of a direct substitution effect away from the exportable that has risen in price toward other markets.

Much the same story can be told if, instead of a price rise in one traded goods sector, there is technical progress (as illustrated in Chapter 4 for the Ricardian model) or there are new discoveries (such as North Sea oil).

The role of the doctrine of *comparative advantage* is crucial in understanding the phenomenon of the Dutch Disease. A country exports commodities in which it possesses a comparative advantage. It may lose such an advantage in some commodities even if the technology in that sector is unchanged, if in another sector its technology (or price) improves. In the present model the route through which traditional sectors get squeezed is a rise in the wage rate. Although the model is not explicitly geared to handle the phenomenon at this stage, another avenue through which traditional traded sectors can be affected is the exchange rate. British manufacturers of commodities enjoying an export market were hit at the end of the 1970s by a strengthening of the British pound, caused in part by anticipation of future oil revenues from North Sea discoveries. These same discoveries caused concern in Norway that wages might rise and threaten the competitive position of other Norwegian industries. The Dutch were not alone in their concerns.

5.9   Summary

This chapter presents one of the classic models of production—a model in which diminishing returns describe the attempt of any sector to increase output by applying more labor to a fixed quantity of another factor specific to that sector. Commodities differ in their factor demands, clothing makes no use of land and food does not require capital. That is, factors of production differ in their degree of mobility: Labor is cost-lessly transferable from sector to sector at a common wage, whereas land and capital are each specific.

This description of an economy is rich in its conclusions for a community engaged in international trade:

1. The internal distribution of income is vitally affected by any change in relative commodity prices. A productive factor specifically tied to some occupation (e.g., land in the production of food) unambiguously gains by an increase in the relative price of the commodity in whose production it is employed. This price increase will cause other specific factors to lose in real terms. This feature of the model, by itself, predicts that any political decision within a community that threatens to affect commodity prices (such as tariff legislation) will arouse ardent support on the part of some and strong opposition from others, as well as fairly widespread apathy from groups not vitally concerned. The mobile factor is less affected by commodity price changes because it can move from sector to sector. This discrepancy in inter-ests can be read in the historical record of almost any significant move concerning trade. Changes in trade policy are apt to prove divisive, and this chapter shows the lines of division running along the characteristics that distinguish one productive factor from another.

2. Income distribution is also affected by growth. Not surprisingly, greater supplies of a factor tend to depress its return. If commodity prices are largely determined by world markets, there is a natural alliance among specific factors (landlords and cap-italists) to raise their own returns by encouraging immigration of nonspecific labor.

3. The composition of outputs is quite sensitive to changes in a community's under-lying factor endowment base. This is especially true for changes in specific factors. A community relatively heavily endowed with land will tend to have a comparative advantage in producing land-using food; equally, a community heavily endowed with capital will tend to have a comparative advantage in producing capital-intensive clothing. The pattern of world trade is closely linked to wide differences in resource endowments.

4. Trade encourages resources to move into sectors in which an economy enjoys a comparative advantage. Unlike the Ricardian model of Chapter 4, a country may nonetheless still support import-competing industries. The law of diminishing returns helps explain how a small amount of production may prove competitive, even though the community relies on imports to provide the bulk of its consump-tion of some items.

5. All the essential features of the two-commodity model remain for economies characterized by a wide variety of productive activities if in each industry use is made of some factor of production available in nationwide markets (e.g., labor) as well as other productive factors specifically tied to that industry. In particular, any

change in relative prices of traded commodities or change in technology or discoveries of new resources is apt to have radical repercussions in various sectors of the economy.

The Dutch Disease describes how a favorable change in conditions affecting one tradable sector can adversely affect other tradable sectors by squeezing their profits (or returns to specific factors). For a small, open economy, cost increases may successfully be passed on to consumers in sectors protected from foreign competition by high costs of transport, even though such relief is not available in traditional export- or import-competing sectors.

Finally, note that all the changes discussed in this chapter, whether in commodity prices, endowments, or technology, create losers as well as winners within countries. This is what is absent in Chapter 4, where the focus instead was on inter-country gains and losses. The specific-factors model yields many realistic responses of internal income distribution to the forces of globalization. As we see in the next chapter, a somewhat different scenario is similar in suggesting that disturbances in international markets are capable of creating both winners and losers and an attendant disharmony in opinions about trade policy.

CHAPTER PROBLEMS

1. The discussion of the Ricardian model in Chapter 4 introduced the concept of an input-output coefficient, a_{Lj}. The reciprocal of this ($1/a_{LF}$ in the food sector, for example) referred to the average product of labor. In a diagram that shows the marginal product of labor, draw in a curve showing the *average* product of labor. How can land rents as well as total wages be shown in such a diagram?

2. With reference to Figures 5.2 and 5.3 it was suggested that a 10 percent increase in the price of food would shift the VMP_L^F curve upward by 10 percent, and a 10 percent increase in the supply of land would (at constant food and clothing prices) shift the VMP_L^F curve rightward by 10 percent. Do these have equivalent effects on the wage rate? Which kind of change would workers prefer? Which would capitalists prefer?

3. Explain why Australian capitalists and landlords probably favor the same policy toward immigration. Given the traditional export position of Australian wool in world markets, how might owners of sheep stations be expected to react to an increase in domestic prices of manufactures brought about by a tariff? Through what mechanism might land rents be disturbed?

4. Contrast the effect on land rents of an increase in a nation's supply of land coupled simultaneously with a reduction in its supply of capital if:
   a. The country cannot engage in world trade.
   b. The country does trade freely with a much larger world market.
   Answer the same two-part question if the nation's supply of land remains constant while its supply of capital increases.

SUGGESTIONS FOR FURTHER READING

Jones, Ronald W. "A Three-Factor Model in Theory, Trade, and History." In J. Bhagwati, R. Jones, R. Mundell, and J. Vanek, eds., *Trade, Balance of Payments and Growth* (Amsterdam: North-Holland, 1971), Chapter 1, reprinted in R. W. Jones, *International Trade: Essays in Theory* (Amsterdam: North-Holland, 1979). Sets out the basic model and explores some applications to trade and economic theory.

Mayer, Wolfgang. "Short-Run and Long-Run Equilibrium for a Small Open Economy," *Journal of Political Economy,* 82 (September/October 1974): 955–968. Interpretation of the specific-factors model as a short-run version of the Heckscher-Ohlin model in Chapter 6.

APPENDIX

The Transformation Schedule

A four-quadrant diagram can fill in details for the shape of the transformation schedule for an economy possessing fixed overall amounts of three distinct productive factors: labor, land, and capital. Labor is used to produce both food and clothing; land is used only in food; and capital is specific to the clothing sector. These assumptions suffice to rule out the phenomenon associated with the Ricardian model, whereby an industry could expand by hiring more labor without driving up unit costs. Instead, production possibilities reflect increasing costs.

The bowed-out production possibilities curve is displayed in quadrant I of Figure 5.A.1, using the relationships drawn in quadrants II, III, and IV. Note especially:

1. Quadrant III shows a downward-sloping 45° line to illustrate the full employment of the economy's total (fixed) labor resources, either to produce food (shown leftward from the origin) or to produce clothing (measured downward from the origin).

2. The curves showing total labor productivity for the two industries (quadrants II and IV) illustrate diminishing returns to labor as more is applied to the fixed amount of the cooperating factor (land in the case of food and capital in the case of clothing).

The production possibilities schedule in quadrant I reflects increasing opportunity costs. Endpoint *D* shows the maximum amount of food that could be produced if all the economy's labor force were employed in food. (0*D* also is shown by *AC* in quadrant II.) Similarly, endpoint *F* is the maximum clothing output, obtainable if labor force 0*B* is used to produce *BE* units of clothing (quadrant IV). Any intermediate labor allocation, such as *G* in quadrant III, results in food output (*HJ*, quadrant II) and in clothing output (*IK*, quadrant IV), which is shown as point *N* on the transformation schedule

FIGURE 5.A.1

Production Possibilities with Diminishing Returns and Increasing Opportunity Costs

The production possibilities curve in quadrant I is derived by picking a labor allocation along the full-employment line (quadrant III) and displaying the outputs of food (quadrant II) and clothing (quadrant IV) obtainable in quadrant I. Diminishing returns lead to increasing opportunity costs.

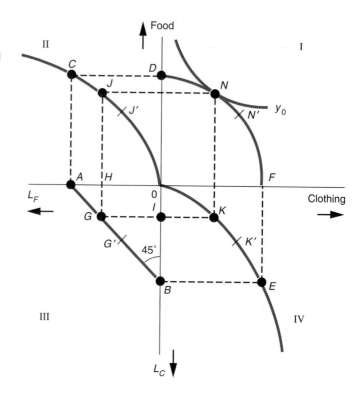

(quadrant I). Other points can be derived in similar fashion (e.g., labor allocation G' yields output bundle N'—just complete the rectangle). Consider the movement from N to N' that accompanies the labor reallocation from G to G'. As extra labor is poured into the clothing sector, diminishing returns decrease labor's productivity (in clothing) at the margin. Meanwhile, the departure of labor from the food industry serves to raise the productivity of the remaining food workers. On both counts, the relative cost of producing clothing increases (the transformation schedule becomes steeper). The transformation schedule bows out because labor is subject to diminishing returns in each sector, and the cooperating inputs (land for food, capital for clothing) are fixed in supply.

CHAPTER 6

Factor Endowments and Trade II: The Heckscher-Ohlin Model

A theory of international trade that highlights the variations among countries of supplies of broad categories of productive factors (labor, capital, and land, none of which may be specific to any one sector) was developed by two Swedish economists, Eli Heckscher and Bertil Ohlin.[1] Their model subsequently has been extended in scores of articles and treatises. Some of the new results were startling: Two countries that share the same general technology but differ in their endowments of the basic factors of production may nonetheless find that free trade in commodities forces wage rates in the two countries into absolute equality. Advocates of protection have found support in another proposition: Even a broad-based factor such as labor may unambiguously gain by the imposition of tariffs.

Most of these propositions were carefully proven and adequately qualified in a simple form of the theory—the *2 × 2 model,* so called because it analyzed an economy producing two commodities with the use of only two productive factors. This model has proved to be immensely popular not only in the area of international trade but also in fields such as public finance and economic growth. We initially follow Heckscher and Ohlin in assuming that countries share the same technological knowledge, an assumption made to highlight a cause for trade (different relative factor endowments) that is distinct from the technological asymmetries emphasized in the Ricardian model. We begin by restricting discussion to the 2 × 2 case, which leads to a pair of key features that deserve to be highlighted here:

1. The pattern of trade reflects the relative endowment of productive factors—relatively labor-abundant countries tend to export relatively labor-intensive commodities.

2. Freeing up trade benefits the relatively abundant factor of production but harms the relatively scarce factor.

The more realistic case in which many countries are trading freely in many commodities is handled later in the chapter.

---

[1] E. Heckscher, "The Effect of Foreign Trade on the Distribution of Income," *Ekonomisk Tidskrift,* 21 (1919): 497–512, retranslated in H. Flam and M. J. Flanders, eds., *Heckscher-Ohlin Trade Theory* (Cambridge, MA: MIT Press, 1991); B. Ohlin, *Interregional and International Trade* (Cambridge, MA: Harvard University Press, 1933). In 1977 Ohlin shared the Nobel Prize in economics for his early work in trade theory.

Once again we label the two commodities, food and clothing. The structure here shares with the two preceding chapters the view that production takes place in a competitive setting in which the technology linking inputs and outputs exhibits constant returns to scale: Doubling all factor inputs exactly doubles output. However, there is an important difference: No longer (as in Chapter 5) does each commodity use an input not required by the other commodity. Instead, both industries compete for the same pair of productive factors, labor and capital. The crucial feature that distinguishes production of food from that of clothing is the *factor intensity* that each requires; the ratio of capital to labor used in food differs from that adopted by the clothing sector.

6.1 If Technology Is Rigid

The basic ideas of the Heckscher-Ohlin theory can be conveyed in a simple scenario in which technology is assumed to be very rigid. By this is meant that there is only one way to produce clothing—a_{LC} and a_{KC} represent fixed input-output coefficients depicting how much labor and how much capital are required to produce a unit of clothing. Similarly, technology is rigid in food production, with a_{LF} and a_{KF} representing the fixed quantities of labor and capital required to produce a unit of food. A direct comparison of a_{LC} with a_{LF} has no meaning because either coefficient can arbitrarily be changed by altering the units in which one of the goods is measured, for example, from pounds to tons (or from grams to kilograms). What is relevant, however, is a comparison of the capital/labor *ratios* used in the two sectors. We henceforth assume (arbitrarily) that clothing is the relatively labor-intensive sector, and by this we mean that:

$$a_{LC}/a_{KC} > a_{LF}/a_{KF} \tag{6.1}$$

One more piece of information is required before output levels (or trading patterns) can be identified: factor endowments. In particular we need to know how these two countries, which are assumed to share a common (rigid) technology, differ from each other in the proportions of capital to labor each possesses. Once again assume that factors of production stay home, and only commodities are traded. This implies that a country's factor endowment bundle, along with its technology, dictates production possibilities. Assume, now, that the home country is the relatively *labor-abundant* country. By this is meant:

$$L/K > L^*/K^* \tag{6.2}$$

A comparison of the production possibilities schedules of the two countries will reveal the bias that endowment differences impart to the likely pattern of trade. Figure 6.1 illustrates the production possibilities schedule for the foreign country. The labor constraint is precisely of the same kind as found in the Ricardian (Chapter 4) model:

$$a_{LC}x_C^* + a_{LF}x_F^* = L^*$$

Unlike the Ricardian case, however, now capital is also required to produce each of the goods, leading to a linear capital-constraint line:

$$a_{KC}x_C^* + a_{KF}x_F^* = K^*$$

FIGURE 6.1

Production Possibilities: Rigid Technology

Inner locus *NAM* is the production-possibilities schedule for the foreign country, with full employment of both factors only at intersection *A*. The home country's full-employment point would be *S* if it had the same technology, the same capital supply, but a 50 percent greater labor force. The home transformation schedule would then be *NSZ*.

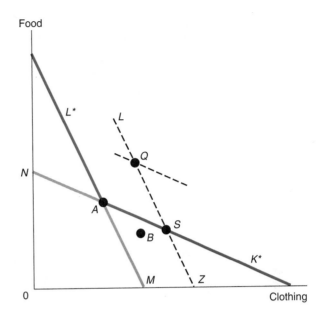

Note that in both these constraint lines the input-output coefficients do not have asterisks. Technology is assumed to be the same abroad and at home. Two features of the way in which this K^* line has been drawn in Figure 6.1 are worth stressing: (1) The capital-constraint line is assumed to intersect the labor-constraint line instead of lying everywhere above (in which case foreign capital is so abundant it is free) or everywhere below (in which case foreign labor is in excess supply). (2) The capital-constraint line has been drawn flatter than the labor-constraint line, a direct consequence of our assumption that clothing is the relatively labor-intensive commodity. (Check this out for yourself by computing the slopes of the lines.) The inner locus *NAM* forms the foreign country's production possibilities schedule; only for production bundles on or below this locus will the economy not be using more of either capital or labor than is available. Intersection point *A* is of particular interest to us; point *A* represents the *only* output combination for which both labor and capital are fully employed.

Because the home country is assumed to share the same (rigid) technology, its constraint lines must be parallel to those in Figure 6.1. But the position of its lines reveals its factor endowments. For example, if the home country were exactly 50 percent larger than the foreign country in both endowments, its constraint lines would lie 50 percent farther from the origin, leading to output bundle *Q* if home labor and capital are fully employed. Instead, let us abide by our assumption that the home country is relatively labor abundant and suppose only its labor force is 50 percent larger. Thus, full employment and home production would lie at point *S* and the home transformation schedule would be *NSZ*.[2] Note that the endowment difference between countries has led to a

---

[2]Figure 6.1 shows that if labor alone expands, the output of capital-intensive food must actually contract, because it must release capital (as well as labor) to the expanding clothing sector. This relationship is known in the literature as the *Rybczynski theorem.* See T. M. Rybczynski, "Factor Endowment and Relative Commodity Prices," *Economica,* 22 (November 1955): 336–341.

magnified or more pronounced difference in the production patterns of the two countries. The generalization that we focus on here for two countries sharing the same rigid
technologies and fully employing both labor and capital can be stated as:

*The relatively labor-abundant country produces relatively larger quantities of the
labor-intensive commodity.*

Thus, if taste patterns do not differ very much between countries,

*The relatively labor-abundant home country will tend to export the relatively labor-
intensive commodity.*

A Numerical Example

A numerical example may help highlight how endowment differences between countries affect production (and trade) patterns. Suppose the following set of input-output
coefficients:

Factor Requirements per Unit of Output

	Labor	Capital
Clothing	$a_{LC} = 3$	$a_{KC} = 1$
Food	$a_{LF} = 1$	$a_{KF} = 2$

The capital/labor ratio in food (2/1) exceeds that in clothing (1/3). If the foreign country possesses 200 units of productive labor and 200 units of capital, the only combination of outputs that will fully employ both labor and capital is a clothing output of
40 units and a food output of 80 units. That is, if x_C^* and x_F^* denote foreign clothing and
food outputs respectively, full employment implies that

$$3x_C^* + x_F^* = 200 \qquad \text{(for labor)}$$
$$x_C^* + 2x_F^* = 200 \qquad \text{(for capital)}$$

or that x_C^* equals 40 and x_F^* equals 80.

Suppose that the home country's labor force is 50 percent higher, 300 units, and
the capital stock is the same. Simple calculation reveals that in order for labor and
capital to be fully employed at home, x_C must be 80 units and x_F must be 60 units. A
comparison with the foreign values shows that the home country, with a 50 percent
higher labor force, has a 100 percent higher output of labor-intensive clothing and a
lower output of food. Such a production comparison supports the presumption that if
these two countries engage in free trade, the home country will export clothing to the
foreign country.

How do commodity price changes alter the internal distribution of income? This
same numerical example can help explain the connections. Because only relative prices
matter, suppose the price of food is $10 in both countries, before and after trade.[3] But

---

[3]We have arbitrarily assumed both countries use the same currency (the dollar) because we have simplified by
letting food's price always be $10.

in the home country the relative abundance of labor supports an equilibrium autarky clothing price of $8, as compared to a higher foreign autarky price of $12. Letting w and r, respectively, denote home wages and rentals on capital, with asterisks showing foreign values, the requirement that in a competitive equilibrium unit costs equal price suggests that:

At home: $3w + r = 8$ (clothing)
           $w + 2r = 10$ (food)

Abroad: $3w^* + r^* = 12$ (clothing)
           $w^* + 2r^* = 10$ (food)

The only pair of wage rates and rents at home that satisfy this requirement is a wage rate of $6/5 and a rental of $22/5. Abroad, because clothing is relatively more expensive in autarky (the foreign country is a relatively labor-scarce country and clothing is relatively labor intensive), it is not surprising to find autarky wages higher, with w^* equal to $14/5 and rentals lower than at home at $18/5. If these two countries trade commodities with each other, equilibrium terms of trade will be established that lie between the autarky price ratios. Suppose this is 1:1—that is, suppose that after trade the world price of clothing is $10 (as is the price of food). Arithmetic manipulation reveals that wages and rents get equalized between countries: At home the wage rate rises to a value of $2 and rentals fall to a value of $4. Abroad, factor prices move in just the opposite direction to yield a value of $2 for the foreign wage rate and $4 for rentals.

Two central features of international trade between countries in the 2 × 2 model have been illustrated:

(1) Free trade benefits the abundant factor of production and harms the relatively scarce factor of production.

(2) If countries share a common technology, free trade in commodities serves to equalize factor returns despite our assumption that factor markets are purely national and no international factor mobility is allowed.

This latter feature of the model is referred to as the *Factor-Price Equalization Theorem.* As we see later, it may not always hold, even if countries do indeed share the same technology.

6.2   Flexible Technology

The preceding account of production and pricing relationships when a technology that is shared in common by both countries is rigid has served to introduce the basic relationships in Heckscher-Ohlin theory whereby countries tend to export commodities that make intensive use of the factor of production found locally in relative abundance, and free trade helps the nation's relatively abundant factor of production but harms the nation's scarce factor. With rigid technology it is unambiguous what is meant by assuming that clothing production is relatively labor intensive. But if technology is flexible, the actual choice of technique depends on market values of wages and rentals on capital equipment; relatively high wages will encourage all sectors to adopt relatively capital-intensive methods of production.

Factor Intensities

One way of illustrating the variety of techniques available when technology is flexible is the *isoquant:* an array depicting the alternative bundles of capital and labor that can be used to produce the same level of output. Figure 6.2 illustrates such an isoquant for each of the sectors of the economy. (This should remind you of indifference curves described in Chapter 2.) If the ratio of wages to rentals is indicated by the slope of the lines tangent at A and B in Figure 6.2, these points (A and B) represent the best choice of technique to produce food and clothing, respectively. Although such a selection reveals that clothing (at B) is produced with relatively more labor-intensive techniques than food (at A), note that it is technologically *possible* for clothing to be produced with more capital-intensive techniques (compare C with A). But if both industries must shop for productive factors in the same national market, Figure 6.2's isoquants show that when costs are minimized in each, clothing is relatively labor intensive. Note that there are many isoquants for each good—depending on the output level illustrated. For each commodity these isoquants will be *homothetic,* reflecting our assumption of constant returns to scale. The quantities of each commodity selected in Figure 6.2 are completely arbitrary.

FIGURE 6.2

Factor-Intensity Comparison

Food is presumed to be produced by capital-intensive techniques compared with clothing. When both industries face the same set of factor prices, the least-cost capital/labor ratio for food (at A) exceeds that chosen for clothing (at B).

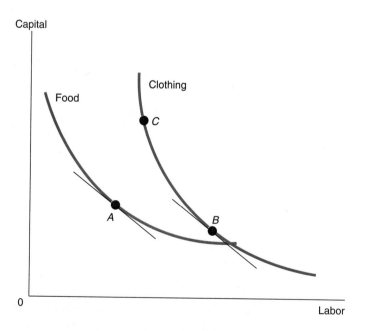

FIGURE 6.3

Factor Intensities and
Factor Endowments

If the capital/labor
endowment ratio at home
is k, the wage/rental ratio
must lie in the range BC.
If the capital-abundant
foreign country has the
endowment ratio k^*, there
is an overlap of possible
wage/rental ratios in the
two countries, DC. Free
trade *may* equalize factor
prices. Should the foreign
endowment ratio be at
the higher value k^{**}, the
relative wage rate abroad
must be higher than at
home.

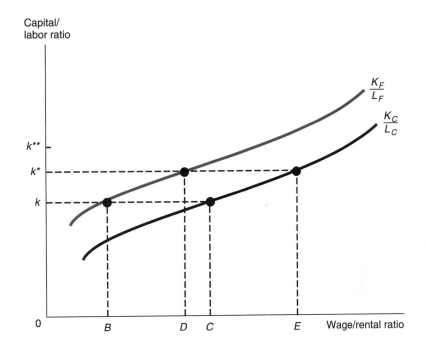

This information about the way in which techniques are flexible can more usefully
be suggested in Figure 6.3. The two curves show how the capital/labor ratios selected in
each sector depend positively on the ratio of wages to rentals; more expensive labor
induces shifts to more capital-intensive techniques in both sectors in order to keep
costs at a minimum. In keeping with our assumption that clothing is the relatively
labor-intensive sector of the economy, the clothing curve lies below that showing capi-
tal/labor ratios in food.[4] Now suppose that the home country's capital/labor endowment ratio is shown by k. Then, even without knowing anything about demand
conditions in autarky or the commodity terms of trade, it is possible to show that the
wage/rent ratio *must* be trapped in the range BC. The reason? If the wage/rent ratio
were to be higher than $0C$, both industries would attempt to use more capital per unit
of labor than is available overall ($0k$). Such an attempt would drive up rentals and
bring the factor-price ratio back within the BC range. Similarly, if wages are too low (a
ratio below $0B$), the attempt to employ more labor-intensive techniques in both sectors
than the endowment labor/capital ratio would serve to drive up the wage rate.

One reason why a diagram such as Figure 6.3 is so useful in our study is that it
allows us to compare the situation in countries sharing the same technology but differing in factor endowments. Given the home country's endowment ratio at k, consider

---

[4]Nothing prevents the possibility that these two curves intersect so that food might be produced with capital-
intensive techniques in one country and labor-intensive techniques in another—a case of *factor-intensity reversal.*

the following two possibilities for the foreign country's proportions, assuming it is the capital-abundant country:

(i) If the foreign endowment ratio is k^*, the ranges of possible wage/rent ratios in the two countries overlap (region DC). This implies that free trade in commodities *may* serve to equate wage rates and rentals in the two countries, but only if commodity prices allow factor price ratios in this range.

(ii) If the foreign endowment ratio is k^{**}, there is *no* overlapping range of possible wage/rental ratios in the two countries, even though they are assumed to share the same technology. This implies that regardless of taste patterns and the equilibrium commodity terms of trade, free trade in goods can never serve to equate factor prices between countries. Furthermore, because foreign relative wages are higher than at home, the relative cost of producing labor-intensive clothing must also be higher abroad than at home. The result: With trade the labor-abundant home country *must* be an exporter of labor-intensive clothing.

A Bowed-Out Transformation Curve

Our previous numerical example for the case of rigid technology can be harnessed to show what happens along a smoothly bowed-out transformation schedule (flexible technology) if a country releases some resources from food to the clothing sector. From an initial equilibrium point such as A in Figure 6.1, with full employment of capital and labor, suppose the country wishes to produce more clothing. At the initial set of techniques, the amount of capital per unit of labor that would be released by the food sector exceeds the ratio required in clothing—from point A labor is the binding constraint if clothing output expands. This relative shortage of labor is precisely what forces the wage rate up and rentals down and causes capital/labor ratios in both sectors to increase. As a consequence the labor constraint at the *extensive margin* (i.e., on outputs) is relaxed and the capital constraint on outputs is tightened. The new constraint lines thus intersect at a point such as B. And the increase in relative wages forces up the relative price of labor-intensive clothing, confirming that the transformation schedule is indeed bowed out.

6.3 Possible Trade Patterns and the Distribution of Income

With reference to Figure 6.3, the pattern of trade between these two countries would be clear if the home endowment ratio were k and the foreign ratio given by k^{**}: The labor-abundant home country *must* be the exporter of labor-intensive clothing. Why? Its transformation schedule is everywhere flatter than the foreign country's curve is at any point. This is what necessarily having a lower wage/rental ratio guarantees. But suppose the foreign country's capital/labor endowment ratio is only k^*. Then in Figure 6.3 there is an overlap of possible wage/rental ratios shown by range DC. If world commodity prices cause factor prices to be in this range, equal in the two countries, then so also must be techniques of production (because they are assumed to share the same technology). Our previous discussion of Figure 6.1 provides the clue for how *production patterns* would then differ between countries. The relatively labor-abundant home country would be at a point such as *S* and the foreign country at *A*. To generalize: If countries that share the same technology have endowment proportions sufficiently close together that factor prices are equalized with free trade, the relatively labor-abundant country *must* produce a relatively larger amount of the relatively labor-intensive commodity.

Go back to Figure 2.9 to see how production patterns are influenced by differences in factor endowments. For a relative price of food such as *OT*, the capital-abundant foreign country would produce a greater relative amount of capital-intensive food (compare point *G** with point *G*). Alternatively, if two countries were to produce the two commodities in precisely the same proportions, capital-intensive food could be produced more cheaply in the foreign country than at home (compare *A** with *A* in Figure 2.9). Does this imply that the foreign country *must* be an exporter of food once trade between these two countries is opened up? Not necessarily. Demand also has a role to play. Food might be relatively expensive abroad in autarky if demand there is heavily biased toward food consumption compared with tastes in the home country. But barring such asymmetries in tastes, endowment differences impart a strong bias in influencing the trade pattern.

Income Distribution in the Move from Autarky to Free Trade

It is now possible to trace the consequences of moving from autarky to free trade for each country. International trade in commodities brings about an equilibrium terms of trade lying between the autarky ratios in the two countries. At home, production of clothing expands (and food contracts) along the production possibilities schedule, with the attendant effect on wages and rents that such a move entails: Expansion of labor-intensive clothing at home raises wages and lowers rents. Abroad, the opposite changes are introduced by trade. As clothing becomes relatively cheaper, both labor and capital leave the clothing sector for the food industry. This move to capital-intensive food production drives up foreign rents and lowers foreign wages.

Before trade, labor-intensive clothing was relatively inexpensive in the labor-abundant home country, and this reflected the relatively low wage at home. International trade allows each country's demand to be freed from its production pattern, which permits home labor *indirectly* to be exported (via clothing exports) and relieves the pressure on scarce foreign labor. As observed, trade consequently raises wages (and lowers rents) at home and lowers wages (and raises rents) abroad. That is, international trade brings wages and rents in the two countries closer together. If countries share the same technology, a remarkable feature of free trade is revealed: Wages and rents *may* be equalized between countries, despite the fact that labor and capital are assumed to be trapped within their own national boundaries.

In this 2 × 2 Heckscher-Ohlin model, a given technology thus implies a strong relationship between prices of commodities (which enter trade) and returns to productive factors (which do not). Figure 6.4 shows this relationship, which is common to both countries *if* each produces both food and clothing. Because clothing is labor intensive, an increase in wages relative to rents must raise clothing's price relative to that of food. Note, however, the magnified effect of a commodity price change on

FIGURE 6.4

Factor Prices and Commodity Prices

The Heckscher-Ohlin theory determines that an increase in the relative price of labor-intensive clothing has a magnified effect on the wage/rent ratio. If countries share the same technology, and if before trade the home country is the low-wage country (0A versus 0A* abroad), clothing must be relatively cheap at home (0P versus 0P*). With free trade the home country exports clothing and factor prices are equalized at 0B if terms of trade settle at 0T.

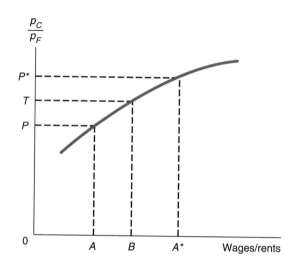

factor prices: A 10 percent increase in clothing's relative price would raise the wage/rent ratio by more than 10 percent. Once again, as discussed in Chapter 5, this reflects the necessary pricing relationship when two factors produce a single product: The relative change in the product price (which equals unit costs) must be trapped between the changes in the components of cost (wages and rents). When trade raises the home clothing price from $0P$ to $0T$, labor benefits in real terms, with relative wages rising from $0A$ to $0B$. Trade equalizes factor prices because the initially high foreign relative wage, $0A^*$, is reduced to $0B$ when clothing's price falls from $0P^*$ to $0T$ abroad.

These observations concerning the effect of trade on the distribution of income support the following pair of results of the 2 × 2 Heckscher-Ohlin theory.

1. *The Factor-Price Equalization Theorem:* Free trade that equalizes commodity prices between countries sharing the same technology *must* equate wages and rents in the home country with those abroad *if* each country actively produces both commodities. This is a big "if." It presumes that factor endowment proportions do not differ all that much between countries. As Figure 6.3 illustrates, if k and k^{**} are the ratios in the two countries, their factor prices *cannot* be equalized with trade. The reason: With free trade at least one of the countries must be completely specialized, and the trade pattern must correspond to the Heckscher-Ohlin dictum that relatively capital-abundant countries export capital-intensive goods.

2. *The Stolper-Samuelson Theorem:* Any interference with trade that drives up the local import price must unambiguously benefit the productive factor used intensively in producing the import-competing good.[5]

---

[5]This relationship was used initially to describe the impact of tariff protection if imports are labor intensive. See W. F. Stolper and Paul A. Samuelson, "Protection and Real Wages," *Review of Economic Studies,* 9 (November 1941): 58–73, reprinted in Alan Deardorff and Robert Stern, eds., *The Stolper-Samuelson Theorem: A Golden Jubilee* (Ann Arbor: University of Michigan Press, 1994), pp. 37–61.

It is important to note that whereas the assumption that countries share identical technologies is crucial for the factor-price equalization result, it is not necessary for the Stolper-Samuelson theorem. The latter reveals that regardless of the technology used at home, if the capital-abundant foreign country protects its labor-intensive clothing imports, it must succeed in raising real wages. This contrasts sharply with the effects described in Chapter 5, whereby a rise in either commodity price produces a more moderate effect on the wage rate: It increases in terms of one good but declines in terms of the commodity that has gone up in price. In the setting described in Chapter 5, labor was the only mobile factor, and specific factor returns (land and capital rents) moved in a more extreme fashion when the relative commodity price changed. In the Heckscher-Ohlin model, both capital and labor are mobile, and changes in commodity prices produce magnified effects on both wages and rents.

Unit-Value Isoquants

Consider the case of a small country facing given world prices for food and clothing. Combine this information about world prices with the two isoquant diagrams illustrated in Figure 6.2 to display, in Figure 6.5, a pair of isoquants showing given amounts of food and clothing that would sell exactly for $1 in world markets. These are known as the *unit-value isoquants*. Also illustrated is the tangent chord to the unit-value isoquants, *BFA*. This chord is useful in part in showing that points on either isoquant lying northeast of the chord (e.g., points *C* and *D*) represent techniques of production (for clothing in this case) that would never be observed at these given world prices.

FIGURE 6.5
──────────

Unit-Value Isoquants

This diagram assumes world prices for food and clothing are given and the isoquants show quantities of each commodity that would sell for $1 in world markets. Producing a combination of the two products if the endowment ratio lies in cone *BOA* is preferable to producing just a single commodity.

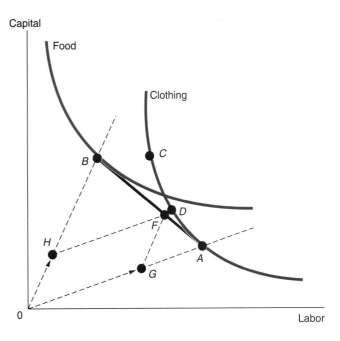

The argument for point *C* is easy because there are ways of producing food instead that could earn \$1 on world markets using less labor and capital (i.e., lying closer to the origin). The argument for a point like *D* is more subtle, in that there is no *single* technique for producing food or clothing that dominates *D*. However, a point such as *F* on the chord is better, and this represents the allocation of labor and capital to a mixture of both commodities: amounts shown by 0*G* to produce, say, around 62 cents worth of clothing and amount 0*H* to produce around 38 cents worth of food. The wage/rental factor price ratio indicated by the slope of the tangent chord corresponds to factor prices associated with the given world commodity prices (e.g., as illustrated in Figure 6.4). That is, if a ray from the origin that indicates the endowment capital/labor ratio lies within the cone *B*0*A*, the country will, with trade, produce positive amounts of both food and clothing. By contrast, if the endowment ray lies outside the cone, the country would have to be completely specialized. For example, if the endowment ray is flatter than 0*A*, the country's transformation schedule would be everywhere flatter than a budget line indicating world prices, and the country would produce nothing but clothing.

6.4   International Trade with Many Commodities

Given this background for the situation of a small country facing given world prices, the possibility that many commodities can be produced and enter world trade is relatively easy to handle. The underlying reason? If labor and capital are the only factors required to produce commodities, international trade allows a country to concentrate its resource base in producing at most two commodities. Recall the Ricardian setting in Chapter 4. With only one factor of production (homogeneous labor), a small country whose technology need not correspond to the pattern of world prices must, in general, produce only a single commodity once it enters trade—the commodity in which it possesses its greatest comparative advantage. Trade allows a massive degree of concentration in production without a sacrifice of a large assortment of commodities available to consumers. If a country has two productive factors, it need produce at most two commodities when it engages in world trade.

Turn, for an illustrative example, to the situation depicted in Figure 6.6 in which the country in autarky has produced five different commodities but with trade can end up producing either one or two. This diagram is a generalization of Figure 6.5 but with unit-value isoquants drawn for five commodities. Note that commodity 5 would not be produced at these prices, regardless of the factor endowments; there would always be a better way of earning a dollar. This reflects the fact that there are other countries in the world with a Ricardian type of technological comparative advantage in producing this commodity. Which one or more of the other commodities the country with this technology would produce would depend on its endowment proportions of capital to labor. If the endowment ray passes through a tangent chord (e.g., at point *I*), the country produces two commodities (*1* and *2* in this instance). But the endowment ray may pass through a point such as *M*, in which case all its resources are focused on producing a single commodity (*3* in this instance).

variety of productive activities than could be sustained in the brisk climate of free trade. This leads to the obvious question: What costs (or benefits) does a nation incur by stimulating this wider productive base? Part III picks up this theme.

Specific Factors: Short Run and Long Run

The Heckscher-Ohlin account of trade often has been referred to as a *long-run* theory.[6] It implicitly assumes that sufficient time has elapsed for factors of production, such as skilled labor, various kinds of capital goods, and entrepreneurs, to avoid becoming trapped in depressed industries if possible returns elsewhere in the economy are superior. It also assumes that these factors cannot successfully beat off competition from new productive factors entering an industry with the required skills. Factors are mobile from industry to industry.

Chapter 5 provided an illustration of *short-run* theory. There capital and land represented separate productive factors. However, alternative scenarios had either capital or labor specifically tied to their occupations only in the short run. Examples abound of workers who can be retrained with new skills to enter new occupations only after a number of months or years, or of textile machines that must be scrapped or allowed to depreciate before they can figuratively be beaten into tractors or lathes. A factor such as capital is not instantaneously shiftable. At any time some traded activities earn higher returns to capital than others. Over time, variations in world commodity prices and/or a country's own technology help account for the presence of production in sectors of the economy whose rationale for existence lies in the past. With the passage of time certain industries disappear from the scene, and new ones emerge. Every period carries with it echoes of the past. However, the *range* of such activities in generally capital-rich countries should differ from that in countries abundant in unskilled labor.

6.6 Changing Comparative Advantage with Economic Growth

Growth experience in today's world varies widely from country to country. In North America and Europe relatively moderate growth rates (2 or 3 percent) alternate with periods of much slower growth (especially for "old" Europe) or faster (as in the United States in the early years of this century). In many parts of Africa the situation appears more grim, with long periods of zero or negative growth. In the past two decades the success stories were to be found primarily in Asia. Japan in earlier years comes readily to mind, but even more rapid rates of growth were being experienced by the so-called tigers of Southeast Asia: South Korea, Taiwan, Hong Kong, and Singapore, all exceeding 6 percent annual rates as an *average* over the past 20 years. These countries were more recently joined by Thailand, Malaysia, Indonesia, and, especially, China and India.

---

[6]For example, see Wolfgang Mayer, "Short-Run and Long-Run Equilibrium for a Small Open Economy," *Journal of Political Economy,* 82 (September/October 1974): 955–968; and Michael Mussa, "Tariffs and the Distribution of Income: The Importance of Factor Specificity, Substitutability, and Intensity in the Short and Long Run," *Journal of Political Economy,* 82 (November/December 1974): 1191–1204.

All these countries are "outward-looking," with export activity fueling the growth process. But more is involved, and Figures 6.6 and 6.7 help tell the story. Growth is accompanied by high rates of capital accumulation, both physical capital and human capital (education).[7] Such capital accumulation raises wage rates, and during this process a country's comparative advantage shifts away from more labor-intensive activities. Thus years ago Japan saw its shipbuilding and textile industries lost to South Korea and Taiwan, which, in turn, lost their comparative advantage to more labor-abundant countries further behind in the growth process. Taiwan lost its grip as the world's leader in umbrellas, as well as its established position in shoes and textiles. The very success of industries like these in raising wage rates in Taiwan now supports a shift toward higher technology and capital-intensive sectors. Taiwanese businesspeople eye wage rates in mainland China that are less than 20 percent of those prevailing in Taipei's tight labor market. As Chapter 8 discusses in more detail, a significant characteristic of modern trade patterns is the great increase in trade in intermediate products, natural resources, and producer goods, facilitating an international fragmentation of production processes whereby more labor-intensive activities get outsourced to low-wage areas.

6.7   Heckscher-Ohlin Theory and Empirical Evidence

A strong attraction of the Heckscher-Ohlin model is its numerous predictions about the relationships among actual trade patterns, factor endowments, and product and factor prices. Nonetheless, this model has caused considerable frustration for empirical researchers seeking to test it formally. Consider the factor-price equalization theorem. Casual observation immediately suggests that wages are not equalized among countries. But are the wage levels those of "comparable" labor? The rewards to capital appear much more nearly equalized among countries, but then capital (contrary to the theory's assumption) is rather mobile among countries (see Chapter 9), and that mobility tends to equalize prices among nations without any reference to the effect of commodity trade. Certainly a given industry does not use the same mixture of factor inputs in different countries, as it would if factor prices were equalized and technologies were identical.[8] Of course it is important to remember that the Heckscher-Ohlin model predicts factor-price equalization only if technologies and factors are comparable between countries and endowment proportions are fairly close to each other.

Testing the Heckscher-Ohlin Theorem

How can we test the Heckscher-Ohlin theorem systematically? Pioneer investigators reasoned as follows. Take a country that appears exceptionally well endowed with some factor, say, capital. Measure the quantities of capital and labor that it uses to pro-

---

[7]For example, according to the *Economist* (November 16, 1991), Taiwan accounted for a full 25 percent of doctorates in engineering at American universities.
[8]David Dollar, Edward J. Wolff, and William J. Baumol, "The Factor-Price Equalization Model and Industry Labor Productivity," in R. C. Feenstra, ed., *Empirical Methods for International Trade* (Cambridge, MA: MIT Press, 1988), pp. 23–47.

duce a unit of each good it exports and each good it produces at home in competition with imports (call such goods "importables"). Add these product-level inputs to obtain the total amounts of capital and labor tied up in producing exports (call them K_x and L_x) and also the total amounts of capital and labor allocated to producing importables at home (K_m and L_m), with actual exports and imports serving as weights. The capital-rich nation should then export a bundle of goods more capital intensive than its bundle of importables: $K_x/L_x > K_m/L_m$. W. W. Leontief proposed that after World War II the United States was a standout capital-rich nation suitable for this test. To everyone's surprise, the test was flunked: Imports were more capital intensive. It turned out, though, that Leontief omitted a big chunk of the U.S. capital stock—education (human capital). With education included in the calculated bundles of factors, the data supported the hypothesis. Even without the human-capital refinement, Leontief's paradox evaporated by the 1970s.[9]

Researchers soon saw serious shortcomings in the form of this test. How can one be sure the chosen country is an outlier in its factor endowment? Guessing won't do: One must measure a country's share of the world endowment of a factor in order to pin down its factor-endowment position. Furthermore, why apply the test to one country, rather than many countries at once? Edward Leamer proposed the following enriched test. Use data on each industry's input requirements to calculate the quantity of a factor of production needed to produce the bundle of goods that the country consumes. Subtract it from the quantity of that factor in the country's endowment (if the difference is positive, the country is well endowed with that factor). Using Leontief's procedure, measure the amount of that factor embodied in the country's net exports (that is, the amount needed to produce its exports minus the amount required for production at home of its importables). If the Heckscher-Ohlin theorem is correct, the amount of the factor embodied in net exports should increase with the excess of its endowment over its consumption needs.

When Edward Leamer, Daniel Trefler, and others performed this improved test, it offered only the weakest support for the hypothesis. Leamer and associates applied this design to no less than 12 factors of production for 27 countries. The results of their statistical test run in the right direction: When a country's net exports use a factor intensively, its endowment tends to be rich in that factor. However, for only one of 12 factors is this association statistically significant.[10]

Looking Elsewhere for Explanations

Daniel Trefler urged that economists, stuck with an attractive but miserably performing model of national trade patterns, should shop around for some new models. He came up with two.[11] The first reaches back to Ricardo: Each factor in Country A might be

[9]Robert M. Stern and Keith E. Maskus, "Determinants of the Structure of U.S. Foreign Trade, 1958–76," *Journal of International Economics,* 11 (May 1981): 207–224.

[10]Harry P. Bowen, Edward E. Leamer, and Leo Sveikauskas, "Multicountry, Multifactor Tests of the Factor Abundance Theory," *American Economic Review,* 77 (December 1987): 791–809. Their test is a restrictive one that assumes all countries have the same technology and tastes in consumption goods.

[11]Daniel C. Trefler, "The Case of the Missing Trade and Other Mysteries," *American Economic Review,* 85 (December 1995): 1029–1046.

10 percent more productive than its counterpart in country *B,* so that countries' shares of the world factor endowment are miscounted without productivity weights. The second recognizes that consumption patterns are dissimilar among countries in a way that is important for the test: Because of transportation costs, tariffs, or simply immemorial custom, a country tends to consume the goods that are cheaply produced with its own factor stock. That hypothesis is particularly attractive in light of Trefler's finding regarding the poor performance of Heckscher-Ohlin: One simply cannot find many instances of a country with a factor content in its net exports that is far out of line with the factor content of its consumption (this is the "missing trade"). Trefler found that both the technology-difference and consumption-bias hypotheses add a lot to the explanatory power of the Heckscher-Ohlin theorem. In short, the Heckscher-Ohlin theorem does explain something of nations' trade patterns, but it needs help from its friends.

Another modern explanation of trade patterns lies in the recent revival of economic geography: This focuses on the power of historical accident to dictate long-lasting patterns of specialization. The geographers note that economic activities concentrate not just in particular countries but in particular regions or cities; one mentions Hollywood, Detroit, and Silicon Valley without even needing to say what goods are produced there. These concentrations seldom depend on any particular natural resource or physical trait of the region that one can detect. Close study indicates that these regional concentrations share two properties. First, their original locations often resulted from some accidental event or institution that could just as easily have occurred in another place. Second, their long persistence rests on many external economies and other self-sustaining factors. A trained, specialist labor force develops, along with specialized auxiliary supply and service firms that do not exist anywhere else. Producers more readily pick up each other's productivity-raising secrets, and they strive to outdo each other for personal esteem as well as profit. Customers can readily compare the wares of competing sellers and, being fussy and demanding from close exposure, they impose high standards on the sellers' products.[12]

Once a successful regional cluster emerges, it becomes a source of exports for its nation. Having happened there first (by luck, perhaps), the cost effectiveness of a region's activities is likely to run ahead of production sites anywhere else, even if other countries' factor endowments could supply the same set of (general) inputs at lower cost. The greater the importance of such agglomerations, the more "noise" is created for the Heckscher-Ohlin and other static explanations of trade patterns.

What Is at Stake: Trade and Wages

The bases for a nation's comparative advantage matter beyond their explanation of its trade pattern. Urgent issues of public policy are also involved. In the United States during the 1980s and 1990s, the differential between the hourly earnings of skilled and unskilled labor increased greatly, with the relative wages of college graduates rising from a 38 percent premium in 1979 to 65 percent in 1993, and the real wages of low-

---

[12]Michael E. Porter, *The Competitive Advantage of Nations* (New York: Free Press, 1990); Paul Krugman, *Geography and Trade* (Cambridge, MA: MIT Press, 1991).

skilled men indeed falling significantly. (The European industrial countries saw a similar development, but there it resulted in high unemployment rates rather than falling wages for unskilled labor.) At the same time U.S. imports from developing countries increased from 0.4 percent of GNP in 1970 to 2.5 percent in 1990.[13] Was the swelling wage differential related to rising capacities of the developing countries to supply low-skill manufactured goods to the United States? If the United States chiefly exports goods intensive in capital and skills and imports goods intensive in low-skilled labor, that could be the answer. The Stolper-Samuelson theorem predicts this relationship as a consequence of U.S. exports using skilled labor in larger proportion to unskilled labor than do the U.S. goods that compete with imports. But other factors vie to provide explanations to this rising wage inequality, and it proves difficult to sort them out.

An obvious competing hypothesis suggests that the supply of low-skill labor (measured by years of schooling) has increased, driving down low-skill wages. Yet it is easily established that the supply of low-skill labor has been falling relative to more highly educated labor. As William Cline pointed out, the relative increase in skilled labor that actually occurred by itself would have lowered the skill differential by 40 percent.[14]

The other competing hypothesis is quite independent of international trade. It springs from the observation that technological change commonly seems to call for the substitution of skilled for unskilled labor. That is, in innovative processes, capital and skilled labor are complements and substitute for less skilled labor and capital embodying traditional technologies. If the outputs of innovative technologies are welcomed in export markets, that tends further to shrink the relative demand for unskilled labor.

Capital-skill complementarity has been confirmed in numerous studies. Furthermore, it is evident in countries other than the United States. It is strong enough to leave only modest room for other explanations of wage inequality. Numerous studies of the effects of increased supplies of low-skill imports give diverse results but typically find only small room for imports as a cause of the increasing inequality of wages.[15] They leave little doubt that these several explanations interact and all make some contribution to explaining increased wage inequality. When Cline added up the various effects on wage inequality, he concluded that international competition made up approximately one tenth of the total forces.[16]

Cline asked whether U.S. policy makers could have preserved unskilled labor's relative wage by means of tariff protection, as the Stolper-Samuelson theorem suggests. He concluded, however, that low-wage labor would actually not benefit. That is because low-skill workers tend to consume relatively large amounts of unskilled-labor-intensive products and transfer payments, and the low savings rates of low-income workers tend to make their share of consumption larger than their share of income.

---

[13]Richard B. Freeman, "Are Your Wages Set in Beijing?" *Journal of Economic Perspectives,* 9 (Summer 1995): 15–32.

[14]William R. Cline, *Trade and Income Distribution* (Washington, DC: Institute for International Economics, 1997).

[15]See Robert E. Baldwin and Glen G. Cain, "Shifts in Relative U.S. Wages: The Role of Trade, Technology, and Factor Endowments," *Review of Economics and Statistics,* 82 (November 2000): 580–595.

[16]Cline introduced immigration to the United States in the international influences and also took account of some other effects such as the erosion of monopoly power in the transportation and metal-fabrication industries, whose excess profits had previously been shared by their low-skill workers.

This conclusion about the fate of unskilled labor fits more comfortably into the specific-factors setting of Chapter 5 if unskilled labor is the factor mobile between sectors. Tariff protection that raises the price of import-competing commodities indeed raises the nominal wage rate but only by a fraction of the price hike. The cost of living index for workers could rise by a higher fraction if their consumption of importables exceeds local production.[17]

6.8 Summary

In contrast to the discussion in Chapter 5 of production in which output in each sector is obtained by combining labor drawn from a national market with a factor specifically tied to that industry, the Heckscher-Ohlin theory assumes no factor is specific. Labor and capital are costlessly transferable from sector to sector.

Some of the Heckscher-Ohlin properties can be compared to similar ones encountered in Chapter 5:

1. Output in any industry cannot expand without driving up relative costs. Costs are bid up because the return to the factor used relatively intensively in that industry is bid up by a magnified amount.

2. Any change in a country's terms of trade is accompanied by a relatively more profound redistribution of factor incomes. Even a broad-based factor such as labor unambiguously gains if the relative price of labor-intensive goods rises. This particular result contrasts with the conclusion in Chapter 5 that a mobile factor such as labor cannot significantly alter its real wage through changes in commodity prices, although specific factors definitely could. The Heckscher-Ohlin model is less applicable to questions of *short-run* impact of policy changes on income distribution than is the specific-factors model of Chapter 5.

3. Differences in factor endowments influence the direction of trade. A relatively ample endowment of capital leads to exports that intensively require capital.

Perhaps the most striking conclusion of the simple Heckscher-Ohlin model is one not shared by the specific-factors model: Free trade in commodities *may* completely substitute for international mobility of capital and labor in the sense of driving wages and rents to equality for countries sharing the same technology. The sharp contrast between this factor-price equalization result and observed international comparisons of wage rates and returns to capital has contributed much to discredit Heckscher-Ohlin propositions as a whole. In defense of Heckscher-Ohlin theory, the following can be pointed out:

1. If countries differ in technological knowledge (or climate and other influences on the relationship between inputs and outputs), any presumption that free trade brings about absolute factor-price equalization disappears.

---

[17]This argument is spelled out in R. Ruffin and R. Jones, "Protection and Real Wages: The Neoclassical Ambiguity," *Journal of Economic Theory* (April 1977): 337–348.

2. Even if countries differ in technological knowledge, many propositions of Heckscher-Ohlin theory are unaffected. For example, the impact of a tariff on real wages at home depends only on home technology and not at all on how commodities are produced abroad.

3. When viewed in a multicountry, multicommodity setting, factor-price equalization is less likely to occur even between countries sharing the same technology. Instead, any significant difference between countries in basic capital/labor endowment proportions would be reflected in countries producing different sets of commodities. If they were to produce a commodity in common, the capital-rich country would be likely to adopt more capital-intensive techniques precisely because its labor force was more productive and better paid.

The pattern of trade in a Heckscher-Ohlin world of many countries and many commodities shares much in common with a Ricardian world. Countries concentrate their productive activities around a few commodities whose demands for factors closely reflect total factor availability and import commodities representing a wide dispersion in factor requirements (if they were to be produced at home) compared with those adopted for the export sectors. Factor intensities in a nation's aggregate *output* bundle reflect that country's factor-endowment proportions. Factor intensities in a nation's aggregate *consumption* bundle reflect average world factor endowments if countries have similar tastes. Because trade flows represent the difference between output and consumption, relatively capital-abundant countries, on the average, import relatively labor-intensive commodities. This is an *average* result, however; the wide dispersion in imports still remains.

As countries grow over time, the range of goods produced for export changes systematically. Growth in physical and human capital leads to higher real wage rates, which alters comparative advantage away from traditional labor-intensive commodities toward commodities reflecting higher capital/labor ratios and superior quality. This pattern was strongly reflected in the particularly high-growth economies of Southeast Asia.

Transport costs and tariffs serve to widen a country's range of productive activities. Resources specific to certain activities also convey a comparative advantage not captured solely by capital/labor rankings. In the short run, many types of capital (and perhaps skilled labor) are not mobile between sectors. This tends to lessen the concentration of production. The spirit of the Heckscher-Ohlin theory still remains to suggest that differences between countries in their endowment of broad classes of productive factors such as capital and labor will be reflected in differences in patterns of production and trade.

In a famous empirical test of the Heckscher-Ohlin theorem, Leontief investigated whether the exports of the United States—a capital-rich country—embody more capital relative to labor than do the goods that the United States produces in competition with imports. To everyone's surprise, he found that U.S. exports were labor intensive compared to import-competing goods. Subsequent research has partly resolved this paradox by showing that U.S. exports are intensive in human capital, and the capital intensity of import-competing goods is associated with the prevalence of raw materials.

Empirical tests of the theorem have shifted recently to a global level. Countries rich in a particular factor generally have been found to make net exports of goods requiring that factor intensively, but the relationship is weak and leaves room for other explanations (economic geography, home biases in consumption patterns).

The relative decline of wages of unskilled U.S. labor invites an explanation based on expanding trade with other countries, especially developing nations, with larger endowments of unskilled labor. This force has been at work, although technological change favoring the substitution of skilled for unskilled labor is much more important.

CHAPTER PROBLEMS

1. Suppose only one technique can be used in clothing production. To produce a unit of clothing requires four labor-hours and one unit of capital; in food production each unit requires a single labor-hour and one unit of capital. At an initial equilibrium suppose the wage rate and the capital rental are each valued at $2. If both goods are produced, what must be their prices? Now keep the price of food constant and raise the price of clothing to $15. Trace through the effects on the distribution of income. Rank the relative changes in the wage rate, the price of clothing, the price of food (unchanged by assumption), and the rent on capital. Relate your results to the Stolper-Samuelson theorem.

2. Retain the assumptions about technology in Problem 1:

$$a_{LC} = 4 \qquad a_{KC} = 1 \qquad a_{LF} = 1 \qquad a_{KF} = 1$$

Draw a diagram with capital on the vertical axis and labor on the horizontal. Draw a ray through the origin with a slope of unity and show how outputs of food can be measured along this ray. Draw a flatter ray, with a slope of $\frac{1}{4}$, and show how outputs of clothing can be measured along this ray. Suppose the economy possesses 1000 units of labor.

   a. Find the full-employment levels of output of each good if the capital stock is 500 units.

   b. Find the lowest and highest capital stocks that still allow full employment of both factors.

   c. Draw the transformation schedule for each of the cases in 2a and 2b.

3. Assume that input-output coefficients are fixed. The table shows capital requirements per unit output (a_{Kj}) and labor requirements per unit output (a_{Lj}) to produce one unit each of commodities 1 through 5. Also shown are prevailing world prices for each commodity.

	Commodity				
	1	2	3	4	5
a_{Kj}	4	2	1	1	1
a_{Lj}	1	1	1	2	4
Price	$16	$14	$10	$14	$16

    a. If the economy has a labor/capital endowment ratio of 3:1, what does it produce? What are the wage rate and rents on capital?

    b. If the world price of commodity *1* should triple, would there be any change in this country's production pattern? Factor prices? Real income?

    c. At the initial prices shown in the table, how would factor prices differ in an economy with the same technology but a capital/labor endowment ratio of 3:1?

    d. For the economy with the original labor/capital endowment ratio of 3:1, how would production patterns and factor prices change if commodity *3*'s price on world markets should rise by 40 percent?

    e. Describe the pattern of trade for an economy with a capital/labor endowment ratio of 1:1.

4. Using Figures 6.6 and 6.7, show how an increase in the world price of commodity *2* would affect real wages in two countries sharing the same technology, both of them producing commodity *2*, but with the home country having an endowment ratio 0*I* (Figure 6.7) and the foreign country with endowment ratio 0*M*.

5. In Figure 6.A.1 the production box diagram shows that a country with given endowments of capital and labor could not produce food by capital-intensive techniques at one set of outputs while switching to labor-intensive techniques at another. Show the inconsistency involved if the contract curve crosses the diagonal.

6. The text describes an example in which a country with the same capital endowment as another, but a greater endowment of labor, must actually produce less of one good if they both face the same terms of trade (this is the Rybczynski theorem). Establish this result by superimposing the box diagrams of the two countries so that they share a common food origin (lower-left corner). How do the two contract curves compare?

SUGGESTIONS FOR FURTHER READING

Cline, William R. *Trade and Income Distribution* (Washington, DC: Institute for International Economics, 1997). Major study of the role of international trade in lowering the relative wages of unskilled U.S. workers.

Heckscher, Eli. "The Effect of Foreign Trade on the Distribution of Income." A translation is provided by H. Flam and M. J. Flanders, eds., *Heckscher-Ohlin Trade Theory* (Cambridge, MA: MIT Press, 1991). This article originally appeared in Swedish in *Ekonomisk Tidskerift*, 21 (1919): 497–512. It discusses the effect of trade on factor prices in a nonmathematical format.

Helpman, Elhanan. "The Structure of Foreign Trade," *Journal of Economic Perspectives,* 13 (Spring 1999): 121–144. Reviews empirical research on the factor-proportions model of trade.

Jones, Ronald W. "Heckscher-Ohlin Trade Models for the New Century," Chapter 16 in Ronald Findlay et al. (eds.), *Bertil Ohlin: A Centennial Celebration* (Cambridge, MA: MIT Press, 2002), pp. 343–362. A general appraisal of the basic Heckscher-Ohlin approach.

————."The Small Country in a Many-Commodity World," *Australian Economic Papers* (December 1974): 225–236, reprinted in R. W. Jones, *International Trade: Essays in Theory* (Amsterdam: North-Holland, 1979), Chapter 2. A more general treatment of the material in Section 6.4.

Leamer, Edward E. *Sources of International Comparative Advantage: Theory and Evidence* (Cambridge, MA: MIT Press, 1984). An interesting application of the Heckscher-Ohlin framework to a setting with three factors (land, labor, and capital). Traces the development of a number of countries.

Ohlin, Bertil. *Interregional and International Trade* (Cambridge, MA: Harvard University Press, 1933). Together with the Heckscher article, this book forms the basis for the modern theory of trade.

Rybczynski, T. M. "Factor Endowment and Relative Commodity Prices," *Economica*, 22 (November 1955): 336–341. A statement and proof of the Rybczynski theorem, using production box diagrams.

Samuelson, Paul A. "International Factor-Price Equalization Once Again," *Economic Journal*, 59 (June 1949): 181–197, reprinted in J. Stiglitz, ed., *The Collected Scientific Papers of Paul A. Samuelson,* Vol. 2 (Cambridge, MA: MIT Press, 1966), Chapter 68. A restatement of Samuelson's factor-price equalization theorem.

Stolper, W. F., and P. A. Samuelson. "Protection and Real Wages," *Review of Economic Studies,* 9 (November 1941): 58–73, reprinted in A. Deardorff and R. Stern (eds.), *The Stolper-Samuelson Theorem: A Golden Jubilee* (Ann Arbor: University of Michigan Press, 1994). The original statement of the Stolper-Samuelson theorem.

APPENDIX

The Production Box

The concept of a consumption box diagram was described in the appendix to Chapter 2. The analogy that now proves useful is that of the production box diagram shown in Figure 6.A.1. The dimensions of the box are the home country's fixed total endowments of capital and labor. Any point inside the box represents a possible allocation of capital and labor to the food sector, whose origin is the lower-left corner of the box, and to clothing, whose origin is the upper-right corner. The *contract curve* $0_F AB0_C$ shows all capital and labor allocations for which isoquants for food and clothing have the same slope. Points A and B are two such allocations. Points along the contract curve are efficient—for example, for given output X_F^A of food, the allocation that maximizes clothing output is shown by A. Each point on the contract curve shows not only (efficient) allocations of capital and labor to each sector, it also shows total food and clothing outputs (by the values of the two isoquants tangent at that point). Thus the points on the contract curve map into the outputs along the country's production possibilities schedule. That is, each point on the home country's transformation schedule corresponds to an allocation of labor and capital to the two industries shown by a particular point on the contract curve.

FIGURE 6.A.1

The Production Box Diagram

Points on the contract curve $0_F AB0_C$ show efficient, competitive allocations of the economy's fixed overall endowments of labor and capital.

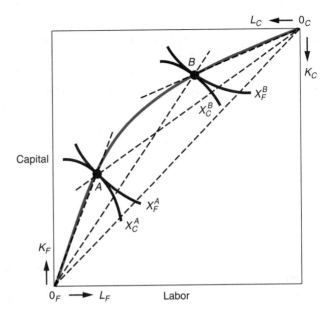

Consider the background adjustments in factor proportions and income distribution that would accompany a move from point *A* to point *B* in Figure 6.A.1; this corresponds to an increase in food production and a reduction in the quantity of clothing produced along the production possibilities schedule. The diagram shows (by the slopes of rays from each origin to *A* and *B*) that such a move lowers the capital/labor ratios used in *both* industries because it drives up the ratio of rents to wages. Such a relative cheapening of labor encourages firms in *both* sectors to adopt more labor-intensive techniques. Thus, at *B*, food is produced with a lower capital/labor ratio than at *A*. At *B* the pair of tangent isoquants are flatter than at *A*, the lower slope reflecting a lower wage/rent ratio.

How can both sectors change factor intensities in the same direction if the economy's overall factor supplies remain unchanged? By changing the composition of output. At *A* both industries adopt a *higher* capital/labor ratio than at *B*, but this is made possible by *lowering* the output of capital-intensive food relative to clothing. Not only is it *possible* that capital/labor ratios move in the same direction (despite the fact that the endowment ratio is fixed), they *must* move in the same direction because techniques in both sectors respond to the same change in factor prices.[18]

---

[18]Suppose you have taken two exams and received a 70 on one and a 90 on the other—with an announced average of 80. You know that because your professor is somewhat of a wimp and susceptible to pressure, by complaining you might raise these two grades, respectively, to a 74 and a 93. However, your wimpy professor may have the last word and keep your average at 80 by raising the weighting of your first test score.

CHAPTER 7

Imperfect Competition, Increasing Returns, and Product Variety

The preceding chapters have developed three different models dealing with production and international trade. Whereas the Ricardian model emphasized the possibility that countries might differ in their effective technological knowledge, including the skills of productive factors and asymmetries in climate, the Specific-Factors model and the Heckscher-Ohlin model both emphasized the role of countries possessing relatively different endowments of productive factors. Although different in these respects, all three scenarios shared something in common: Commodity markets were assumed to display purely competitive conditions in that all firms are assumed to be price-takers and entry into any activity was open so competition would drive prices down to the level of unit costs. Constant returns to scale characterized all productive activity. That is, there were assumed to be no *scale* effects wherein large firms could develop a cost advantage over smaller firms.

Not all commodity markets exhibit purely competitive behavior, and not all production processes are characterized by constant returns to scale. The development of international trade theory based on imperfectly competitive behavior has made great strides in recent years, and such work has developed along two different lines. First has been the analysis focused on international competition between large firms, say monopolists in each country or oligopoly behavior wherein entrance by new firms is made difficult and firms make profits in equilibrium. The role of governments is important in that they may champion their local firm, trying to pass on a strategic advantage in their competition with the national champions of other countries for profits that could be made in international markets. Issues arising from such a setting are discussed in later chapters in which a nation's commercial policy (tariffs, subsidies, and other ways in which countries interfere with free trade) is appraised.

The second line of investigation, discussed in the present chapter, stems from an observation that some real trade patterns seemed not to be well captured by the purely competitive models, namely, that a high fraction of international exchange is of the form of intra-industry trade, wherein countries often export and import commodities that are part of the same industrial classification. We start by describing the importance of such trade and then turn to a type of imperfect market behavior, that of *monopolistic competition*, that has been put forth to explain such behavior. A natural role is found in this model for the importance of scale effects as providing an explanation for international trade patterns that is additional to the relevance of asymmetries in technologies and relative factor endowments we previously examined.

7.1   The Prevalence of Intra-Industry Trade

The traditional theories of a nation's comparative advantage in international trade imply that a traded good is either imported or exported, but not both. However, economists have come to realize that many very similar commodities are both exported from and imported into most industrial countries. This phenomenon was first noticed empirically among the European countries as they eliminated trade restrictions among themselves to form the European Common Market (now European Union). It soon became clear that two-way trade is a fairly general phenomenon.

The simplest way to measure intra-industry trade is by means of the following formula, where X indicates exports of some class of goods and M indicates imports of items in this same class:

$$1 - (|X - M|)/(X + M)$$

If a country only exports or only imports an item in this class, the second term reduces to X/X (or $M/M) = 1$, and the whole expression equals zero. If X equals M, the second term equals zero and the whole expression equals one. Thus the index ranges from zero, where no intra-industry trade occurs, to one (or 100, if expressed as a percentage) when exports and imports are balanced and intra-industry trade is at its maximum. Table 7.1 illustrates the amount of intra-industry trade that takes place. It was calcu-

TABLE 7.1

Average Levels of Intra-Industry Trade, All Commodities, Selected Countries, 1964–1985 (percentages)

Country	1964	1967	1973	1979	1985
Canada	37	49	57	56	68[a]
United States	48	52	48	52	72[a]
Japan	23	22	24	21	24
Belgium/Luxembourg	62	66	69	73	74
Netherlands	65	66	63	65	67
Germany	44	51	60	60	65
France	64	67	70	70	72
Italy	49	45	54	48	55
United Kingdom	46	55	71	80	76
Australia	18	17	29	22	25
Mean of above countries	46	49	55	55	60

[a]These unusually high values probably reflect the enormous volume of trade in automobiles and parts between the United States and Canada under a special free-trade arrangement for this sector.

Source: Organization for Economic Cooperation and Development, Structural Adjustment and Economic Performance (Paris: OECD, 1987), p. 273.

lated by applying a version of the formula to each standard statistical classification of commodities and then averaging the values over all classes for each country (and year). The amount of intra-industry trade evidently rose by approximately a third over the years 1964 to 1985. It is over half for all the countries shown except Japan and Australia, which differ from the others in having very sharply distinguished comparative advantages or disadvantages in wide ranges of commodities.

The extent of intra-industry trade varies a good deal from industry to industry. Casual examination of intra-industry trade ratios for U.S. industries suggests that they are low for simple, undifferentiated products in which the country has either a strong comparative advantage (corn) or disadvantage (crude petroleum). They are high for nearly all complex, differentiated goods (photographic equipment), whatever the apparent state of our comparative advantage. They are also high for some simple goods (fertilizers, inorganic chemicals) for which the country seems to neither have a strong advantage nor disadvantage.

7.2   Consumer Behavior and the Demand for Product Variety

Many commodity groups contain a number of varieties. Consumers differ in the varieties they most prefer. Some men have a preference for suits and ties, whereas others would rather have a more casual look in clothing; some consumers prefer brie to cheddar and others the reverse. A nation could well be populated by consumers with a wide range of preferences in clothing (or cheese), so that if some types are produced at home and others abroad, the country would have to be both an exporter and an importer of each class of commodity to satisfy such a spectrum of demand. Such trade is referred to as *intra-industry*. Other individuals may exhibit a love for variety—sometimes with an appetite for Chinese cooking, other times for an Italian pasta dish. To the extent that both types of individuals are found within the nation's borders, a basis is provided for healthy intra-industry trade, even if endowment differences suggest, say, that overall the home country is a *net* exporter of clothing and the foreign country a *net* exporter of food. Gross trade flows encompass both intra-industry exchanges for commodities in similar categories as well as inter-industry trade of different products.

Return to our earlier discussion of trade in two commodities, clothing and food. There we *assumed* the type of food or clothing available in one country was identical in the two countries. This certainly makes the discussion and the diagrams simpler. But suppose, now, that each country's variety is distinct from that in the other country, so that international trade allows consumers in each country to have variety introduced into their consumption possibilities. That is, in each country, consumption of four distinct varieties (two in each industry) instead of two is made possible in the move from autarky to free trade. Assume varieties in each commodity group can be added up (more on this later). Then, as Figure 7.1 reveals, if indifference curve y_0 for the home country (say) expresses a given level of satisfaction at home for all the consumption bundles along the curve when there is autarky at home, this *same* level of satisfaction can be achieved by the indifference curve, y_T, when free trade between countries allows a wider selection of varieties. Some consumers at home may now just consume

FIGURE 7.1

Trade and Welfare

Point *A* on indifference curve y_0 before trade yields the same level of utility as any point on indifference curve y_T if after trade the variety of clothing and/or food available for consumption increases.

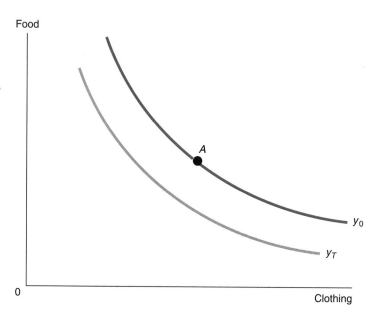

the foreign variety (say of food), if that comes closer to their ideal; others, exercising their love of variety, demand both the home and foreign offerings. The aggregate bundle, *A*, on indifference curve, y_0, would yield a higher level of satisfaction if after trade it were available in either (or both) of each country's variety.

Those individuals who prefer variety to consuming only one type of commodity can have their preferences illustrated by the indifference curve for food drawn in Figure 7.2. Note how such an indifference curve (for a given consumption of clothing) is drawn such that it hits each axis. This is necessary, for it allows the individual to survive with consumption of only one variety or to select some of both. If restricted to consuming only one variety and if the relative price of the first variety is higher than illustrated by the slope of the dashed line, the individual would consume only the second variety. But note that in this event the individual could attain the same level of satisfaction at a lower cost if allowed to consume a combination of the two varieties of food (say at point *A* in Figure 7.2). Similarly, if the relative price of the first variety were lower than illustrated by the dashed line, the individual would prefer to consume only the first variety if only one could be consumed, but a love of variety is revealed by the fact that a point such as *B* achieves the same level of satisfaction at a lower overall cost.

The addition of variety increases the gains from trade already possible by exchanging food for clothing. Indeed, if two countries had identical endowments of food and clothing, intra-industry trade could improve real incomes even in the absence of any inter-industry trade. Furthermore, there need be no losers with trade—everyone benefits by having a wider selection of each type of commodity from which to choose or blend.

FIGURE 7.2

Love of Variety

Individuals consume a given amount of clothing and have available two varieties of food. The indifference curve for these two varieties hits the axes, showing that individuals can survive consuming only quantity *C* of the first variety or only quantity *D* of the second variety. However, for given prices of the two varieties, a mixture of varieties shown by *A* or by *B* could be obtained more cheaply and yield the same level of utility.

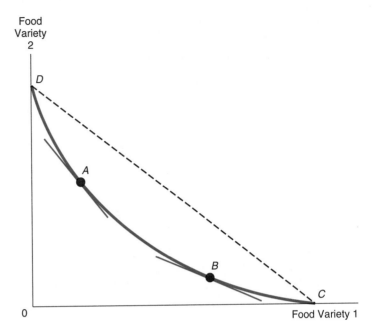

7.3 Increasing Returns in Production

Very little has been said about production in the preceding account or, for that matter, about the nature of competition. If firms in each country produce only a single variety, one that differs from country to country, and if outputs are held fixed, as in Figure 2.4(a) in Chapter 2, intra-industry trade can take place between countries without increasing returns in production and with purely competitive behavior.

Suppose, now, that in one industry, clothing, production exhibits increasing returns to scale in the sense that if all inputs were to increase in the same proportion, output would expand by a greater relative amount. In such a case a large firm would have a scale advantage over a smaller one, and it is easy to imagine that the resulting market would consist of a single large monopolistic supplier. However, suppose that in the clothing sector, individual tastes range over a wide variety of types of clothing. Furthermore, assume that each variety entails two different types of costs: a fixed-cost element (such as the costs of styling as well as capital) plus constant marginal production costs so that total *variable* production costs increase in proportion to output. The consequence: to produce each variety of clothing the average costs of production decline as output expands. From a cost point of view, it would be cheaper just to produce a single variety, but this would neglect the value that consumers place on being able to select from a wide menu of types of clothing. The type of market that results when there is an interplay between declining costs to produce each variety and a demand for variety is called *monopolistic competition.*

FIGURE 7.3

Monopolistic Competition

A firm in a monopolistically competitive equilibrium produces at q_A, with marginal revenue equal to marginal cost. Free entry wipes out all positive profits at price p_A, equal to average costs.

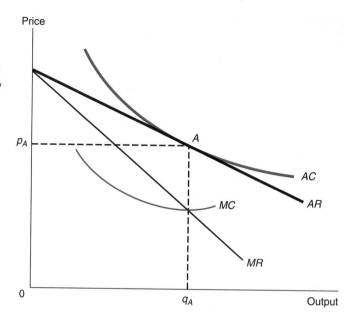

Monopolistic Competition

Figure 7.3 illustrates the type of market equilibrium that would emerge for each firm in monopolistic competition. Two cost curves are drawn: the marginal cost curve showing the extra costs involved in producing an extra unit of output, and the higher average cost curve, which is declining because it includes, for each unit of output, not only marginal costs but also that output's share of fixed costs. Demand conditions have been illustrated as well: a downward sloping demand curve for this variety, the AR curve (for average revenue, which is price). Such a demand curve facing any single firm is assumed to be quite elastic because there are large numbers of firms (each with its own variety), but not to exhibit the strictly horizontal shape that typifies a firm in a competitive environment in which all firms produce identical commodities. A critical feature of monopolistic competition is that new firms are assumed to be able to enter the market in case existing firms are making profits. These new firms will position themselves so as to produce new varieties instead of adding to the output of existing varieties. Such entry causes demand curves for each existing variety to shift to the left until equilibrium is obtained when entry squeezes out all profits. Point A depicts such an equilibrium: Each firm is maximizing profits when marginal costs equal marginal revenue, but such profits are reduced to zero when entry forces average revenue down to the level of average costs—at the tangency point between the two average curves.

To keep the analysis simple, strong assumptions have been made: Each firm produces a separate variety in which the cost structure is the same for all firms. In addition, the configuration of demand is identical for all varieties. The resulting equilibrium price and quantity for each firm is the same, as illustrated by p_A and q_A in Figure 7.3.

FIGURE 7.4

Size and Number of Firms

The *RC* curve shows how in each country sharing a common technology, larger firm size goes hand in hand with the production of a greater number of varieties. In autarky, the smaller home market is served by firms (at *H*) that are fewer in number and smaller in size than in the larger foreign market (*F*). With trade, if the same resources are devoted to clothing as in autarky, producers concentrate (at *H'* and *F'*), all firms are the same (larger) size, and a larger number of varieties is available for consumers (at *W*).

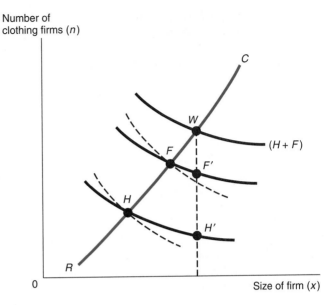

Firm Size and Product Variety in Autarky

The equilibrium illustrated in Figure 7.3 could represent the situation in the home country in autarky. How might such an equilibrium differ in the foreign country when it also must rely only on its own production to satisfy demand in autarky?

Suppose the technology required to produce any variety is not only the same for each variety at home but also is shared by firms abroad. Similarly, suppose demand conditions are the same in both countries. If the foreign country is larger and devotes more resources to the clothing sector, its firms in autarky will not resemble exactly the firms at home. Figure 7.4 helps identify the differences. The horizontal axis measures the size (x) of a firm in the clothing sector, whereas the vertical axis measures the number of clothing firms (n), each producing a distinct variety. The upward-sloping *RC* curve is assumed to be common to both countries.[1] In autarky the home country is positioned at *H* and the foreign country at *F*. The total size of the market is larger for points farther out along the *RC* curve, which suggests that any one firm will face stiffer competition as more brands are introduced. Assuming demand becomes more elastic and profits once again are squeezed out by the entry of new firms, as in the tangency solution of Figure 7.3, the size of a typical firm also expands. (That is, the tangency point in Figure 7.3 slides farther down the average cost curve.) As a consequence, the number of varieties changes positively with the size of the representative firm. With the expansion in market size, any one brand faces closer substitutes and firms become

---

[1]A discussion of this curve is found in Elhanan Helpman and Paul Krugman, *Market Structure and Foreign Trade* (Cambridge, MA: MIT Press, 1985), pp. 153–157.

larger. If the two countries share a common technology, in autarky the smaller market will be served by a smaller number of firms, each similar in size to any other firm in that country but smaller in size relative to firms in the larger foreign market. Thus differences in country size are reflected in differences in firm size.

Differentiated Products in a World Market

A common theme running through all the previous chapters is that the possibility of trading in world markets frees local consumers from a lockstep dependence on the output of national firms. Such a theme is especially relevant to countries producing differentiated products once the countries move from autarky to engage in world markets. The composition of trade depends on cost conditions and tastes for both the clothing and food sectors at home and abroad. Postpone for the moment a full analysis of free-trade patterns by considering only how each country's consumers and producers of clothing respond to the possibilities of international trade *if* each country makes the same commitment of total resources to the clothing industry as it did in autarky. (It will then be asked how this allocation of resources can be altered by trade.)

In Figure 7.4 the curves HH' and FF' show, for home and foreign country, respectively, a given allocation of resources to the clothing sector—the same level as in autarky positions H and F. A move toward the southeast represents, for each country, a cutback in the number of varieties produced but an increase in the scale of operations for each variety. Now add these curves vertically to obtain the $(H + F)$ locus, which cuts the RC curve at W. Consider the consequences of trade for consumers and producers in each country: (1) For consumers, opening up trade with the other country establishes a larger market in which more varieties are made available. As discussed earlier, the possibility of widening the number of varieties from which to choose (singly or in combination) raises the utility gained from purchase of any aggregate bundle of clothing. (2) As for producers of clothing, in each country firms now face greater competition. As a consequence of the change to a single, larger, world market, elasticities of demand increase and, for the assumed given allocation of resources to clothing in each country, the number of firms in each is reduced, with each firm becoming larger. Indeed, in the run-up to the Canadian national elections in 1988, where the possibility of a Free-Trade Agreement with the United States (followed five years later by the inclusion of Mexico in NAFTA) was the burning issue, pro-agreement forces in Canada emphasized the gains to be had by Canadian firms having longer production runs with freer access to American consumers. In Figure 7.4 we illustrate that free international trade allows both home and foreign firms to produce for the same larger world market, thus increasing the size of foreign firms from F to F' and home firms by a larger amount, from H to H'.

This type of reaction of producers in a setting of monopolistic competition suggests that our earlier discussion in Chapter 2 of the gains to be had when a country moves from autarky to free trade can be widened. (Already discussed is the downward shift in indifference curves shown in Figure 7.1, in the case in which both the clothing and food sectors contain a number of varieties). Each country's transforma-

FIGURE 7.5

Trade and the Shift in the
Transformation Schedule

If clothing is available in autarky for
a given number of varieties, a certain
allocation of resources can support
production at point A. If the same
allocation of resources after trade is
made to the entire clothing sector,
production point B is attainable if
clothing varieties exhibit increasing
returns to scale. The reason is that
fewer varieties will be produced locally,
and thus have longer production runs
and lower average costs.

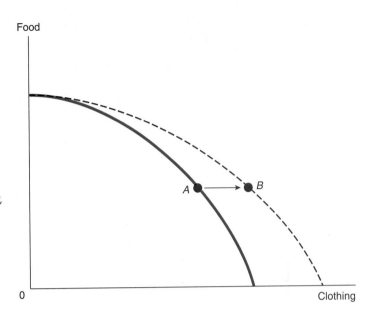

tion schedule shifts outward, in a manner captured in Figure 7.5. Consider an arbitrary assignment of resources to the two industries represented by point *A* for the home country in autarky. After trade, the same total output of food would be produced from the same set of inputs into food production.[2] But a greater aggregate output of clothing is achieved (at point *B* in Figure 7.5). The reason? The greater competitive forces in the larger world market for clothing with trade force a reduction in the number of firms producing clothing at home, with each surviving firm producing a greater output with the same fixed costs. In Figure 7.4 a dotted curve is drawn through point *H* (and one through foreign point *F* as well). This curve is a rectangular hyperbola (the fancy mathematical name), a curve along which the number of firms, (*n*), times the output size of the firm, (*x*), is a constant. That is, total home clothing output would be a constant along such a curve. The clothing output at *H'* exceeds that at *H* because of the increasing returns found in clothing firms. Note there is an asymmetry in the effect of trade on firms in the two countries: In autarky foreign firms are larger than home firms because of the assumed larger foreign market. Such a distinction gets obliterated with the creation of a single world free-trade market, and firm size between countries becomes the same. This, of course, assumes away transportation costs or human-made obstacles that would persist to keep foreign firms larger than those at home.

---

[2]Recall that here we assume food is a homogeneous product and the food market is perfectly competitive. For the development of a model in which one sector is monopolistically competitive, and the other is purely competitive, see especially Elhanan Helpman, "International Trade in the Presence of Product Differentiation, Economies of Scale, and Monopolistic Competition: A Chamberlin-Heckscher-Ohlin Approach," *Journal of International Economics* 11 (1981), pp. 305–340.

The Combination of Intra-Industry Trade and Inter-Industry Trade

There is no reason why the resources allocated to the clothing sector in each country in autarky should still indicate resource use after trade has been opened up. Although we have assumed that all varieties of clothing in each country are produced in the same way (and that consumer demand is such that all have the same price and thus can be aggregated into an industry total), we retain the assumption that food is produced differently, by capital-intensive techniques compared with clothing. Therefore the bias in production imparted by countries possessing different relative factor endowments carries over to indicate the extent of *inter-industry* trade, of net clothing exports from the relatively labor-abundant home country. As the figures in Table 7.1 indicate, intra-industry trade is indeed important but so also is inter-industry trade. The causes of trade explored in the preceding chapters, namely, technology differences and/or differences in factor proportions, often serve well to indicate the pattern of inter-industry trade, but two-way trade in varieties within an industry classification takes place as well, and this kind of trade is encouraged by the increasing returns to scale found in markets characterized by monopolistic competition.

Quality Differences and Intra-Industry Trade

Does this kind of model setting, with the emphasis on increasing returns in production and imperfect competition, rule out the importance of factor endowments and factor intensities in determining the nature of intra-industry trading patterns? The answer would have to be in the affirmative if we literally stick with the assumption that the capital/labor ratios used in producing any variety of clothing is the same as for any other variety, for then there is no opening for factor endowments to make a difference. What, then, does determine which varieties of clothing get produced at home and which abroad? The theory is silent on this point or argues that the pattern makes no difference because this is *horizontal* intra-industry trade. But it is also possible that two-way trade takes place in varieties that differ in quality, a kind of *vertical* intra-industry trade.[3] Japan or Germany may produce automobiles that are of higher quality than South Korea or Spain. If higher quality varieties are produced, say, with more capital-intensive techniques than are lower quality varieties, we might expect the higher quality varieties to be produced by more capital-abundant countries.

There is, however, an added effect stemming from asymmetry between countries in relative capital abundance. Per capita incomes tend to be higher in more capital-abundant countries, and such income differentials may find expression in the difference in the quality of varieties demanded in such countries. Factor endowments have an influence both on the supply side and the demand side. It may be the case that relatively capital-abundant countries tend to export capital intensive commodities in inter-industry trade. However, if a labor-abundant country produces a number of varieties of

---

[3]See especially the article by Rod Falvey and Henryk Kierzkowski, "Product Quality, Intra-industry Trade, and (Im)perfect Competition," in H. Kierzkowski, ed., *Protection and Competition in International Trade* (Oxford: Blackwell, 1987), pp. 143–161.

a commodity, differing in quality, the varieties that get exported to capital-rich countries may well be more capital intensive than those varieties consumed at home.[4] In the United States in discussions leading up to the NAFTA treaty with Mexico and Canada, American tomato producers were concerned with the fact that Mexico often exports its quality tomatoes, well packaged, to the American market.

7.4 Summary

Industries in which consumers' tastes support a wide variety of qualities are often characterized by monopolistic competition. The demand curve facing the producer of any given variety is slightly downward sloping; in equilibrium such a firm will produce in the range where average costs are declining (increasing returns to scale in the technology). If differences in technology among varieties is ignored, and if it is further supposed that demand is evenly balanced over all varieties produced, it is possible to model both autarky and free-trade positions in a Heckscher-Ohlin framework. Conclusions that emerge include:

1. In autarky larger countries tend to produce more varieties of products than do smaller countries, and firms tend to be larger.

2. With free trade and a commonly shared technology, each country may produce a range of different product types, as well as a homogeneous product that differs in its required capital/labor ratio from that adopted by other firms in an industry of differentiated products.

3. Firm size in each country will be larger with trade than under autarky and will be comparable among countries. Consumers everywhere enjoy a larger menu of varieties in a world market than with autarky. Producers, however, face stiffer competition, which encourages longer production runs and a more limited range of varieties produced.

4. Factor endowments affect the pattern of trade in Heckscher-Ohlin fashion. The relatively labor-abundant country, with output levels relatively higher in the labor-intensive industry, will tend to be a net exporter of that industry's output. If the industry is characterized by differentiated products, such a net export position reflects an underlying mutual interpenetration by each firm of the other country's markets.

5. Gross trade exceeds net trade. In situations where some products are differentiated and some are homogeneous, both comparative advantage (as imparted by relative factor endowments) and increasing returns help explain nations' trading patterns.

---

[4]This possibility, that a labor-abundant country may be an exporter of labor-intensive commodities in inter-industry trade but an exporter of more capital-intensive items in intra-industry trade, is discussed in R. Jones, H. Beladi, and S. Marjit, "The Three Faces of Factor Intensities," *Journal of International Economics*, 48 (1999): 413–420.

CHAPTER PROBLEMS

1. Suppose that in autarky the decomposition of food and clothing aggregates reveals that ten varieties of each are produced, with each variety requiring 200 units of resources for setup costs, regardless of scale of output. In addition, each unit of food of any variety produced requires one unit of resources, and each unit of clothing requires two units of resources. The autarky output levels are 400 units of each variety of clothing and 200 units of each variety of food. With trade, competition from the world market narrows the number of varieties produced in each industry (food, clothing) to four. If resources are allocated to food and clothing industries exactly as in autarky, by how much has trade allowed each industry aggregate to expand? Why did the number of varieties produced not get cut back to four in each industry before trade?

2. In Figure 7.4 points H' and F' show each country devoting the same resources to the differentiated clothing sector as it did in autarky. Suppose that the home country is relatively labor abundant and clothing is labor intensive relative to food. How would this alter the number of firms devoted to clothing in each country? Could the home country produce a wider variety of clothing with trade than the (larger) foreign country?

SUGGESTIONS FOR FURTHER READING

Helpman, Elhanan, and P. Krugman. *Market Structure and Foreign Trade* (Cambridge, MA: MIT Press, 1985). A more advanced monograph; Chapter 7 describes trade in a setting of monopolistic competition.

Krugman, Paul R. "Increasing Returns, Monopolistic Competition, and International Trade," *Journal of International Economics*, 9, 4 (November 1979): 469–479. An early discussion of trade with monopolistic competition and increasing returns.

Lloyd, Peter, and Hyun-Hoon Lee (eds.). *Frontiers of Research in Intra-Industry Trade* (New York: Palgrave, Macmillan, 2002). Chapters 1 and 2 especially review the development of intra-industry trade theory.

Smith, Alasdair. "Imperfect Competition and International Trade," Chapter 3 in David Greenaway and L. Alan Winters (eds.), *Surveys in International Trade* (Oxford: Blackwell, 1994). A survey both of monopolistic competition in trade theory and monopoly, duopoly, and other variants of imperfect competition.

CHAPTER 8

Resource Trade, Outsourcing, and Product Fragmentation

Most items traded among countries are not final consumer goods. Typically, they are raw materials, such as coal, oil, or bauxite; or producer goods; or processed materials, such as steel, textiles, or aluminum; or machinery. We estimate that goods passing into consumption without significant further processing account for only approximately a third of the value of world exports. The strong distinction made by David Ricardo between commodities that can be traded on world markets (final consumer goods) and productive inputs that cannot is at best an extremely qualified view of trade. As will become evident, the fundamental Ricardian concept of comparative advantage must increasingly be modified in a world where trade cuts ever more deeply into the production process.

The term *outsourcing* has entered the media's vocabulary. The term is used in a variety of ways, for example, to suggest that a commodity previously produced at home is now only produced abroad or that an item previously produced by a particular firm is now produced by a different firm. Here we apply it to a more focused event: Suppose it becomes possible to break up, or *fragment*, an originally vertically connected production process so that some parts of it (or fragments) can be produced in a different locale—perhaps by a different firm (but not necessarily), and perhaps nearby or, instead, in another country. If the latter, we refer to *international fragmentation* of the production process, for example, the transfer of an unskilled labor-intensive part of production to a developing country where the wage rate for unskilled labor is lower (relative to its productivity). As we discuss, the phenomenon of international fragmentation reveals a natural role for increasing returns (or decreasing costs) that differs from that encountered in Chapter 7's analysis of intra-industry trade and monopolistic competition. Indeed, a natural role is established for any of the competitive production and trade models discussed in Chapters 4 through 6. We discuss as well the consequences of outsourcing for the distribution of income within a country. Does outsourcing of a previously labor-intensive fragment of the production process at home to a developing country such as Malaysia or India necessarily endanger labor's local real wage rate? As we shall argue, the answer could well be in the negative. But first we turn to a discussion of international trade based on resources.

8.1   Given Resources and Footloose Production Processes

Most final goods reach consumers after passing through a series of intermediate stages of production. For example, bauxite ore becomes alumina, then aluminum, electrical wire, and finally a component of your house. Often these successive conversions are performed by different industries, which may be located in different countries. The country with a cost advantage in aluminum wire may be poorly equipped to produce aluminum (an activity that is drawn to low-cost sources of electric power), in which case the aluminum enters into international trade. Nations should be thought of as specializing in activities or processing stages, not products.

Natural Resource Endowments

One of the factors that governs the allocation of production processes among nations is the uneven distribution of natural resources. Saudi Arabia, richly endowed with petroleum, is apt to find most of its factors drawn into the production of crude petroleum. Saudi Arabia may have no comparative advantage in producing petrochemicals, not to mention undertaking activities that require little or no crude petroleum as an input. Less obviously, natural resource abundance can explain major changes in the long-run trade pattern of the United States. A century ago, the United States was, compared to its principal trading partners, rich in natural resources. Over the years some American natural resources, such as forests, metallic ores, petroleum, and natural gas, were partially depleted, and other nations were drawn into world trade to supply these primary products. Applying the models discussed in Chapters 5 and 6, we expect that land (natural resources in general), which was abundant, is now the scarce factor in the U.S. endowment and that American trade switched from predominantly exporting resource-intensive products to principally importing them.

Gavin Wright analyzed the long-run trend in natural resources' role in U.S. comparative advantage from 1879 to 1940.[1] The United States was long a net exporter of resource-intensive products, and the importance of natural-resource inputs in U.S. exports relative to U.S. goods competing with imports actually kept rising until 1914. The United States remained a net natural-resource exporter until 1940, although by 1955 the country had become a net importer. Wright argued that the importance of natural resources in U.S. comparative advantage was even greater than these figures suggest. First, resource-intensive production tends to be strongly capital intensive. For this reason, from 1879 to 1928, before the United States came to appear a capital-rich country, U.S. exports were more capital intensive than import replacements. Exports' resource intensity and capital intensity declined hand in hand after 1928. Second, Wright argued that the predominant role of natural resources in U.S. comparative advantage extended to the mass production industries (automobiles, machinery) that were the high-tech exports of their day and depended on low-cost sources of both energy and resource-intensive inputs (steel). Third, Wright thought the U.S. advantage

---

[1]Gavin Wright, "The Origins of American Industrial Success, 1879–1940," *American Economic Review*, 80 (September 1990): 651–668; Jaroslav Vanek, *The Natural Resource Content of United States Foreign Trade 1870–1955* (Cambridge, MA: MIT Press, 1963).

rested not so much on the endowment of resources as the efficiency with which they were exploited. Other trading nations had rich resource endowments but not the cheap transportation and internal free trade needed to exploit them effectively. Only later did those countries develop their resource endowments, setting the scene for the cheapened world prices of resource outputs that led to the displacement of U.S. domestic resources.

Today most industrial countries share the U.S. position in drawing on other nations to supply many of their raw materials. They still differ a great deal, however, in the prevalence of final and intermediate goods in their international trade. Some, such as Norway and Canada, still export a lot of processed materials and intermediate goods as well as goods for final use. Japan, a crowded island devoid of most natural resources, exports mostly finished goods to pay for its mostly resource-based imports, and Germany's situation is similar, if less extreme. For several countries we calculated the share of primary and intermediate goods in their exports and imports:

	Exports	Imports
Japan	5.0%	66.2%
Germany	7.2	43.0
United States	10.7	32.4
Canada	27.0	31.1
Norway	66.8	41.7

Primary and intermediate goods are defined here as products of the agriculture, fishing, forestry, and mining sectors, plus wood products and basic metals. Economists have debated inconclusively whether Japan's position simply reflects that nation's lack of indigenous raw materials or some abnormal disinclination to purchase manufactured imports from other countries.[2]

Scarce Natural Resources and the Terms of Trade

For countries such as Japan that live by turning imported intermediates into final goods, the terms of trade vitally affect their welfare. Rising prices of primary materials squeeze their "processor's margins" and impoverish their factors of production. Countries such as Kuwait that obtain most of their final goods by exporting raw materials are in the opposite situation. Every so often in the history of international commerce, a controversy arises over how long-term trends affect terms of trade and relative incomes in countries that mainly export intermediate goods compared to those that mainly import and process them. This concern is no surprise given the short-run variability of the prices of many primary products. For example, in 1999 the world price of crude petroleum rose 42 percent while that of tropical beverages fell 21 percent and vegetable oilseeds and oils declined 23 percent.

This controversy has surfaced over and over in the industrial countries; it arose at the end of World War II and again in the 1970s following the major increase in the

---

[2]See Edward J. Lincoln, *Japan's Unequal Trade* (Washington, DC: Brookings Institution, 1990), especially Chapter 2.

price of crude petroleum. Another episode occurred in 2005, when the world price of crude petroleum rose 50 percent during the year. The world's stock of nonrenewable natural resources—metals, energy sources, and so on—is a factor that ultimately limits the real incomes of those who consume them. The most readily available resources—those that require the application of the fewest other inputs—are utilized first. As these resources are exhausted, the margin of extraction moves to resources that are lower in quality, farther away, deeper in the earth, or otherwise more costly in terms of the additional inputs needed to convert them into useful intermediate goods. In the 1970s episode, projections of the Club of Rome[3] focused on the limit that would be reached as fossil energy sources grow scarcer, to the point where securing another unit output of energy requires the input of just that much energy. Then no income would remain to allocate to other factors of production, resulting in the ultimate worsening of one's terms of trade. Most economists were not impressed by the Club of Rome's alarmist stance (and that of its earlier counterparts). It is not that nonrenewable resources lack this potential for shifting the terms of trade against other factors of production. Rather, the forecast neglects technological change, which has shown a remarkable ability over the course of history to cheapen the extraction of natural resources, make it easier to find previously undiscovered ones, and facilitate the substitution of other inputs for resources that have grown more expensive.[4]

Indeed, at other times spokespersons for the developing countries have argued that primary products face long-term deterioration in their terms of trade, presumably reflecting productivity gains in their production. During the period 1900 to 1986, the prices of primary commodities relative to manufactures did indeed decline at a rate of about 0.5 percent a year (a little faster, if fuels are left out of the primary commodities).

The decline in the terms of trade of nonfuel primary products continued at about the same rate for the period 1970 to 2000, although agricultural primary products showed diverse individual patterns but on average did not decline. The fates of the less developed countries are decreasingly tied to the terms of trade for the primary commodities in which they have traditionally specialized. The share of manufactures in exports of developing countries rose from 3.7 percent in 1899 to 21.1 percent in 1979, and many developing countries themselves are losers when energy prices rise.[5]

The Newly Industrializing Countries and Footloose Production Processes

If nations can import intermediate goods to feed their processing capabilities, the processing activities can themselves migrate from country to country. The nations that developed successfully in the last three decades took up processing activities suited to

---

[3]D. H. Meadows et al., *The Limits to Growth* (New York: Universe Books, 1972).
[4]In the nineteenth century when the horse was a principal source of motive power, concern arose over where enough land could be found to raise oats to feed all the horses required for transportation. The internal combustion engine, of course, spared us the need to raise oats in window boxes.
[5]Enzo R. Grilli and May Cheng Yang, "Primary Commodity Prices, Manufactured Goods Prices, and the Terms of Trade of Developing Countries: What the Long Run Shows," *World Bank Economic Review*, 2 (January 1988): 1–47.

their factor endowments—efficient if low-skilled labor, good infrastructure—importing intermediate goods or parts (textiles, electronic components) and exporting finished goods (apparel, consumer electronics). Because these activities demand no elaborate or highly specialized capital goods or labor skills, they are easily expanded in any country where they prove profitable. By the same token, they are quickly contracted in a location where they prove unprofitable. They are sometimes referred to as footloose. (The athletic-shoe industry is, happily, an example.)

Which industries are footloose and have gravitated to the developing countries can be explained by the Hecksher-Ohlin theorem. They are typically industries that generate low value-added per worker when carried out in the United States. Value-added is the sum of all payments to an industry's primary factors of production. It can be high (per worker) because the industry uses a lot of physical capital, pays rents for the use of natural resources, or employs workers with heavy investments in skills. Low value-added per worker thus is a good indicator of low capital intensity of each type. Furthermore, in the absence of factor-intensity reversals, an industry with low value-added per worker in the United States will have that status in the developing countries.[6] These industries have swarmed to the Asian newly industrializing countries (NICs) (Singapore, Hong Kong, Taiwan, Korea), the ASEAN group that followed them (Malaysia, Indonesia, Philippines, Thailand), and now China. These economies accounted for 5 percent of global exports and 5.2 percent of imports in 1965, 16.9 percent of each by 1994. Their share of global manufactured exports rose from 1.6 to 19.9 percent, and the Asian NICs shifted their processing activities from low to increasingly high-technology manufactures.[7]

8.2 Footloose Inputs: The Joint Role of Comparative and Absolute Advantage

The doctrine of comparative advantage points out that the absolute level of efficiency of inputs does not determine a nation's trade pattern. Poor climate and technology at home may make labor less efficient both in producing food and making clothing, but if such inefficiency is relatively less pronounced in the clothing sector, the home country exports clothing. This basic truth is thus strongly linked to the vision of trade offered in the classical paradigm: International markets are limited to final goods, and inputs are trapped within a nation's boundaries. Suppose, however, some productive inputs are footloose: They can be attracted to the country offering the highest return. In such a case, production and trade patterns internationally are determined by absolute advantage as well as comparative advantage.

To construct a model that can handle the importance of absolute advantage jointly with comparative advantage, we adapt the Ricardian model of Chapter 4. Stick to the two-commodity food and clothing scenario, but now introduce an asymmetry in the

---

[6]This was first shown by Hal B. Lary, *Imports of Manufactures from Less-Developed Countries* (New York: National Bureau of Economic Research, 1968).
[7]Sylvia Ostry, *The Post-Cold War Trading System* (Chicago: University of Chicago Press, 1997), Chapter 5.

way these two commodities are produced. As before, let food require labor only, with a_{LF} and a_{LF}^* denoting fixed unit requirements in the two countries. By contrast, clothing requires not only labor (a_{LC} and a_{LC}^*) but also the services of some internationally footloose factor, which we simply call A. To keep matters simple, suppose the pair of input coefficients (a_{LC} and a_{AC} at home; a_{LC}^* and a_{AC}^* abroad) is constant but allows for inter-country differences not only in labor skills but also in the technology whereby A is used in clothing production. Input A is footloose in the sense it is attracted to the country that can offer it the higher return (denoted by R_A if at home, or R_A^* abroad).

Some of the lessons of the simple competitive Ricardian model are applicable here as well. Each country must produce something in a free-trade equilibrium—food, clothing, or both. Competition ensures that unit cost equals price for any activity actually undertaken and does not fall below price (suggesting profitable opportunities that would be bid away in a competitive equilibrium) for activities not undertaken. Suppose world prices of food and clothing are determined in a large world market. Which of these two countries is in a better position to attract the services of footloose factor A? Here we restrict our attention only to these two countries as potential employers of A; later we ask whether A would be attracted to either of these countries if a larger world market exists. Technology for producing food in each country puts a floor on the wage rate. Thus, at home, Equation 8.1 reveals the minimum value for the home wage rate, w:

$$a_{LF}w = p_F \tag{8.1}$$

If the wage rate were higher, the home food sector would prove noncompetitive in world markets. For the home clothing sector, the prevailing world price of clothing, home technology, and this minimal level for home wages help determine the maximum amount, R_A, that the home country could bid to obtain the services of footloose factor A. These are formally related by Equation 8.2:

$$a_{LC}w + a_{AC}R_A = p_C \tag{8.2}$$

Now divide Equation 8.1 into Equation 8.2 to obtain:

$$(a_{LC}/a_{LF}) + a_{AC}(R_A/p_F) = p_C/p_F \tag{8.3}$$

This expression reveals, with given world commodity prices of food and clothing, the maximum amount that the home clothing industry could pay to obtain footloose input A. Of course, if the wage rate were even lower than the breakeven point for food production shown by Equation 8.1, more could be paid to attract input A, but the existence of profitable activity in the food sector would bid up wages again.

Technology differs abroad, so that although foreign producers face the same prices for traded food and clothing, the maximum amount their clothing sector could pay to obtain A without incurring losses is R_A^*, shown in Equation 8.4:

$$(a_{LC}^*/a_{LF}^*) + a_{AC}^*(R_A^*/p_F) = p_C/p_F \tag{8.4}$$

A comparison of Equations 8.3 and 8.4 clearly reveals that the ability to attract the footloose input required to produce clothing depends both on potential *comparative* advantage in labor costs (a_{LC}/a_{LF} vs. a_{LC}^*/a_{LF}^*) as well as on *absolute* superiority in the productivity of footloose input A (literally the inverses of a_{AC} and a_{AC}^*). We follow our earlier assumption in letting the home country possess a comparative labor cost advan-

FIGURE 8.1

Comparative and Absolute Advantage

For relatively high world prices of clothing (above 0D), the foreign country could outbid the home country to attract the internationally footloose input used to produce clothing. Below 0D, relative labor costs become more important and production patterns switch, so that the home country produces clothing.

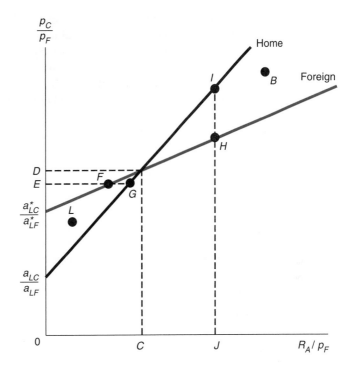

tage in producing clothing, but now suppose that the foreign country has an absolute advantage in employing the footloose factor in clothing (a^*_{AC} is smaller than a_{AC}). In Figure 8.1 relative world prices of clothing and food are shown on the vertical axis, and the maximum amount each country could pay to attract footloose input A is shown on the horizontal axis. The vertical intercepts of each line reveal comparative labor costs; the slopes of the lines reflect absolute costs of the footloose input A in clothing production; the formal expressions for these lines are given in Equations 8.3 and 8.4.

Armed with this apparatus, it is now possible to discuss issues concerning trade and production patterns that arise when not all inputs have strictly national markets.

Who Produces What?

The answer to the question, "Which country is better able to attract footloose factor, A, and thus actively produce clothing?" is, "It depends." In particular, it depends on whether clothing's price is relatively high, in which case the return to footloose factor A is also high. With such payments looming as important in the cost picture, the high-bidding country for A is the country with the superior technology for using A. In Figure 8.1, for any p_C/p_F exceeding 0D, the foreign country can outbid the home county in attracting A. Conversely, low relative prices for clothing imply a low return for A, in which case relative labor costs loom as more important, just as in standard Ricardian theory. For example, at a clothing relative price given by 0E, the home country can offer EG for the use of A and still break even producing clothing; the foreign country, with a comparative disadvantage in labor costs, could offer only *EF* for *A*. The vertical comparisons for any given value of R_A/p_F are also instructive. If, in world markets, the payment required for footloose factor *A* is $0J$, the home country's relative cost of producing clothing, *JI*, exceeds that in the foreign country, *JH*, and the foreign country would be the producer of clothing.

It is perhaps more instructive to imagine both home and foreign countries embedded in a multicountry trading nexus in which the commodity prices *and* the rate of return to footloose input *A* are determined by world market forces. That is, these prices are shown by some point in Figure 8.1. Suppose this is point *B*. The home country cannot compete in the clothing sector. By contrast, the foreign country can successfully pay the going rate for input *A* and establish a competitive clothing industry. But point *B* lies above the foreign relative cost curve in Figure 8.1. This reveals that the foreign wage rate would be bid above the level that would allow foreign food production. In sum, at point *B* the foreign country is specialized in clothing and the home country in food. Should clothing and the return to footloose *A* become cheaper with the passage of time, moving, say, to point *L*, clothing production would shift to the home country as relative labor costs become more important.[8]

National Tax Treatments and Absolute Advantage

The doctrine of comparative advantage recognizes that differences between countries that affect some industries differentially have an impact on trade patterns. This doctrine, however, denies the role of countries' characteristics that affect all local sectors uniformly. Once international trade invades the markets for inputs into the production process, such a neglect of national characteristics is no longer appropriate.

For example, suppose tax rates on earned incomes are uniformly higher in one country than in another. If inputs are *not* internationally mobile, such a difference in national tax treatments does not affect production patterns. But if some inputs are footloose, their location will be influenced by taxes. Other things being equal, footloose inputs will be attracted to countries with low tax rates on earnings. Similarly, differences between governments in attitudes toward expropriation of firms or differences in overall levels of social overhead capital can steer footloose inputs toward some countries and away from others. Pollution controls provide another example. South Korea and Hong Kong have recently been under pressure to tighten up their controls on dirty industry. As a consequence, some of these processes have been shifted to countries like Thailand.[9]

---

[8]In the past half century, the location of the American textile industry has shifted from the North to the South. Southern climate (especially high humidity and temperature) does not naturally favor textiles, but this disadvantage can be overcome by air-conditioning if electricity is cheap enough. In Figure 8.1 associate footloose input *A* with energy (or electricity) and associate the South, where higher energy inputs are required, with the home country. Of course in recent years much of the South's textile industry has been bid away to countries such as China.

[9]The *Economist* of November 16, 1991, cites an increase from 25 to 55 percent of total applications for foreign investment "whose activities would produce significant amounts of hazardous wastes" in Thailand in the two-year period from 1987 to 1989.

Suppose, in Figure 8.1, that the home country is uniformly a "better" place in which to work than the foreign country, in a sense that can be translated into an absolute lowering of all input requirements in all sectors. The vertical intercept of the home curve is unaffected because it reflects only *comparative* labor costs. The home schedule becomes flatter, however, and, if world commodity prices initially did not allow home production of clothing (e.g., at *B*), such a change in home national characteristics could alter its production pattern. That is, uniform tax reduction could serve to attract the footloose input to the clothing sector as the home country becomes a relatively more attractive locale.

Comparative Advantage and the Dutch Disease

Finally, the enduring role of comparative advantage can be revealed in the following example. Suppose that the home country initially produces both goods and that a new innovation that lowers labor requirement, a_{LF}, is introduced into the national food industry. The home country's schedule in Figure 8.1 then shifts upward, possibly wiping out its clothing sector. Despite the fact that no change has taken place in the production techniques for clothing or in the world prices of clothing and food, the country has developed a stronger *comparative* advantage in producing food. The wage rate rises, and footloose input *A* leaves the country for other parts of the world where wages have not risen. This is the Dutch Disease once again, with some inputs (*A*) now escaping the penalty of a shift in comparative advantage through international mobility.

8.3 Outsourcing and the International Fragmentation of Production

Even before David Ricardo (1817) explained the advantages of international trade—advantages based on each nation having a certain range of commodities in which it has a comparative advantage—Adam Smith expounded on the benefits that arise from an enlarged scale of operations and the division of labor. That is, as scale expands, resources (especially labor) can increasingly be focused on a narrower class of activities in a manner that improves productivity. The economist Allyn Young was prescient in remarking as early as 1928 that "over a large part of the field of industry an increasingly intricate nexus of specialized undertakings has inserted itself between the producer of raw materials and the consumer of the final product."[10]

This is even more true now. One of the defining characteristics of the growth in international trade and incomes in the past few decades has been the steady rise in trade in intermediate goods and goods in process, indicative of a phenomenon we call *fragmentation* of production. As the scale of activity in an originally vertically integrated production process expands, costs get reduced by outsourcing some parts of the process, perhaps to other firms, perhaps to different locales, including, as suggested

---

[10]Allyn Young, "Increasing Returns and Economic Progress," *Economic Journal*, 38 (1928): 527–542.

earlier, to foreign countries where different productivities relative to factor prices could lower the costs of producing the outsourced parts. The Swedish furniture firm Ikea has for years outsourced the actual manufacture of items to Poland, retaining the design work in Sweden. In the United States the firm Nike does its design work and advertising at home but outsources its manufacturing of footwear to many developing Asian countries. Many other industries are characterized by production processes featuring international outsourcing of parts of production (e.g., automobiles, cameras, and pharmaceuticals).

A simple model setting in which to discuss this issue is that laid out in Jones and Kierzkowski.[11] Consider, first, a small-scale process whereby local resources are combined in a simple *production block* to produce an output in a manner such as described in Chapters 4, 5, or 6, with, perhaps, technology exhibiting constant returns to scale. More extensive ways of production can also be considered, whereby the process is split up into more production blocks, with their locale being outsourced to other regions of the country or, perhaps, to another country. The attraction would be the possibility of a better fit of the factor proportions required in each block to relative wages and rents found in different areas. Perhaps, instead, outsourcing is encouraged because labor is relatively more productive in some countries than in others, à la the Ricardian model set out in Chapter 4. However, such outsourcing requires additional costs, of what we call *service links*, and these encompass the costs of coordinating the production of separate production blocks, which involves costs of transportation, communication, insurance, and so on. These are areas in which strong increasing returns are to be found. For example, the costs of communication in arranging a shipment of 1000 units of a product are about the same as arranging a shipment of 10,000 units. The extent of outsourcing that will be selected depends on the nature of these costs as well as the scale of total output.

Figure 8.2 illustrates how minimal total costs of producing final output increase with the scale of output but at a diminishing rate. If there is a vertically integrated single production block, costs are shown by ray *1*. An alternative of two blocks, both located within the country, is illustrated by line *2*. This line illustrates the trade-off between lower marginal costs of production achieved by the better fit of locating each block in a locale in which factor prices and productivities match the particular factor intensities required in each block, on the one hand, and the extra service link costs required to coordinate the two blocks, on the other. For simplicity we adopt here the extreme assumption that these costs are constant, level 0*A*. Line segment *3* illustrates an alternative, one in which one of the production blocks is moved overseas, thus achieving even lower marginal costs but at the expense of greater costs of coordinating service links, 0*B*. As output grows, note the switch to greater and greater degrees of fragmentation and outsourcing: None takes place until output level 0*C* is reached. In the range *CD*, it pays to outsource locally, but if output expands beyond level 0*D*, inter-

---

[11]Ronald W. Jones and Henryk Kierzkowski, "The Role of Services in Production and International Trade: A Theoretical Framework," ch. 3 in R. Jones and A. Krueger, eds., *The Political Economy of International Trade* (Oxford: Blackwell, 1990). See also Ronald W. Jones, "Immigration vs. Outsourcing: Effects on Labor Markets," *International Review of Economics and Finance*, 14 (2005): 105–114.

FIGURE 8.2

Costs and Fragmentation

At low levels of output, production might take place in a single production block exhibiting total costs rising proportionally with output, as in ray *1*. An alternative technique fragments the production process into a pair of blocks by placing one of them in a locale more suited to its factor requirements, but this involves service link costs of coordinating the blocks (line *2*). Line *3* illustrates fragmentation that outsources one production block overseas to obtain even lower marginal costs, although the costs of service links become larger (*0B*). The heavy broken lines show how fragmentation leads to a lowering of average costs as output expands.

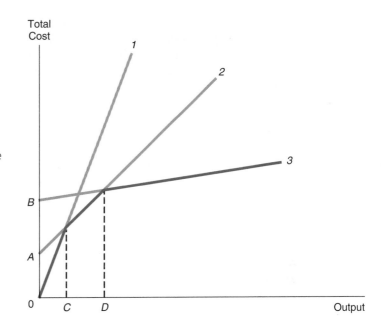

national outsourcing is required to minimize costs. Note that along the lower locus (heavy broken lines) average costs diminish with scale of output, and this happens despite the presumed absence of increasing returns to scale for any given production block. The necessity of service link activities for achieving lower costs with outsourcing is responsible for the overall pattern of increasing returns to scale.

Three major changes in the past few decades help explain why international trade in parts and components has increased more rapidly than world incomes or than overall world trade. First, with incomes rising there is a natural tendency for larger scales of output to result in greater degrees of international fragmentation. This is illustrated in Figure 8.2. Second, one of the most striking changes in technology in recent years has been the great reduction in the costs of service link activities. This is especially the case for the costs of communication, which have been driven down almost to the vanishing point. As well, costs of transportation have been reduced. Greater information about operating abroad, coupled with a larger range of possible suppliers of components abroad, have lowered the costs of outsourcing to arm's-length firms with reduced risk that such supplies will not meet timing schedules. This means that for any given level of output, a greater degree of fragmentation and outsourcing can be expected. Finally, there has been a steady postwar reduction in tariffs and other barriers to international trade as well as a freeing up of domestic restrictions and regulations on service activities.

Although getting good data on the extent of fragmentation and outsourcing is difficult, Francis Ng and Alexander Yeats at the World Bank provided estimates.[12] For the

---

[12]Francis Ng and Alexander Yeats, "Major Trade Trends in Asia—What Are the Implications for Regional Cooperation and Growth?", World Bank Policy Research Working Paper 3084, June 2003.

period 1990 to 2000, they calculate a yearly expansion in world GDP of 3.7 percent. Not surprisingly, overall levels of world trade have been expanding more rapidly, at a 6.5 percent yearly rate. However, the subsector of trade in parts and components (indicative of the degree of international fragmentation) has been expanding at a 9.1 percent rate, even greater than the rate for intra-industry trade.

8.4 Outsourcing and Advanced Country Wage Rates

The recent outsourcing phenomenon has stirred considerable attention in the United States and European countries because of its supposed strong adverse effect on local wage rates and employment, especially of the unskilled.

To investigate the possibilities, we make use of the unit-value isoquant map introduced in Chapter 6. In Figure 8.3 we focus on the possibilities of fragmentation in some commodity, say commodity 2, assumed to be produced in the home country. Production for the second commodity is assumed not to allow substitutability between capital (physical or human) and labor (interpreted as relatively unskilled labor if "human" capital is used to represent skilled labor), and therefore has the right-angled shape of the unit-value isoquant for commodity 2. Its production is made up of two fragments: The one indicated by point *a* is the more capital-intensive one, and the other is indicated by point *b*. The slope of line *AB* is presumed to represent the ratio of the wage rate to the rental on capital. Before international trade in separate fragments is made possible by a reduction (not shown) in service link costs, the capital and labor bundles indicated by *A* and *B* would indicate, respectively, $1 worth of factors that are required initially to produce the capital-intensive and labor-intensive fragments when these are valued at initial home wages and rents.

FIGURE 8.3

Fragmentation in Industry 2

The unit-value isoquant for the second industry shows that a $1 value of output can be produced by a combination of capital-intensive fragment, *a*, and labor-intensive fragment, *b*. Line *AB*'s slope indicates the factor-price ratio before the fragments can be traded. A reduction in service link costs allows such world trade, and the world price of the labor-intensive fragment falls so that point *B'* shows the new input bundle required to earn $1, and *A'* reveals that the price of the capital-intensive bundle has risen compared to initial costs.

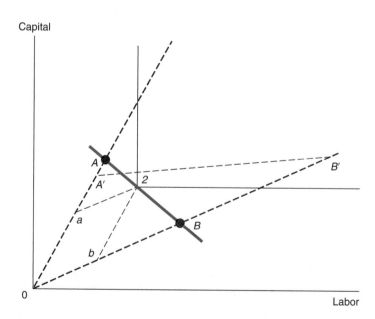

Once fragmentation leads to the possibility of international trade in the two separate fragments, the finer degree of association of factor intensities to various countries' factor prices leads for the first time to world prices for the separate fragments. In Figure 8.3 we have assumed that the world price of the labor-intensive fragment has gone down from its initial home cost (represented by point B), suggesting that although this country could initially meet world competition in producing the second commodity, it was not very good at producing the labor-intensive fragment. Once international fragmentation takes place and world prices for the two fragments are established, the price for the labor-intensive fragment has been reduced from its initial cost in the home country. (Point B' relative to point B indicates a halving of world price relative to initial cost). By contrast, the home country is an efficient producer of the capital-intensive fragment relative to other countries, and its world price has been assumed to increase compared with initial local costs so it now takes only the bundle A' to produce a unit of the capital-intensive fragment at new world prices.

With these details in mind, turn to Figure 8.4, which adds to the initial unit-value isoquant for commodity 2 those for commodities 1 and 3, whose prices are assumed not to be altered. Thus before international fragmentation in industry 2 became possible, the composite unit-value isoquant was given by the broken line $3D21$. After fragmentation the country can no longer compete in producing an integrated second commodity, but the more capital-intensive fragment shown by the isoquant whose corner is A' does emerge as a competitive tradable item at the new world prices. The new unit-value isoquant is the broken line $3CA'F1$. What has happened to the wage rate (or the wage/rental ratio)? That depends on the country's endowment proportions, which help determine its production pattern. If such a ratio were shown by a ray (not drawn) through point F, the home country would originally have produced commodities 1 and 2, and after fragmentation the capital-intensive fragment of commodity 2 as well as

FIGURE 8.4

Fragmentation and a Higher Wage Rate

The prefragmentation unit-value isoquant is the broken line *3D21*; after fragmentation in industry *2* (as shown in Figure 8.3), only the capital-intensive fragment, shown by *A'*, survives, and the new unit-value isoquant is *3CA'F1*. If the economy is relatively capital abundant (as shown by the endowment ray), the wage rate has increased as a consequence of outsourcing the labor-intensive fragment used to produce commodity *2*.

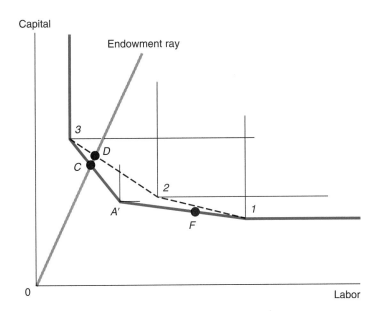

commodity *1*. Its wage/rental ratio would have fallen. However, if the home country were more capital/abundant, say with endowment ratio shown by the ray through point *C*, its wage rate would actually *increase* as a consequence of international fragmentation. It would produce commodity *3* both initially and after fragmentation, but it substitutes the fragment shown by *A'* for the entire commodity *2* produced initially. For such a capital-abundant home country, commodity *2* was the labor-intensive item of the two goods produced initially, and international fragmentation (that substitutes *A'* for *2*) represents a technological improvement in the home country's labor intensive item produced. Such technological progress in the economy's labor-intensive item produced must raise the wage rate (just as a price increase would do).

Popular discussion of outsourcing often focuses on the factors (especially labor) thrown out of work when a labor-intensive fragment of production is sent to foreign shores. What to make of this argument? These trade models all assume that factor markets are flexible in the sense that excess supply in the home labor market would lead to a readjustment of the equilibrium wage rate. Thus in Figure 8.4 there is full employment before and after international fragmentation. But consider what happens to the labor employed in the surviving fragment in the second industry: More labor is employed in this fragment after the new trading pattern than was employed in the entire second industry in the initial situation! In Figure 8.4 point *C* (showing input allocation after fragmentation) is relatively closer to point *A'* than point *D* was initially close to point *2*. The labor-intensive fragment in producing the second commodity was dragging down the home country's competitive position in producing commodity *2*, and its disappearance after international fragmentation puts the remaining fragment in commodity *2* in a stronger position, and it increases its resource inputs.

This result, whereby outsourcing improves the real wage, is just a possibility. But it does serve to emphasize that outsourcing has a positive aspect—it works like an improvement in productivity. Note that in countries such as the United States there is *insourcing* as well. According to Walter Wriston, in the past few years more jobs have been created by foreigners' activities in the United States than have been lost by outsourcing.[13] To concentrate only on jobs outsourced by trade and to ignore insourcing would be like saying that imports generally cause a country to lose jobs (and ignoring jobs created in export sectors).

The illustration just cited associates the outsourcing phenomenon with the loss of production blocks. Much has been made recently about call centers, a kind of service link activity, being outsourced to India. India obviously has a much lower wage rate, and widespread knowledge of English is a necessary characteristic. A partial answer to critics of such outsourcing from the United States is that in America these are not very high-paid jobs and would probably have been phased out anyway by automatic answering services, such as are common now in making airline reservations. As for production blocks, the main worry in advanced countries now is China. Its wage rate is less than 4 percent of the American wage rate. Some of this is related to an undervalued level of the Chinese yuan. Admittedly, its labor productivity is also lower (approximately 9 per-

---

[13]Walter B. Wriston, "Ever Heard of Insourcing?", *Wall Street Journal*, March 24, 2004.

cent of the American level), but this still leaves Chinese labor in a strong competitive position.[14] Indian labor is fairly comparable to that in China in terms of wages, but the infrastructure, such as roads and harbors that would allow India to be as competitive with China in terms of production blocks, is distinctly inferior. Call center activity can bypass such infrastructure.

8.5   Summary

The location of natural resources is spread rather unevenly around the globe, which has a large influence on trade patterns. A country such as Japan is highly dependent on foreign sources for its supplies of coal, steel, and oil and is a heavy exporter of high-quality finished consumer goods to obtain these resources. With such asymmetries, shifts in the terms of trade between resource-intensive primary products and final goods can greatly alter the relative income among countries. When some inputs become internationally mobile, the classical Ricardian concept of comparative advantage needs to be joined by the concept of absolute advantage in order to explain trading and production patterns. Comparative advantage is relevant for productive factors such as labor that are generally considered to be trapped behind national borders, but inputs such as some intermediate goods or capital have much more international mobility and will seek to be used in countries where their returns are maximized. All countries have a comparative advantage in some items, but high levels of taxation and low levels of productivity relative to factor prices make it difficult for some countries to attract internationally footloose inputs.

The recent striking improvements in technology such as in communication and, to a lesser degree, in transportation have encouraged an increase in fragmentation of the production process, whereby some production blocks are relocated to other areas, internationally as well as in the same country. For example, design activities or research and development could be located in advanced countries such as the United States, but more labor-intensive activities such as furniture or footwear production are nowadays often outsourced to locales in Eastern Europe or Asia. Higher levels of income and production, as well as deregulation internally or reductions of trade barriers internationally, also encourage greater degrees of international fragmentation. Although marginal costs of production can be lowered by the closer association of required factor intensities of production blocks with relative factor prices and productivities when outsourcing takes place, service link costs are generally greater when the production activity spreads over several countries. Service link costs tend to be characterized by increasing returns to scale, so that even if production blocks are not, increases in output leading to more fragmentation result in lower average costs of production.

Concerns about the effects of international outsourcing on the internal distribution of income, especially of wage rates in the more advanced countries, tend to stress

---

[14]These figures were supplied by Stephen Golub of Swarthmore College. In particular, see the paper by Janet Ceglowski and Stephen Golub, "Just How Low Are China's Labor Costs?" (2005), unpublished. The figures refer to the year 2002.

the downward pressure on wages and employment of losses of productive activities to developing countries. Some of these concerns may be justified, but often lost in the argument is that outsourcing is like an improvement in technology—it lowers the costs of the remaining productive sectors in a country and thus creates greater incomes for some. We provided an illustration of how this can work to the advantage of workers in advanced countries.

CHAPTER PROBLEMS

1. In Figure 8.1 suppose that labor becomes 10 percent more efficient in the foreign country in producing food. Compare the alteration necessary in the diagram with the case in which foreign labor becomes 10 percent more efficient in producing both food and clothing.
2. Suppose, in Figure 8.3, that this country has an advantage, relative to the rest of the world, in producing the labor-intensive fragment, B, instead of the capital-intensive fragment, A, so that after world prices adjust to separate fragments becoming tradable on world markets, it is fragment B that survives and not A. Show how a revision of Figure 8.4 could still result in showing an increase in real wages for a capital-abundant country.
3. With reference to the discussion of footloose factors in Section 8.2, suppose the fixed foreign labor costs for producing a unit of clothing and a unit of food are four hours and one hour, respectively, and comparable labor requirements in a home country are each one hour. Clothing production requires, as well, fixed units of some footloose productive input A. Suppose the foreign country has an absolute advantage in its use of A: Only one unit of A is required to produce a unit of clothing, whereas two units of A are required at home. Let the world price of food be $1. What is the pattern of production and the wage rate in each country if:
   a. The world price of clothing is $5.50 per unit and footloose factor A commands $2?
   b. The world price of clothing rises to $8 per unit and footloose factor A rises to $4?
   In case (b) suppose that labor in the foreign country becomes more efficient in its production of food. Describe the impact on the production pattern abroad, and link the result to the phenomenon of the Dutch Disease.

SUGGESTIONS FOR FURTHER READING

Baumol, William J., Sue Ann Batey Blackman, and Edward N. Wolff. *Productivity and American Leadership: The Long View* (Cambridge, MA: MIT Press, 1989). Natural resources and technological diffusion in the U.S. international economic position.
Jones, Ronald W. *Globalization and the Theory of Input Trade* (Cambridge, MA: MIT Press, 2000). Chapter 2 contains a more complete discussion of the material in Section 8.2.

————. "Immigration vs. Outsourcing: Effects on Labor Markets," *International Review of Economics and Finance,* 14 (2005): 105–114. Discusses the possible effects of outsourcing on real wages.

Jones, Ronald W., and Henryk Kierzkowski. "The Role of Services in Production and International Trade: A Theoretical Framework" (1990), in R. Jones and A. Krueger, eds., *The Political Economy of International Trade* (Blackwells), Chapter 3, pp. 31–48. The original discussion of international fragmentation, including a discussion of Figure 8.2.

Wright, Gavin. "The Origins of American Industrial Success, 1879–1940," *American Economic Review,* 80 (September 1990): 651–668. Role of natural resources in long-run changes in U.S. comparative advantage.

CHAPTER 9

International Factor Movements: Labor and Capital

Our focus so far has been on the international movement of goods and services. However, some of the most dramatic changes in the international economy have been caused by international movements of factors of production—labor and capital. In the nineteenth century the countries of Europe sent forth their workers and capital in great quantities to develop nearly empty regions. The United States remains a destination for migrants, but today mainly from developing countries. Capital movements remain very important, especially as foreign direct investment by multinational corporations. (Part V considers financial capital movements.)

9.1 Factor Movements, Efficiency, and Welfare

Gains from trade occur because goods move from where their relative prices are low (in the absence of trade) to where they are high. Trade in intermediates, discussed in Chapter 8, can expand a country's production and consumption possibilities by letting it swap other goods abroad for intermediates that have greater resource cost if produced at home. Or a country may specialize in intermediates as a cheaper way to obtain final consumption goods than producing them at home. For the world as a whole, efficiency is further served to the extent that primary factors such as labor can migrate from regions of relatively low returns to regions of higher returns. Production may contract in some countries and expand in others, but for the world as a whole such an international movement of factors serves to increase output. As discussed further in Chapter 11, such a conclusion presupposes that factor returns in various countries accurately reflect the productivity of factors. By contrast, if some countries use tariffs, subsidies, or taxes to attract foreign capital, such flows may be detrimental to world outputs and, indeed, may actually harm the countries into which the capital flows.

The Heckscher-Ohlin model, introduced in Chapter 6, illustrates how trade confined to final commodities may be sufficient to bring about the full equalization of factor prices without any international mobility of capital or labor. The severity of the assumptions, however, suggests the potential for further efficiency gains through factor mobility. For trade in commodities alone to bring about factor-price equalization, countries must share the same technology and differ relatively little in the structure of their factor endowments, so that they also produce similar commodities. Certainly the most casual of observations reveals that these conditions are not obtained in many cases.

Effect of Factor Movements on Commodity Trade

One of the underlying themes of standard Heckscher-Ohlin theory is that international trade in commodities goes at least part way in substituting for international mobility of productive factors. Thus world efficiency would be enhanced if capital, for example, could flow from capital-abundant to labor-abundant countries. Barring such a possibility, though, discrepancies in the returns to capital among countries are lessened by a trade pattern that allows relatively capital-abundant countries to export capital-intensive commodities. That is, the volume of international trade in commodities could be reduced if productive factors are freed to move to locations where their returns are higher. This view suggests that trade in commodities and international mobility of factors can be interchangeable.

Freeing primary factors to move internationally could cause trade in commodities to *expand* instead of contract. James Markusen analyzed this possibility by considering two countries differing in only one of the many ways that could encourage commodity trade.[1] Suppose, as in Heckscher-Ohlin theory, that two countries share the same technology but differ in relative factor endowments. If factors of production could move internationally, the basis for commodity trade would be eroded; trade and factor movements are interchangeable. Now suppose factor endowments are identical but trade is encouraged because the home country has a Ricardian technological superiority in producing the labor-intensive good. With trade, the home country is encouraged to increase its production of the labor-intensive good (so as to export it), which serves to drive up home wages compared to foreign wages. If, now, factors can move between countries, foreign labor is attracted to the home country, which serves to *expand* trade in commodities. The reason: Home exports of labor-intensive goods are encouraged by the inflow of labor.

The general results are clear. If the basis for the international exchange of final commodities resides in differences in factor endowments, allowing these factors to move directly between countries obviates the need for commodity trade. However, if the basis for trade lies in other reasons (technological differences, as in Ricardo, increasing returns to scale, etc.), trade by itself will tend to raise the return to factors used intensively in each nation's export sector.[2] Factor mobility that responds to such differentials adds a factor-endowment basis for expanded commodity trade.

Sometimes the international mobility of factors is a prerequisite for the development of commodity trade. Proponents of this view often point to the extraction and export of natural resources in many developing regions, extraction made possible by foreign investment undertaken by Europe and the United States. On the other hand, deliberate protectionist policies may reduce trade significantly if they encourage the inflow of capital to avoid the tariff barriers. In such a case, factor mobility has enhanced the antitrade nature of protection. Foreign investment may serve to expand production

---

[1]See James Markusen, "Factor Movements and Commodity Trade as Complements," *Journal of International Economics,* 14 (May 1983): 341–356.

[2]This distinction need not always hold. For further discussion, see Ronald Jones, *Globalization and the Theory of Input Trade* (Cambridge, MA: MIT Press, 2000), Chapter 1.

of a nation's exportables or, as above, to encourage production of import-competing products. Much of the large flow of American foreign investment to Europe during the 1960s was viewed as a response to the unified tariff walls of the newly created European Community, and capital flows similarly anticipated further internal unification in 1992.

Migration and Income Distribution

Although factor movements can increase the efficiency of the world economy, they often are restricted by governments serving what they see as their national interests. Immigration of labor in particular is always under strict control, partly from concern over the distribution of income. The models presented in Chapters 5 and 6 showed that this concern has a cogent basis. Immigration acts like a natural increase in the nation's endowment of labor and is predicted to drive down wages and benefit the specific factors of production (Chapter 5) or the other general factor of production (Chapter 6). Under some circumstances all the native factors and the immigrants together can be shown to benefit from immigration.[3] Nonetheless, it is the issue of redistribution that rules the public discussion. Will immigration impoverish native labor? The theoretical predictions are ambiguous, just like those about migration and the volume of trade. Suppose our country produces a single good for consumption and export, using native labor and capital. Immigrants who are perfect substitutes for native labor simply increase the labor working with each unit of capital, driving down labor's marginal product and the real wage. Suppose instead that our country matches the Heckscher-Ohlin model, producing two goods with labor and capital. Ours is a small country, so its terms of trade are fixed on the world market. Relative factor rewards are correspondingly locked to these commodity prices. Increasing the labor supply through immigration will expand domestic production of the labor-intensive good and contract capital-intensive production, but it will not affect the wage rate (or returns to capital). If immigrant and native labor are imperfect substitutes, additional considerations become important, such as the relative ease of substitution between immigrant labor and the two domestic factors, native labor and capital. In short, the theoretical expectation that immigration depresses domestic wages is plausible but not inevitable.

Let us turn to the empirical setting. In the 1960s the European countries faced what they perceived as shortages of unskilled labor. They devised programs for "guest" workers to come from lower-income European countries, presumably for temporary stays and without a change in their basic national allegiances. If the excess demand for unskilled labor should abate, it was thought, these guests could be hustled back to their homelands in order to avert any unemployment problems in the host countries. The guests' stays proved a lot more permanent than had been anticipated, and in the latter 1970s they made up 10 to 20 percent of the workforces of some European nations.

In the United States both legal and clandestine immigration have been heavy. In 2000 11.1 percent of the total population was foreign born, up from 6.2 percent in 1980.

---

[3]Harry G. Johnson, "Some Economic Aspects of the Brain Drain," *Pakistan Development Review,* 7 (August 1967): 379–411.

From 1991 to 2000 the inflow of legal immigrants was 28.2 percent of the increase in the total population. The number of unauthorized immigrants who reside in the United States in 2000 was estimated to be approximately 7 million. Researchers have explored the degree to which immigrants, mostly low-skill workers, have reduced the real wages or employment opportunities of closely competing low-skill natives. Some redistribution occurs, but fortunately it appears small. A doubling of immigrants in a typical U.S. industrial city would drive down native unskilled workers' wages by about 4 percent (and the immigrants' own wages by 3 percent). The labor-force participation of low-skilled natives has not fallen in areas with large influxes of immigrants, as it would if job opportunities for natives were foreclosed in the long run.[4]

Immigrants increase the U.S. supply of low-skill labor. Because industries that use low-skill labor intensively tend to be import-competing in the United States, we might expect them to enlarge the import-competing sector and possibly reduce the nation's overall participation in international trade. Indeed, in 1980 immigrants made up 10.4 percent of the labor forces of import-competing industries but only 7.5 percent of the industries exporting most heavily. That pattern is consistent with immigration's having a negative effect on the real income of labor while increasing the incomes of other factors of production (including the human capital of skilled workers).[5]

9.2   International Capital Movements: Selected Issues

International capital movements are commonly divided into two classes, depending on whether the lender acquires or possesses decision-making control over the borrowing entity. Portfolio capital transfers occur when individuals or institutions purchase bonds or other liabilities issued by foreign enterprises or governments, or acquire equity shares in foreign companies in blocks too small to give the purchasers voting control over the companies. Direct investment, which does imply control over the borrowing entity, is mainly the domain of the multinational company, discussed in Section 9.3.

British Foreign Investment in the Nineteenth Century

Net portfolio capital transfers nowadays are usually small. Norway borrowed 14 percent of its GNP in the 1970s to finance its oil industry, and Singapore loaned double-digit percentages in the 1990s, but the major industrial countries rarely exported capital totaling more than 1 percent annually of their gross national products. However, between 1870 and 1913 Great Britain placed 5.2 percent of its GNP in net foreign

---

[4]John M. Abowd and Richard B. Freeman, eds., *Immigration, Trade, and the Labor Market* (Chicago: University of Chicago Press, 1991), especially Chapters 6, 7, 10.
[5]Peter Kuhn and Ian Wooton (in Abowd and Freeman, ibid., Chapter 10) argue, however, that the story may be more complicated. Skilled labor is used heavily in U.S. exporting industries, whereas the non-traded-goods sector (cement, electricity) relies heavily on physical capital, which is also the middle factor in the traded-goods industries. Increases in the stock of unskilled labor (through immigration or otherwise) could then increase the returns to physical capital while lowering those to both unskilled and skilled labor.

lending, France 2 to 3 percent, and Germany somewhat less than 2 percent. Large flows of migration also occurred in those years. The experience is still instructive as an example of the economics of large-scale international factor movements. The focus here will be on the British economy, which experienced the largest outflows.

It is expected that capital will flow abroad whenever it can earn a higher return than at home. Indeed, from 1870 to 1913 British portfolio investments abroad did earn higher rates of return than did domestic securities held by British investors. What long-run changes opened these gaps in returns to capital, and how did the capital transfers go about eliminating them? The bulk of British portfolio investments went to the United States and to the overseas dominions, such as Australia and Canada. Ultimately, the capital flows served to complement the labor services of Europeans who emigrated to these areas in the development of the new countries' vast quantities of land and natural resources. This long-run adjustment process can be seen as occupying three centuries—from the initial voyages of discovery and settlement to the beginning of the twentieth century.

The period 1870 to 1913, in particular, shows the rhythms of this massive process of factor movement. British foreign investment moved in a somewhat cyclical fashion during this period. Capital flowed abroad heavily when capital formation was depressed in Britain's home economy; when home investment revived, foreign investment fell off. These switches between home and foreign investment responded to shifts in rates of return in Britain and abroad, which, in turn, reflected shifts in Britain's international terms of trade for its manufactured exports relative to its imports of food and raw materials. When the country's terms of trade were poor, primary-product prices were high and so was the profitability of expanding the capital stocks of the recently settled regions. British funds poured into railroad investments in the United States and Australia. Emigration to these areas also went in waves, but the timing was not closely related to the timing of the capital outflows. International capital flows depended not so much on the raw stocks of land and labor in the overseas regions as on the large-scale social capital investments being made there and the degree to which local savings could finance them.[6]

Another aspect of this large flow of capital exports is the transfer process that was explained in Section 3.4. Will a transfer of purchasing power disturb the equilibrium terms of trade between the lending and borrowing countries? It depends on how the borrower spends the proceeds and how the lender cuts back on expenditure that would otherwise be made. The changes in their spending decisions determine whether, without a change in the terms of trade, the balance of trade changes by the amount of the transfer. From the casual observation that people spend most of their incomes on locally produced goods, it is probable that the propensities are too low to adjust trade flows to the transfer without a deterioration of the lender's terms of trade. However, Britain was a major supplier of machinery and other manufactures to the borrowing

---

[6]Most of the analysis in this section is taken from these sources: A. K. Cairncross, *Home and Foreign Investment, 1870–1913: Studies in Capital Accumulation* (Cambridge, UK: Cambridge University Press, 1953), Chapters 7 and 8; Michael Edelstein, *Overseas Investment in the Age of High Imperialism: The United Kingdom, 1850–1914* (New York: Columbia University Press, 1982).

TABLE 9.1

Average Ratios of Wage to Land Rent, 1870 and 1910, in Selected Groups
of Old and New World Countries (Indexes, 1900 = 100)

Country Group	1870	1910
Average of New World countries (Argentina, Australia, United States)	195	57
Average of Old World free traders (United Kingdom, Denmark, Ireland, Sweden)	32	99
Average of Old World protectionists (France, Germany, Spain)	77	95

Source: Kevin H. O'Rourke, Alan M. Taylor, and Jeffrey G. Williamson, "Factor Price Convergence in the Late Nineteenth Century," *International Economic Review,* 37 (August 1996), Table 2.

countries, as well as a major importer of raw materials from them. The borrowing countries' marginal propensities to import must have been high enough to change trade flows roughly by the amounts of the transfers, because history reveals no obvious evidence of terms-of-trade disturbances or their short-run monetary counterparts. Also, in a broader sense, the transfer of capital was surely smoothed by the simultaneous movement of labor from Britain. The exit of both factors from Britain reduced the pressure for changes in British wages relative to capital rents that otherwise might have arisen.

Recent research has found more links between economic development in the late nineteenth century and the Heckscher-Ohlin theory. Land in Britain and North America was the fixed factor of production, and labor and capital migrated in response to their high marginal products when combined with abundant American land. This shift in endowments should have lowered the premium of American over British wages; indeed, between 1870 and 1895 it fell from 67 to 44 percent. Relative American land rents rose. The ideal way to illustrate this adjustment process is by means of the ratio of wages to land rents in the various countries involved in the adjustment process. Over the period of 1870 to 1913, it should have fallen in the New World countries because of immigration and risen in the Old World nations that lost labor relative to their (fixed) supplies of land. Indeed, we can add another wrinkle to this hypothesis. Some European countries (Britain, Sweden) followed a policy close to free trade over this period; others (France, Germany) protected their import-competing, land-intensive industries. The protecting countries should have retarded the increase in their domestic wage/rent ratio that would otherwise have resulted from emigration. The data in Table 9.1 strongly confirm these predictions and illustrate the process of convergence of relative factor prices.

Recent Flows of Portfolio Capital

In modern times international flows of portfolio capital have played smaller and rather different roles. A major flow of international lending went to the developing countries in the 1970s and 1980s (and again in the early 1990s). The larger and better-off of them

TABLE 9.2

Total Foreign Capital Stock Placed in Developing Countries, 1980 and 2000,
Current Dollars and Relation to Country Groups' GDPs

Foreign Capital Stock Component	Billions of U.S. Dollars		Percentage of Developing Countries' Combined GDP		Percentage of G-10 Combined GDP	
	1980	2000	1980	2000	1980	2000
Total foreign capital stock	770	4,937	26.3	72.6	10.9	23.2
Long, medium-term debt	457	2,192	15.6	32.2	6.4	10.3
Official	182	977	6.2	14.4	2.6	4.6
Private	275	1,215	9.4	17.9	3.9	5.7
Short-term debt	147	352	5.0	5.2	2.1	1.7
Portfolio investment	60	959	2.0	14.1	0.8	4.5
Foreign direct investment	106	1,434	3.6	21.1	1.5	6.8

Source: Wendy Dobson and Gary Clyde Hufbauer, *World Capital Markets: Challenge to the G-10* (Washington, DC: Institute for International Economics, 2001), Table 1.4. The G-10 are the ten leading developed countries.

had enjoyed faster rates of economic growth than the industrial countries, and the infusion of capital made obvious sense given their abundant labor. The main lenders in the 1970s were the large international banks, located in the industrial countries. A large portion of the transferred funds, however, no doubt was the wealth of the countries belonging to the Organization of Petroleum Exporting Countries (OPEC—see Chapter 12). Lending to developing countries has continued to encounter crises (see Chapter 24), but nonetheless it has occurred in large volumes. Table 9.2 shows the stocks of foreign capital that they received in 1980 and 2000. The total volume more than doubled in relation to the combined GDP levels of both the developing countries and the largest industrial countries (G-10). The mix has shifted from short- to long-term lending (including both portfolio and foreign direct investment) and away from official and syndicated bank loans.

In the 1980s international capital flows increased perhaps threefold among the developed nations. The pattern of these flows differed greatly from that of the late nineteenth century, described earlier. Rather than being driven by differences in investment opportunities between lenders and borrowers, it mainly reflected differences in rates of saving. A major example was the large flows of lending from high-saving Japan to the low-saving United States; as a result, the United States, once a major international creditor, became a large international debtor. Another key driver was efforts by holders of financial wealth to diversify portfolios internationally, taking advantage of many innovative securities and falling transaction costs in international capital markets. In short, capital flows were dominated by considerations of managing existing wealth rather than creating new capital.[7]

---

[7]For a survey, see Philip Turner, *Capital Flows in the 1980s: A Survey of Major Trends* (Basel: Bank for International Settlements, 1991).

9.3 Multinationals and Foreign Direct Investment

Direct investment is a unique form of international capital flow because it affects both the nation's stock of productive factors and competitive conditions in its markets. Its uniqueness lies in two traits.

1. Direct investment represents a capital movement, but the lender both transfers resources and takes control of the project. Most direct investment passes through or gives rise to *multinational enterprises* (MNEs), defined as firms that control and operate business units in more than one nation.

2. The MNE presumably makes investments abroad to increase its profit. It establishes a distribution firm abroad to market its exports, a factory to supply its foreign customers with locally produced goods, or a mine or an intermediate-goods factory to provide inputs for its operations back home. The factors that explain foreign direct investments are therefore *industry-specific* conditions in particular markets.

MNEs are very important in the international economy.[8] By 1990 they accounted for more than 75 percent of total U.S. merchandise trade, and 40 percent of U.S. merchandise trade passed between domestic and foreign branches of MNEs. The United States in 1995 owned 25 percent of the world's foreign direct investment and served as host for another 22 percent. Table 9.3 illustrates several features of the world distribution of MNEs. More than 60 percent of MNE trade emanates from a handful of major industrial countries, and 70 percent is placed in industrial host countries.

Causes of Direct Investment

Why should a firm invest in production facilities abroad? It does not know the language, the laws, the customs, the local markets. The foreign government may not be its friend. There must be a general explanation as to why profit-maximizing firms, at least in certain industries, establish foreign subsidiaries in the face of these obstacles.

The explanation draws on the theory of industrial organization and is just one application of the concepts used to explain any complex, multiactivity business firm. Many transactions (like buying lettuce at the supermarket) take place simply and effectively as arm's-length deals between a seller and buyer who are anonymous to each another. Other transactions, however, tend to tie the parties together in complex dealings for long periods of time. Consider a Japanese automobile producer that has grown skillful at producing durable, low-cost vehicles for the Japanese market and now considers selling them in the United States. It cannot simply take orders over the phone from

---

[8]For summaries of the large literature on MNEs and the policy issues they raise, see Richard E. Caves, *Multinational Enterprise and Economic Analysis,* 3rd ed. (New York: Cambridge University Press, 2007); and Edward M. Graham and Paul Krugman, *Foreign Direct Investment in the United States,* 3rd ed. (Washington, DC: Institute for International Economics, 1994).

TABLE 9.3

Stock of Foreign Direct Investment by Region,
1990 and 2004 ($ billion)

Region or Country	1990	2004
Outward		
World total	1785	9732
Developing countries	147	1036
Major developed countries	1123	5370
United States	431	2018
Japan	201	371
United Kingdom	229	1378
France	110	769
Germany	152	834
Other countries	515	3326
Inward		
World total	1769	8895
Developing countries	364	2226
Major developed countries	807	3226
United States	395	1474
Japan	10	97
United Kingdom	204	772
France	87	535
Germany	111	348
Other countries	598	3443

Source: United Nations Conference on Trade and Development, *World Investment Report, 2005* (New York: United Nations, 2005), Table B.2. Differences in inward and outward totals reflect discrepancies in the underlying data.

American customers; it must establish a dealer network to market and service its cars. That distribution system requires a substantial investment, and the firm has become a MNE. (It could contract with an independent U.S. firm to provide these services, but it will have trouble writing a contract that motivates its partner's marketing efforts so that they bring in the maximum profit for the Japanese firm.)

Instead of exporting cars, the Japanese firm might establish a plant in the United States to serve the U.S. market. Such a choice could result from reasons familiar from the theory of international trade: High transport costs might favor local production, or Japan's comparative advantage (vis-à-vis the United States) might shift away from automobiles. There are also organizational explanations. By making its vehicles locally, the Japanese seller can more readily adapt them to U.S. tastes, operating conditions, legal requirements, and the like. Finally, a subsidiary might be established in the United States to provide inputs to Japan, such as a design studio that draws on American talent for automotive styling. The Japanese car maker chooses to control both the U.S. plant and the U.S. design studio because their importance to and intricate ties with the parent make dealing with an independent firm infeasible.

Notice the affinity of this explanation for MNEs to elements of trade theory noted in previous chapters. MNEs that produce the same or similar goods in different countries—*horizontal* MNEs—show an affinity for product differentiation. Its role in international trade was treated in Chapter 7. MNEs that produce intermediate goods and services in one country for assembly into final goods in another—*vertical* MNEs—undertake a type of trade examined in Chapter 8. A vertical MNE can be regarded as a production block that is divided into components but minimizes the cost of service links through common ownership.

This sketch illustrates the microeconomic factors that explain foreign direct investment. In any of these forms, it occurs in the first instance because a firm (the Japanese car maker) acquires some rent-yielding skill, some *proprietary asset*. The amount and type of foreign investment are a result of the firm's effort to make the most profitable use of that proprietary asset. Industries vary greatly in the prevalence of foreign direct investment, and the ones dominated by MNEs are not the ones we consider purely competitive. Instead, they are industries in which research and innovation are important, in which successful firms acquire reputations with customers that are valuable goodwill assets, and in which the firm's basic task or production process requires the intricate and large-scale cooperation of many diverse physical assets and human skills.

This explanation for MNEs is consistent with many facts about their activities and international distribution. MNEs spring up especially in industrial countries that are enjoying rapid economic growth, which brings proprietary assets into the hands of many native firms. Examples include Japan in the 1970s and 1980s, European firms after the recovery from World War II, and the United States, still earlier, during its period of industrial dominance. Most direct investment passes between industrial countries. The wealthy nations have similar tastes for sophisticated goods, and a firm successful in serving one national market could well profit as a MNE from serving others as well. Foreignness has its costs and disadvantages, however. MNEs tend to go first to countries most familiar and nearby: U.S. firms go to Canada or Britain, German firms to European neighbors, Spanish firms to Latin America. They tend to locate in large countries because establishing a manufacturing plant or a distribution network always involves some scale economies. They interpenetrate each other's national markets; intra-industry foreign direct investment is mainly an extension of the intra-industry trade described in Section 7.5.

The developing countries are not left out of the loop. They long have been hosts to foreign investment that developed and extracted their natural resources. Before Toyotas ever appeared on U.S. highways, firms in resource-short Japan were big foreign investors in natural resource development. The footloose production activities that were swept into the newly industrializing countries (NICs) sometimes arrived as foreign direct investments, although many of them flourished as arm's-length dealings between foreign and local firms. The NICs' own development successes led them to sprout foreign investments of their own, and multinationals in developing countries have attracted attention as natural outcomes of industrial success in conditions peculiar to these countries.[9]

MNEs and Merchandise Trade

MNEs are widely active in international trade, both as arm's-length exporters and importers and in trading inputs and finished goods between their national branches. There is widespread interest in how foreign direct investment is related to trade. Foreign direct investment from a country could be either a substitute or a complement for its exports. The MNE has an incentive to move production abroad in response to lower real costs of production. But the MNE's capital also seeks to produce exports wherever unit labor cost is the lowest, and we saw that such investments expand trade overall. MNEs that produce complex goods or product lines commonly source their inputs and specialized products in many locations and engage heavily in intrafirm trade. The empirical evidence suggests that overall foreign direct investment expands trade. The complementarity seems to reflect the process of development: The successful firm begins exporting to a foreign market through a local agent; if export sales prosper, it finds it can do better by investing in its own distribution subsidiary; it discovers enough opportunities in the foreign market to warrant starting production there. However, the foreign subsidiary both imports components from its parent and also uncovers new market opportunities, so the parent's total exports to the host country might well continue to increase.

Although foreign direct investment can complement or substitute for trade, like any other capital flow, it does have a distinctive sensitivity to international differences in production costs. Even short-run international differences in costs of production strongly affect flows of foreign direct investment. An appreciation of a country's currency on the foreign exchange markets, even if temporary, can send its firms scurrying to invest abroad, as can the depreciation of the currency of a promising host country. During the 1980s direct investment inflows to the United States strongly reflected swings in the foreign currency value of the dollar.

One factor that makes foreign investment a substitute for trade is the influence of a potential host country's tariff.[10] The historical record is awash with cases in which a foreign enterprise develops a market in a country by selling exports. Then a tariff is imposed, and the foreign enterprise shifts to serving the market through a direct investment. We can enjoy the paradox that domestic producers seeking tariff protection only

---

[9]Louis T. Wells, Jr., *Third World Multinationals* (Cambridge, MA: MIT Press, 1983); and his "Mobile Exporters: New Foreign Investors in East Asia," in Kenneth Froot, ed., *Foreign Direct Investment* (Chicago: University of Chicago Press, 1993), pp. 173–195.

[10]Exports and production abroad are in one sense clearly substitutes for the MNE. The higher the costs of shipping its goods to a foreign market, the higher the trade barriers surrounding that market, and the less scale economies deter decentralized production, the more the MNE serves the market by local production. See S. Lael Brainard, "An Empirical Assessment of the Proximity-Concentration Trade-off between Multinational Sales and Trade," *American Economic Review*, 87 (September 1997): 520–544.

make their problem worse when the foreign tiger comes prowling in their own back-yard (consider the investments by Japanese auto producers in response to U.S. import restrictions), but quite possibly too much foreign direct investment results from such made-to-measure trade restrictions.

MNEs and Technology Transfer

Some models of international trade assume that the same technology is costlessly available to all trading nations; other models (the Ricardian approach) explore the effect of differences. What trade theory neglects is the process by which technological improvements, originating somewhere in the world, are diffused to other sites where they prove useful. Many channels exist: the direct diffusion of nonproprietary scientific knowledge through journals, conferences, and the like; international trade in new machinery and equipment that embodies process improvements; the activities of international engineering firms that transfer technology when they build plants around the world; the licensing of proprietary industrial technology by owners to other firms willing to pay for its use; and the processes by which proprietary technology slips informally from the hands of its discoverers to those who capture it through direct observation, "reverse engineering," or even industrial espionage. The MNE is an important agent in this transmission process. The proprietary assets that launch successful firms on their international journeys consist prominently of industrial knowledge: product and process technologies in the narrow sense; repertories of skills and routines that serve as organizational technology and are no less important for resource productivity than is technology in an engineering sense. One reason why MNEs are so widespread is that firms holding these proprietary intangibles find it impossible to write contracts to license their technology to independent firms abroad that will extract the maximum value from the licensee's use of the technology yet protect it from appropriation by the licensee or other parties.

International technology flows are hard to observe directly, but they can be measured by the flows of revenue they generate. The royalties and license fees that U.S.-based MNEs earn abroad grew rapidly from $4.2 billion in 1985 to $23.3 billion in 1999. We know large companies commit resources to research and development with heed to the possibility of using or licensing it abroad and they would cut research back sharply if denied this opportunity. The newer a technology and the faster it changes, the more likely the firm is to use it abroad only in its subsidiaries; mature technologies tend to be licensed instead to independent firms abroad. Although most transfers of proprietary technology through licensing and foreign investment pass among the industrial countries, one factor promoting multinationals in developing countries is the exploitation of technologies and products suited to the labor-intensive conditions and small markets typical in developing countries.

Direct Investment and Economic Welfare

MNEs have long attracted a storm of controversy in the realm of public policy. Economic analysis detects some welfare effects of foreign direct investment that should trigger government actions. However, economists and other would-be policy makers sometimes disagree sharply on what policy should be. We start with the message of economics, then turn to the public policy debate.

Consider the MNE that earns a profit on its proprietary assets through a successful foreign direct investment in a host country. The firm's host-country customers get something of value from the services of these proprietary assets, but they also pay for this benefit. They are not necessarily better off, on balance. The MNE does earn some additional profit, which belongs to its owners (equity shareholders) in the source country. The profit is a real benefit to the source country.

The host nation may benefit directly from the services of the MNE's proprietary assets if that firm—facing competition with other firms in the host-country market—is unable to charge its customers a price high enough to exact all of their consumers' surplus. The spillover benefits that attract the most attention, however, are those that might pass from the foreign subsidiary to other producers in the host country. These are numerous. If the foreign subsidiary draws on local suppliers and/or business customers (distributors, say), it may benefit from expending efforts to raise the efficiency of these partners, even though some of the gains likely stick to them. It trains local employees, letting them in (as it were) on the workings of its proprietary assets and organizational skills. These employees may pay for their training by receiving only apprentice wages at the start, but the foreign subsidiary likely cannot prevent them, once their training is complete, from quitting and taking their skills to other (domestic) firms. Host-country firms competing with the foreign subsidiary may be able to observe and copy its proprietary assets and business methods. Economists have tried to measure these spillover benefits to host countries, both statistically and through case studies. The spillovers to suppliers and customers clearly occur, although not in every setting. Spillovers to local competitors have proved more elusive; the best statistical evidence on spillovers to competitors confirms their existence, but only in host countries sufficiently advanced in development and organization to absorb the available lessons.

Recent evidence indicates that spillovers in the setting of MNEs can run in both directions. A MNE may invest abroad not to exploit but to augment its proprietary assets by pitching a tent near other firms (which may or may not be MNEs), the better to copy their proprietary assets. A recent study used patent statistics to confirm this. A patent document cites previous patents to indicate the nature of its innovation, thereby indicating knowledge spilled by holders of the previous patents. It turns out empirically that, on the basis of citation counts, foreign subsidiaries "fish" more spillovers from a host country's domestic firms than the domestic firms do from them. (MNEs are even better at snatching spillover from other MNEs.)[11]

Multinational Firms and Public Policy

How do governments treat these rents and surpluses that may be associated with the activities of MNEs? A very important branch of policy is the taxation of corporate income. The host country's tax collector gets first crack at the profits that foreign subsidiaries earn. Rates of taxation on corporate profits naturally vary from country to

---

[11]Jasjit Singh, *Multinational Firms and Knowledge Diffusion: Evidence Using Patent Citation Data*, Ph.D. dissertation, Harvard University, 2003, Chapter 1.

country but commonly lie in the neighborhood of 30 percent. Foreign subsidiaries' profits are also subject to tax by the source country when they are remitted to the parent, but they are not "double taxed." Source countries' tax collectors let the MNE deduct from its liability to the source the taxes already paid on these profits to the host country. Other source countries exempt corporate income earned abroad from any further taxation. In terms of welfare economics, these tax arrangements give the host country a cut of the rents earned by MNEs operating in the host country. To the extent that the host government provides unpriced infrastructure-type facilities and services to foreign affiliates, these taxes may function partly as user charges.

The torpid details of taxation much understate the intensity of the controversies over MNEs. Host countries long regarded MNEs, especially those facing few competitors and those engaged in the extraction of host countries' natural resources, as exploiters. In the two decades after World War II, nationalizations of foreign subsidiaries were common. Foreign direct investment was severely restricted until the MNEs and host governments learned to work out deals whereby the government paid a project's fixed costs (that were at hazard of expropriation) and the MNE provided only managerial services (that were not). Source countries were often no less happy about MNEs' effects. "Exporting jobs" was a rallying cry. In the 1970s U.S. labor unions unsuccessfully launched a major campaign to restrict U.S. direct investment abroad. In the early 1990s the North American Free Trade Agreement (a preferential trading arrangement among the United States, Canada, and Mexico) was feared to draw jobs to Mexico. Economists point out that jobs lost when a MNE invests abroad (or, for that matter, jobs gained when a foreign MNE alights at home) seldom have any substantial or sustained *net* effect on national employment levels—jobs are continuously gained and lost throughout the economy.

The general hostility that MNEs encountered several decades ago has sharply reversed, especially in developing countries and in the economies in transition from central planning. The newfound love for MNEs recognizes the spillover benefits just mentioned, but it raises concern for misconceived policies of an opposite sort. Countries hoping to attract foreign direct investment may fall into competition with one another, bestowing subsidies or giving "tax holidays" to MNEs with major investments to place. The foregone revenues might otherwise have financed worthwhile public expenditures. There is, of course, something to be said for competition to attract investments: The jurisdiction in which an investment creates the greatest spillover value should be the one willing to make the highest bid. That logic falters, though, when a government overvalues the economic benefits. For example, to attract a Mercedes-Benz plant, the state of Alabama spent an amount equal to $168,000 per job created in the plant, hardly a credible benefit.

9.4   Summary

International trade in factors of production potentially increases world welfare. When factor prices are not equalized between countries, factors that move internationally raise both their productivity and their incomes. Factor migration tends to cause income redistribution, however. The industrial countries have been fearful that immigration impoverishes domestic low-skilled labor, but in the United States the effect seems to be small.

Capital moving internationally is direct investment when the investor controls the receiving enterprise and portfolio investment when it does not. Portfolio investment moved in large flows from England and other European countries from 1870 to 1913. Bursts of foreign investment flowed to the overseas regions that supplied Britain's imports when import prices were high (i.e., Britain's terms of trade were poor). Capital stayed at home when Britain's terms of trade improved. There was no obvious transfer problem because the overseas recipients naturally spent most of the proceeds on British capital goods. Portfolio capital flowed heavily but erratically to the developing countries in the 1970s and early 1990s, subject to financial shocks and crises. Recent portfolio capital movements among the industrial countries have been related to differences in rates of saving and the diversification of wealth rather than to differences in investment opportunities.

Foreign direct investment typically involves the creation or acquisition of a subsidiary abroad by a corporation. It is sector specific and usually occurs in certain market structures. Some companies invest abroad to obtain sources of raw materials or other inputs; others acquire subsidiaries that can produce the same product line as their parent. When a foreign subsidiary's production replaces exports, capital and commodity flows are substitutes, but for several reasons they may be complements. A country's tariff that restricts imports, though, is likely to cause foreign producers to set up shop within the protected market. The MNE is an important conveyor of new technologies across national borders. Two features of MNEs' operations drive their encounters with public policy. The first is the profit that many of them earn on proprietary assets that give rise to their multinational status. Countries' corporate income tax provisions affect the distribution of these profits between source and host countries. The second is the spillovers of their proprietary assets and business methods to domestic firms. These can explain why governments nowadays compete to attract foreign direct investments. Unfortunately, they seem sometimes to misconceive these benefits as "creating jobs."

CHAPTER PROBLEMS

1. Suppose that factor-price equalization prevails in the world but a large migration takes place from country A to country B (because of some political disturbance, for example). Describe the adjustments that will occur if capital is also mobile internationally. What will happen if it is immobile?

2. Research by David M. Gould showed that the bilateral trade between the United States and other countries increases substantially in tandem with the number of a country's citizens who have migrated to the United States. What mechanisms could account for this relationship? Might it apply to flows of foreign direct investment as well?

3. Some observers have noted the occurrence of intra-industry flows of foreign direct investment, like the intra-industry trade discussed in Chapter 7. Given the nature of the multinational company, why might this happen?

4. Recent research indicates that those U.S. multinational firms expanding their outputs and/or capital stocks abroad tend to be expanding them in the United States as well. Is that consistent with the microeconomic theory of MNEs? Is it consistent with equilibrium for the U.S. economy as a whole?

SUGGESTIONS FOR FURTHER READING

Borjas, George J. "The Economics of Immigration," *Journal of Economic Literature*, 32 (December 1994): 1667–1717. Survey of data and issues.

Caves, Richard E. *Multinational Enterprise and Economic Analysis,* 3rd ed. (Cambridge, UK: Cambridge University Press, 2007). Survey of concepts and evidence relating to multinationals.

Engerman, Stanley L., and Ronald W. Jones. "International Labor Flows and National Wages," *American Economic Review,* 87 (May 1997): 200–204. Reviews trade theory bearing on migration and wages.

Gould, David M. "Immigrant Links to the Home Country: Empirical Implications for U.S. Bilateral Trade Flows," *Review of Economics and Statistics,* 76 (May 1994): 302–316. Links between migration and trade flows.

Graham, Edward M., and Paul R. Krugman. *Foreign Direct Investment in the United States,* 3rd ed. (Washington, D.C.: Institute for International Economics, 1994). Survey of issues.

Moran, Theodore H., et al., *Does Foreign Direct Investment Promote Development?* (Washington, DC: Institute for International Economics, 2005). Extensive studies of spillovers from foreign direct investment.

O'Rourke, Kevin H., and Jeffrey G. Williamson, *Globalization and History: The Evidence of a Nineteenth-Century Atlantic Economy* (Cambridge, MA: MIT Press, 1999). Extensive application of Heckscher-Ohlin model to economic history.

Wright, Gavin. "The Origins of American Industrial Success, 1879–1940," *American Economic Review,* 80 (September 1990): 651–668. Role of natural resources in long-run changes in U.S. comparative advantage.

PART III

The Theory and Practice of Commercial Policy

Chapter 10 ■ Protection and the National Welfare
PAGE 169

Chapter 11 ■ The Political Economy of Protection
PAGE 187

Chapter 12 ■ Trade Policy and Imperfect Competition
PAGE 203

Chapter 13 ■ Trade Controls in Practice
PAGE 227

Chapter 14 ■ Preferential Arrangements and
Regional Issues in Trade Policy
PAGE 245

CHAPTER 10

Protection and the National Welfare

Free trade supposedly brings benefits to all nations. So why do countries interfere so much with this trade? For centuries most countries have felt compelled to block the smooth flow of commodities by erecting tariff barriers or other obstacles to trade. In the next few chapters we examine the nature of such impediments, ask how they may benefit special groups, and discuss attempts at cooperation in commercial policy, both at the regional level (regional free-trade areas such as the North American Free Trade Agreement or customs unions such as the European Union) and in larger groupings.

The primary weapon of commercial policy used to be the tariff, although successive rounds of GATT (the General Agreement on Tariffs and Trade) negotiations in Geneva and elsewhere lowered the average rate of duty on manufactured goods from more than 40 percent in 1947 to less than 4 percent at the conclusion of the Uruguay Round in 1994. Partly because of these reductions, those interested in protection have cleverly introduced other means of achieving similar ends such as quotas, voluntary export restraints, stringent rules concerning dumping, and so on. Even in the European Union, famous for eliminating most trade barriers among its members, other protective devices discriminate against foreign investment and trade in items such as bananas and genetically modified foods.

In this opening chapter we pay attention to *tariffs*, in full recognition of their relative decline in the arsenal of protective instruments. Nonetheless, tariffs encapsulate the essence of all protective devices—introducing a wedge between prices found in world markets and market prices faced by producers and consumers at home when making choices about purchases and sales of commodities and inputs into production. As well, efforts are being made to reduce some forms of protection devices, for example, quotas on allowable import quantities, by first changing them into the equivalent tariff values, thus making the degree of protection more transparent.

Our focus in this chapter is on the welfare of a nation as well as of the world. The following chapters take a closer look at the set of other rationales for restrictive policies, especially those aimed at helping particular special interests within the country.

10.1   Protection by a Small Country

A *tariff* is a tax on the importation of a commodity from abroad. If the country levying the tariff is small, the tariff has little effect on the world price of the commodity. Instead, the foreign commodity becomes more expensive behind the tariff wall at home, both to producers of the commodity (who can be expected to support the tariff) and to local consumers (who will likely oppose the duty). In general, a tariff attracts resources to the protected sector and shifts demand away from foreign goods. On both counts a tariff reduces a small country's imports.[1]

Tariffs and Partial Equilibrium

We start our discussion of tariffs with a diagrammatic approach often used when focusing on the effect of protection on a single commodity—the so-called partial-equilibium approach. Figure 10.1 shows a small country's downward-sloping demand curve and rising supply curve for some commodity that is being imported. Initial world price, which is also the domestic price in a free-trade equilibrium, is indicated by the horizontal line at P_w, which indicates that unlimited supplies are available to the small country at this price. Points K and L indicate the quantities of this commodity that would be locally supplied and demanded, respectively, at this price; quantity KL would thus represent initial imports. If the country introduces a tariff of height $P_t - P_w$, the world price remains unchanged (the country is too small to affect world prices), and domestic price increases to P_t. Imports are reduced to level MN. In Figure 10.1 four different areas are isolated:

1. The reduction in consumer surplus: This is shown by areas $1 + 2 + 3 + 4$—the loss in the area under the demand curve and above the initial market price when that market price rises.

2. The increase in producer surplus: By analogy, this is area 1—above the supply curve and lower than the new market price.

3. The government revenue: This is area 3—the amount collected as tariff revenue.

4. The triangular areas $2 + 4$ represent a *dead weight loss:* This is the excess of what consumers have lost over and above what producers gain and what the government receives.

We turn now to a discussion of the effect of a tariff using the tools familiar from our earlier work—transformation schedules and indifference curves. The partial equi-

---

[1]It will usually be assumed that the tariff rate is quoted on an ad valorem basis; that is, the domestic price of imports, p_F, equals a multiple, $(1 + t)$, of the world price p_F^*. The tariff rate is sometimes quoted as a percentage of the foreign price (e.g., $100t$ might be 28 percent). For a given tariff rate, t, the absolute wedge separating home and foreign prices would increase if the foreign price rises. A different kind of tariff is the *specific* tariff—a rate quoted in absolute dollars per physical unit (e.g., $2.10 a ton). If t' denotes this amount, p_F would equal $(p_F^* + t')$. An inflation of world prices would, in such a case, leave the absolute tariff wedge unchanged (and diminish its relative significance).

FIGURE 10.1

Effects on Welfare and Government
Revenue of Tariff on Individual Product

Domestic demand is DD', domestic supply is SS',
world price is P_w. Imposing tariff P_tP_w/P_w0 leaves
world price unchanged, raises domestic price
to P_t, and causes a welfare loss (net) measured
by triangular areas 2 and 4.

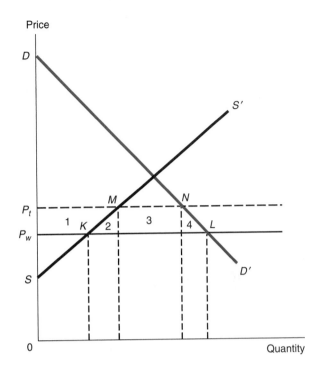

librium techniques displayed in Figure 10.1 can be augmented to ascertain the effects
of protection on other parts of the economy. What happens to production and consumption of *exportables* as a tariff on imports is imposed? We start with the effect on
production, then turn to the more subtle analysis of demand.

Tariffs and Production

Figures 10.2 and 10.3 are designed to highlight separately the impact of a tariff on production and on demand. Curve TT' in Figure 10.2 shows full-employment production
possibilities for a small country initially producing food and clothing at point A and
facing free-trade relative prices shown by the slope of line 1. Suppose the country
imports food and proceeds to levy a tariff on food imports, thus raising the domestic
relative price of food by the amount of the tariff because the country is assumed to be
too small to affect *world* prices. The posttariff *domestic* price ratio is shown by line 2.
The tariff attracts resources to food, driving up the opportunity cost in this sector until
local costs reflect the new higher domestic food price at B.

In terms of domestic prices, production point B maximizes the value of national
production. Yet output evaluated at *world* prices has fallen: Line 3 is parallel to line 1,
showing that national income in food units at world prices is *reduced* from $0F$ to $0D$.
This is a signal that a small country in competitive world markets harms itself by levying a tariff on imports.

FIGURE 10.2

The Effect of a Tariff on Production

The initial free-trade prices are shown by line 1; production is at *A*, and national income, measured in units of food, is *OF*. A tariff on imports of food raises the domestic relative price of food, as is shown by line 2. Resources are shifted into food; production moves to point *B*. At world prices national income in food units has been reduced to *OD* (line 3 is parallel to line 1).

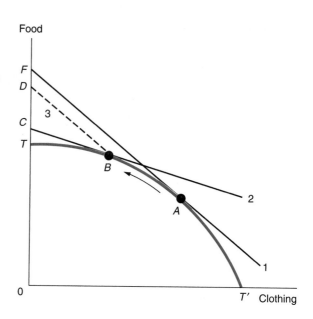

Tariffs and Demand

The analysis of the impact of tariffs on demand is more difficult. Why? Because a tariff not only drives up the relative price of food imports to consumers, it also raises revenue. The assumption typically made about the tariff revenue is that it is redistributed back to the public. This may take the form of reductions in other taxes (for example, income taxes) sufficient to balance the budget. In any case, it is assumed that the public's disposable income (and expenditure) consists now not only of produced income but also of tariff revenue.[2] This means, however, that import demand depends partly on how much tariff revenue is raised, and the amount of tariff revenue raised depends on the quantity of imports demanded. Despite this complication, the bottom line is that a tariff reduces the country's demands for imports.

Details of the argument are provided by Figure 10.3. We abstract from production changes by assuming the production possibilities schedule is the right-angled box *TAT'*, with production fixed at point *A*. The initial free-trade terms of trade are shown by line 1, with the community's best consumption point at *G*. Distance *GK* represents the free-trade level of food imports, matched by clothing exports of amount *KA*.

A tariff raises the relative price of food imports to consumers and also results in tariff revenues being collected and redistributed. The dotted line *0NJH* has been constructed to connect all possible consumption points consistent with the higher relative

---

[2]An alternative procedure has the government keeping the tariff proceeds and spending them according to its own taste patterns, which may differ from those of the private sector. Having the tariff proceeds redistributed makes it possible to consider a single set of preferences for the entire community.

FIGURE 10.3

The Effect of a Tariff on Demand

Production remains at A on the right-angled TAT' transformation schedule. A tariff raises the relative domestic price of food to line 2 (parallel to lines 3 and 4). Food consumption falls by the substitution effect (from G to H) plus an income effect (from H to J). Distance EC measures the tariff revenue in terms of food. The trade triangle shrinks from GKA to JLA.

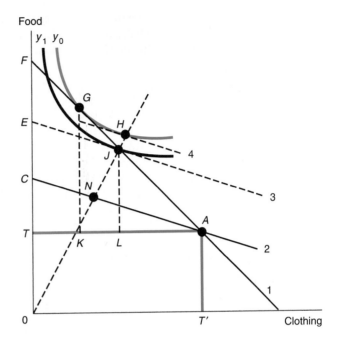

domestic price of food. (This locus is called an income-consumption line. For example, points N, J, and H are consumption bundles demanded at the new posttariff domestic prices when incomes are shown by lines 2, 3, and 4, respectively.) If consumers could stay on initial indifference curve y_0, the rise in food's price would evoke the substitution effect involved in moving from G to H. Income level y_0 cannot be maintained, however. Why not? The value of consumption at world prices must exactly match the value of production. Thus point J is the consumption point chosen after the tariff is imposed because it is the only point on $0NJH$ that also lies on line 1 through production point A. All points on line 1 satisfy the requirement that quantities of clothing exported match demand for food as imports *at world prices*.

In terms of domestic prices, line 3 is the posttariff budget line. It is above a parallel line, 2, through production point A. This reflects the fact that consumers' disposable income exceeds the value of production by the amount of the tariff revenue (EC in units of food). However, note that the tariff has harmed consumers—pushing them to consumption point J, which lies on a lower indifference curve than does G.

To summarize, the effect of a tariff on the demand for imports is tricky to analyze because tariff revenues form part of income, and income is one of the determinants of the demand for imports and thus tariff revenues. To cut through this simultaneity problem, Figure 10.3 shows that demand must satisfy two requirements in equilibrium: (1) The indifference curve must be tangent to a budget line reflecting *domestic* prices, and (2) the value of consumption must match the value of production at *world* prices.

In Figure 10.3 this implies that the consumption bundle must lie both on ray $0NJH$ and on line AJF. Note that, *despite* the fact that a tariff raises revenue, it lowers real income. Thus demand for importables falls both because price rises and real income is reduced.

Tariffs and Imports

Now we combine the production and demand responses because a nation's imports reflect both its demand for the importable commodity and its domestic production of that same commodity. Figure 10.2 shows how a tariff encourages greater production of the importable commodity. Production was kept fixed in Figure 10.3 to highlight the effect of a tariff in cutting demand for importables. These two strands are brought together in Figure 10.4. The free-trade equilibrium production and consumption points are represented by points A and G, respectively, with the slope of line 1 indicating the fixed relative world price of clothing to food. A tariff on food raises the relative domestic price of food and encourages greater local production. This effect is shown by the move from A to B, where line 2 shows posttariff domestic prices. Line 4 is parallel to line 1 and shows combinations of clothing and food that have the same value at world prices as the production point B. The home country's consumption bundle after the tariff must lie somewhere along line 4; specifically, it must rest at J, where indifference curve y_1 has a slope equal to the *domestic* price ratio (line 3 is parallel to line 2). The home country's demand for imports has been reduced from GK to JL—a combination of greater production and lessened demand for food. Thus Figure 10.4 adds details about production and consumption of both commodities to the partial-equilibrium reduction of imports to level MN in Figure 10.1.

FIGURE 10.4

The Effect of a Tariff on Imports

A tariff raises the domestic relative price of food (shown by lines 2 and 3) above the fixed world price (shown by lines 1 and 4). Domestic production of food rises from A to B. Domestic consumption of food falls from G to J. The trade triangle shrinks from GKA to JLB.

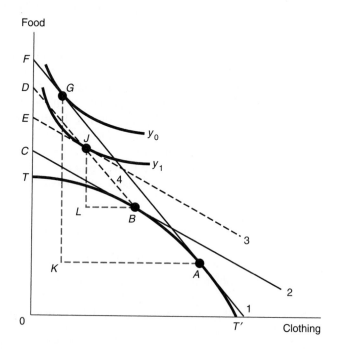

Tariffs and Welfare

In Figure 10.4 the tariff lowers real income, illustrated by the move from curve y_0 to curve y_1. At given world prices, the tariff has lowered the aggregate value of production (compare $0F$ with $0D$). Furthermore, point J is not even the best consumption point along line 4 because the tariff causes domestic prices (line 3) to be distorted away from world prices (shown by the slope of line 4).

Both domestic prices and world prices have a welfare significance that helps reveal why a tariff for a small country facing competitive foreign suppliers lowers national well-being. *Domestic* prices reflect the community's relative evaluation of commodities. (Marginal rates of substitution are equated to domestic price ratios.) *World* prices reflect costs of obtaining a commodity via trade. If a tariff is erected, the cost to the community of obtaining another unit of food imports (as measured by the required export of clothing at world prices) is lower than the value to the community of consuming another unit of food (as measured by the slope of indifference curves or by the domestic price of food). This discrepancy between value and cost indicates that the purchase (at world prices) of another unit of food would yield more in satisfaction than would be sacrificed in cost. Yet the tariff moves consumption the other way; it has *reduced* imports and thus has lowered welfare. It has reduced imports by reducing demand *and* by increasing local production. (In Figure 10.4 food imports have been reduced from GK to JL.) This loss of welfare is also reflected in the sum of areas 2 and 4 in Figure 10.1—the *deadweight loss*. It is approximated by the reduction in imports times the tariff wedge.

If tariffs reduce imports, what is the effect on exports? As Figure 10.4 reveals, exports have also been reduced, from KA to LB. Popular discussions of commercial policy often focus on the desirability of cutting back on foreign imports, perhaps because of the supposed benefit to employment in that sector of the economy. However, if exports are also cut back by such a move, the benefit via total employment or any other measure is clearly questionable. One of the real advantages of analyzing commercial policies in a manner that makes explicit the consequences for *all* sectors of the economy is avoiding the misleading conclusion that protection is beneficial just because it might favor the sector being protected—misleading because there are changes in other sectors that such an argument ignores.

Tariffs and Export Taxes

An export tax is an instrument of commercial policy that raises the foreign price of exportables above the domestic price. Although barred by constitutional provision in the United States, it is sometimes used by other nations. Indeed, in 1987 Canada levied a 15 percent export tax on shipments of softwood lumber to the United States as part of an arrangement whereby a threatened American import duty of 15 percent on softwood imports was recalled. The net effect: The Canadians pocketed the tax revenue.[3]

---

[3]Chapters 11 and 12 discuss in more detail the rationale behind the choice of protectionist instruments that, as in this case, divert tariff revenue to foreign hands.

Application: Harmonization and the Environment

These issues have taken on great importance lately in countries' evolving efforts to achieve efficient international trading arrangements (discussed in Chapters 13 and 14). If a nation restricts trade heavily, trade controls and other industrial policies affect mainly its own welfare. As natural processes of globalization and the removal of tariffs knit national markets more tightly, countries perceive their welfare to be affected by other countries' policies toward their own domestic markets.

Consider industries whose activities tend to generate local pollution, in a trading universe consisting of two countries, the "Cleans" and the "Toughs." The Cleans prefer tight controls on polluting industrial processes, whereas the Toughs select less stringent controls. Any pollution controls raise production costs for polluting industries, and the Cleans penalize the polluters more heavily than do the Toughs. The policy difference changes the comparative-advantage pattern of the two nations so that polluting industries' outputs and exports are larger in Tough and smaller in Clean than would otherwise be the case. If we accept each country's choice of public policy as a reflection of its welfare, this outcome (with no restrictions on trade) is efficient. It can lead to policy conflicts, however, in two ways.

1. The dirty industries in Clean perceived themselves to be unfairly penalized by the lower costs of their less restricted competitors in Tough. They demand redress in the form of tariff protection; such pleas based on perceived fairness often receive sympathetic political responses.

2. Clean's most ardent environmentalists not only favor stringent environmental policies at home but also believe their Tough trading partners should feel the same way. When the United States, Canada, and Mexico were negotiating the North American Free Trade Agreement to eliminate most trade barriers among themselves (Section 14.2), environmentalists opposed the pact on the ground that the Mexicans should be required to adopt policies that met their own elevated tastes.

Pollution and environment problems can be either local (assumed so far) or global (global warming and greenhouse effects). Assume that the burning of a given amount of fossil fuel contributes the same amount to global warming, regardless of where it takes place. Even if each country requires the local abatement of pollution to the degree that its citizens desire, each still fails to recognize the harmful effect of its fuel-consumption level on all the other countries. The only solution is international agreement to restrict the total amount of pollutants. Trade policy stays in the picture, however. For global warming, it does not matter where pollution arises, but countries may differ in their marginal cost of cutting back. The efficient solution is a global version of the one that economists propose for dealing with local pollution problems: The government should create a given amount of "rights to pollute," which can be traded among industrial polluters. That is, firms in a polluting industry may choose between incurring the cost of reducing their pollution and buying a right to go on polluting. The price set by competitive bids and offers for such rights then causes abatement to take place where it is least costly. International pollution abatement through rights trading has been discussed but with much heat. There is a distributional question of who should be given the rights to pollute when the auction starts (the developing countries?). Also, environmentalists are prone to see immorality in something called a "right to pollute," although it simply reflects the fact that eliminating all pollution is neither feasible nor economically desirable.[4]

10.2 Protection by a Large Country

It has been shown that a tariff must reduce import demand and the supply of exports at the initially prevailing world prices. If the tariff-levying country is not small in relation to competitive world markets, its tariff will drive down the world relative price of imports or, equivalently, raise the relative world price of its exports. The tariff can improve a country's terms of trade.

This point can be illustrated by the home net import demand curve, M, and the foreign export supply curve, X^*, in Figure 10.5. The vertical axis measures the world relative price of food (thus the asterisks). Section 10.1 showed that at any given terms of trade a tariff would cut back home demand for imports—from Q to A at the initial terms of trade in Figure 10.5. That is, the home demand curve for imports, M, shifts leftward to M'.

FIGURE 10.5

A Tariff Improves the Terms of Trade

The initial free-trade equilibrium is at Q, with the relative *world* price of food shown at B on the vertical axis. A tariff shifts the home import demand schedule down from M to M' and lowers the world relative price of food to that indicated by Q'.

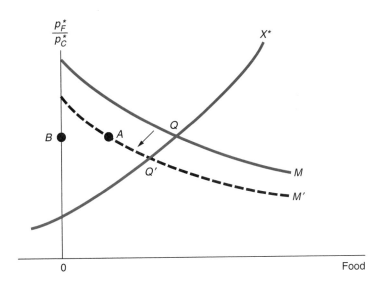

[4]Many other national policies toward production and consumption get tangled with trade policy. Discussion among policy makers has recently turned to these problems of "deeper integration," how countries can coordinate their policies to achieve efficiency in their domestic production and consumption levels without distorting trade patterns. See Pietro S. Nivola, ed., *Comparative Disadvantages? Social Regulations and the Global Economy* (Washington, DC: Brookings Institution, 1997).

The home country is not small in Figure 10.5. This is revealed by the fact that the new world trade equilibrium at Q' shows that the home country's tariff has lowered the relative price of imported food on world markets. That is, a country can use a tariff to improve its terms of trade. It acts like a seller of a commodity that finds itself with some monopoly power. By controlling supply, the seller can exercise some influence over price. Just as a tariff reduces the home country's import demand at given world terms of trade, so does it reduce the quantity of exports supplied. Looked at in this way, a tariff is a means of forcing up the relative price of a country's exports on world markets. An improvement in the terms of trade means either a reduction in the world relative price of imports or an increase in the relative price of exports—they are the same thing. Remember that although the government of the tariff-levying country can act like a monopolist, it is still assumed that private firms are numerous enough to act competitively.

If a tariff depresses the *world* relative price of imports, the *domestic* relative price of imports cannot rise by the full extent of the tariff. This relationship points to a conflict in the motives lying behind the use of a tariff. Tariffs often aim to protect local import-competing industries that wish to raise the domestic price of the commodities they produce. The more inelastic is the foreign supply curve, the more the foreign price of imports will be driven down by the tariff. The consequence: the greater the improvement in the terms of trade, the less the protective effect of a tariff.[5]

10.3   Taxing Trade: Domestic Welfare

If a large country can improve its terms of trade by commercial policy, why is it not always beneficial to keep levying higher and higher tariffs to obtain ever better terms of trade? The analysis of the small-country case in Section 10.1 provides a warning that there is more to the argument than this. If a country cannot improve its terms of trade, a tariff will actually harm welfare. There are two conflicting forces regarding the impact of a tariff on domestic welfare.

Figure 10.6 shows how welfare is linked to the height of the tariff for a country able to improve its terms of trade by trade restriction. Assume there is some rate of duty, t_1, large enough to choke off all trade. If such a tariff were applied, all gains from trade would be wiped out. (Imposing tariff rates higher than t_1 would have no further effect on real incomes because dutiable imports have already been reduced to zero.) Free trade (a zero tariff) is superior to no trade (with a tariff equal to t_1 or higher), so the curve in Figure 10.6 is lower after t_1 than initially at A. Furthermore, the terms-of-trade improvement that would occur when a small tariff is first levied must improve welfare. Obviously, there must be some intermediate tariff rate, t_0, that is optimal in that it maximizes the level of domestic welfare.

---

[5]A tariff might depress the foreign price of imports so much that the domestic price actually falls. The appendix illustrates the possibility geometrically and the supplement provides an algebraic account.

FIGURE 10.6

Domestic Welfare Depends
on the Tariff Rate

Free trade leads to a level of real income
indexed by 0A. For a country with some
influence on world prices, a tariff can improve
its terms of trade and lead initially to a gain
in real income. Rate t_0 is the optimum tariff.
Higher rates of duty cost more in forgone
opportunities to import than is gained by
a lowering of import prices. Rate t_1 cuts off
all imports and leads to a level of real income
identical to that of the no-trade state, which
is lower than the free-trade level, 0A.

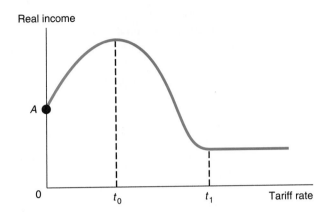

Here we are not concerned with computing the value of the "optimal tariff."[6] Instead, we wish to understand the nature of the conflict between the two effects of a tariff on welfare. A tariff improves the terms of trade, thus serving to raise welfare. However, the terms-of-trade improvement has been deliberately engineered by having the tariff choke off local import demand, and any reduction in imports must serve to lower domestic welfare if the *cost* of obtaining these imports (as shown by *world* prices) is lower than their *value* at home (as shown by *domestic* prices). A tariff is a wedge that raises domestic price above world price. Too high a tariff rate causes a greater loss through forgone opportunities to import than can be compensated for by the favorable price drop on remaining imports.

This discussion has assumed that the foreign country retains a policy of free trade, passively allowing the home country to pursue whatever commercial practices it pleases. This assumption overlooks the very real possibility that the foreign country will retaliate with its own tariff. Any foreign tariff worsens the terms of trade for the home country. If the foreign country does retaliate because of a tariff levied at home, it is no longer clear that the home country can benefit. Many outcomes of such a tariff war are possible. As related in Chapter 13, much of the tariff history of the major trading nations for the past sixty years has been characterized by multilateral attempts to reduce tariff barriers, in full awareness of the dangers of escalation when a single country begins to pursue an active commercial policy on its own.

10.4 Taxing Trade: World Welfare

Supporters of the free-trade doctrine point to the loss in *world* efficiency entailed by taxing trade. Although the protectionist countries might gain, others stand to lose *more*. This argument focuses on the deadweight loss introduced by the *distortion* that a

---

[6]This is carried out in the supplement to Chapter 10 and is illustrated by means of the offer curve diagram in the appendix.

tariff creates between prices in one country and another. To probe further, the argument will be presented in two stages: the effect of a tariff on world production, and the
effect of a tariff on world consumption possibilities *given* the levels of production.

Protection and World Production

A tariff on food in the home country raises the relative price of food above its level in
the foreign country. This higher price is reflected in a difference in the slopes of the two
countries' transformation curves. Figure 10.7 superimposes the point showing production on the foreign transformation schedule (drawn upside down) on the point showing
production at home. The production point is Q for both countries, and the tariff wedge
separating relative prices at home and abroad causes price line 1 at home to be flatter
than price line 2 abroad. The point 0* shows posttariff *world* outputs of food and clothing relative to the axes through 0. If the tariff were removed, resources in each country
would be shifted into the commodity in which that country possesses a comparative
advantage—clothing at home and food abroad. Points A and B represent possible free-
trade production points. The slope of TT' at A equals the slope of $T*T*'$ at B, and if B
were to be superimposed on A, total world outputs would expand from 0* to C.

Protection and World Consumption Losses

The imposition of a tariff on food creates a discrepancy between relative prices in the
home market and those abroad. The fundamental message of Chapter 2 was that both
home and foreign countries can gain by exchanging commodities at a common world

FIGURE 10.7

A Tariff and World Production

Point Q represents production at home and
abroad after a tariff has been imposed. The
foreign transformation schedule, $T*T*'$ is
upside down, so that total world production
is shown by 0*. The home country's tariff
on food imports leads to a higher relative
price of food at home (shown by line 1)
than abroad (shown by line 2). If the tariff
is removed, both countries face the same
price ratio (e.g., the common slope at A
and B). If B is superimposed on A, total world
production expands from 0* to C (measured
from home origin, 0).

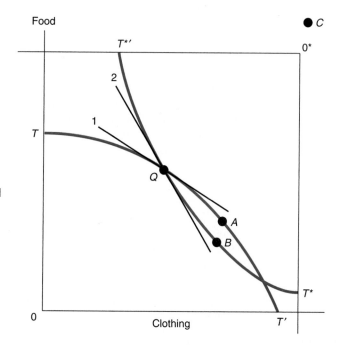

price ratio if initially price ratios differ between countries. By creating such a difference, a tariff leads to losses in real incomes in both countries, even out of a *given* set of world outputs. The appendix to this chapter illustrates this by use of the box diagram.

10.5   Summary

Import protection has both positive and normative aspects. The positive aspects refer to the effects of a tariff on prices, consumption, production, and trade. Proceeding first with a small country's tariff, it was shown that resources are shifted into the import-competing sector of the economy and demand is drawn away from the imported commodity. On both counts the country's demand for imports falls at the given world terms of trade. If a country is large enough for its actions to influence world prices, the contraction in import demand induced by the tariff will lower the country's relative price of imports and thus improve its terms of trade. There was a more ambiguous result concerning the relative domestic price of imports. Typically a tariff is protective because it raises the local price of the dutiable item, but if foreign response to price changes is sufficiently inelastic, the relative world price of imports could fall by a lot, perhaps even more than the tariff itself. (In that case a tariff on food would, paradoxically, lower the relative price of food behind the tariff wall.)

The normative aspects of a tariff deal with its effect on welfare at home and abroad. The foreign country is hurt by the tariff—its terms of trade deteriorate. For the home tariff-levying country, however, there is more to consider than the possible improvement in the terms of trade. Once the domestic price of imports is higher than the world price, any further tariff increases may reduce imports of a commodity for which the cost of purchase abroad is less than the valuation at home (as measured by domestic prices). This loss in trade volume must be set against a terms-of-trade improvement in measuring the net benefits of a tariff. The extreme case of a tariff sufficiently high to choke off all trade shows that the optimal tariff must fall short of this. Furthermore, if the foreign country retaliates, the home country may end up with a lower level of real income than it obtained with free trade.

A tariff is an inferior way to redistribute income between countries. The reason? It introduces a distortion between domestic and world prices and causes world outputs to settle at a suboptimal level and lower real incomes for any given levels of output. In this sense, a tariff is a *second-best* instrument from a world point of view. Other means of redistributing income internationally (e.g., a direct gift from the foreign country to the home country) might allow both countries to emerge with a higher level of real income than a distorting tariff provides. This second-best concept has wider applicability to other arguments for protection, as you will see in Chapter 11.

CHAPTER PROBLEMS

1. A "small" country is one with no power to affect the world prices of commodities. Redraw Figures 10.5 and 10.6 for such a country.

2. The foreign supply curve of exports in Figure 10.5, X^*, has been drawn with a positive slope. This implies that foreign import demand for clothing is elastic. Suppose that for prices near the initial equilibrium point Q, foreign import demand is inelastic. Draw the new X^* foreign supply curve of food exports. What is the effect of a tariff on imports of food? Would local food producers favor such a tariff?

3. In Figure 10.5 the tariff has shifted the demand curve for imports. Does the extent of the downward shift fall short of, equal, or exceed the amount of the tariff? (*Hint:* Ask what would happen to demand if world price were to fall by exactly the amount of the tariff—and decompose between substitution and income effects.)

4. Draw an initial free-trade equilibrium (for a small country facing given world prices) with a transformation schedule and indifference curves. Indicate in such a diagram the rate of the tariff that would completely wipe out trade. What happens to production and consumption if legislators are overzealous and the tariff rate is higher than this rate?

5. In the text it was assumed the government redistributes tariff proceeds back to the private sector. Instead, suppose the government spends the tariff revenues in a manner that differs from that of private citizens. Consider the two extreme forms of public spending: (a) The tariff revenue is spent only on clothing, the commodity exported, or (b) the tariff revenue is allocated, instead, to purchases of food. Which scheme is more likely to be favored by producers who have clamored for protection? What might happen to the terms of trade in case (b)?

SUGGESTIONS FOR FURTHER READING

Irwin, Douglas. *Free Trade Under Fire,* 2nd ed. (Princeton: Princeton University Press, 2005). Chapter 2 provides a good background to the free-trade arguments.

Jones, Ronald W. "Tariffs and Trade in General Equilibrium: Comment," *American Economic Review,* 59 (June 1969): 418–424. A brief analysis of basic tariff theory.

APPENDIX

Tariffs and the Offer Curve

The offer curve construction described in the appendix to Chapter 3 is particularly useful in illustrating the impact of a tariff and the concept of the optimal tariff.

The Optimal Tariff

To pursue the geometry it is useful to introduce a simplifying assumption: The home country is completely specialized in producing its export commodity, clothing. The constant level of clothing output is shown in Figure 10.A.1 by distance 0_T0_C. (0_T refers to the *trading* origin and 0_C to the *consumption* origin.) The home offer curve, 0_TR, intersects

FIGURE 10.A.1

The Optimal Tariff

A tariff that shifts home offer curve $0_T R$ to $0_T R'$ is optimal. Home real income at point A is greater than at any other point on the foreign offer curve, $0_T R^*$.

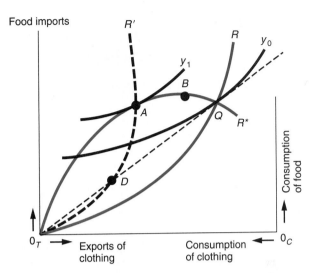

the foreign offer curve, $0_T R^*$ at point Q, establishing the slope of ray $0_T Q$ as the equilibrium terms of trade (the world relative price of clothing). That part of clothing production not exported is available for consumption at home; thus, relative to the 0_C origin, any point in the diagram shows the home consumption bundle of food and clothing.

Two indifference curves have been drawn. The curve y_0 is tangent to ray $0_T D Q$; this is why point Q was selected at those prices. Clearly, other points on the foreign offer curve $0_T R^*$ would represent more favorable trades for the home country. Point B lies on a higher indifference curve (not drawn). The curve tangent to the foreign offer curve, curve y_1, shows the *maximal* utility level possible for the home country.

How does the home country get to point A on the foreign offer curve, $0_T R^*$? By levying a tariff. As illustrated in the text, a tariff decreases the demand for imports and the supply of exports at any given world terms of trade. That is, it *shifts* the home offer curve in toward the origin. The *optimal tariff* rate that maximizes the national welfare is that which leads to the home tariff-ridden offer curve $0_T R'$. Such a tariff has caused the relative *world* price of food, the commodity imported at home, to fall. This is shown by the greater slope of a ray from 0_T through point A. The relative *domestic* price of food has increased slightly; the slope of indifference curve y_1 at its point of tangency with the foreign offer curve at A indicates the domestic relative price of clothing. The wedge between the two prices shows the optimal tariff rate. (A formula for this rate is provided in the supplement.)

The Protective Effect of a Tariff

As previously suggested, a tariff may fail to protect the home import-competing industry by improving the terms of trade so much that the relative domestic price of importables falls. The offer curve diagram and yet another concept—*the income-consumption curve*—can usefully illustrate this possibility.

FIGURE 10.A.2

The Tariff May Not Protect

IC is the income-consumption curve for the home country, which cuts the foreign offer curve at *E*. A tariff that leads to an equilibrium in the *EQ* range of the foreign curve (e.g., at *G*) serves to lower the relative domestic price of importables, as shown by the slope of the indifference curve at *G*. A tariff in range *EQ* fails to protect.

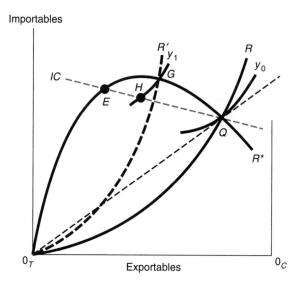

Importables

Exportables

Figure 10.A.2 follows Figure 10.A.1 in illustrating the foreign offer curve, $0_T R^*$, with initial free-trade equilibrium at point Q along an *inelastic* section of the offer curve. The home indifference curve tangent to ray $0_T Q$ has been drawn. The *income-consumption curve* for the home country, *IC*, is the locus of points along home indifference curves for which slopes are the same as at Q (e.g., at point H). This *IC* curve has been drawn so as to cut the foreign offer curve at point E.

As previously illustrated, a tariff levied on home imports of food shifts the home offer curve so that it cuts the foreign offer curve at a point such as G. A higher tariff would shift the home offer curve even more. The principal conclusion is that a home tariff, leading to a new equilibrium anywhere in the stretch EQ along the foreign offer curve, fails to protect the home food sector. The reason: At a point such as G the home indifference curve is steeper than at H (equal to the slope at Q). Therefore, the relative domestic price of food at G is less than the pretariff price at Q. This is called the *Metzler paradox*.[7] However, a tariff sufficiently high to place the new equilibrium point along the $0_T E$ stretch of the foreign offer curve must raise the home relative price of food.

If the income-consumption curve is steeper than the foreign offer curve at Q, any tariff, no matter how small, must be protective. The condition for this, as is proved in the supplement to Chapter 10, is

$$\varepsilon^* > 1 - m$$

---

[7]The argument that a tariff may fail to raise the price of the protected commodity behind the tariff wall is found in Lloyd Metzler, "Tariffs, the Terms of Trade, and the Distribution of National Income," *Journal of Political Economy,* 57 (February 1949): 1–29, reprinted in Caves and Johnson, eds., *Readings in International Economics* (Homewood, IL: Irwin, 1968), Chapter 2. The logic of the argument is explained algebraically in the supplement to this chapter.

FIGURE 10.A.3

The Tariff Pulls Consumption Off the Contract Curve

Initial free-trade equilibrium is on the contract curve at D. The home country's tariff improves home welfare (to y_0) and reduces foreign welfare (to y_0^*) but pulls the consumption point off the contract curve (to A). A point such as B would improve *both* countries' welfare compared with tariff point A.

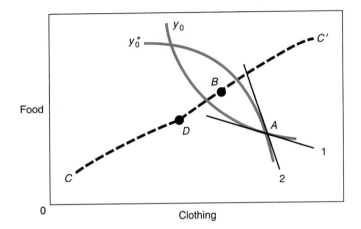

where ε^* is the elasticity of foreign demand for imports along $0_T ER^*$ at Q, and m is the home marginal propensity to import (food). Obviously, if foreign demand is elastic, this condition must be satisfied (as long as both commodities are normal at home, that is, the IC curve is negatively sloped).

The Tariff and the Box Diagram

One consequence of a tariff is a reduction of world outputs below the free-trade level. From a world point of view, however, this is not the only consequence. Recall from the appendix to Chapter 2 the discussion of the box diagram and the contract curve (Figure 2.A.1). For convenience, the box is reproduced as Figure 10.A.3, which shows a *given* world total of food and clothing.

The imposition of the tariff on food in the home country causes domestic prices (as shown by the slope of line 1) to differ from foreign prices (given by the slope of line 2). Therefore, the tariff leads to a consumption allocation *off* the contract curve (such as point A). World welfare has been reduced in that A is worse for *both* parties than some point, such as B, on the contract curve.

CHAPTER 11

The Political Economy of Protection

It would be naive to suppose that nations pursue commercial policy only after carefully weighing the pros and cons for the entire community. Instead, special sections or groups often find that their interests can be served by interfering with free trade despite a loss to others in the economy. Indeed, these groups often find that the potential gains from protection are worth a substantial investment of resources and lobbying efforts. The political process frequently rewards a minority with strong convictions, accompanied by relatively mild losses to each member of a majority. In addition, special circumstances may seem to warrant restrictive trade policies, although deeper analysis would reveal that other weapons in a nation's fiscal armory are more effective or impose lower social costs. Protection is frequently a second-best device in achieving social goals.

11.1 Protection as a Device for Raising Revenue

Long before the progressive income tax and other sophisticated instruments were devised to provide governments with necessary revenues, the government agent at the port of entry typically extracted a toll on the inflow of merchandise from abroad. Any tariff rate that is not so high as to be prohibitive is a source of revenue. Although modern industrial states rarely rely on customs duties to provide government income (less than 1 percent in the United States), developing regions often do.

The relationship between a tariff's impact on real income and on tariff revenue is expressed in Figure 11.1. A zero tariff yields no revenue. Tariff rate t_1 is assumed to be prohibitive, so higher rates of duty also yield no revenue. In the diagram it is assumed that revenues rise continuously, reaching a peak at rate t_2, and fall continuously to zero at rate t_1 as imports dwindle. The crucial point to notice is that the revenue maximizing rate, t_2, exceeds the optimal tariff rate, t_0. An algebraic proof is provided in the supplement to Chapter 11. The geometric argument is provided in Figure 11.2.

Production in Figure 11.2 is assumed to be locked in at corner point A along the TAT' transformation curve. This simplifies the argument.[1] Consumption point B along

---

[1]The argument is strengthened if production responds along a smoothly bowed-out transformation schedule.

FIGURE 11.1

Tariff Revenue and Real Income

The curve showing tariff revenue reaches a peak at a higher tariff rate than does the curve showing real income.

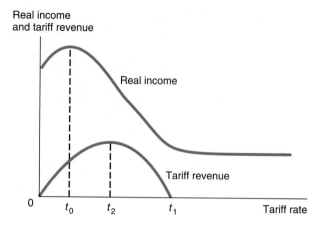

indifference curve y_0 shows equilibrium with a tariff that has driven the *domestic* relative price of food imports to the height shown by lines 1 and 2.[2] Therefore distance *CA* measures the tariff revenue in food units. Suppose the existing tariff rate maximizes tariff revenue (at rate t_2 in Figure 11.1). Note what this implies: A slight increase in the tariff rate would leave tariff revenue (virtually) unaltered—at *AC* in Figure 11.2. If the relationship between real income and tariff revenue illustrated in Figure 11.1, where real income is falling at rate t_2, is to be confirmed, an increase in the tariff rate in Figure 11.2 must push consumers onto a lower indifference curve. This it does—they move from *B* on curve y_0 to *D* on curve y_1. Therefore the tariff rate that maximizes revenue (t_2) must exceed the optimal tariff rate (t_0).

That these two critical rates are not equivalent underscores the point that pursuing commercial policy for revenue purposes is not optimal strategy. Thus, if at current tariff levels an increase in the rate would lower tariff revenues, the current levels are too high for optimal welfare. Furthermore, if the rate should lie between t_0 and t_2 in Figure 11.1, a *reduction* in the tariff rate would raise real income even though it would also reduce tariff revenue. This remark was relevant to the discussion in the U.S. Congress when approval was given to the tariff reductions embedded in the Uruguay Round of GATT agreements that led to the establishment of the World Trade Organization. Partly at issue was the loss of tariff revenue that such trade liberalization would create. Such a loss is not indicative of a loss of real income, especially when the tariff cut is in conjunction with other countries reducing their barriers.

It is well at this point to recall that for a small country that cannot influence the world prices of what it buys and sells, the optimal tariff rate is zero. A tariff to raise revenue must then be rationalized by other arguments, such as the ease of collection on international commerce as compared with local sales or income taxes.

---

[2]The relative *world* price of clothing would be shown by the slope of a line connecting production point *A* with consumption point *B*.

FIGURE 11.2

The Maximum Revenue Tariff
Exceeds the Optimal Tariff

Tariff revenue is shown by distance *CA*.
Near a tariff that maximizes revenue,
a small increase in the tariff rate will
not change tariff revenue. Consumption
point *D* is on a lower indifference curve
than point *B* and corresponds to a higher
tariff.

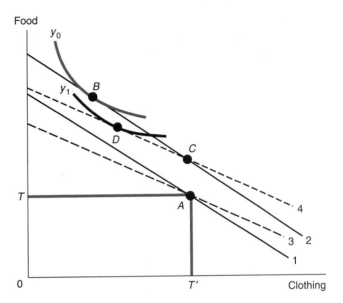

11.2 Commercial Policy as a Second-Best Device

Just as a tariff is not the only instrument of commercial policy, interference in trade via
quotas, tariffs, or other devices does not represent the only set of tools to attain *other*
ends that some governments deem socially useful. That is, commercial policy might be
utilized to affect the general pattern of prices, outputs, and employment where other
noncommercial policies such as production subsidies or sales taxes could more directly
achieve desired ends. Is a subsidy to production better or worse than a tariff? It
depends very much on the policy objective. The tariff can often be used to help imple-
ment some social objective, but it proves frequently to be *second best* to some alternative policy instrument. The following three cases suffice to make the general point.

1. *Production goals.* Suppose the free-trade level of production of some commodity is thought to be too low. Perhaps labor receives special valuable training in the production of this item, or perhaps the community feels it should rely more on its own
production should foreign supplies be threatened in the future. (Witness the arguments
about American dependence on foreign energy sources.) What is the optimal policy for
encouraging greater domestic production?

The stage is set in Figure 11.3. The country is initially in a free-trade equilibrium at
world prices reflected by the slope of line 1: Production is at *A*, consumption at *B*, and
thus the country imports food. Now suppose the country wants to increase *production*
of food. Compare the two alternative policies available to accomplish this end—a *tariff*
on imports of food or a *subsidy* to producers of food. Assume the desired production
target is to raise food output from $0I$ to $0J$.

FIGURE 11.3

Tariffs vs. Production Subsidies to Achieve a Production Goal

Free-trade production is at *A* and consumption at *B*. If *OJ* level of food production must be undertaken, a tariff that raises food's relative price at home to line 2 is sufficient. Consumption is then at *E*. A production subsidy could yield the same result for producers but at a lower cost in welfare. Consumption is at *H*.

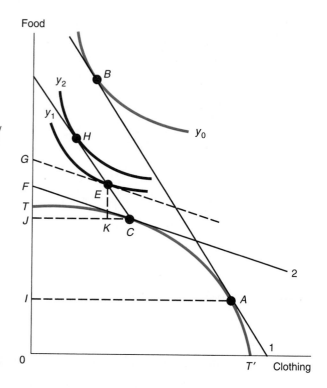

A tariff on food can be analyzed as in the preceding chapter. A duty high enough to move production to point *C* raises the domestic relative price of food to that shown by line 2. What is consumption behind this tariff wall? The consumption bundle must lie on an indifference curve whose slope reflects relative *domestic* prices, and it must have the same value as production point *C* at *world* prices. This is point *E*, and restricted imports are *EK*, matched at world prices by clothing exports *KC*.

The alternative strategy involves providing a subsidy to food producers sufficient once again to reach production point *C*. World food prices are reflected in line *HEC*, parallel to line 1, and food producers receive the higher (subsidized) price shown by line 2. But now home consumers are free to buy at world prices, and the best such point for them is *H* on curve y_2, which represents a higher level of satisfaction than does *E* on indifference curve y_1.

The moral of this comparison is clear. The objective is assumed to be a production goal. This can be achieved at a lower cost in terms of forgone real income if the instrument used focuses precisely on this goal. A production subsidy does exactly that, whereas a tariff (needlessly) distorts prices to consumers.[3]

2. *Consumption goals.* Analogous remarks can be made about the desire that some governments express to restrict consumption of some items below the levels that

---

[3]This analysis can be found in W. M. Corden, "Tariffs, Subsidies, and the Terms of Trade," *Economica,* 24 (August 1957): 235–242.

the community would voluntarily choose in a free-trade situation. For example, the government may wish to restrict the private sector's consumption of automobiles or other items it deems to be unnecessary luxuries.

A tariff can accomplish the purpose, but so could a direct tax on consumption of the luxury item. These are different instruments. A tax on consumption raises the price to consumers above the world level but leaves producers to face world competition at world prices. By contrast, a tariff raises the domestic price to producers as well as consumers and encourages a transfer of domestic resources away from exportables and toward production of the luxury item. If the government's desire is solely to restrict *consumption,* needless losses are involved by using a tariff, for the production shift away from exportables causes the value of income produced at world prices to fall below its free-trade level.

Arguments for tariffs are often aimed at altering the production or consumption pattern of a free-trade regime. Heeding the pleas of special consumer or producer interests involves a loss of welfare to the nation as a whole. Because the tariff affects both consumption and production, using it to alter either the former or the latter makes this loss larger than necessary. A more efficient instrument is a production tax or subsidy to change production or a consumption tax or subsidy to control consumption. In each case the instrument that works most directly on the objective should be used.

3. *Domestic distortions and environmental considerations.* Market prices are not always perfect indicators of social costs and benefits. Occasionally elements of monopoly or of externalities in production or consumption distort market prices away from levels that represent social opportunity costs and values. For example, a commodity that enters a country's export lists may appear to have a low cost of production—and thus be exported—because pollution damage involved in the production process is not taken into account. (Firms may be dumping effluents into the country's streams and harbors at no cost to themselves but at considerable damage to the community.) In such cases it is possible to argue that levels of free trade are not optimal. Instead, those who would attempt to restrict exports (and imports) seem to find natural allies in ecologists and environmentalists. Once again, however, it can be shown that trade restrictions offer only a second-best solution to a problem that is better met directly by consumption or production taxes that attempt to remedy the distortion.

The notion of "fair price" for such items as coffee imported from Latin America has become popular, especially on college campuses. Basically the notion is that the manner in which commodities are produced, and the wages received by labor, affect the utility of the consumers of such commodities. For example, the wages of coffee laborers may be considered too low, so that higher prices would willingly be paid by consumers if it could be ascertained that the coffee beans were grown in situations in which laborers received a higher ("fair") wage. However, such interference in prices can be shown to be second best relative to direct transfers to the underpaid laborers.[4]

---

[4]For a simple discussion of the so-called fair price issue making use of transformation curves and indifference curves such as in Figure 11.3, see Dennis Yanchus and Xavier de Vanssay, "The Myth of Fair Prices: A Graphical Analysis," *Journal of Economic Education* (Summer 2003): 235–240.

If social and private costs differ, there is not only the danger that export levels may be too high or too low; it is also possible that the *pattern* of trade itself is distorted. To return to the pollution example, suppose that private marginal production costs, excluding pollution costs, fall short of costs in the rest of the world by less than the costs of pollution abatement. In such a case, forcing producers to bear these costs would entail that the industry shift from being net exporters to becoming importers.

The reason export taxes (or import tariffs) are second-best devices in these examples is that it is either production or consumption levels that are distorted from their socially optimal level, *not* trade levels. Commercial policy, which affects both domestic consumption and production, is usually inefficient as a device for controlling either separately.[5]

11.3 Protection and Rent-Seeking Activities

The automobile industry and the steel industry in the United States are among many that feel threatened by foreign competition. What attitude toward tariffs or other protective devices would be expected from an autoworker trained in tasks that have little application outside the auto industry, or from the owner of a specialized machine that cannot be used for any purpose other than making autos? Productive factors tied to one industry or occupation are very much affected by trade and commercial policies. Special interests and specific factors employed in import-competing industries usually favor trade restrictions.

If protection favors inputs specific to import-competing production, a counter-argument for free trade can be mounted by factors tied to the nation's export industries. With many industries making up the economy, each import-competing industry that gains protection demands more of each general factor of production, such as unskilled labor, which tends to raise the price of that factor and squeeze the earnings of specialized factors of production in all exporting industries. Somewhat different implications for interest groups come from the Heckscher-Ohlin model of production and trade. Suppose that production in any industry requires only the services of two broad-based factors, capital and labor. Further, suppose that a capital-rich country takes advantage of trading opportunities to import commodities that would be produced by labor-intensive techniques at home. A tariff that drives up the domestic price of these items serves to drive up the real wage as well. As shown by Stolper and Samuelson (a result discussed in Chapter 6), a change in relative commodity prices gets transmitted into magnified changes in the returns to the two productive factors. In their setting one factor—labor—unambiguously gains from the tariff; the other factor—capital—loses.[6]

---

[5]As remarked by Alan Deardorff of the University of Michigan, employing tariffs to attain a consumption goal or a production goal is like performing acupuncture with a fork.

[6]For research on the question of whether employed factors tend to support protection for the industry in which they are employed (as would make sense for specific factors), see William A. Brock and Stephen P. Magee, "The Economics of Special Interest Politics: The Case of the Tariff," *American Economic Review,* 68 (May 1978): 246–250. A model describing how tariffs in a democratic system can reflect factor ownership patterns (whether of the Heckscher-Ohlin variety or the specific-factors type) is developed by Wolfgang Mayer, in "Endogenous Tariff Formation," *American Economic Review,* 74 (December 1984): 970–985.

Tariffs and Political Choice

Several general models of policy choice in a democratic society can be linked directly to these economic models of trade restrictions and income distribution.

1. *Voting model.* One model addresses the democratic voting process. Its core could not be simpler: Each citizen gets one vote, so the economic policy chosen should be the policy expected to raise the welfare of a majority of the voters. On its face this model suggests a political preference for only those tariffs that maximize national welfare. The majority should certainly favor a policy that yields the greatest possible increase in national income (for example, by eliminating inefficient tariffs) and then divides up the gain so all the voters (or a majority, in any case) are better off. The trouble with this interpretation is that in actuality, losers are seldom compensated. Voters rationally size up a policy for its effect on their own real income if they keep the winnings or suffer the losses that come their way. A tariff proposal then wins if it redistributes income from a minority to a majority. For example, assume that the United States is a capital-rich country and that capital income is more concentrated among voters than is labor (wage) income. Then a majority will vote for tariffs to redistribute income from capital to labor. This voting model has an obvious affinity for the Heckscher-Ohlin approach.

2. *Lobbying model.* Another model of tariff determination stresses interest groups. It assumes that groups lobby, support friendly candidates for office, and in other ways invest in securing political action favorable to the interest group. Sellers making up an industry are such a group. They rationally invest in securing tariff protection up to the point where the present value of the last benefits gained just equals the investment needed to secure them. Spending resources to gain access to a protected income stream is called *rent-seeking.*[7] One problem then is to explain which interest groups succeed in buying policies that advance their interests. This leads to the theory of collective action, which stresses the difficulty of organizing a group to secure benefits that are a collective gain to the group. It is difficult because group members can expect to enjoy the benefits even if they do not contribute to meeting the costs of securing them. The most effective groups are already organized for another purpose (professional and trade associations), or they consist of small numbers of beneficiaries (a concentrated industry with few sellers), so the problem of "free riders" is more easily solved. Members of geographically dispersed groups (bankers and steel fabricators) can readily catch the ears of many members of Congress. Consumers, in contrast, have

---

[7]Anne O. Krueger, "The Political Economy of the Rent-Seeking Society," *American Economic Review,* 44 (June 1974): 291–303, emphasizes the magnitudes of rent-seeking outlays in some developing regions, where they may take the forms of bribery, putting relatives of government officials on the payroll and passing out lucrative subcontracts to individuals with ties to persons important in the public sector. Expansion of plant capacity can be stimulated, even if it leads to excess capacity, if licenses for importing inputs are tied to a plant's capacity. Krueger quoted rough estimates that rent-seeking expenditures equal 7 percent of national income for India (1964) and about 15 percent of GNP for Turkey (1968). Rent-seeking is discussed more generally in James Buchanan, Gordon Tullock, and Robert Tollison, eds., *Towards a General Theory of the Rent-Seeking Society* (College Station: Texas A&M University Press, 1980); and Jagdish Bhagwati, "Directly Unproductive Profit-Seeking (DUP) Activities," *Journal of Political Economy,* 90 (October 1982): 988–1002.

the dice loaded against them: They are numerous, and each has only a small monetary stake in the policy that affects them. The interest-group approach is closely aligned with the specific-factors model, and it clearly can explain the persistence of tariffs that do not contribute to national welfare. A modern extension of the lobbying model has the government maximizing a combination of the support it can gather from lobbying groups and the votes it can get from the general public by maximizing the nation's social welfare.[8]

3. *Conservative social welfare function.* Yet another approach notes that the government's job is to maintain certain collective goods, including a social sense that people are being treated fairly and not suffering unreasonably from economic misfortunes. This approach suggests that tariffs will protect low-income persons, such as unskilled labor. It also predicts that tariffs will be raised when an industry's competitive position is significantly undermined, causing unanticipated losses and unemployment. The hypothesized conservative social welfare function is not a decision mechanism but an attitude or value that might explain where and when voters will support a given policy proposal or lobbyists will most readily find a sympathetic ear.

Political scientists have explored the factors that decide whether voting or lobbying dominates the setting of a particular policy, such as controls on international trade. With an election coming, each political party seeks to get itself elected. It selects a package to offer the voters that it hopes will appeal to a majority. The voters do not expend much effort informing themselves about the parties' positions, so the parties choose to emphasize only a few issues that many voters believe make a lot of difference to their welfare. Trade policy will become a party platform highlight only if a large group (a majority?) shares a common interest. If broad interests conflict (say, capital versus labor), the political parties take opposed positions, with one favoring "labor" and one serving "business."

Suppose the electorate responds to no such broad appeals but that the specific factors in individual industries each have strong interests in gaining protection for themselves or warding off the grabs for protection by other industries (their suppliers, for example). The government needs some mechanism to deal with such demands and conflicts. It likely organizes some regulatory bureau that is instructed to "do the right thing" and respond to the special interest demands so that they do not clutter the desks of top elected officials.

In the United States until the 1930s, the political parties did offer the voters conflicting general positions on tariffs—the Republicans promised high tariffs to import-competing capital and industrial labor, and the Democrats pledged low tariffs to export-oriented agriculture. Since then, trade policy has largely fallen out of the parties' competition for votes. Decisions come increasingly under bureaucratic determination subject to lobbying influences.[9]

---

[8]Gene M. Grossman and Elhanan Helpman, "Protection for Sale," *American Economic Review*, 84 (September 1994): 833–850.

[9]The preceding analysis draws on Daniel Verdier, *Democracy and International Trade: Britain, France, and the United States, 1860–1990* (Princeton: Princeton University Press, 1994).

TABLE 11.1

Characteristics of Industries in Relation to Levels of Protection Given by U.S. Tariffs, Nominal and Effective, After Kennedy-Round Reductions

Industry Characteristics and Tariff Measure	Industries Ranked by Level of Protection			
	Highest Quarter	Second Quarter	Third Quarter	Lowest Quarter
Labor intensity (measured by payrolls as percentage of all factor payments)				
Nominal	46%	50%	53%	45%
Effective	47%	48%	52%	44%
Level of labor skill (measured by payroll per worker)				
Nominal	$6,000	$6,700	$7,200	$7,100
Effective	$6,000	$6,600	$7,500	$6,900
Size of manufacturing establishment (measured by value added per establishment in $M)				
Nominal	$1.8[a]	$1.4	$2.2	$3.6
Effective	$1.5[a]	$1.6	$3.2	$2.6

Source: Tariff rates—Robert E. Baldwin, *Nontariff Distortions of International Trade* (Washington, DC: Brookings Institution, 1970), pp. 163–164; other data—U.S. Bureau of the Census, *1967 Census of Manufacturers: Summary and Subject Statistics* (Washington, DC: Government Printing Office, 1971), Table 3. Effective protection takes account of tariffs on an industry's inputs.

[a]The "ordinance and accessories" sector was omitted from this class. The large establishments producing military wares hardly seem relevant to testing the effect of tariff protection.

Evidence on U.S. Tariff Structure

Pending our review of trade policy decisions in Chapters 13 and 14, it is helpful to examine patterns in the height of tariff protection given to various U.S. industries for what they suggest about tariff determination processes. Table 11.1 shows the results of a simple test on the levels of protection that prevailed in the 1970s.[10] For each manufacturing industry, the average levels of both nominal and effective rates of protection were measured (including nontariff barriers, discussed in Section 13.3). Industries were ranked from the most protected to the least protected, and the ranked list was divided into quarters. Some traits of the industries included in each of the four quarters were then averaged.

Does the tariff protect labor-intensive industries? The labor intensity of an industry can be measured roughly by the share that payrolls constitute of payments to all the factors of production it employs (the industry's value-added). The top two lines of

---

[10]We go back to these old rates because they should reflect voting-based determinants more than later U.S. tariffs, which are increasingly affected by broad international agreements we describe in Chapter 13. In fact, the relative protection given to different goods changed little between the 1930s and 1970s; see Real P. Lavergne, *The Political Economy of U.S. Tariffs* (New York: Academic Press, 1983).

Table 11.1 show that the least-protected industries are indeed the least labor intensive. For the other three quarters, however, the hypothesis fails. The most heavily protected industries are not very labor intensive. This does not strongly confirm the prediction of the majority of voters that tariffs favor labor-intensive industries.

Does the tariff protect low-skilled labor? If the political process aims in part to redistribute income to the less fortunate or to those who have suffered reductions in their incomes, high tariffs should protect industries that employ low-skill and low-wage labor. The next part of Table 11.1 shows that the low-wage industries do get the highest protection. Evidence cited in Chapter 13 confirms that products of low-wage labor receive high levels of protection in many countries. However, there is an awkward qualification to this apparent widespread indication of social concern. Although the jobs and wages of low-wage households may benefit from protection, their real incomes as consumers suffer seriously. That is because groups of goods prominent in the purchases of low-income households pay high tariffs (8.7 to 13.8 percent); groups of luxury goods pay much lower rates. Does a tariff on low-wage imports benefit the poor as workers more than it taxes them as consumers?[11]

Does the tariff protect small (or big) business? The lobbying, or interest-group, model suggests that industries with small and widely dispersed production units can influence political decisions at low cost, thus securing high protection. But the collective character of tariff benefits suggests that high protection goes to large, concentrated sellers. Thus the theoretical predictions conflict. In any event, Table 11.1 suggests rather strongly that protection favors small establishments.

That U.S. tariffs protect low-wage and small-scale industries emerges from other, more sophisticated versions of Table 11.1. The finding indicates that tariffs redistribute income toward the less fortunate, but it may also support the lobbying model: Industries with the greatest comparative disadvantage also have the most incentive to invest in high tariffs.[12] Whatever the basis for their clout, industries that secure high tariffs also win heavy nontariff protection. So do geographically dispersed industries, consistent with the way congressional voting on tariff legislation reflects the interests of industries in congressional home districts.[13] The evidence does support the political economy approach to explaining levels of nontariff protection.

Interconnections Among Special Groups

A general theme running throughout our discussion of international trade theory is that the various parts of the economy are interconnected. Thus a resource discovery or technological breakthrough that benefits one part of the economy is apt to harm some other sectors—this is the phenomenon of the Dutch Disease. It suggests that any use of the political process to favor the real income of some special interest may cause other

---

[11]Edward Gresser, "Toughest on the Poor: America's Flawed Tariff System," *Foreign Affairs*, 81 (November 2002): 9–14. Furthermore (in terms of Figure 10.1), domestic production of low-wage goods tends to be small and declining, making area 1 small relative to area 3.

[12]Edward John Ray, "The Determinants of Tariffs and Nontariff Trade Restrictions in the United States," *Journal of Political Economy*, 89 (February 1981): 105–121.

[13]Ray, "The Determinants of Tariffs," Table 4; Robert E. Baldwin, *Trade Policy in a Changing World Economy* (Chicago: University of Chicago Press, 1988), Chapter 3.

sectors to lose and indeed to mount counterefforts. The political maneuvering surrounding the vote on the NAFTA accord in the U.S. Congress in the fall of 1993 well illustrated the point.

In particular, consider the market in durum wheat. This is a hard wheat used to make pasta and certain cereals, and in the United States it is grown in the north-central states such as Montana and the Dakotas. It is also grown in Canada, and the Canadians have obtained approximately a 20 percent share of the American market, enough to encourage politicians in the north-central states to try to obtain quotas on Canadian imports in exchange for their support in letting Mexico into a NAFTA agreement when it came to a vote in the U.S. Congress in the fall of 1993. But at that time the price of durum wheat was high in the United States, partly as a consequence of a federal crop-restriction program for American producers, and partly because, at the same time, the Department of Agriculture was subsidizing exports of durum wheat to other countries. Thus the restriction program coupled with export subsidies led Canadian exporters to enter the U.S. market. The interconnections did not stop there. Foreign pasta producers (primarily in Italy and Turkey) who obtain durum wheat at lower prices than their American counterparts then had an advantage in exporting pasta to the United States—such exports roughly doubled between 1985 and 1993. Furthermore, subsidized wheat exports threaten exports of unsubsidized American corn.[14] This kind of tangled web has been repeated in other markets. American garment makers used to complain that foreign firms had an unfair competitive advantage; they were able to obtain American cotton at lower prices than American firms because of our program to subsidize cotton exports.

11.4 Growth, Protection, and Welfare

If a country devotes newly available resources to its traditional export sectors, won't this encourage a drop in export prices? In any country in which growth is biased toward exportables, that country's terms of trade will tend to worsen.

This kind of argument loses its force if the country under discussion is too small to affect world prices of its export commodity. Suppose this is the case, but nonetheless the developing country has imposed tariffs on imports to support an import-competing industry over and above its free-trade level. It was argued in Chapter 10 that such a diversion of resources entails real income losses. More can be said, however. As this country grows, the more resources it devotes to the protected import-competing sector, the more its potential real income gains from growth are cut back. In extreme cases, growth at home could even result in a loss of welfare.

Figure 11.4 illustrates these possibilities. Line 2 indicates world prices. The country has protected its import-competing sector, food. Thus line 1, showing domestic prices behind the tariff wall, is flatter than line 2. At these protected prices, the community's optimal production point along transformation schedule TT' is at tangency point A and consumption is at A'.

---

[14]See James Bovard, "Our Wheat War with Canada," *Wall Street Journal* (October 15, 1993).

FIGURE 11.4

Growth with Protection

With a tariff on food imports, line 1 showing domestic prices is flatter than line 2 showing world prices. *A'* is the initial consumption point corresponding to production along *TT'* at *A*. Growth to any of points *B*, *C*, *D*, and *E* shows a 25 percent increase in produced income at domestic prices. But corresponding consumption points *B'*, *C'*, *D'*, *E'* are not equivalent.

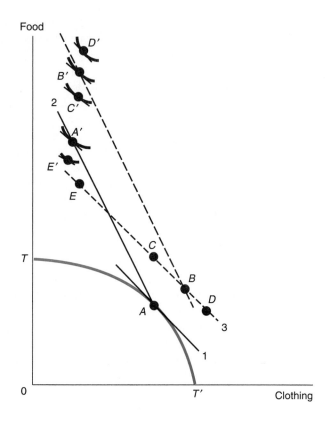

Now suppose that world prices remain unchanged and the country's tariff structure is unaltered, but the value of produced income at domestic prices rises by 25 percent. That is, at domestic prices the country grows by 25 percent. But which industries have expanded? It makes a big difference, even for a small price-taking country. Points *B*, *C*, *D*, and *E* represent four possible alternative production points for which aggregate output at domestic prices would be 25 percent larger than at *A*. Point *B* is a point of fairly balanced expansion relative to initial point *A*. For such a case, home consumption lies on a line through *B*, with slope showing world prices (i.e., parallel to line 2) at consumption point *B'*. Growth has increased real income. Now suppose instead that only the import-competing sector had been allowed to grow (point *C* lies directly above point *A*). The real income gains would have been cut back, an outcome underlined by comparing it to the alternative of letting only the export sector expand (point *D* lies to the right of *A*). Consumption point *D'* is preferable to *B'* (which is preferable to *C'*). These two alternative patterns of expansion, to point *C* and point *D*, share with point *B* an increase in production at *domestic prices* of 25 percent. But they differ in valuation at *world prices* and, consequently, in their real income gains.

The composition of output might have been altered even more radically by growth. Point *E* shows such a possible skewed growth point. Growth has been so biased in favor of the commodity (food) that is artificially high priced at home that the seemingly higher valued production point (E has a 25 percent higher value than A at domestic prices) represents an actual *loss* at world prices. This phenomenon could occur only if the import-competing sector is protected.[15] These comments serve to emphasize that in a growth context, protection may impose costs that go well beyond those described for a static economy.

Protection as an Attraction to Foreign Investment

An argument sometimes raised in favor of protection is that it may encourage foreign investment in home markets. A tariff can affect the pattern of investment. If a country is initially importing a commodity, a protective tariff wall forces foreign firms either to cut prices, lose sales, or, alternatively, to try to produce the commodity directly in the home market and thus avoid the tariff.

Studies of the multinational corporation show that a tariff often causes it to invest in a country. Previously it has exported to the market in question, investing in advertising and customer goodwill but not in physical production facilities. When its exports to the market are struck with a tariff, direct investment becomes more attractive than the only alternative—writing off the firm's investment in goodwill and leaving the market entirely.

There is, however, something ironic about such a policy. Suppose a country is attempting to limit its dependence on foreign sources of supply by following a protectionist policy. It may also be anxious to diversify its productive structure by protecting its local industries from foreign competition. Keeping out foreign-made goods, however, may just encourage the foreigner to come in. In the years before NAFTA, Canada seemed bedeviled by a desire both to protect a whole panoply of secondary industries and to limit the incursion of American direct investment, which such a protected market seemed to attract. In the United States, Japanese automobile companies such as Toyota and Honda for years have invested in production facilities in the Midwest. Protective devices to help American-owned automobile producers have merely encouraged foreign-owned producers to invade the market directly.

Chapter 9 discussed various advantages and disadvantages to host countries of allowing foreign investment. Yet what can be said about using higher degrees of protection to attract more foreign investment? Chapter 10 argued that a country too small to improve its terms of trade by means of a tariff actually harms itself by protection. A tariff or other restriction on trade inserts a wedge between the cost of obtaining importables in world markets and the (higher) value of those importables to local consumers; cost is measured by world price, value by domestic price behind the tariff wall. Any action serving to cut back a nation's imports when an existing tariff wedge causes value to exceed cost must lower welfare at home. An increase in the tariff rate is one such action; such a rise causes a contraction in imports. If foreign investment responds to changes in degrees of protection, the response, a further cut in imports, is apt to exacerbate the damage such protection inflicts on the host country.

---

[15]The possibility of welfare loss with growth if an industry is protected was pointed out by Harry G. Johnson, "The Possibility of Income Losses from Increased Efficiency or Factor Accumulation in the Presence of Tariffs," *Economic Journal,* 77 (March 1967): 151–154.

11.5 Protection and Unemployment

In popular discussions of commercial policy, the issue of unemployment is often raised. An increase in a tariff rate or quota that protects firms in a given industry saves jobs in a fairly obvious way. Less obvious, of course, is the range of jobs that could have been created in export activities if the policy of protection had not been adopted. Thus protectionists who base their case on the threat to jobs that free trade creates always have an advantage in popular discussions because there is a fundamental asymmetry between job losses, which can be identified, and job creation, which is harder to specify.

The effect of any policy change on aggregate levels of employment is a macroeconomic issue that awaits Part IV's analysis. But is there any evidence that commercial policy is useful for protecting overall employment? Very little. And even if there were, two further questions should be raised. First, it may be the case that protection is second best to other policies that aid employment, such as adjustment assistance to workers who may be displaced. Once again, as in our discussion in Section 11.2, trade policies may be inferior to policies aimed more directly at the problem. Second, suppose it is the case, at least in the short run, that some unemployment ensues as resources readjust to the new set of domestic prices when tariffs are reduced. Does this necessarily imply a loss of welfare? No. The gains from trade could easily outweigh losses related to temporary unemployment.[16] To economists the argument linking protection to higher levels of employment is extremely tenuous, despite the fact that it attracts attention in the popular media.

11.6 Summary

Protectionism has become a political issue in most countries. It is possible to argue about the aggregate gains to a nation of opening commodity markets to free trade, as we have done in earlier chapters. But commercial policy can have an important effect on the distribution of income and allocation of resources. Thus it is not surprising that special sectors or interest groups use the political arena in an attempt to foster policies that raise incomes in some sectors but are unfavorable to the economy overall. As well, it is often the case that even if tariffs and quotas can achieve some sought-for objective, other instruments of public policy may achieve the same goal at lower cost. The primary use of commercial policy, which may have some validity for certain large countries, is to improve a country's terms of trade by controlling the volume of demand or supply. This line of reasoning, the so-called optimum tariff argument, is somewhat fragile because of the danger that other countries will retaliate with protective devices of their own. Countries sometimes adopt a protectionist stance as part of a policy to promote growth. We have pointed out the dangers inherent in such a policy, as well as in the use of protection to attract foreign capital. In all this discussion we have maintained the assumption that producing units are relatively small and competitive, so it is only governments that are capable of altering prices and resource allocation. In the

---

[16]Recall the discussion of unemployment in the Ricardian model in the appendix to Chapter 4 and Figure 4.A.1.

next chapter we broach directly the possibility that economic agents deal in imperfectly competitive world markets where their own private actions can affect the terms of trade and the welfare of the whole community.

CHAPTER PROBLEMS

1. Use the kind of diagrammatic argument represented by Figure 11.3 for the case of production subsidies to present the case that a nation wishing to restrict consumption of some item below the free-trade level would do better to levy a consumption tax instead of a tariff.

2. Suppose a capital-abundant country levies a tariff on its labor-intensive imports. (The country's productive structure is that of Chapter 6's Heckscher-Ohlin model.) Show why this must improve workers' real wage. What further changes in the country's real wage would be brought about if foreign countries counter with tariffs of their own on home exportables?

3. To expand on Section 11.4's discussion of the relationship between protection and foreign investment, suppose the home country exports clothing, which is produced by labor and capital, and imports food, which is produced locally by labor and land. That is, assume the specific-factor production structure of Chapter 5. Let some of the capital used in the clothing sector be provided by foreign investment. If the home country protects its food industry with a tariff, trace through the following scenarios:
   a. What is the effect on factor prices, production, consumption, and trade volumes if no more foreign capital enters or leaves the country?
   b. What is the further impact on factor prices, production, consumption, and trade if returns to capital in the clothing sector adjust to a given world rate of return via changes in the quantity of capital foreigners wish to place in the protectionist country?
   c. What is the effect on net home welfare in each case?

SUGGESTIONS FOR FURTHER READING

Bhagwati, Jagdish. *In Defense of Globalization* (Oxford: Oxford University Press, 2004). Critique of present-day arguments for protection.

Brock, William, and S. Magee. "Tariff Formation in a Democracy." In J. Black and B. Hindley, eds., *Current Issues in International Commercial Policy and Diplomacy* (London: Macmillan, 1980), pp. 1–9. Brief survey discussion of features of democratic governments that influence the formation of tariff policy.

Corden, W. M. "Tariffs, Subsidies, and the Terms of Trade," *Economica,* 24 (August 1957): 235–242. A lucid treatment of alternative protective devices.

Irwin, Douglas. *Free Trade Under Fire,* 2nd ed. (Oxford: Oxford University Press, 2005). A spirited attack on protectionism.

Johnson, Harry G. "Optimal Trade Intervention in the Presence of Domestic Distortions." In R. E. Baldwin et al., eds., *Trade, Growth and the Balance of Payments* (Chicago: Rand McNally, 1965). A general discussion of trade taxes and production and consumption subsidies, relying heavily on diagrammatic analysis.

Krueger, Anne. "The Political Economy of the Rent-Seeking Society," *American Economic Review,* 44 (June 1974): 291–303. The classic exposition of the loss in welfare as resources are devoted to obtaining import licenses.

———. "Asymmetries in Policy between Exportables and Import-Competing Goods." In R. W. Jones and A. O. Krueger, eds., *The Political Economy of International Trade* (Cambridge, UK: Blackwell, 1990), pp. 161–178. An interesting discussion of why import-competing industries receive governmental support more frequently than do export industries.

Krugman, Paul. "Import Protection as Export Promotion: International Competition in the Presence of Oligopoly and Economies of Scale." In H. Kierzkowski, ed., *Monopolistic Competition and International Trade* (Oxford, UK: Oxford University Press, 1984), pp. 180–193. A variation on the infant industry argument when trade is of the monopolistic competition intraindustry type.

Stolper, Wolfgang, and Paul A. Samuelson. "Protection and Real Wages," *Review of Economic Studies,* 9 (November 1941): 58–73. The analysis of the effect of a tariff on wages and rents.

CHAPTER 12

Trade Policy and Imperfect Competition

In this chapter the focus on trade policy shifts in two ways. We depart from the assumption that markets for goods, services, and factors of production are purely competitive and allow for elements of monopoly and oligopoly. The effects of these market structures are studied mainly in individual markets (partial equilibrium) rather than in the economy as a whole (general equilibrium). Second, because many practical issues of trade policy, both old and new, turn on imperfect competition, we align the theory closely with its empirical applications.

12.1 Monopoly and the Gains from Trade

The most basic connection between imperfect competition and international trade lies in the ability of international competition to limit distortions caused by monopolies in a nation's product markets. We show this theoretically; then we consider evidence from real-world markets.

Monopoly and Import Competition

"The tariff is the mother of the trusts" was a charge heard often in the United States at the end of the nineteenth century. It meant that domestic producers who had worked out collusive agreements among themselves could not raise prices and exploit consumers without help from tariffs, which kept import competition away. Indeed, the gains from trade are amplified when foreign competition undercuts a monopoly's ability to raise its price above long-run marginal cost (the benchmark for an efficient, competitive price). This is illustrated in Figure 12.1, which shows not the monopoly's demand and cost curves but the effect of its behavior on resource allocation for the economy as a whole. If the economy were closed and both the clothing and food industries competitive, production and consumption would be at point C_1, and the slope of a tangent at that point would indicate the equilibrium price. It is assumed, however, that the food industry is monopolized. The monopoly maximizes its profits by producing less than the competitive output and charging a price higher than its marginal cost. Thus, in the two-good model of the economy, it restricts its output to some level such as F_M or F_M', causing too many factors of production to be shifted into the clothing industry. The monopoly price distorts the economy's relative prices to some value

FIGURE 12.1

Trade Breaks Up a Monopoly: Importables

Without trade, monopolized food production at F_M or F_M' is below the closed-economy competitive level. When trade is opened, food's price falls from P_M or P_M' to AC_2; the welfare gain is greater than that from y_1 to y_2.

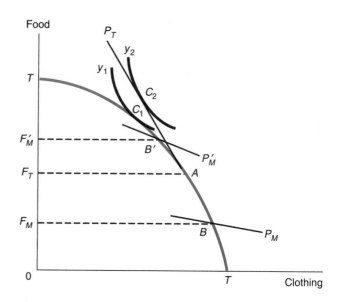

indicated by a truncated price slope, such as P_M or P_M'. (The diagram does not show exactly how the monopoly's profit-maximizing quantity is determined, but price lines such as these will be tangent to community indifference curves.)

Suppose that the economy is now opened up to trade and the monopoly finds itself facing cheaper imports of food with a world market price shown by AC_2 (price slope P_T). Suppose further that the country is too small to influence world prices. The monopoly has now been turned into a pure competitor on the world market because it can only sell whatever output is profitable at the given world price. It chooses output F_T, the same output that a purely competitive food industry would select. It might contract its output from F_M' because of the cost disadvantage against foreign producers of food, or it might even expand output from F_M if its cost disadvantage is not too great because it no longer pays to restrict output to raise price.

The economy gains more from trade in this case than if food production had been competitive. The economy's initial welfare was represented by a community indifference curve tangent to the price line that intersects the production possibilities curve at B or B'. This indifference curve (not shown) would lie below point C_1 and represent a lower level of welfare than community indifference curve y_1, which corresponds to a competitive economy without international trade. The overall welfare gain when trade is introduced can thus be decomposed into two parts: the movement from an indifference curve tangent to P_M (or P_M') to C_1 related to eliminating monopoly, and the gain from C_1 to C_2 related to the advantages of international specialization.

Monopoly and Export Opportunities

It may be surprising that the gains from exposing a monopoly to international trade are essentially the same if the monopoly becomes the exporter; export opportunities change its behavior toward the home market in the same way as does the discipline of

FIGURE 12.2

Trade Breaks Up a Monopoly:
Exportables

Without trade, monopolized clothing
production at C_M or C_M' is below the
closed-economy competitive level.
When trade is opened at world prices
P_T, the monopolist must trade as a pure
competitor on the world market and
produces C_T. Domestic price of clothing
can either rise (from P_M') or fall (from P_M).

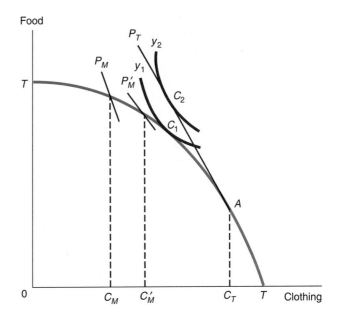

import competition. Figure 12.2 shows the effect of monopoly in the clothing industry.
(The food industry is now assumed to be competitive.) In the absence of trade, output
might be restricted to C_M or C_M', corresponding to relative prices P_M or P_M', and higher
than would prevail in the competitive closed economy at C_1. Exposing the monopoly to
world price ratio AC_2 (shown by the slope of line P_T) induces it to expand its output.
Because it is assumed there is no restriction on imports of clothing at these same world
prices, the monopoly can no longer exploit the downward-sloping domestic demand
curve. Instead it must sell on the foreign and domestic markets at the world price.
Paradoxically, the actual domestic price of clothing could either rise or fall when the
economy is opened to trade. If the nation's comparative advantage is very great, the
high closed-economy monopoly price might be pulled up to a still higher world price
(P_M' is flatter than P_T), but the force of international competition could also make the
price fall (P_M is steeper than P_T). Once more, the economy's total gain in welfare consists of the conventional gains from trade plus an extra gain that arises from elimination of the monopolistic distortion of production.

Monopoly and Exports in Practice: U.S. Steel in 1900

Time and again, trade has reduced the power of national monopolies. Still, its practical
effect is both more limited and more complex than the preceding theory would suggest.
Consider as an example the early years of the United States Steel Corporation, formed
in 1898 by a consolidation of many previously independent companies. It controlled
approximately two thirds of U.S. production of major steel products, and it also enjoyed
tight control over the iron ore deposits in Minnesota and Michigan, thereby gaining
protection from the threat of entry by new domestic competitors. Just at the time of

U.S. Steel's formation, the prices of pig iron (an intermediate product in steelmaking) and the major finished products nearly doubled. That increase itself was not the handiwork of the newly dominant firm because it took place in British markets as well. However, outside the United States, prices quickly retreated, whereas at home they were kept at this newly elevated level. Indeed, during the next decade the domestic pig iron price stayed about 40 percent above the U.K. price plus the U.S. tariff. Transportation costs were apparently high enough that this differential led to substantial imports only in boom years, when the U.S. price became 70 to 80 percent higher than the U.K. price plus the U.S. tariff, setting off a burst of imports.

The United States had in fact become a significant exporter of iron and steel by this time, and U.S. Steel's elevated domestic price was a dire threat to its export sales. The problem had a simple solution: U.S. Steel charged its monopoly price on domestic sales while selling abroad for whatever price it could get. Prices of steel rails for export were sometimes only 75 percent of their domestic level. Transport costs and tariffs were high enough that it did not pay domestic rail buyers to bid these bargain goods away from favored foreign buyers. (This practice of selling cheaply abroad, known as dumping, is considered in Section 12.3.) Thus, although international trade did limit U.S. Steel's monopoly power as theory suggests it would, the presence of high tariffs and transport costs and the feasibility of dumping left the company with access to generous monopoly profits in its early years.[1]

Economists studying trade and market competition in present-day industries often use statistical methods to compare the situations of different industries—those with substantial or little import competition and those with few sellers (perhaps approaching monopoly) or many sellers (close to pure competition). What they find repeatedly—not just in the United States, but for many countries and periods of time—is that freedom from import competition is a necessary condition for such excess profits, as is a small enough number of competitors that they behave in a monopolistic fashion. A monopoly-elevated price pulls in more imports, which erode the monopoly's profits.[2]

Every industrial country maintains some type of antitrust or competition policy that seeks to avert monopoly-type distortions in domestic markets. It has been argued, quite properly, that applications of these policies should take international competition into account. The United States, for example, maintains "merger guidelines" to determine when rival firms that merge can be presumed to obtain market shares high enough to threaten monopoly. These guidelines now take account of import competition. Whereas large countries whose domestic markets are only moderately affected by international competition tend to take competition policy seriously, most small ones with highly open markets count on trade to do the job.

---

[1]This information is taken from Donald O. Parsons and Edward John Ray, "The United States Steel Consolidation: The Creation of Market Control," *Journal of Law and Economics,* 18 (April 1975): 181–219.

[2]Examples of these studies are Thomas A. Pugel, "Foreign Trade and U.S. Market Performance," *Journal of Industrial Economics,* 29 (December 1980): 119–129; and Michelle M. Katics and Bruce C. Petersen, "The Effect of Rising Import Competition on Market Power," *Journal of Industrial Economics,* 42 (September 1994): 277–286.

12.2   Cartels and the Interests of Producing and Consuming Countries

That international trade pays dividends by enforcing market competition and enlarging the gains from trade is a simple message—simple because each country's gains are independent of its neighbors' actions. Noncompetitive markets present a more complex issue, however, when monopoly overflows into international trade. The problem that arises is exactly that identified with the optimal tariff (Section 10.3). When a national monopolist earns profits on exports sold to foreigners, those profits both enrich the monopolist and enter into the exporting country's national income. When the monopolist snatches profits from domestic customers, these represent a redistribution of national income. (The deadweight loss that occurs when buyers cut back on purchases of monopolized goods is a real cost in either case.) Just as countries' interests clash when they attempt to monopolize their trade through tariffs, they may also clash over monopoly prices in international trade.

This section considers this issue in a traditional context—that of international cartels and the divergent interests of producing and consuming countries. Section 12.3 reviews some new thinking about national policies designed to capture monopoly gains or to fight off such raids.

The Organization of Petroleum Exporting Countries

We start with the best known and most successful cartel in history, the Organization of Petroleum Exporting Countries (OPEC). For at least a dozen years starting in 1973, OPEC kept the price of crude oil far above what a competitive market would set. The excess profits are indirectly apparent in the cash buildups that corresponded to the OPEC members' export surplus of $60 billion in 1974 and of almost twice that in 1980 after another price increase. These riches resulted from the members' agreement to charge a common high price for oil. Of course, that price reduced the world's consumption of oil, not only because any price increase tends to cut the quantity demanded, but also because the disturbance reduced employment in the industrial economies, thus reducing their demand for all imports, oil included. For the cartel to hold together, its members had to accept a reduction in the quantities they produced and sold; the leading members made these cuts. However, in the 1981–1983 recession, the cartel began to crumble after appropriating vast wealth for its members and inflicting further heavy indirect costs (unemployment, inflation) on the consuming countries. Three forces finally weakened OPEC's grip on the world's oil consumers. First, many oil users made the investments necessary to shift to the use of other fuels or to reduce their fuel usage overall. Second, other would-be producers went searching for oil, and many succeeded. In 1983 OPEC's share of Western production was one third, down from two thirds a mere five years earlier. Third, some members of the cartel themselves began to cheat on its agreed price; in early 1983 OPEC had to reduce its posted price from $34 to $29 a barrel to acknowledge that some of its members were making spot sales at prices much below list. The decline continued, bringing the price down to $11 a barrel in 1998, little more in real terms than the price prevailing before 1973. Then, aided by heavy world demand, OPEC recovered some of its punch and pushed the price back above $30 a barrel. OPEC has followed classical cartel strategies to sustain some cooperation among its members. Producers with small reserves (and the greatest incentive to cheat) got proportionally large output quotas. Saudi Arabia, the largest producer and chief enforcer, sometimes tolerated cheating and absorbed disturbances by cutting its own output, but it sometimes punished cheaters with a "tit for tat" strategy.[3]

Despite OPEC's apparent departure from classic cartel status, in 2006 petroleum consumers found oil prices soaring above $70 a barrel. The causes seem numerous and present a "supply and demand" aspect rather than monopoly behavior. They include strongly growing demand because of increased use in large successfully developing countries such as China and India but also demand in the industrial countries—notably the ever-decreasing fuel efficiency of the U.S. motor vehicle stock. They also include supply factors such as constraints on the capacity of the world's oil-refining facilities and restricted crude-oil extraction in Iraq and other suppliers.

Commodity Agreements

OPEC's role follows a long history of attempts by countries or producer groups to manipulate their terms of trade. Primary-product cartels first became prominent after World War I. Most of them soon failed for reasons evident from the theoretical requisites of a successful cartel: It must face a price-inelastic demand (no actual or potential close substitutes). All important producers must join the arrangement. Members must be willing to cut back production, and an enforcement mechanism must be found that can curb their incentive to cheat once price has been elevated above their marginal costs. Last, buyers must be unable (or at least disinclined) to organize to ward off the exaction of monopoly rents. Most cartels soon collapsed for want of one or another of these conditions, even after producer governments became active participants in the 1930s.

Fortunately, commodity agreements have commonly sought a different goal, more meritorious than monopoly profit, that is, the stabilization of product prices prone to high volatility. Their demands tend to be inelastic, if only because a primary product often accounts for a small fraction of the cost of the finished product that incorporates it. Supplies also tend to be inelastic because of the sunken status of producers' costs. With both demand and supply price-inelastic, a given disturbance produces a large change in price. The developing countries that supply many such products are commonly quite specialized, so fluctuations of a major export's price translate into large swings in the country's national income—a source of personal disutility, badly blurred signals about investment decisions, a disaster-prone banking system, and various other problems. A case can be made for a so-called buffer-stock scheme: creating an authority with funds to buy and stockpile the commodity when its price is low and sell off its stocks when the price is high. Indeed, buying cheap and selling dear, the buffer-

---

[3]James M. Griffin and Weiwen Xiong, "The Incentive to Cheat: An Empirical Analysis of OPEC," *Journal of Law and Economics,* 40 (October 1997): 289–316; M. A. Adelman, "Scarcity and World Oil Prices," *Review of Economics and Statistics,* 68 (August 1986): 387–397.

stock agency should make a profit. However, with the competitive market-clearing price neither readily known nor agreed upon, observers may well disagree on whether price-raising efforts on a given day carry the market price toward or above that equilibrium price.

The operation of international commodity agreements since World War II shows this ambiguity of objectives and also illustrates the ways in which the agreements can fail. Reflecting their unclear objectives, the agreements have employed a mixture of policy instruments—buffer stocks (usable mainly for price stabilization) and export quotas (needed to secure monopoly prices). Even those agreements that succeeded for some periods of time collapsed through the failure of one or the other mechanism. An agreement of tin producers worked for a time because the producers were few and production was stable (unlike most agricultural crops). However, the buffer stock effectively ran out of funds and collapsed. The international coffee agreement, like others, failed because producers could not agree on reallocating quotas among themselves toward suppliers who were raising their efficiency (lowering marginal cost) or producing varieties in growing demand. After maintaining high and stable prices from 1980 to 1989, the agreement collapsed, and wholesale prices fell 40 percent when Brazil left it; Brazil, a large but not high-quality producer, was unwilling to accept a reduced output quota and market share.[4]

Despite this checkered experience, in the 1970s the developing countries demanded through the United Nations Conference on Trade and Development (UNCTAD) an international program of commodity agreements as the keystone of a "new international economic order." It would involve agreements covering eighteen commodities, along with a Common Fund to finance the agreements and to assist exporters in developing countries in diversifying their economies. A much reduced version of the Common Fund was agreed to in principle in 1983, but ratification faltered. The International Monetary Fund has devised several facilities to assist countries operating buffer-stock arrangements, but they have done little business.

Economic analysis offers several points to clarify the debate over the Common Fund proposal. It was originally intended to promote not just commodity-price stabilization but also income transfers from consumers to producers through increased average prices. Unfortunately, transferring income to producers by having them restrict supply and raise their selling price is an inefficient procedure: It costs more real resources than if the buyer simply hands over an equivalent transfer of real income.

12.3 Monopoly and Policies of Exporting and Importing Countries

The world would be better off without monopolies unless they have an unavoidable "natural" basis, but most countries are happy to maximize their own incomes by using any monopoly power they may possess (or acquire through international cartels). This

---

[4]See Christopher L. Gilbert, "International Commodity Agreements: Design and Performance," *World Development,* 15 (May 1987): 591–616; Robert H. Bates, *Open-Economy Politics: The Political Economy of the World Coffee Trade* (Princeton: Princeton University Press, 1997).

section considers how nations can use their market power effectively—by exploiting foreign consumers or by snatching monopoly rents away from foreign exporters. The discussion also examines the monopolistic practice of selling more cheaply abroad than at home (dumping) and the reactions of importing countries to this practice.

Exploiting Monopoly Power over Exports

The interest of an exporting country in exploiting its monopoly power in trade is obvious enough. The optimal tariff lets it achieve that goal, as was demonstrated in Chapter 10 for a general-equilibrium model with purely competitive industries. The same problem is now considered in a broader context, where each industry or market is thought of as one of many making up the economy. If the U.S. passenger aircraft industry consisted of many small firms that failed to recognize their joint monopoly power, the government would maximize national welfare by imposing an export tax. The right tax rate in this case is one that "marks up" the export price over the industry's marginal cost by the same amount that a profit-maximizing monopolistic seller of aircraft would select.

If the aircraft industry consisted instead of a single monopolistic seller (call it Boeing), the government would presumably find the private firm more than willing to set a price to maximize its profits from export and domestic sales alike. The government still has a welfare problem on its hands, however, because the excess of price over marginal cost to domestic buyers causes an undesirable loss to home consumers. The optimal policy is to compel the firm to sell domestically at a competitive price—that is, one equal to the monopolist's marginal cost. The only problem is to find a practical policy instrument that will effectively control the domestic price while allowing the producer to monopolize the overseas markets. In practice, governments have some means to regulate the degree of competition in an industry but not much leverage for making it more competitive in its domestic than in its foreign sales. That shortcoming makes the government face a trade-off: The more monopoly it allows in the industry overall, the more monopoly profits are lifted from foreign pockets but also the more surplus is lost by domestic buyers. The government can make a second-best choice—with the right degree of monopoly, a slight increase adds just enough income from exporting profits to offset the consequent extra deadweight loss of domestic consumers' surplus. Other things being equal, the welfare-maximizing degree of monopoly corresponds to the proportion of its output that the domestic industry exports.

Manipulating the degree of monopoly in an exporting industry to attain this second-best outcome seems impractical and much more complicated than simply setting an optimal tariff (tax) on exports—and it is. Nonetheless, countries can be observed casting about for second-best ways to garner export profits without using export taxes. For the United States, at least, the explanation is easily found in the U.S. Constitution, Article I, Section 9, which prohibits taxes on exports. One substitute device, useful when the exporting industry consists of many competitive suppliers, is to allow them to form a cartel to manage their export sales while forbidding them to collude in selling to the domestic market. The United States permits such cooperative export agreements under the Webb-Pomerene Act, and other countries employ similar policies. Indeed, just as theory predicts, the more important an exporting activity is for a country, the more generously does the country allow collusion among its exporters (at the risk that this collusion will spill over onto the domestic market and cause deadweight losses to domestic consumers).[5]

National Welfare and International Oligopoly

In the years since World War II, the number of important trading countries in the world economy has grown continuously. The European nations and Japan recovered from the war and then proceeded to narrow the gap in average productivity with the United States. More recently, the emergence of the newly industrialized countries has further enlarged the cast of significant trading nations. With more nations competing, situations in which individual countries, let alone single firms, possess substantial worldwide monopoly power over significant products have grown refreshingly less common. For that reason, OPEC has had no imitators, and in practice the exploitation of single-nation monopoly power is a minor issue. Nonetheless, some important industries are highly concentrated, with few significant sellers worldwide. Automobiles, semiconductors, large computers, large passenger aircraft, turbine generators, and aluminum are a few examples of world oligopolies.

Economists have recently addressed the policy problem of how a country maximizes its welfare when it serves as the home base for only part of a world oligopoly. If it takes a leaf from OPEC's book, it simply works out an agreement with the other producing nations to run a joint monopoly at the expense of consuming nations. For reasons suggested in Section 12.2, this solution is seldom used. Rather, countries define the policy problem as a search for the best method of boosting the home producer's position relative to other members of the international oligopoly. Policy proposals all too often pass up economic reasoning for sporting metaphors: "How can we strengthen our 'national champion' so that the firm can do battle more effectively with its international rivals?" Admittedly, driving the rivals out of business and enjoying a full-blooded monopoly has its economic attractions. Nonetheless, slaughtering one's oligopolistic rivals is usually infeasible, and even if feasible, it may still be unprofitable.[6]

Here some recent theories about national policy-making enter the picture. Suppose that a national firm faces just one competitor, located in a foreign country. That is, the market structure is an international duopoly, with both firms exporting to the rest of the world. Can the government do anything to help the national champion to a larger slice of the duopoly profit or to enlarge the world profit to be sliced? The scope available for national policy depends very much on how the two duopolists compete with one another. If they have formed an OPEC-style cartel to extract maximum joint profit from the world economy, there is probably little that the home government can do unless it can help the home firm bargain for a larger share of that profit.

---

[5]A. A. Auquier and R. E. Caves, "Monopolistic Export Industries, Trade Taxes, and Optimal Competition Policy," *Economic Journal*, 89 (September 1979): 559–581.

[6]Unprofitable because to drive a rival from the market, the aggressor must charge low prices in the short run or otherwise run losses to inflict large (fatal?) losses on the victim. Even if the attack succeeds and monopoly profits then flow in abundance, they lie in the future; their present value may not offset the profits forgone in the initial period of warfare. And the future profits themselves might induce new competitors to enter.

The two duopolists might be less cooperative, however, and in that circumstance recent theoretical models become relevant. The theory of oligopolistic markets in general is indeterminate, meaning that the sellers can interact with one another in any of several ways. We can define some theoretical possibilities but cannot predict in general what output an oligopoly will produce between the reference points of the outputs that purely competitive and purely monopolistic producers would select in the same circumstances. Despite this fundamental ignorance, a popular strategy for modeling oligopoly markets is to assume that the rival sellers do not cooperate in a joint monopoly; indeed, they do not cooperate at all but instead act as if each expects no changes in its rivals' prices or outputs in response to its own moves in the market. Each duopolist knows that increasing its output will drive down the world price because it is a big player on the world market, but it anticipates no reply from its foreign rival. This assumption is implausible for a duopoly, but it makes more sense in oligopolies with enough firms that any one rival holds no systematic expectation about competitors' responses. Also, the assumption is neither particularly optimistic nor pessimistic: At best, when the home firm expands output, it might hope its rival would "move over," reducing output to keep the world price from falling; at worst, it might fear that the rival will come out swinging and expand its own output to maintain its market share, further depressing world price. The assumption that a rival's output will not react to a competitor's output change is called the *Cournot assumption*, and it yields definite conclusions about what output the duopoly will produce and how much monopoly profit its members will earn. As expected, the output is greater than a cartel or joint monopoly would select, and the profit is less, because no collusion occurs.

Profits obtained by the home duopolist go into the national income. What can the government do to enlarge them? The appendix to this chapter shows that by subsidizing the home firm's output, it is possible to increase the profit it obtains (and thus national income) and to reduce the profit of the foreign rival (and its homeland's national income). The intuition behind the result is simple. If the duopolists' behavior follows the Cournot assumption, then an increase in the home firm's output in response to the subsidy causes its rival to contract output. World output still increases, and world price and profit fall, but the firm's enlarged market share gives it a sufficiently bigger share of the shrunken profit pie to make it—and the country—better off.

The Cournot model of duopoly (or oligopoly) is bothersome because sellers in many markets seem to compete by quoting prices rather than setting outputs. The duopoly model can be reconstructed by assuming that each seller sets price on the assumption that its rival's price will remain unchanged—called the *Bertrand assumption*. The market equilibrium is similar to the Cournot equilibrium, if it is also assumed that the duopolists' products are differentiated from one another, and leads to a similar conclusion—that the market price will be set at a level lying above the pure-competition price and below the pure-monopoly price. (Without differentiation, the Bertrand assumption implies that duopolists will settle on the purely competitive price, which is implausible.)

If the world duopoly consists of Bertrand players, can the government once more maneuver the home champion into a superior position? The answer is again affirmative, but—because the Bertrand assumption implies more aggressive behavior than

Cournot's—the appropriate policy this time is to tax rather than subsidize the home company's exports. When the firm, hit with a tax, raises its price and supplies the smaller output that is demanded, its rival will respond by also raising its price and probably lowering its output. Thus the objective in each case is to induce the foreign firm to behave less aggressively.

At this point, the policy maker asks this hard question: "How do I know whether the Cournot or the Bertrand assumption fits a given market, so I can tell whether to subsidize or to tax?" The answer, unfortunately, is that neither assumption can be confirmed by direct observation; in fact, neither approach comes very close to characterizing the behavior of any particular oligopoly. At this point, the policy advice stemming from these models of international duopoly tends to evaporate into nothing more than an engaging curiosity.[7]

Fighting Off Monopoly Power over Imports

So far the discussion has concentrated on how a country might benefit from monopoly power over its exports. The importing country, however, faces the symmetrical problem of how to fight off raids on its economic welfare by monopolists of the goods that it imports. Although recent theoretical research supplies some new insights, it is necessary to recall the message of the optimum tariff for a single importing industry. If a country faces an upward-sloping supply curve for imports, it can benefit from purchasing them as a *monopsonist* (which is what a sole buyer is called). Each additional unit bought (per period of time) drives up the price and thus the cost of every other unit bought. The monopsonist cuts back the quantity bought to the point where the total extra cost due to the last unit is just equal to its marginal value to the user (normally the price that customers pay for a unit of the import).[8] The country could accomplish this cutback either by allowing some import agent to serve as the monopsony buyer or by setting a tariff rate that would achieve the same restriction of imports. The resulting gain is quite consistent with the imports being supplied competitively by their foreign producers. The essential condition is simply that when less is purchased, the asking price goes down.

However, what if the foreign supplier is a monopolist? When OPEC quadrupled the price of oil in 1973–1974, some people urged the United States to impose a tax on imported crude oil. They advanced, among other reasons, the likelihood that OPEC would react by backing off partially from its price increase. That prediction has some logic behind it, as can be seen in Figure 12.3, which shows the U.S. demand for imported petroleum as DD. It is assumed that OPEC can produce petroleum at a constant marginal cost of CC. That assumed constancy is important: In this model the buyer's gains do not depend on an upward-sloping cost or supply curve, as they do in the traditional

---

[7]Simple and judicious accounts of these and related models can be found in Paul R. Krugman, ed., *Strategic Trade Policy and the New International Economics* (Cambridge, MA: MIT Press, 1986).

[8]This decision is symmetrical with the action of a monopolistic seller, which equates its marginal cost to the net gain in total revenue (i.e., marginal revenue) received when it pushes another unit onto the market and lowers the price.

FIGURE 12.3

Using Import Duty to Reduce Foreign Monopolist's Price

Import duty reduces demand for monopolized import from DD to $D_T D_T$. Monopoly reduces its price (net of tariff) from P to P_{NT}.

monopsony model summarized in the preceding paragraph. The marginal revenue curve corresponding to the U.S. import demand is MR. A profit-maximizing OPEC would set price P, and quantity Q would be imported. Now suppose that the government imposes an import duty of $\$X$ per barrel. U.S. consumers' willingness to pay for oil *net* of the newly imposed tax is described by demand curve $D_T D_T$, which is shifted downward uniformly by the amount DD_T (= $\$X$). The profit-maximizing before-tax price charged by OPEC now falls to P_{NT}. U.S. consumers now pay a higher price gross of the tax of P_{GT} and, accordingly, they purchase less than before (Q_T). Although the consumers themselves are worse off than before the tax, the country as a whole is better off because the tax revenue, $(P_{GT} - P_{NT})Q_T$, is part of the national income and could be rebated to consumers or used to buy public goods.

This policy model shares one unhappy property with the model of international duopoly presented previously. Its policy prescription is sensitive to something of which little is known—in this case the exact shape of the demand curve. Figure 12.3 supplied a clear answer because it assumes that the demand curve is a straight line. If it had been assumed only that the curve slopes uniformly downward, however, local "wiggles" in the demand curve (and corresponding, but enlarged, wiggles in marginal revenue) could make a subsidy rather than a tax appropriate, depending on the exact point of equilibrium on the demand curve.[9] Once again, a seemingly confident policy prescription turns on empirical conditions that can be assessed only with difficulty, if at all.

[9]See Homi Katrak, "Multi-National Monopolies and Commercial Policy," *Oxford Economic Papers*, 29 (July 1977): 283–291; James A. Brander and Barbara J. Spencer, "Trade Warfare: Tariffs and Cartels," *Journal of International Economics*, 16 (May 1984): 227–242; Ronald W. Jones, "Trade Taxes and Subsidies with Imperfect Competition," *Economics Letters*, 23 (1987): 375–379.

The analysis of international duopoly applies as well to the country that imports supplies that compete with the output of the domestic duopolist. The duopoly once more offers a profit-shuffling opportunity to the home government. Home consumers buy at a price that incorporates monopoly profits—some going to the domestic duopolist, some to the foreigner. If sales are shifted to the domestic seller, consumers still suffer the deadweight loss, but the profit slice remains in the national income rather than vanishing across the border.[10]

In conclusion, the analysis indicates that the importing country should probably consider restricting imports whose foreign suppliers possess monopoly power. Such restrictions provide a less-than-optimal solution to the problem, however, because they increase the deadweight loss to domestic consumers even when they shift some profits away from foreign monopolists (or oligopolists). Lost from sight among these strategies for exploiting and combating monopoly power is the global interest of all participants in competitive prices (equal to long-run marginal costs). Such a global solution requires countries to agree that each will do its best to keep its domestic producers competitive, whether they sell at home or abroad.

A Monopoly Practice: Dumping

We introduce here a business practice associated with monopoly that plays a major role in trade policy. Its customary name is *dumping*, and its formal theoretical base is price discrimination. The idea is simply that a monopoly selling in two separable markets can profitably charge different prices to them, setting the higher price in the market with the less elastic demand. The term *dumping* refers to the situation of the market with more elastic demand where the monopolist sets a lower price. As a consumer, one obviously enjoys being dumped on. Why the pejorative term? Obviously, the competing producer does not enjoy facing a rival with a self-interest in charging a low price. We see in Chapter 13 that antidumping laws have become a popular way to protect domestic producers. Here we pave the way with a simple model of the seller employing price discrimination.

First of all, notice that a purely competitive firm would not sell identical goods in two different markets at different prices. Because the competitive firm perceives the market price to be unaffected by the quantity it sells, there is no reason to sell any output at less than the best price available. Therefore, dumping must be associated with departures from pure competition. Consider the domestic monopolist illustrated in Figure 12.4. Demand in the home market is given by D, marginal revenue by MR_d. If marginal cost is MC, the firm selling only in the home market maximizes profits by charging P_m, the sale price of the output for which $MC = MR_d$. The world price P_w is lower than P_m, but it still lies above MC over a substantial range of output, so the monopolist can profitably produce for export. Now suppose that different prices can be charged in the home and foreign markets, perhaps because a tariff protecting the

---

[10]An allegedly successful example of such a policy was studied by Richard Baldwin and Harry Flam, "Strategic Trade Policies in the Market for 30–40 Seat Commuter Aircraft," *Weltwirtschaftliches Archiv,* 125, 3 (1989): 484–500. Canada restricted imports from Brazil, shifting profits toward its domestic producer, while Brazilian export subsidies benefited world consumers.

FIGURE 12.4

Dumping and Discrimination Between Domestic and Foreign Markets

Monopoly faces demand curve D at home and world price P_w. If it can charge different prices at home and abroad, it sets P_d and P_w, respectively, selling $0B$ at home and BC abroad.

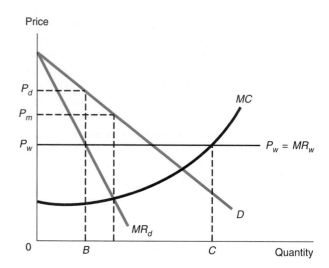

home market keeps goods sold cheaply abroad from being reimported and undercutting the higher domestic price. A monopolist maximizes profits by setting a price that equates its marginal cost to the marginal revenue it can earn in each of its markets: If the marginal revenues were not equal, it would shift sales from the lower to the higher until the two are equalized. In Figure 12.4 the marginal revenue from foreign sales is equal to the world price P_w because that price is unaffected by the monopolist's level of exports. After it begins to export, the monopoly will sell in the domestic market at price P_d, which equates marginal revenue derived from the domestic market, MR_d, to that earned from foreign sales, MR_w. If total production is $0C$, marginal cost MC is equated to the common value of marginal revenue, and profits are maximized. Exports are BC, domestic sales $0B$. Notice that this discrimination between the domestic and foreign markets has caused a higher price to be charged in the domestic market than if no trade were occurring (P_d exceeds P_m).

Whereas the welfare effects of dumping on the *exporting* country are ambiguous, dumping's effects on the importer are clear. As long as the exporter finds that overseas markets are more competitive than the sheltered domestic market, the export price is set lower than the price to the exporter's home customers and lower than it would be in the absence of discrimination. The importing country therefore benefits from being offered a lower price. The welfare-maximizing importing country would encourage dumping. Evidently, importer governments view the practice through very different eyes.

Boeing versus Airbus

We close this section with a case study of a prominent international oligopoly: the rivalry between Boeing, now the sole U.S. producer of large passenger aircraft, and Airbus, a European consortium and Boeing's only rival. Boeing is the long-lived survivor of the U.S. industry, following the exit of McDonnell Douglas and Lockheed

Martin, its last two rivals. Airbus was assembled from a group of European companies with heavy involvement by the governments of France, Germany, and (later) the United Kingdom and Spain. In its early days Airbus received general and open development and production subsidies, which made it feasible for it to develop a series of aircraft models, most of which competed closely with Boeing's designs. In addition Airbus was quite skillful in both the advanced technology of its designs and the efficiency of its production process. Its share of the world market steadily increased, and since 2003 its annual deliveries have exceeded Boeing's. The latest round in their rivalry involves the market for very large aircraft to serve long-distance international routes—Airbus's gigantic A380 (555 passengers) and Boeing's 787 (a smaller craft efficient for very long distances). The two designs bet on somewhat different predictions about the evolution of the air travel market, but they are clearly close rivals. Either one of them would likely be a profitable venture for the manufacturer. Whether both can be profitable is much less clear.

The economic properties of the large-aircraft market are very distinctive. Fixed costs for design and setup for production are very high. Airbus had spent $12 billion on the A380 even before its first test flight. Development of a new model seldom starts without some firm orders from airlines, but it falls far short of the number needed for ultimate profitability. Once production starts, unit costs decline, thanks to a steep learning curve; each doubling of cumulative output leads to a reduction of 20 percent in unit production costs. The manufacturer thus sinks a huge investment before gaining assurance that an aircraft design will be profitable (technically successful and commercially attractive). The buyers' side of the market adds another complication. Consider a large airline or aircraft leasing firm that contemplates a major purchase of either a Boeing or a competing Airbus model. It can stage an auction between the aircraft producers. The sunk development costs provide no floor for these bids, only the seller's (declining) marginal cost of production. Indeed, even the two rivals' marginal costs need not provide a price floor for an order that is critical for preserving a steady flow of production. In short, the market has a potent "winner-take-all" property. The faltering seller cannot finance new models and suffers higher production costs for extant ones.

The U.S. and European Union (E.U.) governments have been at each other's throats over the question of whether each has supported its champion with inappropriate or illegal subsidies. Airbus's production subsidies and debt write-offs were quite evident at the outset. Nowadays they principally take the form of low-interest loans to cover the cost of developing a new model. Furthermore, these launch loans shift much of the downside risk to the member governments. When attacked for these policies, the European Union in rejoinder points to the extensive development contracts Boeing has received from the U.S. government. These contracts, of course, trigger large outlays by Boeing, but they are cost-plus and (Airbus argues) give Boeing substantial contributions toward joint costs of its passenger-aircraft business as well as spillover benefits from its government-funded research. The subsidy components in these contracts (and in similar types of assistance to Airbus by the European Union) are hard to measure but undoubtedly substantial. The United States counts $17 billion in E.U. launch loans over the past thirty-five years; the European Union spots $23 billion research and development (R&D) subsidies to Boeing over the past thirteen years.

The U.S.-E.U. dispute has simmered for a number of years. In 1992 the parties agreed to rule out production subsidies and to limit subsidy components in launch loans. The United States agreed to limit indirect aid through Defense Department and NASA contracts to 4 percent of Boeing's civil-aircraft revenues. The rivalry between the A380 and 787 models and their huge launch costs returned the political pot to a boil, especially when Airbus announced it would adapt one of its existing models to compete with the 787. The United States demanded the removal of subsidy elements from the government aid to the launch; the European Union held out for a limitation that left considerable subsidy in place. In May 2005 the United States terminated bilateral negotiations and brought a case against the European Union before the World Trade Organization (WTO) set up to resolve just such commercial conflicts (see Section 13.2). The European Union countersued, and the machinery for adjudicating the charges started to turn. The dispute settlement panel's task is formidable because the WTO's founding document contains a general provision restricting governments' production subsidies. It contemplated the later agreement on rules suitable to the government-involved aircraft industry, but this never happened.

Why have the U.S. and E.U. governments fought so tenaciously for their corporate champions? Initially the Europeans were concerned with maintaining some capability for producing military aircraft. However, economists have suggested a purely economic motive for the European Union. Without Airbus, there was little prospect of averting a worldwide Boeing monopoly. Especially given the stiff price competition that occurs even between aircraft duopolists, that would have spelled much higher prices for aircraft (and air travel). The United States would gain—Boeing's profits exceeding U.S. consumers' losses. But the Europeans (and others) would have lost. If the E.U. subsidies "bought" this freedom from monopoly prices, they could well have achieved a net benefit for the E.U. countries.

12.4   Intellectual Property Rights

Monopoly and conflicting national interests come together on the issue of intellectual property rights (IPRs)—patents, copyright, and trademarks. These intangible assets, forms of knowledge or information, are "public goods," nonrivalrous in consumption (my use of an intangible leaves unimpaired the amount of it available to you) and nonexcludable (you cannot keep me from using it). They pose a dilemma for economic welfare. Without a legal property right in a discovery, the innovator has no way to prevent others from copying it, and thus no source of income to cover R&D costs. Given that property right, however, the innovator charges a monopoly price for the new product.

Society hence faces a trade-off. Giving innovators generous property rights maximizes the incentive to produce new knowledge and also to reveal it for further development by others (without a property right, the innovator tries to keep the discovery a secret). But the monopoly price imposes deadweight losses. In the international economy this dilemma generates a clash of interests between countries that are heavy R&D spenders and innovators and those that mainly import innovations. The former countries' national incomes benefit from strong IPRs; the latter benefit from refusing to recognize such rights and free-riding on the valuable knowledge. Large sums are at issue. In the pharmaceutical industry, which depends heavily on patents, a new drug may take $200 million and 15 years to develop; without patent protection, such investments could not be recovered, and R&D outlays would shrivel. Lack of effective copyright enforcement in some foreign countries costs the U.S. computer software industry an estimated $7.2 billion annually, computer games producers $3.1 billion, cinema filmmakers $2.3 billion, and recording labels $1.3 billion.[11]

Public Policy

Intellectual property rights raise two major questions for public policy. First, whether a country benefits from offering only weak IPRs depends on its own level and pace of development. Capable domestic firms want IPRs of their own to enhance their revenue productivity. Also, they can benefit from knowledge spillovers from foreigners' intellectual properties—especially from subsidiaries of foreign multinational enterprises—and hence favor national IPR properties that attract foreign subsidiaries. In the 1990s dozens of countries strengthened their IPRs. Along with their expected developmental benefits, though, there is no denying that IPRs bring large static international redistributions of wealth. The United States is the biggest winner, Brazil and Canada the biggest losers. (Japan, interestingly, is a large loser.) Second, IPRs pose a case for collective action among nations, so that the benefits spilled abroad by one country when it strengthens its IPRs tend to be offset by spills from other countries tightening theirs. An international agreement on Trade-Related Aspects of Intellectual Property Rights (TRIPS) came into force as part of the World Trade Organization (discussed in Chapter 13). It set minimum standards for national IPRs and mandated mechanisms for their enforcement. It caps a large number of narrower international agreements—bilateral agreements promoted by the United States and regional trading agreements such as the North American Free Trade Agreement (Chapter 14).

Counterfeit Goods

A contentious issue of intangible property rights is the counterfeiting of trademarked goods. A trademark is a valuable intellectual property because it establishes a maker's mark or guarantee of the design or performance of the trademarked good. The consumer unaided by trademarks must either make greater investments in testing or inspecting potential purchases or take more chances on the performance of the good purchased. It is estimated that counterfeit goods account for 5 to 7 percent of all merchandise entering into international trade. China is the origin of nearly two thirds of these goods. China has lately shown great skill at producing manufactures that are well made to foreign buyers' specifications. The counterfeiter lives by these same skills. The maker of fakes may be an independent local enterprise or a firm under contract to a

---

[11]Most information contained in this section is drawn from Keith E. Maskus, *Intellectual Property Rights in the Global Economy* (Washington, DC: Institute for International Economics, 2000).

foreign importer or marketer, perhaps even making unauthorized sales of the very same trademarked goods that it produces under license. The counterfeiter's skills are devoted to making its goods indistinguishable from genuine trademarked goods for the buyer.

Indistinguishable is not the same as functionally equivalent—the counterfeit automobile part may fail in half the time of a genuine one, and the counterfeit pill may contain none of the genuine drug's active ingredient. The counterfeiters' prowess increases steadily. Devices or designs developed by the trademark owner to make genuine goods harder to imitate are themselves promptly imitated, and some fakes are close enough that the trademark owner must resort to scientific testing to tell which is which. The counterfeiters also have honed their skills at getting their fakes into distribution channels overseas, where complaisant distributors (with a cut of the counterfeiter's handsome profit) may intermingle them with genuine merchandise.

Trademark owners make significant expenditures running down counterfeiters and urging governments to prosecute. They also devise market strategies to repel fakes, such as a Yamaha motorcycle model designed to be made and sold cheaply in China—cheaply enough to leave little or no profit margin for the faker.

The Chinese government, appreciating its manufacturers' profits from successful fakes, at first took a very relaxed attitude toward punishing counterfeiters. As Chinese production skills have rapidly improved, however, native manufacturers have developed their own brands and stocks of customers' goodwill. The national interest thus swings away from turning a blind eye to local fakers. Similarly, approximately 92 percent of computer software used in China is said to be pirated, and the government became aware that a local computer software industry would never develop under those conditions. This change in national interest is furthered by China's accession in 2005 to the WTO, which commits it to adhere to the rules mentioned previously, including the enforcement of intellectual property rights.[12]

12.5 Summary

International trade helps make national markets competitive when the number of domestic producers is small. This gain can occur whether the noncompetitive domestic producer faces import competition or has a comparative advantage and exports to competitive foreign markets. Either way, the gains from curbing monopoly are a dividend atop the usual gains from trade for a small country.

Conversely, a country also can gain if its export activity enjoys monopoly status, either alone or in collusion with other producers. The OPEC cartel annexed enormous monopoly profits, although these were ultimately limited by the existence of substitute energy sources, competition from independent oil producers, and the incomplete cooperation of cartel members. International commodity agreements, even with the ostensible goal of stabilizing rather than raising prices, have nonetheless usually collapsed from attempts to hold the price above a market-clearing level in the short run.

---

[12]Carol Matlack et al., "Fakes!" *Business Week* (February 7, 2005): 54–64.

A nation can extract available monopoly profits on its exports either by letting its national monopolist do the job or by setting an optimal tax on competitively produced exports. The former method has the disadvantage that the monopolist also imposes an undesirable loss on domestic consumers. When it shares monopoly power with a few other producers, its first objective is to collude with them for maximum joint profits (as with OPEC). If this proves infeasible, the government may be able to nudge the home producer into a more profitable position in the international oligopoly. Symmetrically, a country can increase its welfare when sellers of its imports enjoy some monopoly power. A tax on imports may cause the monopolist to reduce its price, or policies can be used to shunt business toward a competing domestic oligopolist (whose excess profits *are* part of the national income).

Dumping is a form of price discrimination between a competitive foreign market and a less competitive domestic market. One might expect importing countries to welcome the practice, but instead it is generally restricted for being unfair to domestic producers.

The market rivalry between Boeing and Airbus has its counterpart in the wrangling between the U.S. and E.U. governments over each other's subsidies to its national firm. This rivalry is owing to the "winner-take-all" structure of this industry (very high fixed costs and a steep learning curve affecting production costs).

Intellectual property rights (IPRs)—patents, copyrights, trademarks—allow producers to cover the costs of their investments in technological and cultural innovations and consumers' goodwill. This benefit comes at the cost of monopoly pricing of outputs embodying their IPR. These monopoly profits cause a conflict between countries that are big generators of IPRs (United States) and those that make large payments abroad for the use of others' IPRs (Brazil). Nonetheless, more and more countries see their interests best served by awarding strong IPRs.

China, a fecund and skillful producer of counterfeit goods, finds its interests shifting toward enforcement of trademarks as its own manufacturers grow skillful in producing high-quality trademarked goods that attract fakes.

CHAPTER PROBLEMS

1. The effect of import competition on a domestic monopolist was illustrated in Figure 12.1 in terms of general equilibrium. It can be illustrated equally well in terms of the standard graphical treatment of the monopolist in partial equilibrium. Draw this diagram, indicating the closed-economy monopolist's output and price determined by the intersection of its marginal revenue and marginal cost curves, and then show what happens when it is confronted by a fixed world price for its output.

2. Economists discussing the feasibility of international commodity-price stabilization agreements have pointed out that price stabilization is easier if the commodity can be stored at low cost. Why should that be so?

3. A country can exert its monopoly power over an export good either by organizing its competitive producers into a single monopoly seller or by imposing an export tax that

corresponds to the monopoly's profit-maximizing markup of the export price over its marginal cost. Which policy yields the higher level of welfare, and why?

4. Suppose that a nation could tackle a monopoly over imported goods either by persuading the World Court to transform the monopoly into a competitive industry or by banning imports of the monopoly's goods and giving the business instead to a domestic monopolist. Could the latter policy increase the nation's welfare? Why would it be inferior to the former?

5. A trademark gives a legal monopoly over the brand name of a product. Controversies arise because counterfeits of trademarked goods are sold in international trade. Suppose that a Taiwanese counterfeit of a Swiss watch is imported to the United States and sold at a low price; it may or may not be equivalent to the Swiss product in physical quality. How is U.S. economic welfare affected by the practice? What difference would it make if the trademark's owner were American rather than Swiss?

6. In the case of Boeing versus Airbus, evaluate the effects on welfare of the policy chosen by the United States in its dealings with Boeing and with the European Union.

7. A foreign manufacturer of a differentiated good is considering whether or not to export it to the United States. The manufacturer has a monopoly at home, but in the U.S. market it faces close competition and would have to sell at a price lower than the one that maximizes profits in its home market. Nonetheless, such export sales would be profitable for it. However, if it charges different prices at home and abroad, it is sure that its U.S. sales agency will be penalized heavily under U.S. antidumping laws. Explain why the manufacturer might choose, under those circumstances, not to export to the United States at all.

8. In 1988 the Ivory Coast, producer of a third of the world's cocoa, was upset by the decline of the world price from $3.00 to $1.50 a kilogram over the preceding two years. That fall had resulted from heavy planting of cocoa trees in the late 1970s. The president of the Ivory Coast announced that his country would sell no cocoa at a price less than $2.00 a kilogram. Other cocoa-producing countries, however, were clearly willing to sell their available supplies at the world market price. Assume that cocoa supply is fixed (in the short run) and that marketwide demand elasticity is one (that is, world sales must be reduced by 1 percent to effect a 1 percent increase in price). What fraction of its crop must the Ivory Coast hold off the market to make $2.00 the equilibrium world price? What fraction must it withhold if the elasticity of demand is only one half?

SUGGESTIONS FOR FURTHER READING

Bhagwati, Jagdish, and Hugh T. Patrick, eds. *Aggressive Unilateralism* (Ann Arbor: University of Michigan Press, 1992). Experience with retaliation and strategic trade policy.

Gilbert, Christopher L. "International Commodity Agreements: Design and Performance," *World Development,* 15 (May 1987): 591–616. Review of recent experience.

Goldstein, Andrea E., and Steven M. McGuire. "The Political Economy of Strategic Trade Policy and the Brazil-Canada Export Subsidy Saga," *The World Economy*, 27 (April 2004): 541–566. Another case study of governments' rivalry over duopolistic aircraft firms.

Griffin, James M., and David J. Teece. *OPEC Behavior and World Oil Prices* (London: Allen & Unwin, 1982). OPEC as a cartel.

Krugman, Paul R., ed. *Strategic Trade Policy and the New International Economics* (Cambridge, MA: MIT Press, 1986). Summarizes theoretical research.

Lawrence, Robert Z., and Charles Schultze, eds. *An American Trade Strategy: Options for the 1990s* (Washington, DC: Brookings Institution, 1990). Debate over strategic trade policy for the United States.

Maskus, Keith E. *Intellectual Property Rights in the Global Economy* (Washington, DC: Institute for International Economics, 2000). Thorough treatment of national and international interests in intellectual property rights.

Mutti, John, and Bernard Yeung. "Section 337 and the Protection of Intellectual Property in the United States: The Complainants and the Impact," *Review of Economics and Statistics*, 78 (August 1996): 510–520. A potentially legitimate form of import restriction: excluding imports that violate domestic firms' patents, copyrights, and trademarks.

APPENDIX

International Duopoly and National Strategy

The following is a simple formal analysis of the model used by most researchers to identify a country's opportunity to gain from profit-shifting. Suppose that the home firm (H) produces output Q while its foreign rival (F) produces Q^*. They do not collude with each other but make their decisions independently. Specifically, each selects the quantity of output that it expects will maximize its profits on the assumption that the other's quantity is given and unaffected. Each has the same average unit costs, which are independent of its output (no scale economies or diseconomies).

Their behavior is illustrated in Figure 12.A.1, which shows the foreign firm's output on the horizontal axis and the domestic firm's on the vertical axis. The device used to derive the market equilibrium is a *reaction function,* constructed as follows: Consider H's choice of output, given whatever quantity F has decided to produce. If F were producing nothing, H would maximize profits by producing the output that maximizes monopoly profits from the world market. This is indicated by Q_M on the vertical axis. Now suppose instead that F had chosen to produce the competitive world output. The best response of H is to produce no output (point Q_C^*). When F selects any quantity that lies between nothing and the world competitive output, H's best responses will lie along the line between Q_M and Q_C^*. This is H's reaction function.

FIGURE 12.A.1

Possible Equilibria with Home and Foreign Duopolists

Duopolists might reach a Cournot equilibrium (*K*), or government may help the home duopolist to attain the more profitable Stackelberg equilibrium (*S*).

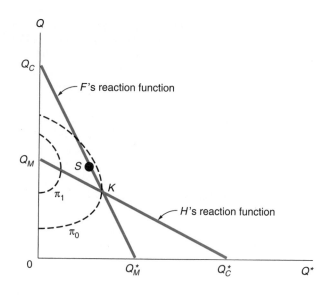

So far the discussion has not explained *F*'s choice of output, only explored its consequences for *H*'s output. Constructing *F*'s reaction function is exactly symmetrical with constructing *H*'s. If *H* was producing the world competitive output, Q_C, *F* would choose to produce nothing; if *H* was producing nothing, *F* would select Q_M^*. *F*'s reaction function is the line connecting these two points. The industry equilibrium output for this duopoly is indicated by point *K*, where the two reaction functions intersect. This is called a *Cournot equilibrium*. It has the property that each duopolist is producing its most profitable output, consistent with the output choice made by the rival. Each makes some profit because (it can be shown) the industry output is less than the world competitive output. It is also greater than the world monopoly output, so the duopolists together make less profit than would a world monopolist.

To understand the government's options for profit-shifting, we must consider the firms' profits more closely. *H* makes the maximum possible profit if production lies at Q_M, with *H* producing the world monopoly output and *F* producing nothing. Points farther to the right along *H*'s reaction function yield lower and lower profits, going to zero at Q_C^*. Consider some profit level arbitrarily lower than the world monopoly profit. It could be attained at some point on *H*'s reaction function, but also by other pairs of duopolist outputs not lying on the reaction function. Those points would lie on a locus such as π_1, which can be shown to have the shape illustrated in the figure. π_1 is called an *isoprofit locus* because every point on it yields the same profit. An important property is that at its intersection with *H*'s reaction function it is tangent to a line perpendicular to the horizontal axis; indeed, that property defines the reaction function itself.

Now consider *H*'s profit at the Cournot equilibrium, which lies on isoprofit locus π_0. Notice that a stretch of *F*'s reaction function lies within π_0, meaning that if *H* selected a higher output than that corresponding to the Cournot equilibrium (but not too much higher), not only would *F* reduce its output but *H*'s profits would increase.

Should *H* now seize this new strategic opportunity, it maximizes profit by committing to select an output that corresponds to point *S* on *F*'s reaction function. When *H* takes the initiative and picks its best point on *F*'s reaction function, the result is known as a *leader-follower* or Stackelberg equilibrium. Although *H*'s profit is higher at *S* than at *K*, the opposite holds for *F*; the meek do not inherit the earth.

With this apparatus in hand, we return to the question of public policy toward international duopoly. *H*'s profit is part of the home country's national income; *F*'s is not. Therefore, some points lying above *K* on *F*'s reaction function have the clear potential for increasing the home country's welfare. Profit is shifted from the foreign to the domestic duopolist, and home consumers also gain (because total output increases and price falls). The question is, what can the home government do to achieve this result? In the Cournot model, as noted in the text, a subsidy can have this effect. What determines whether equilibrium *K* or *S* materializes? Economic theory has no general answer to this because it depends on assumed perceptions of the market rivals. There has been much interest, however, in the possibility that government might make some binding commitment, such as a subsidy to *H*'s research and development spending, that would effectively shift *H*'s reaction function upward (increase the output it selects given any output of *F*) and make the Cournot equilibrium coincide with point *S*.[13]

---

[13]Barbara J. Spencer and James S. Brander, "International R&D Rivalry and Industrial Strategy," *Review of Economic Studies,* 50 (October 1983): 707–722.

CHAPTER 13

Trade Controls in Practice

How prevalent are government restrictions on international trade? How have these restrictions evolved over time? Why do they change when they do? In Chapter 11 we suggested that trade controls should be considered an act of public choice. Here we explore the ups and downs of actual trade restrictions in the United States. Actually, make that downs and ups. The United States and its major trading partners have undertaken a long collaborative effort to lower the general level of restrictions. However, the very success of this process bred a reactive swing toward *managed trade*, in which lowered tariffs are replaced by other types of restrictions to shelter important (and politically powerful) industries.

13.1 Tariffs: Levels and Trends

Without doubt, tariffs and other governmental restraints on trade have curbed international specialization and reduced world economic welfare. It is known, for example, that regions of the United States, trading freely with one another, are far more specialized in production than independent industrial nations of comparable size.[1] We consider the long-run pattern in the United States, then refer briefly to broader patterns.

Makers of public policy in the United States were little impressed with the virtues of international trade until the last six decades. As Figure 13.1 shows, the American tariff through much of the nineteenth century averaged 40 percent or more on dutiable imports. It reached its high point in 1932 as a result of the Smoot-Hawley Act of 1930, then began a substantial decline that was caused in part by American participation in the multinational tariff reductions. The average duty paid on *total* imports declined even more than did customs revenue on dutiable imports as duty-free imports (often raw materials) became more important. The decreased reliance on tariffs as a source of federal governmental revenue was striking. Customs revenues, now less than 1 percent of the federal government's budget receipts, were 89 percent in 1821 (when they were the only tax that was easy to collect).

The history of tariff legislation is fascinating for its insights into the process of public decision making. Early in the nineteenth century, America became a high-tariff country mainly for two reasons. One was acceptance of the infant-industry argument that tariffs actually would raise real income by promoting economic development. The other

---

[1]John McCallum, "National Borders Matter: Canada–U.S. Regional Trade Patterns," *American Economic Review,* 85 (June 1995): 615–623.

FIGURE 13.1

Long-Run Trend in U.S. Tariffs

Average duty collected on dutiable imports was high until the 1930s, then fell sharply. Average duty on total imports has fallen more because a larger proportion of imports has become duty-free.

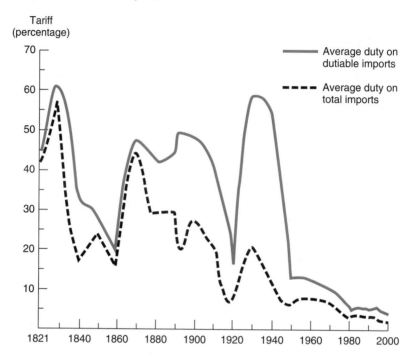

reason was nationalism and a collective distaste for things British, notably imported British goods. Throughout the nineteenth century, changes in the tariff reflected shifts in regional political strength—the manufacturing states in the Northeast benefited from tariffs while the primary-product exporters of the South suffered. The Civil War swung the power balance decisively toward the manufacturers and enshrined a high tariff for the rest of the century.

The process that brought this drastic reduction of average tariffs for the United States has worked for other industrial countries as well. Industrial countries' average tariffs on manufactures are now typically just a few percent. They tend to be very low for differentiated goods and for the products of science-based industries, higher and more variable in mass production industries, and highest for labor-intensive products and some processed natural resources. This pattern is close to the one seen in U.S. tariffs, analyzed in Chapter 11. Whatever the political mechanism that has produced this sectoral pattern, it seems common to most of the industrial countries.

If many manufactures coast past the tariff collectors in industrial countries, agricultural produce is not so lucky. The following data show the size of the advantages over foreign producers conferred on domestic farmers by the United States, Japan, and most European countries (members of the European Union):

	Wheat	Sugar	Beef
United States	40.7%	68.4%	9.0%
Japan	99.7	69.7	61.9
European Union	31.0	32.8	43.5

These figures encompass the combined effect of tariffs and other direct restrictions on imports, plus subsidies given to domestic farmers.[2]

13.2   Multilateral Tariff Reduction

What accounts for the *90 percent* drop in U.S. tariffs between the early 1930s and the present day? The answer to this question lies in the policy change that accounted for half of the decline—a program initiated by the United States, whereby nations join in simultaneous reductions of their tariffs.

Evolution of the Trade Agreements Program

In the face of mountainous tariff rates imposed by the Smoot-Hawley Act of 1930, it was no wonder that the U.S. share of world trade dropped from 16 to 11 percent in the next five years. The world total also declined as international trade shriveled in the face of the Great Depression of the 1930s. The combined effect on U.S. exports of the depression and of retaliatory increases in other countries' tariffs prompted a major shift in trade policy in 1934. Congress authorized the president to negotiate agreements with foreign trading partners to lower tariffs hampering American exports. In return, U.S. tariffs would be cut on selected goods exported by the partner. The president could offer to cut the rates of duty set by the Smoot-Hawley Act up to 50 percent. By 1940 the United States had entered into bilateral trade agreements with twenty partners, thereby establishing a ritual for these accords.

If the tariffs reduced by the agreement were not offsetting some specific failure of the market, their reduction should have increased world welfare. Did they also increase the welfare of each participating country? How were they consistent with the setting of tariffs through a process of political choice? One possible answer comes from the role of tariffs in extracting monopoly profits from international trade (the optimal tariff). If the tariff-cutting importer is large enough to influence its terms of trade, or if it merely *thinks* it gives benefits to foreigners by reducing its tariff, the reciprocal trade agreements make some sense. A tariff reduction now raises the world price of the imported good to the exporter's benefit. The size of this benefit depends on the initial volume of trade (as well as on the size of the tariff concession). This terms-of-trade

---

[2]U.S. Department of Agriculture estimates for 1982 to 1987. Summarized by Joachim Zietz and Alberto Valdes, "The Growth of Agricultural Protection," in Takatoshi Ito and Anne O. Krueger, eds., *Trade and Protectionism* (Chicago: University of Chicago Press, 1993), pp. 115–143.

gain to the exporter is a loss to the importer unless its tariff was higher than optimal. The importer might not gain from cutting a single tariff (even though the world does), but the importer's terms-of-trade loss on one product can be offset by its gain as an exporter when a reciprocal agreement is signed. In addition, these gains and losses are more likely to cancel each other out if each party cuts tariffs on the same initial volume of trade.[3]

That all parties might gain through reciprocal tariff-cutting agreements is consistent with the political economy of tariffs. Suppose that a country has high tariffs in place, the result of the political processes described in Chapter 11. The government knows that national economic welfare has been impaired; it would like to reduce the tariffs and raise national welfare but cannot get rid of tariffs one at a time. Therefore, it proposes a broad tariff-cutting agreement with its trading partners, which will benefit most of its export producers as well as consumers generally. Enough voters might perceive that they benefit significantly from the package that a majority coalition forms in favor of it. Both this process of forming coalitions in favor of freer trade and the monopoly-tariff story probably help explain the success of reciprocal trade agreements.

The bilateral trade agreements program was running out of steam by the end of the 1930s. It was replaced in the postwar period by a process of multilateral bargaining in which countries increasingly bundled together their offers to reduce tariffs. Ultimately, the cuts took the form of consent on a common, across-the-board reduction in all tariffs. In the so-called Kennedy Round of multilateral tariff bargaining, completed in 1967, the chief industrial countries agreed on a target of a 50 percent across-the-board cut in all tariff rates. Each country could propose to except some of its tariffs from the cut, presumably where unacceptable injury to domestic industries would result. Bargaining proceeded over the size of the exceptions lists, rather than over the 50 percent cut itself. The participants agreed to weighted-average tariff cuts of approximately 35 percent, making the Kennedy Round the most sweeping tariff reduction since these rounds began.

The Tokyo Round (1973–1979) continued the procedure of the Kennedy Round but also tackled the thorny problem of nontariff barriers to trade. In the tariff-cutting part of the agreement, the industrial countries agreed to reduce their tariffs, on average, by another third over an eight-year period. Most of the major countries lowered individual tariffs by a formula that shaves more off those tariffs that were higher initially.

The Uruguay Round (1986–1994) featured another general reduction in tariffs of 40 percent. Also, the industrialized nations agreed to eliminate tariffs among themselves on the products of ten important industries, including construction equipment, farm machinery, furniture, medical equipment, paper, pharmaceuticals, and steel. Overall, it brought trade-weighted average tariffs in the developed economies down from 6.3 to 3.9 percent; in the developing countries from 15.3 to 12.3 percent; and in the

---

[3]Elements of monopoly and product differentiation in individual product markets probably contribute to causing the prices of a country's imports net of tariff to rise when a tariff is reduced. A study of U.S. tariff reductions in the 1950s found that nearly half of the price effects took the form of increased external prices, rather than reduced prices (including tariff) to domestic consumers. See M. E. Kreinin, "Effect of Tariff Changes on the Prices and Volume of Imports," *American Economic Review,* 51 (June 1961): 310–324.

Eastern European economies in transition from 8.6 to 6.0 percent.[4] The Uruguay Round's major accomplishment, however, was to attack other types of restrictions and distortions. It encouraged uniform national laws protecting intellectual property—patents, copyrights, and trademarks. These property rights mitigate an important market failure: If the pharmaceutical firm's new wonder drug or the writer's literary creation can be freely copied by others, their incentive to invest in developing these products is greatly reduced. However, a nation heeding the welfare of its own consumers lets them copy foreigners' intellectual property (see Section 12.4). The Uruguay Round made a start at reducing the heavy protection given (by various devices) to agriculture, textiles and apparel, and certain other sectors. These were to be converted to tariffs—which makes the severity of the restrictions plain to hapless consumers—and were then supposed to undergo reduction at targeted rates.

The Doha Round was launched in 2001 with an agreement focused on the developing countries, which had by and large sat out the earlier rounds—maintaining heavy protection of their domestic industries but also facing heavy protection in markets for their agricultural products and labor-intensive manufactures. Approximately 150 nations including many developing countries are involved in the Doha Round discussions, and the agenda is slanted toward their interests. The industrial countries agreed to discuss the protection and subsidies given to their farmers, and services (business services, international air travel) are on the agenda. Agricultural subsidies of the developed countries have been the most bitterly contested issue. They are extensive in the United States, and indeed subsidies for agricultural exports have been a central policy of the European Union. At the end of 2005, the United States and European Union formally reached a conditional commitment to end these subsidies by 2013. The firmness of that commitment is unclear, and in any case export subsidies (cotton from the United States, dairy products and sugar from the European Union) are a small part of the protection given industrial countries' agriculture (production subsidies, price supports, high tariffs on imports).[5] Also included in Doha's agenda are national policies that can indirectly distort trade—either by their use or disuse: competition policy, government procurement, and so on.

World Trade Organization

One of the Uruguay Round's accomplishments was to create the World Trade Organization (WTO), an international organization. It replaced the General Agreement on Tariffs and Trade (GATT), a network of international agreements that had been in place since 1947–1948. Apart from managing the trade agreements program, the WTO's key function is to provide a framework for resolving alleged violations of GATT/WTO rules. Suppose that country *A* raises a tariff that it had previously committed in a trade

---

[4]United Nations, *World Economic and Social Survey, 2001*, Table V.2. Average tariff rates understate their true values when they are weighted by the imports that get in over the tariff rather than the imports that are kept out.

[5]Also promised in late 2005 was duty-free access to industrial countries' markets for most exports from a group of the world's poorest countries. This pledge discriminates against the *next* poorest countries and runs counter to the commitment to nondiscriminatory reduction in trade barriers.

agreement to "bind." Exporting country B believes its interests are harmed and lodges a complaint. If conciliation efforts fail, a panel of other WTO members hears the two parties' cases. The disputants are obligated to work out a solution within the framework of the panel's decision, although there is a formal appeals procedure. A solution to the dispute might involve A cutting its tariff on some other product(s) imported from B. If A declines to "make good," as a last resort the WTO panel authorizes B to make specific retaliatory increases in its tariffs on goods imported from A. The key feature of this procedure is that via their WTO membership, countries are committed to accept whatever agreement is worked out before the WTO panel. This averts escalating tit-for-tat rounds of trade restriction that were commonplace in the 1930s. In the WTO's first decade of operation, the plaintiffs (both the United States and others) won quite large proportions of the cases they brought. In a majority of cases, the losing defendant brought itself into compliance. The WTO is "democratic" in the sense that all countries have equal standing before the organization; in 2001 developing countries filed approximately 80 percent of the complaints. Their typical small sizes, however, limit their ability to use the WTO's procedure of retaliating. They are unlikely to find in their imports goods in which they have the market influence to inflict significant punishment on the defendant.[6]

The United States has been a fairly active plaintiff before the WTO, and sometimes a defendant as well. In 2000 the United States was charged by the European Union with maintaining an illegal export-subsidy arrangement in the form of a tax exemption for income from export sales booked through an organization called a Foreign Sales Corporation (FSC). With the United States facing WTO-authorized sanctions on $4 billion of U.S. exports, Congress passed a bill ending the FSC arrangement—but recasting the tax benefit in another form. The European Union agreed to withhold retaliation until 2001 when the WTO was expected to rule on this new arrangement. The United States in 1999 had assailed E.U. policies that favored bananas imported from the Caribbean over imports from U.S.-owned plantations in Central America. The United States imposed 100 percent tariffs on $300 million a year of European products (mostly luxury goods) until the dispute was resolved (2001).

Gains from Trade Liberalization

Trade liberalization is always controversial. With the progressive reduction of tariffs by the industrial countries, some observers have begun to wonder whether the real welfare gains warrant the political effort involved. To discuss this and other problems of quantifying the welfare effects of trade controls, economists commonly rely on the partial-equilibrium analysis displayed in Figure 10.1. A number of economists have estimated the deadweight losses expected to be recovered from the Uruguay Round.[7]

---

[6]Anne O. Krueger, ed., *The WTO as an International Organization* (Chicago: University of Chicago Press, 1998); Jeffrey J. Schott, *WTO 2000: Setting the Course for World Trade* (Washington, DC: Institute for International Economics, 1996).

[7]Summarized by Alan V. Deardorff, "Economic Effects of Quota and Tariff Reductions," in Susan M. Collins and Barry P. Bosworth, eds., *The New GATT: Implications for the United States* (Washington, DC: Brookings Institution, 1994), pp. 7–27.

The estimated increases in world gross domestic product range from 0.7 to 1.3 percent; these are permanent gains expected to be realized by the time the changes are fully phased in. Although not every country necessarily gains (there can be terms-of-trade losses from reducing tariffs for countries that exploited monopoly power), no losers are identified, although the gains range from 0.6 percent for the least developed countries to 2.1 percent for some European countries that are not yet members of the European Union. As we expect from Figure 10.1, the proportional increase in trade (5 to 20 percent expected) is larger than the expected increase in welfare.

13.3 Devices for Special Protection

The rounds of trade agreements seem to benefit from a welcome mechanism of "political economy" within the participating countries, in the form of coalitions of the majority of a country's economic interests that obtain shares of the gains from removing trade restrictions. Symmetrically, we rarely see countries choosing to tighten their trade restrictions across the board. We do, however, observe particular import-competing interests that hang on to protection, or even gain more of it, evading the general move toward freer trade. Some instances apparently involve plain and simple political clout strong enough to evade the majority coalition. Others exploit special forms of protection that permit concealment of the true incidence of protection from the general public.

We start with some descriptive statistics that expose the magnitude of the problem. Although successive rounds of largely across-the-board tariff cutting took place under the GATT and WTO, many countries were providing special deals for selected import-competing sectors.

One study[8] estimated that the proportion of countries' trade subject to nontariff barriers had risen as follows:

	1966 (%)	1986 (%)
United States	36	45 (12)
European Union	21	54 (19)
Japan	31	43 (14)
All developed countries	25	48 (16)

Although the increase shown here is evident on any reckoning, the levels may prompt an overpessimistic interpretation. Nontariff barriers are defined to include both nontariff measures specifically intended to restrict trade and various domestic policies (technical or health and safety standards, border tax adjustments, etc.) that incidentally impose extra costs on foreign suppliers. If only the former restrictions are considered, the lower figures shown in parentheses apply for 1986. These are still high, however, and they have increased greatly.

---

[8]Sam Laird and Alexander Yeats, "Trends in Nontariff Barriers of Developed Countries, 1966–1986," *Weltwirtschaftliches Archiv,* 126, 2 (1990): 299–326.

Theory of Quantitative Restrictions

A quantitative restriction (QR) has basically the same effect as a tariff, yet its incidental differences are important. The similarity is shown when we turn back to Figure 10.1. Given domestic demand and supply and the world price P_w, a tariff of P_t imposed by the government will shrink the volume of imports from KL to MN. This outcome could equally well be obtained by the government's allowing only MN imports to enter the market. With the market purely competitive, this volume of imports will allow the market to clear only at the price P_t. The Uruguay Round obligated countries to perform this calculation and reveal to consumers the tariff-equivalents of the highly restrictive quotas in use for agricultural products. E.U. quotas have the effect of tariffs of 178 percent on dairy products, 152 percent on sugar. United States tariff-equivalents for these products are 93 and 92 percent, respectively. Japan imposes a tariff-equivalent of 326 percent on dairy products and 152 percent on wheat.

Given this basic equivalence, tariffs and quotas can have important differences in practice. Some of these depend on what happens to the revenue representing the gap between the foreign and the domestic price. The tariff generates government revenue equal to area 3 in Figure 10.1. When imports are limited by quota, ordinarily no tariff is collected, yet the privilege of buying abroad at P_w and selling domestically at P_t is obviously valuable. The government might auction off licenses to import to the highest bidder. Competitive bidding by would-be importers would wipe out this potential profit and hand the government the same revenue as if it levied the tariff equivalent. Conversely, the government might give away import licenses to the domestic importers, in which case they capture the proceeds. If the government awards the licenses to foreign exporters, their country gains the scarcity rent. Note that the world welfare cost of the restriction is the same in each case. The method of administering a quota only redistributes income.[9]

Voluntary Export Restraints

A special type of quantitative restriction now in widespread use is the so-called voluntary export restraint (VER), whereby the importing nation induces the exporting countries to curtail their shipments. This device simply hands over area 3 to the exporters, who are expected to charge the price that clears the market for the restricted volume of sales. It is equivalent to an export tax. A VER obviously maximizes the cost to the importing country's real income of restricting imports. We will speculate on why the choice of VERs has been so popular among importing-country governments.

Another difference between tariffs and quotas arises if the domestic industry is not perfectly competitive because a tariff and quota that let in the same volume of imports have different effects on the domestic price. We consider the case of a single, monopolistic domestic seller, shown in Figure 13.2. The world price is P_w, the monopoly's marginal cost is MC, and domestic demand is D. A quota of Z causes the

---

[9]At one time the Japanese government was financing its entire international commercial intelligence network (JETRO) from its cut of the profits of importers licensed to bring quota-restricted bananas into Japan.

FIGURE 13.2

Tariffs and Quotas with Monopoly

The same quantities of imports Z would enter with an import quota of Z and a tariff of $P_t - P_w$. However, the fixed quota gives the monopoly more power, with the domestic price raised to P_z, higher than the tariff that would let in the equilibrium volume of imports Z.

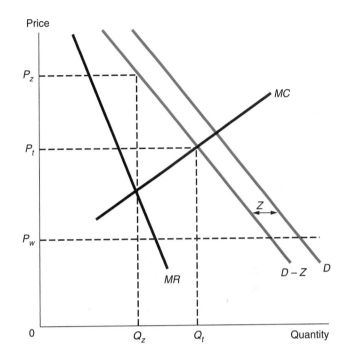

monopoly to select its most profitable output by ceding this much of the market and maximizing its profit on the residual demand of $D - Z$. MR is marginal revenue corresponding to this residual demand. The monopoly selects a quantity of output Q_z that equates marginal revenue to marginal cost and commands a price of P_z. Now we must find the tariff that makes Z the equilibrium volume of imports. The country (and the monopoly) are price-takers on the world market, so that a tariff raises the world price inside the country but still leaves the monopoly facing an exogenous price. If that price were P_t, the monopoly would select output Q_t, which equates MC to the constant marginal revenue indicated by the tariff-ridden world price P_t. Q_t and Z satisfy domestic demand at P_t, which is therefore an equilibrium price. P_z considerably exceeds P_t. The intuition behind this difference is that the quota caps the amount of imports and leaves the monopoly facing a (net) domestic demand that is imperfectly elastic. The tariff, however, allows the quantity of imports to expand when the monopoly raises its price.

Management through VERs

The United States seldom imposed quotas unilaterally on imports of manufactured products, but it has used VERs extensively to regulate the quantities of goods that exporters ship to the United States. The VERs began with an informal agreement with Japan in 1957 to limit exports of cotton textiles in order to protect that U.S. industry. It proliferated into the Multifiber Arrangement, an umbrella agreement covering bilateral quotas negotiated among a number of exporting and importing countries. We pick up the story of the Multifiber Arrangement in the next section.

The restrictiveness of VERs can be assessed by calculating export-tax equivalents of these quotas, like the import-tax equivalent of a quota administered by the importing country. Hamilton, however, used the even more direct method of obtaining data from Hong Kong on the market values of quota allocations. That is, what competitive Hong Kong producers will pay for the privilege of exporting a given lot to a particular destination should equal the difference between their costs and the goods' sale value at the destination. He found tariff equivalents of 27 percent for the United States and 14 percent for the European Union; added to the conventional tariffs that continue to apply to these imports, the combined trade barriers are 56 percent for the United States, 33 percent for the Union.[10]

VERs have been very popular with the United States and other developed-country governments. Besides the thicket surrounding the Multifiber Arrangement, by 1986 at least 99 additional VERs covered other exports (steel, electronics, footwear, transportation equipment). Why their popularity? The answer probably lies in the bargaining power possessed by foreign exporters. When a large customer such as the United States raises its trade barriers, it certainly inflicts short-run losses on foreign exporters and may permanently worsen their terms of trade. Exporting countries often have ways of retaliating, such as restricting imports from the United States. In addition, the United States may appear to be less protective if foreigners "voluntarily" restrain their exports than if U.S. quotas are imposed.

One outcome of the Uruguay Round was an agreement that members should convert their quantitative restrictions and VERs into standard tariffs. It is unlikely, though, that the last of them will be seen any time soon.

13.4 Special Protection in Action

The U.S. government like other trading nations keeps open several channels for domestic interest groups seeking protection. One (the escape clause) provides temporary relief for domestic industries that suffer owing to protection reduced in one of the GATT rounds. Another (countervailing duties) permits a domestic industry to obtain increased tariffs to offset subsidies provided to their foreign competitors. In this section we examine several in detail.

Antidumping Measures

Clearly the most important form of special protection is antidumping policy. On its face this policy addresses price discrimination (see Section 12.3) by exporters who charge lower prices abroad than at home. Specifically, it provides relief to domestic producers competing with imports sold at a lower price than in the exporter's home market. The

---

[10]Carl Hamilton, "An Assessment of Voluntary Restraints on Hong Kong Exports to Europe and the USA," *Economica*, 53 (August 1986): 339–350.

relief available to the injured producers takes the form of a tariff equal to the difference between the imports' sale price and their "normal" selling price abroad. A producer's charge of dumping triggers an investigation by both the U.S. Department of Commerce to determine whether dumping is taking place and by the U.S. International Trade Commission to determine whether the domestic industry is thus being harmed. If each agency makes a positive finding, duties to offset the dumping margin (which are imposed provisionally as soon as the determination of dumping is made) become permanent subject to periodic review. Another possible outcome is a negotiated agreement with the exporters to raise their prices. In the abstract the effect of dumping on welfare is equivalent to that of price discrimination. That practice in general can either raise or lower the welfare of all parties affected by it. In the country that is "dumped on," the gain from lower prices to consumers exceeds the loss of rents to competing producers.

Antidumping (AD) cases have become the main systematic route to obtaining special protection in the United States and other countries as well. They sprang into prominence in the 1980s, with 29 countries adopting antidumping legislation from 1987 to 1997. The most prolific sources of antidumping complaints have been import-competing producers in the United States, the European Union, Canada, New Zealand, and Australia. The United States has generated more AD cases than any other country (in excess of 700 from 1980 to 1994).

This epidemic of AD cases may seem surprising. Economic theory says that only monopolies undertake price discrimination. Are that many monopolies sending dumped goods across the high seas? The administration of U.S. (and probably that of other countries) AD laws provides the answer to that question. Exactly how does the Department of Commerce measure the exporter's home price? It may take the price in the exporter's home market or in another export market. Or it may determine "fair value," a constructed price that would cover all fixed and variable costs and provide a generous profit margin.[11] The Commerce Department is free to use information provided by the plaintiff. The fair value is obviously prone to a stacked outcome, and indeed the Commerce Department almost always finds dumping (98 percent of cases brought from 1995 to 1998) regardless of the method used. A finding that dumping occurs may rest on only a single export transaction, which could well be a random event. The International Trade Commission usually finds injury (83 percent of 1999 to 2002 cases). Another procedural quirk is important. Approximately a fourth of U.S. AD cases are settled informally, through some agreement between the import-competing plaintiffs and their competitors abroad (perhaps with the U.S. government lending a hand). The natural outcome of such an agreement is a price set collusively by the firms or some sort of VER.

Let us consider the outcomes of U.S. AD cases. Over a fifteen-year period, an estimated quarter of them were settled before reaching a decision. The remaining three quarters divided about equally between rejection and imposition of an AD tariff. In the cases that proceed to a decision, the levels of the resulting AD duties are high. The

---

[11]Constructed fair values are used mainly although not only in cases involving economies in transition, where many prices may make no claim to market-clearing status.

average "fair value" in the exporters' home market exceeds the export price by more than 40 percent. In the cases that involve an AD duty actually levied (that is, the domestic industry is found to be injured), the average duty is approximately 16 percent (but 50 percent or more in a fifth of the cases).[12] Imports naturally retreat: When the AD duty exceeds 50 percent, imports on average decline 73 percent, and their prices (after paying duty) rise 3 percent. The quarter of cases that were withdrawn also call for scrutiny. These include so-called innocent cases such as the plaintiff deciding that its case looks too weak. However, a substantial number of withdrawals stemmed from agreements being reached between the plaintiffs and accused import suppliers to adhere to higher (collusive) prices in the U.S. market. Sometimes the government intervened, so the result was essentially a VER. One study found that the restriction of the offending imports was as large in these privately settled cases as when the AD duty was formally imposed.

Considerable evidence indicates that firms act strategically to game the AD system. The exporter who loses an AD case finds its export demand shrunk, and its best move is to raise its export price. When the AD duty is reviewed by the regulators, it will likely be reduced. In fact, AD duty rates in force on average clearly shrink over time, indicating that the exporters reduced their price discrimination margins. A study of AD plaintiffs in the European Union found that they raised their price-cost margins by as much as 50 percent on average following an AD case. Governments also behave strategically in deciding whether the domestic industry has suffered injury. When the U.S. International Trade Commission decides whether the complaining domestic industry has suffered injury, it looks over its shoulder at the likely wrath the United States will encounter with the foreign government in question. Thus a finding of injury is less likely when the exporting country is a large importer of American goods and when it has shown itself prone to take trade disputes to the WTO or its GATT predecessor.[13]

The annual welfare cost to the United States of the AD policy has been placed at $4 billion, an impressively large loss although smaller than the $10 billion charged to the next trade restriction we examine, the Multifiber Arrangement.

Multifiber Arrangement

The Multifiber Arrangement (MFA) was a broad system of quantitative restrictions and tariffs that regulated trade in textiles and apparel. It was terminated at the beginning of 2005, but its experience conveys important lessons about quantitative trade restraints in labor-intensive and footloose industries. The main lesson that comes from the MFA's experience is the tangle of regulations that results from attempting to manage trade in a footloose industry by quantitative measures. The MFA's origin in 1961

---

[12]Thomas J. Prusa, "On the Spread and Impact of Anti-Dumping," *Canadian Journal of Economics,* 34 (August 2001): 5911–6611.

[13]Bruce A. Blonigen and Jee-Hyung Park, "Dynamic Pricing in the Presence of Antidumping Policy: Theory and Evidence," *American Economic Review,* 94 (March 2004): 134–153; Josef Konnings and Hylke Vandenbussche, "Antidumping Protection and Markups of Domestic Firms," *Journal of International Economics,* 65 (January 2005): 151–165; Bruce A. Blonigen and Chad P. Bown, "Antidumping and Retaliation Threats," *Journal of International Economics,* 60 (August 2003): 249–273.

lay in the U.S. industry's pleas for relief from competition with imports from Japan, which were growing rapidly despite long-standing high U.S. tariffs (Japan's period of rapid economic development was just beginning). One quantitative restriction led to another. Restrictions were placed on (say) cotton fabric for men's shirts, raising the price of that fabric in the U.S. market. That increase squeezed the shirt-making sector of the U.S. apparel industry, leading to a quantitative restriction on imports of men's cotton shirts from Japan.[14] Other countries (Hong Kong, say) could now profit by exporting cotton fabric and shirts to the United States. To sustain the higher U.S. prices owing to the restrictions on Japan, Hong Kong fabric and shirts came under quantitative restrictions. Higher prices on cotton fabric and shirts raised the profitability of selling fabric and shirts of manufactured fibers to the United States, so the quantitative restrictions were extended to those as well. Some manufacturers moved their plants from Japan and Hong Kong to countries not yet under control. Finally, the low-cost Asian producers, fenced off from the U.S. market, tended to increase their exports to European countries, which then imposed their own quantitative restrictions. This chain of substitutions led to a labyrinthian international network of quantitative controls, the MFA.

How were the benefits and costs of the MFA divided? The exporting countries were handed the task of administering the quotas, so they (or their citizens) picked up the rents created by the quotas (area 3 in Figure 10.1). Furthermore, U.S. domestic producers' share of the U.S. apparel market is fairly small, so that the welfare loss to U.S. consumers was offset only by a small gain picked up by the protected domestic producers (area 1 in Figure 10.1).

A given country's textile production might flourish not because it offers the world's lowest cost location but because it has not yet been snared in the network of controls. In recent years the organization of the U.S. apparel market has changed, with large retailers ordering their stocks of goods electronically and expecting delivery of their orders within a short period of time. This innovation gave a large advantage to producers located near the United States—Mexico and the Caribbean. Those countries' quotas came to be strongly constraining while a number of Asian export categories no longer filled their quotas.

The MFA may be gone, but the urge of industrial countries to protect their textiles and apparel industries has not. The MFA's end naturally coincided with a large increase in exports from China's efficient and low-cost factories; the value of imports of Chinese textiles and apparel to the United States in the first half of 2005 was 58 percent greater than in the first half of 2004. The U.S. government imposed quantitative restrictions on several categories of Chinese goods. This action was not without some legal basis; when China joined the WTO, an agreement was made that other countries could impose safeguards if Chinese goods caused "material injury" to their domestic industries.

---

[14]This effect of protection on vertically related production processes is of quite general importance. The incidence of a tariff on a finished good depends on the elevation of its selling price. If tariffs are also imposed on inputs into the finished good, its producers' variable costs are elevated and its *effective protection* is reduced. Another way to look at effective protection is that what matters is the effect of tariffs on a production process's slice of value added—the difference between the selling price and the cost of intermediate inputs.

Conversely, trade restraints applied to particular exporters violate basic WTO principles of nondiscrimination. In response, China itself first quintupled the (small) export tax it had imposed on these goods, no doubt as a political signal but also to ensure China a cut of any trade restriction rents. However, China soon removed the export tax and pursued a more aggressive posture regarding the U.S. quotas. The United States has continued to make more textiles categories subject to quotas. European countries have joined the procession, placing their own import quotas on Chinese textiles. The MFA takes on zombie properties—dead but not departed.[15]

U.S. Sugar Market

The next case deals with the protection of sugar producers in the United States. The special protection of sugar typifies the protection given to several other agricultural sectors in the United States and other countries (notably the European Union). These agricultural products share several properties unattractive to producers. The price in the international market for sugar is highly variable, making its production a risky business. The risk is compounded by the product's high fixed cost, especially cane sugar.[16] The sugar refiners with whom sugar growers deal are large concentrated firms. Sugar producers evidently can present themselves as deserving a governmental helping hand. The United States imports approximately 15 percent of the sugar it consumes. Domestic production is substantial—cane in the South, beet in the Upper Midwest—a distribution that bolsters the sector's political influence. The protection regime thus can take the simplest form. The government sets a target domestic price. In recent years it has been approximately double the world price (20 cents vs. 10 cents a pound). The government estimates the quantity of imports that, marketed along with domestic sugar, would make 20 cents a pound the market-clearing price.[17] The quota has been imposed by means of a two-step tariff—a low rate for sugar quantities up to the target import quantity, 150 percent of the world price for quantities greater than the quota. It is a valuable opportunity to export sugar bought or produced at 10 cents to the United States to sell at 20 cents. The United States chooses to dole out this rent to each of some forty sugar-producing countries, by giving each the right to supply some share of the quota quantity. The annual cost to U.S. consumers (deadweight loss plus the rent transferred to foreign and domestic producers) is approximately $11 billion.

The U.S. sugar protection regime can usefully be compared to that of the European Union, which produces enough beet sugar to make it a net exporter. E.U. authorities' target support price, higher than that of the United States, is maintained by assigning each producer a (maximum) quota for its sales on the domestic (E.U.) and foreign markets. The target price much exceeds the world price, so the European Union dips

---

[15]Both under the MFA and recently, quotas were set to constrain the rate of growth of imports rather than their level. This feature suggests that the importing government sought to limit its domestic industries' rates of contraction rather than ensuring its output level.

[16]An identical product can also be obtained from sugar beets, which involve less fixed costs.

[17]The government protects itself against forecasting errors by means of the right to impose marketing quotas on U.S. sugar processors, limiting what they can sell if imports are larger than expected.

heavily into general tax revenue to subsidize these exports. (The United States as a net importer avoids any cost to the government.) In late 2005 the European Union announced a major change in its sugar policy—the end of its export subsidy. The domestic price would remain much higher than the world price, and government funds would assist the exit of approximately a third of E.U. sugar producers. This policy change, to be phased in over four years, responded to the intense criticism of the export subsidy by WTO members.

We have seen that schemes of special protection always generate incidental distortions and costs. The largest single input cost for cheap candy is sugar, and U.S. producers (once concentrated around Chicago) have moved much of their production to Canada and Mexico, where they can buy sugar at the world price. Although the United States and Canada have joined in a free-trade area that eliminates nearly all tariffs between the two countries (see Chapter 14), a special provision keeps the Canadians from buying 10-cent sugar on the world market and reselling it to Americans at 20 cents. Finally, a large share of the U.S. domestic sugar market has been taken by a new product, high fructose corn syrup. Produced from domestic corn, it is a perfect substitute for sugar in beverages (although not in other uses). Its production costs less than the government-supported domestic sugar price but more than the world price (and cost of efficient cane-sugar producers). These excess production costs add to the total economic costs of the sugar price-support scheme.

13.5   Prospects for Special Protection

What can we say about the prospects for the world trading system, taking these patterns of general and special policy into account? The extensive reduction of tariffs through the GATT/WTO has inevitably squeezed a number of import-competing sectors. Some of these do (and others do not) enjoy sufficient lobbying and rent-seeking resources to hang on to their protection. So the existence of some loopholes such as antidumping and countervailing power is inevitable in the behavior of the public-choice process. The coalitions of beneficiaries from freer trade that have sustained the successive GATT/WTO rounds have probably been as successful as one could hope on limiting the amount of entrenched special protection. Furthermore, although some of the special protection is deeply entrenched and long lived, much of it (MFA, for example) has functioned to limit the rate of expansion of an efficient supplier's exports rather than permanently stalling or repelling it.

In Chapter 14 we consider another general force for trade liberalization: free-trade areas (generally, preferential trading arrangements) among selected country groups. Although these conflict in important ways with the central principles of the GATT/WTO arrangements, they are on balance complements in pursuit of the general goal of removing inefficient protection.

Some entrenched forms of protection will hang on indefinitely. The protection of low-skill labor-intensive industries is a nearly universal policy preference. A study of nontariff barriers in forty-one countries found them higher where real wages per worker were low and declining, and tariffs (although high) were capped by commitments under GATT.[18] A social preference for helping the poor may be at work, and helping them through tariff-created job opportunities may be a more attractive policy than handing over cash. Indeed, the ongoing debate over trade policies has become entangled with several other policy objectives in the disputes over globalization. Protection warranted by a preference for helping the poor is at least a coherent economic policy position. Less coherent is the antiglobalists' proposal that the United States should restrict imports from developing countries to punish the corporations operating in those countries for not treating their employees more generously. Another tangle has arisen between trade policy and environment policy. Standard economic analysis (Chapter 10) regards environmental quality as a costly good, like any other. The possibility then arises that some producing locations incur lower (marginal) costs of pollution abatement than others, opening up an opportunity for mutually beneficial trade with other countries afflicted with higher marginal abatement costs. Some environmentalists, however, take the position that economic activity in general harms the environment, and we should be seeking less rather than more real output from the economy, for the sake of the environment. Standard economic analysis points out that greater potential economic output offers us the opportunity to consume more public and private goods of all sorts, including (if we choose) heavy spending on improving the environment.[19]

13.6   Summary

Over the last sixty years, tariffs imposed on manufactured goods by the United States and other industrial countries have been reduced greatly, but governmental restrictions still substantially restrict world trade (for example, the exchange of primary products for manufactures between the industrial and developing countries). Little of the remaining protection has any obvious justification in terms of economic models of national welfare.

The industrial countries' success in reducing tariffs came through a series of reciprocal reductions initiated by the United States in the 1930s. These reductions were broadened into multilateral and increasingly across-the-board reductions. The recent Uruguay Round went far, not only in lowering tariffs but also in protecting intellectual property rights, seeking to curb special protection, and improving the governance of international trading relations. Two interpretations are offered of how multilateral tariff reductions were able to raise world economic welfare. The reductions might have effected a truce in nations' mutually destructive efforts to improve their terms of trade. Or the multilateral reductions might have aided domestic political alliances able to defeat protectionist interests in import-competing industries.

---

[18]Jong-Wha Lee and Philip Swagel, "Trade Barriers and Trade Flows across Countries and Industries," *Review of Economics and Statistics,* 79 (August 1997): 372–382.

[19]For an attempt to clarify the anti-globalization position, see Alan V. Deardorff, "What Might Globalism's Critics Believe?" *The World Economy,* 26 (May 2003): 639–658. The analysis of trade and environmental quality is developed in Section 14.6.

Running counter to the multilateral reduction of tariffs, countries have retained avenues through which certain industries could seek protection. It often comes in the form not of tariffs but quantitative restrictions and voluntary export restraints (VERs). A quantitative restriction can be stated as a tariff equivalent, but its magnitude is more easily concealed from the consumers who are harmed by it. VERs are in essence export taxes collected by the producing country, a transfer from the importer's treasury.

Restrictions on dumping (price discrimination in favor of the importing country) have become a highly popular form of special protection. U.S. producers enjoy easy access to them because the government almost always finds that dumping has occurred and usually that the domestic industry has suffered injury. An antidumping duty on one source of imports often causes other countries to expand their exports. This (likely inefficient) shift of production was a major drawback of the Multifiber Arrangement (MFA), a recently lapsed network of quantitative restrictions on textiles and apparel. In 2005 strong signs indicated that the network of controls was being reassembled. The U.S. sugar industry gets protection by means of a target domestic price picked by the government, which then imposes a quantitative restriction on imports. The quota imports plus the domestic production supplied at the target price should yield a market equilibrium.

CHAPTER PROBLEMS

1. You are asked to estimate the welfare cost of a tariff imposed in a market like that depicted in Figure 10.1. You are told that imports were $100 million before the tariff and $50 million (valued at world prices) after it was imposed; the tariff rate is 20 percent. Can you estimate the approximate loss in national welfare because of the tariff?

2. Suppose the trade restriction described in the preceding problem were related not to a tariff but to a voluntary export restraint. Then what would the welfare loss be?

3. Exporting countries sometimes administer export restraints by creating transferable rights to export to the restricted market, which domestic manufacturers can trade among themselves. Suppose you learn that Hong Kong shirtmakers pay $20 for the privilege of exporting a dozen shirts to the United States and the shirts have a world market value of $60. What conclusions can you draw about the tariff equivalent of the export restraint?

4. You are a domestic manufacturer persuading the government to protect your industry. You can secure either a 20 percent tariff or a fixed quota that is equivalent to it. You expect the market to grow in real terms. Will that fact affect whether you choose the tariff or the quota?

5. Governments in some European countries are believed to make substantial use of industrial subsidies to avert the contraction of some industrial sectors. What difference does it make for national welfare whether the subsidy applies to domestic sales, export sales, or both? Governments do not find it easy to raise tax revenues to finance such subsidies. Does that fact help explain why such governments would rather subsidize an industry's export sales than its sales in the domestic market?

6. In 1986 the United States and Japan reached an agreement setting minimum prices on Japanese semiconductor chips sold by Japanese manufacturers not just directly to the United States but also to all other export markets. At the time, producers in both countries had considerable excess capacity because demand was unexpectedly low. Explain why chip prices in Japan plummeted and why chip buyers in developing countries started to obtain their supplies from intermediaries and brokers in Japan.

7. The United States manages its protection of the sugar industry without (ordinarily) restricting domestic producers' production. The European Union in its similar arrangement finds such restrictions necessary. Why the difference?

SUGGESTIONS FOR FURTHER READING

Bhagwati, Jagdish, and Hugh T. Patrick, eds. *Aggressive Unilateralism* (Ann Arbor: University of Michigan Press, 1990). Papers on the U.S. campaign to force other countries to reduce trade barriers in the name of fairness.

Destler, I. M. *American Trade Politics*, 4th ed. (Washington, DC: Institute for International Economics, 2005). Detailed account of political decision making on trade.

Feenstra, Robert C., ed. *The Effects of U.S. Trade Protection and Promotion Policies* (Chicago: University of Chicago Press, 1997). Sophisticated studies of various specific sectors and issues involved in U.S. trade policy.

Irwin, Douglas A. *Free Trade under Fire*, 2nd ed. (Princeton: Princeton University Press, 2005). Clear treatment of U.S. policies for general and special protection.

Krueger, Anne O. *Economic Policies at Cross-Purposes: The United States and the Developing Countries* (Washington, DC: Brookings Institution, 1993). Reviews of the many ways in which U.S. trade and aid policies affect the developing countries.

———. *The Political Economy of American Trade Policy* (Chicago: University of Chicago Press, 1996). Extensive studies of protection in eight U.S. industries.

———, ed. *The WTO as an International Organization* (Chicago: University of Chicago Press, 1998). Essays on policy issues related to WTO.

Ostry, Sylvia. *The Post–Cold War Trading System* (Chicago: University of Chicago Press, 1997). Long view of policy development in the international trading system.

Schott, Jeffrey J. *WTO 2000: Setting the Course for World Trade* (Washington, DC: Institute for International Economics, 1996). Early evaluation of WTO's performance.

CHAPTER 14

Preferential Arrangements and Regional Issues in Trade Policy

C hapter 13 reviewed the mutual efforts of countries to remove impediments to trade. Their efforts have been largely global (though with the developing countries and formerly centrally planned economies participating only recently). A key principle underlying these efforts has always been to avoid discriminatory trade restrictions—a country's imports from A pay higher duties than comparable imports from B. Another approach to liberalizing trade, however, flies in the face of this no-discrimination or "most favored nation" rule. That is the formation of preferential trading arrangements by which a group of countries eliminate trade restrictions among themselves while maintaining them against the outside world. Such arrangements are clearly discriminatory, but they are thought to have offsetting virtues, and hence were allowed as an exception to the antidiscrimination rules of the General Agreement on Tariffs and Trade.

14.1 Regional Preferences and Regional Trade

Preferential arrangements have long been around, but they have recently enjoyed a spectacular boom. Japan is now the only major country that does not belong to at least one such arrangement. With a few exceptions these groupings are regional, involving countries with common borders, sharing a continent, and often with common ties of culture and language. Casual observation might suggest that these "neighborly" arrangements serve diplomatic rather than economic objectives. Whether or not that perception is accurate, trade flows themselves have a strong regional bias: Neighbors tend to trade heavily with one another, so the restrictions that they maintain or (instead) remove will be important for the efficiency of world trade.

The models of trade presented in Parts I and II of this book all focus on explaining the pattern of a country's trade—why, as David Ricardo first posed it, England exports cloth to Portugal and imports wine. The trading world consists of many countries, however, and we also need an explanation of why, say, England exports its cloth to Portugal whereas Japan ships its cloth exports to Australia. The amounts and composition of these bilateral trade flows require some new modeling considerations. Suppose we want to explain the total volume of trade (exports plus imports) flowing between various pairs of countries. The volume should clearly depend on two factors. The first is the economic size of each country. The larger a country, the more numerous the types and the greater the volumes of goods it is capable of supplying, and the more goods it does demand when it spends its income. The bilateral trade flow should increase with both partners' economic sizes; indeed, it is likely to increase with the product of their sizes. Second, the bilateral flow should decrease with the cost of transportation between them. Transportation costs depend on the mode used (ocean shipping, for example, is cheap but slow). They increase with distance, although less than proportionally. There is a fixed cost of loading the freight at the source and unloading it at the destination, and a variable cost that increases with the distance shipped. This fixed-plus-variable cost structure explains why total shipping costs increase less than proportionally with distance.

These propositions have led economists to employ the empirical "gravity model," which explains bilateral trade flows very well indeed. Frankel summarized his extensive investigation with the following equation.[1] It is a statistical regression equation in which T_{ij} is the sum of exports and imports flowing between countries i and j, GNP is the gross national product of country i or j, pop is the population of country i or j, and $dist$ is the distance between the two countries. Logarithms are taken of all the variables, so that the coefficients quoted in the equation (which are typical results of estimates based on different time periods and different groups of countries) can be interpreted as elasticities with which the dependent variable responds to a change in each exogenous variable:

$$\log(T_{ij}) = 0.7 \log(GNP_i GNP_j) + 0.3 \log\left[(GNP/pop_i)(GNP/pop_j)\right] - 0.7 \log(dist_{ij}).$$

This equation has several important implications. If both countries' GNPs increase because of an increase in population, so that GNP/pop remains constant, bilateral trade will increase 70 percent as fast as the product of the two countries' GNPs. If both GNPs increase related to an increase in productivity, however, trade will increase proportionally with the product of the two GNPs (because $0.7 + 0.3 = 1$). Among countries, then, there is a tendency for those of a given size with higher incomes per capita to trade more extensively with each other than do poorer countries with the same total size. The role of product differentiation in trade (Chapter 8) explains why this might happen: Wealthier consumers buy more types of goods, including more foreign "specialties," and not just the bread-and-butter necessities likely to be produced at home. Finally, trade declines with distance but less than proportionally, which is consistent with the fixed-plus-variable cost structure of transportation charges.

In sum, regional trade is indeed important, and regionally organized preferential trading arrangements hence may matter a great deal for economic welfare.

---

[1]Jeffrey A. Frankel with Ernesto Stein and Shang-Jin Wei, *Regional Trading Blocs in the World Trading System* (Washington, DC: Institute for International Economics, 1997), Chapter 4.

14.2   Welfare Effects of Trade Preferences

Preferential arrangements may be assumed to involve the elimination of tariffs and nontariff barriers on trade among member countries in all or nearly all goods and services. Even with these restrictions, several important distinctions need to be made. The following terms have come into fairly standard usage:

1. *Free-Trade Area.* Members eliminate tariffs among themselves but keep their original tariffs against the outside world. The North American Free Trade Agreement (United States, Mexico, Canada) provides an example.

2. *Customs Union.* Members not only eliminate all tariffs among themselves but also form a common tariff against the outside world.

3. *Common Market.* Members proceed beyond a customs union to eliminate restrictions on movements of factors of production among themselves. The European Union began as a customs union but is committed to achieving a full common market.

4. *Economic Union.* Members proceed beyond a common market to unify their fiscal, monetary, and socioeconomic policies. Belgium and Luxembourg formed an economic union in 1921.

These preferential arrangements are analytically interesting—and complex—because they both distort and liberalize trade. Trade is freed because some flows face lower restrictions than before. However, trade is also distorted because goods coming into a member country pay different tariffs depending on their origin—the external tariff if from outside the group, a preferential or zero rate if from a partner. The distortion amounts to price discrimination—that is, charging or (in this case) paying different prices for identical goods at a given market location. Because preferential arrangements have this two-faced character, they can either improve or worsen the economic welfare of their members or of the world as a whole.

Trade Creation and Trade Diversion

Jacob Viner first showed that preferences could either improve or worsen allocation, by leading either to *trade creation* or to *trade diversion*.[2] Suppose that A and B form a customs union, leaving C (the rest of the world) outside. Previously, A inefficiently produced part of its requirements of good x at home behind its tariff wall. Partner B is the most efficient producer of x and the sole world exporter. When A abolishes tariffs against B (and all the necessary market adjustments have taken place), A's inefficient x industry is partly competed down as A's imports from B expand. Trade has been *created*. The gains are the same as if A had eliminated its x tariff completely.

---

[2]Jacob Viner, *The Customs Union Issue* (New York: Carnegie Endowment for International Peace, 1950), Chapter 4.

FIGURE 14.1

Welfare Effects of Trade Creation

PP' is the partner-country supply curve. Tariff removal cuts domestic price from $0T$ to $0P$, expands imports to $M'N'$, and raises welfare by areas $2 + 4$.

Because trade creation works just like the removal of a tariff against all foreign suppliers, the analysis of it is a replay of Figure 10.1. In Figure 14.1, A's demand and domestic supply curves for x are shown as D and S, respectively. Suppose that x is produced in B under conditions of perfectly elastic supply, so that an unlimited quantity is available at price $0P$. A's external tariff is set at the rate $PT/0P$. Before the customs union was formed, the supply function for imports after payment of tariff was TT'; thus A produced amount $0M$ of its consumption $(0N)$ of x, importing MN from B. Elimination of the tariff against B now makes PP' the relevant import supply schedule and causes consumption to expand to $0N'$, imports to expand to $M'N'$, and domestic production to shrink to $0M'$. The four numbered areas in the diagram measure the welfare gain. A's consumers of x enjoy a gain in surplus measured by the whole area $1 + 2 + 3 + 4$, but not all of this is net gain to the country. Area 1 formerly was profit to A's protected producers of x, so this gain to consumers is offset by the loss to producers. Likewise, area 3 formerly represented tariff revenue collected by A's government that is now lost when the preference is given to B. If the government was spending its revenues on useful things, such as parks and schools, there is no presumption that any net social benefit derives from (in effect) giving the revenue measured by area 3 to the consumers of x; therefore, it is assigned no net welfare significance. Two triangles remain, both measuring net gains to A. Area 2 formerly represented part of the real cost of securing $0M$ of domestic production; it is assumed that those resources are now put to other uses, so the extra surplus measured by 2 is a net benefit. Likewise, area 4 represents a pure gain in consumers' surplus not subject to any offset. The net benefit is areas $2 + 4$.

Trade diversion can occur for another good, y, if A's consumption of y was formerly supplied by outsider C and if C is the world's most efficient producer. Suppose that B can also produce y—not as efficiently as C, but efficiently enough to undercut C in A's market when C pays A's tariff but B does not. In Figure 14.2 A's demand for y

FIGURE 14.2

Welfare Effects of Trade Diversion

P_B indicates pretariff supply price in partner country and P_C pretariff supply price in rest of the world. Tariff preference lowers internal price from T_C to P_B. Welfare loss occurs if area 5 exceeds area 4.

appears as DD. Suppose C's supply of y is perfectly elastic at a domestic cost (and price) of P_C; likewise, B can supply y at the higher constant cost (and price) of P_B. Before the customs union is formed, A imposes an ad valorem tariff on imports of y equal to $P_C T_C / 0 P_C$ or $P_B T_B / 0 P_B$—they are the same. A would buy from the less costly source after paying the tariff and thus would import $0 M_C$ at price $0 T_C$. Forming the customs union allows B's exports of y to enter duty-free, and A's consumption expands to $0 M_B$. Areas in the diagram are labeled to illustrate the significant effects on welfare. Once again, lowering a tariff (even preferentially) allows a gain to A's consumers of y (areas $3 + 4$). The meanings of these areas match their counterparts in Figure 14.1: Area 3 shows tariff revenue formerly collected on imports from C, its loss offsetting the congruent gain in consumer's surplus; and area 4 depicts the remaining pure gain in consumer's surplus that is not subject to any offset. A loss occurs, however, in the form of area 5. Areas $3 + 5$ measure the total tariff revenue formerly collected on imports $0 M_C$. This revenue now is lost to A's government, and the part denoted by 5 is instead paid by A's consumers to the higher-cost producers of y in B. It is pure social loss.[3] A *net* welfare loss from trade diversion occurs if area 5 is larger than area 4. It need not be, of course: The loss from switching to a less efficient source of supply could be more than offset by the gain from reducing a distortion of consumers' spending. If a supply curve for domestic producers had been incorporated in Figure 14.2, another gain would have resulted because protected output falls when the domestic price declines from $0 T_C$ to $0 P_B$ (an area of gain like 2 in Figure 14.1). Also, notice that welfare increases in the trade-creation case, even if the former tariff sheltered no protected production. (The welfare gain is just area 4.)

---

[3] No welfare gain for country B is involved because the resources drawn into the production of y presumably were engaged in other activities where their value productivity was just as high.

Net Gains or Losses?

What can be said about the net influence of these forces? If *A* and *B* consume and trade many commodities, is it possible to establish any presumption that a union leads to net gains? An accurate evaluation depends on the trade pattern for every good. Nonetheless, some rough tests can suggest whether trade creation (which must raise welfare) is likely to prevail over trade diversion (which may or may not). For trade creation to predominate, the economies of *A* and *B* should be *actually competitive* (before the union) but *potentially complementary* (after it comes into effect). Trade-creation gains are greater when protected production is reduced because protective tariffs have made the output pattern of the two economies look similar before they join in a customs union. Thus they should appear actually competitive. However, each member must also be the most efficient producer of goods protected and inefficiently produced by its partner—this condition guarantees trade creation rather than trade diversion.

Other simple tests for a union's welfare significance can also be used. Higher initial tariffs mean greater potential benefit. Higher initial tariffs enlarge area 4 in Figures 14.1 and 14.2. If a common external tariff is formed (as in a customs union), the chances of benefit are enlarged if the new common tariff is lower than the previous individual ones—making trade diversion less likely, reducing the distance $P_C T_C$ (in Figure 14.2) and lowering the probability that P_B will fall within it. A larger preferential arrangement is more likely to be beneficial. This condition is obvious if we imagine enlarging a hypothetical customs union until it includes nearly all the world's economic activity. The less production taking place outside, the more likely is the union to include the most efficient producer; trade diversion is therefore curtailed.

Another factor affecting the balance of welfare effects works in a different way. When countries form a customs union, they must decide on a common external tariff. Of the many possible methods, they usually choose to average the members' previous national tariff rates. Because of the averaging process, there is less variation of the resulting rates among the different classes of imported commodities than existed in the previous national schedules. That reduced dispersion is itself a source of welfare gain because the relative prices of commodities inside the tariff wall are then less distorted from those in the world at large. If each of two products is subject to a 10 percent tariff, both domestic prices are raised 10 percent, and the relative price is the same as in the outside world.[4] Thus, the more tariff schedules are homogenized, the greater the welfare gain.

Distribution of Gains and Losses

One more building block is needed for this analysis of the effects of tariff preferences. The technique for measuring the welfare effects of trade creation and diversion set forth in Figures 14.1 and 14.2 assumes that the country's terms of trade remain unchanged. That assumption is built into the perfectly elastic supply of imports. If the

---

[4]Both theory and evidence on this point were developed by Pan A. Yotopoulos and Jeffrey B. Nugent, *Economics of Development: Empirical Investigations* (New York: Harper & Row, 1976), pp. 352–355.

partner's terms of trade with the outside world change, or if one member's terms of trade with its partner change, redistributions of real income take place. The total effect of preferences on any one country's welfare is the sum of effects related to trade creation or diversion and any redistribution stemming from changed terms of trade.

You might suppose that a country would pick its partners for a preferential arrangement so that it would get a terms-of-trade gain, or that the members would select each other to extract a gain from the rest of the world. Countries seem to pick their partners primarily on political grounds, not from economic motives or calculations. Still, whether intended or not, a preferential arrangement is likely to change its members' terms of trade with the outside world and with each other. The possible results are diverse, but consideration of preferential arrangements in the context of general equilibrium reveals some likely outcomes.

Start with a question that has a simple answer. Suppose that A and B decide to form a preferential arrangement, excluding C (the outside world). What tariff structure will maximize their joint gain from the venture? In the absence of any special market distortions, A and B should clearly adopt free trade with each other and levy the optimum tariff against the outside world (that is, the tariff that maximizes their joint monopoly gain). Even if each member's tariff was optimal before, from its own viewpoint, each gains from the expansion of previously restricted trade with the other. If their individual tariffs had not been optimal, a further gain accrues from switching to the optimal tariff. Notice that their joint monopoly power in trade could well be greater than that of each separately. If they are sole exporters of a product and each previously calculated its optimal tariff by taking the other's as given, further monopoly gains should accrue to them from setting a higher external tariff jointly. Should A and B form a free-trade area without changing their former external tariffs, the elimination of internal tariffs is still apt to improve their terms of trade with the outside world. The only requirement is the occurrence of some trade diversion. The switch of trade away from C, as A and B adopt preferences and increase their mutual trade, has the same effect on C as if A's and B's demand curves for imports from C were shifted inward. (Conversely, the preferential arrangement gains from trade creation with no corresponding loss for the outside world.[5])

14.3 Preferential Arrangements in Practice

Customs unions and free-trade areas have been popular in the last several decades among both industrial and developing countries, and more than a hundred now exist. The primary ancestor was the European Union (formerly the European Community), formed in 1957 by France, (West) Germany, Italy, the Netherlands, and Belgium-Luxembourg. By 1995 fifteen Western European nations belonged, with only Norway

---

[5]This terms-of-trade improvement was analyzed and estimated by Howard C. Petith, "European Integration and the Terms of Trade," *Economic Journal,* 87 (June 1977): 262–272. He suggested that Germany's terms of trade may have improved as much as 7 percent, France's as much as 9 percent, when the European Union was initially formed.

and Switzerland staying out. Upon the collapse of the Soviet Union's empire of centrally planned economies, its former members sought E.U. membership, and in 2004 a group of them were admitted—Estonia, Latvia, Lithuania, Poland, Czech Republic, Slovakia, Hungary, and Slovenia. The initial members moved to eliminate tariffs among themselves by staged reductions completed in 1968, and 1992 was the target year for removing many remaining types of nontariff restrictions. The E.U. members also adopted a Common External Tariff, its rates set (with some exceptions) by averaging the rates for individual products that previously appeared in the member nations' tariff schedules.[6]

Trade Creation and Diversion in the European Union

We saw that the welfare effects of a preferential arrangement are related to trade creation and diversion. Consider the effect of the European Union on international trade in manufactures. It would be insufficient simply to look at the sizes of trade flows—external and internal—before and after the European Union was formed. They changed in response to forces other than tariff rates, such as the growth of national incomes. One reasonable way to estimate trade creation and diversion, however, is to look at changes in the sources of supply of manufactures to the E.U. countries, as Mordechai Kreinin did.[7]

The reduction of internal tariffs resulted in trade creation that was reflected in a reduced share of each E.U. country's consumption of manufactures supplied by its domestic producers. Trade diversion was detected in the increased share of E.U. countries' imports coming from exporters in E.U. partner countries. Even without the European Union, these shares would have changed because of movements in prices and incomes that differed between the European Union and the rest of the world. Kreinin experimented with various adjustments to control for these movements; finding that none was clearly superior to the others, he suggested taking an average of their results. He concluded that, as of 1969 and 1970, the European Union had caused trade diversion of $1.1 billion, but trade creation in the amount of $8.4 billion. For another test of trade creation's prevalence, if a country had the European Union's lowest price for a line of goods before internal tariffs were removed, then it tended to gain a large share of E.U. exports to other E.U. countries by 1966 when internal tariffs were 80 percent eliminated. Tests based on the gravity model suggest that from 1970 to 1990 the E.U. members traded with each other 36 percent more than otherwise identical countries not members of the European Union.[8]

To the static welfare analysis of customs unions set forth here, and that of trade liberalization in Chapter 13, many students respond, "Is that all there is in it?" Are

---

[6]For a review of the European Union's development and prospects, see Mike Artis and Norman Lee, eds., *The Economics of the European Union: Policy and Analysis,* 2nd ed. (Oxford: Oxford University Press, 1997).
[7]Mordechai E. Kreinin, *Trade Relations of the EEC: An Empirical Investigation* (New York: Praeger, 1974), Chapter 3.
[8]Jeffrey A. Frankel et al., *The Regionalization of the World Economy* (Chicago: University of Chicago Press, 1998), p. 97.

there no gains from greater scale economies, more vigorous competition, new incentives to invest and innovate? To which the economist answers, "If you believe that markets are competitive and always pretty much in equilibrium, yes, that's all there is." If that assumption fails to hold, however, the gains from tariff reduction, whether preferential or general, may be greatly enlarged. Consider these alternative assumptions:

1. Most producers (outside the primary sector) make goods that are specialized and differentiated, so each faces a downward-sloping demand curve for its own output.

2. Elements of oligopoly may be present (especially in pre-E.U. Europe), so that producers' efforts to maintain and share out their collusive profits divert them from making major plant expansions or otherwise getting an innovative jump on their rivals.

Either of the two assumptions suffices to predict that trade liberalization (preferential or general) will induce producers to make a dash for larger-scale and more efficient plants. Under the first assumption, each individual producer foresees the possibility of enlarged export markets that will absorb a substantially increased quantity of output. Under the second assumption, collusion gets harder to sustain when tariff barriers fall, and foreign producers not in the cartel offer their wares at more competitive prices; erstwhile loyalists of the cartel abandon that ship and try instead to make their activities as efficient as possible within a larger and more competitive market.

Evidence indicates that these competitive gains occur and are important. Producers in the original E.U. countries rationalized their product lines, concentrating on what they could make most efficiently, and plant sizes were increased to more efficient scales. Productivity growth in E.U. industries reflects spillover benefits from economic growth in the aggregate, and in the same industry elsewhere in the European Union. If the output of a given industry grows 10 percent elsewhere in the European Union, apparently it will grow by 1 to 2 percent in that industry's branch within any of the core member countries without any growth at all of its inputs.[9]

Economists recognize another productivity gain from enlarging a market that depends on consumers' tastes. Consider an economy that displays all the standard competitive properties, except that each product is differentiated and potentially available in many varieties. To make a new variety available (to produce or import it), its distributor must incur a fixed cost. The larger the market, the more likely it pays to incur this fixed cost. Consumers in a larger market—a country that has joined a customs union, or simply one that has grown—will enjoy a dividend in real income.[10] These additional sources of gain from expanding the scope for unrestricted trade clearly have relevance beyond preferential trading arrangements. In Section 14.5 we report some estimates of their magnitudes.

---

[9]Riccardo J. Caballero and Richard K. Lyons, "External Effects and Europe's Integration," in L. Alan Winters and Anthony J. Venables, eds., *European Integration: Trade and Industry* (Cambridge, England: Cambridge University Press, 1991), pp. 34–51.

[10]Paul Romer, "New Goods, Old Theory, and the Welfare Costs of Trade Restrictions," *Journal of Development Economics,* 43 (February 1994): 5–38.

Despite these gains, the European Union has its less-than-rosy side. A keystone of the organization is a scheme to provide massive protection to European agriculture. This protection has imposed large costs of trade diversion, especially on Great Britain, which before joining had a relatively efficient policy toward agriculture. High food prices in the European Union have fostered excess supplies of crops that could be disposed of only through massive export subsidies, which came to squander 70 percent of the European Union's budget (now below half). These outlays financed an elaborate program of production and export subsidies. E.U. consumers bore the burden of high food prices and taxes used to finance the subsidy system. Other losers were efficient agricultural exporters (including developing countries) that were denied the opportunity to sell to the European Union, and indeed were forced to compete with subsidized E.U. exports. As we saw in Chapter 13, the complaints of these frustrated agricultural exporters were a major source of contention in both the Uruguay and Doha rounds, and the European Union finally made a commitment (of unknown firmness) to end export subsidies by 2013.

"Europe in 1992"

Although the E.U. nations long ago removed tariffs on trade among themselves, in 1988 they attracted considerable attention by agreeing to remove many nontariff restrictions—all internal economic barriers and customs posts—by 1992. In 1985 the European Commission compiled a list of three hundred remaining national nontariff restrictions on intra-E.U. trade. Some of them were no doubt erected as substitutes for the tariffs previously removed. These barriers include inconsistent product safety standards (children's toys, oxygen tanks), national differences in professional licensing requirements (for professions such as accounting); and restrictions on the entry of firms into certain sectors, such as financial services. Not the least of these barriers is so-called administrative protection—the sheer cost of documenting imported goods at the customs post: Intra-E.U. highway trucks had to file up to 75 forms to comply with border-crossing regulations.

The year 1992 came and went with some of the targeted restrictions removed but others still on the books. Energy sales and public-sector procurement resist liberalization. National governments pressed by powerful lobbies continue to invent clandestine forms of protection, such as national technical standards that imports can meet only at a cost. Even with some restrictions remaining, the economic gain merely from eliminating the administrative costs of customs frontiers to shippers and governments is large, estimated at no less than 1.8 percent of the value of goods traded within the European Union.

In 1992 the E.U. members also signed the Maastrict Treaty, committing to a prospect of long-run political unification and limited centralization of political decision making in the Union. A constitution embodying these objectives and codifying many previous agreements among E.U. members was duly prepared and submitted to the member nations for ratification. It required unanimous consent, and negative majorities among voters in France and the Netherlands appeared to leave it stranded. It is not obvious that its defeat will threaten the economic unification already achieved.

Free-Trade Agreements in North America

In 1987 the United States and Canada negotiated a free-trade arrangement. Starting in 1989, the arrangement called for removal during the following decade of all tariffs and quotas between the two countries on most categories of goods and services. The Canadians expressed concern that the U.S. government would take away—via ad hoc trade restrictions—what it gave in the agreement, and so provision was made for international dispute-settlement panels to replace U.S. courts in final appeals of administrative decisions. Although the agreement left various forms of special protection in place, it did eliminate others in each country. U.S. trade with Canada already constitutes 21 percent of total U.S. trade, and the Canada-U.S. bilateral trade flow is by far the world's largest. The geographical proximity of the two countries and the substantial levels of protection previously in force (especially Canada's) mean that this free-trade agreement could have very important effects.

The Canadian economy is roughly a tenth the size of the U.S. economy. That difference implies that Canada gets proportionally larger benefits, for two reasons. First, the established trade restrictions have caused different sets of relative prices to prevail within the two countries. Free trade will bring these prices together, but with most of the change coming in Canada's prices. As the smaller country, Canada gets the advantage of trading at an "alien" set of prices.[11] Second, when a small country protects its domestic market (and its exports are limited by foreign tariffs), it not only forgoes the usual gains from trade but also suffers because production units in some industries cannot grow large enough to exhaust the available scale economies when serving only the domestic market. Thus the combined effect of the Canadian and U.S. tariffs has been an estimated cost to Canada of approximately 6 to 10 percent of its potential welfare.[12] Over the long run, the free-trade arrangement ought to retrieve that loss. Thus, relative to the United States, Canada will experience a very large reallocation of its resources, but it will also get proportionally much larger benefits in the form of productivity increases because of greater economies of scale.

During 1992 the United States and Mexico negotiated a similar free-trade agreement; Canada and Mexico also reached a bilateral agreement, so the resulting North American Free-Trade Agreement (NAFTA) wraps around the U.S.-Canadian bilateral arrangement and links the three North American economies. The U.S.-Mexico agreement links an industrial with a large developing nation. Because the two countries have quite different factor endowments, the scope for trade diversion would seem large. In Mexico, for example, sophisticated U.S. industrial machinery is likely a better substitute for machinery from Japan or Germany than for machinery produced in Mexico—which sets the stage for trade diversion. However, the scope for inefficient diversion in U.S. imports from Mexico seems small. U.S. trade with Mexico is already very heavy compared to U.S. trade with other Latin American countries. Indeed, before NAFTA the United States already had a preferential arrangement with several Caribbean

---

[11]This point was made in the basic argument for gains from trade in Chapter 2.
[12]Richard G. Harris, "Applied General Equilibrium Analysis of Small Open Economies with Scale Economies and Imperfect Competition," *American Economic Review,* 74 (December 1984): 1018–1032.

nations (Caribbean Basin Initiative), with its own trade-diverting potential that is countered by NAFTA. And in 2005 the United States formed a free-trade area with a group of Central American nations plus the Dominican Republic (CAFTA), that put them on the same footing as Mexico.

NAFTA's Effects

There was a general consensus among early assessments of NAFTA that the net benefit to the United States would be positive but small, the effect on Mexico positive and large.[13] The evidence from aggregate trade data is hard to interpret, mainly because Mexico experienced other major disturbances around the same time NAFTA came into effect: a large unilateral reduction of its tariff protection between 1985 and NAFTA's start (1994) and a large devaluation of the peso. The share of U.S. exports going to both Mexico and Canada had been increasing since 1980 and continued to increase to the late 1990s; the same is true of imports from Mexico. This supports the theory that NAFTA creates additional trade. The shift of U.S. import sources toward Mexico coincided with a shift away from East Asia, which suggests trade diversion. A closer look, though, indicates that commodity categories in which Mexico strongly expanded its exports to the United States also saw strong expansion of Mexican exports to other countries.[14] NAFTA's political economy probably benefited Mexico by locking in economic reforms that were already under way and supporting the rapid expansion of industrial activity along the U.S.-Mexico border.

Researchers on trade creation and diversion associated with NAFTA have developed a new microeconomic approach. For two countries joining in a free-trade area, the eliminated tariffs on the goods they trade with each other are high in some cases, low in others. A greater fall of imports from third parties for high-tariff goods indicates trade diversion. A greater increase in trade between the partners in high-tariff goods suggests trade creation. Indeed, a cut of 1 percent in U.S. tariffs on Canadian goods corresponded to a 10 to 11 percent increase in imports from Canada. U.S. imports from sources other than Canada increased significantly with any cut in U.S. non-Canada tariffs, but those imports were unrelated to the preference margin of Canadian goods.[15] Thus there was no evidence of trade diversion. However, a similar approach to Mexican exports did expose trade diversion. For imports from Mexico gaining a high preference at the U.S. border, Mexico's share of U.S. imports rose 224 percent; low-preference items gained only 24 percent. Compare these figures to changes in Mexico's share of E.U. imports, which dropped 77 percent for high-preference goods and rose 64 percent for low-preference goods. Thus some Mexican exports were diverted to U.S. buyers with lower valuations than their former European purchasers.[16]

---

[13]Mary E. Burmeister, Sherman Robinson, and Karen Thierfelder, "The Impact of NAFTA on the United States," *Journal of Economic Perspectives*, 15 (Winter 2001): 125–144.

[14]Anne O. Krueger, "NAFTA's Effects: A Preliminary Assessment," *The World Economy*, 23 (June 2000): 761–775.

[15]Kimberly A. Clausing, "Trade Creation and Trade Diversion in the Canada-United States Free Trade Agreement," *Canadian Journal of Economics*, 34 (August 2001): 677–696.

[16]John Romalis, "NAFTA's and CUSFTA's Impact on International Trade," National Bureau of Economic Research, Working Paper No. 11059 (2005).

14.4 Trade Problems of the Economies in Transition

The centrally planned economies of Eastern Europe and the former Soviet Union were long studied as a regional trading group. They chose to do much of their trading with each other. Furthermore, because of both ideology and the operating methods of their planned economies, they effectively discriminated against trade with the rest of the world. Their principal trading association, the Council for Mutual Economic Assistance (CMEA), was called a trade-destroying customs union: Economic planners pursued the goal of self-sufficiency for each nation, closing off efficient trade with outside nations and generating what often appeared to be inefficient trade among CMEA members.[17] To everyone's surprise, the political regimes that kept central planning in place vanished almost overnight, leaving their stranded economic systems to find their own paths of transition toward Western-style market economies.

The Legacy of Central Planning

The managers of the centrally planned economies made no use of prices for allocating resources among activities and uses. State-owned production units were told what and how much to produce on the basis of a central plan. This plan selected a mix of final outputs—consumption goods, investment goods, military equipment, and so on—and then devolved detailed instructions for the state enterprises to deliver all the various inputs required to satisfy the planned final output. In addition to the suppression and distortion of international trade already mentioned, the system suffered from three grave defects that are being painfully removed as these economies make their transition to market organization:

1. The capacities to produce various products bore no relation to what would be the final demands for them if the planned economies' consumers were free to make their choices. Some sectors were "large" because the planners "liked" their outputs: steel and other basic materials, capital goods. At world prices, supplies of these goods would have exceeded demands.

2. Suppliers of goods and services did not bargain with their users or seek directly to respond to the customers' qualitative wishes; instead, they just produced the planners' quotas. Poorly functioning products in clunky and outdated designs were the rule.

3. The state enterprises had little or no incentive to be efficient. Labor could not be discharged, and managers could capture no personal benefit from properly maintaining plants or making them run better. Productivity hence was very low.

When the planning regimes withered away, in essence nothing worked well and nobody knew exactly what reallocations of resources would be viable. It is no wonder that outputs plunged and unemployment swelled as the transition began.

---

[17]Franklyn D. Holzman, "Comecon: A 'Trade-Destroying' Customs Union?" *Journal of Comparative Economics*, 9 (1985): 410–423.

Trade among the CMEA countries themselves was both constricted and distorted. Little effort was made to coordinate the countries' plans so as to exploit comparative advantage within the CMEA group. Trade of CMEA members with the market economies was distorted because of the necessities of central planning: This trade was regarded as a way to make up shortages of actual from planned domestic outputs, exporting for payment whatever outputs the planners felt they could currently spare. Quantity-based planning made it infeasible for the CMEA traders to quote prices in the manner of a market economy and let the world's buyers go shopping among the wares they produce. One study measured this suppression by fitting the gravity model to bilateral trade among the market economies around 1985; CMEA members' actual trade with the European Union was then only 19 percent of the level predicted for market economies with the same incomes and location.[18]

Trade Patterns Transformed

With the collapse of central planning, the administered trade among the CMEA members also collapsed, and the newly independent "countries in transition" scrambled to reorient their trade toward the market economies. In 1980, 50.3 percent of their exports (54.7 percent of imports) had been with their CMEA partners. By 1992, early in the transition, the export share had fallen to 19.1 percent (imports to 17.2 percent). Table 14.1 shows how the transition evolved. It distinguishes three groups of transition economies—the Central European and Baltic nations that subsequently joined the European Union, a group of less developed economies in Southeast Europe, and a group of former members of the Soviet Union.[19] The shift away from trading with other transition economies continued, especially for exports and especially for the more distant countries in other transition groups. The shift toward trade with the European Union kept increasing, especially for exports from the transition economies. Trade with the rest of the world behaved irregularly.

The transition economies immediately abandoned the accounting prices used in the CMEA and relied instead on Western market prices. This left some of the state-owned enterprises running heavy losses and reducing output. However, it also revealed patterns of comparative advantage. Early in the transition, economists tried to predict the sectors that would realize an advantage on export markets. They used various strategies, such as the trade pattern between the transition economies and market economies before the transition actually began. Also, they attempted (in the spirit of Heckscher-Ohlin) to identify elements in the factor endowments of the transition economies. The predictions, borne out subsequently, were that the transition economies would generally find their advantage in goods requiring much technical and engineering skill and produced efficiently at large scales. These were exactly the traits that appealed to the CMEA planners, including the emphasis on engineering and technical

---

[18]L. Alan Winters and Zhen Kun Wang, *Eastern Europe's International Trade* (Manchester, England: Manchester University Press, 1994), Chapter 2.

[19]The distribution of the trade of the former Soviet bloc nations is not shown in the table, but they are included as trading partners in the Other Transition Countries column.

TABLE 14.1

Changes in Distribution of Trade, Countries in Transition, 1995–2002 (percentages)

Country Group	Year	Own Group	Other Transition Countries	European Union	All Other Countries
		Exports			
Central Europe, Baltic states	1995	16.4	20.7	53.4	9.6
	2002	15.2	9.5	62.9	12.3
		Imports			
	1995	10.3	19.4	54.9	15.4
	2002	8.9	17.5	59.6	13.9
		Exports			
Southern, Eastern Europe	1995	10.7	12.5	54.0	22.9
	2002	9.4	7.2	64.6	18.8
		Imports			
	1995	12.3	17.6	52.2	17.8
	2002	7.8	18.7	58.4	15.0

Source: European Bank for Reconstruction and Development, *Transition Report 2003: Integration and Regional Cooperation,* Table A.4.1.1. Central European and Baltic states include Estonia, Hungary, Latvia, Lithuania, Poland, Slovakia, and Slovenia. Southern and Eastern European states include Albania, Bosnia, Croatia, Macedonia, Romania, and Serbia/Montenegro.

education. The other advantage lay in exports intensive in natural resources. Resource-intensive exports flowed because of plentiful resource stocks, obviously, but also because of the CMEA's notorious indifference to industrial pollution.[20]

The transition also has its interesting organizational side: How does a nation join the market economy when it has eschewed many tasks and functions important for flourishing in the market? These include minimizing costs, deal-making and contracting practices, development of labor resources and relations, marketing, and product design. Many Western European enterprises have subcontracted the making of parts and components to the transition economies, making use of their skills while dodging their shortcomings. Foreign direct investment by Western European enterprises has also flourished. Some foreign investors have drawn upon low-cost skilled labor for producing traditional manufactured goods and components for export; for example, the nation that produces the most motor vehicles per member of its population nowadays is Slovakia! Other multinationals serve local markets in the transition economies. These firms' proprietary assets (Section 9.3) could not be exploited in the East

---

[20]Peter Murrell, *The Nature of Socialist Economies: Lessons from Eastern European Foreign Trade* (Princeton: Princeton University Press, 1990); Thomas C. Lowinger, Mudziviri Nziramasanga, and Anil K. Lal, "Economic Transition in Central and Eastern Europe: The Consequences for Trade Structure and Trade Volume," *International Trade Journal,* 14 (Spring 2000): 53–76.

European home markets during the CMEA regime. Now, entrant multinationals find not only unserved current demand but also the prospect of rapidly growing per capita incomes and demands for diversified products.[21]

14.5   Trade and Growth: China and the Asian NICs

Although the relationship between trade and development is a vital question for all developing countries, the East Asian region provides a striking case. China is particularly in the news, but its successful development follows the experience of the "Asian NICs" (newly industrialized countries: Korea, Taiwan, Hong Kong, and Singapore) and, before them, Japan. China might be regarded as one of the economies in transition from central planning. However, the economic geography of its transition calls for viewing it in the context of its Asian neighbors.

China

Since China's modern development began in 1979, its national income has grown at a rate of 9 percent annually and its international trade has grown at more than 20 percent a year. The striking feature is that such rapid growth in a country this large has been heavily concentrated in just a few coastal provinces located adjacent to Hong Kong in the southeast part of the country. This could occur because the Chinese economy had been quite decentralized, without much internal (interregional) trade except in raw materials. Furthermore, most state-owned enterprises were locally administered. In 1984 the central government thus could experiment with economic openness by letting coastal cities set up their own economic and technological development zones outside the reach of central planning.

In Hong Kong and various other Asian locations dwell large numbers of Chinese with entrepreneurial skills, access to capital, and a close familiarity with the international market economy. It proved a relatively easy matter for these entrepreneurs to import to China the machinery needed to make a wide variety of relatively simple manufactures, train the local Chinese workforce to use it, and sell the output on the world market. Furthermore, the relatively low opportunity cost but high potential productivity of Chinese labor meant that the manufactured products competed strongly with goods from countries already integrated into the international economy. Once these lines of simple manufactures were established, China's vast population made them readily expansible. This is evident in the population growth of cities that were central in this development process. The population of one of them, Shenzhen, grew from 320,000 in 1980 to more than 7 million in 2000. The distribution of new lines of manufacturing among the region's cities was far from random: Local specialization is strongly evident, so economies of agglomeration have been one source of advantage.

---

[21]Saul Estrin, Kirsty Hughes, and Sarah Todd, *Foreign Direct Investment in Central and Eastern Europe: Multinationals in Transition* (London: Pinter, 1997).

The national government's policies were not uniformly benign during this period. The apparatus of central planning and the state-owned enterprises largely remained in place. The state-owned enterprises were only gradually unleashed from the regime of government-controlled prices; once a quota of output was delivered at the official price, output exceeding this could be sold at whatever price it would fetch. (The European transition economies, in contrast, made a dash to the reorganization of their economies on a market basis.) Only since 2000 has the government moved to encourage modernization in some other parts of the country. This choice seems astute because the resources needed to expand this development process more broadly across the country were simply not available.[22]

The Asian NICs

Although China is immense and important, it is anything but typical of the developing countries. Most others have chosen policies with important impacts but nothing close to central planning. China's Asian neighbors who preceded it in successful development provide an apt case of trade policy and development. Korea, Taiwan, Hong Kong, and Singapore rapidly increased their national incomes per capita (now half that of Japan) and their shares of world trade. Four other nations are apparently following the Asian NICs: Thailand, Malaysia, Indonesia, and the Philippines, called the ASEAN 4 (for their membership in the Association of Southeast Asian Nations). The following data from their period of most rapid growth illustrate the dramatic development of these Pacific Basin countries:

	Per Capita Income (1980 U.S. Dollars)		World Trade Share (%)	
	1963	1988	1963	1988
Asian NICs	974	5162	1.9	7.7
ASEAN 4	606	1546	1.1	2.1

Protection and Import-Substituting Industrialization

These nations once shared with most other developing countries a strategy for achieving economic development through the heavy protection of domestic manufacturing industries, or import-substituting industrialization.[23] In Taiwan, for example, nominal tariffs remained, on average, in the 40 to 50 percent range until the 1980s. In the 1960s, the Philippines levied average tariffs of 70 percent on consumer manufactured goods, 55 percent on intermediate-good inputs into construction, and 27 percent on other

[22]Michael J. Enright, Edith E. Scott, and Ka-mun Chang, *The Greater Pearl River Delta and the Rise of China* (Singapore: John Wiley, 2005).

[23]See Marcus Noland, *Pacific Basin Developing Countries: Prospects for the Future* (Washington, DC: Institute for International Economics, 1990), for a general treatment of the Asian countries' development. For an account of these countries' trade policies in the context of their other public policies, see World Bank, *The East Asian Miracle: Economic Growth and Public Policy* (New York: Oxford University Press, 1993).

intermediate goods. The Philippines had also used the policy of imposing heavy effective taxes on its two main agricultural exports, sugar and coconuts, to wring out funds for investment projects and industrialization.

The developing countries once placed faith in the infant-industry argument for tariff protection. This argument holds that a viable import-competing industrial activity might fail to take root in a country because it requires large-scale production to be efficient, demands organizational and technical skills that its workforce has not yet acquired, or depends for efficiency on learning that occurs only after production is under way. Another strand of the infant-industry argument maintains that an unskilled workforce needs to acquire skills, but these are costly for the enterprise employing them. The firm has no assurance that it can recoup its investment in training because the trained employees are free to quit and take their valuable new skills elsewhere.

Both arguments have their analytical flaws, but the point we stress here is that infant-industry protection worked badly in practice. Most developing countries have small domestic markets. Thus the domestic producers springing up behind tariff walls were usually few in number. Unless dynamic gains were forthcoming from learning and experience, local producers were doomed to high costs. (When public policy intervened to attract numerous producers, as in the automobile industries of some Latin American countries, the problem of inefficiently small scale grew that much worse.) Furthermore, little benefit appeared in the form of development gains. Instead, the protected local monopolies and oligopolies showed a pattern often seen in industrial countries as well: When an enterprise has few actual competitors and government assurance against potential rivals, its prime sin appears to be inefficiency and sloth rather than monopoly profits. Besides nurturing inefficiency, protection applied to capital goods and machinery raised the real costs of investment for local producers and reduced rates of capital formation and hence economic growth.[24] Many developing countries further suffered a general-equilibrium consequence of their protection policies: By taxing or otherwise turning the terms of trade against their resource-based export industries, they discouraged investment by farmers and other primary producers and undermined the basis for their gains from trade.

From Import Substitution to Export Orientation

Lately the developing countries in general (and the Asian NICs in particular) have turned away from import-substituting industrialization. The Asian NICs shifted to export-oriented policies that support the expansion of simple labor-intensive manufacturing for export. Part of these burgeoning exports stemmed from the capture of offshore processing activities, described in Chapter 8. Attuned to these countries' resource endowments and not cramped by the small sizes of domestic markets, these lines of exportable production (footwear, clothing, consumer electronics, and other simple consumer goods and components) expanded rapidly. By 1988 manufactures accounted for

---

[24]Colin I. Bradford, Jr., "NICs and the Next-Tier NICs and Transitional Economies," in Colin I. Bradford, Jr., and William H. Branson, eds., *Trade and Structural Change in Pacific Asia* (Chicago: University of Chicago Press, 1987), pp. 173–204.

more than 90 percent of the exports of each Asian NIC except Singapore, whereas in 1963 manufactures' share had been less than 47 percent for all except Hong Kong. Capital formation proceeded apace, with physical capital expanding at 8 to 12 percent annually and human capital also growing fast (the Asian NICs have high literacy rates and have trained large numbers of engineers).

These gains, of course, did not emerge just because tariff protection was reduced, but rather because a wide range of economic policies were adjusted to support the expansion of exports. Policies to encourage capital formation were especially important. Nor were all export-oriented policies well chosen: Up to the 1980s Korea continued to promote capital-intensive, large-scale export activities ill-suited to its factor endowment.

The exports-based growth of the NICs is no less impressive for occurring in the face of import restrictions of the United States and other industrial countries. The proportion of Korean exports subject to U.S. nontariff barriers rose from 37.5 percent in 1976 to 43.3 percent in 1985, then fell to 19.7 percent in 1989—not because U.S. controls were being relaxed but because of the rapidly changing commodity composition of Korean exports. Korea had to absorb substantial declines in the values of its exports when these goods were subjected to various forms of administered protectionism.[25] Development for the Asian NICs has involved shifting exports toward more sophisticated goods—partly because of the industrial countries' trade controls but also because of increased competition from the ASEAN 4 and now China.

Openness and Economic Growth

Partly from reflecting on the Asian economies' success, economists have intensively studied the relation between the openness of national economies and their rates of economic growth. Inefficient restrictions on a country's trade, like distortions (natural or policy-induced) in domestic markets, lower the level of a country's national income relative to its potential. For the distortions also to lower the growth rate, there must be some connection between openness to trade and the sources and mechanisms of economic growth. The candidate mechanisms are exactly the ones we discussed in Section 14.3 as sources of productivity gain from enlarging the market through forming a customs union. For a developing nation, foreign goods, international travel, and foreign direct investment (the presence of foreign business units) tend to increase the stock of human capital and reduce transaction costs.

Research testing this proposition is not unanimous, but productivity growth does seem to increase with openness to the international economy and freedom from price and allocative distortions in the domestic economy. For 78 developing economies Sachs and Warner analyzed the relation between openness and "convergence" during the 1970s and 1980s. They defined openness by the absence both of controls on international trade and payments and intensive regulation of the domestic economy via planning regimes. By convergence they meant the relation between a country's income

[25]Chong-Hyun Nam, "Protectionist U.S. Trade Policy and Korean Exports," in Takatoshi Ito and Anne O. Krueger, eds., *Trade and Protectionism* (Chicago: University of Chicago Press, 1993), pp. 183–218.

growth over a period of time and its shortfall from the most productive economies at the start of the period; economies that are the furthest behind enjoy the greatest opportunity to grow through diffusion and catching-up. Sachs and Warner found no evidence of catch-up among the closed economies in their sample, but strong catch-up processes among the open economies. The following simple averages of annual growth rates of incomes per capita tell the story:

	Open	Closed
Developing economies	4.5%	0.7%
Developed economies	2.3	0.7

The open economies overall outran the closed ones, and the developing open economies enjoyed substantial convergence, whereas the closed economies showed none.[26] In a parallel line of research, economists have sought to estimate the relation between a country's trade ratio (exports plus imports divided by GDP) and its income per capita. Trade ratios vary among countries and for a given country over time. Those data allow them to estimate (say) what effect a long-run increase of 10 percent in the trade ratio and the associated change in income per capita—at least 2 percent. This figure covers the productivity and efficiency gains in production, mentioned in Section 14.3. It does not include consumers' gains from the availability of an enhanced array of varieties of differentiated goods; that might be as large as the gain in production efficiency. The long-run gain available to the United States from removing all of its remaining trade restrictions came up with the impressively large magnitude of $1,500 to $2,000 per capita annually.[27]

14.6   Preferential Arrangements: New Policy Issues

Spillovers and Harmonization

Negotiations over preferential arrangements have spotlighted several policy issues that, although affected by these deals, arise in a different context. One group of issues concerns countries' domestic policies such as environmental policies, labor standards, and the like. Negotiations over NAFTA, the World Trade Organization, and other such settings flush out public sentiments that Americans should not trade (or should not trade *more*) with countries whose domestic policies Americans feel are unfair or inappropriate. We should not, some urge, consume goods whose production polluted the

---

[26]David Dollar, "Outward-Oriented Developing Economies Really Do Grow More Rapidly: Evidence from 95 LDCs, 1976–1985," *Economic Development and Cultural Change,* 40 (April 1992): 523–544; Jeffrey D. Sachs and Andrew Warner, "Economic Reform and the Process of Global Integration," *Brookings Papers on Economic Activity,* 1 (1995): 1–95.

[27]Scott C. Bradford, Paul L. E. Grieco, and Gary Clyde Hufbauer, "The Payoff to America from Global Integration," in C. Fred Bergsten, ed., *The United States and the World Economy* (Washington, DC: Institute for International Economics, 2005), pp. 65–109.

environment at their site of production or involved poor working conditions—child labor or a harsh or hazardous workplace.

Let us consider pollution controls in the context of international agreements on trade liberalization—either preferences such as NAFTA or global deals such as the World Trade Organization. Each country chooses its own set of pollution taxes to restrict outputs that cause local environmental damage (that is, confined to the country in question). Indeed, the optimal tax effectively adds to producers' marginal cost an amount equal to the value of the extra output's environmental damage. Producers are induced to contract their polluting outputs. Now, several such countries come to the bargaining table to negotiate (say) a free-trade area. The negotiators and the public immediately notice that any given polluting industry is subject to a different tax in each country. Should the low-tax country's polluting industry be allowed that cost advantage? Isn't that unfair to the producers who face higher tax rates? The answer is that the low-tax country's advantage is a real one and should be allowed to stand. A lower optimal tax reflects at least one of two factors. First, natural conditions may cause a given volume of pollutants to do less damage in one location than another—think of one producer group located in Beverly Hills, the other in the middle of the Sahara Desert. Second, a lower subjective valuation might be assigned to the effect of a given quantity of pollutants in one country than another. Citizens of higher-income countries are thought to place higher valuations on environmental quality; in a poor country, a pristine environment competes weakly against the provision of life's necessities—food and shelter. Pollution taxes on any given industry in each country should indeed reflect these differences in "technology" and taste for environmental quality. To charge that one country gains an unfair advantage from a lower optimal tax is equivalent to charging that the Caribbean's sunshine and beaches give it an unfair advantage as a vacation spot.[28]

So far, we have assumed that the environmental degradation associated with any good's production is local—specifically, confined within the producing country. Pollution may spill across national boundaries, however, as with the sulfur emissions of midwestern U.S. coal-burning electricity generators, which the prevailing winds carry as acid rain into eastern Canada as well as the northeastern United States. Similar problems arise along the U.S.-Mexican border. Whether as part of a preferential trading arrangement or otherwise, these negative externalities are an appropriate subject for international bargaining. Suppose that the U.S. government taxes sulfur emissions at a rate that is optimal for mitigating acid rain's damage within the country but does not take into account the additional damage done in Canada. Canada might use trade agreement negotiations as an occasion for seeking redress. For that matter, Canada might be better off if it subsidized the relevant pollution-abatement expenditures in the United States. The connection between a trade agreement and redress for international spillovers is tenuous. Lacking a better arrangement, Canada might tax imports of

---

[28]Jagdish Bhagwati and T. N. Srinivasan, "Trade and the Environment: Does Environmental Diversity Detract from the Case for Free Trade," in Jagdish Bhagwati and Robert E. Hudec, eds., *Fair Trade and Harmonization: Prerequisites for Free Trade?* (Cambridge, MA: MIT Press, 1996), Vol. 1, Chapter 4.

electric power from the United States as an indirect and inefficient way of reducing the spillovers of environmental damage.

Negotiations over preferential arrangements sometimes raise a different issue of harmonization of trading partners' domestic policies. Many policies involve not a simple (presumed) optimal rule such as a pollution tax. Some are simply longstanding conventions. We measure in inches, you measure in centimeters. One works about as well as the other, but harmonization on a single system would increase our gains from trade by reducing the cost of adapting products to a foreign measuring system. Transition costs apart, we could agree both to use the same measuring system and permanently avoid these incompatibility costs. This issue of harmonization has been pursued extensively in the European Union. There, for example, each country has developed different standards for qualifying professionals such as accountants, but there is room for bargaining because no country maintains that its qualifications are uniquely optimal. With a single qualification system, professionals could be mobile among the E.U. countries—another source of potential gains from trade. Harmonization is not a necessary part of an agreement on a preferential arrangement. Also, harmonizing with one trading partner or group might mean deharmonizing with other trading partners. Harmonization nonetheless offers the possibility of mutually beneficial agreements. Harmonization between two trading partners might pay even without a preferential arrangement, but such an arrangement that expands trade is likely to raise harmonization's benefits.[29]

Preferential versus Multilateral Trade Liberalization

Another policy issue raised by preferential arrangements is their relation to the process of multilateral reduction of trade barriers. If we agree that most trade barriers impair the efficiency of the world economy, and indeed usually the welfare of the countries maintaining them, we look with favor on any strategy for removing them. The track record of multilateral reduction is impressive (Section 13.1), but it has already lowered most tariffs of the developed countries enough to question whether further rounds are worth the negotiating costs. Preferential arrangements provide an opportunity to sweep out trade barriers across the board, though only among particular countries.

Some economists worry, though, that the good (preferential tariff reductions) is the enemy of the best (multilateral free trade). Theoretically, that is possible. If all countries start with a common positive level of tariffs, preferential reduction among a subgroup will raise welfare initially, but welfare declines as the preference margin gets larger and larger. Conversely, any group of countries could in principle form a customs union with a common external tariff that would benefit themselves while leaving the rest of the world just as well off as before. Theory alone cannot resolve the issue.[30]

---

[29]Many aspects of harmonization are addressed in Bhagwati and Hudec, eds., *Fair Trade and Harmonization*.
[30]Jagdish Bhagwati, David Greenaway, and Arvind Panagariya, "Trading Preferentially: Theory and Practice," *Economic Journal,* 108 (July 1998): 1128–1148.

Some economists have argued more pragmatically that regional preferential arrangements often unite neighboring countries with large potential gains from trade thanks to low costs of transport and communication. It is difficult, though, to make this argument rigorous (neighbors also have large trade-diversion potential). Much turns in practice on the pattern of political choices made by trading countries inside and outside of preferential arrangements. Are countries grouped in preferential arrangements prone to maintain and raise protection against the outside world, refuse new members, and get into trade wars with others? Or do preferential groups tend to expand, and their members to seek membership in other groups as well? The pattern prevailing in the last few years suggests the latter. But no easy judgment can be reached.[31]

14.7 Summary

Preferential trade arrangements eliminate controls on trade among member countries while maintaining restrictions against the outside world; they desirably reduce trade barriers, but they undesirably create discrimination between sources of supply. They usually link up regional neighboring countries, which raises their importance: Transport costs cause a bias in bilateral trade toward regional neighbors, as the gravity model predicts.

Preferential arrangements can either raise or lower economic welfare, in that they both free trade (among their members) and distort trade (with the outside world). Beneficial trade creation results when protected production is competed down and trade expanded between members. The effects are like those of the nondiscriminatory removal of tariffs. Trade diversion occurs when a preference causes a country to switch its purchases from a more efficient to a less efficient supplier. That switch itself imposes a welfare cost, but that cost might be offset by a gain for consumers. A preferential arrangement is most likely to benefit the world when a lot of protected production is competed down, when very high tariffs are lowered, and when the membership comprises a large proportion of the trading world.

A preferential arrangement is likely to shift the terms of trade of each party. The members would maximize their joint welfare by freeing trade among themselves and levying the optimal tariff against outsiders. A member who gives a preference to its partner loses (and the partner gains) if the member's terms of trade with the outside world fail to improve; if they improve, however, the member and the partner may both benefit. Speaking broadly, preferences seem likely to improve their members' terms of trade and welfare and to impose a cost on the outside world.

The European Union seems to have created a good deal of trade in manufactures and diverted little. Its welfare gains were probably much enlarged by the opportunity to raise the productivity of imperfectly competitive industries, but they were shriveled

---

[31]Anne O. Krueger, "Are Preferential Trading Arrangements Trade-Liberalizing or Protectionist?" *Journal of Economic Perspectives,* 13 (Fall 1999): 105–124.

by its expensive system of agricultural subsidy. The removal of nontariff barriers in 1992 brought significant gains in reduced transaction costs. In the Canada-U.S.-Mexico NAFTA arrangement, a small country such as Canada should gain from access to a new set of relative prices as well as to scale economies that increase its productive efficiency. With Mexico, trade diversion is a more serious concern, but developmental benefits seem substantial.

The centrally planned economies of the former Council of Mutual Economic Assistance (CMEA) nations extinguished trade with the market economies without effectively pursuing comparative advantage among themselves. Their centralized planning apparatus eschewed the use of prices in allocating resources among sectors and created great disincentives for efficiency, innovation, and the provision of high-quality, reliable goods. The collapse of their socialist regimes caused these economies in transition to rush to reestablish trade with the industrial market economies while the administered trade among themselves dried up. The trade of these economies in transition quickly shifted toward the market economies, especially the E.U. members, and that process continued to its denouement in eight Central European countries joining the European Union.

The successful development of newly industrialized countries in Asia is closely related to their participation in the international economy. China's development has concentrated in the coastal provinces near Hong Kong, which gained access thereby to sources of entrepreneurship, capital, and connections to international markets for simple manufactured goods. Before China's rise developmental success was enjoyed by the Asian Newly Industrialized Countries (NICs) (and before them Japan) by the same process of finding export specialties suited to their factor endowments. Formerly, they promoted industrialization by excluding manufactured imports. That policy brought them inefficient, small-scale manufacturing activities often ill-suited to their factor endowments; it also strangled their existing natural-resource-based exports. By contrast, export-oriented policies have allowed the Asian developing countries to industrialize rapidly by exporting manufactures well suited to their endowments of low-skill labor. Success of the NICs typifies the general conclusions of recent research on openness and economic growth: Increases in international commerce bring a nation in contact with new goods, production methods, and techniques of economic organization that let it reduce the gap between its own and the highest attained levels of productivity and income.

Regional arrangements raise two urgent policy issues. First, is there a problem of harmonizing partners' domestic policies toward the environment, labor, and the like? A country with low costs of environmental protection or weak preferences for environmental equality efficiently tends to specialize in polluting activities, although this seems unfair to its more onerously regulated competitors in other countries. Second, does the proliferation of preferential arrangements impede the multilateral liberalization of trade? Neither theory nor empirical evidence gives a clean answer, but preferential trading groups have been notably open toward new members and a source of attraction to those members.

CHAPTER PROBLEMS

1. Why is it that, as a customs union encompasses a larger proportion of the trading world, its formation becomes more likely to promote net welfare gains for the world at large?

2. A form of economic integration used occasionally is the elimination of trade barriers among countries in the goods produced by a particular sector; an example is a free-trade arrangement in automobiles and parts between the United States and Canada. If the parties keep their tariffs on all other goods, why might freeing trade in one sector cause the wrong country to specialize and export?

3. Suppose that a customs union causes a substantial expansion in its members' real incomes and output through the attainment of scale economies. How does this gain affect the chances that the rest of the world will lose from worsened terms of trade with the customs union?

4. What balance of trade creation and trade diversion will result from the addition of eight Central European countries to the Economic Union? From the evidence on the transition economies (and your general knowledge), suggest some hypotheses about the extent of these two outcomes.

5. The standard analysis of purely competitive markets does not incorporate seemingly important processes by which reduced barriers to international trade can increase welfare. Taking Figure 14.1 as a framework, describe (qualitatively) what sources of welfare gain are omitted.

6. Economists have debated the political economy of regional preferential arrangements in relation to the goal of removing all of the world's inefficient trade restrictions. What ways can you think of, grounded in the political economy of trade policy, by which preferences could pave the way toward world trade liberalization? How could they retard it?

SUGGESTIONS FOR FURTHER READING

Artis, Mike, and Norman Lee, eds. *The Economics of European Union: Policy and Analysis,* 2nd ed. (Oxford: Oxford University Press, 1997). Review of the European Union's policies.

Bergsten, C. Fred, ed. *The United States and the World Economy: Foreign Economic Policy for the Next Decade* (Washington, DC: Institute for International Economics, 2005). Many papers on current issues in U.S. trade policy.

Frankel, Jeffrey A. *Regional Trading Blocs in the World Economic System* (Washington, DC: Institute for International Economics, 1997). Analysis of effects of trading blocs on trade flows and welfare.

Hufbauer, Gary Clyde, and Jeffrey J. Schott. *NAFTA Revisited: Achievements and Challenges* (Washington, DC: Institute for International Economics, 2005). Summary of evidence on the results of NAFTA.

Ito, Takatoshi, and Anne O. Krueger, eds. *Regionalism versus Multilateral Trade Arrangements* (Chicago: University of Chicago Press, 1997). Research papers on this topic.

Krueger, Anne O. "Are Preferential Trading Arrangements Trade-Liberalizing or Protectionist?" *Journal of Economic Perspectives,* 13 (Fall 1999): 105–124. Good review of the debate over this issue.

———. *Foreign Trade Regimes and Economic Development: Liberalization Attempts and Consequences* (Cambridge, MA: Ballinger, 1978). Summarizes a large study of the transition away from import-substituting industrialization.

Pomfret, Richard. *The Economics of Regional Trading Arrangements* (Oxford: Clarendon Press, 1997). Extensive treatment of theory and evidence.

Winters, L. Alan, and Zhen Kun Wang. *Eastern Europe's International Trade* (Manchester, England: Manchester University Press, 1994). Research on comparative advantage and trade patterns of the transition economies.

PART IV

Money, Income, and the
Balance of Payments

Chapter 15 ■ The Balance of Payments Accounts
PAGE 273

Chapter 16 ■ The Foreign Exchange Market
and Trade Elasticities
PAGE 291

Chapter 17 ■ National Income and the Trade Balance
PAGE 307

Chapter 18 ■ Spending and the Exchange Rate
in the Keynesian Model
PAGE 327

Chapter 19 ■ The Money Supply, the Price Level,
and the Balance of Payments
PAGE 353

Chapter 20 ■ Developing Countries and Other Small
Open Economies with Nontraded Goods
PAGE 391

CHAPTER 15

The Balance of Payments Accounts

P arts I through III of this book concentrated on the behavior of "real" variables in the international economy—on the quantities of goods produced, consumed, and traded. Prices were crucial in securing equilibrium, but only as the relative prices of goods (the terms of trade) or of factors of production. The focus now turns to the macroeconomic side of international economics.[1] This requires an examination of the behavior of monetary magnitudes—the quantity of money itself and various prices that are measured in currency units. These include overall price levels, wage rates, and the foreign exchange rate, which is the price at which currencies exchange for one another.

The subject of international monetary economics has grown rapidly in interest and importance over the last 40 years. Much has happened over this period in the world economy. In 1973 the major industrialized countries moved from a system under which exchange rates were fixed by governments—a system that had held sway since World War II—to a new system in which exchange rates are determined in the marketplace.

Meanwhile, both goods markets and financial markets have become highly integrated, forcing even previously insular American macroeconomists to recognize the importance of the foreign sector; oil price changes have induced economists to build back into their view of the macroeconomy some of the real factors that had been left behind; developing countries have become integrated into the global economy; European countries have achieved monetary integration with each other; and large new macroeconomic policy disturbances, unprecedented trade imbalances, and currency crises in some countries have tested the limits of the modern financial system. Exchange rate flexibility has continued to spread, including to major developing countries. At the same time, thinking on the subject has been stimulated by new developments in the macroeconomic theory of closed economies: Intellectual revolutions that introduced such concepts as rational expectations in financial markets, credible commitment in monetary policy, and intertemporal optimization in saving behavior.

This half of the book will introduce eight or ten factors, or variables, that received little or no attention in the first half of the book. The variables include the exchange rate, output and employment (emphasizing the cyclical components of each), the interest

---

[1]The term *international finance* applies as well, particularly to the material covered in Parts V and VI.

rate, stocks of money and reserves, the aggregate price level, the relative price of non-traded goods, international flows of portfolio capital, and expectations. Understanding how the macroeconomic system works can be quite difficult if one tries to consider all ten variables simultaneously. These variables will be introduced one at a time, so that each can be assimilated—understood in terms of its interaction with the other variables—before the next is introduced. Thus we need not discard what we have used at each stage as we move on to the next stage and the next variable. Rather, we can consider what came before to be the right answer when the variable in question is held constant; we will then examine the corresponding change in the results when the new variable is allowed to change.

Before proceeding, however, we briefly explain the sequence of the different variables. Chapter 16 will introduce the exchange rate and show how it helps determine a country's balance of trade. The effect of the exchange rate on the trade balance will be examined first in the most controlled environment, in which price levels, income levels, and all other variables are held constant. Then Chapter 17 will allow for cyclical fluctuations in income. Unlike changes in output considered previously, these fluctuations will represent changes *relative* to potential output, changes associated with unemployment of labor and unutilized capacity. They are the consequence of wages and prices that are rigid, or at least "sticky"—that resist moving to equilibrate the labor and goods markets. This represents a sharp departure from the first half of the book, in which all prices were assumed to be flexible enough that they adjusted to ensure that supply always equaled demand. Some of the results, such as the existence of unemployment and excess capacity, are familiar from standard macroeconomics textbooks. However, much will be new and different in the open economy. For example, when prices are not free to adjust, the exchange rate can sometimes be used to restore equilibrium.

In the last part of Chapter 18 the money supply and the interest rate will make their appearance. At this point we will address how five variables—trade balance, exchange rate, level of income, money supply, and interest rate—all interrelate. Here, and throughout the last half of the book, a key question concerns the effects of monetary and fiscal policy on the open economy. In Chapter 19 two more factors are added. The first half of the chapter introduces the stock of international reserves (e.g., gold) that is held by the central bank. The second half of the chapter examines, for the first time, the overall price level. Chapter 20 distinguishes between traded and nontraded goods, providing a particularly useful model for developing countries and other countries that are small in world trade.

The core of Part V concerns the international flow of capital, the most powerful new factor in the modern world macroeconomy. To simplify: Parts I through III concentrated on the international flow of *goods,* with the net trade balance generally constrained to zero; Part IV introduces the international flow of *money,* allowing nonzero payments balances; and Part V introduces the international flow of *portfolio capital*—assets such as stocks and bonds. Because an asset is a claim to future consumption, international trade in assets is what allows countries to spend more than they earn in some periods, then make up for it by spending less than they earn in other periods. Finally, Part VI examines the determination of exchange rates in international asset markets, where expectations also arise as a key variable.

We will see that two particular aspects of the structure of the world economy as it evolved since the 1970s—the great ease of international capital movements and the system of market-determined exchange rates—have completely altered how policy changes and other macroeconomic disturbances operate. These aspects of the modern economy have important implications for the resolution of international payments imbalances and other policy problems that the world faces.

Before we begin exploring the operation of the international macroeconomy, it is necessary to go through the mechanics of balance-of-payments accounting in the present chapter. This tool would be necessary even if the subject were as tedious as matters of accounting sometimes appear. Balance-of-payments accounts, however, have attained a new fascination. Some measures of the balance of payments are closely watched by the press and policy makers.

Considerable insight into present international payments imbalances can be gained simply from the accounting identities, even before the discussion turns to the more interesting questions of economic causality. An accounting identity is an equation that must hold precisely, as a matter of definition or arithmetic, as opposed to behavioral equations, which represent theories of economic behavior that are not expected to hold precisely.

15.1 Breakdown of the Accounts

A nation's balance-of-payments accounts is the statistical record of all economic transactions taking place between its residents and the rest of the world. These are most conveniently broken up into three accounts, as shown in Table 15.1. First, the *current account* (*CA*) is the record of trade in goods and services and other current transactions, as opposed to trade in *assets,* which are obligations regarding the future. Trade in assets appears in the capital accounts. If the asset is traded among private citizens of the countries, then it appears on the *private capital account* (*KA*). If the buyer or seller of the asset is a central bank—that is, the monetary authority of either the domestic or foreign government—then the transaction appears on the *official reserve transactions* account (*ORT*).

Breakdown of the Current Account

Each of these three accounts is in turn divided into subaccounts. Within the current account the first subaccount is merchandise trade, consisting of exports and imports of goods, which includes all movable goods either sold, bought, or otherwise transferred between domestic and foreign owners.

The second subaccount within the current account is services (also known in the United Kingdom as "invisibles," as opposed to "visibles," which refer to merchandise). Some of the important international service transactions are as follows:

1. Transportation services include freight and insurance charges for the international movement of goods and also the expenditures on international travel of tourists and other passengers.

TABLE 15.1

Schematic Representation of the Balance of Payments

Accounts and Subaccounts	Cumulative Balances
CURRENT ACCOUNT (CA)	
Merchandise	Merchandise balance
Services	
• Transportation	
• Tourism	
• Business and professional services	Balance of goods and services
Investment income.	Balance of goods, services, and income
Unilateral transfers	
• Government grants	
• Private remittances	Current account balance
PRIVATE CAPITAL ACCOUNT (KA)	
Direct investment	
Portfolio investments (securities and banking flows)	
• Long term.	Basic balance
• Short term	Overall balance of payments
OFFICIAL RESERVE TRANSACTIONS (ORT)	
Changes in foreign central banks' holding of domestic assets	
Changes in the domestic central bank's holding of foreign assets	
• Gold	
• IMF credits and SDRs	
• Foreign exchange reserves	

Note: Each balance at the right is the sum of the previous balance and the additional items listed before the dotted line.

2. Tourist services include all expenditures by a country's citizens in foreign countries (on food, lodging, local transportation, etc.).

3. Business and professional services make up a diverse class of international transactions, which has come to public prominence under the name "overseas outsourcing." International trade in the services of engineer firms, management consultants, computer programmers, telephone receptionists, and so forth, is a rapidly growing component of trade. Royalties and license fees paid for the use of a work or invention, when the copyright or patent is held by a resident citizen of another country, are also counted as payments for a service.

A third subaccount within the current account is investment income. Interest payments or dividends appear here because they are considered payments for the services of capital that is "working" abroad. The profits earned by a factory owned by a foreign resident, for example, are payments for the services of the capital embodied in that factory. It is important to distinguish these yearly payments for the *services* of capital, which appear in the current account, from the original investment itself, which appears in the capital account.

Unilateral transfers are a fourth subaccount. This subaccount consists of government grants (foreign aid) and private remittances (from emigrant workers to their families, from pensions to retired people living abroad, etc.). Transfers appear in the current account rather than in the capital account because they do not create any obligation for repayment in the future, as a loan does.

Breakdown of the Capital Account

Within the capital account,[2] the key distinction is between direct investment and portfolio capital. Portfolio investment in turn can be divided into long term and short term.

1. *Foreign direct investment* occurs when the residents of one country acquire control over a business enterprise in another country. The acquisition may involve buying enough stock in an existing enterprise to become a controlling shareholder (defined for this purpose as 10 percent ownership), taking over the enterprise outright, or building a new factory or enterprise from scratch (including, as well, the purchase of real estate). When an investor buys only a small fraction of the shares of a foreign company, however, it is an example of long-term portfolio investment.

2. *Long-term portfolio investment* involves international transactions in financial assets with an original term to maturity greater than one year. Such investment consists of purchases of securities (stocks, also called shares or equities, and bonds) and long-term bank loans. Often the distinction between long-term and short-term capital flows is arbitrary, as when an investor buys a 10-year government bond, intending to resell it in a short time, or buys a bond that has already been held for 9½ years and is about to mature.

3. *Short-term capital flows* involve assets with original terms to maturity of less than one year. Examples are Treasury bills, commercial paper, and certificates of deposit (short-term claims on the government, corporations, and banks, respectively). Also included as short-term capital flows are any international shifts in the ownership of liquid funds, such as an interest-earning deposit or even a check or cash that does not pay interest. For example, British pound notes, or deposits in a British bank, are assets giving a claim on future British goods and services, just as surely as British treasury bills. The distinction between short term and long term is still reported in Japan, Germany, and some other countries, but not in the U.S. accounts, mainly because it is difficult to disentangle the two types of portfolio investment in the data.

Finally, the ORT account consists of central bank transactions in international reserve assets: gold, foreign exchange reserves, credits issued by the International Monetary Fund (IMF), and Special Drawing Rights (SDRs).[3] Central banks hold these reserve assets to back up the liabilities they issue (domestic currency and other assets that add up to the monetary base), much as commercial banks hold reserves to back up the liabilities that they issue (checking account deposits and other assets that add up to the total money supply).

---

[2]"Capital account" is generally used here to refer to the private capital account, as distinct from the transactions of central banks. (It does include, however, any international transactions undertaken by government agencies other than the central bank—for example, credits to U.S. armed forces stationed abroad.)
[3]Special Drawing Rights, sometimes described as "paper gold," are an asset created by the IMF. Their value is defined in terms of four currencies: the dollar, yen, pound, and euro.

15.2   How Individual Transactions Are Recorded

The key rule for recording transactions is as follows: Whatever enters the country, such as an import, is recorded as a debit; whatever leaves the country, such as an export, is recorded as a credit. The examples that first come to mind concern trade in merchandise (goods). An import of an automobile appears as a debit in the merchandise account because something is entering the country; the export of jet engines appears as a credit because something is leaving the country. Of course, the country that exports the automobile earns a credit on *its* merchandise account; and the country that imports the jet engines receives a debit.

There are many other examples for exports and imports of various services, and for each of the other subaccounts as well. When an American importer arranges transportation with a Greek shipping company or American tourists cross the Atlantic on a foreign airline, the import of the service is recorded as a debit in the U.S. transportation service account. When foreign firms hire American ships to carry goods or when foreign tourists come to the United States, the export of the service is recorded as a credit. The spending of American tourists in Europe is recorded as a debit, again on the service account, and the spending of Japanese tourists in the United States as a credit. When an American firm contracts out to a call center in India, a service import of the United States again appears. When a foreign student comes to an American university to study or a foreign medical patient comes to an American hospital for surgery, it appears as a U.S. service export.

The convention is that gifts and other transfers are recorded under unilateral transfers. Even though a transfer from another country does not create any obligation for future monetary repayment, as does a loan, a device for remembering that it appears as a credit might be to think of the transfer as the export of a political or moral IOU. In 1991 the United States received large payments from Japan and other allies to finance Operation Desert Storm in Kuwait. These credits did not appear on the services account because they were not *literally* exports of military services but appeared instead as transfers. Emigrants' remittances are an important source of credits for Mexico, the Philippines, and countries around the Mediterranean; the corresponding debits are incurred in the United States, northern European countries, and Persian Gulf states that host the immigrant workers.

Credits and Debits on the Capital Account

The acquisition of a foreign asset counts as a debit on the capital account because the asset, or at least the claim to the asset, is entering the home country. As a device for remembering that an investment abroad counts as a debit, think of it as the "import" of an asset. (The equivalent term—"capital outflow"—may be less helpful here, in that it may not sound like an import, even though it is one.) When General Electric builds a factory in China, an outflow of direct investment, a debit equal to the value of the equity that GE acquires in the factory, is recorded in the U.S. balance of payments. In this sense the purchase of machine tools bolted down to a factory floor in Scotland is similar to the purchase of Scottish machine tools imported into the United States, but in the former case the debit appears on the capital account and in the latter case it appears on the merchandise trade account. An American purchase of the bonds of a Canadian provincial government is recorded as a portfolio capital outflow, a debit on the long-term portfolio capital account. The American acquisition of a short-term asset in another country—whether it is a Treasury bill, corporate IOU, certificate of deposit, check, or currency—counts as a debit on the short-term portfolio capital account. This point should be emphasized because it will be important for understanding the accounting to follow. Remember that the reason this acquisition counts as a debit is that an American has increased individual holdings of a foreign asset, even if the asset is only foreign currency.

Ever since 1982, the U.S. capital account has shown many more credits than debits. Foreign citizens have been acquiring assets of every sort in the United States: currency, Treasury bills, bank loans, bonds, stocks, and direct investment. The term *credit* makes it sound like a good thing for the receiving country. In one sense this is true: It can be viewed as a vote of confidence when foreigners decide to invest in the United States. The downside, of course, is that U.S. citizens will have to service the debt (i.e., pay interest, and eventually repay the principal) in the future; or, in the cases of sales of stocks and inward direct investment, dividends and profits will have to be repatriated abroad in the future.

If American citizens resell to a foreign resident a bond originally issued by a foreign corporation, or any other foreign asset they acquired in the past, that too counts as a credit. There is no economic difference between an increase in your obligations to a foreigner or a decrease in a foreigner's obligations to you. Both contribute to a decrease in the net foreign investment position of the United States, which is simply one more way of saying "capital inflow" or "credit on the capital account." Similarly, if an American buys back a U.S. Treasury bill from a foreign resident who acquired it in the past, it counts as a debit in the U.S. capital account in the same way as when the asset the American purchases from the foreign resident is one that was originally issued by some foreign government or institution.[4]

The final place where credits and debits can appear is the Official Reserve Transactions account. When the domestic central bank buys foreign currency or gold, its purchase counts as a debit, just as it does when a private investor makes the purchase, but here it appears on the ORT account rather than the private capital account. As a device for remembering that it counts as a debit, the purchase can be thought of as an import of gold or foreign currency by the central bank. In this sense it is like the import of gold jewelry or shares in a foreign gold mine, except that in the jewelry case the debit appears in the merchandise trade account and in the gold mine case in the capital account. Only when the central bank makes the purchase does it appear on the ORT account.

---

[4]As a matter of fact, increases in U.S.-held assets issued abroad and decreases in foreign-held assets in the United States are reported separately in the detailed balance-of-payments accounts published every quarter by the Department of Commerce. Economic discussions of the balance of payments usually focus only on the net capital flows, however. (Incidentally, since 1999, U.S. capital flows appear on what is now technically called the "financial account.")

Another example arises if the country in question is one whose currency is used by other central banks as a reserve asset (as are the dollar, euro, and several other currencies[5]). When a foreign central bank buys some of the domestic currency, its purchase counts as a credit in the domestic balance-of-payments accounts, just as it does when a private foreigner buys some.

15.3 Double-Entry Bookkeeping

Note a critical point: As a matter of accounting, every complete economic transaction is recorded twice, once as a debit and once as a credit. The reason is that in every complete transaction there is something leaving the country in exchange for something entering the country. If there were not, then one party or the other would be giving up something for nothing.[6] One case where this is easy to see is barter. If, for example, Argentina exports wheat to Russia in exchange for tractors, then both the credit for the wheat export and the debit for the tractors import appear on the merchandise trade account. Similarly, if Russia accepted the claim to some Argentine farmland in payment for the tractors, the Argentine balance-of-payments statistics would show a debit to the trade account and a corresponding credit under foreign direct investment.

Paying for Imports

Usually, however, transactions are paid for in an immediate sense through the banking system.[7] Argentina pays for the tractors by writing a check on a bank. The credit that corresponds to the debit on the trade account appears on the short-term capital account. Recall that any time a foreign resident acquires an asset or a claim on the domestic country, even if it is a bank deposit rather than a more tangible investment, it counts as a credit on the domestic capital account. It is quite likely that the Russian tractor manufacturer will quickly cash in its check, which is a claim on an Argentine bank, to buy something more directly useful to it than Argentine pesos (perhaps that Argentine wheat), but this would count as an entirely separate transaction and would appear in the accounts as a new credit-debit pair.

---

[5]Only *convertible* foreign currencies are held as foreign exchange reserves. Central banks do not hold Tajikistani rubles as reserves because neither the government nor private banks will freely convert them into gold, dollars, or other international reserve assets.

[6]The unique case where one party does in fact give up something for nothing is the unilateral transfer. When the United States donates grain to an African country, for example, a debit is assigned to the trade account of the African country (or to its capital account if the donation consists of money) because something is entering the country. A credit is assigned to the United States because something is leaving the country. As already noted, the unilateral transfers account is where accountants, by convention, also assign a corresponding credit to the recipient country and a debit to the donor country.

[7]In a type of international transaction called *countertrade*, the exporter of goods to a country promises to import a corresponding value of goods from that country. However, most countertrade transactions are still paid for through the banking system. Relatively little of it is outright barter for goods, as this is awkward. Dalia Martin, "Tying in International Trade: Evidence on Countertrade," *The World Economy*, 13, no. 3 (1990): 445–462.

Other than paying for transactions by cash or check, the only other common method is trade credit: The tractor manufacturer extends to the Argentine importer the credit needed to buy the tractors (i.e., the importer does not have to pay until a later date) or else a bank extends the credit to the importer. In this case the credit item again appears in the short-term capital account: A foreign resident has acquired a short-term claim against an Argentine resident. In this sense paying for an import on short-term credit looks just like paying cash; both appear as credits in the same line of the balance of payments.

Paying for Asset Purchases

As a final set of examples, consider how the purchase of an asset is paid for. If a Japanese company buys an office building in Los Angeles and pays by check, the U.S. balance of payments registers a credit under direct investment (a foreign company has increased its holdings of U.S. real estate) and a debit under banking flows (an American company has increased its holdings of short-term claims on foreigners—it has the Japanese check). If an American firm buys a Mexican bond and pays by check, the U.S. balance of payments shows a debit to portfolio capital (the firm has increased its holdings of foreign securities) and a credit under banking flows (a foreign firm has increased its holdings of short-term claims on Americans). If an American buys a 90-day Certificate of Deposit in the United Kingdom and pays by check, both the credit and the debit appear under banking flows (two short-term assets have been exchanged). In some cases it is difficult to say which side of the transaction is paying for the other. There is nothing wrong with this; both parties have to get something out of it.

It may be clearer now why it makes accounting sense to enter a payment abroad as a credit to the capital account at the same time that a debit is entered for the other half of the transaction (e.g., on the trade account in the case of an import of merchandise). Take the case of an American company paying for an import in dollars, either cash or a check on its bank account. If the foreign company were to hold on to the dollars rather than cashing them in, in exchange for its own currency—that is, if there were no second transaction undoing the capital flow— this would have to mean that the foreign company had made a deliberate decision to increase its holdings of dollars. This *should* count as a capital-account credit; it constitutes foreign investment in U.S. assets, just as if the foreign company had increased its holdings of U.S. stocks or bonds. Again, normally the foreign company would be expected to cash in the dollars for something more useful, but doing so would count as a separate transaction. If the foreign company sells the dollars to the central bank, the second transaction consists of a debit to the U.S. short-term capital account (a foreign private company has now reduced its holdings of short-term U.S. assets) and a credit to the ORT account (the Federal Reserve has exported some foreign currency reserves).

What If the Importer Pays in *Foreign* Currency?

It has been assumed so far that the U.S. importer can make payment in dollars. The story is similar, however, if it pays in foreign currency. Assume first that the U.S. importer has on hand a stock of foreign currency just for such purposes. Initially the current account debit is paid for by a short-term capital-account credit: A U.S. company has reduced its holdings of foreign assets, which represents a capital inflow just as if it had sold off a security. (Recall that when the U.S. company decreases its credit position vis-à-vis foreign companies, it is as if foreign companies had increased their credit position vis-à-vis U.S. companies.) However, if the importer obtained the foreign currency by drawing down some transactions balances that were kept on hand for the purpose, subsequently it will probably want to replenish its stock of foreign currency by buying some in the foreign exchange market. If the importer does not have a stock of foreign currency to begin with, then again it has to go into the foreign exchange market to obtain some. Either way, the importer needs foreign currency, and there will be a second transaction in which it is obtained. If the importer obtains the foreign currency from its central bank, the second transaction consists of a debit to the short-term capital account and a credit to the ORT account, exactly as in the first example.

Conversely, if the importer allows its stock of foreign currency to remain lower at the end of the period than it was at the beginning (or goes into debt in foreign currency), then it must have decided deliberately to decrease its (net) holdings of foreign assets. The net credit then remains on the capital account—as when foreign companies increase their claims on domestic companies—rather than being transferred to the ORT account.

15.4 The Balances

Every year, the country adds up the debits and credits arising from the international transactions that have taken place. For most purposes in macroeconomics, the only concern is *net* flows, or total credits minus total debits. Within any given line of the balance of payments, there will be many credits and debits that cancel each other out. For example, short-term banking flows are typically very high in gross terms as banks buy and sell short-term positions in foreign currency and send checks back and forth for collection. But the net flow is much smaller.

The country then adds together the net flows, or subtotals, from different lines in the accounts to determine various balances, such as the trade balance. If credits outweigh debits, then the balance in question is positive. A positive balance is commonly referred to as "favorable." If debits outweigh credits, the balance is negative, or "unfavorable."

Note the subtle implication of the semantics. The export side owns all the positive words—and has done so ever since the eighteenth-century mercantilists made a national virtue of selling abroad more than one bought to "store up treasure." Although economists from Adam Smith on have proclaimed that economic welfare ultimately depends on the goods available for the nation's use and not on the money earned from exporting, they have never conquered this linguistic remnant of mercantilism. When the term *unfavorable* is used in reference to a negative trade balance, remember that it may be perfectly appropriate for a country to run a trade deficit, depending on the circumstances. For example, developing countries sometimes run large trade deficits. This practice can be perfectly appropriate if they are growing rapidly and need, typically, to import capital goods to invest in plants and equipment. Such countries are necessarily borrowing from abroad to finance their current-account deficits. If they are spending the funds well, they will in the future have the capital stock, particularly export capacity, necessary to generate export earnings with which to repay that debt.

The Adding-Up Constraint

Because every debit has an offsetting credit somewhere, $CA + KA + \text{ORT} \equiv 0$. (Three bars are used in the equality sign to indicate this is an accounting identity.) Because it is always zero, the three-account sum is not a very interesting statistic! Two interesting statistics are (1) the current-account balance and (2) the sum of the current and capital accounts, which is what is generally meant by the overall balance of payments (BP): $BP \equiv CA + KA$. These statistics reveal whether the country is spending beyond its means, and whether there is a net supply of, or demand for, its currency. A country that is running a current-account deficit—for example, the United States since 1982—is borrowing from abroad to do so, running down its net foreign asset position. Ever since 1917, the United States had been accumulating claims on the rest of the world, but in a few years the enormous deficits of the 1980s wiped out that accumulated investment position. The official statistics show that the country passed from net credit status to net debtor status in 1989.[8]

A country running a current-account surplus—Japan, for example—is accumulating claims on foreigners and building up a positive net foreign asset position. If the foreign assets are acquired by the private residents of the domestic country, then the capital-account deficit can offset the current-account surplus and the overall balance of payments can be zero. In this case, $KA = -CA$, so $\text{ORT} = 0$.

If a country is running a current-account surplus and its private residents are *not* acquiring foreign assets, however, then it must be the central bank that is acquiring foreign assets. In this case, $KA = 0$, so $\text{ORT} = -CA$. Such a country is running a surplus, not just on its current account, but also on its overall BP, which is sometimes called the *official settlements balance*. Note that it is the *negative* of the sum of the items on the ORT account: $\text{ORT} \equiv -BP$. The overall balance of payments is the net supply of foreign currency (or the net demand for domestic currency, which is the same thing), after the private sector has made all its desired current-account and capital-account transactions. If it is a positive number, the ORT is negative, which means that the central bank is adding to its foreign exchange reserves (or is supplying the domestic currency that private agents in the foreign exchange market want, which is the same thing). If BP is a

---

[8]This may be the appropriate place to introduce the distinction between *stocks* and *flows*. Flows have a "per unit of time" dimension, whereas stocks are absolute and dimensionless. Examples of stocks are the level of reserves held by a central bank and the level of assets held by private investors, whether money, bonds, equities, or physical capital. Examples of flows are the balance of payments, the current account, income, spending, and saving. A flow is the rate of change of a stock. The current account is the rate of change of the net international investment position, with the proviso that the latter also changes discretely when there is a change in the price of the assets (e.g., because of a change in the value of the currency). Such *valuation effects* have been important in recent years for the United States.

negative number, then ORT is positive, which means the central bank is selling foreign exchange reserves (or is buying the domestic currency that private agents in the market want to sell).

Where to Draw the Line?

There used to be a presumption of causality running from items reported higher in the accounts shown in Table 15.1 to items reported lower. Trade, for example, logically came first. Suppose a line is drawn under the entries for trade in goods and services. Then, if the balance is in deficit, it could be financed by transfers, by borrowing (KA), or by reserve loss (ORT). All items "above the line" would be considered *autonomous*—they cause the items below the line, which are financing or accommodating. There was much debate as to where to draw the line. Obvious places are the CA balance, with KA and ORT as accommodating, or at BP, with ORT alone as accommodating. However, there are other places to draw the line, as shown in the right-hand column in Table 15.1.

Monthly merchandise trade balance numbers historically received more attention than any other measure of the balance of payments. They become available more quickly than financial components of the U.S. balance of payments because they are reported directly to the Commerce Department by the Customs Service. They are subject to short-term fluctuations and sometimes have to be substantially revised at a later date, related in part to lags before imports arrive in port to be counted. This means that the merchandise trade balance for any one month is not a very good indicator of future trends.

There is no reason, conceptually, to focus on exports and imports of merchandise while ignoring services. Thus a better measure than the merchandise trade balance is the *balance on goods and services*. The Commerce Department began to report service exports and imports on a monthly basis in 1994, in recognition of their growing importance.

The balance on goods and services is a point of juncture between the international payments statistics and national-income accounts. Gross domestic product, the chief measure of a nation's economic output in one year, consists of goods and services produced at home for consumption, investment, government use, and export. The national accountants measure these flows of goods, however, not as they are *produced* but as they are *purchased*. Some purchases (whether by households, firms, governments, or foreign residents) consist of imports—goods that are produced abroad. Therefore, after all purchases are added up, the statisticians must then subtract out imports to arrive at the desired measure of domestic production. The import total is often shown as a subtraction from exports. Thus

$$GDP \equiv C + I + G + (X - M)$$

The term in parentheses is the balance of goods and services. In the national-income accounts it is called "net exports of goods and services."[9]

---

[9]The U.S. trade balance numbers differ from "net exports" in the national income and product accounts in a number of minor technical ways, such as the treatment of gold.

Another place to draw the line is to include interest payments and other investment income. This total is referred to as the *balance of goods, services, and income*.[10]

Next comes the current-account balance, the measure of the balance of payments that adds transfers in with goods, services, and investment income. We have already explained that the current account is important because it represents the net acquisition of foreign assets, whether by private citizens of the home country or by the central bank. Also discussed was the overall balance of payments (also called the official settlements balance), which adds to the current account all private capital-account transactions and is important because it represents the net acquisition of foreign reserve assets by the central bank. Some economists have argued that the line should be drawn between these two, that "exports" of claims to factories, along with other forms of foreign direct investment and sales of long-term assets, should count above the line—as do exports of goods. Thus the *basic balance* adds these long-term capital inflows to the current account. The accounting shows that this balance must be financed, or accommodated, either by short-term private capital flows or by official reserve transactions. The basic balance is no longer reported for the United States. Indeed, it cannot even be computed because the statistics collected no longer distinguish between long-term and short-term portfolio investment. The balance is still reported for Japan and some other countries.

Are There Really Accommodating Transactions?

Originally, the reason for drawing the line—whether at the merchandise trade balance; goods and services; goods, services, and income; current account; basic balance; or overall balance of payments—was so that transactions below the line could be thought of as financing or accommodating (being caused by) transactions above the line. This reasoning is now somewhat out of date.

A more modern view of causality in the balance-of-payments accounts evolved out of the transition to floating exchange rates. The definition of (pure) floating is $ORT = 0$: The central bank does not buy or sell foreign exchange, so there are no official reserve transactions to record. Obviously, in this case BP is not an interesting statistic because it is now always equal to zero.

Currently, most central banks at times *do* participate in foreign exchange markets to try to influence the exchange rate. This is *managed floating*, rather than pure floating.[11] Yet there is no clear sense in which central bank sales or purchases of international reserves necessarily accommodate (i.e., are caused by) private trade and capital flows, rather than the other way around. For example, in the late 1960s, under fixed

---

[10]The distinction among (1) the balance of goods and services; (2) the balance on goods, services, and income; and (3) the current-account balance is roughly similar to the distinction between (1) gross domestic product, which includes only income from domestic production; (2) gross national product, which also includes profits from abroad (net factor income); and (3) total national income, which also includes income from transfers. The U.S. government began to emphasize GDP over GNP in 1991.

[11]The United States is one of the few countries that seldom intervenes in the foreign exchange market. Mexico, Brazil, and Chile are three middle-income countries that joined the ranks of the floaters in the 1990s.

exchange rates, it made some sense to say that large U.S. balance-of-payments deficits caused foreign central banks to buy up unwanted dollars. In the case of the deficits run by the United States in recent years, however, it was as correct to say that the voluntary decision by foreign central bankers to buy dollars allowed, or even "caused," the U.S. deficits.

This point is even more applicable when assets are sold to foreign private residents rather than to foreign central banks. A surplus in the private capital account is what allows, or even causes, a country to run a deficit on the current account, as much so as the deficit in the current account giving rise to the surplus in the capital account. The most prominent example is the large U.S. current-account deficit. To say that the decision by private foreigners to increase their holdings of U.S. assets caused the U.S. current-account deficits is as correct as saying that the decision by Americans to import more goods and services caused the current-account deficits, which then had to be financed by borrowing from abroad. The important point is that no clear presumption exists as to the direction of causality. In reality, the various accounts are generally determined simultaneously.

In fact, even the figures for the overall balance of payments are no longer explicitly reported for the United States, as can be seen from the actual balance of payments statistics reproduced in Table 15.2. The net capital-account balance has to be computed. In 1983 it turned sharply from deficit into surplus as foreigners began to acquire U.S. assets in record amounts. We must add the capital-account number to the balance on current account (a large deficit since 1983) to find the overall balance of payments. At first, the private capital inflow was sufficient to finance the U.S. current-account deficit. In 1986–2000, however, the private capital inflow has usually fallen short of the current-account deficit. Foreign central banks make up the difference, as evidenced in Table 15.2 under "foreign official assets." The United States runs a deficit, not just on its current account, but also on its overall balance of payments.

Making these calculations can be instructive even though we have abandoned the presumption that the U.S. balance-of-payments deficit was necessarily *causing* central banks to buy up unwanted dollars, rather than the other way around.

15.5 Statistical Errors in the Payments Accounts

When government statisticians assemble the record of a nation's international transactions, they do not observe directly the two sides of every transaction. Errors creep in for two reasons: Some transactions are valued incorrectly, so the quantity recorded for one side of the transaction fails to equal that for its compensating transaction, or one side of a transaction is omitted entirely. Although the authorities measure each class of transaction as accurately as possible, because of these and other errors the sums of credit and debit items do not come out equal. Therefore, the accounts include an item called "statistical discrepancy," or "errors and omissions," equal to this difference. These measurement errors are no small problem. The errors in the U.S. statistics began to run wild in the 1980s, indicating an unmeasured net inflow of money, as can be seen in Table 15.2. This inflow was due in part to turmoil in some foreign countries that

TABLE 15.2

U.S. Balance of Payments Statistics in Summary Form (Billions of Dollars)

Year	Merchandise[a] Exports	Imports	Net Goods Balance	Net Services	Balance on Goods and Services	Investment Income (Net)	Balance on Goods and Services and Income	Unilateral Transfers (Net)[b]	Balance on Current Account	Net foreign-owned Assets in U.S. Excluding Official[c] (increase)	U.S. Official Reserve Assets Abroad[d] (decrease)	Foreign Official Reserve Assets in the U.S. (increase)	Statistical Discrepancy (sum of the items with sign reversed)
1981	237.0	−265.1	−28.0	11.9	−16.2	32.9	16.7	−11.7	5.0	−27.7	−4.1	5.0	21.8
1982	211.2	−247.6	−36.5	12.3	−24.2	35.2	11.0	−16.5	−5.5	−29.9	−5.0	3.6	36.6
1983	201.8	−268.9	−67.1	9.3	−57.8	36.4	−21.4	−17.3	−38.7	17.7	−1.2	5.8	16.2
1984	219.9	−332.4	−112.5	3.4	−109.1	35.1	−74.0	−20.3	−94.3	77.4	−3.1	3.1	16.7
1985	215.9	−338.1	−122.2	0.3	−121.9	25.7	−96.2	−22.0	−118.2	106.3	−3.9	−1.1	16.5
1986	223.3	−368.4	−145.1	6.5	−138.5	15.5	−123.0	−24.1	−147.2	82.3	0.3	35.6	28.6
1987	250.2	−409.8	−159.6	7.9	−151.7	14.3	−137.4	−23.3	−160.7	114.8	9.1	45.4	−9.0
1988	320.2	−447.2	−127.0	12.4	−114.6	18.7	−95.9	−25.3	−121.2	104.1	−3.9	39.8	−19.3
1989	359.9	−477.7	−117.7	24.6	−93.1	19.8	−73.3	−26.2	−99.5	66.3	−25.3	8.5	49.6
1990	387.4	−498.4	−111.0	30.2	−80.9	28.6	−52.3	−26.7	−79.0	28.6	−2.2	33.9	25.2
1991	414.1	−491.0	−76.9	45.8	−31.1	24.1	−7.0	9.9	2.9	23.3	5.8	17.4	−44.8
1992	439.6	−536.5	−96.9	57.7	−39.2	24.2	−15.0	−35.1	−50.1	51.9	3.9	40.5	−45.6
1993	456.9	−589.4	−132.5	62.1	−70.3	25.3	−45.0	−39.8	−84.8	11.1	−1.4	71.8	4.6
1994	502.9	−668.7	−165.8	67.3	−98.5	17.1	−81.3	−40.3	−121.6	82.1	5.3	39.6	−3.7
1995	575.2	−749.4	−174.2	77.8	−96.4	20.9	−75.5	−38.2	−113.7	−13.8	−9.7	109.9	28.3
1996	612.1	−803.1	−191.0	86.9	−104.1	22.3	−81.7	−43.1	−124.9	4.3	6.7	126.7	−12.2
1997	678.4	−876.5	−198.1	89.8	−108.3	12.6	−95.7	−45.2	−140.9	203.3	−1.0	19.0	−79.4
1998	670.4	−917.1	−246.7	81.7	−165.0	4.3	−160.7	−53.3	−214.1	96.4	−6.8	−19.9	145.0
1999	684.0	−1030.0	−346.0	82.6	−263.4	13.9	−249.5	−50.6	−300.1	183.9	8.7	43.5	68.8
2000	772.0	−1224.4	−452.4	74.1	−378.3	21.1	−357.2	−58.8	−416.0	443.9	−0.3	42.8	−69.4
2001	718.7	−1145.9	−427.2	64.5	−362.7	25.2	−337.5	−51.9	−389.5	377.1	−4.9	28.1	−9.6
2002	682.4	−1164.7	−482.3	61.1	−421.2	10.0	−411.2	−64.0	−475.2	388.1	−3.7	115.9	−23.7
2003	713.4	−1260.7	−547.3	52.5	−494.8	46.3	−448.5	−71.2	−519.7	280.9	1.5	278.3	−37.8
2004	807.5	−1472.9	−665.4	47.8	−617.6	30.4	−587.1	−80.9	−668.1	187.1	2.8	394.7	85.1
2005*	657.9	−1224.2	−566.3	41.4	−524.8	−0.5	−525.3	−62.3	−587.6	416.4	9.3	146.3	20.6

*2005 figure is between Quarter I and IV.

[a]Excludes military.

[b]Includes transfers of goods and services under U.S. military grant programs.

[c]The number reported here shows net private capital account. It is computed as nonofficial financial inflows (the increase in private foreign assets in the United States, minus the increases in U.S. private assets abroad and U.S. government assets abroad, other than official) plus a new category of miscellaneous capital account transactions.

[d]Consists of gold, Special Drawing Rights (SDRs), convertible currencies, and U.S. reserve position in the IMF.

Source: Department of Commerce (Bureau of Economic Analysis).

impelled funds to seek a safe haven in the United States. The acquisition of such claims by foreigners, called "capital flight," often is clandestine and goes unrecorded. Subsequently this net flow reversed, suggesting that this flight capital was returning home. The absolute magnitude of the discrepancy is still large.

Another major discrepancy appears when the net current-account positions of all countries are added together. Because every export is some country's import, these accounts would sum to zero if all countries got their measurements right. The discrepancy has run as large as $100 billion in recent years. It appears as though the world were running a deficit with other planets.

15.6 Summary

The study of international monetary economics begins with the balance-of-payments accounts. The current account adds up all credits and debits arising from trade in goods and services and from transfers, the private capital account covers the purchase and sale of assets, and the official reserve transactions account consists of changes in international reserve holdings by central banks.

We will now turn from rules of accounting to models of economic behavior. Throughout most of the book, the subaccounts will usually be ignored and the focus will be on the *CA/KA/ORT* level of aggregation. For example, the discussion will often abstract from transfers to speak interchangeably of the trade balance (TB) and current account (CA).

CHAPTER PROBLEMS

1. In this question you must play balance-of-payments accountant.

   The Rules
   - On the current account, exports are credits; imports are debits.
   - On the capital account, capital inflows are credits (exports of stocks, bonds, etc.); capital outflows are debits (imports of stocks, bonds, etc.).
   - On the official reserve transactions account, reserve losses are credits (exports of gold, foreign currencies, etc.); reserve gains are debits (imports of gold, foreign currencies, etc.).
   - Every autonomous debit (e.g., a merchandise import) must have an accommodating credit (e.g., an inflow of short-term capital to pay for the import), and vice versa.

   For each of the following transactions indicate (a) on which account the debit occurs, and (b) on which account the credit occurs. Your choices are merchandise, services, income, transfers, direct investment, long-term capital, short-term capital, and official reserve transactions. Also, in each case indicate (c) the effect on the current-account balance ($+, 0,$ or $-$), and (d) the effect on the overall balance of payments ($+, 0,$ or $-$).

Answer only the implications of the transaction specified for the U.S. balance of payments. Do not assume that the recipients of payments from abroad necessarily exchange foreign currency with the central bank as would be the case if capital flows were assumed to be zero.

1. U.S. imports BMWs from Germany; pays by check in euros.
2. U.S. exports grain to Japan; paid by check in dollars.
3. U.S. imports coffee from Brazil; agrees to pay in dollars 3 months later.
4. U.S. tourists spend Swiss francs in Geneva.
5. Mexico buys locomotives from U.S. firm, which agrees to let the Mexicans pay in dollars 18 months later.
6. French firms and banks, because they are accumulating more dollars than they want or than U.S. banks will accept, turn them in to the Federal Reserve, which agrees to give them euros.
7. A U.S. investor buys a 2-year Canadian treasury note; pays by check.
8. U.S. firm builds a factory in Mexico; pays for land, local labor, and so on, in pesos.
9. U.S. government sends foreign aid to Pakistan, which Pakistanis hold in the form of dollars.
10. China buys nuclear reactors from the U.S. government; pays in gold. (No central bank is involved.)
11. Portuguese immigrant sends money back to family in Lisbon in the form of a 10-year U.S. savings bond.
12. U.S. firm receives profits in the form of pesos from the factory it previously built in Mexico.
13. Dutch holding company buys a controlling interest in an American firm; pays in dollars.
14. U.S. ship is leased to carry beef from Australia to Britain. Payment for freight charges is in dollars.
15. Federal Reserve sells gold to support the value of the dollar.

2. We hear of financial transfers to "launder" illegally acquired funds. For example, a South American smuggler might deposit income from illegal exports in a Miami bank, and arrange for the bank to re-lend it to the smuggler to invest in a legitimate activity.

   a. How would this transaction appear in the U.S. balance-of-payments accounts if it were recorded correctly? How would it appear in the accounts of the South American country?

   b. What error will it create in the accounts if the exporter's earnings and claim on the Miami bank are not recorded in the exporter's home country but the transactions are recorded in the United States? (This could be the case if the commodity exported is legal, but the exporter leaves the dollar proceeds in the Miami bank to evade taxes.) What will this do to the worldwide current-account discrepancy?

   c. What error will be created in the two countries' accounts if the exporter's claim on the bank is not recorded in either country, but the export is reported in both? (To minimize the chances of getting caught, the exporter simply fails to inform the Miami bank that he or she is not a U.S. citizen.) What would this error do to the worldwide current-account discrepancy?

CHAPTER 16

The Foreign Exchange Market and Trade Elasticities

The foreign exchange market is where domestic money (for example, dollars) is traded for foreign money (for example, pounds sterling). The exchange rate is usually defined as the price of the foreign currency in terms of the domestic currency, although it could as easily have been the reverse.[1] This convention will be followed here. Note that a *depreciation,* a decrease in the value of the domestic currency, is an *increase* in the exchange rate because it is an increase in the price of foreign currency. Some find it counterintuitive that a decrease in the value of the currency is called an increase in the exchange rate. Yet just as economists often talk about an increase in the prices of commodities rather than the equivalent depreciation of money's purchasing power over commodities, so it is often intuitive to talk about an increase in the price of foreign currency rather than the equivalent decrease in the value of the domestic currency.

We are simplifying when we speak of *the* exchange rate for a country. In reality, each country has many exchange rates, one for every other currency in the world. The United States, for example, has the dollar/yen rate, the dollar/pound rate, and so on. Although these exchange rates tend to be correlated, the measure of the movements in the home country's currency depends on which exchange rate is used. To get a good idea of the value of the currency overall, it is necessary to use an exchange rate index, known as the *effective exchange rate,* which computes a weighted average of the exchange rates against each of the individual countries. Typically the weights used are the countries' shares in trade.

16.1 The Flow of Supply and Demand for Foreign Exchange

In the foreign exchange market, as in other markets, supply and demand are central. The proceeds from exports, and other credit items in the balance of payments, generate the supply of foreign exchange or foreign currency. Import spending and other debit items generate the demand for foreign exchange. In Figure 16.1 we measure the quantities of foreign exchange supplied and demanded on the horizontal axis, and the price

---

[1] In the United Kingdom, for example, the practice is to speak in terms of the dollar/pound rate, an exception to the general rule because the pound is the domestic currency.

FIGURE 16.1

Increase in Demand for Foreign Currency

When the demand for foreign currency shifts out from D to D', the result depends on the exchange rate regime. Panel (a) illustrates a floating exchange rate: An increase in the price of foreign currency is necessary to equilibrate the private market. Panel (b) illustrates a fixed exchange rate: The central bank intervenes by supplying the excess amount demanded, out of its foreign exchange reserves.

of foreign exchange—the exchange rate E—on the vertical axis. We can think of the supply and demand for foreign exchange as functions of the currency's price—the exchange rate—just as the supply and demand for any commodity are functions of its price. Unless otherwise specified, supply and demand refer to private sources (i.e., transactions on the current account and private capital account, not official reserve transactions by the central bank). In Figure 16.1 the supply curve and demand curve are (for the moment) simply assumed to slope the conventional ways: upward and downward, respectively.

The behavior of the exchange rate varies considerably depending on which *regime* is in effect: floating exchange rates or fixed exchange rates. Under pure floating, the exchange rate is whatever it must be to equilibrate supply and demand in the private market. Consider an increase in the demand for foreign exchange, an outward shift of the curve in Figure 16.1(a) from D to D'. Such an outward shift in the demand for foreign currency could result, for example, from an increase in demand for imports or from an increase in investors' demand for foreign assets. Under floating, the increased demand for foreign currency causes an increase in its price, the exchange rate, just as an increase in demand for a commodity causes an increase in the price of the commodity. E goes up.

With a completely fixed or "pegged" exchange rate, conversely, the central bank stands ready to buy or sell foreign currency whenever private supply and demand are not equal at the fixed rate. The official exchange rate would only by coincidence be the rate that precisely equates private supply and demand. Under this regime, an increase in demand, illustrated in Figure 16.1(b), would result in an excess demand for foreign currency that must be met by sales of foreign currency by the central bank. From our discussion of the balance-of-payments accounts, we know that the country runs a balance-of-payments deficit. The central bank keeps the domestic currency from depreciating by buying up the excess supply of the domestic currency. Obviously, the central bank can continue this only as long as it has foreign exchange reserves. (The other country's central bank also could use its own currency to buy up the unwanted domestic currency, if it were willing to do so.) There are policy changes, which will be examined later, that the domestic government can make to reduce the deficit instead of financing it, but such policies generally take time to have an effect. If the deficit continues, eventually the central bank will run out of foreign exchange reserves and will be forced to withdraw support from the domestic currency. The central bank must then either (1) set a new, higher exchange rate at which it will stand ready to sell foreign exchange from then on, or (2) cease foreign exchange operations and allow the market to determine the rate. The first option constitutes a *devaluation* of the currency, the second the floating of the currency.[2]

Deriving Supply and Demand for Foreign Exchange from Exports and Imports

What determines the supply and demand for foreign exchange? Three assumptions together will provide a preliminary answer to this question. We are, in effect, going to derive the shapes of the curves in Figure 16.1.

Assumption 1.   Assume (until Part V of this book) that *there are no net capital flows* ($KA = 0$). Thus the private supply and demand for foreign exchange are determined entirely by the trade account. Most of the results in this part of the book would be unaffected if it were assumed that capital flows were constant or exogenous, without necessarily being zero. In the 1950s capital flows indeed consisted largely of government loans (e.g., lending to Europe under the Marshall Plan after World War II) and foreign direct investments that were not very responsive to short-term factors such as the interest rate.

Furthermore, assume now that two goods are traded: an importable good and an exportable good. Thus the first assumption is that the balance of payments is simply sales of the export minus spending on the import.

Assumption 2.   Assume (through the remainder of this chapter) that *domestic residents look only at prices expressed in domestic currency*. Thus, in the case of domestic consumers, the demand for imports depends only on the price of the import expressed in domestic currency. In the case of domestic firms, the supply of exports depends only

---

[2]The appendix to this chapter shows how stability in the foreign exchange market depends on the slopes of the supply and demand curves in Figure 16.1(a). This analysis holds whether or not the curves are derived from exports and imports, as in the next subsection. Chapter 21 will discuss the mechanics of how foreign exchange is actually bought and sold, most of it by banks.

on the price of the export expressed in domestic currency. Similarly, assume that *foreign residents look only at prices expressed in foreign currency* when choosing the demand for the home country's exports (in the case of foreign consumers) or the supply of imports to the home country (in the case of foreign firms). Changes in demand arising from changes in income are ignored. This assumption, representing the defining characteristic of the "elasticity approach" to devaluation, will be relaxed in Chapter 17.

Assumption 3.   Finally, assume for now that firms set a price for their product and then meet any forthcoming demand. In other words, assume that *supply is infinitely elastic.* This assumption can be regarded as a special case that is only a realistic description of the short run. In light of Assumption 2, the price at which domestic firms supply exportables with infinite elasticity must be set in domestic currency—call it P—and the price at which foreign firms supply the home country with importables must be set in foreign currency—call it P^*. Assumption 3 will be relaxed later as well.

By Assumption 3, output levels are determined by demand. The demand for imports, M_D, is a decreasing function of the import's price expressed in domestic currency, which is the fixed price in foreign currency times the exchange rate.

$$M = M_D(E\overline{P}^*)$$

If a Range Rover costs £20,000 and the exchange rate is $2.00/£, then the price to an American is ($2.00/£)(£20,000) = $40,000. Americans will buy fewer Range Rovers when the dollar price goes up, without distinguishing whether it is the exchange rate or the pound price that has changed. Figure 16.2 graphs prices in terms of foreign currency to facilitate calculation of export revenue and import spending. Thus the import demand curve is drawn for a given exchange rate, E. A change in E would shift the entire M_D curve. The demand for exports, X_D, is a decreasing function of their price expressed in foreign currency, which is the fixed price in domestic currency divided by the exchange rate.

$$X = X_D(\overline{P}/E)$$

If a Ford costs $20,000 and the exchange rate is $2.00/£, then the price in Britain is $20,000/($2.00/£) = £10,000. British buyers will buy fewer Fords when the pound price goes up, regardless of whether it is the dollar price that rose or the exchange rate that fell.

A devaluation, an increase in E, lowers the price of exports to foreigners. This is a movement down the curve, increasing the quantity of exports demanded, X_D, in Figure 16.2(b). The devaluation also raises the price of imports to domestic residents, reducing their demand, M_D. This is represented in Figure 16.2(a) as a proportionate downward shift of the entire import demand curve because the curve was drawn contingent on the exchange rate.[3]

---

[3]If the vertical axes had been expressed in domestic currency instead of foreign currency, the devaluation would have been an upward movement along the import demand curve and an upward shift of the export demand curve, instead of the other way around. (The effect on the quantities would have been the same as in Figure 16.2.) The general rule is that a devaluation is a movement *along* the curve that describes the behavior of the people (domestic or foreign residents) whose currency is on the vertical axis; it *shifts* the curve that describes the behavior of the people whose currency is not on the axis.

FIGURE 16.2

Effect of a Devaluation on Trade

Panel (a) shows how a devaluation lowers the quantity of imports. Panel (b) shows how the devaluation raises the quantity of exports. The effects on import spending and export revenue, respectively, are shown by the areas of the shaded rectangles.

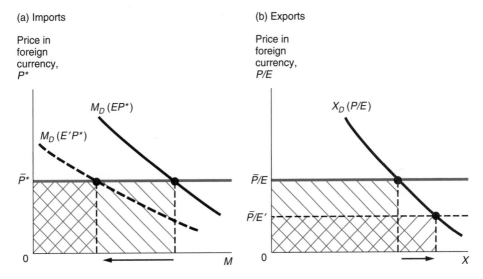

Now consider the market for foreign exchange. Assumption 1 means that the demand for foreign exchange is identical to import spending: In the absence of borrowing, foreign exchange must be obtained on the market to pay for imports. Import spending is quantity times the foreign currency price. The supply of foreign exchange is identical to export revenue: All foreign exchange earned through exports is cashed in on the foreign exchange market. Export revenue is export quantity times foreign currency price. So the demand for foreign currency prior to the devaluation is P^*M, the shaded rectangular area in Figure 16.2(a), and the supply is $(P/E)X$, the shaded area in Figure 16.2(b). The net supply of foreign exchange is

$$(\bar{P}/E)X - \bar{P}^*M$$

which is also the trade balance measured in foreign currency, TB^*.

The appendix to this chapter considers the question of stability in the foreign exchange market: Does an increase in the exchange rate increase the net supply of foreign exchange? This question is identical to this one: Does a devaluation improve the trade balance? The two questions are the same because no capital flows have been assumed. Domestic consumers cannot borrow abroad to get the foreign exchange they need for imports, so the trade balance is the same as the net supply of foreign exchange. We will now derive the condition under which the answer to the two questions is yes.

The Marshall-Lerner Condition

The effect of a devaluation on the trade balance can be decomposed into three factors. (1) A devaluation reduces the real quantity of imports (the number of Range Rovers imported, in the example) and, because their nominal price is fixed in foreign currency, clearly reduces the amount of foreign exchange spent on imports. The rectangular area in Figure 16.2(a) shrinks. This factor helps improve the trade balance. (2) The devaluation also increases the real quantity of exports. This factor also helps the trade balance. (3) Any given quantity of exports earns less foreign exchange than before because their nominal price is set in domestic currency. This factor *hurts* the trade balance.

The net effect on foreign currency export revenue is unclear. The size of the rectangular area in Figure 16.2(b) may either increase or decrease, depending on the elasticity of export demand. If the demand response (factor 2) is small enough, export revenue may actually fall. This will be the case if the elasticity of export demand is less than 1. Export revenue could fall, and yet be outweighed by a reduction in imports, so that the total trade balance would still improve. However, if the demand response on the import side (factor 1) is also small enough, the trade balance will actually worsen: The net supply of foreign exchange will fall. (The various cases are explored further in the appendix.)

At this point a fourth assumption is added to those required by the elasticities approach.

Assumption 4.   Assume that *the economy is initially in a position of balanced trade* ($TB = 0$). Given this, the necessary and sufficient condition for the devaluation to improve the trade balance, or for the foreign exchange market to be stable, is the Marshall-Lerner condition. The supplement to Chapter 3 includes a derivation of the Marshall-Lerner condition. Here, with price levels fixed in each country, the exchange rate plays the role of the price of foreign goods in terms of domestic. The condition is

$$\varepsilon_X + \varepsilon_M > 1$$

where ε_X and ε_M are the elasticities of demand for exports and imports, respectively. For example, if exports have an elasticity of exactly one, a devaluation leaves export revenue unchanged in foreign currency (the second and third factors just described cancel out); then, if import demand has any elasticity, the devaluation reduces imports, thereby improving the trade balance. Alternatively, if imports are more-than-unit elastic and exports have any elasticity, or if both elasticities are greater than half, then the third factor will be outweighed by the first two and the trade balance again will improve.[4]

We have discussed the supply and demand for foreign exchange, but we could as easily have discussed the demand and supply of *domestic* exchange. Assuming again that the starting point is a position of balanced trade, the Marshall-Lerner condition applies unchanged to the question of the trade balance expressed in domestic currency.[5]

---

[4]The proof of the Marshall-Lerner condition in the present context (i.e., where the exchange rate takes the role of the relative price) is given in the supplement to this chapter.

[5]The proof of the Marshall-Lerner condition in terms of domestic currency is left to the student in Problem 5a at the end of the chapter.

The model can be generalized in two directions. First, Assumption 4 can be relaxed. In particular, note that in practice a country seldom devalues unless it starts from a position of deficit, rather than balanced trade: $TB < 0$, or $EP^*M > PX$. Now, it makes a difference whether the trade balance is measured in terms of domestic currency or foreign currency. If trade is measured in terms of domestic currency, the necessary condition for a devaluation to improve the trade balance is more stringent: The elasticities must be higher than those given by the Marshall-Lerner condition.[6] The economic reason is that, given the relatively large initial value for imports, M, the valuation effect on import spending is more negative. For example, the import elasticity could be almost as high as one, and yet if the export elasticity—even though positive— is not high enough, the trade balance could worsen. A 10 percent devaluation may raise exports, yet this accomplishes little if exports initially were a small number; meanwhile, the already large import bill falls.

Another generalization involves relaxing Assumption 3—that firms exhibit infinitely elastic supply. The supplement to this chapter (second half) considers this general case.

According to general equilibrium theory, consumer demand should be a function not of nominal prices but of *relative prices and real income*. The elasticities approach is frequently criticized for the partial equilibrium nature of Assumption 1. (Partial equilibrium means that some important variables are held constant.) For example, an increase in demand for a country's exports should raise its real income and thus raise its demand for imports, but in the elasticities model there are no such effects. Chapter 17 begins to remedy this deficiency by introducing income as a variable in the import demand function.

16.2 Empirical Effects of Devaluation on the Trade Balance

Clearly, much depends on the magnitude of the import and export elasticities. Are they large enough in practice for a devaluation to improve the trade balance? It is now time to turn to the empirical evidence.

Elasticity Pessimism

A view known as elasticity pessimism suggests that actual trade elasticities are too low to satisfy the Marshall-Lerner condition. Several factors have contributed to this view historically. First, floating exchange rates in the 1930s were unstable, in that they were highly variable. The appendix to this chapter shows that the Marshall-Lerner condition is also the necessary condition for a stable foreign exchange market under floating rates. Thus highly variable exchange rates seemed to imply low trade elasticities. Second, many countries on fixed exchange rates have found their trade balance worsening after a devaluation, rather than improving.

---

[6]You are asked to show this in Problem 5b at the end of the chapter.

This is especially true of oil importers. Because the demand for oil is relatively inelastic in the short run, many small countries discover that a devaluation against the dollar raises their oil import bill proportionately when expressed in domestic currency, thus worsening their trade balance. When a deficit country is advised to devalue its currency, it often argues that its elasticities are too low for a devaluation to help.

A third factor that originally contributed to the rise of elasticity pessimism was that early econometric estimates of the demand elasticities were low, frequently less than half. However, there were a number of problems with these estimates. They ignored the possible simultaneous existence of an upward-sloping supply relationship, problems of aggregation, errors in the measurement of the variables, and the crucial role of *time lags*.[7] Some studies measure only relatively short-run elasticities, but abundant evidence indicates that the factor of time is important. Elasticities are higher in the long run, which makes the Marshall-Lerner condition more likely to hold.

The J-Curve

Some studies that allow for lags of import demand in response to changes in relative prices have found that only about 50 percent of the full quantity adjustment takes place in the first three years; 90 percent occurs in the first five years. For example, the dollar depreciated substantially between 1985 and 1987, but because of these lags, the favorable effect on the quantities of exports and imports did not begin to show up until the end of 1986, and the effect on the dollar trade balance did not begin to show up until the end of 1987.

In this case, contrary to what we have assumed, dollar prices of imports did not respond immediately or fully to the exchange rate. Many importers, rather than passing exchange rate changes immediately through to import prices, at first absorbed in their profit margins much of the difference between foreign currency prices and domestic currency prices. The delayed pass-through to import prices added an extra lag at the beginning, before the elasticities could even begin to come into play. The United States is unusual in how small a portion of an exchange rate change tends to be immediately passed through to import prices.

There are a number of reasons why demand elasticities rise over time, and why the quantities demanded are slow to respond even after the change in the exchange rate is passed through to import prices. First, there is a lag because of the imperfect dissemination of information, during which importers recognize that relative prices have changed.

Second, there is a lag in deciding to place a new import order. In the case of firms' imports of inputs, it may take months or years before inventories are depleted or machinery is worn out and replacements are needed. Also, a firm may be tied to a particular supplier, through implicit or explicit contracts. In the case of consumers' imports,

---

[7]Faulty measurement of prices is particularly common in foreign trade. For example, importers in some countries underinvoice, that is, they understate the price of their imports so as to minimize the import duty they must pay. Also, where laws require exporters to turn over all their foreign exchange earnings to the government, exporters might understate their prices to retain some of the scarce foreign exchange for themselves. Such measurement errors in the price data make it more difficult to discern a statistical relationship.

changing habits takes time. For example, when the price of energy jumps, continued strong demand causes many observers to assert that energy demand is essentially inelastic. With the passage of time, however, energy demand falls considerably. The adjustment process requires not only overcoming the momentum of old patterns of consumption but also changing where people live and what kind of cars they drive.

Third, after a new import order has been placed, there may be production and delivery lags before it is filled. Much internationally traded merchandise is still transported by ship, requiring weeks or months in transit. Payment is typically not made before delivery, even though the contract may have been signed months earlier.

The fourth reason why trade quantities respond more fully with the passage of time, and the reason that can potentially draw out the process the longest, is that producers sometimes relocate their factories to the country where costs are lower because of an exchange rate advantage, regardless of whether it is the home country of the producer or the country where the goods are sold. For example, when the yen appreciated strongly from 1985 to 1995, some Japanese firms that had previously been exporting with great success found that they were losing out to competition from countries with lower cost. To compete more effectively, they moved some operations to other countries with lower-valued currencies. Sales in the world market that were previously counted under Japan's exports came to be counted under the host countries' exports.

Thus the response of export and import quantities after an exchange rate change is greater in the long run than in the short run because companies are able to relocate their plant and equipment. The transition costs are large. For this reason, a company is unlikely to relocate until the change in the exchange rate has lasted long enough to convince the company that the fluctuation is not transitory. Such an endurance test may take as long as five or ten years. Indeed, even after the exchange rate has returned to old levels, a company that decided to move operations abroad when the dollar was high might never move back, after having incurred the costs of moving. The word *hysteresis* is used to describe such not-easily-reversed reactions.

The tendency of the elasticities to rise over time results in the commonly observed phenomenon of the J-curve. The trade balance following a devaluation is observed first to worsen and then to improve, in the J-like pattern of Figure 16.3. (The figure assumes an initial trade balance of zero.) At the moment of the devaluation, quantities have had no time to adjust and the Marshall-Lerner condition fails. In fact, if quantities do not respond at all initially, then only the negative valuation effect remains: The trade balance worsens by the initial level of exports times the percentage decrease in their foreign currency value caused by the devaluation.[8] However, as time passes, export demand begins to pick up and import demand begins to fall. A point is reached where the curve crosses the zero axis, which means that the elasticities are high enough to sum to one and the trade balance is back at zero. After that point, the Marshall-Lerner condition holds and the trade balance moves into surplus. The surplus must run for a

---

[8]If it takes time before the exchange rate change is passed through to domestic prices of imports, the initial worsening in the trade balance is spread over a longer period. The downward sweep of the J would then be more round than as shown in the figure.

FIGURE 16.3

The J-Curve

In the aftermath of a devaluation, the trade balance (1) worsens initially because of the perverse valuation effect, then (2) gradually improves over time as the elasticities rise, and finally (3) surpasses its starting point when the Marshall-Lerner condition is satisfied.

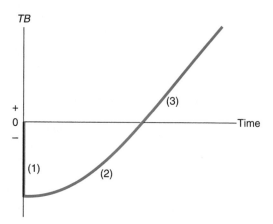

while if the reserves accumulated are to outweigh the reserves lost during the initial period of deficit.

All this assumes that exporters in the home country continue to supply whatever quantity is demanded at the same fixed price. This may get increasingly harder, especially if they are operating close to full capacity. The exporters in the devaluing country will be tempted to raise their prices in response to the increasing demand. Alternatively, their workers may demand higher wages in response to the greater cost of imported consumer goods, and the firms will be "forced" to pass through the higher labor costs in the form of higher prices. However, we will stay with the fixed-price assumption until Chapter 19.

16.3   Summary

The *exchange rate* is defined as the price of foreign exchange in terms of domestic currency. Under a floating exchange rate system, the central bank does not intervene in the foreign exchange market, and the exchange rate is determined by supply and demand in the market: An increase in the demand for foreign exchange causes an increase in the price of foreign exchange (a depreciation of the domestic currency). Under a fixed exchange rate system, an increase in demand for foreign exchange means that the central bank has to supply the difference—the net demand for foreign exchange, which is the balance-of-payments deficit—out of its foreign exchange reserves.

This chapter adopted the first and simplest model of what determines the balance of payments. Part IV does not include capital flows; this chapter looked only at the effect of the exchange rate on the trade balance, holding constant the level of income, interest rate, price level, and other macroeconomic variables that we introduce in subsequent chapters. A devaluation of the currency (or, under floating exchange rates, a depreciation) increases the quantity of exports demanded by foreign residents and decreases the quantity of imports, working to improve the trade balance. A third effect that works to worsen the trade balance, however, is the higher cost in domestic currency of any given quantity of imports that have prices set in foreign currency. Only if the sum of the import and export elasticities is high enough, as in the Marshall-Lerner condition, will the quantity effects dominate and the trade balance improve after the devaluation.

Empirically, the elasticities do appear to be high enough for a devaluation to improve the trade balance, but only after enough time has passed. In the short run, the trade balance often worsens, which gives rise to the J-curve pattern of response.

CHAPTER PROBLEMS

1. The newspaper reports that the dollar/euro exchange rate has risen.
   a. Does this news mean that the value of the dollar has risen or fallen? The value of the euro?
   b. Does this mean that the dollar/yen rate is more likely to have gone up than down?
   c. Does this mean that the euro/yen rate is more likely to have gone up than down? (*Hint*: If neither the dollar/yen rate nor the euro/yen rate has changed, what does that imply for the dollar/euro rate?)
2. Assume that the United States is currently exporting 10 million calculators at a price of $10 apiece and importing .002 million BMWs at a price of 100,000 euros apiece, and that the current exchange rate is 50 cents per euro. Calculate in a table the effect of a 10 percent devaluation of the dollar on each of 12 variables under each of four sets of assumptions about the elasticities (assuming infinitely elastic supply and no income effects). Round off.

		BEFORE THE DEVALUATION (a)		AFTER THE 10% DEVALUATION			
				(b)	(c)	(d)	(e)
			Export Elasticity:	0	$\frac{1}{2}$	1	4
			Import Elasticity:	0	0	$\frac{1}{2}$	1
(1) Export quantity		10m					
(2) Import quantity		.002m					
Expressed in $	(3) Export price	$10					
	(4) Import price						
	(5) Export earnings						
	(6) Import spending						
	(7) Trade balance						
Expressed in euros	(8) Export price						
	(9) Import price	100,000 euros					
	(10) Export earnings						
	(11) Import spending						
	(12) Trade balance						

3. **a.** In the example from Problem 2, comment on the trade balances in (b) and (c) versus those in (d) and (e).
   b. In which case is spending on imports in dollars very close to what it was before the devaluation? Why?
   c. In which case are earnings from exports in euros very close to what they were before the devaluation? Why?
   d. Starting from a position of importing .003 million BMWs, with everything else remaining the same, what would be the initial trade balance in dollars? For given elasticities, for example, (d), would the devaluation cause the trade balance to improve (i.e., the trade deficit decrease) by more than, less than, or the same amount as in Problem 2? (A numerical answer is not necessary but is fine if you can't do it intuitively.)

4. The trade balance expressed in domestic currency, with prices normalized to 1, is $TB = X(E) - EM(E)$.
   a. Illustrate the effect of a devaluation graphically; that is, repeat Figure 16.2, but with domestic-currency prices on the vertical axis.
   b. If the import elasticity is greater than 1 and the export elasticity is greater than 0, then the Marshall-Lerner condition holds. Is this condition sufficient to imply that TB, the trade balance expressed in domestic currency, improves? (You may assume the starting point is $TB = 0$.) Explain why, in terms of export revenue and import spending.

Extra Credit

5. **a.** If you know calculus, prove that the Marshall-Lerner condition is still the correct condition necessary and sufficient for a devaluation to improve TB, the trade balance expressed in *domestic* currency, starting from $TB = 0$.
   b. Starting from $TB < 0$, is the Marshall-Lerner condition too strong or too weak for a devaluation to improve the trade balance?
   c. The trade balance expressed in domestic currency is equal to the exchange rate times the trade balance expressed in foreign currency: $TB = E\ TB^*$.
      i. Does it follow that if the trade balance is in surplus when expressed in foreign currency, then it is also in surplus when expressed in domestic currency?
      ii. Does it follow that $dTB/dE = E\ dTB^*/dE$? Why not?
      iii. If initially $TB < 0$, which is greater: the left-hand side in the preceding question or the right-hand side?
      iv. Which side is greater if initially $TB > 0$?
      v. Which is greater if initially $TB = 0$?
   d. Assume we start from a position of deficit, and the elasticities sum approximately to one.
      i. Notice from the supplement to Chapter 16 that if $E\ M > X$ initially, the Marshall-Lerner condition is more than sufficient to imply $dTB^*/dE > 0$. For example, if both elasticities are half, that is enough for a devaluation to improve the trade balance in foreign currency. Conversely, from 5(b) we know that $dTB/dE < 0$ under these conditions. Can the trade balance improve in

terms of foreign currency while worsening in terms of domestic currency? (Refer to your answers to Questions c (ii) and c (iii).)

    ii.   If a devaluation brings the trade deficit back to zero in terms of foreign currency, then it must also do so in terms of domestic currency, because E times zero is zero. There is an apparent contradiction between this fact and the answer to (i). What is it? How do you reconcile the apparent contradiction?

6. It is possible (if old-fashioned) to stay within the partial equilibrium elasticities approach and yet relax the assumption that supply is infinitely elastic. The Bickerdicke-Robinson-Metzler condition for a devaluation to improve the trade balance is

$$\frac{\varepsilon_M \varepsilon_X (1 + \sigma_M + \sigma_X) - \sigma_M \sigma_X (1 - \varepsilon_M - \varepsilon_X)}{(\sigma_M + \varepsilon_M)(\sigma_M + \varepsilon_X)} > 0$$

where σ_M and σ_X are the supply elasticities of imports and exports, respectively.

    a. Prove that in the limit, as σ_M and σ_X go to infinity, the formula reduces to the Marshall-Lerner condition.

    b. Does the presence of the supply elasticity terms make the condition more or less stringent than the Marshall-Lerner condition?

SUGGESTIONS FOR FURTHER READING

Bergsten, C. Fred, ed. *International Adjustment and Financing, The Lessons of 1985–1991* (Washington, DC: Institute for International Economics, 1991). Did the 1985–1897 dollar depreciation reduce international trade imbalances as promised? At least one contributor, Paul Krugman, answers yes.

Mussa, Michael. "Exchange Rate Adjustments Needed to Reduce Global Payments Imbalances." In C. Fred Bergsten and John Williamston, eds., *Dollar Adjustment: How Far? Against What?* (Washington, DC: Institute for International Economics, 2004), pp. 113–138. The same issue, with respect to the sharp rise in U.S. deficits after 2001.

APPENDIX

Stability of the Foreign Exchange Market

The focus now turns from the comparative statics of the foreign exchange market, considered in Section 16.1, to the question of stability under a floating exchange rate. The theoretical question of whether a market equilibrium is stable (as in Chapter 3) is not the same as the question of whether the market price moves around a lot. The theoretical question is the following: If an equilibrium price is displaced slightly, will it tend to return to its original value?

(a)

(b)

(c)

FIGURE 16.A.1

Stability in the Foreign Exchange Market

The market is stable if the increase in the price of foreign exchange that results from an increase in demand for foreign exchange works to eliminate the excess demand. In cases (a) and (b) the market is stable, but in (c) it is not.

Think of foreign exchange traders as individuals who buy from and sell foreign exchange to each other on the floor of centralized exchanges in New York and elsewhere, or, in the case of the trading divisions of banks, on a network of telephones and computer terminals. Assume that whenever foreign exchange traders find that demand exceeds supply, they raise the exchange rate; whenever supply exceeds demand, they lower it. Consider the following three cases.

1. Assume that the demand curve slopes down and the supply curve slopes up, as in Figure 16.A.1(a). If the curves are derived from import spending and export earnings, respectively, this first case is the one where the elasticity of demand for exports is greater than one. In response to an increase in demand, from D to D', the traders raise the exchange rate. This raises export revenue, reduces the excess demand for foreign exchange, and thus constitutes a move toward the new equilibrium. The market is stable.

2. Next, assume that the demand curve slopes down and the supply curve slopes down also, but more steeply, as in Figure 16.A.1(b). Again, in response to an increase in demand, the traders raise the exchange rate, causing a move toward equilibrium.

Again the market is stable. This is the case where the elasticity of demand for exports is less than one (so the increase in the exchange rate *lowers* export revenue) but the sum of the two elasticities is nevertheless high enough to satisfy the Marshall-Lerner condition.

3. Finally, assume that both curves slope down, but the supply curve is less steep, as in Figure 16.A.1(c). This is the case where the Marshall-Lerner condition fails. This time, when the traders respond to the increase in demand by raising the exchange rate, they cause a move *away* from the new equilibrium. At the higher exchange rate, excess demand is even greater, so the traders raise the exchange rate again, and the situation is farther still from equilibrium. The market is unstable.

These examples show that the required condition for stability is that the supply curve slopes up or, if sloping downward, is steeper than the demand curve.

As a practical matter, a floating exchange rate usually will not shoot off to infinity. One possibility is that there are two stable equilibria surrounding an unstable one, much as is shown in Figure 3.A.1. Even if the market is stable in the technical sense, however, it may be unstable in the sense that the market-clearing price is highly variable. Very small changes in demand may produce large jumps in the exchange rate. High variability in the exchange rate may create uncertainty and imply high costs for importers and exporters. These are cited as an argument against floating exchange rates. This chapter showed that if the demands for exports and imports are relatively inelastic, then the curves representing the supply and demand for foreign exchange will be relatively steep. Resulting exchange rates may be highly variable if the exchange rate is called on to clear the trade balance.

CHAPTER 17

National Income and the Trade Balance

This chapter examines the interaction of income and the trade balance. We use the simple Keynesian multiplier model familiar from introductory macroeconomic textbooks but open up the model to international trade. This will turn out to make quite a difference.

Here *Keynesian* means simply that prices are assumed to be fixed (in terms of the currency of the producing country, as in Chapter 16) and therefore that changes in demand are reflected in output instead of price. This assumption is realistic for the short run, especially in an economy with unemployed labor and excess capacity. Empirical observation shows that prices are not perfectly flexible (to come in Chapter 19). In addition to the short-run realism, a second reason for continuing to hold prices fixed here concerns the structure of the remainder of the book. It helps to encounter new variables one at a time. Chapter 16 focused on the effect of changes in the exchange rate. This chapter adds the effect of changes in income. Only in Chapter 19 will we be ready for changes in the price level, followed by international capital flows and other factors. The introduction of all these variables at once would be quite confusing, so they will be introduced one by one.

17.1 The Small-Country Keynesian Model

In contrast to our assumption in Chapter 16, this section recognizes that import demand depends on more than just relative prices. (We continue to assume that suppliers fix prices in terms of their own currencies, so that the relative price of imports is simply the exchange rate, E.) Here we see that import demand also depends on income, Y.

$$M = M_d(E, Y) \tag{17.1}$$

The marginal propensity to import out of income[1] is represented by m.

$$M = \overline{M} + mY \tag{17.2}$$

---

[1]From this point on, imports are defined in domestic, not foreign, units. In other words, if the economy is the United States, M (like Y and the other variables) is expressed in dollars. Because the price level is assumed to be fixed, this is the same as expressing everything in units of U.S. output: number of automobiles, bushels of wheat, and so on.

This linear import function is analogous to the standard Keynesian consumption function

$$C = \overline{C} + cY \tag{17.3}$$

where c is the marginal propensity to consume. The essence of the Keynesian consumption function is that households' consumption increases, but less than proportionately, in response to an increase in households' disposable income.

Equation 17.2 does not show the exchange rate explicitly because the first step will be to consider the case of a fixed exchange rate. Although many countries have highly variable exchange rates, there are several reasons for beginning with the case of a fixed exchange rate. First, it will provide a greater understanding of the 1950s and 1960s, when almost all countries had fixed exchange rates. Second, it will aid in understanding the many countries that, today, still have fixed exchange rates. Twelve European countries, for example, have adopted the ultimate mechanism for fixing their exchange rates (vis-à-vis each other) by joining the European Economic and Monetary Union (EMU) and adopting the euro as their currency, created in 1999. Third, it will make it easier to evaluate the frequently heard proposals to restore stability in exchange rates—from ambitious schemes for a complete return to firmly fixed rates to more moderate proposals for target zones.[2] Finally, with the exchange rate held fixed, it is easier to understand how the economy operates—before proceeding to what happens when the exchange rate can change.

The demand for exports (foreigners' imports) should be a function (analogous to Equation 17.1) of relative prices and foreigners' income, Y^*.

$$X = X_d(E, Y^*) \tag{17.4}$$

Most countries are small enough that, although developments in the rest of the world have important implications for the domestic economy, any impact of the domestic economy on the rest of the world can be safely ignored. Thus this section begins with the Keynesian small-country assumption that foreign income is exogenous. (This is in contrast to the very different *classical* small-country assumption, which is that relative prices are exogenous. That assumption is ruled out when export prices are set in domestic currency.) Now we have the simplified export demand function,

$$X = X_d(E)$$

or, staying with a fixed exchange rate for the moment,

$$X = \overline{X}. \tag{17.5}$$

In other words, exports are given exogenously. Thus, from Equations 17.2 and 17.5, the trade balance is given by

$$TB = X - M = \overline{X} - (\overline{M} + mY) \tag{17.6}$$

---

[2]Discussed in Section 27.6.

The Determination of Income

The definition of equilibrium in the Keynesian model is that output supplied, Y, is equal to output demanded. In the closed economy, demand comes from three sources: consumption by households (C), investment by firms (I),[3] and spending on various goods and services by the government (G). In the simple Keynesian version with which this chapter begins, investment, like government expenditure, is taken to be exogenous (which is shown by a bar over the letter), even though consumption is endogenous. The open economy factors a fourth source of net demand for domestic goods—that coming from foreign residents—into the total demand for domestic goods. Net foreign demand for domestic goods is the trade balance, or net exports ($TB = X - M$). So the equilibrium condition is as follows:

$$Y = C + I + G + X - M$$
$$= \overline{C} + cY + \overline{I} + \overline{G} + \overline{X} - (\overline{M} + mY)$$

Solving for the equilibrium level of income,

$$Y = \frac{\overline{A} + \overline{X} - \overline{M}}{s + m} \tag{17.7}$$

where, for notational simplicity, we have defined the exogenous component of aggregate demand as $\overline{A} \equiv \overline{C} + \overline{I} + \overline{G}$, and the marginal propensity to save as $s \equiv 1 - c$. (The part of each additional dollar of income that is not consumed must be saved.)

If government spending goes up by \$1 billion ($= \Delta \overline{G} = \Delta \overline{A}$), by how much does income go up? $\Delta Y = \$(1/(s + m))$ billion. The parameters s and m are fractions totaling less than 1 because imports are a subset of total consumption. It follows that the multiplier is greater than 1: An autonomous increase in spending of a given amount raises income by a greater amount. The explanation is that those who produce the goods and services to which the spending goes see an increase in their income and so raise their spending; this, in turn, raises the incomes of other producers, who raise their spending, and so forth. The infinite series has a finite sum for the same reason as in a closed economy: At each round of spending, some "leaks out" of the system through saving, so each round is smaller than the previous round. Notice that in the special case of a closed economy, where $m = 0$, the multiplier reduces to the familiar $1/s$, or $1/(1 - c)$. In general, however, the open-economy multiplier is less than $1/s$ because of a second leakage from the spending stream: through imports.

17.2   The National Saving-Investment Identity

To look at the Keynesian model graphically, it will be easier to work in terms of saving, which is equal to disposable income minus consumption, than in terms of consumption itself. To do so, first recognize that, in addition to decomposing GDP into the sectors to

---

[3]Investment includes not only additions to plant, equipment, and inventories by firms but also residential construction.

which the output is sold $(C + I + G + X - M)$, an alternative is to decompose income from the viewpoint of those who earn it and dispose of it: consumption (C), saving (S), and taxes (T).[4]

$$C + S + T \equiv \text{GNP} \equiv \text{GDP} + \text{NFI}$$

$$= C + I + G + X - M + \text{NFI}$$

NFI is net factor income, which includes investment income from abroad. Subtract C from both sides and rearrange.

$$S + (T - G) - I = X - M + \text{NFI}$$

Think of the government budget surplus $(T - G)$ as government saving or, inasmuch as the number is often negative, think of the government budget deficit $(G - T)$ as government "dissaving." Define total national saving as $NS = S + (T - G)$. Then the equation is

$$NS - I \equiv CA \qquad (17.8)$$

Equation 17.8 is called the National Savings Identity. It is described as follows: National saving exceeds investment by an amount equal to the current account balance, which is the rate of accumulation of claims on the rest of the world. Intuitively, all national saving, NS (whatever is left over after financing the government), goes into building up either the stock of capital or the stock of foreign claims. For example, beginning in the 1980s, a very low rate of U.S. national saving, consisting especially of high federal budget deficits, translated into high deficits in the current account balance, as Table 17.1 shows. In the late 1990s U.S. national saving increased because the federal budget deficit was eliminated, and indeed was turned into a surplus. But private saving remained low and investment rose faster than national saving. The result, by definition, was a rising current account deficit. Since 2001, record current account deficits have been associated with a return to large government deficits and low national savings.

Another way of viewing Equation 17.8 is in terms of the funds available to finance domestic investment, I. Investment must be financed either by the nation's domestically generated savings, NS, or by funds made available for the use of the home country by the rest of the world, that is, foreign lending to finance the domestic trade deficit. In Italy most investment is financed domestically, whereas in the United States more investment is in effect financed abroad.

17.3   Multipliers

Now consider Figure 17.1, where the horizontal axis represents income, Y. The saving gap, $NS - I$, is an increasing function of Y, with slope s. Higher income means higher

---

[4]If we wish to include government transfers such as unemployment compensation and social security in the model, then T should be defined as taxes *net* of these transfers. If there are *international* transfers, they should also be added in along with NFI.

TABLE 17.1

U.S. National Saving, Investment, and Current Account

	Net Private Saving (% of GDP) (1)	Government Saving (% of GDP) (2) = (3) + (4)	State and Local Saving (% of GDP) (3)	Federal Saving (% of GDP) (4)	Net National Saving (% of GDP) (5) = (1) + (2)	Net Domestic Investment (% of GDP) (6)	Current Account (% of GDP) (7) ≈ (5) − (6)
(average)							
1961–1964	9.9	1.4	0.9	0.5	11.2	10.4	0.8
1965–1968	10.6	0.7	0.9	−0.2	11.3	11.3	0.5
1969–1972	9.4	−0.4	0.8	−1.3	8.9	9.6	0.1
1973–1976	10.2	−1.6	0.6	−2.2	8.6	8.8	0.7
1977–1980	9.4	−0.9	0.6	−1.4	8.6	10.1	−0.1
1981–1984	10.3	−3.5	0.2	−3.7	6.8	8.2	−0.7
1985–1988	8.6	−3.1	0.4	−3.5	5.5	8.6	−2.8
1989–1992	7.5	−3.3	0.1	−3.4	4.2	6.2	−0.8
1993–1996	6.5	−2.7	0.2	−2.9	3.8	6.7	−1.3
1997–2000	4.9	1.2	0.5	0.7	6.1	8.5	−2.6
2001–2004	4.4	−2.4	−0.1	−2.2	2.0	6.6	−4.5

Note: "Net" means net of depreciation of the capital stock.
Source: National Income and Product Accounts, Bureau of Economic Analysis, U.S. Department of Commerce.

FIGURE 17.1

Fiscal Expansion in the Keynesian Model

The saving-investment line slopes up because higher income, Y, means higher national savings, NS. An increase in government spending of ΔG shifts the line down. Point D is the new intersection with the $X - M$ line.

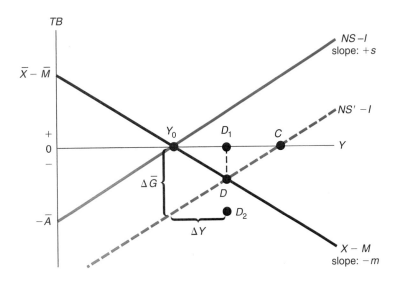

saving.[5] The other line in the figure represents the trade balance, $X - M$, a decreasing function of Y, with slope $-m$ as given by Equation 17.6: Higher income means higher imports. Equation 17.8 states that equilibrium occurs where the two lines cross. Figure 17.1 shows the initial intersection as occurring when saving equals investment and exports equal imports. But the choice of this location is arbitrary; equilibrium could occur as easily above or below the zero axis.

The Multiplier Effect of a Fiscal Expansion

Let us consider as our first experiment a fiscal expansion $\Delta \overline{G}$. It shifts the $NS - I$ line down by that amount because $NS = S + (T - G)$. It raises equilibrium income to point D, the intersection on the new line $NS' - I$ in Figure 17.1. Notice in the graph that the change in income is less than in the closed-economy case: A closed-economy equilibrium would occur where the $NS' - I$ line crosses the zero axis at point C, which lies farther to the right than D.

The multiplier for government spending, or for other autonomous components of spending, follows from Equation 17.7:

$$\frac{\Delta Y}{\Delta \overline{A}} = \frac{1}{s + m} \tag{17.9}$$

Again, $\Delta Y / \Delta \overline{G}$, the multiplier effect on income, is smaller in the open economy than in the closed economy because there is leakage through imports in addition to the leakage through saving. The multiplier formulas could also be derived geometrically. (See Problem 3 at the end of the chapter.)

The convenient aspect of this graph is that it depicts not only income, Y, measured on the horizontal axis, but also the trade balance, $TB = X - M$, measured on the vertical axis. In Figure 17.1, the fiscal expansion pushes the trade balance into deficit because the higher income draws in more imports. Algebraically,

$$\Delta TB = -\Delta M = -m\Delta Y$$

Now use the multiplier, from Equation 17.9, to substitute for ΔY.

$$\Delta TB = -\frac{m}{s + m}\Delta \overline{G} \tag{17.10}$$

Equation 17.10 shows that the effect of a fiscal expansion on the trade balance is clearly negative.

In short, the trade balance has been *countercyclical* in the United States, as in most countries. Historical swings in the U.S. trade balance reflect the economy marching up and down the $X - M$ line in Figure 17.1. In the macroeconomic expansions of the

---

[5]If it is recognized that tax revenues, T, depend positively on income, then the slope of NS is higher than s (by the amount of the marginal tax rate). For simplicity in what follows, taxes will be treated as if they were exogenous. The marginal tax rate is introduced, however, in problem 1 of Chapter 18. We also ignore the distinction between the current account and trade balance in Figure 17.1; that is, we assume away investment income and international transfers.

1976–1978, 1983–1989, 1992–2000, and 2002–2005 periods, imports rose and the trade deficit widened (as at point D). In the recessions of 1980, 1990–1991, and 2001, the trade deficit shrank.

The Multiplier Effect of an Increase in Exports

Now consider the effect of a devaluation. Assume that the Marshall-Lerner condition is satisfied. This analysis could apply equally well to other exogenous sources of improvement in the trade balance, such as a shift in tastes away from foreign goods or an exogenous increase in foreign income. Algebraically, these changes are represented as an increase in $\overline{X} - \overline{M}$. Graphically, they are represented as an upward shift in the $X - M$ line by the distance $\Delta\overline{X}$ in Figure 17.2.[6] If changes in income could somehow be ignored (as in Chapter 16), the trade balance would improve by the vertical distance $\Delta\overline{X}$. The magnitude of $\Delta\overline{X}$ depends on the magnitude of the devaluation and of the elasticities. An elasticity of 1, for example, would imply that exports increase by the same percentage as the devaluation.

In addition to the obvious effect of raising the trade balance, however, the devaluation stimulates income. Algebraically, from Equation 17.7,

$$\Delta Y = \frac{1}{s + m}\Delta\overline{X}$$

FIGURE 17.2

Devaluation in the Keynesian Model

The devaluation shifts up the $X - M$ line (assuming the Marshall-Lerner condition is met). Income, Y, rises. The trade balance also rises, but less than it would if income were held constant.

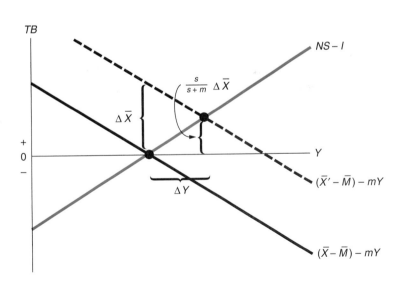

---

[6]For simplicity, the exogenous increase in net exports is represented by $\Delta\overline{X}$, even though it could be a fall in imports as well as a rise in exports. One might want to think of the special case where the import elasticity is 1, so total import spending is unaffected by changes in the exchange rate, and the entire improvement in the dollar trade balance comes from export earnings X.

The higher income means higher imports, according to the marginal propensity to import, and so the improvement in the trade balance is less than if income were held fixed.

$$\Delta TB = \Delta \overline{X} - m\Delta Y$$

$$= \Delta \overline{X} - m\frac{1}{s+m}\Delta \overline{X} \qquad (17.11)$$

$$= \frac{1}{s+m}\Delta \overline{X}$$

The key point is that $\frac{1}{s+m} < 1$; the trade balance improves by less than the full exogenous increase in net exports because of the higher imports that are drawn in by higher income. Yet the effect is still positive: Imports do not go up as much as exports.

17.4 The Transfer Problem

Our model can be applied to an old problem in international macroeconomics. As was discussed in Section 3.4, the transfer problem originated with war reparations payments, such as those from Germany to France after World War I; yet it can be applied whenever there is a transfer of income from one country to another. More recent examples abound. The OPEC price increase at the end of 1973 could be modeled as an exogenous transfer from the oil-importing countries to OPEC. The 1982 international debt crisis could be modeled as an exogenous transfer from debtor countries to creditor countries (the transfer is the increase in debt-service requirements). The 1991 payments from Japan, Germany, Saudi Arabia, Kuwait, and other countries to the United States in connection with military operations against Iraq constitute the best example because they were literally unilateral transfers in the balance of payments.

The important issue is the extent to which the recipient country will spend the transfer on imports and the transferor will cut back on its imports. Recall that the current account is defined as the balance of trade on goods and services *plus* transfers received (or minus transfers paid). Let us consider a small country that has just received a transfer. If it spends the entire transfer on imports and its trade balance worsens by precisely this amount, then the overall current account is unchanged at the existing exchange rate. In this case, the transfer is considered "fully effected," meaning that the *financial* transfer leads to the intended matching transfer of *real goods*. If the recipient spends most of the money on its *own* goods, its overall current account will improve at the old exchange rate—the negative effect on the trade balance will be smaller than the transfer. In this case the transfer is "undereffected."

Now consider a country making a transfer T, say Saudi Arabia in 1991.[7] We saw in the model of Chapter 3 that a transfer may or may not be undereffected. In the

---

[7]Here it is assumed for simplicity of notation that the money for the transfer is raised by taxation of the public, T.

Keynesian model, however, the transfer is *necessarily* undereffected.[8] The change in the trade balance is less than the transfer. Why?

Recall the National Saving Identity, Equation 17.8:

$$NS - I \equiv CA$$

If the government finances the transfer with taxes, the budget balance is unchanged. Given that I is exogenous, if S were also unchanged it would follow from the National Saving Identity that the trade balance would increase by exactly the transfer, T. But disposable income falls by the amount of the transfer. In a Keynesian model, that leads to a fall in S. Therefore the trade balance must rise by less than the transfer.

The point is demonstrated graphically in Figure 17.3. Note that the horizontal axis is disposable income Y_d, not output GDP, because both saving and imports depend on Y_d, not Y, once the distinction is acknowledged. The current account, CA, depends on disposable income with the same slope as the trade balance ($-m$, the marginal propensity to import). If there is no transfer, then the trade balance coincides with the current account. An outward transfer, T, shifts the CA line down. Saving-investment equilibrium is given at point R, where the new CA line intersects $NS - I$. At this lower level of disposable income, imports have fallen and thus the trade balance is in surplus at point S. Yet the trade balance, TB, is not as large as the outward transfer, T. The overall current account, $CA = TB - T$, necessarily goes into deficit at point R. So long as the $NS - I$ curve is not flat—that is, so long as the marginal propensity to save is greater than zero—the transfer is undereffected.

FIGURE 17.3

Transfer Worsens the Total Current Account

A transfer, T, to a foreign country improves the domestic trade balance, $X - M$, because imports fall when domestic disposable income falls. Nevertheless, in the Keynesian model the overall current account, $X - M - T$, falls.

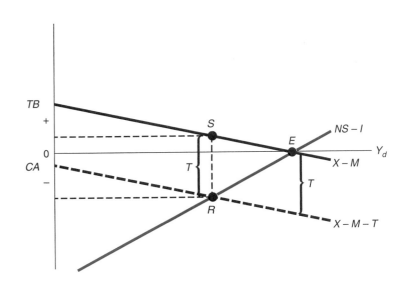

[8]The first to show this was not Keynes, but Lloyd Metzler, "The Transfer Problem Reconsidered," *Journal of Political Economy* (June 1942): 397–414.

17.5   For a Large Country: The Two-Country Keynesian Model

So far we have assumed exports to be exogenous with respect to income. This section relaxes that assumption, taking into account how exports depend on developments in the rest of the world. In the examination of a large country, developments in the rest of the world, in turn, depend on developments in the home country. The rest of the world, which we aggregate into a single foreign country, and the home country are interdependent.[9]

Repercussion Effects

If income, Y^*, increases in the foreign country, foreigners import more from the home country.

$$X = \overline{X} + m^*Y^*$$

The foreign marginal propensity to import is represented by m^*. In Equation 17.7, $\overline{X}$ is replaced by the new expression for exports, resulting in the new formula for equilibrium income.

$$Y = \frac{\overline{A} + \overline{X} - \overline{M} + m^*Y^*}{s + m} \tag{17.12}$$

Obviously, domestic income depends positively on foreign income. Figure 17.4 graphs this relationship. The slope $\Delta Y/\Delta Y^*$ is $m^*/(s + m)$, which is less than 1 unless the foreign country is much more open to imports than the home country.

    The relationship explains how expansion in one country is transmitted to its trading partners through the trade balance. For example, in 1977–1978 the United States pressured Germany and Japan to expand their economies. The plan, known as the locomotive theory, was to help pull the rest of the world out of recession. Often the United

FIGURE 17.4

Transmission from Foreign Income to Domestic Income

When foreign income, Y^*, rises, imports into the foreign country rise—that is, exports from the domestic country rise; as a result, domestic income, Y, also rises.

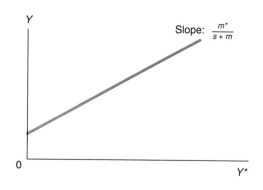

Slope: $\frac{m^*}{s+m}$

[9]The Keynesian two-country model was developed by James Meade, *The Theory of International Economic Policy*, Vol. I: *The Balance of Payments* (London, Oxford University Press, 1952), Chapters 4 and 5.

States has been the locomotive pulling the world out of recession. In each episode, the smaller, more open, and developing countries were anxious for the big industrialized countries to expand because the economies of the smaller countries depend particularly on foreign income. Of course, contraction is transmitted across countries, as well. The prime example is the Great Depression of the 1930s, when declining income in one country would result in declining imports, and thus declining income, among its trading partners.

Now we are ready to drop the assumption that foreign income is exogenous. The rationale has been that the domestic economy is too small to affect foreign income. However, when a country as large as the United States (or the European Union or Japan) expands, and consequently imports more from its trading partners, those imports are a large enough component of world demand to raise income and expenditure significantly among the trading partners. Then a large enough fraction of the foreign expenditure is spent on domestic goods, so that foreigners' imports from the home country in turn rise significantly. In other words, part of the spending that leaks out, flows back. The result is that income increases in the home country, the place that began the expansion, by more than one would expect based on its spending alone (the model in Section 17.1). The feedback through the trading partner can be called a repercussion effect. To model the repercussion effect, we now consider two countries that are each large enough to affect the other's income.

The Solution to the Two-Country Model

To make foreign income endogenous, the foreign country is modeled analogously to the home country, recognizing that its exports are the home country's imports. That is, they are a function, $\overline{M} + mY$, of the home country's income. Similarly, its imports are the home country's exports; they are a function, $\overline{X} + m^*Y^*$, of the foreign country's income. Then the solution for equilibrium foreign income is

$$Y^* = \frac{\overline{A}^* + \overline{M} + mY - \overline{X}}{s^* + m^*} \tag{17.13}$$

where $\overline{A}^*$ represents the autonomous components of foreign expenditure and s^* the foreign marginal propensity to save. This is simply the other country's version of Equation 17.12.

Equilibrium income for each country is indicated algebraically by solving the two equations simultaneously.[10] The multiplier for a domestic expansion turns out to be

$$\frac{\Delta Y}{\Delta A} = \frac{1}{s + m - \dfrac{m^*m}{s^* + m^*}} \tag{17.14}$$

The important point is that it exceeds the small-country multiplier $\frac{1}{s+m}$ derived in Section 17.1. (In terms of either Figure 17.5 or the appendix figure, the expansion

---

[10]You are asked to do this in Problem 8a at the end of the chapter. Also see the appendix.

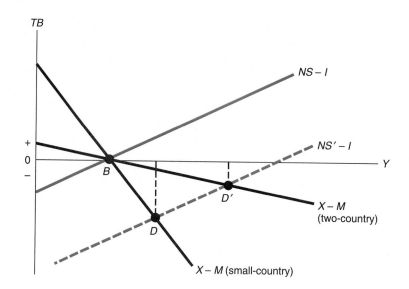

results in a move to the new intersection at D', whereas the intersection would be at point D if foreign income, Y^*, were kept constant.) Why? Some of the expenditure stream that leaks out as imports now returns as exports. For every dollar increase in domestic income, imports go up by m; because the other country's exports go up by m, its income goes up by $\frac{m}{s^* + m^*}$, and so it imports more from the home country. This effect is represented by the term $(m^*m)/(s^* + m^*)$ in Equation 17.14. Because it reduces the denominator, it increases the multiplier. The small-country multiplier is the special case where a negligibly small proportion of foreign expenditure falls on domestic goods ($m^* \approx 0$), so this term can be ignored. Conversely, the multiplier is still necessarily *less* than the closed-economy multiplier, $1/s$, as long as m and $s^* > 0$. It is not possible for all of the expenditure that leaks out through the trade balance to come back, as long as any foreign income is saved.

We can continue to use a version of the $X - M = NS - I$ graph of Figure 17.1. Because

$$\Delta TB = m^*\Delta Y^* - m\Delta Y \qquad (17.15)$$

we can substitute

$$\Delta Y^* = \frac{m}{s^* + m^*}\Delta Y$$

from Equation 17.13 and so find the new slope of the $X - M$ line:

$$\Delta TB = \left(m^* \frac{m}{s^* + m^*} - m\right)\Delta Y$$

$$\Delta TB/\Delta Y = -\frac{ms^*}{s^* + m^*} \qquad (17.16)$$

Notice that the slope is close to $-m$, the slope of the TB line in the small-country case, if m^* is small. In general, however, the slope is less in absolute value than $-m$, as evidenced in Figure 17.5. It is possible to see from the intersection with the $NS' - I$ line at point D' the proposition already shown algebraically: An expansion (rightward shift of $NS - I$) has a greater effect on domestic income in the two-country model than in the small-country model because there is less leakage through the trade deficit.

Empirical Evidence on Growth and Import Elasticities

Figure 17.6 shows the U.S. balances for goods and services and the current account (as shares of GDP) for the last half century. In the 1970s the trade balance went into deficit for the first time since World War II, but it was small enough that the current-account balance still averaged zero. More recently, however, the trade deficit has far exceeded its previous record. These large trade deficits have generated concern throughout the U.S. economy. They represent lost output and employment in those sectors or firms that rely on overseas customers for a rising share of their sales, as well as in those sectors or firms that face tough competition from rapidly rising imports. Furthermore, the equally large current-account deficits mean that the country is rapidly going into debt to foreign investors. Members of Congress and editorial writers rail against the deficits, some adopting protectionist views. Why have these deficits occurred?

FIGURE 17.6

U.S. Trade Balance and Current Account Balance, 1946–2005

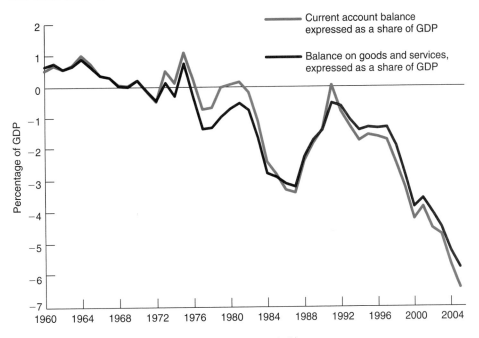

Source: Department of Commerce (Bureau of Economic Analysis).

Part of the answer is that in 1983–1984, and again in 1992–2000 and 2002–2005, the United States was expanding more rapidly than were its trading partners. As is seen from Equation 17.15, if the home country expands faster than the foreign country, the home country suffers a worsening trade balance—assuming that the two countries have the same marginal propensity to import.

What happens if both countries expand together, i.e., if income growth is equal? If the two countries have the same elasticities of import demand with respect to income, then there is no effect on the trade balance. The elasticity of demand with respect to income is the marginal propensity to import ($m = \Delta M/\Delta Y$) divided by the ratio of imports to income: $(\Delta M/\Delta Y)/(M/Y)$. The usual way to think of it is the *percentage* change in imports that results from a given *percentage* change in income, $(\Delta M/M)/(\Delta Y/Y)$. There is evidence that imports are more elastic with respect to income in the United States than they are in many of its trading partners.[11] The developing countries and Japan have lower income elasticities.

One implication that follows for developing countries and any other countries exporting goods that face highly income-elastic demand is that their incomes tend to be procyclical: When the world is in recession, demand for their goods tends to fall more than demand for goods produced by other countries, and so their incomes fall more than proportionately. The high variability in income is particularly severe for developing countries producing a single commodity, such as copper or oil, that serves as an intermediate input in other countries' production processes with little scope for substitution.

A second implication would also follow if these elasticities were assumed to apply to long-run, as well as short-run, changes in income: There will be a long-run secular trend in the trade balance in favor of these countries and against the United States, and other producers of manufactured goods, who face demand that is less income-elastic. Indeed, this could be part of the explanation for the long-term trend toward deficit in the U.S. trade balance reported in Figure 17.6.

It has been suggested, however, that the long-term income elasticities are in reality not as high as the short-term elasticities when care is taken to separate long-term growth in income from exogenous trends such as increased supply capacity in the newly industrialized countries. Some have discerned a secular trend in trade adverse to the raw materials produced by developing countries. The NIEs, such as Hong Kong, Singapore, South Korea, and Taiwan,[12] have achieved strong trade positions through policies of growth led by exports—not of traditional raw materials but of manufactured goods, beginning with labor-intensive manufactures such as textiles and elec-

---

[11]Some empirical evidence on how the income elasticities of import demand vary across countries was presented in a famous paper by Hendrik Houthakker and Stephen Magee, "Income and Price Elasticities in World Trade," *Review of Economics and Statistics,* 51, no. 2 (1969): 111–124.

[12]These four entities are sometimes called newly industrialized economies, or NIEs, instead of NICs, in deference to the People's Republic of China, which retook responsibility for the British colony of Hong Kong in 1997 and has never recognized the independence of Taiwan.

tronics. The pattern that fits them best—and now China—is the product cycle.[13] For any given technology, a secular trend exists against the United States and in favor of those countries able to adopt the technology to produce the same goods at lower cost. Yet the United States and other technological leaders have always innovated and stayed one step ahead, at least up until now.

17.6 Summary

This chapter added a second factor, national income, or GDP, to the exchange rate in the determination of the trade balance. When income increases, the demand for imports increases, and that, in turn, works to decrease the trade balance. Because the trade balance is a component of income, the determination of both variables must be considered simultaneously.

Because we have maintained the assumption that the prices of domestic goods are fixed (in terms of domestic currency), the resulting model is Keynesian: Changes in demand are reflected in output, not in prices. This assumption is more realistic in the short run than the long run.

The most important conclusions were evident even in the simplest form of the model where the level of foreign income is held constant. This form is realistic given the assumption that the domestic country is too small to affect foreign income. The first conclusion concerned changes in government spending: (1) Such changes have a multiplier effect on national income because at each round of spending some proportion of the income earned is passed on in a new round of spending; but (2) the effect on income is smaller than in closed-economy textbooks because at each round of spending some income leaks out of the country in the form of higher import spending and a higher trade deficit. Feedback effects via foreign income, which only need be taken into account if the home country is large, work to increase the effect of an expansion on domestic income.

The next conclusions concern devaluations: (3) If the Marshall-Lerner condition is met, a devaluation will raise the trade balance, as in Chapter 16,[14] and this in turn will improve income because of the multiplier, but (4) because the higher income means higher imports, the increase in the trade surplus will be less than it was when income effects were omitted.

Other important questions can also be explored with the simple Keynesian model. (5) When a country makes an exogenous transfer to its trading partner (reparations, foreign aid, or interest payments), it will generally experience an improvement of its trade balance that is smaller than the amount of the transfer; thus, its total current account will deteriorate (at a given exchange rate). Chapter 18 will consider further applications.

---

[13]See the discussion of the product cycle in Chapter 9.
[14]The appendix to Chapter 18 explores a qualification to this conclusion that arises if saving depends on the terms of trade the "Laursen-Metzler-Harberger" effect.

CHAPTER PROBLEMS

1. In the Keynesian multiplier process, at each round of spending some proportion of the income is passed on by its recipients as a new round of spending. The number of rounds is infinite. Does this mean that the total effect on income is infinite? Why not?

2. The multiplier is greater than 1 if $s + m < 1$. Does this condition hold? Do you think $M < C$ or $M > C$? Why?

3. Look carefully at the geometry of Figure 17.1.
   a. What is $\Delta \overline{G}$ divided by $Y_0 C$, that is, by the horizontal distance from point Y_0 to point C? (Remember the definition of the slope of a line.) Then what is $Y_0 C / \Delta \overline{G}$? What have you just shown about the fiscal multiplier in a closed economy?
   b. What is the vertical distance $D_2 D$, expressed relative to ΔY? What is the distance $D_1 D$, expressed relative to ΔY? Now take the sum of the two vertical distances: What is $D_1 D_2 / \Delta Y$? Then what is $\Delta Y / \Delta \overline{G}$? What have you just shown about the multiplier in an open economy? How does it compare to the answer in (a), and why, intuitively?

4. Would you expect the multiplier to be highest in Australia, Luxembourg, or Singapore?

5. Consider an increase in a country's budget deficit.
   a. What must happen to private saving, investment, or the current account, according to the national saving identity?
   b. In the Keynesian model (leaving out any interest rate effects on investment), which of these alternatives, or what combination of them, results from a tax cut? What is the answer if investment is allowed to depend on the interest rate (as at the end of Chapter 18)?

   (For parts c–e, assume tax revenue depends on income, as in footnote 5 or Problem 1 of Chapter 18.)

   c. If there is a recession because of an exogenous fall in C, what is the effect on the budget deficit? Are the effects on private saving and the trade balance the same as in 5b?
   d. If there is a recession because of an exogenous fall in exports, what are the effects on the budget deficit, saving, and the trade balance?
   e. Are your answers to question b consistent with your answer regarding the national saving identity in question a?

6. This question concerns the Keynesian model.
   a. Recall that the definition of equilibrium is that output supplied is equal to output demanded:

   $$Y = A + TB$$

   where Y = Output
   A = Aggregate Demand, and
   TB = Trade Balance

Assume that Aggregate Demand is given by

$$A = \overline{A} + cY_d,$$

$$TB = \overline{X} - \overline{M} - mY_d$$

and disposable income is given by

$$Y_d = Y - \overline{TP}$$

where $\overline{TP}$ = tax payments, here assumed exogenous.

Solve for equilibrium output.

b. What is the tax multiplier $\Delta Y / \Delta \overline{TP}$? In this Keynesian model, how does the effect of a tax cut compare to the effect of an increase in government spending? Why?

c. In the mid-1990s, the U.S. government advised Japan to cut taxes, to revive economic growth. The Japanese government rejected the advice, arguing that the multiplier effect would be very small. What do you think were the grounds for its argument?

7. Consider a new transfer ΔT made by a small country to abroad, say by Saudi Arabia in 1991. The question posed by the transfer problem is the net effect on Saudi Arabia's current account.

The three lines in Figure 17.3 are represented by three equations:

$$NS - I = -\overline{A} + sY_d$$

where $\overline{A}$ includes all exogenous components of domestic spending;

$$TB = \overline{X} - \overline{M} - mY_d; \text{and}$$

$$NS - I = CA = TB - T$$

Solve for:

a. ΔY_d. This is the change in disposable income, equal to the change in output minus the change in the transfer.

b. ΔTB.

c. ΔCA. Is the transfer undereffected or overeffected, or does it depend on the parameters?

8. This question concerns the two-country model.

a. Solve Equations 17.12 and 17.13 simultaneously, to determine Y.

b. Use Equations 17.16 and 17.14 to solve for the effect of a spending rise on the trade balance:

$$\frac{\Delta TB}{\Delta \overline{A}} = \frac{\Delta TB}{\Delta Y} \frac{\Delta Y}{\Delta \overline{A}}$$

c. Compare your answers in b with the analogous expression in the small-country model. In which case is the fall in the trade balance greater and why?

9. In Section 17.4 we applied the transfer problem to a small country, but the problem is more often applied to two countries of approximately equal size (such as France and Germany).

   a. The transfer, ΔT, can be viewed as an exogenous decrease in the income of the transferring country *and* an exogenous increase in the income of the recipient country. The answer to 8b gives the effect of the first factor on the trade balance, and the analogous equation for the foreign country gives the effect of the second factor. Show that

   $$\frac{\Delta TB}{\Delta T} = \frac{ms^* + m^*s}{s^*s + ms^* + m^*s}$$

   b. Is the ratio necessarily less than 1? What if the marginal propensities to save are zero? How would the special case when the domestic country is so small that the foreign country spends almost nothing on its goods look?

   c. Show the effect on the current account, $\Delta CA = \Delta TB - \Delta T$. Does the current account of the transferor improve or worsen?

SUGGESTIONS FOR FURTHER READING

Goldstein, Morris, and Mohsin Khan. "Income and Price Effects in Foreign Trade." In Ronald Jones and Peter Kenen, eds., *Handbook of International Economics,* Vol. II (Amsterdam: Elsevier, 1985), Chapter 20, pp. 1041–1105. Econometric estimates of the elasticities of demand for imports and exports, including the distinction between short- and long-run elasticities of demand with respect to income.

Hooper, Peter, and Jaime Marquez. "Exchange Rates, Prices and External Adjustment in the United States and Japan." In Peter Kenen, ed., *Interdependence and the Macroeconomics of the Open Economy* (Princeton: Princeton University Press, 1995). Empirical analysis of the U.S. trade deficit and Japanese surplus.

Sachs, Jeffrey. "The Current Account and Macroeconomic Adjustment in the 1970s," *Brookings Papers on Economic Activity,* 1 (1981), pp. 201–268. A clear exposition of the current account as the outcome of a two-period saving decision (as in the appendix to Chapter 22), with special reference to the oil shocks of the 1970s and countries' responses.

APPENDIX

The Two-Country Model in Graphical Form

Figure 17.A.1 presents graphs of the two simultaneous equations: Equation 17.12, which gave Y as a function of Y^*, and Equation 17.13, which gave Y^* as a function of Y. The latter graph is analogous to Figure 17.5. It must be turned on its side in Fig-

FIGURE 17.A.1

Simultaneous Solution for Both
Countries' Incomes

A relationship runs from domestic income,
Y, to foreign income, Y^*. A domestic
expansion shifts the domestic line up so
that the new intersection occurs at D'.
The increase in Y is greater than in the
small-country model—which ignored
the repercussion effect of higher income
abroad (point D).

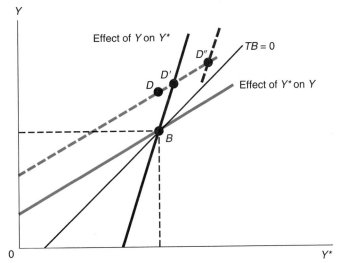

ure 17.A.1 to show it on the same axes as Figure 17.5. Equilibrium income for each
country is indicated graphically at the intersection of the two lines, point B.

Consider now an increase in domestic spending. In terms of Figure 17.5, the domestic income line shifts up vertically by the amount of the simple open-economy multiplier (the amount Y would rise if we were still holding Y^* constant). The expansion
results in a move to the new intersection at D', whereas the intersection would be at
point D if foreign income, Y^*, were kept constant. Why? As we learned in Section 17.5,
the multiplier is larger in the two-country model because of the repercussion effect.

Figure 17.A.1 can also be used to illustrate the point about an adverse trend in the
U.S. trade balance. The line that gives U.S. income, Y (as a function of foreign income,
Y^*), shifts out faster than the line that gives foreign income (as a function of U.S.
income). In terms of Equations 17.12 and 17.13, $\overline{A}$ increases faster than $\overline{A}^*$. The intersection moves up faster than it moves to the right. At point D'' it lies above the trade
balance equilibrium schedule (the slope of which is m^*/m, as we can see by setting
$\Delta TB = 0$ in Equation 17.15). The United States goes into deficit because its imports go
up faster than do those of its trading partners.

CHAPTER 18

Spending and the Exchange Rate in the Keynesian Model

Chapter 17 developed the Keynesian model for determining income and the trade balance in an open economy. In this chapter we consider some further applications of the same model, including how governments can change spending in pursuit of two of their fondest objectives—income and the trade balance. We begin with the question of how changes in spending are transmitted from one country to another. Throughout, we focus particularly on the role that changes in the exchange rate play in the process. We bring together the analysis of flexible exchange rates from Chapter 16 with the analysis of changes in expenditure from Chapter 17.

18.1 Transmission of Disturbances

Section 17.5 showed how income in one country depends on income in the rest of the world, through the trade balance. The effect varies considerably, depending on what is assumed about the exchange rate. This section compares the two exchange rate regimes, fixed and floating, with respect to the international transmission of economic disturbances. This comparison is one of the criteria that a country might use in deciding which of the regimes it prefers.

Transmission Under Fixed Exchange Rates

Our starting point will be the regime of fixed exchange rates. For simplicity, return to the small-country model of Section 17.1. In other words, ignore any repercussion effects via changes in foreign income. As Equation 17.9 implies, an internal disturbance, such as a fall in investment demand $\Delta \bar{I}$, changes domestic income by

$$\frac{\Delta Y}{\Delta \bar{I}} = \frac{1}{s + m} \tag{18.1}$$

in the small-country model. Recall that the multiplier here is smaller than in the closed-economy multiplier because some of the change in aggregate demand "leaks out," or is transmitted to the rest of the world. An external disturbance such as a fall in export demand, $\Delta \bar{X}$, changes income by the same amount.

$$\frac{\Delta Y}{\Delta \bar{X}} = \frac{1}{s + m} \tag{18.2}$$

In this case some of the *foreign* change in aggregate demand is transmitted through the trade balance to the *home* country.

The two-country model would serve as well here. The domestic spending multiplier would be a little higher, as in Equation 17.14, because some import leakage returns in the form of exports. The same applies to the export multiplier. The important point is that under fixed rates, disturbances are generally transmitted positively from the country of origin to the trading partners via the trade balance.

Transmission Under Floating Exchange Rates

Now assume that the central bank does not participate in the foreign exchange market. Thus the exchange rate adjusts automatically to ensure $BP = 0$. Continue to assume no capital flows (or transfers), so $TB = 0$ as well. In the case of an internal disturbance, a fall in investment demand $\Delta \bar{I}$ would cause a fall in income and a consequent trade surplus under a fixed exchange rate. The $S - I - G$ line shifts up, as is seen in Figure 18.1(a). However, under floating exchange rates a surplus is impossible because the central bank is no longer in the business of buying or selling foreign exchange. In response to what would otherwise be an excess supply of foreign currency, the price of foreign currency automatically falls—that is, the domestic currency automatically appreciates. The effect of an appreciation of the currency is the same as it would be if the government deliberately increased the value of the currency: Imports are stimu-

FIGURE 18.1

Insulation Under Floating Exchange Rates

Panel (a) shows how domestic disturbances are "bottled up" inside the country. A fall in investment, I, has a greater effect on income under a floating rate than under a fixed rate because the currency appreciates and discourages net exports. Panel (b) shows how the country is "insulated" from foreign disturbances. A fall in foreign demand causes the domestic currency to depreciate, which stimulates net exports.

(a) Internal Disturbance Under Floating Rates   (b) External Disturbance Under Floating Rates

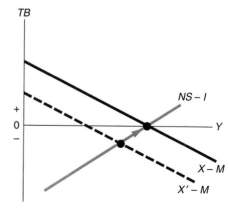

lated and exports discouraged, and the $X - M$ line shifts down. The shift will be whatever is required to restore the trade balance to equilibrium. The required change in the
exchange rate could be computed if the trade elasticities were known.

Whatever the exchange rate change, the ultimate effect is such that the trade balance remains at zero: $\Delta TB = 0$. From Equation 17.6,

$$\Delta TB = \Delta \overline{X} - m\Delta Y$$

So floating exchange rates imply that

$$\Delta \overline{X} = m\Delta Y$$

The downward shift in the component of net exports attributable to the appreciation
must be sufficient to offset the decrease in imports attributable to lower income. To
compute the change in income, note from Equation 17.7 that

$$\Delta Y = \frac{\Delta \overline{I} + \Delta \overline{X}}{s + m}$$

$$= \frac{\Delta \overline{I} + m\Delta Y}{s + m}$$

$$\Delta Y = \frac{\Delta \overline{I}}{s} \tag{18.3}$$

Compare this to the multiplier under fixed rates shown in Equation 18.1. The internal
disturbance has a greater effect under floating rates than under fixed rates. The disturbance induces an exchange rate change that reinforces the effect on aggregate
demand. In fact, the disturbance has the full closed-economy multiplier effect. The reason is that when the exchange rate fluctuates to keep the trade balance at zero, it
reproduces the effect of a closed economy. *All disturbances are bottled up inside the
country rather than being partially transmitted abroad.* The point can also be shown
graphically. The $X - M$ line becomes irrelevant. Equilibrium income is determined
wherever the $NS - I$ line crosses the zero axis because the floating exchange rate automatically ensures that the $X - M$ line crosses there as well. Because the $NS - I$ line
has slope s, a disturbance that shifts it up by $\Delta \overline{I}$ reduces income by $\Delta \overline{I} / s$.

Now consider the case of an external disturbance. A downward shift of the $X - M$
line, as in Figure 18.1(b), would cause a fall in income and a trade deficit on a given
exchange rate. The incipient trade deficit causes the currency to depreciate automatically, however, shifting the $X - M$ line back up until balanced trade is restored. At this
point the effect on income is eliminated as well: $\Delta Y = 0$. *The floating exchange rate
insulates the economy against foreign disturbances.* Again, by adjusting to keep the
trade balance at zero, it reproduces a closed economy.

To sum up, floating rates (in the absence of capital flows) restrict the effects of disturbances to the country of origin. This result suggests one possible basis on which a
country could choose between fixed and floating exchange rates. If the goal is to minimize the variability of domestic output, then the absence of international transmission
is desirable to the extent that disturbances originate abroad because the home country
is insulated from them. Floating would be better than fixed. However, the absence of

transmission is undesirable to the extent that disturbances originate domestically; the floating rate prevents these disturbances from being passed off to the rest of the world. Fixed is better than floating.

Conversely, if the goal is to allow each country to pursue its own independent policies, then the absence of transmission constitutes an argument for floating exchange rates. In the late 1960s when the world was still on fixed rates and excessive expansion in the United States was transmitted to the European countries as unwanted inflation, floating rates were suggested as the ideal solution. They would allow each country to pursue its preferred policies independently.

The conclusion that floating rates prevent transmission extends to the two-country model. As long as the trade balance is always zero, income must be determined by domestic demand. Chapter 25, however, will show that this conclusion does not extend to models with capital mobility, as then the trade balance need not equal zero. Furthermore, although foreign disturbances have no effect on domestic output and employment in the model of this chapter, they do affect domestic real income. The currency depreciation illustrated in Figure 18.1(b) turns the terms of trade against the home country: The price of imports rises in domestic terms, causing a fall in the real purchasing power of a given quantity of domestic output. Domestic residents will feel poorer even though national output is unchanged. Such changes in the terms of trade can have further implications; they are considered in the chapter appendix.

18.2 Expenditure-Switching and Expenditure-Reducing Policies

Chapter 17 explained the use of the Keynesian model in determining income and the trade balance. This section uses the model to show the most effective ways for government policy makers to combine the tools at their disposal to achieve their policy goals.

Adjustment to a Current Account Deficit

Consider a country running a current account deficit. It has two broad choices: *financing* the deficit or *adjustment*. By financing we mean that the country chooses to continue running the deficit for the time being, either by borrowing from abroad (on the private capital account) or by running down its central bank's holdings of reserves (on the official reserves transactions account). Let us say that the country instead wishes or is forced to adjust—that is, to change macroeconomic policies in such a way as to eliminate the current account deficit. How, specifically, can it do this?

Expenditure-reducing policies and expenditure-switching policies are alternative ways to reduce a trade deficit. Measures to reduce overall expenditure, such as reductions in government expenditure or increases in taxes, work to reduce a trade deficit because some of the eliminated expenditure would have fallen on imports. Conversely, measures to increase expenditure increase the trade deficit, as was evidenced in the prior chapter (for example, in Figure 17.1 and Equation 17.10). There are also expenditure-reducing policies other than fiscal contraction, in particular monetary contraction. Monetary policy will be covered at the end of the chapter.

Expenditure-switching policies are those that, for any given level of expenditure, work to improve the trade balance by switching expenditure away from foreign goods and toward domestic goods. In the case of domestic expenditure, the result is a fall in imports. In the case of expenditure by foreigners, the result is a rise in exports to them. The expenditure-switching policy focused on so far is devaluation, as in Figure 17.2 and Equation 17.11.

Expenditure-reducing and expenditure-switching policies are equally valid ways of eliminating a trade deficit. The most important difference between the two is that the former accomplishes this by reducing income and employment, whereas the latter does so by—or, more precisely, with the effect of—raising income and employment.

Types of Expenditure-Switching Policies

There are several possible expenditure-switching policies. One is price deflation, which makes domestic goods more attractive to residents of both countries. In practice, price deflation can usually be achieved only by expenditure reduction. The period of low income and high unemployment that must be endured before wages and prices come down can be long and painful. We continue to assume, in the Keynesian model, that because of the existence of minimum wage laws, unions, contracts, implicit contracts, money illusion—for whatever the reason—wage and price deflation is so difficult in the short run as to be ruled out.

Devaluation is the expenditure-switching policy on which we will continue to focus: Taking rigid prices as given, it works to cheapen domestic goods on world markets.

Direct trade controls can also be expenditure-switching policies. A common form of direct trade control is a tariff, which raises the price of imports and thus discourages domestic residents from buying them. An export subsidy, which lowers the price of exports and encourages foreign residents to buy them, is also sometimes used. A uniform 10 percent import tariff combined with a uniform 10 percent export subsidy would have the same effect on the relative prices facing each country as a 10 percent devaluation. The devaluation analysis would apply, in large measure unchanged.

In practice, tariffs and subsidies are enacted more often to help specific industries that are in trouble or that have sufficient political clout than to further macroeconomic purposes. Pure trade theory provides some persuasive microeconomic arguments against them, as explained in Part III. Nevertheless, these measures are sometimes imposed for macroeconomic reasons. In the 1930s the United States adopted the Smoot-Hawley tariff in an effort to switch expenditure toward domestic goods generally. Policies of this type, which are designed to switch spending to domestic products at the expense of other countries, are called "beggar-thy-neighbor."[1] The consequences in that case were disastrous, as was seen earlier in this text. Trading partners responded by putting up tariffs of their own to protect their trade balances, and the result was a global collapse in trade. Following World War II, the GATT was set up to negotiate reductions in tariffs.

---

[1]"Beggar" is used as a verb here, meaning "to impoverish."

Partly as a consequence of the success of the GATT (now the WTO), protection has shifted emphasis away from tariffs and toward other direct controls on trade, that is, toward nontariff barriers. One nontariff barrier is the quantitative restriction or quota. Some quotas, those imposed on industrialized countries on imports of textiles from labor-abundant countries, were abolished in 2005 under the terms of the Uruguay Round of negotiations concluded in 1994.

The economic analysis of an import quota is similar to the analysis of a tariff, in that a quota raises the domestic price. The two would be practically equivalent if the government auctioned off the licenses to import, so that the revenue accrued to the domestic government instead of to the importers fortunate enough to get the licenses. In practice, governments rarely auction off quotas. In the case of a tariff, the fact that the revenue goes to the domestic government is an obvious advantage from the national viewpoint, relative to a voluntary export restraint where the "revenue" goes to the foreign country. If the alternative is a domestically imposed quota, then the revenue generally accrues to domestic residents, as with a tariff. From a macroeconomic viewpoint, however, there is still an important difference between a tariff, under which the revenue accrues to the domestic government, and a quota, under which the revenue accrues to the domestic private sector. An increase in tariffs, like any tax increase, reduces the private sector's disposable income and constitutes a contractionary fiscal policy. Thus it has an expenditure-reducing side in addition to the expenditure-switching side and may have a bigger effect on the trade balance than would a domestically imposed quota.

Another nontariff barrier used sometimes when a government has a pressing trade balance crisis is advanced deposits on imports. An importer must place on deposit with the government a certain amount of money for a certain length of time, such as six months, without interest. The effect is the same as a tariff equal in amount to the interest on the deposit lost by the importer. Like a tariff, this barrier withdraws money from circulation and thus has an expenditure-reducing effect, in addition to the expenditure-switching effect.

The topic here is barriers to trade; barriers to capital flows will be discussed later. Nevertheless, one device for discouraging the outflow of money bears mentioning: the two-tier exchange rate. Suppose that South Africa is experiencing a substantial outflow of capital and downward pressure on the price of its currency. Because it wants to avoid worsening its inflation, as would follow if it devalues the South African rand, the central bank maintains its fixed exchange rate for current-account transactions but requires parties making capital-account transactions to use the competitive foreign exchange market. There the exchange rate is left free to find its own level. Those clamoring for foreign currency to buy foreign assets—that is, to export capital from South Africa—find the supply limited to the flow of currency made available by foreign residents desiring to export capital to South Africa. Capital exports and imports would be equated by the market-determined exchange rate for capital transactions, and no *net* international capital transfers could take place. This device could similarly be used to avert a revaluation when a country is experiencing capital inflows. The two-tier foreign exchange market is difficult to administer because it requires elaborate controls. If the price of the South African rand is higher in the competitive market for capital-account transactions, those exporting capital to South Africa have an incentive to gain access to its currency at the cheaper rate for current-account transactions. In addition, South African importers who must buy foreign exchange at the (for them) less favorable current-account rate have an incentive to sell South African rand to buyers in the capital-account market. Controls must keep these parties apart if the system is to work.

Capital controls can impair economic efficiency because they keep capital from moving to where it earns a higher return. If the difference in returns faced by the lender is also a difference in real social productivity, the control imposes a welfare cost. One cannot be dogmatic, though, about the welfare costs of capital controls because governments use the interest rate—the return to capital—extensively as a policy variable. When the central bank is influencing the price of credit, the connection between the market price and social productivity of capital is no longer certain.

Another barrier that has been used by developing countries is multiple exchange rates. The government charges a higher price for foreign exchange when it is used to purchase luxury consumer goods than when it is used to purchase, for example, capital goods or—considered most essential of all—spare parts and fuel.

The Swan Diagram

Assume that the government authorities have two policy goals. First, they want to attain external balance: for example, a trade deficit equal to zero. Second, they want to attain internal balance: output equal to full employment or potential output. (The situation in which demand exceeds potential output, $\overline{Y}$, can be considered undesirable because it leads to inflation.) There is a general principle that attaining two different policy goals requires two independent policy tools. In this case the two policy tools are expenditure-switching and expenditure-reducing policies, or, for concreteness, devaluation and government expenditure.[2] Each policy will be considered in isolation before we consider the use of both at once.

As already seen, government fiscal expansion raises output but worsens the trade balance. If the government were restricted to the use of fiscal policy, this would represent a dilemma. The government could adopt a contractionary fiscal policy to achieve external balance ($TB = 0$) at the expense of unemployment ($Y < \overline{Y}$), at point X in Figure 18.2(a), or could adopt an expansionary fiscal policy to attain internal balance at the expense of a trade deficit ($TB < 0$), at point N. The government cannot, however, attain external and internal balance simultaneously, except by coincidence. Such simultaneous balance demands another policy tool.

A devaluation also raises output, but it improves the trade balance. This presents another dilemma: whether (1) to choose a low exchange rate—that is, revalue to achieve internal balance ($Y = \overline{Y}$) at the expense of a trade deficit ($TB < 0$) at point N in Figure 18.2(b); or (2) to choose a high exchange rate—that is, devalue, to achieve external balance ($TB = 0$) at the expense of excess demand ($Y > \overline{Y}$) at point B.

---

[2]The general principle originated with Jan Tinbergen. The application to the open economy was developed by James Meade. The application of the principle to an economy with international capital mobility, which we study in Chapter 22, was developed by Robert Mundell. All three won Nobel Prizes.

FIGURE 18.2

Dilemma: External Balance or Internal Balance?

Panel (a) shows how the government, using just fiscal policy, can attain either a zero trade balance at point X or full employment at N, but not both. Panel (b) shows how the government, using just exchange rate policy, again can attain either one goal at B or the other at N, but not both.

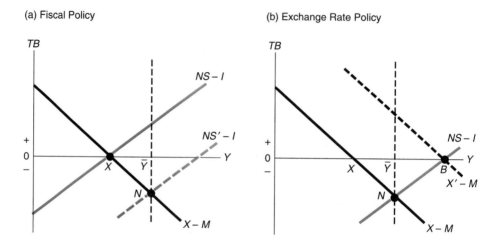

(a) Fiscal Policy   (b) Exchange Rate Policy

Obviously, to attain balance in both sectors, both policies must be used together. The case depicted in Figure 18.2 requires an intermediate exchange rate policy together with an intermediate fiscal policy.

Heavy use has been made of Figure 18.2, the diagram of income and the trade balance, with one schedule that holds for a given level of government expenditure and another that holds for a given level of the exchange rate. Now the situation will be inverted, shifting to a diagram of expenditure and the exchange rate, with one schedule that holds for a given level of income and another that holds for a given level of the trade balance. Same model, new graph.

Assume that, by coincidence, the starting point is a position of both external and internal balance, point A in Figure 18.3(a). To begin, consider external balance. If the government increases expenditure, it must also devalue to maintain external balance, as at point B. Otherwise, it will go into deficit. For trade balance equilibrium to hold, G and E must vary together: Higher expenditure must be accompanied by a higher exchange rate. This means that the combinations of G and E that imply external balance in Figure 18.3(b) are represented by an upward-sloping line: the BB schedule.

It is quite likely that the economy is at a point off the line BB. At any point, F, that is below and to the right of BB, E is too low or G too high for external balance. This is a point of trade deficit. Total expenditure is too high, or too large a fraction of expenditure falls on foreign goods. It is necessary to reduce expenditure (cut G) or switch expenditure toward domestic goods (raise E) to return to balanced trade. Similarly, at any point, S, above and to the left of BB, E is too high or G too low, for external bal-

FIGURE 18.3

Policy Combinations That Give External Balance

After a fiscal expansion, there must also be a devaluation if the trade balance is to be restored to its original level. In panel (a), the axes represent the policy goals. In panel (b), the axes represent the policy instruments.

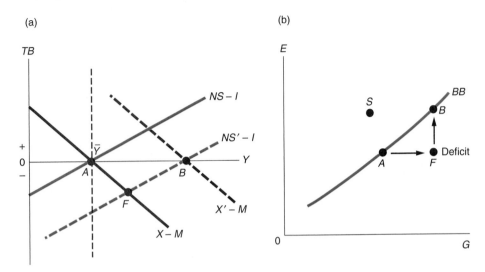

ance. This is a point of trade surplus. G would have to be increased or E reduced, to return to balanced trade. Only under a floating exchange rate regime will the economy necessarily be on the BB line. In that case, the exchange rate adjusts automatically, so as to maintain an external balance. Under fixed rates it is possible to be anywhere on the graph.

Now consider internal balance. Return in Figure 18.4(a) to point A and the exercise of an increase in government expenditure. Now observe, however, that the government will have to *revalue* if it wants to maintain internal balance, as at point N. Otherwise, the economy will suffer from excess demand. To stay at the same level of demand, output, and employment, G and E must vary inversely: Higher expenditure must be accompanied by a lower exchange rate. This result yields the YY schedule in Figure 18.4(b). The combinations of G and E that imply internal balance are represented by a downward-sloping line.

Again, it is perfectly possible that the economy is off the line YY. At any point, F, above and to the right of YY, the exchange rate E is too high, or too large a fraction of expenditure falls on domestic goods. It is necessary to reduce expenditure (cut G) or switch expenditure toward foreign goods (reduce E) if the country is to return to potential output. Similarly, at any point, U, below and to the left of YY, E is too low or G is too low for internal balance. This is a point of excess supply or unemployment. G or E would have to be increased to return to full employment. In general, there is no reason necessarily to be on the YY line.

FIGURE 18.4

Policy Combinations That Give Internal Balance

After a fiscal expansion there must also be a revaluation of the currency if the level of output is to be restored to its original level. In panel (a), the axes represent the policy goals. In panel (b), the axes represent the policy instruments.

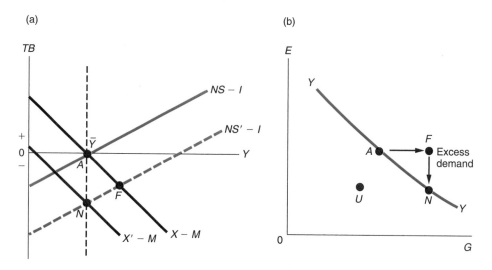

Figure 18.5 shows the BB and YY schedules together, in a graph known as the Swan diagram.[3] There are four zones. Zone I indicates a combination of trade deficit and excess demand, Zone II a deficit and unemployment, Zone III a trade surplus and unemployment, and Zone IV a surplus and excess demand. There is only one point of full equilibrium, A. Again, both tools are needed to attain it. For example, many countries find themselves at a point like P_1: deficit and unemployment. They could raise G to reach full employment at the expense of a greater deficit or cut back G to attain balanced trade at the expense of greater unemployment. The correct strategy is to cut G and devalue, attaining internal and external balance simultaneously at A. Of course, policy-making is not always this easy in practice. For example, the symptoms at point P_2 are the same, deficit and unemployment, and yet the correct strategy here is to devalue and *raise* G. In practice, this might only be discovered by experimentation: devaluing and then waiting to see what happens before deciding whether to change expenditure. (Appendix B carries this analysis further.)

---

[3]The Swan diagram was invented by Trevor Swan, "Longer-run Problems of the Balance of Payments," 1955; reprinted in R. Caves and H. Johnson, eds., *Readings in International Economics* (Homewood, IL: Richard Irwin, Inc., 1968): pp. 455–464. It was further developed in W. Max Corden, "The Geometric Representation of Policies to Attain Internal and External Balance," *Review of Economic Studies*, 28 (1960): pp. 1–22.

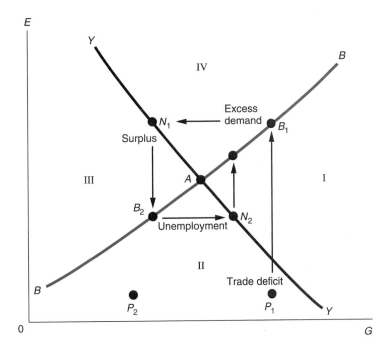

FIGURE 18.5

The Swan Diagram of Internal and External Balance

The *BB* schedule shows the combinations of spending, *G*, and the exchange rate, *E*, that give the desired trade balance. The *YY* schedule shows the combinations that give the desired level of output. Only by deliberately using both independent policy instruments could the government attain both policy goals at point *A*.

18.3 Monetary Factors

The discussion of policies to change the level of expenditure has so far focused on fiscal policy. However, it is easy enough to put monetary policy into the Keynesian model. The mechanism of transmission from the money supply to income is the interest rate. Assume that expenditure, in particular, investment—which has been treated previously as exogenous—is now a decreasing function of the interest rate. The interest rate is the cost of borrowing to firms. If it falls, firms are more likely to undertake investment projects. Households may raise their expenditure as well and so reduce savings. Residential construction and purchases of consumer durables (automobiles, household appliances, and so forth) are often particularly sensitive to interest rates.

Figure 18.6 shows how a decrease in the interest rate shifts the $NS - I$ line down. Equilibrium occurs at a higher level of income, $Y_2 > Y_1$. Thus an inverse relationship between the interest rate and income is traced out, describing equilibrium in the goods market. This relationship is none other than the *IS* curve, from the familiar closed-economy *IS-LM* analysis of intermediate macroeconomics courses.

What would make the interest rate fall to begin with? The obvious answer is monetary policy. The central bank usually sets the interest rate directly. In the 1980s, however, it was more common to treat the central bank as setting the money supply. The interest rate then adjusted to equilibrate the money supply with money demand.

Individuals balance their portfolios between money and other assets, such as stocks and bonds. Their demand for money is a decreasing function of the rate of return on

FIGURE 18.6

Effect of a Fall in the Interest Rate, *I*

If monetary policy lowers the interest rate from i_1 to i_2, then it stimulates investment from I_1 to I_2. The saving-investment line shifts out, raising the level of income from Y_1 to Y_2. This inverse relationship between i and Y is the *IS* curve.

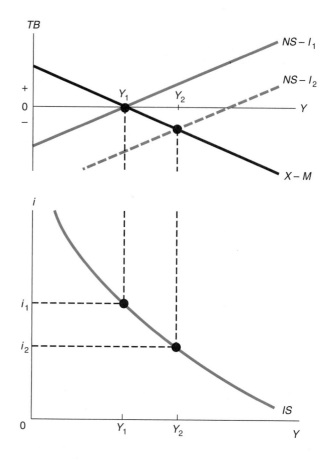

alternative assets, represented by the interest rate. Yet even though money pays no interest, people must hold some to undertake transactions. The demand for real money balances is thus an increasing function of real income. If income were to go up, and nothing else changed, the demand for money would go up. For a given real money supply, to maintain equilibrium in the financial markets (demand equals supply) something else must change: The interest rate must rise to make bonds more attractive and money less attractive. Only then will money demand be equal to the existing money supply. Thus the lower part of Figure 18.7 traces a positive relationship between the interest rate and income, describing equilibrium in the financial market. For a given real money supply, the two variables must move together, precisely because they have offsetting effects on money demand. This relationship is the familiar *LM* curve. The intersection of the two curves, *IS* and *LM*, gives the equilibrium level of income and interest rate.

Notice that there is a unique critical level of income that implies a zero trade balance, Y_1, in the upper panel of Figure 18.7. Anywhere to the right of Y_1 is a point of trade deficit because imports are too high. Anywhere to the left of Y_1 is a point of surplus because imports are too low. An expenditure-switching policy that shifts the $X - M$ line will change the critical level of income consistent with $TB = 0$.

FIGURE 18.7

Monetary Expansion

The upward-sloping *LM* curve gives equilibrium in the money market. An increase in the money supply shifts the *LM* curve out, driving down the interest rate, *i*, at point *M*, and as a result increasing income, *Y*. The trade balance worsens.

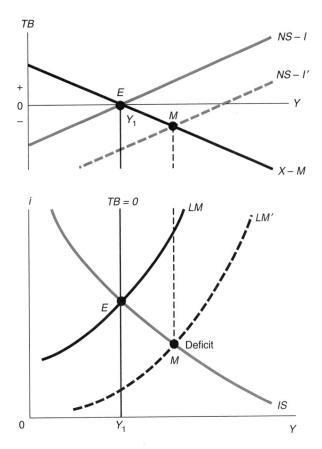

Monetary Expansion

The following analysis will begin from a point where the equilibrium level of income given by the *IS-LM* intersection also implies a zero trade balance, point *E* in Figure 18.7. We will consider in turn the effects of three policy changes: a monetary expansion, a fiscal expansion, and a devaluation.

The monetary expansion shifts the *LM* curve to the right. For the higher money supply to be willingly held, either the interest rate must fall or income must rise. In fact, both happen; the interest rate falls and stimulates investment and thus income. The new equilibrium occurs at point *M*. Because this is to the right of the *TB* = 0 point, clearly the higher level of expenditure stimulated by the expansion has pushed the country into trade balance deficit.

Fiscal Expansion and Crowding-Out

Figure 18.8 depicts an increase in government expenditure, ΔG. The fiscal expansion shifts the *IS* curve to the right: Any given interest rate and consequent level of investment, which previously implied a particular level of income, now imply a higher level of

FIGURE 18.8

Fiscal Expansion with Crowding-Out of Investment

An increase in spending shifts the *IS* curve to the right by the amount of the simple Keynesian multiplier. However, the actual increase in income is somewhat less than this, at point *F*, because an increase in the demand for money drives up the interest rate and crowds out investment.

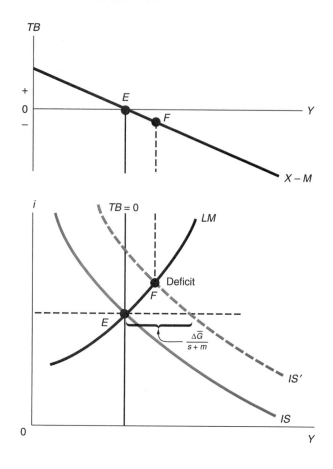

income. In fact, the distance that the fiscal expansion shifts the *IS* curve to the right can be precisely stated. The simple Keynesian multiplier analysis of Section 17.1 showed that, for a given interest rate, income increases by $\Delta Y = \frac{1}{s+m}\Delta \overline{G}$ (Equation 17.9). Previously, that formula was the complete answer to the question of how much income increases because the interest rate was assumed to be constant. Now it only answers the question of how much the curve shifts because the interest rate is no longer necessarily constant. The increases in expenditure and income raise money demand, forcing the interest rate up, which in turn discourages private investment. The new equilibrium occurs at point *F*. Income is still higher than at point *E*, but some of the effect of the fiscal expansion has been offset by the crowding-out of investment. The overall effect on income is somewhat *less* than the full open-economy multiplier effect.[4]

_____

[4]The $NS - I$ schedule has not been explicitly drawn in the upper half of Figure 18.8. It initially runs through point *E*. Then the fiscal expansion shifts it to the right, by $\Delta G/(s + m)$, and the increase in i immediately shifts it part of the way back to the left. It ends up intersecting the $X - M$ line at point *F*.

Notice that the economy is again in trade deficit at point F because of higher imports. In this model, monetary and fiscal expansions operate in the same way. Both raise expenditure, thus raising income and worsening the trade balance. They differ only in their implications for the composition of the given level of output, a monetary expansion favoring private investment and a fiscal expansion favoring government spending (or, in the case of a tax cut, favoring consumer spending).

The Liquidity Trap and Japan in the 1990s

The Keynesian model omits such concerns as inflation and government borrowing. Many a country has justified a fiscal expansion as a supposedly temporary measure aimed at counteracting a recession, only to be stuck for years thereafter with an unsustainable buildup in debt, entrenched inflation, and high interest rates. For such reasons, the Keynesian model is generally regarded as a poor guide to fiscal policy-making in practice, perhaps even as obsolete.

The example of Japan in the 1990s, however, illustrates that the Keynesian model is still relevant. Bubbles in the Japanese stock and real estate markets in the late 1980s collapsed after 1990, leading to a period of deflation, unemployment, and slow growth. Despite a decade of recession, almost reminiscent of the Great Depression of the 1930s, goods prices in Japan did not decline enough to restore equilibrium.

Furthermore, the response of the Japanese economy to monetary and fiscal policy suggested that it may have been caught in a rare case of a liquidity trap. In an effort to stimulate the economy, the Bank of Japan lowered interest rates, virtually to zero. After that, further reductions in interest rates were not possible. This is the definition of a liquidity trap; further increases in the money supply are simply absorbed by the public without bringing about a reduction in the interest rate. In terms of Figure 18.8, the LM curve becomes completely flat, like the horizontal dotted line that runs through point E.

The liquidity trap has two strong implications for policy. First, monetary policy becomes ineffective. A monetary expansion still "shifts the LM curve to the right," but because the curve is flat in this range, there is no stimulus to the demand for goods. Thus the Bank of Japan declared in the late 1990s that no further stimulus to output was possible. Second, fiscal policy becomes *more* effective. Because the LM curve is flat, there is no increase in the interest rate to crowd out private spending as at point F; instead the full multiplier effect shows up.

In 1997 the government of Japan raised taxes, out of concerns that accumulating fiscal deficits were saddling the next generation with rising levels of debt. Unfortunately the immediate effect was to reduce consumption and send the economy into a renewed recession. The multiplier effect was alive and well.

Devaluation and Crowding-Out

We now turn from the two kinds of policies affecting the level of expenditure to an expenditure-switching policy, devaluation. Figure 17.2 showed that, assuming the Marshall-Lerner condition holds, a devaluation shifts the $X - M$ line up by some

FIGURE 18.9

Devaluation with Crowding-Out

A devaluation shifts the *IS* curve to the right by the amount of the simple Keynesian multiplier (at point *L*). However, the actual increase in income is somewhat less than this because investment is crowded out at *D*. The trade balance improves.

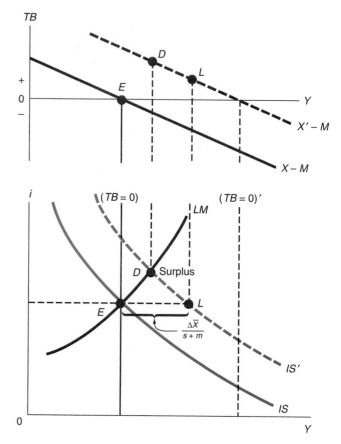

positive amount, called $\Delta\overline{X}$. For any given level of investment, equilibrium occurs at a higher level of income. Thus, for any given interest rate, the equilibrium point in the lower panel of Figure 18.9 shifts to the right. From Section 17.1, it is even possible to state by how much it shifts to the right: For a given interest rate, $\Delta Y = \frac{1}{s+m}\Delta\overline{X}$. The actual overall effect on *Y* is less, as can be seen at the new *IS-LM* intersection, point *D*.[5] Like the increase in demand from the government sector, the increase in demand from the foreign sector raises output, but the effect is partly offset by the investment crowded out by higher interest rates.

Despite the move to the right, point *D* brings a trade surplus, not a trade deficit. As shown in the upper panel in Figure 18.9, the critical level of income that implies a zero trade balance has shifted to the right. Furthermore, the *TB* = 0 line has shifted to the right by *more* than the *IS* curve. How do we know this? Imagine for a moment a per-

---

[5]In terms of the upper panel, the *NS* − *I* schedule has shifted to the left (again because of the increase in *i*), so that it intersects *X'* − *M* at *D*.

fectly flat *LM* curve (the liquidity trap), such that the devaluation causes a move to point *L*. Section 17.1 showed that the trade balance would improve, by

$$\Delta TB = \Delta \overline{X} - m\Delta Y$$

$$= \Delta \overline{X} - m\frac{1}{s+m}\Delta \overline{X}$$

$$= \frac{s}{s+m}\Delta \overline{X} > 0$$

The marginal propensity to import times the increase in income is only a partial offset to the improvement in the trade balance. When the *LM* curve has some slope, the change in the trade balance is still $\Delta TB = \Delta \overline{X} - m\Delta Y$, but now crowding-out means that ΔY is smaller than the simple multiplier formula indicates. The marginal propensity to import has even less of an offsetting effect on the trade balance. If there is a surplus at *L*, there is an even greater surplus at *D*. This proves that the vertical *TB* = 0 line shifts right by more than income increases, leaving *D* to the left of the new line.[6] Intuitively, income would not have increased in the first place if devaluation did not, on net, stimulate the trade balance.

This section has shown how the effectiveness of fiscal expansion or devaluation in stimulating demand is reduced by crowding-out, and how monetary expansion is an alternative policy for stimulating expenditure. Most of this closely resembles material covered in an intermediate, closed-economy macroeconomics course. Opening the economy up to foreign trade has merely appended the trade balance as a function of income.

18.4 Summary

This chapter used the Keynesian model developed in Chapter 17 to study two types of exogenous policy changes: expenditure-switching policies such as devaluation, and expenditure-reducing (or expenditure-increasing) policies such as government spending. It also examined the effects of changes in such policy instruments on the two policy targets: internal balance (GDP at the full-employment level, for example) and external balance (the trade balance at zero, for example). A general principle was demonstrated: If a country is to attain both policy targets, the government must use two independent policy instruments, such as fiscal policy and the exchange rate.

A second lesson concerned the regime of floating exchange rates, in which the value of the currency adjusts automatically to equilibrate the balance of payments. Under a regime of fixed rates, disturbances are transmitted from one country to another. However, a regime of floating rates helps insulate countries from each other's disturbances because the exchange rate ensures that the balance of payments is zero.[7]

---

[6]The *TB* = 0 schedule shifts to the right by $\Delta \overline{X}/m$. (In other words, only if $m\Delta Y = \Delta \overline{X}$ is *TB* unchanged.) However, as can be seen in the figure, the *IS* curve shifts to the right by a smaller amount: $\Delta \overline{X}/(s+m)$.

[7]This chapter continues to assume the absence of international financial flows, so the overall balance of payments is the same as the trade balance. Part V will introduce capital flows; one consequence will be that floating exchange rates do not provide complete insulation.

A third lesson was that crowding-out effects via the domestic interest rate, which must be taken into account if the central bank keeps the money supply constant, decrease the effect of a fiscal expansion on domestic income.

The chapter concluded by introducing monetary policy into the model for the first time, thus leading to the subject of Chapter 19.

Chapter 19 will return to the *IS-LM* graphs to analyze the effects of reserve flows, and Chapter 22 will explore the effects of international capital mobility. Chapter 22 will also present greater synergy between the financial markets and the foreign sector. The existence of a balance-of-payments surplus or deficit will ultimately have much wider implications for the entire economic system in those chapters.

CHAPTER PROBLEMS

1. Output is given by

$$Y = C + I + G + TB$$

where consumption (C), disposable income (Y_d), investment (I), government expenditure (G), and the trade balance (TB) are given as follows:

$$C = \overline{C} + (1 - s)Y_d$$

$$Y_d = Y - tY$$

$$I = \overline{I}$$

$$G = \overline{G}$$

$$TB = \overline{X} - (\overline{M} + mY_d)$$

This model differs from Section 17.1 by the introduction of t, the marginal tax rate.

a. i. Solve for the equilibrium level of income Y_0 as a function of exogenous variables.

ii. What is the open-economy fiscal multiplier, $\Delta Y_0/\Delta \overline{G}$? Is it larger or smaller than the multiplier in a closed economy, $1/s$? What is the intuitive explanation?

iii. Is the multiplier larger or smaller than the open-economy multiplier in Section 17.1? What is the intuitive explanation?

iv. What is the effect on the trade balance, $\Delta TB/\Delta \overline{G}$?

b. Assume that export demand increases exogenously by $\Delta \overline{X}$—for example, because of a devaluation that raises exports by $\Delta \overline{X} = \varepsilon \Delta E$ (think of ε as the export elasticity times $\overline{X}/\overline{E}$)—and has no direct effect on imports in domestic currency (import elasticity is 1).

i. What is the effect on income, $\Delta Y/\Delta \overline{X}$?

ii. What is the effect on the trade balance, $\Delta TB/\Delta \overline{X}$? How does this answer compare with the elasticities approach and why?

iii. Assume (just for this question) that floating exchange rates are in effect so that E always increases by the amount necessary to guarantee $TB = 0$. What is the floating-rate fiscal multiplier, $\Delta Y_0/\Delta G$? How does it compare with the fixed-rate and closed-economy multipliers in Problem a(ii)? What is the effect of a fiscal expansion on the exchange rate, $\Delta E/\Delta \overline{G}$?

2. This question concerns the relative virtues of the regimes of fixed and floating exchange rates in automatically stabilizing real growth in the economy. Assume that the goal is to minimize Variance (ΔY) in the presence of domestic disturbances $\Delta \overline{A}$ and foreign disturbances $\Delta \overline{X}$ (which are assumed to be independent of each other). The variance is a measure of variability that has the following three properties in general.

$$\text{Variance } (au) = a^2 \text{ Variance } (u)$$

$$\text{Variance } (b + v) = \text{Variance } (v)$$

$$\text{Variance } (u + v) = \text{Variance } (u) + \text{Variance } (v)$$

where a and b are parameters, or exogenous variables, and u and v are independent disturbances. Assume the simple Keynesian model of Section 17.1.

a. i. How does Variance (ΔY) depend on Variance $(\Delta \overline{A})$ and Variance $(\Delta \overline{X})$ under fixed exchange rates?

ii. Under floating exchange rates?

b. i. Which regime would be preferable if the variance of foreign disturbances is much larger than the variance of domestic disturbances?

ii. Which would be preferable if the two kinds of disturbances are similar in magnitude, and the country is very open (m is large)? Which is a better candidate for a fixed exchange rate, Australia or Luxembourg?

3. Compute the ratio of the slope of the internal balance line, YY, to the slope of the external balance line, BB:

$$\frac{(\Delta E/\Delta \overline{G})\big|_{Y=\overline{Y}}}{(\Delta E/\Delta \overline{G})\big|_{TB=0}}$$

(*Hint:* The numerator refers to the change in E that is required to offset a given change in G, in such a way as to leave Y at the original level of $\overline{Y}$; it is given by

$$-\frac{\Delta Y}{\Delta \overline{G}}\bigg/\frac{\Delta Y}{\Delta E}$$

The logic applies analogously to the denominator.) How is this ratio relevant to the assignment problem of Appendix B?

4. Choose a country. Read recent articles about its macroeconomy in the *Financial Times* or the *Economist*. Where on the Swan diagram (Figure 18.5) do you think this country falls?

Extra Credit

5. In this question the interest rate is allowed to vary. (Think of it as having been held constant by monetary policy in the preceding problems.) In the preceding model, replace

the exogenous specification for investment, I, with an equation in which it depends inversely on the interest rate, i:

$$I = \overline{I} - bi$$

and add an equation for the demand for money. (We now use M to stand for money.)

$$M/P = KY - hi$$

a. Derive the *IS* curve, giving Y as an inverse function of i. [For notational simplicity, use α to denote the answer to 1a(ii).]
b. Combine your answer to 1a with the *LM* curve (the money demand equation, with real money demand M/P equal to the exogenous real money supply $\overline{M}/\overline{P}$) to solve for Y as a function of exogenous variables. Solve for i as well.
c. What is the fiscal multiplier $\Delta Y/\Delta \overline{G}$ now? How does it compare with the answer to 1a(ii) (call it α), and why? What happens if h is very high (i.e., money demand is very sensitive to i)?
d. What is the monetary multiplier $\Delta Y/\Delta(\overline{M}/\overline{P})$? What happens if h is very high?

SUGGESTIONS FOR FURTHER READING

Johnson, Harry. "Toward a General Theory of the Balance of Payments" (1958). Reprinted in Jacob Frenkel and Harry Johnson, eds., *The Monetary Approach to the Balance of Payments* (Toronto: University of Toronto Press, 1976). The first half interprets the absorption approach ($TB = Y - A$) as pointing the way to the monetary approach to the balance of payments by emphasizing reserve flows. The second half develops the distinction between expenditure-switching and expenditure-reducing policies.

Krugman, Paul. *Adjustment in the World Economy,* Occasional Paper No. 24 (New York: Group of Thirty, 1987). Argues, using the logic of the transfer problem, that the U.S. trade deficit should not be eliminated by U.S. fiscal contraction alone, or even together with foreign fiscal expansion. Depreciation of the dollar is also needed.

Posen, Adam. *Restoring Japan's Economic Growth* (Washington, DC: Institute for International Economics, 1998). The experience of Japan in the 1990s suggests that the Keynesian model is not dead.

APPENDIX A

The Laursen-Metzler-Harberger Effect

When a devaluation worsens the terms of trade, there may be real consequences beyond the simple fact that purchasing power has fallen. This observation leads to the Laursen-Metzler-Harberger effect.

Expenditure and the Terms of Trade

Up to now, we have assumed that the marginal propensities to save and consume are specified in domestic terms. (In Equation 17.3, C and Y were both defined in *domestic value units*.) This has meant that a change in the terms of trade between domestic output and foreign output has had no effect on the $NS - I$ schedule when the horizontal axis measures income in domestic terms, as in Figure 17.2. An increase in the exchange rate has affected only the $X - M$ line, shifting it up if the Marshall-Lerner condition is satisfied. One implication has been that the Marshall-Lerner condition is the necessary and sufficient condition for a devaluation to improve the trade balance. The change in income, and therefore imports, reduces the effect on the trade balance but does not reverse it.

However, there is little justification in theory for measuring income in domestic terms when determining saving. When the exchange rate rises, the terms of trade worsen. (The terms of trade are defined as the price of exports divided by the price of imports.) Any level of income given in domestic terms translates into less when measured in terms of foreign goods, or in terms of the appropriate consumption-weighted basket of domestic and foreign goods. If consumption, saving, and imports were proportional to income, it would not matter what numeraire we used for measurement. In the Keynesian model, however, a fall in income is hypothesized to induce consumers to reduce their consumption *less than proportionately*. In other words, the elasticity of consumption with respect to income is less than 1:

$$\frac{\Delta C / \Delta Y}{C / Y} = \frac{c}{(\overline{C} + cY)/Y} < 1$$

It is argued that a fall in real income, even if it results from a worsening in the terms of trade rather than from a fall in domestically measured income, should be reflected in a similar less-than-proportionate fall in real spending. If measurements are made in domestic terms, this is reflected as an increase in spending, or a decrease in saving, for any given level of income domestically measured. In other words, an increase in the exchange rate, in addition to shifting the $X - M$ schedule up, shifts the $NS - I$ schedule down, as in Figure 18.A.1. Consumers reduce their savings to maintain living standards in the face of the worsened terms of trade. This terms-of-trade factor is called the Laursen-Metzler-Harberger effect.

The Condition for a Devaluation to Improve the Trade Balance

There are two implications of the Laursen-Metzler-Harberger effect. The first is that the fall in saving, or increase in expenditure, has a negative effect on the trade balance. Thus the trade balance could go into deficit (depending on the elasticities) even if the Marshall-Lerner condition is satisfied. That is the way Figure 18.A.1 is drawn. If we recall that the trade balance is equal to saving minus investment, it is intuitively clear why the Laursen-Metzler-Harberger effect would work to reduce the trade balance when it works to reduce saving.

Evidently the necessary condition for a devaluation to improve the trade balance is more stringent than

$$\varepsilon_X + \varepsilon_M > 1$$

FIGURE 18.A.1

Increase in the Exchange Rate with the Laursen-Metzler-Harberger Effect

As usual, the devaluation shifts the $X - M$ line up. If the saving rate depends not just on income measured in domestic terms, Y, but also on the terms of trade, then the $NS - I$ line shifts down as households seek to protect their standard of living.

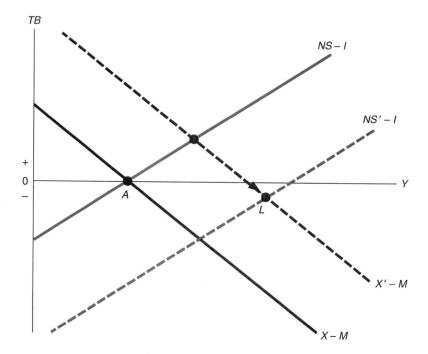

In the two-country context the necessary condition is

$$\varepsilon_X + \varepsilon_M > 1 + m + m^*$$

This condition will not be derived.[8] Note, however, that in addition to the price effects of the devaluation, the stimulus to domestic real income from increased exports will raise imports to an extent that depends on the domestic marginal propensity to import, and the fall in foreign real income from the fall in foreign exports will lower their imports to an extent that depends on the foreign marginal propensity to import. Thus the effect of the devaluation depends on the magnitudes of the elasticities compared to the marginal propensities to import.

Implications for Transmission Under Floating Rates

The second implication of the Laursen-Metzler-Harberger effect has to do with the question considered in Section 18.1, of the international transmission of disturbances.[9] This is illustrated in Figure 18.A.2, with the economy initially at point A. It is no longer

[8]The condition for a devaluation to improve the trade balance was originally derived by Arnold Harberger, "Currency Depreciation, Income and the Balance of Trade," *Journal of Political Economy* (February 1950): 1147–1160.
[9]The transmission of disturbances that occurs despite floating exchange rates was the motivation behind the original paper, Svend Laursen and Lloyd Metzler, "Flexible Exchange Rates and the Theory of Employment," *Review of Economics and Statistics,* 32 (November 1950): 281–299.

FIGURE 18.A.2

External Disturbance
Under a Floating
Exchange Rate

In the presence of the
Laursen-Metzler-Harberger
effect, a fall in foreign
demand can actually raise
domestic output. The
reason is that the domestic
currency depreciates,
which causes saving to
shift down.

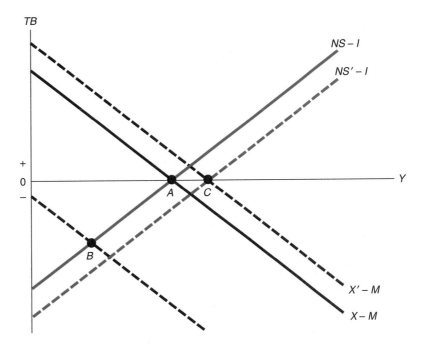

true that a floating exchange rate completely insulates domestic output and employment from foreign disturbances. As before, a fall in exports due, for example, to a foreign contraction, leads to a depreciation to prevent the trade deficit that would otherwise emerge at point *B* in Figure 18.A.2. In the standard Keynesian model, the depreciation would increase exports and reduce imports, causing a return (instantaneously) to point *A*. With the Laursen-Metzler-Harberger effect, however, the worsened terms of trade cause saving to fall. Thus the $NS - I$ line shifts down, and a further depreciation is necessary if the trade balance is to avoid going into deficit. Equilibrium occurs when the depreciation is sufficient to restore the trade balance to zero despite the fall in saving, point *C* in Figure 18.A.2. This point occurs at a higher level of income than *A*, even though the chain of events began with a contraction of foreign income. The disturbance is transmitted in reverse.

Temporary Versus Permanent Shifts in the Terms of Trade

The Keynesian consumption function on which the Laursen-Metzler-Harberger effect is based cannot be applied to long-run permanent changes in real income. When there is an adverse shift in the terms of trade, or any other reduction in real income, consumers can only reduce saving (or borrow) to maintain expenditure levels *if* conditions are expected to improve in the future, allowing the consumers to make up the lost savings (or pay back the loan). It has long been recognized that the marginal propensity to consume out of a permanent change in real income is higher than the marginal propensity to consume out of a temporary change in income. The latter will be close to zero in the limit of a very short-lived change in real income, which has no effect on a rational individual's expectation of lifetime wealth or permanent income, and thus no effect on consumption plans.[10]

It is reasonable to think of standard Keynesian propensities to consume and save as applying in the intermediate case, in which a change in real income is observed but is not known to be necessarily either temporary or permanent. Thus the Laursen-Metzler-Harberger effect applies in this general, intermediate case. It should be modified, however, if there is additional information on the permanence of the change.[11]

One illustration was the sharp increase in the price of oil in 1973. For an oil-importing country, this was an adverse shift in the terms of trade analogous to a devaluation. One might have expected all oil-importing countries to incur large trade deficits because of the increase in their oil import bills. Yet the industrialized country that ran the largest deficit was Norway, which had North Sea oil reserves it could develop in the future. The Norwegians knew that their real income loss was temporary and that they would be wealthier in the long run. Accordingly, they reduced saving relative to investment, borrowing from the rest of the world to finance the development of their oil reserves. Norway's current-account balance declined by 7 percent of GDP from the period 1965 to 1973 to the period 1974 to 1979. Other oil importers who had little prospect that their loss in real income would be temporary had no choice but to adjust. The United States and Germany each had no change in their current-account positions between the two periods. They increased exports of other goods to pay for the higher oil import bill.

APPENDIX B

The Assignment Problem

Imagine a decentralized government in which the central bank determines the exchange rate and the treasury determines fiscal policy, and the two bodies do not coordinate policy effectively. Which agency, the central bank that sets E or the treasury that sets G, should be responsible for external balance and which for internal balance? This question is known as the assignment problem.

---

[10]These ideas regarding the consumption function began with Milton Friedman's *permanent income hypothesis* and Franco Modigliani's *life-cycle hypothesis*. The appendix to Chapter 21 shows that a country of optimizing consumers will borrow from abroad if it can expect income to be higher in the future than today.
[11]The theory is updated to include explicit intertemporal utility maximization by consumers in Maurice Obstfeld, "Aggregate Spending and the Terms of Trade: Is There a Laursen-Metzler Effect?" *Quarterly Journal of Economics,* 96 (May 1982); and Lars Svensson and Assaf Razin, "The Terms of Trade and the Current Account: The Harberger-Laursen-Metzler Effect," *Journal of Political Economy,* 97, no. 1 (February 1983): 97–125. The first paper makes strong enough assumptions to rule out the Laursen-Metzler-Harberger effect.

Consider the consequences of assigning external balance to the central bank and internal balance to the treasury. Call this assignment Rule 1. Whenever the trade balance is in deficit, the bank raises E; whenever it is in surplus, the bank lowers E. Whenever output falls short of full employment, the treasury raises G; whenever it exceeds full employment, the treasury lowers G. The analysis will be pursued here in discrete time. Assume that the two agencies take turns. For example, the budget is drawn up and enacted only at yearly intervals, and the exchange rate is changed only in periodic devaluations or revaluations.

Start from point P_1 in Figure 18.5. Let the central bank go first. Because of the trade deficit, Rule 1 tells the bank to devalue until balanced trade is reached at B_1. Now the stimulus to net exports has moved the economy into the region of excess demand. When it is time to set the annual budget, Rule 1 tells the treasury to contract until internal balance is attained at N_1. However, the reduction in expenditure has created a trade balance surplus. The rule tells the central bank to revalue until balanced trade is restored at B_2. Now, however, unemployment means that the treasury will expand until reaching full employment again at N_2. Once again, a trade deficit tells the central bank to devalue, and the counterclockwise cycle repeats.

As the graph is drawn, the line spirals in on the equilibrium point, A, where the goal of simultaneous balance in both sectors is achieved. The reason for spiraling in rather than spiraling out is that the YY schedule is steeper (in absolute value) than the BB schedule. This claim can be demonstrated by making the slopes more extreme. Try this yourself: Draw the external balance schedule to be much steeper than the internal balance schedule. When Rule 1 tells the treasury to contract because of excess demand at point B_1, the trade surplus that opens up is larger than the initial imbalance. When the central bank revalues, the country moves farther away from internal balance than it was previously. This system is unstable, moving farther and farther from full equilibrium.

Now try Rule 2. External balance is assigned to the treasury. Whenever the trade balance is in deficit, the treasury cuts G; whenever it is in surplus, the treasury raises G. Internal balance is assigned to the central bank. Whenever output falls short of full employment, the central bank raises E; whenever it exceeds full employment, the bank lowers E. Starting from a point such as P_1, a reduction in G leads to unemployment, an increase in E, and so forth. The path now progresses around the graph clockwise, not counterclockwise as under Rule 1. If the YY schedule is the steeper one, as in Figure 18.5, there is a spiral *out*. Rule 2 does not work. Yet if the BB schedule is steeper, there is a spiral in to equilibrium. Rule 2 works.

Thus the selection of the assignment rule should be based on the relative slopes of the schedules. Which case is more likely, a YY schedule that is steeper than the BB schedule, or one that is flatter? Problem 3 at the end of the chapter involves computing the relative slopes of the two lines. It turns out that the YY line is steeper only if the economy is not very open to imports. In that case Rule 1 should be used: Fiscal policy should be used for internal balance. Otherwise—that is, for an economy that is highly open—fiscal policy should be assigned to external balance. Intuitively, if the marginal propensity to import is high, then expenditure-reducing policies are an effective way of improving the trade balance because a high proportion of the eliminated expenditure would have gone to foreign goods. Mundell's principle of "effective market classification" states that policy tools should be assigned responsibility for those policy variables on which they have a relatively greater effect.

In practice, it may take time for policy makers to enact major policy changes. They should monitor economic conditions continuously and try to update their policies accordingly. If they are unable to do so, policy activism may exacerbate macroeconomic fluctuations rather than dampen them.

CHAPTER 19

The Money Supply, the Price Level, and the Balance of Payments

I n Chapter 16, we considered the impact of changes in the exchange rate alone on the balance of payments. In effect, income was held constant. In Chapter 17 we allowed income to vary. Similarly, the interest rate was held constant in Chapter 17; then it too was allowed to vary in Chapter 18. Chapter 19 will continue this pattern of letting additional macroeconomic variables vary by introducing the price level, which was assumed constant in the preceding chapters.

The determination of the price level, a monetary variable, had been relatively neglected until its central importance was pointed out by economists of the monetarist school of thought. This chapter considers not only changes in the price level but also changes in a second monetary variable: the central bank's holdings of international reserves. These two variables are fundamental to the monetary approach to the balance of payments. The monetary approach was originally developed in the 1960s, in large part at the University of Chicago but also at the International Monetary Fund. Its central point was that the balance of payments is a monetary phenomenon. The monetary approach to the balance of payments was and is often used by the IMF staff when they must figure out why a country is running a balance-of-payments deficit and what should be done about it.

19.1 The Nonsterilization Assumption

The monetary approach to the balance of payments is sometimes presented as an object of controversy, a model in conflict with the previously discussed elasticity and Keynesian approaches. The controversy is more apparent than real. This chapter will show that no necessary connection exists between the *monetary* approach to the balance of payments and *monetarism*. The debate between monetarists (or their successor, the new classical macroeconomists) and Keynesians *is* a proper object of controversy, but it is not directly at stake here. The beginning of this chapter will apply the monetary approach within the context of the Keynesian model of Chapter 17. The second half will show how the price level is determined in the monetarist model.

The Definition of Sterilization Operations

What *is* at stake here is "sterilization." It is important to understand the difference between what happens when the central bank practices sterilization of international reserve flows and what happens when it does not. This distinction is relevant for understanding the difference between how major industrialized countries, especially the United States, conduct monetary policy today, and how it was conducted under the classical gold standard of the nineteenth century and is to an extent still conducted today in many small, open economies.

To begin, consider the definition of a country's *monetary base* (sometimes called high-powered money to distinguish it from broader definitions of money such as M1). The monetary base consists of currency plus other liabilities issued by the central bank—particularly deposits that government agencies or commercial banks hold at the central bank. A checking account that an individual holds at his or her commercial bank is included in M1, but not in the monetary base.

When a country runs a balance-of-payments deficit, its central bank is necessarily buying the country's own currency and selling international reserves.[1] If the bank takes no other action, then the monetary base is decreasing. One way of thinking of this is that there is less domestic currency in the hands of the public.

Another way of thinking of the effect is to recognize an alternate definition of the monetary base. Define it in terms of the assets held by the central bank: international reserves (claims against the rest of the world) plus net domestic assets (the central bank's holdings of claims against its own government or citizens).

$$MB \equiv Res + NDA$$

where MB is the monetary base, Res is reserves, and NDA is net domestic assets, also known as domestic credit. This definition of the monetary base is identical to the first because the assets on the bank's balance sheet must—by the rules of accounting—add up to the same sum as the liabilities. (As noted earlier, the equality sign is drawn with three lines for accounting identities.) As detailed in Chapter 15's discussion of the balance-of-payments accounts, a country's overall balance of payments is the same thing as the current period's change in the central bank's international reserves.[2]

$$BP \equiv \Delta Res$$

If reserves fall in a given year (because the balance-of-payments deficit, ΔRes, is negative), and net domestic assets, NDA, are unchanged, then the monetary base, MB, falls by the same amount.

---

[1]The effect on the level of reserves is the same whether the balance-of-payments deficit arises in the trade balance or in the private-capital account. That is why we talk of the monetary approach to the balance of payments, rather than the monetary approach to the balance of trade. Nevertheless, this chapter will continue to omit capital flows and so will restrict the discussion to the determination of the trade balance. Chapter 22 will show how the monetary approach to the balance of payments changes in the presence of international capital movements.

[2]Assume here that the country's currency is not held by other countries' central banks, so their actions are not relevant.

The central bank *sterilizes* the reserve outflow if it prevents it from reducing the domestic money supply. The most standard way of doing this is to create money by expanding domestic credit at the same rate as the reserve outflow is contracting the money supply, so there is no net effect. If $\Delta NDA = -\Delta Res$, then $\Delta MB = 0$. In the United States, when the Federal Reserve wishes to expand domestic credit, it does so through open market operations in which it buys U.S. Treasury securities on the private market. In this way, any changes in the Federal Reserve's holdings of reserves are sterilized immediately.

When a country runs a balance-of-payments *surplus,* its central bank is necessarily selling its own currency in the foreign exchange market, thus adding to its stock of international reserves. Again, the central bank sterilizes the reserve inflow if it prevents the increase in reserves from increasing the domestic money supply. The most obvious way of doing this is to extinguish money by contracting domestic credit so that no net effect on the total monetary base results. In the United States, the Federal Reserve sells U.S. Treasury securities on the private market.

Most countries do not have as highly developed bond markets as does the United States, and open market operations are less feasible. For these countries, expanding domestic credit may be accomplished by buying securities directly from the treasury, and so monetizing the budget deficit, or else by extending credit to domestic commercial banks or other enterprises, especially any that may be owned by the government. In some developing countries, the central bank lends money directly to such enterprises as public utilities, industrial development banks, and agricultural cooperatives.

Contracting domestic credit means cutting back on loans to the government, state-owned enterprises, or the banking system. However, it is usually difficult to control the budget deficit of the government or state-owned enterprises on short notice. In developing countries and other countries where the central bank is obligated to finance these deficits, domestic credit is not a viable tool for sterilization, that is, for offsetting reserve flows on a short-run basis. An alternative possibility is to allow the high-powered money supply or monetary base—the liabilities of the central bank—to change, but to offset the effect on monetary aggregates such as M1. M1 represents the liabilities of the entire consolidated banking system, including not only claims on the central bank (such as currency) but also claims on commercial banks (such as checking accounts). Even on a relatively short-term basis, the central bank can regulate the amount of credit banks extend to the public—for example, by varying the reserve requirements to which banks are subject.

In many countries where the central bank has little short-run control over domestic credit, reserve flows simply are not sterilized. In the nineteenth century this was mostly true of countries that participated in the gold standard. If money is directly backed with gold, then balance-of-payments deficits are necessarily financed by gold sales that reduce the domestic money supply: They cannot be sterilized via offsetting changes in the liabilities of either the central bank or the private banking system.[3] A handful of economies—Hong Kong, Estonia, Lithuania, and Bulgaria—have adopted a

---

[3]Appendix A to this chapter explains the gold standard at somewhat greater length.

monetary institution, called a currency board, which is a sort of modern equivalent of a strict gold standard. This arrangement requires 100 percent international reserve backing for domestic currency. Thus reserve flows, by legislation, cannot be sterilized.[4]

If reserve flows are not sterilized, then a balance-of-payments deficit or surplus implies that the money is, over time, decreasing or increasing. (If $\Delta NDA = 0$, then $\Delta MB = \Delta Res$.) This is bound to have effects on expenditure and the entire system, and it is the essence of the monetary approach. The monetary approach to the balance of payments is less applicable to the United States or other major industrialized countries under the current system than it is to many smaller countries, to which it is sometimes applied by the IMF.

Hume's Price Specie-Flow Mechanism

The monetary approach to the balance of payments can be traced back to eighteenth-century philosopher and economist David Hume. Hume attacked the mercantilists, who believed that a country's power depended on amassing gold and silver (specie), and who thus restricted trade to maximize the inflow of specie through the balance of payments. Hume, like Adam Smith and other writers of the Enlightenment, believed in maximizing the welfare of free, atomistic, rational individuals, not the power of an autocratic state. He believed further that the welfare of the individuals residing in a country depended on the economy's productive capabilities, not on the country's stock of gold or money. Money goes where it is demanded, which is where goods are being produced and sold. Assume that a country acquires a new stock of gold but is not especially productive. (Hume mentioned the example of tribute brought to Spain from the New World.) Then the country will spend the gold on the goods of countries that are productive. (Hume had in mind the England of the Industrial Revolution.) The gold flows out through the balance of payments and will continue to do so until the country's gold stock returns to what it was originally.

Hume attributed this process to the *price specie-flow* mechanism. If a country, previously in equilibrium, experiences an increase in its gold supply, then in the short run its price level will be driven up. However, the higher price level will discourage export demand and stimulate import demand, worsening the trade balance. The corresponding outflow of specie will continue until it, and thus the price level, returns to its original level and the trade balance returns to zero. The automatically equilibrating process is described by Hume in terms that evoke the tendency of physical systems toward equilibrium.

> *All water, wherever it communicates, remains at a level. Ask naturalists the reason; they tell you that, were it to be raised in any one place, the superior gravity of that part not being balanced must depress it, till it meet a counterpoise; and that the same cause, which redresses the inequality when it happens, must for ever prevent it, without some violent, external operation.*

---

[4]For a balanced description, see John Williamson, "What Role for Currency Boards?" *Policy Analyses in International Economics,* 40 (Washington, DC: Institute for International Economics, 1995).

Can one imagine, that it had ever been possible, by any laws, or even by any art or industry, to have kept all the money in Spain, which the galleons have brought from the Indies? Or that all commodities could be sold in France for a tenth of the price which they would yield on the other side of the Pyrenees, without finding their way thither, and draining from that immense treasure? What other reason indeed is there why all nations, at present, gain in their trade with Spain and Portugal; but because it is impossible to heap up money, more than any fluid, beyond its proper level?

—David Hume: *On the Balance of Trade*

Mundell's Income Reserve-Flow Mechanism

Harry Johnson and Robert Mundell revived Hume's view in the 1960s under the name, "the monetary approach to the balance of payments." They were more specific about price determination than Hume had been. First we consider Mundell's income flow mechanism, under which prices were assumed fixed for Keynesian reasons. This is simply the Keynesian model of Chapter 18, plus an analysis of the effects over time under the assumption of nonsterilization of reserve flows. One way to think of the Keynesian model is with a perfectly flat aggregate supply curve, so that outward shifts of demand are reflected entirely in output and not at all in price. As already mentioned, the assumption of a constant price level will be relaxed later in the chapter. At that point we will consider the opposite extreme—a perfectly vertical aggregate supply curve—in which increases in demand are reflected entirely in prices and not at all in output. Chapter 26 will examine more closely where the aggregate supply curve comes from and how its slope might be determined at some intermediate position between flat and vertical.

We consider the effects of a monetary expansion. Given the Keynesian assumption of fixed prices, the monetary expansion does not alter the price level. Instead, the expansion shifts out the *LM* curve and raises expenditure and income, thus raising imports and worsening the trade balance, as was detailed at the end of Chapter 18. Figure 19.1 is a reproduction of Figure 18.7. The monetary expansion moves the economy from point *E* to point *M*. The deficit at point *M* means that reserves are declining over time.

If the central bank sterilizes the reserve outflow, the money supply remains at the new, higher level. The effect would be to keep income high and the trade balance in deficit. The central bank could keep the economy at point *M* indefinitely, or at least until it exhausts its international reserves. However, assume now that the central bank is either unable or unwilling to sterilize the reserve outflow. Over time, the reserve outflow reduces the money supply. The *LM* curve gradually shifts back. The effect is that expenditure and income fall, and the trade balance improves. The process continues as long as the trade balance is in deficit, which is until the economy returns to *E*. Once the trade balance is back at zero, no reason exists for reserves or any other variables to be changing. Notice that in the long-run equilibrium, income has not changed from what it was before the monetary expansion. Thus we have a central result under the monetary approach to the balance of payments: A monetary expansion, although it raises income and worsens the trade balance in the short run, has no effect on either in the long run.

FIGURE 19.1

Effects of a Monetary Expansion over Time

In the short run, an increase in the money supply raises output and worsens the trade balance. If the loss of reserves is not sterilized, however, then the money supply falls over time and output returns to its original level at E.

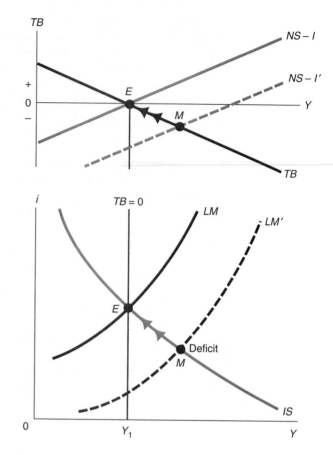

Conversely, a monetary contraction reduces income and improves the trade balance in the short run but has no effect in the long run. Only continuing growth in the money supply (in excess of growth in money demand) could cause a continuing deficit.

19.2 The Purchasing Power Parity Assumption

The previous section defined the monetary approach to the balance of payments by the assumption of nonsterilization. There is a second proposition often associated with proponents of the monetary approach, however. It is called *purchasing power parity* (PPP) and requires the assumption that goods prices are perfectly flexible. Thus the time has come to consider the determination of the price level.

Unlike the nonsterilization assumption, which is simply appropriate or inappropriate depending on what the central bank does, the assumption of price flexibility is a bigger issue, one that generates ideological controversy. The issue is similar to the old Keynesian–monetarist debate in closed-economy macroeconomics. Some writers continue to confuse the monetary approach (nonsterilization) with monetarism (perfectly flexible prices). However, the difference is clear in a passage written by two of the central figures in the area:

> *The monetary approach to the balance of payments . . . can be readily applied to conditions of price and wage rigidity and consequent response of quantities— employment, output, consumption—rather than money wages.*[5]

Indeed the application to price and wage rigidity constitutes Mundell's income mechanism, developed in the preceding section.

The alternative view, entailed by PPP, is that prices are perfectly flexible and so markets clear. This assumption is shared by the monetarists and their successors— those who believe in real business cycles and proponents of other branches of new classical macroeconomics. These believers in price flexibility adopt the nonsterilization assumption, but they have a slight quarrel with Hume's price specie-flow mechanism. Hume said that a monetary expansion will raise prices and worsen the trade balance, which will lead to an outflow that in the long run returns the prices to their original level. The alternative view asks how prices can be higher in one country than another even in the short run. Why would consumers buy any goods at all from the country with the higher prices? Would it not suffer an instantaneous trade deficit of unlimited size?

PPP: Definitions

Purchasing power parity, or PPP, is simply the name for the following equation:

$$P = EP^*$$

where E is the exchange rate, and P and P^* are the domestic and foreign price levels, respectively. It could also be written,

$$E = P/P^*$$

We are not ready to draw any conclusions about causality, about whether changes in E cause changes in P or the other way around. PPP is just a condition, not in itself a complete theory of determination of the price level or the exchange rate.

The equation has a long history. Many economists consider it discredited. Certainly it is inconsistent with the Keynesian model, in which price levels are not free to adjust whenever the exchange rate changes. However, some consider it a necessary and logical consequence of economic rationality. The right answer depends on how one defines P and P^*.[6]

---

[5]Jacob Frenkel and Harry Johnson, "The Monetary Approach to the Balance of Payments: Essential Concepts and Historical Origins," in Jacob Frenkel and Harry Johnson, eds., *The Monetary Approach to the Balance of Payments* (Toronto: University of Toronto Press, 1976), p. 25.
[6]For a survey of PPP, see Kenneth Rogoff, "The Purchasing Power Parity Puzzle," *Journal of Economic Literature,* 34, no. 2 (1996): 647–648.

Arbitrage and the Law of One Price

If P and P^* are defined to be the price, in domestic and foreign currency, respectively, of the identical good, and if tariffs and transportation costs are low, then the formula is indeed a logical consequence of economic rationality and competitive markets. Under this interpretation, the equation is called the *law of one price*. It is practically a definition of what it means to be a single good. The law of one price should hold because of international *arbitrage*.

When the price of the good in one country begins to rise above the price in another country (expressed in a common currency), it will become profitable for intermediaries to buy the good in the low-price country, sell it in the high-price country, and pocket the difference. Such activity is what is meant by arbitrage.

For example, in 1985, when the dollar had appreciated to roughly double its 1980 value against the mark, luxury German automobiles were selling for higher prices in the United States than in Germany. A so-called gray market developed rapidly, in which people bought BMWs, Mercedes, and Porsches in Germany and shipped them to the United States, either to use themselves or to resell. Another example of arbitrage arose in 1995, when the dollar had depreciated and it was the yen that was at its highest level in 40 years. Then arbitrage consisted of Japanese visitors to California loading up on consumer goods that were cheaper than the same goods back home.

Arbitrage will tend to drive the price up in the low-price country, by adding to demand there, and down in the high-price country, by adding to supply. The process should continue until the price is equalized in the two countries. Hence the law of one price.

An interesting question is why the arbitrage in 1985 was not powerful enough to force retailers of German autos in the United States to lower their prices to match the lower dollar prices of the autos sold in Germany. Evidently the costs involved in buying an auto in Germany and shipping it to the United States are large enough that most American customers preferred to continue buying from authorized dealers despite the higher price. Part of the explanation is that a BMW bought in Germany is not precisely the same commodity as a BMW bought from an authorized U.S. dealer. Even leaving aside the shipping costs, some changes must be made in pollution control equipment to satisfy U.S. regulations. Furthermore, when consumers buy automobiles from an authorized dealer, one thing they get is a warranty, the ability to have mechanical problems fixed at no cost. Needless to say, this is difficult to do if the dealer is in Munich.

Such frictions in the arbitrage process sometimes allow exporters to set different prices in different customer countries. This phenomenon of the firm "pricing to market"—setting prices with an eye more on prices of competing products in the customers' market than on the price of the good in its country of origin—is especially a phenomenon of the U.S. market. In other countries, exchange rate changes tend to be somewhat more fully and rapidly passed through to the prices of imports. A possible reason is that foreign firms in U.S. markets tend to be heavily outnumbered by domestic firms.

Because the law of one price is so basic, we have been implicitly assuming all along that it holds. In the preceding two chapters even though we assumed that the price of BMWs produced in Germany was set rigidly in terms of euros (refer to the discussion of Assumption 3 in Section 16.1), we took as given that the price of BMWs in the United States was simply the euro price times the dollar/euro exchange rate. In other words, we assumed that arbitrage enforced the law of one price for BMWs, and we will continue to do so, notwithstanding the anomaly just noted.

This is not as strong as the assumption that the price of *American-made* automobiles is equal to the euro price of German automobiles times the exchange rate. Buicks and BMWs are, after all, different products. Arbitrage between the two does not operate, given the reasonable assumption that consumers view American and German automobiles as different products. This fact allows U.S. manufacturers to set their prices in dollars with some degree of rigidity (at least in the short run), and at the same time allows German manufacturers to set theirs in euros.

Reasons for Failure of PPP

The term *purchasing power* connotes a basket of goods rather than a single good. If identical goods entered the domestic and foreign consumption baskets with identical weights, and the law of one price held for each good, then PPP would necessarily follow.

We will use P and $P*$ to refer to actual price indices in use, such as the producer price index (PPI) or consumer price index (CPI). Such indices inevitably refer to different baskets of goods in different countries, which immediately allows the possibility that the equation $P = EP*$ will fail to hold. Note that aggregate price indices are expressed relative to a base year (e.g., 2000 = 100) rather than in absolute dollar or pound terms. Thus the concept here is known as "relative PPP," rather than "absolute PPP."[7] Relative to the base year, the domestic price goes up by the same percentage as the foreign price level plus the percentage change in the exchange rate. If a bushel of wheat or a ton of steel is now—and in the past has always been—more expensive in France than China, this will not show up in the calculations of relative PPP. In other words, the equation $P = EP*$ holds only up to a multiplicative constant. For convenience, the multiplicative constant usually is not shown explicitly. Another way of stating the proposition that relative PPP holds is to say that the *real exchange rate*, defined as $EP*/P$, is constant over time.

There are four reasons why purchasing power parity can fail to hold. Each is associated with its own typical pattern of movement in the real exchange rate.

1. *Tariffs and transportation costs* create a band in which prices can fluctuate before arbitrage becomes profitable. Only if the price in one country exceeds the price in the other by more than the size of any tariffs, other trade barriers, and shipping costs, will arbitrage start to operate. We might rescue the law of one price by claiming that a

---

[7]It is difficult to get the data necessary for computing absolute PPP; we cannot use standard statistics on price indices that governments publish as we can when computing relative PPP. It means sending a team of researchers to different countries to sample the prices of a standardized set of goods. Absolute price indices are reported in the Penn World Tables. See Irving Kravis and Robert Lipsey, "Toward an Explanation of National Price Levels," *Studies in International Finance*, 52 (1983).

bushel of wheat delivered in New York City at noon on a particular day is a different good than a bushel of wheat delivered in London, or delivered on a different day. (Contracts for spot or forward delivery of agricultural and mineral commodities do, in fact, specify time and place, and the price can vary accordingly, especially if there are substantial tariffs or transportation costs.) In any case, PPP is defined to apply to price indices that aggregate together, not only wheat, but all goods, so these geographical factors clearly allow deviations from PPP. Figure 19.2(a) represents these deviations as fluctuations of the real exchange rate within a band. The width of the band should be twice the magnitude of tariffs and transportation costs.

2. *Permanent shifts in the terms of trade* between traded goods take place, such as the upward shift that occurred between oil and manufactured goods in 1973 and 1979, the reverse shift that occurred in 1986 and 1998, or the return of high oil prices after 2004. Oil and manufactured goods can have very different weights in the price indices of the two countries, particularly if we consider producer price indices rather than CPIs. An oil-producing country, for example, will experience a real appreciation of its currency when the relative price of oil goes up, whether in the form of a nominal appreciation of the currency or in the form of an increase in the producer price index, P. If the oil price goes up by 50 percent and oil has a weight that is 20 percentage points higher in an oil-exporting country than in another country, then the effect on the real exchange rate will be 10 percent. To take another example, automobiles could have the same weight in two countries' price indices, but if Japan produces smaller, more fuel-efficient cars, then it is likely to experience a real appreciation in the event of an oil price increase that causes demand to shift toward its products.

In the case of tariffs and transportation costs, when the real exchange rate nears the top of the band it cannot go much farther. However, in the case of permanent shifts in the terms of trade, no natural limit exists on how far the real exchange rate can drift in one direction or the other. In the absence of any particular theory predicting changes in the terms of trade, the real exchange rate can move up from its current position as easily as down. Accordingly, in Figure 19.2(b), the shifts in the terms of trade are shown as "permanent": When a change in the real exchange rate is observed, there is no way to know whether it will in the future continue to move further in the same direction or will reverse itself. When changes in a variable such as the real exchange rate are not predictable, we say that the variable follows a "random walk," like a drunken reveler walking down an empty street. This description is just a statement of our ignorance of what the real exchange rate will do, however; it does not take the place of an economic theory.

3. Even if the traded goods baskets are identical in both countries, if the indices include prices of *nontraded goods and services,* which cannot be arbitraged internationally, PPP may fail. If the prices of nontraded goods in each country happen to move proportionately to the prices of traded goods, then PPP will still hold. If there are shifts in the relative prices of traded goods and nontraded goods, PPP will fail. (Models with nontraded goods are discussed at greater length in Chapter 20.)

Consider the real exchange rate defined in terms of consumer price indices.

$$E_{\text{real}} = E(\text{CPI*}/\text{CPI}) \tag{19.1}$$

FIGURE 19.2

Patterns of Deviation from Purchasing Power Parity

(a) Tariffs and transportation costs create a band within which the real exchange rate can fluctuate. (b) Permanent shifts in the terms of trade move the real exchange rate unpredictably. (c) A long-term trend in the relative price of nontraded goods (e.g., upward in a rapidly growing country) will cause a trend in the real exchange rate. (d) The real exchange rate works its way back to equilibrium after a devaluation as goods prices adjust, but the process can be slow.

In each country, a weighted average of nontraded goods and traded goods constitutes the CPI. The real exchange rate will change if the *relative* price of non-traded goods (i.e., the price of nontraded goods in terms of traded goods) changes in either the foreign country or the domestic country.[8] For example, the Japanese yen had come to appear highly overvalued in real terms by 1995. The long-term trend in the yen over the preceding half century had shown a strong real appreciation, in part because of an increase within the Japanese price index of the prices of housing and other nontraded goods and services (including golf-club memberships, a nontraded good particularly important in Japan!).

Bela Balassa and others have identified a pattern based on differential economic growth (the famous "Balassa-Samuelson effect").[9] Growth of a country's income is associated with increased productivity in traded goods, which then fall in price relative to nontraded goods. In other words, the relative price of nontraded goods in terms of traded goods rises. Growth also may cause a rise in the relative price of nontraded goods and services if they are superior goods in consumers' demand functions.[10] Either way, because the prices of traded goods are tied to world prices, a rise in the relative price of nontraded goods can only mean an increase in the price of nontraded goods relative to world prices. Therefore, the CPI, which includes nontraded goods, rises relative to world prices. The domestic currency will appear to appreciate by PPP calculations. The real exchange rate, $E(CPI^*/CPI)$, will appear to fall (i.e., either E will fall or CPI will rise). That is why countries with strong growth rates tend also to have upward trends in their relative prices and therefore in the real foreign exchange value of their currencies, as is shown in Figure 19.2(c). In other words, such countries often show downward trends in their real exchange rates.[11]

4. In Chapter 16, lags caused by *imperfect information, contracts, inertia in consumer habits,* and so forth, rendered elasticities lower in the short run than in the long run. This implies that two goods that are highly substitutable in the long run may be very imperfect substitutes in the short run. This low degree of substitutability allows prices to be "sticky" and allows large deviations from PPP in the short run without inducing large-scale international arbitrage. For example, following a devaluation or revaluation, firms do not readjust their prices fully but absorb the (finite) increase or decrease in demand by varying the quantity sold. If the goods are close substitutes in the long run, then prices will adjust to PPP eventually; if they did not adjust, demand

---

[8] Refer to Problem 2c at the end of the chapter.

[9] Bela Balassa, "The Purchasing Power Parity Doctrine: A Reappraisal," *Journal of Political Economy,* 72 (1964): 584–596; Paul Samuelson, "Theoretical Notes on Trade Problems," *Review of Economics and Statistics* (May 1964): 145–154. This is the sort of "real trade theory" explanation for changes in the real exchange rate that we would like to have, as opposed to the agnostic position that is content with describing the real exchange rate as following a random walk.

[10] "Superior" goods are goods that experience a relative increase in demand when real income increases. Jeffrey Bergstrand, "Structural Determinants of Real Exchange Rates and National Price Levels: Some Empirical Evidence," *American Economic Review,* 81, no. 1 (March 1991): 325–334.

[11] Evidence in time-series data is found to support the Balassa hypothesis in Jose De Gregorio, Alberto Giovannini, and Holger Wolf, "International Evidence on Tradables and Nontradables Inflation," *European Economic Review,* 38, no. 6 (June 1994): 1225–1244. Such studies look at relative PPP. Cross-country evidence on absolute PPP is summarized by Irving Kravis and Robert Lipsey, "National Price Levels and the Prices of Tradables and Nontradables," *American Economic Review,* 78, no. 2 (May 1988): 474–478; it too shows that the price of non-traded goods relative to traded goods increases with the level of the country's per capita income.

levels might rise or fall without limit. Figure 19.2(d) illustrates the process. If a sudden increase in the nominal exchange rate occurs, with prices fixed in the short run it translates fully into an increase in the real exchange rate. This real depreciation stimulates the demand for domestic goods, putting upward pressure on prices. As prices gradually rise, the real exchange rate comes back down toward its long-run equilibrium. However, it is always possible that before equilibrium is reached, another sudden exchange rate change will occur.

The precise nature of the microeconomics of sticky prices is not well understood, but the empirical evidence is clear, as we will see in the following section. Of these four ways in which PPP can fail, all contain some truth, but the last is the one with the most macroeconomic content. From now on, any reference to the possibility of short-run failure of PPP will usually be a reference to the macroeconomic, sticky-price interpretation. Although permanent changes in the real exchange rate because of productivity differences and other real factors do occur, they tend to be slow long-term trends. Short-run deviations from those trends are the sort of PPP failure that we will be examining at length.

Empirical Evidence on PPP

Any empirical study of PPP shows very large deviations, at least in the short run. Relative to the Bretton Woods period of fixed exchange rates, most countries' real exchange rates have been especially variable in the years since 1973, including Great Britain and the United States. This is reflected in Figure 19.3, which graphs the real pound sterling/dollar rate. A useful measure of variability is the standard deviation.[12] The standard deviation of the real pound/dollar rate was 22 percent over the period 1973 to 2005. In general, it takes a band of two standard deviations either way to encompass 95 percent of the fluctuations in a variable (assuming a normal distribution). These numbers imply that departures from PPP as large as 44 percent occur (2 times 22 percent = 44 percent). These are large swings to be occurring regularly in the relative prices of countries' goods. In comparison, the standard deviation of the real pound/dollar rate was only 9 percent over the fixed-rate period of 1945 to 1972. Some of the variation in the real exchange rate during the earlier period was caused by differences in inflation rates between the two countries, but much of the variation was accounted for by a few discrete devaluations of the pound. The exchange rate was not literally "fixed" permanently; it was "fixed, but adjustable."

The 1973 increase in the variability of the real exchange rate against the United States was particularly great for Japan. This is clear in Figure 19.4, which shows monthly changes in the real yen/dollar rate.[13] The pre-1973 versus post-1973 comparisons suggest strongly that fluctuations in the nominal exchange rate may be a cause of fluctuations in the real exchange rate.

---

[12]If you are familiar with the statistical concept of the *variance*, the standard deviation is simply the square root of it.

[13]Monthly variability in major exchange rates tripled after 1973. We have concentrated here on the U.K. case rather than the Japanese one, or others, because the time series of data extends unbroken much further back in history.

FIGURE 19.3

Two Hundred Years of Purchasing Power Parity Between the Dollar and the Pound

Changes in the real exchange rate are not purely random. Rather, it tends to regress slowly toward its long-run equilibrium (until a new disturbance comes along). In the case of the United States and United Kingdom, the long-run equilibrium appears to have been constant.

Sources: 1790–1990 James Lothian and Mark Taylor, "Real Exchange Rate Behavior: The Recent Float from the Perspective of the Past Two Centuries," *Journal of Political Economy* 104, 484–509 (1996); and for 1990–2005: IFS (International Financial Statistics) and Federal Reserve.

Another explanation is that the greater variability in real exchange rates after 1973 was related to the greater magnitude of real worldwide disturbances, such as oil shocks, and would have happened even under a regime of fixed exchange rates (in which case the variability would have shown up in the price levels). This alternative view holds that changes in the nominal exchange rate do not *cause* changes in the real exchange rate, but that both occur in response to exogenous real disturbances such as productivity changes.[14] One problem with this view is that no one has identified these real shocks. It would seem if there were a change in productivity or consumer tastes that applied to hundreds of different industries in a country, such that all of them experience an increase in price when the currency appreciates (relative to their counterparts in foreign countries), then we should be able to identify what that change is. A few cases, in fact, do suggest explanations. The rapid fall in the value of the yen and the mark against the dollar when the price of oil quadrupled at the end of 1973 surely resulted because those two countries' economies depended more on imported oil than the U.S. economy

---

[14]Such theories have been constructed, for example, by Alan Stockman, "The Equilibrium Approach to Exchange Rates," *Economic Review*, Federal Reserve Bank of Richmond (March–April 1987): 12–31.

FIGURE 19.4

Nominal and Real Exchange Rates Both Became More Volatile After 1973

(a) Monthly Changes in the Nominal Yen/Dollar Rate

(b) Monthly Changes in Real Yen/Dollar Rate

did. It is hard to see what changes in worker productivity or consumer tastes could possibly explain the 50-plus percent real appreciation of the dollar between 1980 and 1985, however, and its reversal over the following three years, or the similar 1990–1995 real appreciation of the yen and *its* reversal over the subsequent three years.

One way to check if the comparison of the fixed-rate and floating-rate periods might be contaminated by larger supply shocks after 1973 than before is to look at Canada, the one country to have a floating exchange rate in the 1950s. The real exchange rate in Canada was highly variable at the time, whereas those in fixed-rate countries were much less so. Evidently the floating-rate regime made the difference.

Another piece of evidence is offered by the case of Ireland. From 1957 to 1970 the Irish currency was pegged to the pound, and thereby to the dollar and mark as well, until the currencies began to float against each other. From 1973 to 1978 the Irish currency was again pegged to the pound, which meant it floated against the dollar and mark. Then from 1979 onward Ireland was in the European Exchange Rate Mechanism, and the currency—the punt—was thereby tied to the mark, which meant it floated against the dollar and pound. In each of the three periods, the choice of *nominal* exchange rate regime for the punt corresponds very well with the observed degree of *real* exchange rate variability vis-à-vis each of the three trading partners. Stickiness of prices explains the pattern. Otherwise it would be quite a coincidence that real variability vis-à-vis the mark, say, should fall and vis-à-vis the pound should rise at precisely the same moment that the nominal variabilities, respectively, fall and rise as well.[15]

A third way of evaluating whether real exchange rate variability is related to the exchange rate regime is to consider earlier historical experience. History demonstrates that the variability of real exchange rates was larger under floating-rate regimes than under fixed-rate regimes, not just during the period after World War II, but before the war as well.[16]

These findings would be difficult to explain with perfectly flexible goods prices. It seems more likely that prices are sticky and that nominal exchange rate variability is indeed a primary source of real exchange rate variability. Estimates on the yearly U.S.–U.K. data indicate that fluctuations in the nominal exchange rate are 84 percent reflected as fluctuations in the real exchange rate (1973–2005).

There have been some studies of PPP, or the law of one price, for disaggregated categories of goods matched across countries that are the smallest, most narrowly defined, SITC (Standardized International Trade Classification) categories. These studies find large deviations even on these disaggregated data. This need not be interpreted as a failure of economic rationality or the law of one price. One partial explanation is that most foreign trade takes place under 30- to 90-day contracts, so prices cannot be readjusted for 30 to 90 days after a disturbance. More fundamentally, manufactured goods of different firms are actually different goods, as was noted earlier.[17]

---

[15]Michael Mussa, *Exchange Rates in Theory and in Reality,* Essays in International Finance, 179 (Princeton: Princeton University Press, December 1990).

[16]Alan Taylor, "A Century of Purchasing Power Parity," *Review of Economics and Statistics,* 84 (2002): 139–150.

[17]Charles Engel, "Real Exchange Rates and Relative Prices: An Empirical Investigation," *Journal of Monetary Economics,* 32 (1993): 35–50.

Even goods that are marketed in the same location and differ in little more than brand name—for example, a Japanese television set and the identical item manufactured by the identical firm but under an American label—violate the law of one price. Different manufacturers vary with respect to reputation or warranty offered, and different retailers vary with respect to their sales and maintenance service. Long-term customer relationships are thought to be particularly important in Japan and give rise to what are sometimes called *implicit* contracts: A Japanese corporation will hesitate before raising prices when there is excess demand, in the anticipation that this will build loyalty among customers, who will continue to buy from it in other periods of excess supply.

This point recalls a distinction between homogeneous "auction goods"—for which the law of one price holds instantaneously and worldwide, and heterogeneous "customer goods"—for which the law of one price fails, at least in the short run. Auction goods are usually basic commodities such as agricultural and mineral products, whereas customer goods are usually heterogeneous manufactured goods that bear brand names. The rapidly evolving semiconductor industry provides an example of each kind of good. So-called commodity chips tend to be all the same regardless of the producer and are sold in perfectly competitive markets resembling those for agricultural or mineral commodities. Specialty chips are designed to fulfill more specific functions and tend to fit better the description of customer goods.

If PPP holds in the long run but not in the short run, the obvious empirical questions become: How long is the short run? How quickly do deviations from PPP disappear? The speed with which the real exchange rate adjusts back toward its long-run equilibrium has been estimated at about 15 percent a year: The best guess in a given year as to what will be the gap between the real exchange rate and its long-run equilibrium is 85 percent of what it was in the preceding year. After two years, 72 percent of the gap will remain ($.85^2 = .72$), and so forth. After four years, 52 percent of the gap will remain ($.85^4 = .52$). In other words, the half-life has been estimated at about four years. This speed of adjustment is not implausibly slow, but it is sufficiently slow as to be difficult to detect statistically in the data, given that large new disturbances come along frequently. This is especially true if only a few years of data are available. We must look at a long time period, such as the 200 years of data in Figure 19.3, for clear manifestation of the tendency of the real exchange rate to return to equilibrium.[18]

19.3 Purchasing Power Parity in a Hyperinflation

Hyperinflation was defined by Philip Cagan as a sustained inflation in which the price level goes up by more than 50 percent per month. Hyperinflations seem to attack like a mysterious disease. They afflicted Central Europe in the early 1920s, a smattering of countries at the end of World War II, Latin America in the 1980s, and several countries

---

[18]Hyperinflation is one context in which PPP in a sense works well empirically (because the long run in effect "telescopes" into a few years). This is explained in Section 19.3.

in the wake of the breakup of the Soviet Union in the early 1990s. The source is usually simple enough: a government that has control of a printing press but controls little else. Often it is a weak government printing money to fight a war.

In January 1994 the inflation rate in what remained of Yugoslavia (essentially Serbia) reached 313,563,558 percent per month, almost equaling the preceding record, which had been set by Hungary in 1945–1946. As with any hyperinflation, residents tried desperately to buy marks or dollars, anything to avoid holding the domestic currency. Reporting at the peak, a Belgrade newspaper described the situation: "Yesterday [morning] the price of the [Deutsche] mark on the black market was 2.0 million dinars, and around 3:00 P.M. it was 2.5 million dinars. Belgrade dealers were reluctant to sell marks, as they expected the exchange rate to reach 5 million dinars (per DM) by the evening."[19]

As mentioned in footnote 18, hyperinflation is one context in which PPP in a sense works well empirically. Table 19.1 reports cumulative increases in the price level and in the exchange rate for some memorable hyperinflations of the twentieth century. They

TABLE 19.1

PPP in Great Hyperinflations of the Twentieth Century

Country	Period	$\dfrac{P \text{ final}}{P \text{ initial}}$	$\dfrac{E \text{ final}}{E \text{ initial}}$
Austria	10/1921–9/1922	93	29
Germany	7/1922–12/1923	179×10^8	141×10^8
Poland	1/1923–1/1924	699	491
Hungary	3/1923–2/1924[a]	44	12
Hungary	8/1945–7/1946	381×10^{25}	304×10^{25}
Nat. China[b]	9/1945–5/1949	105×10^9	119×10^9
Bolivia	4/1984–9/1985	974	2,129
Peru	9/1988–8/1990	7,242	11,600
Argentina	4/1989–3/1990	204	294
Brazil	11/1989–3/1990	12	8
Ukraine	4/1991–12/1993	4,772	799
Belarus	4/1991–2/1992	8	6
The Congo	10/1991–9/1994	237,499	284,519
Tajikistan	1/1992–12/1993	1,088	743
Serbia	2/1992–1/1994	366×10^{20}	8.3×10^{20}
Armenia	9/1993–5/1994	139	99

[a]Cumulative rise in exchange rate in Hungary is from average of March 1923 to average of March 1924.

[b]China's exchange rate change is the change in the price of gold rather than a direct exchange rate.

Sources: P. Cagan, "The Monetary Dynamics of Hyperinflation," in Milton Friedman, *Studies in the Quantity Theory of Money* (Chicago: University of Chicago Press, 1956); Bogetic, Dragutinovic, and Petrovic, "Anatomy of Hyperinflation," *Economic Review* and *International Financial Statistics*, IMF; T. Sargent, "The Ends of Four Big Inflations," in Robert Hall, *Inflation: Causes and Effects* (Chicago: University of Chicago Press, 1982); D. Paarlberg, *An Analysis and History of Inflation* (New York: Praeger, 1993); T. Hu, "Hyperinflation and the Dynamics of the Demand for Money in China, 1945–1949," *Journal of Political Economy* (January/February 1971); International Monetary Fund.

[19]The report was dated January 16, 1994, soon before a successful stabilization. As reported by Z. Bogetic, D. Dragutinovic, and P. Petrovic, "Anatomy of Hyperinflation and the Beginning of Stabilization in Yugoslavia, 1992–1994," World Bank (September 1994).

FIGURE 19.5

PPP in Great Hyperinflations of the Twentieth Century

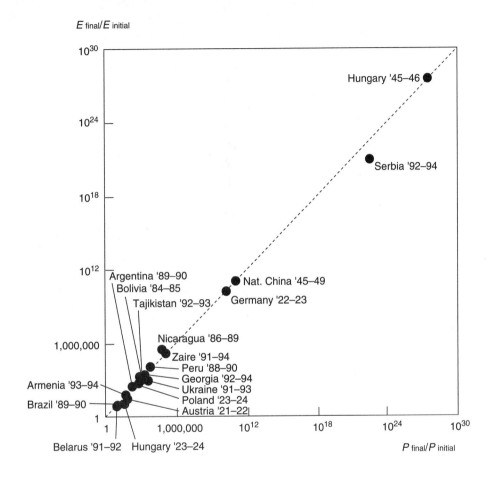

are expressed as multiples—that is, the level at the end of the period divided by the level at the beginning. In most of the hyperinflations reported, the increase in the exchange rate was roughly of the same order of magnitude as the increase in the price level. Figure 19.5 graphs the cumulative change in the price level and exchange rate for each of these hyperinflations. The points lie impressively close to the 45° line, supporting PPP.[20]

Yet there is another sense in which PPP works poorly during a hyperinflation. We can see from Table 19.1 that the cumulative rise in the exchange rate never matches the

---

[20]Similarly, Jacob Frenkel found that an OLS regression testing the time series relationship between the exchange rate E and the relative price level $P/P*$ in the German hyperinflation of 1920 to 1923 produced a coefficient close to one. "Purchasing Power Parity: Doctrinal Perspective and Evidence from the 1920's," *Journal of International Economics*, 8, no. 2 (May 1978): 169–191.

rise in the price level exactly. It is not uncommon for one variable to go up twice as much as the other—a movement in the real exchange rate of 100 percent—or by more.

The explanation for these seemingly conflicting findings is that PPP holds fairly well in the long run, but large short-run errors can push the exchange rate and the price level away from PPP. In a hyperinflation, the long run arrives quickly. In terms of Figure 19.5, the deviations from the 45° line are dwarfed by the magnitudes of the hyperinflations.[21] In short, as an explanation of the level of the *nominal* exchange rate, PPP works well in hyperinflations. As a theory of the *real* exchange rate, it does not. We examine these hyperinflations further in Chapter 27.

19.4 PPP in the Model of the Balance of Payments

We now adopt the assumption that prices are perfectly flexible, so that PPP holds.

$$P = EP^* \qquad (19.2)$$

Why is PPP assumed here, when the empirical evidence just reviewed does not support it? There are several reasons. First, just as assuming fixed prices allowed us to focus on the determination of output in the preceding chapter, assuming flexible prices and full employment is a simplification that allows us to focus on the determination of the price level. (We will relax the assumption of full employment in Chapter 26 to study the complete case, where increases in demand go partly into output and partly into prices.) Second, some economic analysts write as if PPP does hold. It helps to understand their viewpoint. Third, the flexible-price full-employment assumption is fairly realistic for thinking about the *long run,* just as the rigid-price assumption is fairly realistic for thinking about most countries in the short run.

Finally, PPP is more realistic, even in the relatively short run, for thinking about very small, very open economies. Hong Kong and Singapore are examples. Why is PPP a good assumption for some countries but not for others?

The Aggregation of Traded Goods for Small Open Economies

For most countries, even relatively large ones, prices of import goods can be taken as given exogenously in the short run, fixed in terms of foreign currency, as was assumed in the preceding three chapters. The reason is that a typical country constitutes a small fraction of the world demand for any given product and so has very little monopsony power. The situation is more varied when it comes to the country's export goods. Many countries have some monopoly power in their export goods. Even if the country is only one of many that produces, for example, automobiles, foreign consumers will not treat its autos as perfect substitutes for other countries' autos because they are customer goods. This makes it possible for producers to set a price for the product in domestic

---

[21]This is a standard "errors in variables" problem in econometrics. N. Davutyan and J. Pippenger, "Purchasing Power Parity Did Not Collapse During the 1970s," *American Economic Review,* 75, no. 5 (December 1985): 1151–1158.

currency without fearing an instantaneous large loss of demand when there are adverse changes in the exchange rate or in the prices charged by foreign competitors. This was the sort of country we considered in Chapters 16 through 18. But we now consider a different kind of country.

Many countries are so small in world markets that they have little monopoly power in their export goods and must take prices of export goods as exogenous, or fixed in terms of foreign currency. In the case of agricultural and mineral commodities and other auction goods, the output of different countries often can be considered perfect substitutes. Sugar or tin, for example, is basically the same regardless of where it is produced. In addition, if the country doesn't happen to produce a large proportion of the world output of the agricultural or mineral product, then it is safe to assume it accepts the world price. In other words, if it tried to charge more than the going price, it would quickly find itself without customers. In the case of manufactured goods, some labor-intensive products such as textiles are sufficiently similar among a wide range of countries that their prices too can be taken as essentially given on world markets. Then the analysis returns to the definition of a small country used in the first half of the book: a country that is too small in international markets to affect world prices.

As these examples show, developing countries are more likely to take export prices as given than are larger industrialized countries. (Note, however, that the assumption that the country can sell any quantity it wants on the world market at the going price can go wrong for another reason: Major customers may apply country-by-country quotas to purchases of the commodity. Industrialized countries maintain such quotas against sugar, for example.)

If a country is so small that it takes not only its import prices as given but its export prices as well, then it is possible to aggregate the two kinds of goods together at their (given) relative price. The composite commodity thereby created is referred to as *traded goods*. Under the assumption that the small open country can buy or sell all of the traded goods it wishes to, the trade balance becomes the quantity of traded goods it chooses to produce minus the quantity it chooses to buy. With this analysis, the question of how a given trade balance breaks down into imports and exports is left unanswered. The approach just tells us the overall trade balance, which is the variable we are usually interested in.

In reality, the relative prices of some of the goods within this composite commodity—the traded good—will sometimes change. When this happens, it will not be useful to talk in terms of traded goods in the aggregate. Worldwide changes in the relative price of oil, as occurred in 1973 and 1979 (upward), 1986 and 1998 (downward), and 2005 (again upward), are an important example. But such developments are usually taken to be exogenous. For purposes of studying changes that do not affect the terms of trade, such as changes that originate in macroeconomic policy, this aggregation will be useful. The next chapter will also continue to aggregate all traded goods.

The Real Balance Effect

In previous chapters, a devaluation raised the trade balance to the extent that it lowered the price of exports relative to imports. One might think that once we rule out such terms of trade, and indeed assume that purchasing power parity holds continuously, that a devaluation can no longer affect the balance of payments. But this is not correct. Here we briefly consider the *real balance effect* resulting from a devaluation.

Consider a 10 percent devaluation. Not only do the prices of imports follow the price of foreign exchange E up by the same 10 percent, but under the assumption of PPP, *all* prices rapidly go up by the same amount. When the price level P rises 10 percent, if the nominal money supply is unchanged, then the real money supply M/P falls by 10 percent. This is called the real balance effect because M/P is sometimes called real money balances.

Nothing has happened to change money demand, so we now have excess demand for money. Individuals respond by cutting back purchases of internationally traded goods, thereby improving the trade balance. Thus is the improvement accomplished with no change in the terms of trade. (Individuals also cut back purchases of internationally traded assets, if capital flows are in the model. Recall from the opening of this chapter that its subject is the Monetary Approach to the Balance of Payments, not just the Balance of Trade.)

As with the Hume and Mundell flow mechanisms of Section 19.1, the balance of payments surplus sets in motion developments that are self-correcting. The surplus implies that reserves are flowing into the country. Under a system of nonsterilization, the money supply gradually rises. This endogenous monetary expansion, in turn, gradually reverses the fall in purchases of goods (and assets). The balance of payments declines, eventually returning to zero.

Appendix C to this chapter presents this model algebraically and graphically. It illustrates the effects not just of a devaluation, but of three other experiments as well: a monetary expansion, inflation in the rest of the world, and supply-led domestic growth. (The model is useful for thinking about how the global system operated under the gold standard and Bretton Woods systems, the subject of Appendix A.) The common denominator throughout the experiments, and throughout the chapter, is that effects on the balance of payments are temporary and self-equilibrating.

19.5 Summary

This chapter introduced two new concepts into our study of economies that operate under fixed exchange rates. The first concept was the flow of international reserves into or out of a country through the balance of payments. This reserve flow changes its monetary base endogenously over time if the central bank either cannot or does not choose to sterilize (offset or neutralize). Such changes in the monetary base then have further implications over time for the economy. The second concept was purchasing power parity (PPP). The first of the two concepts is the one that defines most the monetary approach to the balance of payments.

We studied the effects of two policy experiments: a change in the money supply and a devaluation. An increase in the money supply creates an excess supply of money, which leads to a higher level of private expenditure and a balance-of-payments deficit in the short run, the same as at the end of the preceding chapter. The difference is that under the nonsterilization assumption, the balance-of-payments deficit implies that the level of the money stock falls over time, which in turn gradually undoes the increase in expenditure and the balance-of-payments deficit. A devaluation leads to a balance-of-payments surplus in the short run, again as in previous chapters. The level of the money stock rises over time, which in turn gradually undoes the balance-of-payments surplus. Whatever the policy experiment, in the long run the balance of payments must be zero under the monetary approach, so that the stock of reserves is no longer changing.

These results apply regardless of what is assumed about the second concept associated with the monetary approach to the balance of payments: purchasing power parity (PPP). PPP states that the domestic price level is given by the exchange rate times the foreign price level. There are a number of reasons why this relationship can fail in theory, why the *real* exchange rate is not constant. The most important, at least in the short run, is that prices are "sticky," meaning that prices require time to adjust after a change in the nominal exchange rate. Thus the fixed-price assumption (which we made in Chapters 16 through 18 and will return to in Chapter 22) is realistic for the short run. Nevertheless, in the last part of the present chapter we explored the implications of the assumption of price flexibility and PPP. One motivation is to think about the long run. Another motivation is to think about very small, open economies.

In the small open economy model a devaluation translates directly into a proportionate increase in the domestic price level, so no change occurs in the real exchange rate. Nonetheless, there is an effect on the balance of payments, through what is called the *real-balance effect*. The increase in the price level reduces the real money balances held by the public. In response to the resulting excess demand for money, people cut back on expenditure, which in turn leads to the improvement in the balance of payments. The next chapter will include some additional effects that devaluations have for small, open countries, especially developing countries. In particular, it will introduce nontraded goods into the monetary model.

CHAPTER PROBLEMS

1. What effect does a revaluation of the currency upward have on income and the trade balance, in the short run and in the long run? Answer diagrammatically for each of the two monetary models.
   a. The monetary model with fixed goods prices (Section 19.1).
   b. The monetarist model with purchasing power parity (Section 19.4).
2. The real exchange rate is defined to be E (CPI*/CPI).
   a. If PPP holds, what is the rate of change of the CPI when the foreign inflation rate is 3 percent per year and
      i.   the nominal exchange rate is fixed?
      ii. the domestic currency is depreciating at 7 percent per year?
      iii. the domestic currency is appreciating at 3 percent per year?
   b. Assume that PPP holds, the foreign price level is fixed, the parameter K measures the sensitivity of desired money balances to nominal income, and the parameter δ measures the sensitivity of the balance of payments to the excess

demand for money, as in Equation 19.5 in Appendix C. In each of the following cases, what is the (short-run) effect on the balance of payments? Assume that nominal GDP is initially $100 billion.

   i.   The central bank decreases domestic credit by $1 billion.

   ii. Domestic output grows by 1 percent.

   iii. The country devalues its currency by 1 percent.

c. Let CPI $= P_n^a P_t^{(1-a)}$, where P_n is the price of nontraded goods, P_t the price of traded goods, and a the weight given to the former in the consumption basket. Define CPI* analogously. Express the real exchange rate as a function of the relative price P_n/P_t in each country. (Assume the law of one price for traded goods.)

d. If the domestic and foreign CPIs each give a weight of two thirds to nontraded goods and one third to traded goods, what is the rate of change of the real exchange rate if

   i.   the relative price of nontraded goods is rising at 3 percent per year in the domestic country (and is constant in the foreign country)?

   ii. the relative price of nontraded goods is rising at 3 percent per year in both countries?

   iii. the relative price of nontraded goods is constant, but within traded goods there is an increase in EP_t^*/P_t—a shift in the terms of trade running against the home country—of 3 percent per year?

3. a. Assume that the gold standard is in effect and that huge new deposits of gold are discovered in California. What happens to the U.S. price level and trade balance, and the world price level?

  b. In *The Wizard of Oz,* Dorothy thinks that powerful men in the Emerald City have the answers to her problems, only to discover at the end of her journey that their power is based on sham and illusion and that she, the girl from Kansas, knew the answers all along. What city do you think this is? (See Appendix A, footnote 24.)

Extra Credit

Problems 4 and 5 deal with the monetary approach to the balance of payments. The rate of change of the money supply is given by the balance of payments.

$$H = TB$$

Problem 4 maintains the fixed-price assumption of the Keynesian model of Chapter 17. Problem 5 goes to the opposite extreme, fixed output.

4. Assume the model of Problem 5 in the problem set for Chapter 18.

  a. Continuing Problem 5b, what is the initial, short-run effect of a fiscal expansion on the balance of payments: $\Delta TB_{SR}/\Delta \overline{G}$? What happens over time? What is the effect on income in the long run, defined as the time when the money supply is no longer changing $(H = 0)$: ΔY_{LR}?

  b. Continuing Problem 5d from Chapter 18, what is the initial effect of a monetary expansion on the balance of payments: $\Delta TB_{SR}/\Delta(\overline{M}/\overline{P})$? What is the effect on income in the long run: ΔY_{LR}?

5. Think of the balance of payments, now equal to the desired rate of accumulation of money balances, as a function of the gap between the actual current money supply, M, and desired (long-run) money, M^d, where the latter is proportional to nominal GDP:

$$H = -\delta(M - M^d)$$

$$M^d = \frac{1}{v}PY$$

   a. Using BP to represent the balance of payments, which is equal to the nominal trade balance in the assumed absence of capital flows, express it as a function of M and PY. What is the effect of ΔM on ΔBP, and why?
   b. Is the effect of a monetary expansion on the trade balance in the Keynesian model of Problem 4b consistent with its effect in the monetarist model of 5a? (Note that the Keynesian model used TB to denote the real trade balance; the nominal trade balance is given by P times it. This made no difference when P was exogenous and normalized to 1.)
   c. For the first time, the assumption of a fixed price level is relaxed and replaced by the assumption of purchasing power parity:

$$P = E\overline{P}*$$

   where the small open economy assumption (that the world price level $P*$ is exogenous) is adopted, along with the assumption that income is exogenous because flexible prices guarantee full employment ($Y = \overline{Y}$).
   Returning to the monetarist notation of Problem 5a, what is the effect of a devaluation, ΔE, on the balance of payments in the short run? In the long run?

SUGGESTIONS FOR FURTHER READING

Dornbusch, Rudiger. "Purchasing Power Parity," in J. Eatwell, M. Milgate, and P. Newman, eds., *The New Palgrave*, Vol. 3 (New York: Macmillan, 1987). A good survey.

Eichengreen, Barry. *The Gold Standard in Theory and History* (New York: Methuen, 1985). Important papers, including Barro, Cooper, Hume, and Triffin, on how the gold standard operated, and whether it did or did not correspond to the idealized version represented by the monetary approach to the balance of payments.

Frenkel, Jacob, and Harry Johnson, eds. *The Monetary Approach to the Balance of Payments* (Toronto: University of Toronto Press, 1976). Includes, among other relevant papers, accounts of the overall monetary approach by the editors.

Mundell, Robert. *International Economics* (New York: Macmillan, 1968). Includes "Barter Theory and the Mechanism of Adjustment" (Chapter 8), a classic reference on the monetary approach; "Growth and the Balance of Payments" (Chapter 9), which makes the argument that real growth leads to a surplus, not a deficit; and "The International Disequilibrium System" (Chapter 15), which develops the model of the income-flow mechanism (although this paper, like much of the book, allows for capital mobility, and thus is most relevant for our Chapter 22).

Wanniski, Jude. "The Mundell-Laffer Hypothesis—A New View of the World Economy," *The Public Interest,* 39 (Spring 1975): 31–52. The author, a former editorial writer for the *Wall Street Journal,* offered a heartfelt proclamation of the view that changes in the exchange rate have no effect on relative prices and therefore no effect on the trade balance.

APPENDIX A

The Gold Standard

The monetarist model is useful for thinking about the gold standard, the subject of this appendix. The two-country version of the model, which is developed formally in the supplement to Chapter 19, is particularly useful for thinking about international flows of money between Britain and the United States under the nineteenth-century gold standard—roughly the period 1880 to 1914.

The Idealized Gold Standard

There are many senses in which the world "lost its innocence" in World War I. The era before 1914 often is recalled with fond, and sometimes overly idealized, nostalgia as an era of unprecedented economic growth and stability under the gold standard. The definition of a gold standard is that central banks fix the value of their currencies in terms of gold. This means that they set a price of gold in terms of domestic currency and then stand ready to buy or sell gold to whatever extent is necessary to maintain that price. They must, of course, hold reserves of gold to meet any fluctuations in demand.

A gold standard is a special case of a system of fixed exchange rates. It is easy to show this: If the Federal Reserve has fixed the price of gold in terms of its currency (i.e., in dollars/ounce) and the Bank of England has fixed the price of gold in terms of its currency (in pounds/ounce), then they have in effect fixed their exchange rate (the ratio of the two, in dollars/pound).

The nineteenth-century gold standard, when visualized in its idealized form as a system of smooth and automatic adjustment to any disequilibrium, has two distinguishing characteristics. They correspond to the two assumptions of the monetary approach to the balance of payments laid out in the chapter.

First is the assumption that wages and goods prices are perfectly flexible and so adjust quickly to maintain equilibrium in the labor and goods markets. In the chapter, this cornerstone of the global monetarist view was discussed at length. Here it is worth noting that the assumption of flexible prices and wages was less unrealistic in the pre-1914 period than it is in the modern era of differentiated brand products, labor unions, and myriad forms of government intervention in the marketplace (such as minimum-wage laws).

The second aspect of the monetary approach to the balance of payments, the emphasis on international reserve flows, takes on an especially simplified form in the case of the idealized gold standard. The idealization leaves out reserves held in the form of foreign currency and thus treats gold as the only form of international reserve.[22] Furthermore, it leaves out net domestic assets—purchases of domestic bonds by the central bank—and thus treats gold as the only component of the monetary base. Finally, it leaves out credit created by the commercial banking system, so that gold is treated as the only component of the money supply. This need not mean that gold literally circulates among the public; it is enough if the banking system always holds exactly the right amount of gold to back up one for one the domestic currency that it issues. (This is called "100 percent reserve backing," as opposed to the modern system of "fractional-reserve backing," under which the monetary base is only a fraction of the money supply in the hands of the public.) It follows that under this idealized version of the gold standard, the central bank could not sterilize international reserve flows even if it wanted to. The money supply necessarily varies one for one with the country's holdings of gold, evaluated at the set price. This appendix will freely use the word *gold* interchangeably with reserves, or money.

In truth, domestic credit creation and fractional reserve backing began long before 1914. Central banks did not in fact always allow reserve outflows to translate fully into monetary contraction as they were supposed to under the *rules of the game*. It is probably true, however, that in the nineteenth century central banks made much less of a practice of sterilizing reserve flows so as to set monetary policy where they wanted it than they do today. It was only after World War I that central banks began to acquire responsibility for the deliberate setting of monetary policy to respond to problems such as unemployment. (One possible interpretation is that the motivation for them to do so stems from the greater degree of rigidity of wages and prices in the modern era.[23])

The Ups and Downs of the Gold Standard

When the world's money was tied to gold, the world price level was determined by the world supply of gold, relative to world real income, precisely as in Equation 19.S.4 in the supplement. This relationship is the key both to arguments in favor of a gold standard and to arguments against it. The pro argument is that it prevents central banks from creating money at an excessive rate and thus generating sustained inflation. Excessive money creation and inflation have sometimes inspired proposals for a return to the gold standard, or some related form of commodity standard.

There are several con arguments. Tying the money supply to gold prevents central banks from responding to cyclical downturns with more expansionary monetary policy. (This is not considered a disadvantage by the gold-standard proponents; they would

---

[22]This ignores the fact that under the gold standard, central banks held much of their reserves in the form of pounds sterling because they knew that the pound was convertible into gold.

[23]See Robert Triffin, "Myths and Realities of the So-called Gold Standard"; and Donald McCloskey and J. Richard Zecher, "How the Gold Standard Worked, 1880–1913," both reprinted in Eichengreen, *The Gold Standard in Theory and History*.

prefer that the government not have such discretionary power because they do not trust that it has the good faith and competence to use the power well.)

A second objection is that tying the money supply to gold also prevents the steady long-term growth in the world supply of money and reserves necessary to satisfy the transactions demand that comes with growing output and trade. If there is no increase in the supply of available gold, then money will get tighter and tighter, creating a drag on world growth. The absence of major discoveries of gold between 1873 and 1896 helps explain why price levels fell dramatically over this period (53 percent in the United States and 45 percent in the United Kingdom).[24] Conversely, the gold rushes in California in 1849 and in South Africa and Alaska in the late 1890s were each followed by upswings in the price level of similar magnitude. Clearly, the system did not in fact guarantee price stability. Opponents of the gold standard ask why one would want to make the world economy hostage to chance gold discoveries and the other arbitrary vicissitudes of supply and demand in the world gold market. They also question the efficiency of a system that requires the use of resources to dig gold out of the ground laboriously, only to bury it back in the ground at Fort Knox.[25]

After World War I, it was considered very important to Britain to restore convertibility of the pound into gold. But at what exchange rate? This is the context in which the idea of purchasing power parity was first debated. A misplaced faith in the ability of wages and prices to adjust downward easily led the treasury minister, Winston Churchill, to peg the pound at too high a value, that is, to set too low a price for gold in terms of pounds. The result was a balance-of-payments deficit and severe contraction that ended in collapse of the system, rather than in smooth adjustment to the disequilibrium.[26]

Officially, gold was also the reserve asset of the Bretton Woods system founded in 1944. World growth would have soon run into the constraint of a basically fixed supply of gold, were it not for the fact that the dollar immediately became the de facto reserve asset. Central banks held much of their reserves in the form of dollars because the dollar was convertible into gold, in the same way that central banks had earlier held much

---

[24]The deflation of these years inflicted economic hardship, in particular, on American farmers, who had debts that were set in dollar terms but who produced commodities and owned land whose prices were falling in dollar terms. This was the era of Snidely Whiplash threatening to foreclose on poor Nell's farm and of the rise of populism in the American Midwest. The populists wanted the United States to abandon the gold standard so as to expand the money supply and get prices up. William Jennings Bryan, their candidate for president in 1896, warned that the farmers would not be "crucified on a cross of gold." Incidentally, the book *The Wizard of Oz* was really an allegory about populism. Oz stands for "ounces" (gold). Dorothy is the "innocent" from Kansas, the Scarecrow represents the farmer, the Tinman is the downtrodden urban worker (with whom the populists might have hoped to make a political alliance), and the Lion is William Jennings Bryan. Their enemies are the Wicked Witch of the East, representing the East Coast bankers (who were suspected of conspiring to keep money tight) and the Wicked Witch of the West, representing drought (only water can kill her).
[25]A good introduction to the topic is provided by Richard Cooper, "The Gold Standard: Historical Facts and Future Prospects," *Brookings Papers on Economic Activity,* 1 (1982): 1–45. It includes the latter-day controversy over proposals to return to the gold standard to restore price stability, and the statistics on the price level swings that in fact characterized the nineteenth century.
[26]John Maynard Keynes accurately predicted this outcome of the return to gold in 1925: "The Economic Consequences of Mr. Churchill," reprinted in his *Essays in Persuasion* (New York: Norton, 1963), pp. 244–270. Much has been written on this interwar period. See Barry Eichengreen, *Golden Fetters: The Gold Standard and the Great Depression, 1919–1939* (New York: Oxford University Press, 1992).

of their reserves in the form of pounds. This is why the Bretton Woods system was sometimes called a gold-exchange standard.

Before long, however, the new system came under increasing strain. The reason was that, beginning in 1958, the United States ran balance-of-payments deficits. Foreign central banks' holdings of dollars rose relative to the gold in Fort Knox, and foreigners (particularly Charles de Gaulle, the gold-conscious leader of France) began to doubt the ability of the U.S. government to redeem its dollar liabilities in gold. This was the beginning of the long, drawn-out breakdown of the Bretton Woods system.

The monetarist model can be used to illustrate the emergence of U.S. balance-of-payments deficits in 1958. Let the countries in the two-country model of the chapter supplement be the United States and Europe. In the 1950s the European economies grew more rapidly than the U.S. economy as they recovered from the devastation of the 1940s. Their rapidly growing levels of income led to rapidly growing demand for money. To acquire international reserves, they had to run balance-of-payments surpluses against the United States. The model was used in the 1960s to show why the emergence of U.S. deficits was a natural consequence of the system that had been set up in 1944.

The world monetary system was faced with the "Triffin dilemma."[27] If the United States was allowed to continue running balance-of-payments deficits, eventually there would be a crisis of confidence as foreigners all tried to cash in their dollars for gold before it was too late, and thereby exhausted the U.S. gold reserves. Conversely, if steps were taken to end the U.S. deficit, then the rest of the world would be deprived of sufficient liquidity in the form of a steadily growing stock of reserves.

Economists and policy makers debated the problem throughout the 1960s. There were two solutions proposed to increase the world supply of reserves, both of them radical departures from the system agreed on at Bretton Woods. The first was to increase the price of gold—that is, to devalue the dollar in terms of gold—thereby raising the nominal value of the world supply of reserves. The second was to create an artificial reserve asset, a sort of "paper gold."

Eventually, both changes were made, although it had not been planned that way. The artificial asset was the Special Drawing Right, which the members of the International Monetary Fund agreed to create in 1968. By the time three batches of SDRs were phased into use (1970–1972), other events had intervened. In August 1971, in response to the worsening U.S. balance of payments.[28] President Nixon unilaterally suspended convertibility of the dollar into gold, not just for private residents, but for foreign central banks as well. When the leading countries met at the Smithsonian Institution in December 1971 to agree on a new set of exchange rates, the realignments included a 10 percent devaluation of the dollar against gold. This attempt to shore up

---

[27]Robert Triffin, *Gold and the Dollar Crisis* (New Haven: Yale University Press, 1960).

[28]The year 1971 was the first time since World War II that the United States ran a deficit, not just on the private capital account, but on the trade account as well. The U.S. trade surplus had been diminishing steadily since 1964. The cause was overly expansionary macroeconomic policies, as the Johnson administration—followed by the Nixon administration—increased military spending on the war in Vietnam and domestic spending at the same time, and were reluctant to raise taxes to pay for it. Some have pointed out parallels between that period and U.S. macro policy from 2001 to 2005.

the system of fixed exchange rates did not last long, and in March 1973 the system was abandoned completely. The market price of gold increased twentyfold (in dollars) over the remainder of the decade.

APPENDIX B

Reserve Flows After Spending Increase and Devaluation

Section 19.1 looked at the implications of reserve flow by focusing on the effects of a monetary expansion. Now consider the effects of a fiscal expansion in the same model (Mundell's "income reserve-flow mechanism"). Figure 19.B.1 is a reproduction of Figure 18.8. The fiscal expansion shifts out the *IS* curve, raising income. The higher income at point *F* causes a trade deficit. The deficit means that reserves are declining over time.

FIGURE 19.B.1

Effects of a Fiscal Expansion over Time

In the short run an increase in spending raises output and worsens the trade balance. If the loss of reserves is not sterilized, then the money supply falls over time and output returns to its original level at *B*.

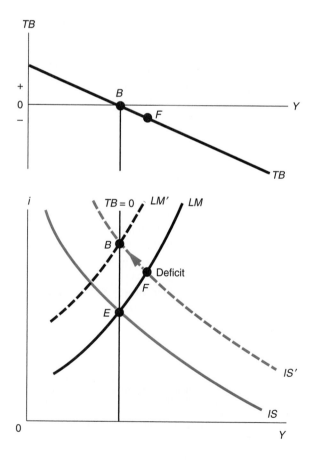

As in the case of a monetary expansion, the central bank could sterilize the reserve outflow to keep the money supply constant and remain at F. Under the assumption of nonsterilization, however, the money supply falls over time. The LM curve shifts back, income falls, and the trade balance improves. Eventually, income and the trade balance return to B, where they were before expansion. There is one difference between the new equilibrium at B and the old equilibrium at E. The interest rate is higher, meaning that a reallocation of output between sectors has taken place: The government sector has expanded at the expense of private investment. We thus have another result under the monetary approach: A fiscal expansion, athough raising income and worsening the trade balance in the short run, has no effect on either in the long run.

Finally, consider the effects of a devaluation. Figure 19.B.2 is a reproduction of Figure 18.9. The devaluation shifts out the IS curve. At point D income has increased. The devaluation shifts the vertical $TB = 0$ line farther out than the IS curve, so the trade balance improves at point D. As a consequence of the trade surplus, reserves are increasing over time. The central bank could sterilize the reserve inflow to keep the

FIGURE 19.B.2

Effect of a Devaluation over Time

In the short run a devaluation improves the trade balance and raises output. If the inflow of reserves is not sterilized, then the money supply rises over time and output rises further to C.

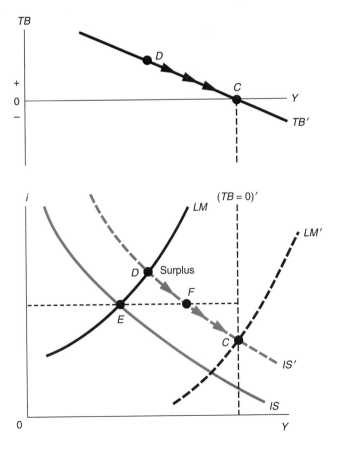

money supply constant and remain at point D, but under the assumption of nonsterilization the money supply rises over time and the LM curve shifts out. Income rises and the trade balance worsens. Eventually, the trade balance returns to zero, at point C. In this case, however, income ends up at a permanently higher level. The TB line in the upper panel of Figure 19.B.2 shows the magnitude of the long-run increase in income. The line's slope is $-m$, so

$$\Delta Y_{LR} = \frac{1}{m}\Delta \overline{X}.$$

Intuitively, we can see that money keeps flowing in through the trade surplus until income has risen enough for increased imports, ΔM, to cancel out the initial stimulus of the devaluation, $\Delta \overline{X}$. This returns the trade balance to where it was before the expansion.[29] It is interesting to compare the effect of the devaluation to what it would be in the simpler Keynesian multiplier model (at point F), that is, in the absence of crowding-out:

$$\frac{1}{s + m}\, \Delta \overline{X}.$$

The former is larger. Under the monetary approach to the balance of payments, the long-run effect is not only greater than the short-run effect, but it is even greater than the short-run effect without crowding-out. The conclusion that a devaluation is an effective means of raising income even in the long run is a very "unmonetarist" conclusion; it stems from the Keynesian assumption that prices are fixed. This assumption is not realistic for the truly long run and is relaxed in Section 19.4.

APPENDIX C

The Determination of the Balance of Payments in the Monetarist Model

This chapter considers only pegged exchange rates. This is probably just as well because most very small, very open economies (such as Hong Kong) do in fact seek to maintain a fixed exchange rate. The monetary approach under floating rates will be taken up in Chapter 27. The goal here is to analyze the effect of monetary policy and devaluation on the two target variables, income and the trade balance. Furthermore, this section considers the small-country version of the monetarist model, which means that the world price level is taken as exogenous.[30] Because both the exchange rate and

---

[29]The way Figure 19.B.2 is drawn, the long-run interest rate is lower, and therefore I is higher, after the devaluation than before. We know that this must be right. Otherwise, with $X - M$ unchanged, $Y = C + I + G + X - M$ could not be higher after the devaluation.

[30]The supplement to this chapter relaxes the small-country assumption to look at the two-country version of the monetary approach to the balance of payments, which is relevant when the country is large enough to affect the world price level. (As long as world prices are perfectly flexible and PPP holds, it continues to be a "monetarist" or "new classical" model, as opposed to the Keynesian model previously examined.)

the foreign price level are determined, by Equation 19.2 the domestic price level is also determined. This method of determining the domestic price level is very different from the Keynesian way in which it was exogenously set. The difference becomes obvious when we consider devaluation as in Section 19.4. PPP states that the devaluation is instantly reflected as a proportionate increase in the domestic price level, whereas in the Keynesian model the domestic price level did not change.

Desired money balances are proportional to nominal income.[31]

$$M^d = KPY \qquad \text{(19.C.1)}$$

Individuals adapt actual money balances to desired money balances through saving (in excess of investment), represented by H. This part of the book ignores assets other than money, such as bonds. (They will enter in Part V.) For this reason, saving can only take the form of additions to holdings of money balances. H is thus equal to the change in the money stock over time: It tells us how much the money supply is going up per year. H is assumed proportional to the current gap between the desired money stock and the actual money stock, M:

$$H = \delta(M^d - M)$$

where δ is the speed with which money balances are adjusted. This equation simply says that individuals act to add to their money balances when money demand minus money supply is positive. Now we use Equation 19.C.1 to substitute for long-run desired money balances, M^d.

$$H = \delta(KPY - M) \qquad \text{(19.C.2)}$$

Under the key nonsterilization assumption of the monetary approach, the rate of change of the money supply, M, is the same as the rate of accumulation of reserves, the balance-of-payments surplus, BP. The equation becomes

$$BP = H = \delta KPY - \delta M \qquad \text{(19.C.3)}$$

Equation 19.C.3 looks unlike any balance-of-payments expression seen before. An increase in the money supply has a negative effect on the surplus, as in the last chapter. Although the Keynesian model was quite specific about the channel through which the increase in the money supply raises spending (it lowers the interest rate and thus stimulates investment), the monetarist explanation is more general. A monetary expansion worsens the balance of payments because individuals, when faced with an excess supply of money, increase spending to adjust their excessive money holdings back down to the level of their money demand. (These two explanations can be made entirely consistent if investment depends linearly on the interest rate.[32])

Another difference between the two models is that the monetary approach says the outflow occurs through the overall balance of payments, without differentiating

---

[31] M here represents the money stock, not imports as in previous chapters. Desired money balances, M^d, refers to a long-run notion of money demand; it differs somewhat from the short-run notion of money demand in $IS - LM$, where the interest rate adjusts so that money demand is always equal to money supply, even in the short run.

[32] The reduced form of the linear $IS - LM$ system (i.e., with the interest rate substituted out) is the same as the monetarist formulation. This is chapter Problem 5b.

between the current account or capital account, whereas the Keynesian approach specifies that it occurs through the trade balance. However, because we have not yet introduced capital flows, it is difficult to tell the difference.

These differences are not especially important. The crucial difference between the monetarist and Keynesian models, remember, is price flexibility.

The assumption of perfect wage and price flexibility in the global monetarist model implies completely inelastic aggregate supply. Because income is always at the full-employment level, $Y = \overline{Y}$, the balance of payments in Equation 19.C.3 varies only with the price level, P, and the money supply, M. Figure 19.C.1 graphs the relationship between the balance of payments and the price level for a given M, with the balance of payments measured on the vertical axis, and refers to it as the H schedule.[33] As the equation says, the vertical intercept is $-\delta M$ and the slope is $\delta K \overline{Y}$. Again, the reason the schedule slopes upward is that a higher price level means a higher demand for money, which causes residents to cut back on spending so they can earn the desired money balances through a balance-of-payments surplus.

The exogenous foreign price level, P^*, and the given fixed exchange rate, E, together determine the domestic price level, $P = E\overline{P}^*$, by Equation 19.2. This price level, P, is represented in Figure 19.C.1 by a vertical line. Point B in the figure is the starting point, a position of balance-of-payments equilibrium. Two policy changes will be considered: monetary policy and devaluation.

FIGURE 19.C.1

Monetary Expansion in the Monetarist Small-Country Model

An increase in the money supply shifts the H schedule. With the price level, P, tied down by PPP, this leads to an excess supply of money and a balance of payments deficit ($BP < 0$ at M). Over time, money flows out of the country and balance is restored ($BP = 0$ at B).

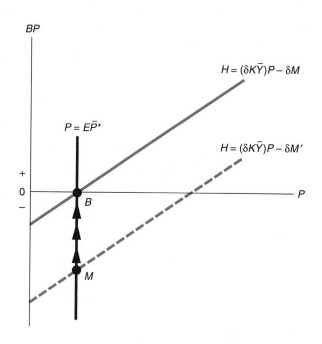

---

[33]The symbol H stands for "hoarding," defined as the accumulation of money through saving.

The Effect of a Monetary Expansion in the Monetarist Model

A monetary expansion shifts the H schedule down. The size of the downward shift is determined by the size of the change in the vertical intercept ($\delta\Delta M$). The economy moves to point M. Any given P implies a certain level of money demand. At the level implied by the exogenously given $P = E\overline{P}*$, an excess supply of money is now evident because money supply is greater than money demand. (*Any* point below the horizontal axis is a point of excess money supply.) People will increase spending or decrease saving. In fact *dis*saving, a balance-of-payments deficit, can be read off the vertical axis at point M.

Recall again the essence of the monetary approach—the identification of the balance-of-payments deficit with the rate of decumulation of the money supply. The H schedule shifts whenever the money supply changes. As time passes and money flows out through the balance-of-payments deficit, the H schedule shifts upward. The intersection with the price level line gradually moves upward from M. As the excess supply of money is worked off, the deficit falls, as can be read off the vertical axis. This process continues until (in the long run) the economy returns to point B, where money supply again equals money demand and there is no further need for dissaving: The balance of payments has returned to zero. Only then, when the reserve stock is no longer changing, has it reached long-run equilibrium.

Conversely, a monetary contraction initially shifts the H schedule upward, improving the balance of payments. However, the payments surplus itself leads to an increasing money supply, which over time shifts the H schedule back down until, again, in the long run it returns to balance-of-payments equilibrium.

In the case of either expansion or contraction, there is no long-run effect on the level of the money supply, but there may be an effect on its composition. Expansion or contraction of domestic credit is permanent. It is the foreign component of the monetary base—international reserves—that changes to offset the change in domestic credit.

The "Real Balance" Effect of a Devaluation

Now consider the effect of a devaluation. An increase in the exchange rate from E to E' means that the exogenous world price level, $\overline{P}*$, translates into a higher domestic price level, $E'\overline{P}*$, represented by a vertical domestic price line that is farther to the right in Figure 19.C.2. The higher value of P implies a higher level of domestic money demand. With an unchanged level of money supply, there is an excess demand for money at point D. (*Any* point above the horizontal axis is a point of excess money demand.) People reduce their spending or increase their saving. A balance-of-payments surplus results. That devaluation leads to a surplus is a common observation, but in this case the cause is not a change in relative prices stimulating exports. There can be no change in relative prices in this model. Rather, the higher price level raises the demand for nominal money balances. This is the *real balance* effect.

The balance-of-payments surplus at D means that the money supply is increasing. Over time, the H schedule shifts down, as the excess demand for money is alleviated by the increasing supply. In the long run it moves to point C, where money supply again

FIGURE 19.C.2

Devaluation in the Monetarist
Small-Country Model

An increase in the exchange rate from E to E'
raises the price level, P, proportionately, leading
to an excess demand for money and a balance
of payments surplus ($BP > 0$ at D). Over time,
money flows into the country and balance is
restored ($BP = 0$ at C).

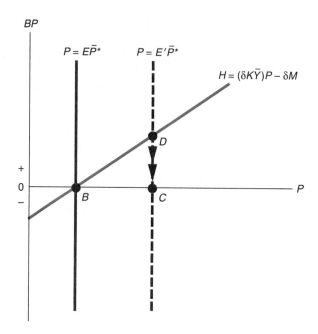

equals money demand and the balance of payments is back at zero. The new equilibrium after the devaluation features not only a higher price level but a higher money
supply, with both nominal variables having increased in the same proportion as the
exchange rate.

Let us now consider an exogenous increase in the world price level, $\overline{P}^*$, as might
result, for example, from an expansion in the world money supply. It is instantly transmitted as a proportionately higher domestic price level, $P = E\overline{P}^*$. It acts just like the
devaluation pictured in Figure 19.C.2 so far as the small country is concerned. The
excess demand for money shows up as a temporary balance-of-payments surplus.
Notice again that the favorable effect of the foreign price increase on the balance of
payments does not take place through *relative* prices, as in the elasticities or Keynesian
approaches, but rather through the effect of the price *level* on money demand.

Finally, consider an exogenous increase in domestic money demand. Such an
increase in money demand might result, for example, from an exogenous increase in
domestic output, $\overline{Y}$. Because this section assumes full employment, the increase in output must come from the supply side: an increase in the capital stock, labor force, or
productivity. In any case, the increase in money demand causes people to cut back
spending so that they can acquire the desired money balances. It acts like the decrease
in money supply previously considered, in that it creates an excess demand for money
and shifts the H schedule up. (More precisely, if the increase in M^d comes from an
increase in Y, then it rotates the H schedule in the counterclockwise direction: Refer to
the slope, $\delta K\overline{Y}$. The point remains: A higher BP now corresponds to a given P.) The
cutback in spending thus leads to a balance-of-payments surplus. Over time money

flows in through the payments surplus, until equilibrium returns with a higher money supply and a zero balance of payments, as always.

Notice the sharp contrast to the Keynesian model, in which an increase in income caused an immediate trade deficit, rather than a surplus. The Keynesian model should be thought of as correct for income growth induced by increases in spending because it is a model in which the economy can be below full employment. The present result—growth causing a payments *surplus* because of higher money demand—is appropriate for exogenous supply-induced growth. A prime motivation for the development of the monetary approach in the 1960s was the observed fact that the fastest growing countries, such as Japan, Germany, and other European countries, ran balance-of-payments surpluses while the United States ran a deficit. That the monetary approach could explain this situation accounted in part for its popularity.[34]

---

[34]The argument was made by Robert Mundell, "Growth and the Balance of Payments," in his *International Economics* (New York: Macmillan, 1968), Chapter 9. For examples from the current era (in which Japan and euroland have floating rather than fixed exchange rates and are growing more slowly than before), consider the cases of China and some other newly industrialized economies of East Asia. They have tended to experience rapid supply-side growth with surpluses in their balances of payments.

CHAPTER 20

Developing Countries and Other Small Open Economies with Nontraded Goods

I magine the dilemma faced by the finance minister of a small developing country that needs to improve its trade balance. Advisers urge that some combination of devaluation and contractionary demand policies be adopted. They base their reasoning on standard macroeconomic models such as the ones developed in the preceding chapters.[1] The finance minister has little faith in these models, believing that they were designed to fit the experience of relatively large industrialized countries, not small developing countries. But the finance minister also does not believe the simple small-country monetarist model developed in Chapter 19.[2] A bit more realism is required. This chapter departs temporarily from the central focus of the text to consider an alternative model that is particularly appropriate for typical developing countries.

If a country were so open to international trade and so small in world goods markets that purchasing power parity held, then, by definition, a devaluation could not change relative prices. As we saw in Section 19.4, a devaluation could affect the trade balance only through the real money balance effect. Hong Kong and Singapore were cited as relatively close approximations of such an economy.

Even countries that are small in terms of world trade often have large internal markets, however. Indonesia and Australia, for example, are probably too small in world markets to affect their terms of trade, but they are certainly not "small" countries in other respects. This chapter will continue to consider countries that are sufficiently small and open that they take the prices of all traded goods (exports and imports) as determined outside the country and fixed in terms of foreign currency. However, the existence of goods that are not internationally traded will also be recognized. The discussion will reveal that, as a consequence, such countries experience relative price effects when they devalue, along with the real money balance effect already explored.

---

[1] Such recommendations are often highly unpopular politically, especially when they are perceived to be imposed by the International Monetary Fund (IMF). See Chapter 24 for more on the unpopularity of devaluations.

[2] Blind adherence to PPP (among other things) got the policy makers of the "southern cone" of Latin America (Argentina, Chile, and Uruguay) into trouble in the late 1970s. Vittorio Corbo and Jaime de Melo, "Liberalization with Stabilization in the Southern Cone of Latin America," *World Development*, Special Issue, 13, no. 8 (August 1985): 893–916.

20.1   Nontraded Goods

We first introduced nontraded goods in Section 4.6. Chapter 19 explained that the existence of nontraded goods is one reason why PPP fails to hold in practice.

The primary examples of nontraded goods are not goods at all, but services. Some services, such as insurance, shipping, tourism, and computer programming, are internationally traded, and these have been growing in importance in recent years, especially with the advent of the Internet. (Witness the public attention to overseas outsourcing.) Nevertheless, most services are too localized to be traded internationally—for example, personal services like those offered by barbershops and dry cleaners. Some larger sectors, such as housing, utilities, and local transportation, also fit in this category.

Some goods are also nontraded, specifically those where the cost of transporting them internationally is prohibitively high. Highly perishable food is a good example. More commodities will qualify as nontraded in a country far removed from the rest of the world geographically, like Australia, than in one centrally located, like Germany. Prohibitively high trade barriers can also render goods nontraded. Particularly in developing countries, transportation costs and trade barriers sometimes insulate much of the economy from the rigors of international competition. In Latin America, for example, high import tariffs and quantitative restrictions on imports of manufactured goods historically have put into the nontraded category some industries that might otherwise be in the category of traded goods. A final case is that in which cultural tastes are such that foreigners are not interested in consuming the good in question. Who but an Australian could love Vegemite?

Output of Traded and Nontraded Goods

We now develop the appropriate model for thinking about a small open economy with nontraded goods.[3] We recall that if the country is too small to affect its terms of trade, then we can aggregate together tradable goods, for the reasons explained in Section 19.4. We begin by drawing the production possibility curve, or transformation schedule, showing the different quantities of nontraded goods versus traded goods that the economy can produce if its labor and other resources are fully employed. Figure 20.1 shows this curve, with traded goods measured on the horizontal axis. The curve has the usual bowed-out shape, meaning that there are diminishing returns as more and more labor is shifted out of nontraded goods into traded goods. Section 4.6 considered the special case of Ricardian production, in which this production possibility curve was flat. In that case the relative price of traded goods in terms of nontraded goods is determined entirely by the relative labor costs of producing the two goods, which is a constant (the slope of the line). In general, however, the relative price will vary and with it the quantities of the two kinds of goods that are profitable to produce (as in Section 2.7).

Assume that the relative prices are given by the slope of the straight line in Figure 20.1. P_N will denote the relative price of nontraded goods. $P_N \equiv P_n / P_t$, where P_n

---

[3]A country's "openness" could be defined as the ratio of its production of traded goods to its total GDP. This chapter focuses on countries that, although small as in the model of Section 19.4, are not *100 percent* open.

FIGURE 20.1

Output and Consumption of
Traded and Nontraded Goods

Production occurs where the
transformation curve is tangent to a
relative price line. Consumption occurs
where the budget line is tangent to an
indifference curve. As drawn, the two
points coincide, so output of traded
goods, *TG*, equals consumption of
traded goods, and the same is true
for nontraded goods, *NTG*.

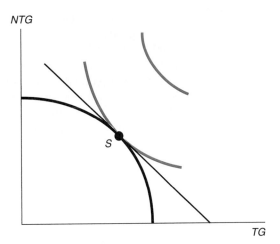

and P_t represent the (nominal) prices of nontraded goods and traded goods, respectively. P_N gives the number of units of traded goods required to buy one unit of nontraded goods. When P_N is low, nontraded goods are relatively cheap and the budget line in Figure 20.1 is steep: A resident can buy a larger quantity of nontraded goods for any given quantity of traded goods.

In the most general case, many combinations of outputs are "fair game," including points that lie inside the production possibility curve. These are points at which the supplies of labor and other resources are not being fully utilized, so that output of both goods is less than it could be. In this chapter, however, the discussion will be restricted to the assumption that labor and other resources are fully employed, as in Chapter 19. In this case, the quantities of output of the two goods, X_N and X_T, are given by the point S, where the line is tangent to the curve. The output quantities are the outcome of supply decisions that firms make when faced with the prevailing prices. Keep in mind that output of traded goods includes not only specific products that the home country might currently be exporting but also specific products that might be *imported* if the demand from domestic consumers exceeds domestic output.

Consumption of Traded and Nontraded Goods

The trade balance is given by the quantity of traded goods produced minus the quantity of traded goods consumed. If some of the output produced remains after domestic residents have bought what they want, it is exported and the country runs a trade surplus. There is no question as to whether there will be sufficient demand for the goods outside the home country because under the small-country assumption, the rest of the world will take all goods that the country has to offer at the going world price. If, however, domestic consumption of traded goods exceeds domestic output, then the difference is imported and the country runs a trade deficit. This way of thinking of the trade balance—as the difference between the output and the consumption of traded goods—is the same as in the small-country model of Section 19.4, the only difference being that there *all* goods were traded goods. It is very different, however, from the way we thought of the trade balance in Chapters 16 to 18—as foreigners' demand for the export goods of the home country minus domestic residents' demand for the imports. In the present model, with all traded goods aggregated together, it is impossible to say what determines the level of exports and the level of imports. Fortunately, it is not necessary to know either level to determine the difference of the two, the trade balance.

What determines the pattern of consumption? Assume, as in Figure 2.7, that we can draw community indifference curves. Along any given indifference curve, consumers are equally happy with the different possible combinations of nontraded and traded goods consumed, C_N and C_T. The slope of the indifference curve is the *marginal rate of substitution* between the two; it tells the amount of consumption of nontraded goods the consumer is willing to give up to get one more unit of traded goods. Indifference curves farther from the origin are better, of course, because more consumption is better than less. The curves are convex because of the diminishing marginal rate of substitution.

To attain the highest level of welfare available to them, consumers will determine their quantities purchased, C_N and C_T at the point on an indifference curve where the given price line is tangent, that is, where the marginal rate of substitution is set equal to the relative prices of the two kinds of goods. It is possible that this will be the same point, S, where production occurs. In that case the quantity of traded goods consumed will equal the quantity of traded goods produced. If this happens, the trade balance is zero. If we were to rule out gaps between expenditure and income, thereby ruling out trade deficits or surpluses, as in most of the first half of the text, we would necessarily be at S. Indeed, under this restriction, the relative price line would have to be determined endogenously by the unique point where the production possibility frontier was tangent to an indifference curve.

Now we allow for countries to "spend beyond their means." We assume expenditure is at some level, A (measured in terms of traded goods: $A \equiv C_T + P_N C_N$), that is greater than the level of income, Y (also expressed in terms of traded goods: $Y \equiv X_T + P_N X_N$). For example, there may have been an income tax cut or an increase in expenditure on the part of the government that raised A. A and Y are measured along the horizontal axis in Figure 20.2. The budget line is the one that passes through point A, with consumers assumed to face the same relative prices as producers. (There are no taxes or subsidies on the goods.) C_N and C_T are located where the budget line is tangent to an indifference curve, at point F. This is where consumers attain the highest level of welfare, given their budget constraint. In Figure 20.2, consumption of both goods exceeds output. In the case of traded goods, the difference $(C_T - X_T)$, which can be measured horizontally on the graph, is simply the trade deficit. Consumers are satisfying their excess demand for traded goods abroad. In the case of nontraded goods, the difference $(C_N - X_N)$, which can be measured vertically, is the excess demand for nontraded goods. According to the definition of nontraded, this excess demand cannot be satisfied abroad but can be thought of as being satisfied out of inventories held by firms (temporarily, until they run out).

FIGURE 20.2

Increase in Expenditure, Followed by Decrease in Relative Price of Nontraded Goods

Assume expenditure exogenously increases to A, beyond income, Y. If relative prices are unchanged, consumption is at F, implying excess demand for *NTG* and excess demand for *TG*. If the relative price of traded goods is increased, it raises output of *TG* at X and may also lower consumption of *TG* at B.

Other conditions could exist in these markets as well: a trade surplus if F occurs anywhere to the left of S, and an excess supply of nontraded goods if F occurs anywhere below S. The next thing to consider is what determines these points of consumption and output.[4]

20.2   Expenditure and the Relative Price of Nontraded Goods

This section will examine the effects of changes in the level of relative prices P_N and expenditure A. Subsequent sections will show how exogenous changes in exchange rate policy and monetary policy bring about changes in relative prices and expenditure. For the moment, take P_N and A as given.

We examine the effect in the traded goods market first. Starting from a position of zero trade balance, S in Figure 20.2, an increase in expenditure with no change in relative prices will move the country into trade deficit because a certain share of the new expenditure falls on traded goods. Remember that importable and exportable goods are aggregated together. It does not matter here whether the additional purchases are

---

[4]Figure 20.2 is known as the Salter diagram because it originated with W. E. G. Salter, "Internal Balance and External Balance: The Role of Price and Expenditure Effects," *Economic Record* (August 1959): 226–238. Salter, like a number of the other authors who developed the model that features both traded and nontraded goods, was Australian. Australia fits the model relatively well because the two categories of goods are fairly clearly drawn. (The model goes by various names: Australian, nontraded goods, dependent economy, and small open economy.)

imports or goods that would otherwise have been exported; in either case the result is a worsening of the trade balance. When the new spending comes from the private sector—for example, in response to a tax cut—the deterioration in the trade balance is the marginal propensity to spend on traded goods times the increase in expenditure. When it is government expenditure that has increased, the import content could be either higher (as it usually is in the case of military weapons, construction equipment, or other capital goods) or lower (as in education or health services). For simplicity, assume that the government's marginal propensity to spend on traded goods is generally the same as that of the private sector.

Maintaining Equilibrium in the Traded Goods Market

Let us now ask what would have to happen, after an increase in expenditure such as that illustrated in Figure 20.2, to restore trade balance, without claiming that this will in fact necessarily happen. To restore trade balance, the relative price of traded goods would have to rise to eliminate an excess demand for traded goods. This could happen if the country decides to devalue, that is, to increase the price of foreign currency. The price of traded goods will rise by the same percentage as the price of foreign currency. If the price of nontraded goods remains the same, or at least fails to rise as much as the price of traded goods, then the relative price of traded goods will have risen.[5] In other words, the relative price of nontraded goods, P_N, will have fallen.[6]

It certainly sounds plausible that an increase in the relative price of traded goods will help eliminate an excess demand for traded goods, just as an increase in the relative price of chocolate will help eliminate an excess demand for chocolate. But we have to see how this would work. In Figure 20.2 the change means that the relative price line has become steeper (line 2 instead of line 1): Each unit of traded goods is now worth more units of nontraded goods. The effect on production of traded goods will clearly be favorable. As resources shift out of nontradables into tradables, we move down along the production possibility frontier from S.

What incentive induces resources to shift from one sector to the other? Within the tradable industry, the higher price at which firms can sell their products means that at S the real wage in terms of traded goods, W/P_T, is now below the marginal product of labor. These firms thus find it profitable to hire more workers. They will continue to hire workers until they reach the point at which the marginal product of labor is down to the level of the new real wage. In a full-employment model with flexible wages, the increased demand for labor from the tradables sector will quickly bid up the nominal wage—not just in that sector, but throughout the economy, assuming that workers are

---

[5]If the price of nontraded goods is fixed in terms of domestic currency because firms supply these goods with infinite elasticity—the same assumption that we made for domestically produced goods in Chapters 16 through 18—then a devaluation is the *only* way that the country can increase the relative price of traded goods. In this case, with nominal prices fixed, we could speak interchangeably of the nominal exchange rate and the relative price of traded goods.

[6]Incidentally, the relative price of traded goods in terms of nontraded goods in small open economies (particularly in Latin America) is sometimes called the *real exchange rate*. Because others use the term "real exchange rate" to denote the price of foreign goods in terms of domestic goods, we avoid this alternative use of the term.

basically the same in both sectors. Firms in the nontraded sector now find that the real wage in terms of *their* product has *risen*. They now find it less profitable to produce on the same scale as previously, so they release labor and contract in size. Under the full-employment assumption, the workers who lose their jobs in the nontraded sector are the same ones hired in the expanded traded sector. We continue to move down the curve until we reach X, the new point of tangency with the relative price line. By reading off the horizontal axis, we can see that the quantity of tradable goods has risen.

The effect of the increase in the relative price of tradables on consumption is not quite as clear as the effect on production. There is clearly a positive substitution effect: The steeper relative price line means a move upward along any given indifference curve to lower levels of consumption of traded goods. However, there is also an income effect that may go the other way. It depends on what is assumed about the level of expenditure. The experiment we are examining is an exogenous increase in expenditure and the associated change in relative prices that would be necessary if balanced trade is to be restored. In this experiment, when the relative price of traded goods rises, the expenditure line remains tied down at its new bottom endpoint (expenditure remains fixed at the new level, A, in terms of traded goods).[7] The expenditure line swivels to its new, steeper slope, the same slope as the new price line facing producers. The new consumption point will be located at a point such as B, where the steeper expenditure line is tangent to a new indifference curve. This point could be located either to the right or left of the old point, F. Thus the consumption of traded goods could either rise or fall.

The trade balance is the difference between the production and consumption of traded goods. Thus, even if consumption fails to fall because of the income effect, the trade balance would still probably improve because of the unambiguously positive effect on production. Assume that the production effect and the substitution effect in consumption are large enough to outweigh the negative income effect in consumption; therefore, the net effect on the trade balance is positive. The new trade balance is the distance, measured horizontally, between X and B. If the increase in the relative price of traded goods is large enough, then it will eliminate completely the trade deficit that opened up when expenditure was increased. This is the case shown in Figure 20.2: B is directly over X.

Now consider, on a graph of its own, the relationship between expenditure, A, and the relative price of nontraded goods, P_N, necessary to maintain trade balance equilibrium. Figure 20.3 shows expenditure on the horizontal axis and the relative price of nontraded goods on the vertical axis. Again, S denotes the initial point of both external balance (a zero trade balance) and internal balance (no excess supply or demand for nontraded goods). Increased expenditure causes a horizontal move to the right (by precisely the same distance as the movement of the expenditure point along the horizontal axis in Figure 20.2). Point F lies in a region of trade deficit because expenditure on traded goods has increased, and a sufficiently large increase in the relative price of

---

[7]Because we are considering changes in relative prices, how we draw the graph depends in part on whether we define expenditure in terms of traded goods or in terms of nontraded goods. In other words, the precise question we are asking is slightly different, depending on whether we hold expenditure constant in terms of one type of good or the other. Naturally, then, the precise answer is slightly different.

FIGURE 20.3

Equilibrium in the Traded
Goods Market

In the aftermath of an increase in expenditure, A, if the relative price of nontraded goods, P_N, is decreased far enough, it will eliminate the excess demand for TG, which is the trade deficit. Thus equilibrium in the TG market gives the downward-sloping BB schedule.

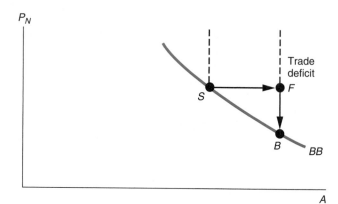

traded goods would be needed to restore balanced trade. This is the same as a sufficiently large decrease in the relative price of nontraded goods, represented by a movement vertically downward from point F to point B in Figure 20.3. For each level of A, there is a corresponding level of P_N that is necessary to maintain balanced trade. We can trace out a whole series of points representing combinations of A and P_N, which is downward sloping, as shown in the graph. We label this curve BB, for balance of trade.

Maintaining Market Equilibrium for Nontraded Goods

There is no reason why an increase in expenditure necessarily *will* be accompanied by a decrease in the relative price of nontraded goods to maintain equilibrium in the market for traded goods. This requires something like a deliberate decision by the government to devalue. Notice in Figure 20.2 that, although the excess demand for traded goods has been eliminated by the change in relative prices, there is now a large excess demand for *nontraded* goods: Point B lies far above point X. Policy makers may be just as concerned about equilibrium in the market for nontraded goods and the related problems of employment and inflation as they are about trade balance equilibrium. We now consider what would have to happen to maintain equilibrium in the market for nontraded goods instead of traded goods.

We return to the initial increase in expenditure that moves the economy to point F in Figure 20.2. Some of the increased expenditure falls on nontraded goods. Thus point F is a point of excess demand for nontraded goods. The excess demand can be measured vertically as the gap between consumption and output, in either Figure 20.2 or its equivalent Figure 20.4. In terms of Figure 20.3 or its equivalent Figure 20.5, the increase in expenditure causes the move rightward from S to F, into a region of excess demand.

Eliminating this excess demand for nontraded goods would require that the relative price of nontraded goods rise. Again there are effects on both production and consumption. The higher price of nontraded goods makes their production more profitable. Resources shift out of the other sector into nontraded goods, causing a move up along the production possibility frontier from S, as shown in Figure 20.4, until reaching a point of tangency, X, with the new, less steep relative price line. Thus X_N rises. The

FIGURE 20.4

Increase in Expenditure, Followed by Increase
in Relative Price of Nontraded Goods

Again, an exogenous increase in expenditure, A, beyond Y, moves consumption to F but leaves
output at S if relative prices are unchanged. If the relative price of traded goods is decreased,
it raises output of NTG at X and lowers consumption of NTG at G.

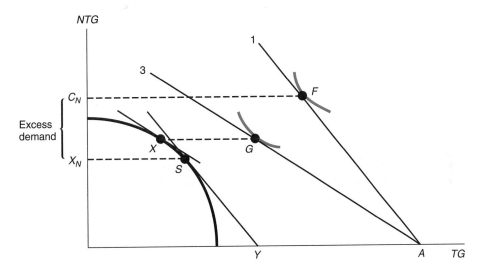

higher relative price of nontraded goods also means that consumers substitute away
from them into the cheaper traded goods. The income effect, like the substitution
effect, reduces consumption of nontraded goods, as is seen when the relative price line
is rotated downward to the new tangency (line 3 instead of line 1). The income effect is
not ambiguous, as it was when considering the demand for traded goods. C_N unambiguously falls at point G.[8]

   If the increase in the relative price of nontraded goods is sufficiently large, then the
upward movement of output and the downward movement of consumption will be sufficiently large that the point X and the point G will be at the same horizontal level: The
excess demand for nontraded goods that opened up when expenditure increased will
have been eliminated. In terms of Figure 20.5, a sufficiently large increase in the relative price of nontraded goods, P_N, returns the country to equilibrium in the domestic
market at point G. There is an entire set of combinations of A and P_N, such as S and G,
that give equilibrium in nontraded goods. These points constitute the upward-sloping
internal balance schedule, NN. To recap the reason for the NN schedule's upward

[8]If expenditure had been set in terms of nontraded goods rather than in terms of traded goods, then a change
in relative prices would have an ambiguous effect on the demand for nontraded goods and an unambiguous
effect on the demand for traded goods. This is the method used in the dependent economy model in Rudiger
Dornbusch, *Open Economy Macroeconomics*, 2nd ed. (New York: Basic Books, 1989).

FIGURE 20.5

Equilibrium in the Nontraded Goods Market

In the aftermath of the increase in expenditure, *A*, if the relative price of nontraded goods, P_N, is increased far enough, it will eliminate the excess demand for nontraded goods. Thus equilibrium in the *NTG* market gives the upward-sloping *NN* schedule.

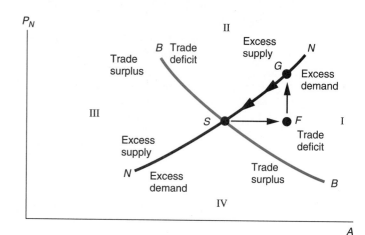

slope, an increase in expenditure *A* must be accompanied by a sufficiently large increase in P_N if the potential excess demand for nontraded goods is to be eliminated.

The external balance schedule, *BB*, and the internal balance schedule, *NN*, together divide the policy instrument space into four quadrants, or four "zones of economic unhappiness." (I) Any point such as *F* has a trade deficit and an excess demand for nontraded goods, as we have seen. Proceeding counterclockwise through the other three regions, we have (II) trade deficit with excess supply of goods, (III) trade surplus with excess supply, and (IV) trade surplus with excess demand. In general, the government would need to set both policy variables, *A* and P_N, to hit both targets. Only at point *S* are both the traded and nontraded goods markets in balance simultaneously. (The graph is conceptually the same as the Swan diagram derived in Chapter 18, although the curves are flipped vertically because that chapter showed increases in the exchange rate as movements up the vertical axis, rather than down.[9])

To take an example, many Latin American countries in the period from 1974 to 1982 were at points like *F*, as the result of high levels of government spending: They experienced excess demand for nontraded goods together with large trade deficits, which they financed by borrowing from foreign banks.[10] Many also had overvalued currencies, and thus were at points like *G*, even farther from external balance than *F*. After 1982, the typical Latin American country was obliged to cut the level of government

---

[9]More substantively, the Keynesian model focused on the price of exports in terms of imports, whereas this chapter uses the price of traded goods in terms of nontraded goods. Swan originally developed his diagram in the context of the nontraded goods model, not in the context of the Keynesian model. Trevor Swan, "Economic Control in a Dependent Economy," *Economic Record* (November 1956): 239–256.

[10]The other major source of financing for government deficits in the Latin American countries was printing money. A point like *G* in Figure 20.5 is shown to correspond to a high rate of money growth and inflation, in Rudiger Dornbusch, "Stabilization Policy in Developing Countries: What Lessons Have We Learned?", reprinted in his *Dollars, Debts and Deficits* (Cambridge, MA: MIT Press, 1986). It would follow that a prerequisite to eliminating inflation is eliminating the budget deficit (while simultaneously undergoing a real devaluation, if seeking to avoid excess supply of domestic goods in zone II, that is, seeking to move to *S*).

expenditure and devalue its currency to generate more foreign exchange earnings, thereby helping to pay the interest bill on the debts that it had incurred. It moved into region III of the diagram, with a trade surplus and an excess supply of nontraded goods. Developing countries in Latin America and some other parts of the world were obliged to increase their trade balances dramatically after 1982 in response to decreased availability of loans to finance their deficits. In the early 1990s, developing countries were able once again to finance large trade deficits. Chapter 24 discusses this phase and its subsequent reversal in the late 1990s.

20.3   The Monetary Approach with Nontraded Goods

Even if the government does not undertake any deliberate policy change in response to a trade deficit or in response to excess demand for nontraded goods at a point like F, two automatic mechanisms of adjustment may be set in motion. First, in response to the excess demand for nontraded goods, producers of these goods would be expected to raise their prices. If the market for nontraded goods operates with sufficient flexibility, the prices of nontraded goods, and therefore P_N, will rise sufficiently quickly to restore equilibrium at G.

In practice this is likely to be a more gradual process. The adjustment process can be especially slow if the country finds itself in a position of excess supply, as at point H in Figure 20.6, because then a *fall* in the price of nontraded goods is required. There may be a prolonged recessionary period, with unemployed labor if wages adjust slowly. In such circumstances, a case can be made for speeding up the process by a change in government policy. One possibility is to devalue the currency, thus accomplishing the required reduction in the relative price of nontraded goods, and immediately jumping downward in Figure 20.6 to equilibrium on the NN schedule. Another possibility is to increase expenditure, moving to the right in the same figure. Unfortunately, a policy change bringing the country closer to internal balance may move it farther from external balance.

Reserve Flows

A second possible automatic mechanism of adjustment, which operates in response to external imbalances, is the flow of international reserves we studied in Chapter 19 under the monetary approach to the balance of payments. As we saw there, the money supply is one of the policy variables that determines the level of expenditure. When the country is running a balance-of-payments deficit, at a point like F in Figure 20.5, its level of reserves is decreasing over time. If the reserve loss translates into a reduction in the total money supply, then it will exert a contractionary effect on expenditure. A declining level of expenditure means a gradual movement leftward over time and a diminishing balance-of-payments deficit. The movement stops at a point on the external balance line, BB, because the rate of change of reserves is zero when the balance of payments is zero. However, if the monetary authorities offset the effect of the reserve loss on the money supply by expanding domestic credit (i.e., sterilize), then there will

FIGURE 20.6

Adjustment with Excess Supply of Nontraded Goods

At a point to the left of *BB*, such as *H*, excess supply of nontraded goods puts downward pressure on the price of *NTG*. Even when the *NN* schedule is reached, however, there is still a trade surplus. If the reserve inflow is not sterilized, expenditure, *A*, increases over time.

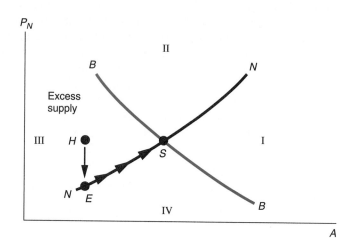

be no leftward movement. However, the country cannot continue to intervene in the foreign exchange market forever. As the central bank's level of reserves approaches zero, the government will eventually be forced to react, either by reducing expenditure or—if it is too late for that—by devaluing the currency.

This is precisely what happened in the Mexican peso crisis of 1994. Sterilization of reserve outflows kept Mexico at a point like *G* for a while. But eventually the Banco de Mexico used up its reserves, and in December 1994 it was forced to undergo a painful devaluation and contraction of the real money supply, to return to *S*.

Similarly, when the country is running a balance-of-payments surplus, at a point like *H* in Figure 20.6, its level of reserves is increasing over time. If the upward effect on the money supply is not offset, then expenditure will be increasing. There is movement rightward in the graph, with the balance-of-payments surplus gradually decreasing over time, until equilibrium is reached somewhere on the *BB* schedule. Again, the government can forestall this process by reducing domestic credit (sterilizing), which it may choose to do if it is politically or emotionally attached to its trade surplus. Indeed, unlike the situation facing a deficit country, there is nothing to force a surplus country to adjust. For example, China has run enormous surpluses and allowed its reserves to pile up to levels that surpass the largest and wealthiest countries in the world.

The Dutch Disease

Reserve inflows can create serious problems, however. One cause of potentially undesirable reserve inflows is the Dutch disease, discussed in Section 5.8: a natural resource boom, as experienced by the Netherlands in the 1960s (a producer of natural gas) and a variety of other countries in the 1970s and again after 2002 (producers of oil, coffee, and various other mineral and agricultural products).

Sometimes the commodity boom takes the form of high export earnings because of high world prices today, perhaps prices that are only temporarily above their long-run equilibrium; in that case the surplus should appear in the current account. On other occasions, the commodity boom takes the form of newly discovered deposits that will take time to develop; in that case the surplus should appear in the capital account, as the country borrows to smooth spending, and in particular to finance imports of capital goods necessary to develop the resource (e.g., equipment for drilling and pumping, in the case of oil). Either way, the commodity boom results in a surplus in the balance of payments.

Sometimes an analogy is drawn between the Dutch disease and other forms of exogenous inflows, such as unilateral transfers, or capital inflows arising from monetary stabilization or other sources. Many developing countries have experienced such inflows intermittently, particularly in three boom periods: 1975 to 1982, 1990 to 1996, and 2001 to 2006, as we shall see in Section 24.1. Whatever the cause of the reserve inflows, the difficulty arises when real appreciation of the currency causes a loss of competitiveness for exports of manufactured goods (or for any other tradable-goods industry)—excluding, of course, the industry experiencing the export boom that is the original source of the reserve inflow.

How does a reserve inflow lead to real appreciation of the currency? There are two possible mechanisms. On the one hand, if the monetary authorities keep the exchange rate fixed, then the monetary approach to the balance of payments indicates that the reserve inflow will cause the money supply to swell, which may in turn lead to increases in wages and the prices of nontraded goods. In this case the real appreciation takes the form of inflation. On the other hand, the monetary authorities may respond to the reserve inflow by allowing the currency to appreciate in *nominal* terms, bringing about the real appreciation directly. To take an example, the value of Colombia's currency tends to move with the international price of its leading export, coffee.

The real appreciation is an increase in the relative price of nontraded goods. In many countries experiencing a commodity boom, revenues accrue to the government, either because it owns the resource directly (the norm among oil exporters) or because it is paid royalties or tax proceeds by the private owners. Typically the government responds by raising spending, which is another source of increased demand and upward pressure on the prices of nontraded goods. Not only are resources pulled into the sector experiencing the commodity boom, but, less obviously, they are pulled into the production of nontraded goods such as construction. Resources are pulled out of the production of manufactures and other tradables—those that lie outside the booming commodity sector.

Even when events like the Dutch disease create difficulties for manufactured exports, this does not mean that the country as a whole is worse off. A country would be foolish to turn down a windfall gain on its commodity exports. After all, no country would welcome a *fall* in the value of an exportable resource. Examples of sudden falls in the price of a basic export commodity that lead to real depreciation and (often) sharp recession include Chile in 1974–1975 (copper), Bolivia in 1985 (tin), and Russia in 1998 (oil).

One of the main respects in which the Dutch disease can indeed be a "disease" is that the boom may turn out to be more temporary than the government had thought. When world prices go back down, the country can be left with an atrophied export sector, "white elephant" investment projects, bloated government payrolls, unwanted real estate construction, and sometimes even large international debts. The cycle of Dutch disease followed by commodity bust, which can be attributed to the combination of volatile world commodity prices and poor institutions susceptible to procyclical government spending, often impairs long-run economic performance. It is one interpretation of what is called the "natural resource curse." This is the observation that countries rich in natural resources can experience lower long-run economic growth than those without.

The Effects of an Increase in the Money Supply in the Nontraded Goods Model

We now formally examine, within the context of the nontraded goods model, the implications of the two assumptions associated with the monetary approach to the balance of payments: Goods prices are perfectly flexible, and reserve flows are not sterilized.[11] The first assumption means that the automatic mechanism of adjustment in the home (nontraded goods) market described earlier not only exists but operates instantly. Whenever the economy finds itself at a point of excess demand for nontraded goods, prices rise rapidly to clear the market, causing a jump vertically upward to the NN line. Whenever the economy finds itself at a point of excess supply of nontraded goods, prices fall rapidly to clear the market, causing a jump vertically downward to the NN line. In short, we assume that the economy is always on the NN line. The second assumption means that the other automatic mechanism of adjustment described earlier, via the balance of payments, is in effect as well. It will not operate instantly, however. As long as large-scale, rapidly responding capital flows continue to be ruled out, the rate of reserve flow is restricted to the same finite scale as the trade balance.

Consider first the effects of an increase in the money supply. Figure 20.5 showed how an increase in expenditure—whatever its causes—resulted in a move from point S to point F, featuring excess demand for nontraded goods and a trade deficit. A monetary expansion is precisely the sort of policy change that would cause such an increase in expenditure. Now that we are incorporating automatic adjustments in the market for nontraded goods, however, we recognize that point F represents an equilibrium that cannot last for long. Producers respond to the excess demand for nontraded goods by raising the nominal price. This is equivalent to raising the relative price, P_N, because the nominal price of traded goods is tied down (by the exogenous foreign currency price of traded goods and the fixed exchange rate). We move vertically upward from point F in Figure 20.5 until we reach point G on the NN line, where the excess demand has been eliminated. We assume that this adjustment takes place very rapidly, so that following the increase in the money supply, we virtually jump from point S to point G.

At point G the country is still running a trade deficit. In fact, the increase in the relative price of nontraded goods has moved the country even farther from trade balance equilibrium than it would be at point F (because the price change discourages the output of traded goods and encourages the consumption of traded goods). The balance-of-

---

[11]The model that follows was developed by Rudiger Dornbusch, "Devaluation, Money and Nontraded Goods," *American Economic Review* (December 1973): 875–880.

payments deficit means that reserves will be steadily flowing out of the country. Under the assumption that the reserve outflow is not sterilized, the money supply is declining over time. As the money supply declines, the level of expenditure, A, declines, so there is a move leftward in Figure 20.5. At the same time, however, P_N must decline, so as to eliminate any incipient excess supply of nontraded goods that would otherwise result from the declining expenditure and keep the country on the NN schedule. In other words, the movement is down and to the left, until eventually we return to balance-of-payments equilibrium at point S. Only when the rate of change of reserves, equal to the balance of payments, is zero will there be long-run equilibrium. In the long run the monetary expansion has changed absolutely nothing except the composition of the central bank's balance sheet: The original expansion in domestic credit has been offset by an equal decrease in the central bank's holdings of international reserves.

The Effects of a Devaluation

The primary motivation for introducing the monetary approach to the balance of payments in the presence of nontraded goods is to use it to study the effects of a devaluation. A devaluation should improve the balance of payments through two independent routes. First is the contractionary effect on expenditure introduced in Chapter 19 (the real balance effect). Second is the effect of the decrease in the relative price of nontraded goods, introduced in this chapter.

Consider an increase in the exchange rate. Under the assumption that the country takes the world price of traded goods as given, this causes a proportionate increase in the price of traded goods, P_t, expressed in domestic currency. The first effect of the devaluation occurs even if, for some reason, there is no change in the relative price of nontraded goods—that is, even if the prices of all goods rise by the same percentage. For example, assume that n stands for nuts instead of nontraded. What would happen if P_n, the price of nuts, along with P_t, the price of tin, rose by the same percentage as the devaluation? In Figure 20.6 this constraint would prevent any movement off a horizontal line through S. The economy moves from S to H. An increase in the price of traded goods reduces the real money supply. The reduction in real money supply (or, equivalently, the increase in nominal money demand) results in an excess demand for money. At H, households and firms cut back their spending to restore their level of real money balances.

In terms of Figure 20.1, the reduction in expenditure means that the budget line shifts inward, with an unchanged slope if relative prices remain unchanged. Thus the consumption point, the point of tangency with an indifference curve, occurs inside the production possibility frontier. Both consumption of traded goods, C_T, and consumption of nontraded goods, C_N, fall. Some of the decrease in spending takes the form of an "excess supply," or surplus, of traded goods. This is the first favorable effect of the devaluation on the trade surplus. The rest of the decrease in spending, however, takes the form of an excess supply of nontraded goods. Inventories of nuts are piling up because demand is lower than producers of nuts anticipated. Only if nuts really were a traded good, so that the excess supply could be unloaded on the world market at the going price, would the relative price of nuts and tin be unchanged (*both P_n and P_t having gone* up in proportion to the devaluation). Nuts are a nontraded good, however. To equilibrate the market for nontraded goods, their relative price, P_N, will have to fall. This means that the budget line in Figure 20.1 will become steeper.

Because we have already derived the NN schedule, it is easier to see the effects by turning back to Figure 20.6. The fall in the relative price of nontraded goods moves the economy from point H to point E on the NN schedule. That is, if nuts are nontraded, then their price does not rise by the same proportion as tin and other traded goods.[12] The decline in the relative price of nontraded goods yields the second favorable effect of a devaluation on the trade balance: As we saw earlier in the chapter, for any given level of expenditure, a lower relative price of nontraded goods means that more traded goods are produced and fewer consumed. The trade surplus is larger at point E, where both effects are operating, than at point H, where only the real balance effect was allowed to operate.[13]

The second aspect of the monetary approach now appears: the nonsterilization of reserve flows. At point E the country is running a trade surplus. If the money flowing into the country through the trade account is not offset elsewhere, then it will increase expenditure, which reduces the trade surplus. We move up steadily along the NN schedule: As expenditure rises, the price of nontraded goods must continuously rise to eliminate what would otherwise be an excess demand for nontraded goods. Money continues to flow into the country and expenditure continues to rise, until as always in the monetary approach, in the long run the country is back at S and the trade surplus has been completely eliminated.

This process illustrates some principles that recur throughout the study of devaluation. First, to have an effect on the trade balance, some variable must be "sticky" in the short run—in other words, it must be restricted from jumping discontinuously. A nominal devaluation reflected as equal increases in all nominal magnitudes would have no real effects. In Chapters 16 through 18, the sticky variable was the price of export goods; thus the devaluation changed the relative price of export and import goods. In the monetary approach to the balance of payments, the sticky variable is the stock of foreign reserves. Because the devaluation changes the real money supply, it has an effect on the trade balance in the short run, even in the absence of slow adjustment in the goods or labor markets.

Second, the sticky variable adjusts over time. When it is the stock of international reserves, it adjusts via the balance of payments. Analogously, when the sticky price variable is the price level, it adjusts via excess demand. In the long run, when all adjustments are complete, all nominal magnitudes have increased by the same percentage as the devaluation, which is to say that no real magnitudes have changed.

---

[12]The nominal price of nontraded goods, P_n, probably stays about the same in the short run, or rises a little (less than the nominal price of traded goods). It is even possible, in theory, that P_n falls. It depends on the elasticities of demand and supply of nontraded goods. All that is certain is that the *relative* price of nontraded goods, P_n/P_t, falls.

[13]To see the increase in the trade surplus graphically, think of successive waves of downward-sloping "iso-trade-surplus" lines emanating from the BB schedule in Figure 20.6, each one corresponding to a different level of the trade balance. Point E lies on an iso-trade-surplus line that is farther from BB than is H, so the trade surplus is larger as a result of the fall in P_N.

20.4   Summary

Most developing countries (and industrialized countries as well) have a substantial internal market where prices do not adjust instantly in response to a devaluation; in such countries the PPP model of Chapter 19 is not applicable. However, many such countries are too small in world markets to be able to set the price of their exports, so neither is the Keynesian model relevant. This chapter examined the effects of exchange rate and monetary policies in such small open countries with nontraded goods.

The trade balance can be thought of as the country's excess supply of internationally traded goods. We focused on two key variables: the level of expenditure and the relative price of nontraded goods (in terms of traded goods). One possibility is that these variables adjust automatically to ensure equilibrium in the two markets. Whenever there is a trade deficit, reserves flow out of the country; under the monetary approach to the balance of payments, the level of expenditure falls until trade balance equilibrium is restored. Whenever there is excess supply of nontraded goods, the price of nontraded goods falls until equilibrium in this market is restored as well.

In practice, these automatic mechanisms of adjustment are likely to work slowly at best. Thus there is an argument for the government to use its available policy tools to speed up the process. The government can adjust the level of expenditure by changing the money supply. The government can adjust the level of the relative price of nontraded goods by changing the exchange rate and thus changing the price of traded goods.

We saw that a devaluation works to improve the trade balance in a small country through two effects. In addition to the real balance effect studied in Chapter 19 (whereby the higher price level creates an excess demand for money and leads to a reduction in spending), there is a second effect. When the price of traded goods goes up in proportion to the devaluation, the relative price of nontraded goods goes down. In response, resources shift out of the production of nontraded goods into production of traded goods. Thus the trade balance improves by more than it would have if the price of nontraded goods had gone up by the same proportion as the price of traded goods. In the long run, however, all nominal magnitudes are likely to go up in proportion to the devaluation, leaving no permanent effect on the trade balance.

CHAPTER PROBLEMS

1. The country of Lampong used to import grain but now produces enough to feed itself. During the last few years imports have been essentially zero (as have exports). Does this mean that grain is a nontraded good?

2. You are the governor of the central bank in the country of Salesia, which is running a large balance-of-payments surplus as the result of recent discoveries of valuable natural resources. You are worried that the inflow of reserves through the balance-of-payments surplus is causing excessive growth in the money supply. Indeed, you have already exceeded the year's money supply target that you and the International Monetary Fund team agreed on at the time of their last visit. But you don't want to allow the currency to appreciate, causing your exporters in the manufacturing sector to lose competitiveness. What can you do?

3. You have just been called in to advise the government of Gondar. The country has been running a large trade deficit for years and is in trouble with its international creditors. Other economic statistics, however, are unreliable. More than the usual number of people seem to be wandering the capital looking for odd jobs. Also, prices for hotel rooms, pedicabs on the street, and the local delicacy in the countryside have all fallen since your last visit. In what quadrant of Figure 20.5 would you tentatively place the country's economy?

4. You are the finance minister of Khakistan. The country has started running a balance-of-payments deficit as the result of a bad harvest in the countryside, but the rest of the economy appears to be booming. Your foreign advisers suggest that you devalue your currency to eliminate the payments deficit. Do you agree with this course of action? If you are worried about inflationary pressures, how should you respond?

5. You are minister of trade in Santa Maria, which is undergoing an acute balance-of-payments crisis. In desperation you are considering cutting off imports of cotton, which is the country's main import because it is used by the large textile industry. Is this a good idea?

6. You are advising the prime minister of Phoenesia. Traded goods constitute half of workers' consumption basket. The other half consists of nontraded goods. The price of nontraded goods, P_n, is a simple proportionate markup to wages, W. Industry and the labor unions have agreed on a contract stipulating that two thirds of any increases in the CPI will be passed through to wages.

    a. For every 1 percent nominal devaluation, what is the effect on the price of nontraded goods?

    b. Assume that firms in the traded goods sector show an elasticity of supply (with respect to P_t/W) of 1.0. If the government wants to increase output of traded goods by 10 percent, how large an increase in P_t/W is required?

    c. Putting together your answers to a and b, how large must the nominal devaluation be to bring about the desired increase in output of traded goods? How large is the resulting increase in the wage, W? In the CPI?[14]

SUGGESTIONS FOR FURTHER READING

Corden, W. Max. *Economic Policy, Exchange Rates, and the International System* (Oxford, UK: Oxford University Press, 1994). Includes a verbal exposition of the dependent-economy model of the balance of payments.

Dornbusch, Rudiger. "Devaluation, Money and Non-traded Goods," *American Economic Review* (December 1973): 871–880. The classic model of the monetary approach to devaluation in small open economies. Nontraded goods are introduced in the second half of the paper.

---

[14]A simple version of the dependent-economy model along the lines of the calculations laid out in Problem 6 is sometimes known as the Scandinavian model. Nontraded goods are called the sheltered sector (sheltered from international competition), and traded goods, the exposed or competitive sector.

PART V

International Financial Markets and Their Macroeconomic Implications

Chapter 21 ▪ **The Globalization of Financial Markets**
PAGE 411

Chapter 22 ▪ **The Mundell-Fleming Model with Partial International Capital Mobility**
PAGE 445

Chapter 23 ▪ **Fiscal and Monetary Policy Under Modern Financial Market Conditions**
PAGE 467

Chapter 24 ▪ **Crises in Emerging Markets**
PAGE 489

Chapter 25 ▪ **Interdependence and Policy Coordination**
PAGE 525

Chapter 26 ▪ **Supply and Inflation**
PAGE 543

CHAPTER 21

The Globalization of Financial Markets

Part IV of this book introduced the international movement of money. It left out, however, the factor that has by now become perhaps the most important aspect of the world monetary system: the international movement of capital. In the 1950s it was possible to ignore international capital flows without seriously endangering the accuracy of the analysis. The world financial system, which had facilitated large volumes of international capital movement in the nineteenth century,[1] had become badly fragmented in the course of two world wars and the Great Depression. Even in the countries where financial markets were the most developed, such as the United States, the United Kingdom, and Switzerland, governments in the 1950s and 1960s maintained controls preventing the free international flow of capital.

Innovative bankers and others began to find ways around these controls. The Euromarkets developed outside the reach of national governments. Then, in the 1970s and 1980s, the larger countries removed their capital controls. Meanwhile, transaction costs were gradually falling because of technological progress in telecommunications and computers. The process of internationalization of financial markets continued as a result of further liberalization by governments and further innovation by the private markets. In the 1990s the scope extended increasingly to emerging markets in developing countries. Chapter 21 traces the process whereby the world's financial markets have become highly integrated over the last 30 years. Then, the primary focus in the remainder of the text is the implications of this financial integration for the operation of the world economy.

The increasing degree of international capital mobility is crucial for macroeconomics in many ways. With large volumes of short-term capital poised to shift back and forth among countries every time investors' preferences change, financial markets are volatile and the prices of stocks, bonds, and foreign exchange are highly variable. Interest rates in each country are increasingly determined by financial conditions abroad rather than by domestic policy alone. Income, employment, and inflation, in turn, are increasingly affected by economic developments abroad.

---

[1]Section 9.2 discusses portfolio capital in the nineteenth century.

The structure of the world's financial markets over the last quarter century has been profoundly affected by a number of trends. From the viewpoint of individual countries' financial markets, the trend has been *internationalization* or *globalization:* National markets are increasingly influenced by foreign investors, foreign assets, foreign financial institutions, and developments in foreign economies.

Integration—the breakdown of the barriers separating nations' financial markets—began with the development of the Euromarkets. The trend continued with *liberalization* and *deregulation* on the part of national governments through the removal of controls, regulations, and taxes, and *innovation* on the part of the private sector resulting from the development of new financial instruments and new ways of issuing and trading them. Innovation in the 1980s and 1990s includes *securitization:* Where previously a borrower would have relied on bank loans, securities such as stocks and bonds are now increasingly sold directly to investors, often without the participation of banks. We examine the Euromarkets in Section 21.1, liberalization in Section 21.3, and innovation in Section 21.4.

21.1 The Postwar Financial System (1944–1973)

After World War II, the steps taken to restore and encourage international trade in goods did not apply to international trade in financial assets. Although the Articles of Agreement of the International Monetary Fund, worked out in 1944 at Bretton Woods, New Hampshire, incorporated a presumption of the desirability of free trade, there was no analogous presumption that free capital movements were necessarily desirable. No mechanism analogous to GATT (WTO) was set up to negotiate reductions in barriers to capital movements. Most countries retained controls on such movements.

One can make a good theoretical case that the free movement of capital maximizes welfare, just as the free movement of trade in goods does. International trade in assets allows countries to reallocate consumption from high-income periods to low-income periods. It also allows the financing of investment in countries with a high rate of return to capital. (These points are developed in the appendix to this chapter.) Furthermore, international trade in assets allows countries to share risk internationally, thereby reducing the amount of risk that each must bear. Some policy makers, however, including the architects of the Bretton Woods system, have always questioned whether capital markets left to themselves would function as efficiently as the theoretical ideal.

Indeed, in the 1960s the United States adopted more stringent controls in an effort to prevent capital from flowing out of the country: U.S. policy makers were concerned that the United States would run out of international reserves, thereby jeopardizing the viability of the Bretton Woods exchange rate system. For example, there was an "interest equalization tax," designed to reduce the rate of return on foreign assets relative to domestic U.S. assets, thus making the foreign assets less attractive to investors. There was also a "voluntary" foreign credit restraint program that placed ceilings on banks' foreign lending. The controls were not entirely effective, in part because of the development of the Euromarkets.

The Euromarkets

The *Euromarkets* (not to be confused with the euro, the currency created by Europe in 1999) began in the 1960s. Deposits were denominated in U.S. dollars but placed in banks located in London and elsewhere outside the United States. The banks, many of which are European branches of major American banks, accept these deposits and use them to make short-term loans to borrowers of any nationality. This market is like any other for bank deposits and bank loans, except that the transaction is not denominated in the currency of the country where it takes place. Indeed, the fundamental purpose of this market is to sever the location of the bank from the nationality of the currency in which it deals.

In the 1960s the markets offered a way to avoid capital controls and other U.S. financial regulations. Banks are required to hold a certain ratio of reserves (that do not pay interest to the bank) against deposits in the United States, whereas there is no reserve requirement for deposits in the Euromarket. From early on, depositors in the Eurodollar markets included U.S. corporations, which earned a higher return on their liquid balances there than at home. Depositors also include many non-Americans who transact large volumes of business in dollars and so prefer to hold funds in dollars.

The Euromarkets grew rapidly after 1973. In the aftermath of the oil price increase of that year, the OPEC countries had far larger dollar earnings than they could usefully spend, and they invested these *petrodollars* in Euromarket bank deposits. The banks in turn "recycled" these dollars by lending them to developing countries and other oil-importing countries that needed to finance current-account deficits.

The Euromarkets expanded along several dimensions in addition to size. First, they began to deal not just in U.S. dollars, but in pounds, yen, marks, and all other major currencies. Second, the geographical location spread, first from London to European capitals such as Zurich, then to the Caribbean such as in the Bahamas and the Cayman Islands, and more recently to rapidly growing Asian financial centers such as Hong Kong, Singapore, and Bahrain. As a result of this geographical extension, the markets are effectively open 24 hours a day. Third, the instruments that the system uses to re-lend deposits to borrowers on a longer-term basis have evolved over time. In the 1970s the money reached developing countries and other borrowers by means of the syndicated bank loan—a large number of banks lending together under the same terms. In the latter part of the decade, innovation was evident in the shift from loans at fixed interest rates at long terms to loans indexed to short-term dollar interest rates, usually the London Interbank Offered Rate (LIBOR) or the U.S. Treasury bill rate. The goal was to protect against the risk of changes in inflation and interest rates. The process of innovation accelerated with the growth of Eurobonds and other new instruments, as we see in Section 21.4.

There has been a steady trend of reduced costs related to improved communications and transaction technology. Between 1930 and 1990, the cost of a three-minute telephone call from New York to London fell from $245 to $3. The *Economist* magazine and *Financial Times* of London are now available in the United States on the day they are published. The revolution in international finance has been pushed even further by information technology—new computer advances merged with new telecommunications technology. Financial news services like Bloomberg's and Reuters provide continuous updates on market-relevant developments. Regardless of home base, an investor can now analyze the day's developments in Washington, monitor reactions in the financial markets in Tokyo, take a position in a foreign currency in London, and make payment through a bank in New York, all with little effort and little time lag. As a result of the reduction in communications and transaction costs, together with the other processes of liberalization and innovation to be discussed in Sections 21.3 and 21.4, the boundaries between the Euromarkets and many countries' domestic financial markets have broken down.

21.2   The Foreign Exchange Market

The foreign exchange market is really a loose network of banks and other financial institutions, linked by telephone and computer, that buy and sell currencies. Because there are so many participants, and the products being traded are so homogeneous (i.e., a yen deposit is the same wherever you buy it), this market fits the classical economists' model of perfect competition.

The daily flow through the world's foreign exchange markets is very large. In April 2004, the world's major central banks surveyed the markets. When the results were compiled by the Bank for International Settlements, they showed that global foreign exchange trading had continued to grow, a 36 percent increase over a similar survey three years earlier. The volume had reached a remarkable $1.9 trillion per day. This figure includes, along with regular spot transactions (35 percent), trading in forward contracts and some other derivative contracts. (The figure does not include the "over the counter" market in derivatives, which is of roughly similar size.) A "spot" purchase of foreign exchange is the purchase of a contract for immediate delivery of the currency (actually within two business days). The other contracts are explained in Section 21.4. They are ways to manage risk.

Trading tends to be focused in major centers. Arguably, there is a natural equilibrium consisting of one major center in each of three 8-hour time zones. London continues to handle the greatest volume of foreign exchange transactions, with the U.K. share of world turnover equal to 31 percent. (Frankfurt, Paris, and Zurich are competitors in the European time zone.) New York is the main center in the Western Hemisphere, with U.S. volume accounting for 19 percent of world turnover. Tokyo has long dominated the Asian time zone, but Singapore and Hong Kong are competitors.

These numbers do not include the many small countries where there is no large organized private foreign market, often because the government owns the banking system and prohibits private trading. In these countries, the government buys and sells foreign exchange. Informal trading may also go on in an illegal black market or an officially tolerated "parallel market," at an exchange rate usually very different from the official rate.

Bid-Ask Spreads and Arbitrage in the Spot Market

One reason for the large volume of foreign exchange transactions is their low cost. The cost of the transaction usually appears in the form of a "spread between the bid and ask," that is, a gap between the price at which the bank is willing to buy a given currency and the price at which it is willing to sell it. The size of the spread is determined by the type of customer. A tourist who buys foreign exchange at a bank will typically pay a large cost, perhaps 1 percent. A firm that conducts a great deal of international business will receive a much better rate from its bank. When banks or brokers deal with each other, the spread is yet another order of magnitude smaller. The quoted spread on the Reuters screen averages around .05 percent; in practice banks and brokers deal with still smaller margins.

These transaction costs are lower than those in the past. Reasons include the technological factors mentioned previously and the economies of scale involved in large transactions and "thick," or highly liquid, markets.[2] However, the bid-ask spread still widens at times, especially for less important currencies that are thinly traded. A major determinant of the bid-ask spread is the volatility of the spot rate itself. Every time a bank buys foreign currency from a customer, it runs the risk that before it can resell the currency, there will be a large movement in the exchange rate and the currency will lose value. Clearly, this risk is higher when exchange rate volatility is higher—one reason why the bid-ask spread is larger at some times than at others.

Exchange rates in different financial centers are kept nearly identical by foreign exchange arbitrage. As we saw in Chapter 19, *arbitrage* is a general term that means buying something where it is cheap and selling it where it is expensive, thus working to reduce the differential by driving the first price up, the second price down, or both, to an equilibrium. In this case, the commodity being bought and sold is currency. If the dollar price of Swiss francs in New York falls below the dollar price of Swiss francs in London by more than the small transaction cost, it pays to buy in New York and sell in London. The arbitrage will bid up the price of Swiss francs in New York and bid down the price in London, until the difference disappears.

Arbitrage also keeps exchange rates among three or more currencies consistent with each other. Suppose you buy $1000 worth of sterling in New York, sell it in London for euros, then sell the euros for dollars in Frankfurt. If you wind up with either more or less than $1000, the exchange rates were not consistent. If you made a profit, you (and other arbitragers) will repeat the transaction until the market rates are forced to be consistent. If you lost in the transaction, you went around the circuit the wrong way; the opposite series of purchases and sales would have yielded an arbitrage profit. This process is called *triangular arbitrage*. Subject to the limits of transaction costs, it maintains consistency among the bilateral "cross rates," connecting all the world's internationally traded currencies. In other words, the $/£ exchange rate times

---

[2]Notice the multiple directions of causality. Higher transaction volume is partly a result of low bid-ask spreads, and low bid-ask spreads are partly a function of high transaction volume (the economies of scale).

the euro/$ rate equals the euro/£ rate (as you can tell by crossing out currencies in the numerators and denominators).

Interbank Trading of Foreign Exchange

The large volume of foreign exchange transactions seems puzzling. The 2004 survey showed that the amount of foreign exchange traded in the major markets was in the area of $2 trillion per day. Of this, most consisted of trading the U.S. dollar for another currency. Cross-currency transactions, foreign exchange transactions not involving the dollar, were only 11 percent of the total.

By contrast, U.S. merchandise imports plus exports totaled roughly $2 trillion for the entire *year*. The volume of foreign exchange trading is roughly 100 times greater than the daily volume of global merchandise trade. Why is this?

Briefly, the answer is that most of the foreign exchange transactions involve trading among banks, rather than providing services for importers, exporters, and other customers: Only 14 percent of the foreign exchange trading reported by dealers was with nonfinancial customers.

Consider a bank that buys Swiss francs from a customer who has just earned them from exporting to Switzerland. The bank will not choose to hold the Swiss francs unless (1) it has good reason to expect that another customer will want to buy them before long, or (2) it expects that the foreign exchange value of the francs is about to go up. Otherwise, it will quickly try to unload the Swiss francs to some other bank. That bank may itself try to unload them on another bank, and so on, until the francs find someone who wants them, either to spend on imports from Switzerland or to hold as an investment.[3]

Vehicle Currencies

In any center of foreign exchange trading, most business is carried on in only a few foreign currencies. This does not necessarily imply that the market discriminates against the smaller trading countries. Rather, it demonstrates the convenience to all parties of picking one or two leading currencies—known as *vehicle currencies*—and using them as focal points for trading. For that reason, a high proportion of transactions in the foreign exchange market is explained by exchanges of U.S. dollars for another currency. In an overseas financial center such as Singapore, foreign exchange transactions in U.S. dollars are much more prominent than Singapore's commercial transactions with the United States would suggest.

To see why there are vehicle currencies, recall why there exists any sort of money at all. In theory, we could go through life without money, bartering our goods and services instead. But this would be awkward; we could not sell a good or service until we

---

[3]Under the existing multiple dealer system, banks must provide quotes on both sides of the markets, both bid and ask, and then must accept a trade offered at the quoted price. An exciting new approach to the foreign exchange market shows how currency is repeatedly passed from one trader to another like a hot potato: Richard Lyons, *The Microstructure Approach to Exchange Rates* (Cambridge, MA: MIT Press, 2001).

found someone who wanted to buy that particular service *and* who happened to have something to sell that we wanted. This is called a "double coincidence of wants." It is much easier to sell our services for money and then use the money to buy what we want from someone else. The same is true about currencies at the international level. Those wanting to exchange South African rand for Malaysian ringgit are too small a group to support an active cross-currency market. Instead, it is more efficient to trade rand for dollars and then dollars for ringgit.

Vehicle currencies are used not only to facilitate foreign exchange transactions but also, to some degree, for invoicing trade in goods and services. This is especially true for homogeneous goods and materials (particularly agricultural and mineral commodities), which are sold on competitive world markets, as opposed to the differentiated finished goods, whose manufacturers control their own prices even if they face substantial competition. This is essentially the same distinction made earlier between auction goods and customer goods.

The widespread use of a currency in one activity will contribute to its widespread adoption in another activity. For example, if all foreign exchange transactions must pass through dollars, then the convenience of settling transactions is an extra incentive to use the dollar for invoicing trade as well. Arguments similar to those made regarding the currency choice for invoicing trade can also be made regarding the choice of vehicle currencies to denominate assets. Another area in which international use of currencies is in evidence, in addition to foreign currency trading, invoicing of merchandise trade, and denomination of assets, is the form in which central banks choose to hold their foreign exchange reserves.

The Dollar and Its Rivals for International Currency Status

Before World War I, the pound sterling was the leading currency in international use. Subsequently, the dollar came to be used more widely, as the United States gained economic power and political prestige relative to Great Britain. Since World War II, the dollar has been the clear choice as the leading international currency. Some observers believe that the dollar might in turn eventually be supplanted in international use by another currency. The mark and yen both gradually rose in prominence in the 1970s and 1980s, at the dollar's expense. This trend leveled off in the 1990s.

Measures of international use of major currencies include both official use (by central banks in other countries, as a currency to peg to or to hold reserves in) and private use (e.g., vehicle currency). The dollar's share remains much greater than the U.S. share in world output or trade.

The world monetary system also features a composite currency—the SDR (Special Drawing Right), created by the IMF. The value of the SDR is determined as a weighted basket of major currencies. However, it has not caught on widely.

A new challenger was created on the first day of 1999: the euro, the currency of the European Economic and Monetary Union (EMU). The euro has now replaced fully the mark, French franc, and ten other European currencies as well. Countries hold reserves in euros and issue debt denominated in it. Because the euro has become the home currency among a set of countries that are collectively almost as large as the

United States, it could aspire eventually to rival the dollar as an international currency. The dollar is still a long way from giving up the number-one position, however. Everyone—banks, importers, exporters, borrowers, lenders, and central banks—tends to use the currencies that other market participants are using. The choice of currency is based not only on the current relative importance of the respective countries in the world economy, but also on the relative use of the various currencies in the recent past. Like the English language, people will continue to use the dollar internationally because everyone else is using it.[4]

What are the pros and cons of being an international currency? The major disadvantage to a country having its currency used as an international currency is that the demand for money may be subject to larger fluctuations than before. The major advantage is that the country earns *seignorage* on the other countries' holdings of its currency: The other countries have to give up real goods and services to add to their currency balances. It has been estimated that roughly 60 percent of U.S. currency, for example, is held abroad. Just as American Express profits whenever people hold its traveler's checks, which they are willing to do without receiving interest, so the United States currently profits whenever people in Argentina or Russia hold dollars that do not pay interest. In the 1960s, the French would complain about America's "exorbitant privilege." Europe would give up goods and factories in exchange for mere pieces of paper (dollar). Today Asia plays the role of dollar accumulator.

Is Most Foreign Exchange Trading "Speculation"?

The dollar's status as a vehicle currency explains why dollar foreign exchange trading is such a high proportion of the total. However, it does not explain why total foreign exchange trading among banks is so large, relative to the foreign exchange sales and purchases required by customers for exports, imports, borrowing, and lending.

A major economic activity for banks is trading with other banks. Many banks and other financial institutions report profits from their foreign exchange business each year. This trading is extremely short term: Most traders are under instructions to close out their open positions—that is, to unwind any sales or purchases of foreign currency—by the end of the day. Longer-term positions are apparently considered too risky by banks.

Most purchases and sales of foreign exchange by traders, those trades not accounted for by the needs of customers, are made in effect as a gamble that the exchange rate will change in the trader's favor by the end of the day. Thus these transactions meet the definition of short-term speculation. (Chapters 27 and 28 will analyze speculation—the holding of assets in expectation of increases in their value.) What is not clear is whether the spot traders in the banks are able to outguess the general public, as many of them claim they can, so that their total profits exceed the transaction costs they charge their customers. The alternative possibility is that, although on any given transaction somebody must gain and somebody lose, the aggregate profits banks

---

[4]Paul Krugman, "The International Role of the Dollar: Theory and Prospect," in J. Bilson and R. Marston, eds., *Exchange Rate Theory and Practice* (Chicago: University of Chicago Press, 1984).

report from foreign exchange trading are nothing more than the normal payment they earn in return for providing foreign exchange services for customers.[5]

The remainder of this chapter discusses the successive waves of liberalization and innovation that over the last 30 years have increasingly broken down the barriers between the various financial markets around the world—not only the markets for money, but also the markets for stocks, bonds, and loans.

21.3 Liberalization

After the system of fixed exchange rates was abandoned in March 1973, the United States and several other major countries no longer needed the capital controls that had been put in place in the 1960s and the early 1970s, and so they removed them.

Liberalization by Countries Controlling Inflows

In Germany and some of its neighbors, the controls in place in the early 1970s were primarily designed to discourage the acquisition of assets in these countries by foreign residents—to discourage the inflow of capital rather than the outflow. The German government essentially prohibited the payment of interest to nonresidents on large bank deposits, taxed any new credits by nonresidents to German banks, and prohibited nonresidents from buying German bonds. A primary motive behind such controls was to limit the flow of capital from the United States to Germany, which was putting unwanted upward pressure on the mark at the same time as it put downward pressure on the dollar. Another, related, motive behind the barriers to capital inflow was concern over possible loss of control over the money supply: If a large volume of reserves flowed in through the balance of payments, the countries' central banks might not be able to sterilize the effects on the money supply, and inflation might result. Both motives were more or less eliminated after 1973, insofar as countries were no longer supposed to be concerned about preventing their exchange rates from fluctuating. Most of these controls were removed in 1974.

One way to determine the extent to which a country's capital controls are effective is to look at the differential between the domestic interest rate and interest rates outside the country. If a higher rate of return is being paid on assets inside the country than outside, this is a good indication that controls are preventing foreign residents from bringing in their capital; otherwise it would be difficult to explain why foreign residents would settle for a lower rate of return in their own countries.[6] Conversely, if the domestic rate of return always moves closely with foreign rates of return, this indicates that financial

---

[5]The view among banks that their spot trading operations make profits *above and beyond* the bid-ask spread is reported by Charles Goodhart, "The Foreign Exchange Market: A Random Walk with a Dragging Anchor," *Economica,* 55 (November 1988): 437–460.

[6]An exception to this rule of thumb, particularly relevant for long-term interest rates, arises if the country has a history of political instability, large budget and international deficits, or defaults on debt. In such cases, a higher rate of return on domestic assets than on foreign assets is probably a premium to compensate investors for risk.

markets are open and that arbitrage is keeping the rates in line with each other—by means of borrowing where interest rates are low and lending where they are high.

For such a test it is important that the two interest rates be expressed in terms of the same currency. The dollar interest rate in the United States is not directly comparable with the mark interest rate in Germany, for example. A differential that appeared in such interest rates would not truly be a difference in expected returns if it simply compensated investors for the likelihood that the dollar would depreciate against the mark during the period in question. Fortunately, the Euromarket allows observations of interest rates on currencies outside the home country.

During the period 1970 to 1974, the mark interest rate in Frankfurt exceeded the Euromark interest rate. In early 1973 the interest differential was as high as 10 percent per annum. We can view this differential as a measure of the magnitude of the barrier discouraging capital from flowing into Germany. The differential fell sharply thereafter, tangible evidence of the government's liberalization.

One country that maintained stringent controls on capital inflows in the period 1975 to 1979 was Japan. Foreign residents were prohibited from holding assets in Japan. The motive, again, was concern over monetary independence. Japan, like Germany and Switzerland, had a reputation for maintaining a strong currency, and potential demand for yen assets by international investors was growing. Sudden, large capital inflows would give the Bank of Japan an unpleasant choice. It could respond by allowing the yen to appreciate, or it could buy up the surplus dollars—in which case the increase in its reserve holdings would, it was feared, have inflationary implications for the money supply. During this period the Japanese were particularly worried that either a nominal appreciation of the yen or an increase in prices would erode their competitive price position on international export markets.

By 1979 the Japanese were more confident of their exporters' ability to compete on world markets, and the government did not consider a depreciation of the yen desirable. There was also political pressure from foreigners seeking to buy Japanese assets. For such reasons, the Ministry of Finance removed the prohibition against foreign investment.

The effect of the liberalization is visible in the differential between yen interest rates in Tokyo and overseas, shown in Figure 21.1. From January 1975 to April 1979, the differential between the three-month interest rate in Tokyo and the Euroyen interest rate in London averaged 2 percent, showing the efficacy of the controls on capital inflow. After 1979, the differential fell sharply. Since a 1984 agreement between the U.S. Treasury and the Japanese Ministry of Finance, the differential has been essentially zero, showing evidence of continued liberalization.[7]

Liberalization by Countries Controlling Outflows

Countries often use capital controls to discourage outflows rather than to discourage inflows. These are usually countries that are concerned about a balance-of-payments deficit or a depreciating currency.

---

[7]Jeffrey Frankel, *The Yen/Dollar Agreement: Liberalizing Japanese Capital Markets* (Washington, DC: Institute for International Economics, 1984).

FIGURE 21.1

Financial Liberalization in Japan

In the 1970s capital controls in Japan prevented foreign residents from acquiring assets that were then paying a higher return than equivalent yen assets offshore. In 1979 these controls were removed, and arbitrage caused the interest differential to diminish.

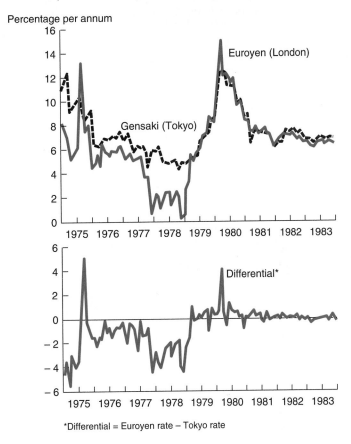

Japanese and Euroyen Interest Rates (3 month)

*Differential = Euroyen rate − Tokyo rate

The United Kingdom maintained controls on capital outflows until 1979. Even though the largest Euromarket was physically located in London (in the old financial district known as "the City"), effective legal restrictions required that British banks keep their offshore accounts separate from their domestic accounts. Again, the effectiveness of these restrictions is shown by the interest differential. In 1978 the three-month Europound interest rate averaged 1.4 percent per annum higher than the U.K. Interbank interest rate. The controls were preventing British residents from getting at the higher-paying assets that were so close at hand. However, as is illustrated in Figure 21.2, the differential fell sharply in 1979 when Margaret Thatcher became prime minister and removed the controls.[8]

The two largest Western countries maintaining effective capital controls into the 1980s were France and Italy. Both France and Italy were members of the European

---

[8]Michael Artis and Mark Taylor, "Abolishing Exchange Control: The UK Experience," in A. Courakis and M. Taylor, eds., *Policy Issues for Interdependent Economies* (London: Macmillan, 1990).

FIGURE 21.2

Financial Liberalization in the United Kingdom

In the 1970s capital controls prevented British residents from acquiring offshore assets, which paid a higher return than equivalent assets in London. In 1979 these controls were removed, and arbitrage caused the interest differential to fall.

U.K. and Eurodollar Interest Rates (3 month)

*Differential = Offshore Eurodollar rate − onshore London rate

Monetary System (EMS) and were periodically threatened with capital outflows. Consequently, they had difficulty keeping their commitments to maintain their exchange rates within the bands of plus or minus 2.25 percent (6 percent in the case of Italy) against stronger member currencies such as the German mark. At such times, France and Italy had the option of raising domestic interest rates to keep capital inside the country. However, they too wanted to maintain some measure of independence in their monetary policies, which would not be possible if their interest rates were completely tied to foreign interest rates. This was their motive for maintaining controls on capital outflow. Indeed, France had to tighten its controls when socialist François Mitterrand was elected president in 1981 and many residents rushed to get their money out of the country.

The differential between the three-month Eurofranc interest rate in London and the most comparable domestic interest rate in Paris was highly variable. Most of the time it was only 1 to 2 percent per annum. Evidently, all along outflows in moderate quantity were possible. For example, there is the technique applicable in many countries with capital controls, of *leads and lags* in trade credit. Exporters request early payment from their foreign customers in foreign exchange, and importers try to delay payment of foreign exchange to their foreign suppliers. If an importer or exporter succeeds in shifting the timing of the payment from what it would normally be by, for example, six months, this is equivalent to a six-month capital outflow.

At times, however, the interest differential on Eurofrancs would shoot up sharply. These episodes occurred when investors suspected that the franc was about to be devalued within the Exchange Rate Mechanism of the EMS. If the capital markets had been free, then franc interest rates would have risen in Paris and London equally, to compensate holders of franc assets for the anticipated loss in value. Instead, a shortage of investors willing to hold Eurofrancs caused the interest rate to be bid up offshore, and most French citizens—because they could not get their money out of the country fast enough—were stuck with the lower domestic rate. These episodes ended as soon as the question of devaluation was resolved, usually when the suspected EMS realignment actually took place and investors decided it was safe to hold French assets again for another year. This same pattern was evident in Italy.

Subsequently, liberalization became more popular. After 1986 France and Italy dismantled their capital controls. By 1990 virtually all industrialized countries had opened their financial markets.

Many other countries still retained serious barriers to international capital movements. Nevertheless, financial liberalization around the world is the continuing trend. Many "emerging market" countries opened up their capital markets in the 1990s. Chapter 24 considers them at greater length.

Changes in Tax Laws

Tax reform can have important effects on international capital flows. Countries' income tax rates may have less of an effect on international investors' decisions concerning where to put their money than one would think, however. The mere fact that the citizens of one country are taxed at a higher rate than those of another does not necessarily create an incentive for portfolio capital flows, assuming that either group of citizens is taxed at the same rate on its foreign interest earnings as on its domestic earnings. Investors sometimes evade taxes by keeping their money in tax havens, however, in the Caribbean or elsewhere. Thus the existence of taxes does give rise to capital flows.

The United States, at times, serves as something of a haven for investors seeking to avoid taxation or the possibility of future controls, or even confiscation in their own countries. Comparisons of the current-account deficits of countries in Latin America and elsewhere with the debt incurred by those countries to foreign creditors suggests there have been at times large increases in unrecorded overseas claims by citizens of those countries, the well-known problem of *capital flight*. Many Latin Americans with wealth seek to hide it in Miami real estate. High corporate taxes, as opposed to personal income taxes, can induce capital outflows. This encourages countries to harmonize corporate tax rates.

Turnover taxes are an altogether different tax, one that affects the amount and location of trading in financial assets rather than the international flow of capital. Stock market participants in Germany, Switzerland, and Japan have to pay a tax on every transaction. Authorities in these countries are under some pressure to remove these turnover taxes, so that Frankfurt, Zurich, and Tokyo do not lose business to other financial centers.

With respect to taxes, the apparent trend is again toward increased international capital mobility.

Liberalization of Domestic Financial Markets

When governments consider liberalizing controls on international capital movements, they often simultaneously consider other types of economic liberalization: those related to domestic capital markets and, perhaps, those related to distortions affecting trade in goods and services.

Domestic financial market liberalization involves the removal of ceilings on interest rates. Regulation Q in the United States, for example, was phased out long ago. The Japanese have also been phasing out their interest rate ceilings. Historically, the interest rates paid to small savers in Japan—through the enormous Postal Savings System, for example—were artificially kept quite low.

Domestic financial liberalization also involves the removal of other restrictions on the permissible activities of banks. Examples of restrictions in the United States are the prohibition against interstate banking, which ended in 1994, and the Glass-Steagall Act, which used to prohibit commercial banks from dealing in securities, as do investment banks.

In countries at an earlier stage of financial development, there may be little resembling a private banking system to deregulate. The government may have to begin by selling off banks it had previously owned (this process is known as privatization) and by abolishing existing prohibitions on private banking. One school of thought states that "repression" of the financial sector in many developing countries retards economic development by keeping the real rate of return low, thus discouraging people from saving, and by interfering with the efficient allocation of available saving among possible uses.[9]

Liberalization of Trade in Financial Services and Direct Investment

Trade liberalization is the removal of tariffs, subsidies, quotas, and other barriers to trade in goods. Its theoretical motivation stems from the argument in the first half of the text regarding the welfare gains from free trade. Firms' losses related to competition with imports are generally outweighed by the gains on the part of consumers, firms that export, and firms that use imported inputs. Nevertheless, for the liberalization arguments to succeed politically usually requires the promise of reciprocal reductions in import barriers by trading partners, as in successive rounds of multilateral negotiations.

---

[9]Ronald McKinnon, *Money and Capital in Economic Development* (Washington, DC: The Brookings Institution, 1973); and Edward S. Shaw, *Financial Deepening in Economic Development* (New York: Oxford University Press, 1973).

The United States formally proposed that trade in services, along with trade in goods, be included in trade liberalization in 1986 (at the meetings held in Uruguay, setting off a seven-year round of multilateral negotiations). The United States was primarily concerned with insurance, banking, and other financial and information services. Not until 1997, however, was a multilateral agreement to open markets to trade in financial services successfully negotiated under the World Trade Organization, which by then had succeeded the GATT. If, like the liberalization of capital controls, this trend becomes more widespread, it will further facilitate borrowing and lending between countries. This is still a U.S. priority area in negotiations such as the Doha Round.

Barriers to foreign direct investment in plant and equipment are common.[10] Some countries place performance requirements on any foreign direct investment (FDI), such as domestic-content legislation that prohibits such plants from importing a high proportion of the final product's value-added—for example, in the form of auto parts that are merely assembled in the host country. Such issues have also sometimes been important in the United States. Americans have begun to show the political sensitivity to inward foreign direct investment that had in the past been more common in other countries. A provision in the 1988 Omnibus Trade Bill empowered the president to investigate and block foreign investment for reasons of national security. U.S. politicians blocked attempts by a Chinese oil company to buy an American oil company in 2005, and by a Dubai company to buy U.S. port facilities in 2006. In truth, direct investment is less likely to be destabilizing than is portfolio investment, which can be cut off at any time. At the same time, Americans have begun to fear outward FDI as well. The concern, for example, in the debates over NAFTA or outsourcing to India, is that jobs are relocating to low-wage countries. In truth, more U.S. FDI goes to high-wage countries than low-wage countries. But multilateral attempts to negotiate reductions in international barriers to FDI have so far made little progress.[11]

The Optimal Order of Liberalization

An important practical question that arises for policy makers undertaking a program of liberalization along multiple fronts is the optimal order of liberalization. Should international capital liberalization proceed more rapidly or more slowly than domestic financial market liberalization? Than trade liberalization? In theory, the optimum (first best) is to remove all distortions immediately, but this strategy is seldom practical. The wrong order of liberalization can misallocate resources and give an unsatisfactory third-best outcome. What order is "second best"?

These questions were considered in the late 1970s when several countries in the southern cone of Latin America embarked on general liberalization plans. Subsequently, the optimal order of liberalization again became an urgent question in the context of plans for economic reform in Eastern Europe in the 1990s.[12] The consensus

---

[10]Refer back to Section 9.3 for a more complete discussion of foreign direct investment.
[11]All these restrictions are examples of so-called TRIMs (trade-related investment measures). The Uruguay Round included efforts to reduce TRIMs, for the first time in GATT negotiations.
[12]Ronald McKinnon, *The Order of Economic Liberalization: Financial Control in the Transition to a Market Economy* (Baltimore: Johns Hopkins University Press, 1991).

seems to be that international capital liberalization should come last. The argument is that if international controls are removed prematurely, massive capital flows might occur in response to distorted incentives. For example, liberalization in Chile resulted in a large trade deficit financed by a large increase in borrowing, leaving the country with a clearly excessive debt in the 1980s.[13] There is also an argument that the removal of capital controls should be postponed until after the reduction of a large existing government budget deficit, to prevent overborrowing while the government deficit is still stimulating demand, and until after the completion of any planned monetary stabilization program, again to prevent foreigners from rushing to buy domestic assets.

Indonesia is an example of a country that reversed the conventional wisdom, pursuing international financial liberalization more rapidly than domestic financial liberalization. One can imagine a possible justification for this reverse sequencing. In an environment where banks, brokers, and the rest of the financial sector are highly protected, regulated, and dependent on long-standing customer relationships, they may lack experience at competing in terms of the fees they charge for their services or at adapting to new ways of doing business. Like any vested interest group, they may be able to oppose liberalization politically. In such an environment, if international liberalization comes first, the "demonstration effect" of seeing foreign financial companies operating in their markets may teach them new ways of doing business. In any case, the argument goes, the political opposition will soon become irrelevant as banks are forced to offer competitively high interest rates to their depositors, and brokers are forced to charge competitively low fees to their clients, to avoid losing business to the foreign newcomers. The severe financial crisis experienced by Indonesia in 1997–1998, however, would seem to support the conventional wisdom of pursuing domestic financial liberalization, along with appropriate prudential banking regulation, *before* international liberalization.

The subject of increasingly competitive financial services markets leads to the next topic: innovation by the private financial sector.

21.4   Innovation

Innovation in domestic financial markets reduces the cost differential between the rate of return paid to the investor and the cost of capital paid by the ultimate borrower. Innovation in international financial markets works similarly and therefore, like liberalization, increases the degree of capital mobility across national borders. The original key innovation was the development of the Euromarkets, out of reach of regulation by national authorities. However, the innovation process accelerated in the 1980s and

---

[13]To be fair, the Chileans did in fact seek to keep liberalization of the international capital barriers for last. Other factors, such as the plummeting of the world price of a key export, copper, and the increase in world interest rates, were the proximate causes in the 1980s of the debt crises in Chile, as in other countries that had borrowed too heavily in the 1970s. See Sebastian Edwards, "Stabilization with Liberalization: An Evaluation of Ten Years of Chile's Experience with Free-Market Policies, 1973–1983," *Economic Development and Cultural Change* (December 1985): 223–254.

1990s. Financial centers in London, New York, Chicago, Tokyo, Singapore, and elsewhere are awhirl with new products and new ways of buying and selling them.

Innovation can be driven by exogenous technological developments, such as those in telecommunications and computers already mentioned. Often, however, innovation is an endogenous response to some new problem in the financial environment, such as uncertainty. Exchange rate variability and interest rate variability have been higher in the decades since 1973. Uncertainty in exchange rates and interest rates creates risk for international investors. In response, a variety of new ways to protect against risk in exchange rates and interest rates were developed.

The Forward Exchange Market

The most standard technique for dealing with exchange rate risk is by means of the *forward exchange market*. This market enables transactors, after they commit themselves to a transaction but before payment is made, to protect themselves against a change in the exchange rate. Saudi Arabian exporters invoicing exports to the United States in dollars run the risk that the value of the dollar in terms of the Saudi riyal will fall before the date comes when they are paid and can convert the dollars into their own currency, which may be three months later. The Swedish portfolio manager who acquires a sterling treasury bill in the United Kingdom runs the risk that the value of the pound in terms of the Swedish krona will fall by the time the treasury bill matures in three months. In each case, if the prospective recipients (Saudi and Swedish) of the foreign currency do not wish to bear this risk, they can protect themselves against it by *hedging,* or "selling the currency forward." This involves entering into a contract with a bank, under which they agree to sell the foreign currency for their own currency, with the exchange to take place in 90 days but with the price set at the time the contract is agreed on. The price received is the current stated forward exchange rate, as opposed to the uncertain spot exchange rate that will prevail in 90 days.

There are other market participants in addition to exporters and investors for whom hedging on the forward exchange market is often beneficial. The Argentine importing a German product invoiced in euros runs the risk that the peso price of the euro will go up by the time payment is required. Similarly, the Australian borrowing in U.S. dollars runs the risk that by the time the debt needs to be repaid, the cost of doing so in Australian currency will have gone up. In each case, the party obliged to pay foreign currency in the future (the Argentine or Australian) can avoid the risk of changes in the exchange rate by hedging, which in this case means *buying* the currency forward. In this way, the future cost of the obligations in terms of domestic currency is locked in today. The ability to hedge risk on the forward exchange market has meant that the high degree of volatility exhibited by exchange rates has not been as costly as it otherwise would have been to firms engaged in international business. Once hedged, they are immune.

The forward exchange market has developed since the advent of floating exchange rates in 1973, as Milton Friedman predicted it would,[14] in that more currencies are

---

[14]Milton Friedman, "The Case for Flexible Exchange Rates," in *Essays in Positive Economics* (Chicago: University of Chicago Press, 1953).

traded more widely around the world. Banks report that as of 2004, about 65 percent of their foreign exchange business consisted of forward transactions.[15] Although most trading is in the pound, euro, yen, and Swiss franc (all against the dollar), many other currencies are traded as well. In addition to the popular 90-day maturity, contracts are also traded at 30 days, 60 days, and one year.

Others participate in the forward exchange market in addition to those importers, exporters, investors, and borrowers seeking to hedge against currency risk. A second group is made up of "speculators," that is, anyone who takes an "exposed" (open or risky) position in the foreign exchange market in hope of gains when the exchange rate changes. Speculators expecting the currency in question to appreciate to a value higher than the going forward rate will buy a forward contract in that currency. A profit will result if the currency does appreciate as expected, but a loss will result if it does not. If the speculator expects the currency to depreciate to a value lower than the going forward rate, then he or she sells a forward contract in that currency. Now profits result only if the currency depreciates in the expected way. Speculators are thus the ones who accept the risk that the hedgers shun.[16]

Covered Interest Arbitrage

The third set of participants in the forward exchange market, after hedgers and speculators, are called *covered interest arbitragers.* Covered interest arbitrage is a powerful force in forward exchange market equilibrium under modern conditions, that is, in well-developed financial markets without barriers to international transactions. Indeed, covered interest arbitrage is sufficiently powerful that it can be considered the sole determinant of the forward exchange rate, provided the spot rate and the interest rate are taken as given.[17] We will now see how it works.

Consider an asset holder facing the choice between putting money into a one-year certificate of deposit (CD) denominated in dollars at a U.S. bank or a one-year CD denominated in pounds at a U.K. bank. If there is a difference between the interest rates on the two assets of 1 percent per annum in favor of the U.K. asset, it might appear that the U.K. asset is the better investment. However, there is the risk that the pound/dollar exchange rate will change during the course of the year. To eliminate this risk, the investor must use the forward exchange market.

Assume that the investor has $1 million to invest. By putting it into the U.S. CD, at the end of the year the investor will get back $(1 + i_{US})$ million, where i_{US} is the U.S. interest rate. Here is the alternative:

---

[15]Counting not only forward transactions but also foreign exchange swap contracts, which constitute the simultaneous execution of a spot and forward transaction (in opposite directions).

[16]The minimum contracts in the forward market are too large for individuals. If you feel the urge to speculate, you should—after considering the large risks involved!—investigate the closely related futures market or the options market, both of which are discussed later in this chapter.

[17]For a country that still has some barriers to international capital movements, it takes all three groups—hedgers, speculators, and covered interest arbitragers—to determine together the equilibrium value for the forward exchange rate (again taking the spot rate and interest rates as given).

1. Take the $1 million and buy pounds on the spot exchange market, getting £$(1/S)$ million, where S is the spot exchange rate in dollars per pound;[18]

2. Then take the £$(1/S)$ million and put it into a British CD, which in one year's time will pay off £$(1/S)(1 + i_{UK})$ million, where i_{UK} is the U.K. interest rate; and finally

3. Sell the £$(1/S)(1 + i_{UK})$ million on the current forward exchange market, where it will fetch $$F(1/S)(1 + i_{UK})$ million, F being the current forward exchange rate in dollars per pound. Because the forward rate is known at the time the initial investment is made, the complete investment strategy is riskless in terms of dollars. The investor has "covered" the holdings of foreign securities, just as a home owner is "covered" when buying fire insurance.

Which should the investor buy, the U.S. asset or the U.K. asset covered (hedged) on the forward exchange market? In both cases, the investor would be putting $1 million in today, and getting back a certain amount of dollars in one year. Assuming that the two investments are the same with respect to taxes, risk of default, and so on, the investor should clearly buy whichever one pays the higher return. If $(1 + i_{US}) < (F/S)(1 + i_{UK})$, then the investor should buy the U.K. asset and cover it. When many investors do this, they will add to the supply of pounds on the forward market, thus driving down the forward price of pounds, F, and reducing the inequality. (If the investors also drive up the spot price of pounds, S, by their purchases of pounds in the spot market, or drive down the British interest rate, i_{UK}, by their purchases of pound CDs, this too will tend to reduce the inequality.) This is covered interest arbitrage at work.

To engage in covered interest arbitrage, it is not necessary to be a wealth-holder with a stock of dollars to allocate. If the U.K. interest rate exceeds the U.S. interest rate on a covered basis, as in the preceding inequality, it is possible to make a profit even without initial capital. Begin by borrowing the $1 million at the relatively low U.S. interest rate, i_{US}, and then proceed as before: Exchange the dollars for pounds on the spot market, invest the proceeds in a U.K. CD, and finally, sell the pounds forward. The dollars received in one year as a result of the forward transaction will be enough to settle the dollar debt incurred at the beginning, with some left over as a profit; the inequality tells us so. Anyone engaging in this form of arbitrage will be adding downward pressure on the forward rate.[19]

If transaction costs are low, such arbitrage will continue until the inequality is eliminated. The result is a condition called *covered interest parity*.

$$(1 + i_{US}) = (F/S)(1 + i_{UK}) \qquad (21.1)$$

---

[18]Previous chapters have designated the exchange rate as E, but now the spot exchange rate, S, must be distinguished from the forward exchange rate, F.

[19]Even though anyone could engage in this sort of arbitrage if the inequality held (i.e., it is not the sort of thing where "it takes money to make money"), one has to incur four transaction costs to do so: borrowing, spot, investing, and forward. In practice, those who already have money and are investing it all the time anyway (or hedgers who are already engaging in forward transactions) have an advantage in covered interest arbitrage because they have fewer additional transaction costs to incur.

If the inequality goes the opposite way, with the right-hand side of the expression being less than the left-hand side, then arbitrage will run in the opposite direction. Investors will convert pounds (which they may have borrowed at the relatively low interest rate, i_{UK}) into dollars (at the relatively favorable spot exchange rate, S), invest them in a U.S. CD (at the relatively high interest rate, i_{US}), and sell the dollar proceeds forward for pounds (at the relatively favorable rate of $1/F$), thereby locking in a riskless profit. Such arbitrage, again, will put upward pressure on F, pushing it back into line with Equation 21.1, until covered interest parity is restored.

Let us define the forward discount: $fd \equiv (F - S)/S$. If F is greater than S, the foreign currency is more expensive—or the domestic currency is less expensive—on the forward market than on the spot market. The forward discount on the domestic currency is the percentage rate at which "the forward market thinks the currency will depreciate." If the current spot rate is $2 per pound, and the one-year forward rate is $2.02 per pound, then the forward discount on the dollar is 1 percent.[20] Thus, in Equation 21.1, F/S can be thought of as "1 plus the forward discount."

$$(1 + i_{US}) = (1 + fd)(1 + i_{UK})$$

Multiplying out,

$$(1 + i_{US}) = (1 + fd + i_{UK} + fdi_{UK})$$

The forward discount and the interest rate are both normally fractions, relatively small numbers such as 0.01 and 0.06. Thus, the last term, the product of these two small numbers, is likely to be very small—for example, 0.0006—and can be omitted, with the approximation remaining relatively accurate.[21] Canceling out the two "1"s that appear as well, the equation becomes an alternate statement of covered interest parity, which may be more intuitive than Equation 21.1.

$$i_{US} \approx fd + i_{UK} \tag{21.2}$$

This equation implies that when the U.S. interest rate is higher than the U.K. interest rate, U.S. assets are not necessarily a better investment. If there are no barriers to capital mobility, then the dollar will be selling at a discount in the forward exchange market at a rate fd that precisely cancels out the interest differential.[22]

---

[20]If the forward rate, F, is less than the spot rate, S, then there is a forward *premium* on the dollar. (Check that you understand the arithmetic of covered interest parity, including the case where the maturity is less than one year, by doing Problem 2 at the end of the chapter.)

[21]The approximation is fairly safe when dealing with stable industrialized countries, where the inflation rate, interest rate, and forward discount are usually in single digits. But when dealing with some developing countries, where these rates can go to 100 percent per annum or higher, one must be very careful how the rates are expressed; one cannot go back and forth readily between equations like Equation 21.1 and Equation 21.2.

[22]There is another way of getting to the approximation of covered interest parity, Equation 21.2, if you know enough about logarithms to apply them to Equation 21.1.

$$\log (1 + i_{US}) = \log F - \log S + \log (1 + i_{UK})$$

Because the log of $1 + i_{US}$ is approximately equal to i_{US}, and the same for i_{UK}, this equation is simply Equation 21.2 with the forward discount expressed in logarithmic terms.

Ever since the 1980s, for example, dollar interest rates have usually been higher than yen interest rates by three or four percentage points per annum. As a result, the dollar has sold at a forward discount of the same magnitude. The dollar often sells at a forward premium against the Mexican peso, reflecting Mexican interest rates that are higher than U.S. interest rates.

The theory of covered interest parity is clear. Does it hold precisely in practice? This depends on where interest rates are observed. If the dollar interest rate, the yen interest rate, and the dollar-yen forward discount are all observed in the same location, such as London, then covered interest parity holds extremely well—to within the very small margins of interbank transaction costs. Indeed, banks in the Euromarket determine the forward rate they offer their customers by calculating it from the spot and Euromarket interest rates using the covered interest parity equation. It is more interesting, however, to see whether the condition holds across national boundaries—for example, with the dollar interest rate observed in New York and the yen interest rate observed in Tokyo. Section 21.3 pointed out that, even for some of the G-7 industrialized countries, nonzero differentials in interest rates remained in the 1970s (the U.K. and Japan as late as 1979, and France and Italy as late as 1986), and they remain today for developing countries. The reason is default risk, capital controls, tax differences, and the other barriers to the movement of capital across national boundaries that have been discussed.

The covered interest differential, the deviation from Equation 21.1 (which Figure 21.2 illustrated for the case of the U.K. liberalization of 1979), is essentially the same as the Eurocurrency onshore interest differential (which Figure 21.1 illustrated for the case of the Japanese liberalization).[23] Statistics on covered interest differentials confirm that only eight industrialized countries (plus Hong Kong and Singapore) began the 1980s with relatively open financial markets, but other countries liberalized significantly thereafter.[24]

Other Ways of Managing Risk in Exchange Rates and Interest Rates

In addition to the market in forward exchange, there is also an active market in foreign exchange *futures*. Like a forward contract, a futures contract is a commitment to buy foreign exchange in the future. One difference is that a deposit must be put down to buy a futures contract. Then, each day, the contract is "marked to market." This means that if the market rate moves the wrong way, the investor receives a margin call requiring payment for any losses. A forward contract, by contrast, does not have to be settled until maturity.

---

[23]This is because covered interest parity holds so perfectly *within* the Euromarket. Consider the yen example illustrated in Figure 21.1. Within the Euromarket we have $i_E^¥ = i_E^\$ - fd$, where $i_E^¥$ is the Euroyen interest rate, $i_E^\$$ is the Eurodollar interest rate, and fd is the forward discount on the dollar. The interesting question is whether there is a covered interest differential across national boundaries. The covered interest differential is $i_T^¥ - (i_E^\$ - fd)$, where $i_T^¥$ refers to the Tokyo rate. Given covered interest parity in the Euromarket this is the same differential as the one discussed earlier: $i_T^¥ - i_E^¥$.

[24]Jeffrey Frankel, "Measuring International Capital Mobility: A Review," *American Economic Review*, 82, no. 2 (May 1992): 197–202.

Another difference is that futures contracts mature on specific dates: the third Wednesday of March, June, September, and December. Forward contracts, by contrast, are tailored to the customer seeking foreign currency, for example, 90 days into the future, regardless of the starting date. Another difference is that futures contracts are traded on centralized exchanges, like the Chicago Mercantile Exchange, whereas forward contracts are arranged through the banking system. A large investor or importer who wants to lock in the rate on foreign currency needed in the future may use the forward market. A small speculator buying or selling foreign exchange on a short-term basis in anticipation of exchange rate changes is more likely to use the futures market.[25]

Foreign currency *options* were introduced in the United States in 1982 and grew rapidly in popularity. When buying an option on pound sterling, an investor acquires the right, but not the obligation, to buy pound sterling in the future at a price agreed on at the time the option is purchased. The buyer has the right to buy the pounds at what is called the *strike price*. It will not be in the buyer's interest to exercise that right until such time as the market price of pounds rises above the strike price. The option gives the investor protection against possible future increases in the spot price of pounds (the exchange rate), protection that could be useful if the investor is planning on buying British goods or securities in the future and will need to pay in pounds. Alternatively, an individual may buy an option because of a desire to speculate in pounds, betting on an increase in the pound's value. Finally, an option is a way for a trader to take a position on the volatility of a currency. The higher the volatility of the currency, the more valuable the option, because the probability is higher that the exchange rate will reach the strike price in the time allotted. The famous Black-Scholes formula relates the options price to volatility.

Whether the motive for buying the option is hedging or speculation, a similar goal could be accomplished by buying pounds in the futures market. In a futures contract, however, the agent would be committed to complete the transaction regardless of whether the spot rate goes up or down. Of course, in buying the option the individual must give up some return for the advantage of not having to buy the pounds if the price goes down in the future. Options are often used for speculation, and as with other derivatives, it is sometimes charged that they add to volatility. (*Derivatives* is the name applied to the general class of instruments or contracts that are written so as to depend on an underlying spot price.) However, they are an effective way for the individual international investor to manage risk arising from exchange rate or interest rate volatility.[26]

Forward exchange contracts (along with futures and options) are widely available only for horizons up to one year at the longest. An investor considering the purchase of a long-term bond in a foreign currency, or a borrower considering issuing a long-term

---

[25]For more on futures, see Norman Fieleke, "The Rise of the Foreign Currency Futures Markets," *New England Economic Review* (March/April 1985): 38–47.

[26]The right to *buy* pounds in the future is a *call* option. The right to *sell* pounds is a *put*. Here the investor is speculating that the value of the pound might fall in the future. An accessible reference on options is Ian Giddy, "The Foreign Exchange Option as a Hedging Tool," in J. Stern and D. Chew, eds., *New Developments in International Finance* (Cambridge, MA: Basil Blackwell, 1988).

bond abroad in a foreign currency, will be exposed to exchange rate risk that cannot be readily hedged on the forward exchange market. Another important innovation is the *currency swap,* although the transactions involved sound somewhat complicated.

To take an example, assume that the Coca-Cola Corporation is sufficiently well known in Switzerland that it can borrow at a slightly lower cost there than it can at home (where investors already have all the Coca-Cola bonds they want)—provided that the debt is denominated in Swiss francs, which is the currency Swiss investors prefer to hold. Coca-Cola, however, may wish to avoid the uncertainty of not knowing what the exchange rate will be in the future, and thus not knowing the cost of debt service in terms of dollars. At the same time, Nestlé Corporation, a Swiss company, may wish to know its debt service ahead of time in terms of Swiss francs. Coca-Cola, or its bank, goes to Nestlé and proposes that each corporation issue bonds denominated in the other's currency and that they then swap the obligations to service each other's debt—Nestlé paying interest in Swiss francs to the investors who bought the Coca-Cola bond, and Coca-Cola paying interest in dollars to the investors who bought the Nestlé bond.[27] This technique has allowed hundreds of corporations to go beyond their own countries' capital markets and borrow internationally when it otherwise might not have been convenient for them to do so.

Securitization

In the 1960s and 1970s, bankers led the assault on international financial barriers. In the 1990s, however, new waves of exotic financial weaponry succeeded the now-mundane bank loan.

International banking was dealt a major blow by the international debt crisis, which first surfaced in August 1982 when Mexico informed its creditor banks that it was unable to service its debts on the original schedule. The crisis spread rapidly to other debtors, and banks became much less willing to put new money into developing countries. Bank lending to developing countries fell from $51 billion in 1982 to $8 billion in 1985 and then turned negative. In the second half of the 1980s, repayment of previous loans exceeded new loans.

At the same time, public concerns regarding the stability of the banking system arose, fueled by reports of problems at financial institutions. The Federal Reserve and other regulatory agencies put pressure on banks to raise the ratio of their capital to their outstanding loans. One consequence of these developments was that banks sought to earn more of their fees through "off balance sheet" activities, like swaps, which do not involve recording a loan on their books. In the Basel Agreement of 1987, central banks of the Group of 10 set common "harmonized" rules (which took effect in 1993) for the minimal capital requirements they impose on their countries' banks, and they also set some reserve requirements to cover off balance sheet items. The East

---

[27]In practice, the corporations do not necessarily have to deal with each other directly. Rather, the bank may swap a dollar obligation for the corporation's foreign currency debt, and it is then up to the bank to match up with another corporate borrower (and to guarantee the other side of the transaction against default).

Asian financial crisis of 1997–1998 prompted efforts to extend such standards to banking in emerging markets, under "Basel II."

Borrowers and lenders have begun to rely less on banks for intermediating between them, and more on the direct selling of bonds and other securities. This is the process of international disintermediation, or *securitization*.[28] We have already covered a number of the innovations, such as swaps, that facilitate issuing international bonds. The new methods of selling bonds have helped them to become increasingly important relative to bank loans.

The majority of international bond issues are by industrialized countries. Nevertheless, in light of disenchantment with bank loans as a vehicle for developing countries borrowing, there has been a trend toward securitization in this area as well. When foreign capital began flooding back into Mexico in the early 1990s, it largely took the form of bond purchases rather than bank flows. Bonds have been tried before as an alternative to bank loans for lending to developing countries. In the nineteenth century and in the 1920s, capital flowed from industrialized countries to colonies and developing countries via this route. Defaults occurred periodically, however, culminating in the widespread defaults of the 1930s.

Capital also reaches developing countries through foreign direct investment. Recipients of FDI are apparently less vulnerable to financial crises than are recipients of loans. China has allowed in large flows of FDI, as a successful industrialization strategy that circumvents deficient domestic systems of finance (too many bad loans by banks) and corporate governance (too big a role of government). However, developing countries value their political independence, and some are reluctant to have foreigners owning controlling shares of their natural resources, land, or plant and equipment. Thus there is interest in devising some new mode of capital flow, other than bonds, direct investment, or bank lending.

An obvious candidate is equity investment. Unlike bonds or bank loans, the cost of such an obligation does not stay fixed in dollar terms when the ability of the country to earn export revenue falls because of a world recession or a collapse in commodity prices. Unlike direct investment, securities do not give the foreigner a controlling interest in investment projects. Another idea is the possibility of tying the repayment terms on bonds to export prices or export revenues, which would give them "risk-sharing" characteristics more like equity: The cost of the obligation automatically falls when the ability to pay falls, thus reducing the risk to the borrower.

Equity markets are, of course, far more developed in the United States and other industrialized countries. The United States (and the United Kingdom) have historically had the largest stock markets. But international equity trading has grown rapidly. One reason for this trend (and for securitization in general) is that in wealthy countries, savings have shifted out of banks and other financial intermediaries, and into securities

---

[28]Disintermediation describes the phenomenon of borrowers (e.g., firms) and lenders (e.g., individual investors) starting to do business directly, rather than via financial intermediaries (e.g., banks). This normally means the borrower sells securities to the lender. (The term *securitization* is sometimes reserved for the transformation of a given bank loan into a security, e.g., debt-equity swaps. Here we are using it more broadly to denote any increased use of securities in international capital markets at the expense of bank lending.)

markets, especially via diversified mutual funds, where they can in turn find their way overseas. Although it will take time for investors everywhere to hold similar, widely diversified portfolios, movement is clearly in that direction. The strengthening links among countries' stock markets are reflected in the increasing tendency for market indices to rise or fall together. The stock market crash of October 1987, for example, was transmitted within hours from the United States to markets in Asia and Europe. Ten years later, in October 1997, Asia was the origin of a sharp decline in securities markets that was again felt around the world. Chapter 24 will discuss the integration of emerging markets into the global financial system.

21.5 Advantages of Financial Integration

Financial integration has both pros and cons. It is important to consider both, in order to make the trade-off. Advantages of financial opening include the following:

- For a rapidly growing country, with a high return to domestic capital, investment can be financed more cheaply by borrowing from abroad than out of domestic saving alone. Most of the remainder of this chapter develops the model to illustrate this advantage.
- Investors in wealthier countries can earn a higher rate of return on their saving by investing in emerging markets than they could domestically.
- Everyone benefits from the opportunity to diversify away risks and smooth disturbances.
- Letting foreign financial institutions into a country with an underdeveloped financial system improves the efficiency of domestic financial markets. Overregulated and potentially inefficient domestic institutions are subject to the harsh discipline of competition and the demonstration effect of having examples to emulate.
- Governments face the discipline of the international capital markets in the event they make policy mistakes.

Some Disadvantages in Practice

Financial integration has disadvantages as well, unfortunately, because financial markets do not always work as well as the perfect textbook theory suggests. In theory, private capital markets should be *countercyclical:* flowing in to countries suffering temporary setbacks, so as to cushion the adverse impact, and flowing out from countries that are expanding. In practice, especially for developing countries, it is more nearly the reverse: In boom times the whole world wants to lend to you, but in recessions it cuts you off. In other words, capital flows are observed empirically to be *procyclical.* Particularly salient are the recurrent disruptions, the busts that follow the booms, such as the 1982 international debt crises, 1992–1993 crisis in the European ERM, 1994 Mexican peso crisis, and 1997–1998 Asian financial crisis, followed by Russia (1998), Brazil (1999), Turkey (2001), and Argentina (2002). Chapter 25 examines the crisis phenomenon in detail. For now, let us note that it has gotten more difficult to argue that investors punish countries when and only when the governments are following bad policies, for three reasons:

- Large inflows often give way suddenly to large outflows, with little news appearing in between that might explain the change in sentiment.
- Second, contagion sometimes spreads to countries that are unrelated, or where fundamentals appear strong.
- Recessions that have hit emerging market countries in such crises have been so big that it is difficult to argue the system is working well.

The Theory of International Capital Flows as Intertemporal Optimization

This section serves three purposes. First, it formalizes the first advantage of financial integration that was listed earlier, showing how the freedom to borrow and lend internationally can leave people better off. Second, it constitutes an important theory of the current account, the intertemporal approach. (Recall that the current account is just the flip side of the capital account.) Third, it leaves us with the prediction that capital flows from the low-interest-rate country to the high-interest-rate country, a proposition that will be a central building block of Chapters 22 and 23. It is nice to have such a key proposition rooted in the economic theory of individual agents who optimize.

The procedure here will be the same as that used to introduce the theory of international trade in Chapters 2 and 3: first taking supply as given and looking at trade that arises from differences in demand, and then introducing supply differences. Rather than discussing the supply and demand for goods, however, the discussion here will be concerned with the supply and demand for *bonds*.

This analysis is necessarily *intertemporal,* meaning that it concerns different periods in time. The purchase of a bond in the present period is the purchase of a claim to consumption in the future, when the bond comes due. Assume two periods: the present, period 0, and the future, period 1.

First consider an economy in which output in the two periods is fixed. Imagine, for example, a country where coconuts fall off the trees with no effort on the part of the population. Figure 21.3 shows the number of coconuts in period 0 on the horizontal axis and the number of coconuts in period 1 on the vertical axis. Point A indicates the number of coconuts that fall off the trees in the two periods.

We draw community indifference curves along which consumers ("representative agents") are indifferent between different combinations of the two kinds of consumption, in this case present and future consumption, C_0 and C_1. The slope of the indifference curve is called the *intertemporal rate of substitution*. It tells how many future coconuts the agent is willing to give up to get one more coconut this period. Thus it reflects how impatient the agent is.

In autarky, where there is no possibility of trade between periods, the point of output A must also be the point of consumption. Point A is located on the graph in such a way that $C_1 > C_0$. There are more coconuts in the second period than in the first. (This is the usual case: Output, like the size of coconut trees, tends to grow over time.) The

FIGURE 21.3

Borrowing from Abroad, with Fixed Output in Both Periods

The horizontal axis represents the current period; the vertical axis the future period. *A* represents given levels of output in the two periods. If the country is relatively impatient to consume, at *B* it can borrow to finance a relatively greater level of current consumption C_0 at the expense of lower consumption C_1 next period.

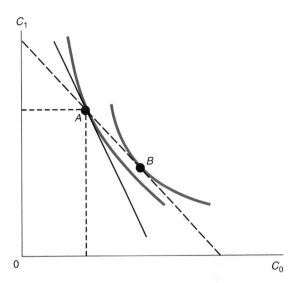

market price of C_0 in terms of C_1 is (the absolute value of) the slope of the indifference curve that passes through *A*. A solid line is drawn through *A* tangent to the indifference curve. As drawn, the slope is greater than 1 (in absolute value): Present consumption must be more expensive than future consumption to induce agents to wait for the next period, when more coconuts will be available.

Another way of expressing the slope is $1 + i$, where i is the market interest rate. Why is $1 + i$ the price of C_0 in terms of C_1? Because an individual saver can take $1 worth of coconuts, buy a one-period bond, receive back the principal plus interest next period, and then consume $(1 + i)$ worth of coconuts. The proposition that the marginal rate of substitution is greater than 1 is thus the same as the proposition that the interest rate i is greater than 0.

Now assume that the country is opened up to international financial markets, that it can borrow or lend at the going world interest rate. Suppose that the world interest rate, i^*, corresponds to the slope of the dotted line in Figure 21.3. It has been drawn less steep than the solid line, meaning that the world interest rate, i^*, is less than the domestic autarkic interest rate, i. The relative price of current consumption, although still greater than 1, is lower in the rest of the world. (Or the relative price of *future* consumption is *greater* in the rest of the world.) Foreign agents are less impatient than domestic agents, less anxious to consume today.

Domestic agents will take advantage of a lower interest rate abroad by borrowing. In terms of the figure, they will slide down the new relative price line to point *B*, where the line is tangent to a new indifference curve that represents a higher level of welfare. At point *B*, domestic agents are giving up some consumption in period 1 in exchange for more consumption in period 0. They gain from this arrangement because it assuages some of the impatience they feel at point *A*. The horizontal distance between points *A* and *B* is the current account deficit, financed by a capital inflow.

To illustrate with a key feature of the world economy, Japan is the perfect example of a country where people have a low rate of impatience: The Japanese have had a high saving rate during the postwar period because they were willing to postpone consumption to the future even for a relatively low interest rate. The United States is a good example of a country with a high rate of impatience: Americans have a low national saving rate because they are reluctant to postpone spending, even for a relatively high interest rate. In autarky, Japan would have a low interest rate and the United States a high one.[29] When nations remove barriers to the international flow of capital, as the Japanese government did in the early 1980s, the Japanese lend and the Americans borrow.

We now consider the possibility that the quantities of coconuts produced in the two periods are not determined exogenously but are the outcome of an economic decision. In the illustration, the coconuts do not fall off the tree but have to be picked. The decision as to how many to leave on the tree (or the decision as to how many trees to plant) is an *investment* decision, of the sort firms make when planning additions to factory capacity. Figure 21.4 draws a production possibility frontier, showing the trade-off between coconuts harvested for sale this period and coconuts available next period.

The point A again represents autarky, determined where the indifference curve is tangent to the production possibility frontier. Again, the graph is drawn so the slope is relatively high at A. Again, the interest rate, i, in autarky exceeds the world interest rate, i^*, and the domestic country will borrow from abroad when it is opened up to international capital movements. Now, however, the international borrowing has two effects. The new one is that the country responds to the lower interest rate by increasing investment (planting more coconuts): Output takes place at point B, with a greater harvest in period 1 in exchange for a smaller harvest in period 0. The second effect is that, as before, the international borrowing allows the home country to reallocate some of its consumption from period 1 to period 0: Consumption takes place at point C, where consumption is higher than output in period 0 and lower than output in period 1.

To return to the example of the United States: the net capital inflow, ever since it began in 1982, has kept interest rates lower than they otherwise would be. The capital inflow thereby has both prevented U.S. investment from being crowded out as much as it would have otherwise been and allowed U.S. consumption to be higher than it would have otherwise been.

---

[29]If the rate of intertemporal substitution for a country like the United States is higher than for other countries, as at point A in the figure, this can be for either of two reasons. First, the high degree of impatience may be inherent in Americans' preferences: Their indifference curves might be steeper than the indifference curves of Japanese would be at the corresponding point in the graph. Second, even if the pattern of indifference curves is the same for all nationalities, if the U.S. economy is growing more rapidly than the Japanese economy, then the autarky point A will be located higher and farther to the left than it would be for the Japanese economy. Because all indifference curves are curved, it would then follow that the indifference curve at A would be steeper in the U.S. case. Either way, the slope of the solid line comes out higher (in absolute value) than the slope of the dotted line that represents the rest of the world.

FIGURE 21.4

Borrowing from Abroad, with Investment

The possibility of physical investment means there is a transformation frontier between output in the two periods. The country can divert resources to future production at *B* and borrow more to finance current consumption at *C*, thereby realizing further welfare gains.

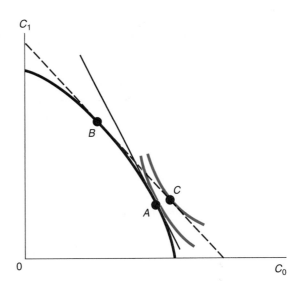

21.6   Summary

This chapter showed how governments' removal of capital controls, the development of new financial instruments, and other forms of liberalization and innovation have all worked to reduce barriers to the international flow of capital. This increase in the degree of international capital mobility makes an enormous difference, not just for those who operate in these markets, but for the entire macroeconomy as well, as the following chapters will show.

CHAPTER PROBLEMS

1. You have acquired an option to buy Swiss francs at a strike price of $.70 per Swiss franc. (At the time you bought the contract, the spot exchange rate was only $.50 per Swiss franc.) In each of the following three cases, would you choose to exercise the option? Answer either "definitely yes," "definitely no," or "maybe yes; maybe no, to wait to see if the spot exchange value of the Swiss franc goes higher."
    a. The current spot exchange rate is $.60 per Swiss franc.
    b. The current spot exchange rate is $.80 per Swiss franc, and the contract is about to expire.
    c. The current spot exchange rate is $.80 per Swiss franc, and the contract still has two months to run.
    d. Would the option be more or less valuable if the Swiss franc is thought to be highly volatile this year?

2. Suppose you are a U.S. exporter expecting to receive a payment of € 100 in 12 months. The one-year interest rate on € deposits is 4 percent per annum. The one-year interest rate on dollar deposits is 6 percent per annum. The present spot exchange rate is $1.20 per €.

   a. What is the one-year forward exchange rate?

   b. Assuming you ultimately need dollars, you have two ways to cover yourself from the exchange rate risk. Describe them and show their equivalence computationally.

   c. Now suppose your claim on € 100 is due in six months. The interest rate on six-month € deposits is 2 percent per annum. The interest rate on six-month dollar deposits is 6 percent per annum. What is the six-month forward exchange rate? (*Hint:* You can't do this one in per annum terms.)

   d. What do a and c imply about "the market's expectations" regarding the future path of the exchange rate?

   e. The Swedish krona (SK) faces a spot exchange rate of 10 SK/€, and obeys the covered interest parity condition as in a. Suppose, however, that investors today discover (with certainty) that the krona will devalue sometime over the next year, to 11 SK/€. Suppose that the U.S. and euro interest rates remain unchanged (because their home countries are large). To what level will investors drive the one-year forward exchange rate? What will that imply for the interest rate on one-year deposits in SK?

SUGGESTIONS FOR FURTHER READING

Bank for International Settlements. *75th Annual Report* (Basel: BIS, June 2005). Yearly review of the global economy, financial markets, and foreign exchange markets.

Edwards, Sebastian. "The Order of Liberalization of the External Sector in Developing Countries," *Essays in International Finance,* 156 (Princeton: Princeton University Press, 1984). An analysis of whether international trade should be liberalized before or after capital markets, and related issues.

Frankel, Jeffrey. "Still the Lingua Franca: The Exaggerated Death of the Dollar," *Foreign Affairs,* 74, 4 (August 1995): 9–16. Is the dollar losing its role as premier international currency?

Mussa, Michael, and Morris Goldstein. "The Integration of World Capital Markets," in *Changing Capital Markets: Implications for Monetary Policy* (Federal Reserve Bank of Kansas City, 1993). Good comprehensive survey of measures and implications of the internationalization of financial markets.

Prasad, Eswar, Kenneth Rogoff, Shang-Jin Wei, and M. Ayhan Kose. "Effects of Financial Globalization on Developing Countries: Some Empirical Evidence," *Occasional Paper No. 220*, Research Department, International Monetary Fund, 2003. The IMF has become less confident of the virtues of high financial integration in emerging markets.

APPENDIX

The Effect of a Budget Deficit Under Intertemporal Optimization

The notion of the twin deficits suggests that an increase in the budget deficit translates into an increase in the current account deficit. But this need not necessarily always be the case, especially if household behavior is derived from intertemporal optimization as in Section 21.5. In the first place, a budget deficit could as a theoretical matter be offset by private saving. In the second place, even if a budget deficit reduces national saving, it is an open empirical question whether it crowds out domestic investment or whether it is instead offset by borrowing from abroad, financing a current account deficit. We consider each of these two questions in turn, under the names "debt neutrality proposition" and "Feldstein-Horioka finding."

The Debt-Neutrality Proposition

This is the place to acknowledge a school of thought associated with the economist Robert Barro. The key proposition, known as Ricardian equivalence, or *debt neutrality,* states that changes in the government budget deficit have no macroeconomic effect on the economy. (This refers to changes in the deficit with government spending held constant, that is, to tax cuts.) The argument runs as follows: A budget deficit implies that the government is accumulating debt. At some point in the future the government will have to raise taxes to service or pay off that debt. If people can see far into the future, and if they intertemporally plan in an optimizing way like the consumers in Figures 21.3 and 21.4, then they will save more today, so that they or their children will have the money to pay the taxes in the future. Their current spending will fall by the same amount as the budget deficit. On net, total national saving will be unchanged. The fiscal expansion will have no effect on total spending. It will not shift the *IS* curve out and thus will have none of the effects on income, the interest rate, the exchange rate, and the current account to be studied throughout Chapter 22.

Many economists, and most other observers as well, find it difficult to believe that households in reality look that far into the future when planning their consumption. A great many theoretical and econometric points have been scored on both sides of this debate. One compelling argument against the debt-neutrality proposition is precisely the massive U.S. experiments of the administrations of Ronald Reagan and George W. Bush. Many of those who supported their tax cuts and countered concerns that it would result in budget deficits predicted that private saving would rise to offset the decline in public saving. What happened, however, was quite the reverse.

The federal budget deficit averaged 2 percent of GDP in the 1970s. It then rose sharply in the 1980s as shown in Table 17.1. Private saving as a share of GDP, far from rising to help finance the budget deficit, actually fell. As a result, the total level of net domestic saving, private plus public together, available to finance additions to the capital stock was down to about 5 percent of GDP by the late 1980s, compared to about 9 percent, on average, in the 1970s. If it had not been for the large-scale borrowing from abroad, investment would have fallen sharply as a percentage of GDP. Events of the 1980s did not seem to have borne out the predictions of Ricardian equivalence. These events have been repeated in the years since 2001. A large swing in the budget, from record surplus to record deficit, was not offset by an increase in private saving. To the contrary, private saving declined further, thereby exacerbating the decline in national saving.

Feldstein-Horioka and Measures of International Capital Mobility

If we take as an established event a fall in national saving, it is interesting to examine how the shortfall is divided between a net capital inflow—that is, a current-account deficit—and a decline in investment. Alternatively, there is the more positive experiment of an increase in national saving as the result of a cut in government spending, an increase in taxes, or a rise in private saving. To what extent are the funds that are generated retained at home to finance additions to the capital stock, and to what extent do they instead go to reduce the capital inflow from abroad?

This question has been examined in a series of papers by Martin Feldstein and others inspired by him.[30] The name *saving-retention coefficient* will be used to describe the effect that an exogenous change in national saving (whether public, i.e., the budget deficit, or private) equal to 1 percent of GDP has on the country's investment, again as a percentage of GDP. The initial finding was that the coefficient for a cross-section of countries was about 0.9. Changes in national saving were reflected almost one-for-one as changes in investment. Feldstein considered this result surprising, in light of the existing consensus that the degree of international capital mobility was close to perfect. According to his logic, perfect capital mobility implies that arbitrage ensures that the domestic interest rate is tied to the foreign interest rate. Thus a fiscal expansion or other shortfall in national saving should be easily financed by borrowing from abroad, with no increase in the domestic interest rate and consequently no crowding-out of investment. According to this logic, the saving-retention coefficient should have been zero![31]

The direct way to test statistically for capital mobility is to examine international differentials in interest rates to see if arbitrage is able to drive them to zero. How should interest differentials be measured? We will continue to define international capital mobility as the absence of transaction costs, default risk, capital controls, risk of future capital controls, or other barriers to financial integration across political boundaries. Chapter 21 showed that interest rate differentials covered on the forward exchange

---

[30]Martin Feldstein and Charles Horioka, "Domestic Saving and International Capital Flows," *Economic Journal,* 90 (1980): 314–329.

[31]To compute the statistics correctly, the changes examined in national saving should be exogenous. The estimate of the saving-retention coefficient will not be accurate if national saving and investment rates are highly correlated because both are responding to some common factor. However, the coefficient appears to be high also for exogenous changes in government budgets or in private saving.

market can be used to test for perfect capital mobility in this sense. The covered differential is expressed as

$$i - i^* - fd \tag{21.A.1}$$

where i is the domestic interest rate, i^* is the foreign interest rate, and fd is the forward discount on domestic currency. As we saw in Chapter 21, this measure of the interest differential is indeed very small for most major industrialized countries. For developing countries, which may lack active forward markets, we can test these factors by looking at the sovereign spread that global investors require to lend to the country in dollars. This spread, or country premium, is not very small.

A somewhat broader measure of the international differential is the difference in expected returns on the two countries' bonds, expressed in terms of a common currency but *not* covered for exchange rate risk on the forward exchange market. This is the *uncovered* interest differential,

$$i - i^* - \Delta s^e \tag{21.A.2}$$

where Δs^e is the rate at which investors expect the domestic currency to depreciate against the foreign currency in the future. The uncovered differential (Equation 21.A.2) is equal to the covered differential (Equation 21.A.1) *plus* the exchange risk premium, defined as

$$rp = fd - \Delta s^e. \tag{21.A.3}$$

The risk premium is the extra expected return that investors demand in compensation for holding a currency that they perceive as riskier than others. It can be small if risk is not important (if uncertainty regarding the future exchange rate is not very large or if investors are not very risk averse). In general, however, even if the covered differential, Expression 21.A.1, is zero, the uncovered differential, 21.A.2, will not be zero because of the existence of the risk premium, Expression 21.A.3.[32]

A still broader measure of the international differential in rates of return is the *real* interest differential. The real interest rate, defined as the nominal interest rate adjusted for expected inflation, is the cost of funds on which investment in each country depends. The real interest differential is

$$(i - \Delta p^e) - (i^* - \Delta p^{*e}) \tag{21.A.4}$$

where Δp^e and Δp^{*e} are defined as the domestic and foreign expected inflation rates, respectively. It is equal to the uncovered differential, Expression 21.A.2, *plus* expected real depreciation of the currency, defined as

$$\Delta s^e - (\Delta p^e - \Delta p^{*e}). \tag{21.A.5}$$

If purchasing power parity held, then expected real depreciation would be zero and there would be no difference between Expressions 21.A.4 and 21.A.2. However, as seen in Chapter 19, purchasing power parity does not in reality hold, and expected real

---

[32] Chapter 28 examines the exchange risk premium at greater length.

depreciation is not always zero. It follows that arbitrage could equalize interest rates across countries when they are expressed in a common currency, not only on a covered basis but even on an uncovered basis, and yet real interest rates will not be equalized.

Even though covered interest differentials have become very small, reflecting low political barriers to the movement of capital across national boundaries, currency variability remains high. Perhaps this is the reason why real interest parity continues to fail, and the saving-retention coefficient, although it seems to have fallen to roughly half, is still well above zero, even for developed countries.

CHAPTER 22

The Mundell-Fleming Model with Partial International Capital Mobility

This chapter adds international capital flows to the basic model, continuing the process of adding new factors one by one to our analysis of the balance of payments. Chapter 16 examined the effects of changes in the exchange rate, holding everything else constant. Then Chapter 17 introduced the level of income, and Chapter 18, the interest rate. Chapter 19 focused on international money flows and the price level.

In Chapter 21 we saw in detail that the degree of international capital mobility has increased steadily over the past 30 years. This chapter and those to follow will demonstrate that international capital mobility has important implications for the operation of macroeconomic policy. For example, the most dramatic shift of the 1980s in the economic interaction of the industrialized countries, the emergence of large trade deficits in the United States, was not primarily caused by changes in trade policy or competitiveness. Rather, it had its origin in the international flow of capital to the United States. This flow of capital, in turn, was caused primarily by fiscal and monetary policies enacted in Washington, D.C. An analogous shift in fiscal and monetary policies in Germany in the early 1990s had similar consequences for that country. In some ways the United States is repeating the experiment in the current decade.

In reality, international capital flows depend on many factors. Perhaps the most important are the rates of return that various countries are offering on their assets. We will simplify and assume that the rates of return on all assets offered by a given country (other than money) move together sufficiently closely within the country that they can be represented by a single nominal interest rate, i. In other words, we aggregate together bonds, stocks, and other nonmonetary assets. It is further assumed here that the differential between the domestic and foreign interest rate is the only determinant of the net capital inflow or outflow. Chapters 27 and 28 will add other determinants of the behavior of the international portfolio investor besides interest rates: in particular, investors' awareness that future changes in exchange rates will affect the returns they earn.

When investors in a low-interest-rate country buy assets in a high-interest-rate country, they exploit the principle of comparative advantage, just as consumers do when buying goods from a foreign country that can produce them at lower cost. Chapters 2 and 3 introduced the concept of autarky—the hypothetical situation that would prevail if a country were closed off from international trade in goods (for example, because of prohibitively high tariff barriers), so that agents could consume only those goods produced domestically. It was shown that once the country opens up to international trade, the pattern of trade is dictated by the prices that would hold in autarky: If one good sells for a lower price in the foreign country than in the domestic country (whether because demand for it is lower or supply higher), then domestic residents will import that good as soon as they have the opportunity.

A similar concept can be applied to international trade in bonds. Autarky now would prevail if a country were closed off from international trade in bonds, that is, from borrowing or lending abroad (for example, because of prohibitively high capital controls). In autarky the interest rate in each country would be determined so as to equilibrate the supply and demand for bonds versus money. The last part of Chapter 18 introduced monetary policy and the interest rate, i, into the model, but did not allow for international capital flows. In Figure 18.7, for example, a high interest rate was required for equilibrium in the home country. There had been an increase in government demand for funds that reduced total national saving, and thus drove up the interest rate and crowded out private investment. (Do not be concerned if your recollection of the graph is hazy; it will be covered again momentarily.)

Imagine now that in autarky a lower interest rate prevails in the foreign country. Once the countries open up to international capital flows, the pattern of trade in bonds is dictated by the rates of return. If the home country has the higher interest rate, then domestic residents will borrow from abroad, where the cost of funds is lower. Equivalently, foreign residents will lend to the home country, where the rate of return is higher. Either way, the point is that capital flows from the low-interest-rate country to the high-interest-rate country.[1]

We represent the net (private) capital account balance by KA. Thus

$$KA = \overline{KA} + k(i - i^*) \tag{22.1}$$

To the extent that the domestic interest rate, i, rises above the foreign rate, i^*, foreign investors will find domestic assets more attractive than their own and will seek to acquire them; domestic residents will be less eager to buy foreign assets and may even borrow abroad at the lower foreign interest rate. Whether foreigners invest in the home country or domestic residents borrow abroad, the transaction counts as a capital inflow and the domestic capital account shows a surplus: KA is positive. Conversely, if the domestic interest rate falls below the foreign rate, domestic residents will buy foreign assets and foreign residents will borrow in the home country; there is a capital outflow and KA is negative.

Why, if one country is offering a higher interest rate than another, would investors be willing to hold *any* assets of the low-rate country? This is a question well worth asking, and there will be an answer to it that holds even under conditions of perfect integration of financial markets (that is, the possibility of future changes in the exchange

---

[1]To carry the analogy with the two-good trade model one step further, the "good" that the foreign country obtains is the ability to consume more in the future in exchange for consumption today. This point was spelled out in Section 21.5.

rate, to be introduced in Chapter 27). For the moment, assume there are still some transaction costs, capital controls, or other impediments to the movement of capital across national borders that prevent investors from completely arbitraging away interest differentials.[2]

This chapter inserts the capital flow equation, Equation 22.1, into the model used to determine national income, Y, in Chapters 17 and 18. The chapter thus returns to the Keynesian assumption made there that the speed of adjustment of goods prices is so slow that it can be ignored in the short run, so that changes in demand are entirely reflected as changes in output. (As before, much of the analysis developed here would also apply in a world of flexible prices, with changes in the price level substituting for changes in output when there are changes in aggregate demand.) Because Chapter 18 assumed a capital account constrained to zero, the model did not look radically different from the *IS-LM* model of traditional closed-economy textbooks. Now, however, international capital flows will change the model radically, particularly regarding the effects of monetary and fiscal policy.

In this chapter we hold the exchange rate constant. Then in Chapter 23 we consider a floating exchange rate regime. At every stage, the discussion explores not just what difference it makes to have *some* degree of capital mobility ($k > 0$) but also the different implications of high versus low capital mobility. Section 23.3 will also consider the limiting case of perfect capital mobility ($k =$ infinity). This logical progression—from no capital mobility to low, high, and finally perfect capital mobility—mirrors the historical evolution of the international financial system as the processes of innovation and liberalization have gradually diminished the barriers between countries.

22.1 The Model

We set down equations for the *IS* and *LM* relationships from Chapter 18:

$$IS: \quad Y = [\overline{A} - b(i) + \overline{X} - \overline{M}]/(s + m) \tag{22.2}$$

$$LM: \quad M/P = L(i, Y) \tag{22.3}$$

The curves appear in the figures used throughout this chapter.

To review, the *LM* curve is the relationship between income, Y, and the interest rate, i, that gives equilibrium in the money market, where equilibrium is defined as real money supply (M/P) equal to real money demand. A given curve represents a given real money supply. The curve slopes upward because i and Y have opposite effects on money demand. An increase in Y raises the demand for money because people undertake more transactions. If there is no accommodating increase in the money supply, then the interest rate will be driven up, reducing the demand for money back to its original level. If the central bank adopts an expansionary monetary policy, under the

---

[2]Again, to point out the analogy with trade in goods, the existence of transportation costs, tariffs, or other impediments to the movement of goods across national boundaries would prevent the prices for the identical goods from being equalized between the two countries.

assumption that the short-run price level is fixed, the increase in the nominal money supply is also an increase in the real money supply. It shifts the *LM* curve to the right so that a higher level of *Y* can be sustained for any given interest rate.

The *IS* curve is the relationship between output, *Y*, and the interest rate, *i*, that gives equilibrium in the goods market, where equilibrium is defined as a point where the amount of goods produced equals the amount of goods demanded. The curve slopes downward because *i* has a second role (in addition to the return paid to households on nonmonetary assets). It is the cost to firms of borrowing funds to finance investment in plant and equipment or the cost to households of borrowing to finance the purchase of an automobile or other consumer durable. An increase in *i* reduces such expenditures, and in turn (through the multiplier effect) leads to a lower level of output throughout the economy. Just as the *LM* curve is drawn contingent on a given level of the money supply, so too is the *IS* curve drawn contingent on a given level of government expenditure, *G*. *G* is subsumed in the intercept term for the equation, along with the exogenous components of consumer spending and business investment. An increase in any of these exogenous components of spending ($\Delta \overline{A}$) shifts the *IS* curve to the right by an amount equal to the simple Keynesian multiplier, which is $\Delta Y = [1/(s + m)]\Delta \overline{A}$. Similarly, a reduction in the tax rate would leave households with more disposable income and would exogenously increase consumption. The multiplier, $1/(s + m)$, is smaller than it would be if the economy were closed to international trade ($1/s$) because some of the spending leaks out into imports from abroad. The effect on income in complete *IS-LM* equilibrium is smaller still because the higher transaction demand for money drives up the interest rate and discourages investment.

The *IS* curve shifts to the right not only when there is an exogenous increase in demand for domestic goods coming from domestic residents (*A*), but also when there is an exogenous increase in demand for domestic goods coming from foreign residents, that is, when there is an increase in net exports (*TB*). This would be the case, for example, if there is a shift in foreign tastes toward domestic products or if quotas are imposed on imports. The same occurs if there is a devaluation (assuming the Marshall-Lerner condition is satisfied). It will often be necessary to take into account these sources of shifts in the *IS* curve.

The Balance-of-Payments Relationship

In Chapter 18 a third line, labeled *TB* = 0, was drawn. At that stage in the analysis the balance of payments consisted solely of the trade balance because there was no capital account. That can be considered the approximate situation of the world economy in the 1950s, when capital flows were not free to respond to rates of return. (This is not to say that the capital account was literally zero. There was an exogenous component, $\overline{KA}$.) The interest rate had no effect on the balance of payments, so the line representing the balance of payments was vertical: A unique level of income *Y* was consistent with balance-of-payments equilibrium. Any point to the right was a point of deficit because higher income means higher imports, and any point to the left a point of surplus because lower income means lower imports. The position of this line, however, like the position of the *IS* curve, shifts to the right when there is a change in the exchange rate. Some points that previously represented a trade deficit now represent a trade surplus.

In this chapter the third line, which we will now call the *BP* line, still represents equilibrium in the overall balance of payments, but this no longer means the trade balance alone. It includes both the trade balance, *TB*, which depends negatively on income and positively on the exchange rate as before, and the capital account, *KA*, which depends positively on the interest differential $(i - i^*)$ as in Equation 22.1:

$$BP = TB + KA = 0$$

$$BP = \overline{X} - \overline{M} - mY + \overline{KA} + k(i - i^*) = 0. \tag{22.4}$$

The third line represents combinations of income and the interest rate that would give an overall balance of payments equal to zero. To help graph it on the same diagram as the *IS* and *LM* curves, we can solve the equation to show the level of the interest differential that corresponds to any given level of income, *Y*:

$$i - \bar{i}^* = -(1/k)(\overline{X} - \overline{M} + \overline{KA}) + (m/k)Y. \tag{22.5}$$

This chapter will assume the home country is relatively small in world financial markets, so it can take the rest of the world's interest rate as given $(i^* = \bar{i}^*)$. Figure 22.1 graphs the relationship shown in Equation 22.5. Notice that an increase in income must be associated with an increase in the interest differential to maintain a zero overall balance of payments. This is because imports increase with income, and the interest rate must be raised to attract the capital inflow to finance the trade deficit. Notice also that the slope of the line depends inversely on the degree of international capital mobility, *k*. The larger is *k*, the flatter is the *BP* = 0 line: The smaller is the increase in the interest rate necessary to attract a given required capital inflow. If *k* is small, the *BP* = 0 line is steep: It would take a large increase in the interest rate to attract the required capital inflow. The previous case of no capital mobility $(k = 0)$ is the case where the line is

FIGURE 22.1

Balance of Payments Equilibrium Schedule

The *BP* schedule appears on the same axes as *IS-LM*. An increase in income *Y* raises imports and causes a trade deficit; it thus requires an increase in the interest rate *i* to attract a capital inflow if the overall balance of payments is to remain at zero.

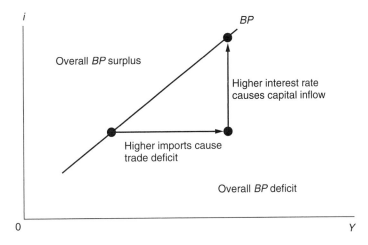

vertical: No finite increase in the interest rate would be enough to attract the capital. The slope also depends positively on the marginal propensity to import, m.[3]

Notice also that an increase in the exchange rate, or anything else that exogenously increases the trade balance, still shifts the BP curve to the right: For any given interest rate, the condition that the balance of payments is zero would now permit a higher level of income. (The BP curve shifts to the right by precisely the same distance as it did in the absence of capital mobility: $(1/m)\Delta\overline{X}$.)

The economy is always at the intersection of the IS and LM curves, under the assumption that there is always equilibrium in the goods and asset markets. The demand for goods equals the output of goods supplied, and the demand for money equals the supply of money. There is not necessarily any reason to be also on the BP curve. The balance of payments will be nonzero, and the economy will be off the BP curve, if the central bank is buying or selling foreign exchange reserves. The following discussion assumes that the starting point just happens to be a point where the balance of payments equals zero, so all three curves intersect.

We now use the model to examine the effects, first, of a fiscal expansion and, second, of a monetary expansion.

22.2 Fiscal Policy and the Degree of Capital Mobility Under Fixed Rates

Consider an increase in government expenditure, beginning with the case of zero capital mobility, shown again in Figure 22.2(a) for convenience. The IS curve shifts right to IS', with the new intersection at point G. Income, Y, increases, and the higher transaction demand for money drives up the interest rate. There are now different implications for the balance of payments, however. In the case of no capital mobility shown in Figure 22.2(a), the only effect on the balance of payments came via imports and the trade deficit. The balance of payments went into deficit, with the central bank buying up the unwanted domestic currency (under the regime of fixed exchange rates, the one considered in this section). But now, when we include the capital account, the higher interest rate attracts a capital inflow into the country, which works to improve the balance of payments. Conversely, the higher level of income still draws in imports and worsens the trade balance, which works to worsen the balance of payments. Which effect dominates? It depends on the degree of capital mobility. If capital flows are not very sensitive to interest rates, then the improvement in the capital account will be small and the trade deficit will dominate. However, if capital flows *are* highly responsive to the interest rate, then the capital inflow will dominate and the overall balance of payments will improve.

Figure 22.2(b) shows the upward-sloping BP curve as relatively steep—steeper than the LM curve. This is the case of low capital mobility. It is the case where the new

---

[3]Most countries have gradually become more open to international trade in the postwar period, so m has gradually been increasing. However, the degree of capital mobility, k, has been increasing more rapidly, so the slope m/k has been gradually diminishing.

FIGURE 22.2

Fiscal Expansion Under Fixed Exchange Rates

(a) Regardless of the degree of capital mobility, a fiscal expansion shifts the *IS* curve out, raising *Y* and *i* at *G* and worsening the *TB*. If capital mobility is low (b), then the capital inflow, *KA*, is smaller than the trade deficit and the overall *BP* is negative. If it is high (c), then *KA* is larger than the trade deficit and *BP* is positive.

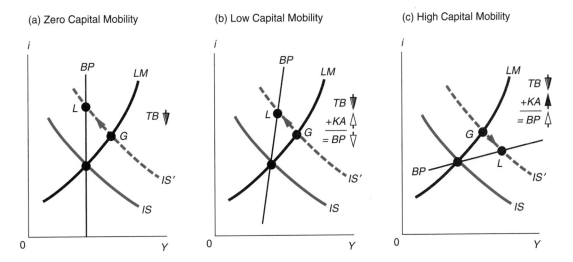

IS-LM intersection at point *G* occurs to the right of or below the *BP* curve. Any point to the right of or below the *BP* curve is a point of deficit: Either the level of income, and therefore imports, is too high for balance-of-payments equilibrium, or the level of the interest rate, and therefore the capital inflow, is too low. Thus the fiscal expansion in Figure 22.2(b) gives a balance-of-payments deficit, as in the case of zero capital mobility, with the central bank buying up the unwanted domestic currency on the foreign exchange market. Yet there is a difference: The deficit is not as large as in Figure 22.2(a) because the capital inflow does partially offset the trade deficit. This is the *only* difference. *Y* and *i* are the same as in the earlier case.

In Figure 22.2(c) the *BP* curve is relatively flat—flatter than the *LM* curve. This is the case of high capital mobility. The fiscal expansion again produces the same increases in *Y* and *i*. Now, however, the new intersection of the *IS* and *LM* curves occurs at a point, *G*, to the left of or above the *BP* curve. The increase in *i* attracts a capital inflow more than sufficient to finance the higher imports resulting from the increase in *Y*. Thus the overall balance of payments is in surplus. Under fixed exchange rates, the central bank is accumulating foreign exchange reserves, not losing them, as with a lower degree of capital mobility.

Which case, (a), (b), or (c), is most realistic in practice? Clearly, all countries have at least some degree of capital mobility. The degree of capital mobility for the United States and Canada has been high enough to put them in category (c) ever since capital controls were removed in 1974. Still, many other countries have lagged behind in liberalizing their financial markets, as we noted in Chapter 21. The United Kingdom was still in category (b) in 1978, and Japan in 1984. By now, these countries are in category (c). None is on fixed exchange rates, so the complete analysis relevant to them will have to await Chapter 23, which deals with floating rates.

Nevertheless, many continental European countries have tried to maintain fixed exchange rates against each other—first, starting in 1979, as part of the European Monetary System (EMS). Since 1999 many have locked their currencies together permanently, in the EMU. So this analysis can be applied to them. Consider the example of France, which undertook an expansion when the socialists were elected in 1981. At the time, capital controls placed the country in category (b). The balance of payments went into deficit, so the French franc was in excess supply (vis-à-vis the German mark) and President Mitterrand was forced to reverse the expansion. In other words, France had difficulty attracting the foreign capital to finance fiscal expansion.

Subsequently, liberalization moved France from category (b) to category (c), where most Western European countries are now. Deficits are easily financed. Germany in 1991–1992 undertook quite a large increase in government spending in an effort to rebuild the economies of the newly reincorporated Eastern länder. The macroeconomic effect was to push interest rates up sharply, which attracted a large capital inflow into Germany and put strong upward pressure on the mark.

Fixed exchange rates are common in small developing countries. However, small countries usually have a high marginal propensity to import, so a fiscal expansion leads to a large trade deficit. Most developing countries naturally have less developed financial markets. As a result, interest rates may not be free to rise in response to a fiscal expansion. Even if interest rates do rise above the level in the rest of the world, the degree of capital mobility is likely to be low enough that the overall balance of payments worsens rather than improves. In other words, they are in case (b).

This analysis has assumed that the central bank holds the money supply constant. The effect of the fiscal expansion would be greater if the central bank at the same time were to follow an expansionary, or "accommodating," monetary policy so as to prevent interest rates from rising. The Federal Reserve generally followed such a policy in the 1960s when expansionary fiscal policies were adopted: the 1964 tax cut originally proposed by President Kennedy and the subsequent increases in spending by President Johnson during the Vietnam era. We now consider the effects of an increase in the money supply itself.

22.3 Monetary Policy and the Degree of Capital Mobility Under Fixed Rates

Figures 22.3(a), (b), and (c) again illustrate the cases of zero, low, and high capital mobility, respectively. From the initial equilibrium, a monetary expansion shifts the LM curve to the right. The effects of the increase in the money supply on the interest rate and income are precisely the same in each of the three cases. The interest rate, i, falls, stimulating spending and raising income, Y, to the new intersection point M. In each

FIGURE 22.3

Monetary Expansion Under Fixed Exchange Rates

(a) Regardless of the degree of capital mobility, a monetary expansion shifts the *LM* curve out, lowering *i* and raising *Y* at *M*, and worsening the *TB*. (b) With low capital mobility, an outflow through the *KA* supplements the trade deficit, so that the overall *BP* deficit and speed of reserve outflow are greater. (c) With high capital mobility, the speed of reserve outflow is greater still.

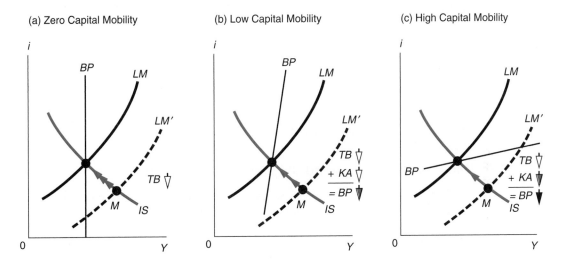

case, higher income means higher imports and a trade deficit. However, the presence of international capital mobility has implications for the balance of payments. This time there is a capital outflow, resulting from the fact that *i* has fallen below the foreign rate, *i**. Because the capital account moves in the same direction as the trade balance, the overall balance of payments is in deficit in each of the three cases. Because the lower interest rate causes larger capital outflows at higher degrees of capital mobility, the overall balance of payments must deteriorate by more in case (b) than in case (a), and by more in case (c) than in case (b).

If a country is running a balance-of-payments deficit, as in Figure 22.3(a), (b), and (c), it is losing foreign exchange reserves continuously over time. Because it has only a certain level of reserves, it cannot continue to do this indefinitely. Eventually, it must adjust. One way would be deliberately reversing the monetary expansion. Yet there is also the possibility of automatic adjustment of the money supply through the balance-of-payments deficit if the central bank does not sterilize reserve outflows. We consider nonsterilized reserve flows momentarily.

A final way to adjust is to let the exchange rate change. A deliberate devaluation would stimulate net exports and shift the *BP* curve to the right. The automatic version of this mechanism of adjustment is to *allow* the currency to depreciate on the foreign exchange market, when the central bank follows a rule of not intervening, as we will see in our discussion of floating exchange rates.

So far in this chapter, capital mobility has affected only the balance of payments, not income. However, under either of these two possible (automatic) mechanisms of adjustment—reserve flows or exchange rate changes—the changes in the balance of payments already derived will, in turn, have implications for the level of income.

22.4   When Money Flows Are Not Sterilized

If the central bank does choose to sterilize reserve flows, the economy can remain at point *M* in Figure 22.3 or at point *G* in Figure 22.2 as long as the stock of reserves holds out. Now, however, the analysis adopts the assumption of the monetary approach to the balance of payments: Changes in the level of reserves are not sterilized and thus are allowed to be reflected one for one as changes in the level of the total money supply. The preceding analysis still explains what happens to income and the interest rate in the short run, but now it is necessary to trace the implications of the money flow over time.

Monetary Expansion and the Capital-Account Offset

We begin by picking up the experiment where the central bank undertakes a deliberate increase in domestic credit. The combination of a lower interest rate and higher level of income at point *M* is only a short-run equilibrium. Even without any capital mobility, as in Figure 22.3(a), the trade deficit at point *M* in itself implies that reserves are flowing out of the country over time. If the central bank does not choose to sterilize this loss in reserves, then the money supply is decreasing, which means the *LM* curve is shifting back to the left over time. The sequence of intersections back along the *IS* curve is shown by the arrows in Figure 22.3(a). They bring to mind the principle illustrated in Figure 19.1 where the monetary approach to the balance of payments was first encountered. As the money supply falls, the interest rate rises, discouraging business investment and other interest-sensitive components of spending. This process continues as long as the balance of payments is still in deficit. In the long run, the economy is back where it started. The entire increase in the money supply has flowed out through the balance of payments, leaving no permanent effect on income.

The story is similar when we add some degree of capital mobility as in Figure 22.3(b). Because the lower interest rate induces a deficit on the capital account as well, the overall balance of payments at point *M* is in greater deficit than it was in the absence of capital mobility. As in the case without capital mobility, if the central bank opts not to sterilize the reserve outflow, then the economy follows the sequence of arrows until in the long run it is back where it started, with no effects. Is this case then identical to the case illustrated in Figure 22.3(a)? The two graphs look quite similar, but there is a difference. Because the balance-of-payments deficit is greater in the case of capital mobility illustrated in Figure 22.3(b), the rate at which the money supply decreases over time is greater, and therefore the economy returns to its starting point more rapidly.

The case of high capital mobility, illustrated in Figure 22.3(c), proceeds in the same way. The balance-of-payments deficit at point *M* means that the addition to the money supply is flowing out of the country over time. In the long run the economy is again back where it started. What difference does the higher degree of capital mobility make? Because the capital outflow is greater for the same differential in interest rates, the rate of reserve loss is even greater in Figure 22.3(c) than in Figure 22.3(b), and so the return to the long-run equilibrium will be that much faster. The speed with which increases in domestic credit flow out through the capital account is called the speed of *offset*.

Fiscal Expansion and Capital Mobility

We now turn from the experiment where the government undertakes a deliberate monetary expansion to the experiment where it undertakes a deliberate fiscal expansion, such as an increase in government expenditure. Figure 22.2 showed an outward shift in the *IS* curve and an increase in income. Recall that the higher level of income resulted in a trade deficit, just as in the monetary expansion.

When a fiscal expansion results in a balance-of-payments deficit, the money supply will gradually decrease over time if the central bank does not sterilize the reserve outflow. The declining money supply will shift the *LM* curve leftward and the interest rate will rise. We now move up the new *IS* curve (*IS'*) in a sequence of *IS-LM* intersections, with interest-sensitive expenditures declining. As expenditure declines, the trade balance improves. This process continues until the economy has returned to a zero balance of payments. Only then are we in long-run equilibrium, because only then is the money supply no longer changing. The arrow in Figure 22.2(a) shows this process for the case of zero capital mobility and reminds us of the lesson learned from Figure 19.B.1: In the long run (point *L*), the fiscal expansion is completely offset by the outflow of money and there is no effect on the level of output. In the case of low capital mobility illustrated in Figure 22.2(b), the balance-of-payments deficit that exists at point *G* again means that reserves will be flowing out over time and that under the nonsterilization assumption the money supply and level of income will be declining over time. In this case, however, the long-run equilibrium at point *L* features a level of income that, although below the short-run level at point *G*, is still somewhat higher than before the fiscal expansion.

What about the case of high capital mobility, illustrated in Figure 22.2(c)? We have already seen that the short-run equilibrium at point *G* is a point of balance-of-payments surplus, rather than deficit. The capital inflow is more than enough to offset the trade deficit. This represents a qualitative departure from the other five cases illustrated. It means that the stock of international reserves is increasing over time, not decreasing. If the central bank opts not to sterilize, but rather allows the total money supply to increase over time, then the *LM* curve will again shift, but to the *right* this time. From point *G*, the economy moves to the right along the *IS'* curve, with the higher money supply driving down the interest rate and stimulating spending. The long-run equilibrium occurs at *L*, where the capital inflow is no more than is needed to finance the trade deficit. Unlike the case with low capital mobility, the level of income in the long run is not just higher than it was before the fiscal expansion, it is also higher than in the short run.

Are Capital Flows and Money Flows the Same Thing?

It is appropriate here to note a pitfall that may be encountered when analyzing international money flows. A capital inflow, such as that resulting from the increase in interest rates shown in Figure 22.2, is sometimes referred to as an "inflow of money." This is permissible terminology because foreign residents are usually paying for the stocks and bonds they buy with money. However, it is important to realize that at the same time that money is "flowing in" through the capital account, it may be "flowing out" through the trade account. It takes money to buy goods, just as it takes money to buy securities. Money is only truly flowing in, on net, if the total balance of payments is in surplus—that is, both the trade account and the capital account—as in the short-run equilibrium at point G in Figure 22.2(c). Even then, the total money supply does not increase unless the central bank allows it to, by refraining from sterilizing the inflow. It is probably safest to avoid altogether using the term *inflow of money* to describe an inflow of capital. Then there will be no danger of confusing it with a change in the money supply. There are many other more suitable synonyms for capital inflow to choose from (borrowing from abroad, foreign financing, foreign investment in the domestic country, decrease in the net international investment position, foreign purchases of domestic assets, etc.).

As we have seen repeatedly, under the monetary approach to the balance of payments, the overall balance is zero in the long run. At point L in Figure 22.2, however, there must be a continuing capital inflow because the domestic interest rate remains above the world interest rate. "Money" is flowing in through the capital account at precisely the same rate as it is flowing out through the current account. Another implication is that in the long run all three curves intersect (at the same point L), not just the *IS* and *LM* curves.

22.5   Other Automatic Mechanisms of Adjustment

Within the context of the monetary approach to the balance of payments, the findings of Figure 22.2(b) and (c) are unfamiliar. As a general rule, it is expected that in the long run, when the economy has had enough time to adjust to a change in macroeconomic policy, there are no real effects left. Yet it has just been shown that under conditions of capital mobility, a fiscal expansion seems to have a permanent effect on real output. It is clear why some effect on output can remain even in the long run in this model: The only automatic mechanism of adjustment is the flow of money through the balance of payments, which is shut off at point L. However, there are other automatic mechanisms of adjustment that have been omitted here.

One is the adjustment of the price level over time in response to an excess demand for goods and labor. Inflationary pressure may exist at points like G in Figure 22.2 or M in Figure 22.3, assuming that the starting point before the fiscal or monetary expansion was near the point at which the economy was at potential output and full employment. Chapter 19 showed that an increase in the price level reduces the real money supply, which works to discourage expenditure and return the economy to its long-run equilibrium. Chapter 26 will add the gradual adjustment of goods prices to the model of this chapter.

Another possible automatic mechanism of adjustment omitted here is changes in the stock of bonds. This point is particularly relevant in Figure 22.2(b) and 22.2(c). At point *L* the government is still running a budget deficit and—as a consequence—the country is still running a current-account deficit, even though the capital inflow is large enough to finance these deficits. When the government runs a budget deficit, the supply of government bonds in the hands of the public increases over time, assuming that the deficit is not monetized (i.e., assuming that the bonds are not bought by the central bank—which they are not, under the assumption that the central bank is holding the money supply constant). Analogously, when the country runs a current-account deficit, the supply of foreign bonds in the hands of the public decreases over time. In other words, the public borrows, or runs down the asset position vis-à-vis foreigners that it has accumulated in the past, to pay for its trade deficit.

The *stock* of bonds (i.e., the accumulated *level* of bonds issued, as opposed to the *flow*, i.e., the deficits), either domestic or foreign, has no role to play in the model developed in this chapter. However, there are possible effects left out of the model. For example, holdings of bonds, along with money and other assets, are a component of the *wealth* or *net worth* of households and thus have an effect on the level of spending. If spending declines at point *L* in Figure 22.2(c) because households are running down their holdings of foreign bonds at the rate of the current-account deficit, then the *IS* curve will shift back to the left, just as it does when there is any exogenous fall in domestic spending. The process may continue until the current account is back to zero and the stock of bonds back to where it started. There is an analogy with the monetary approach to the balance of payments, in which the adjustment process continues until the overall balance of payments is back to zero and the money supply is back to where it started. This added possible mechanism of adjustment will not be pursued here. The discussion, rather, is based on the model in which changes in the stock of bonds have no effect, so that it does not matter whether it is changing over time or not.[4]

22.6   The Pursuit of Internal and External Balance

The last section of Chapter 18 introduced a fundamental principle of policy-making: To attain the two independent policy targets of internal balance (output equal to a desired level) and external balance (the trade balance at a desired level), at least two independent policy instruments are required. In Chapter 18 the two policy instruments were spending and the exchange rate. In this chapter we have been keeping the exchange rate fixed, ruling out one of the instruments. (Chapter 23 will return to the case of flexible exchange rates.) A new policy instrument, the money supply, has been

---

[4]These effects are modeled in the portfolio-balance approach. One statement of the approach under fixed exchange rates is Lance Girton and Dale Henderson, "Financial Capital Movements and Central Bank Behavior in the Two-Country Short-Run Portfolio-Balance Model," *Journal of Monetary Economics* (1976): 33–61. Chapter 28 will explain the portfolio-balance approach in the context of floating exchange rates.

FIGURE 22.4

External and Internal
Balance

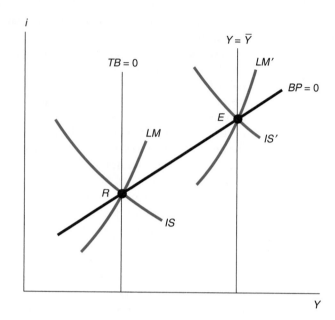

added, however, since the issue was last considered. Monetary and fiscal policy are each thought of as domestic policy instruments. Will the two, used together, nevertheless allow the two targets of external and internal balance to be attained simultaneously? The answer turns out to be yes, but only because the model now allows for international capital movements.[5]

Figure 22.4 repeats the earlier depiction of the Mundell-Fleming model under fixed exchange rates but emphasizes the government's objectives more explicitly. The vertical line labeled $TB = 0$ marks the unique level of income that corresponds to a trade balance of zero, a possible interpretation of the external balance objective. This level of income, however, is incompatible with another objective in this illustration, internal balance. The vertical line labeled $Y = \overline{Y}$ marks the level of income that corresponds to potential output and the natural rate of unemployment. Any point further to the right is assumed to be undesirable because the excess demand for goods leads to inflationary pressures. (Workers are working overtime and demand higher wages; bottlenecks in factory capacity and supplies of inputs lead suppliers to charge higher prices.) Any point to the left of $Y = \overline{Y}$, such as point R, is undesirable because it represents high unemployment and idle factories. There is no way to use our two policy instruments to attain both objectives simultaneously: The two vertical lines don't intersect.

Consider now what happens if the external balance objective is defined as an overall balance of payments equal to zero, rather than a trade balance of zero. Then we are

[5]This section, and especially the elaboration in the appendix, is based on R. A. Mundell, "The Appropriate Use of Monetary and Fiscal Policy Under Fixed Exchange Rates," *IMF Staff Papers,* 9 (March 1962): 70–77. Mundell (a native Canadian) had in mind particularly the example of policy-making in Canada. Capital mobility became crucial for Canada because of the high degree of integration with the United States, earlier than for many other countries.

happy to run a trade deficit, so long as it is offset by a surplus on the capital account. There exists a particular combination of monetary and fiscal expansion, shifting the economy from the *IS-LM* intersection of point R to the intersection of *IS'* and *LM'* at point E, that gives us both internal and external balance. Notice that point E lies on $Y = \overline{Y}$, and so is a point of internal balance. At the same time, it lies on the $BP = 0$ schedule, which Section 22.1 showed to be upward sloping. Intuitively, even though the higher income implies higher imports and therefore a trade deficit at point E, *the interest rate is also higher, implying a capital inflow.* If the capital inflow is large enough to finance the trade deficit, the overall balance of payments is zero. This is the case at point E. Both objectives are attained. In practice, of course, such a carefully calculated combination of policies may be difficult to attain.

Difficulties of Policy-Making

The model and diagrams discussed so far make it sound as if policy-making should be perfectly easy. The government simply ascertains where the economy lies relative to internal and external balance, calculates how much it needs to move the monetary and fiscal policy levers to restore equilibrium, and proceeds. Is it possible that policy-making is this easy in practice?

Four problems make policy-making much more difficult than this. First, there are considerable *lags* between the time a policy instrument is changed and the time the economy responds. Chapter 16 considered a major lag, between an exchange rate change and its effect on the trade balance: the J-curve. There are also important lags between the time that monetary or fiscal policy is changed and the time that households and firms fully adjust their plans for consumer spending and business investment.

If lags were the only problem, it would not be so difficult to select the appropriate policies. The policy makers would simply need to plan ahead so that their policy changes would have the desired effects at the right time. However, the process is complicated enormously by the existence of *uncertainty*. There are three kinds of uncertainty: (1) uncertainty about the current position of the economy relative to the "full employment" level of output and the desired external balance; (2) uncertainty about future disturbances or "shocks" (such as sudden shifts in the demand for money or in private spending); and (3) uncertainty about the correct model (such as the correct value of the marginal propensities to save and import, the slope of the *LM* curve, and other parameters). Any of these three forms of uncertainty can lead to policy errors.

In the 1970s, for example, policy makers saw the United States and the world as being at levels of income substantially below full employment, and therefore they decided to use both fiscal and monetary policy to expand. The expansion began with a tax cut by the Ford administration in 1975 and was continued by the Carter administration from 1977 to 1979. Inflation reached double digits by the end of the decade and—in retrospect—the expansion is considered to have been excessive. One way of interpreting the error is that there were unanticipated shifts in some key economic relationships. There was a sizable downward shift in the demand for money—an outward shift in the *LM* curve—which meant that the planned rate of money growth translated into a higher demand for goods than had been anticipated. In 1979 there was also an unexpected new increase in oil prices associated with the fall of the shah of Iran. (Chapter 26 will examine the effects of such supply shocks.)

The third problem for policy-making is the elusive factor of public *expectations,* particularly as they relate to inflation. If moving into a zone of excess demand caused the inflation rate in the current period to rise but had no further implications thereafter, then policy makers would have the relatively straightforward task of picking the preferred point in their inflation/unemployment trade-off. The internal balance line would be interpreted as the level of demand corresponding to this point, which might not be precisely the same as the level corresponding to full employment. In truth, however, there are future periods to consider as well. The trade-off between output and inflation does not stay put over time, as Chapter 26 will show. If inflation is high this period, then the public—particularly workers—will enter the next period with higher expectations of inflation and higher wage demands, raising the level of inflation (for any given level of output) in the next period. Chapter 26 will show that complications resulting from such expectations, even aside from the problems of lags and uncertainty, offer a reason for policy makers to reduce the frequency with which they adjust their instrument settings in response to new developments in the economy (*fine-tune,* to use a pejorative word). Indeed, some economists believe that government should abandon such discretionary policy-making altogether and instead should follow preset rules for monetary and fiscal policy.

The fourth difficulty for policy makers is that even if a politician or economist feels confident of exactly what policy changes should be made, in practice there are always formidable political constraints that must be overcome before enacting any changes. The government is not a unified, rational agent. Most politicians give at least some weight to their own selfish interests, and even those who might genuinely have the public welfare at heart will disagree over their interpretation of how to maximize that welfare. Most questions are decided more on the basis of simplistic slogans, bureaucratic turf wars, special interest lobbying, congressional politics, and arbitrary historical precedents, than on the basis of sound economic logic.

22.7 Summary

This chapter began to show the difference that international capital mobility makes in the modern world economy in regard to the important questions of policy-making, particularly the effects of monetary and fiscal policy.

The key new assumption is that a country's capital account depends on the difference between its interest rate and foreign interest rates. We considered fixed exchange rates in this chapter. A monetary expansion leads to a balance-of-payments deficit, a loss in reserves, and consequently a loss over time of any expansionary effects on income as the money flows out of the country. In this case, capital mobility simply speeds up the process as the money flows out not just through the trade account but also through the capital account. Although capital mobility changes the results in one direction in the case of monetary policy (giving it a smaller effect on total GDP over time), it changes it in the opposite direction in the case of fiscal policy (giving it a larger effect over time).

A fiscal expansion causes capital to flow into the country in response to a higher interest rate. If capital mobility is sufficiently high, then the overall balance of payments increases rather than decreases. Over time, reserves are gained rather than lost.

Capital mobility will make even more of a difference under floating exchange rates. We turn to this case in the next chapter.

CHAPTER PROBLEMS

1. A country that maintains a fixed exchange rate suffers from unemployment and a balance-of-payments deficit. What combination of G and i is appropriate? (See Appendix.)

2. For this question, it will help to use linearized versions of Equations 22.2 and 22.3:

$$Y = (\overline{A} - bi + \overline{X} - \overline{M})/(s + m)$$

$$M/P = KY - hi$$

The appendix presents an economic argument as to why the YY schedule must be steeper than the BB schedule, as long as the degree of capital mobility, k, is greater than zero. The slope of the YY line is given by the increase in Y resulting from a fiscal expansion, divided by the increase in Y given by a monetary expansion. The slope of the BB line is given by the decrease in BP resulting from a fiscal expansion, divided by the decrease in BP resulting from a monetary expansion. Show that the ratio of the two slopes is greater than 1.

SUGGESTIONS FOR FURTHER READING

Mundell, Robert. "The International Disequilibrium System," *Kyklos*, 14 (1961): 154–227. The original model under fixed exchange rates, including the role of non-sterilized reserve flows.

Swoboda, Alexander. "Equilibrium, Quasi-Equilibrium and Macroeconomic Policy Under Fixed Exchange Rates," *Quarterly Journal of Economics* (February 1972): 162–171. A clear early explanation of the Mundell-Fleming model, emphasizing the adjustment to reserve flows over time.

APPENDIX

Zones of Internal and External Balance

To study further the problem of internal and external balance from the viewpoint of the government policy maker, we view the same model with a different graph than was used in Section 22.6. In Figure 22.4, changes in fiscal or monetary policy showed up as

FIGURE 22.A.1

External and Internal Balance

The *YY* schedule shows internal balance (*Y* at full employment). It slopes upward because an increase in *G* would cause excess demand for goods at *B* (which is inflationary), which would require that the monetary authority raise *i* to eliminate the excess demand at *C*. However, the *BB* schedule is not as steep as the *YY* schedule when an increase in *i* has the added effect of attracting a capital inflow.

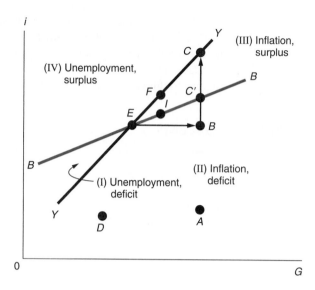

shifts of the *IS* or *LM* curves. Figure 22.A.1, however, shows the two policy instruments directly on the axes. Here the level of government expenditure, *G*, appears on the horizontal axis. The interest rate, *i*, the instrument of monetary policy, appears on the vertical axis.

Why do we put the interest rate on the vertical axis instead of the money supply? In the absence of exogenous shifts in money demand, it makes no difference which we choose: When the central bank sets a money supply, it implicitly determines the interest rate as well. Here we use the interest rate for the policy instrument, so that the implications for international capital flows can readily be seen.[6] Furthermore, innovations in banking, such as payment of interest on checking accounts, have blurred the distinction between money and other assets. Consequently, the money supply is no longer considered the superior measure of monetary policy that it was at the beginning of the 1980s. It has once again become standard to focus on the interest rate as the instrument of monetary policy.

We use Figure 22.A.1 to see the combinations of the two policy instruments consistent with the targets. Assume that internal balance and external balance both hold at the starting point, *E*. Consider an increase in government expenditure, *G*, a rightward movement from point *E*. Figure 22.2 showed that such a fiscal expansion affects both policy targets. It raises income and, as a result, raises imports and worsens the trade balance. (The discussion here is concerned only with the short-run equilibrium at point *G* in Figure 22.2. Endogenous effects of reserve flows on the money supply are not under consideration for the moment because the focus is deliberate changes in monetary and fiscal policy.)

---

[6]Also because this is the way Robert Mundell did it originally.

Consider first external balance. At point B the increase in government spending has moved the trade balance into deficit. To eliminate the balance-of-payments deficit resulting from the trade deficit, the government must generate a surplus on the capital account. It can do this by following a contractionary monetary policy. The higher interest rate for any given level of income will attract a capital inflow into the country. This policy mix, a fiscal expansion with monetary policy kept sufficiently tight to allow interest rates to rise, describes well the United States expansion in the years 1981 to 1984. The predicted result emerged: a large trade deficit, financed by large-scale borrowing from abroad attracted by high interest rates.

If the interest rate rises far enough, the surplus in the capital account will be sufficient to offset the deficit in the current account and the overall balance of payments will be restored to zero. In terms of Figure 22.A.1, if the increase in G (a rightward movement) is accompanied by a sufficiently large increase in i (an upward movement), then overall external balance will be maintained at point C'. Thus the set of combinations of G and i that give external balance constitutes an upward-sloping relationship, which is labeled the BB curve. There is no reason necessarily to be on the BB curve because there is no reason why the balance of payments must necessarily be zero. Indeed, the advantage of the graph is that it shows where the economy is *relative* to the policy goals. Any point below and to the right of the BB schedule is a point of balance-of-payments deficit because policy is expansionary. One way of thinking of it is that the capital-account balance is low because the interest rate is low. The other way of thinking of it is that the current-account balance is low because income is high. Any point above and to the left of the schedule is a point of balance-of-payments surplus because policy is tight. The capital-account balance is high because the interest rate is high, or the current-account balance is high because income is low.

Now consider internal balance. When the government increases G, income goes up. Thus the rightward movement from point E to point B in Figure 22.A.1 causes a move into the zone of excess demand, where the level of income exceeds the full-employment level and creates inflationary pressure. If the government is to restore internal balance, it must undertake a monetary contraction, raising the interest rate to dampen demand. If the interest rate is increased by enough, it will restore income back to the full-employment level. In terms of the graph, if the increase in G is accompanied by a sufficiently large increase in i, to a point like C, then internal balance is maintained. Thus the set of combinations of G and i providing internal balance constitute another upward-sloping relationship, which is labeled the YY curve. Again, there is not necessarily any reason to be on the YY curve because in the absence of instantaneous flexibility in wages and prices there is no reason why output should necessarily be at the full-employment level. Any point below or to the right of the YY schedule is a point of excess demand. Any point above and to the left is a point of excess supply.

What determines the relative slope of these two upward-sloping curves? It might seem, reasoning from the BP curve in the earlier graphs, that the answer to this question depends on the degree of capital mobility. It is true that the higher the degree of capital mobility, the flatter the slope of the BB curve because if k is higher, then it takes a smaller increase in i to attract the necessary capital inflow to finance any given trade deficit. However, it turns out that even if the degree of capital mobility is relatively low, so that the BB curve is relatively steep, it cannot be any steeper than the YY curve. To see this, consider the movement from point E to point C, a simultaneous fiscal expansion and monetary contraction calculated to leave income unchanged at the full-employment level. Is point C a point of balance-of-payments surplus or deficit? There is no reason for the trade balance to have changed, as income is unchanged, but because the interest rate is higher, there is a capital inflow that puts the balance of payments in surplus. Only points above and to the left of the BB schedule are points of surplus. Therefore C must be above the BB schedule, which implies that the YY schedule is steeper.

This logic applies whatever the degree of capital mobility k, so long as it is greater than zero. In the event that k is zero, the balance of payments is no higher at C than at C' or E. In this case the BB curve has the same slope as the YY curve. This is a return to the situation of no capital mobility, as in Chapter 18, in which case monetary and fiscal policy are not *independent* policy instruments. Monetary policy has no extra effect on the balance of payments beyond the same effect that fiscal policy has via income and imports. In general, C lies above C' because the interest rate has an effect on the capital account above and beyond its effect on the trade balance.

Combinations of Monetary and Fiscal Policy

Figure 22.A.1 is divided into four zones. In zone I there is a payments deficit and excess supply (unemployment), in zone II a deficit and excess demand (inflation), in zone III a payments surplus and excess demand, and in zone IV a surplus and excess supply. There is only one point of full equilibrium, E. Both policy tools are needed to attain it.

We can draw conclusions about the proper direction of change in the policy instruments from Figure 22.A.1. Point A lies in zone II. A deficit and inflationary pressure call for both a contraction of public spending and a rise in the interest rate. The same problems at point B, however, would be solved by a policy of fiscal contraction alone; monetary policy is already tight enough to secure overall balance once the appropriate change in fiscal policy is made. At point C' external balance and inflationary pressure coexist. Fiscal policy must be tightened but monetary policy eased somewhat, to keep the contraction from throwing the balance of payments into surplus as inflationary pressures abate. At point D, however, a monetary contraction must be associated with fiscal expansion to secure a relatively large improvement in the balance of payments while removing only a relatively small amount of inflationary pressure. In zone II, and in zone IV as well, the proper direction of change for both instruments depends on the relative sizes of the internal and external disequilibria.

Conversely, in zone I it is possible to tell unambiguously the right direction of change for both instruments. In zone I unemployment and payments deficit are always fought by expansionary fiscal policy coupled with a tightening of monetary policy. The rising interest rate combats the restoration of full employment but does less harm there than the good it does in eliminating the payments deficit, and the interest rate at any point in zone I is lower than it must be if balance is secured at point E. The corresponding statements apply to zone III.

Were monetary and fiscal policy used as independent instruments during the era of fixed exchange rates in the way that this analysis suggests is possible? In the late 1950s and early 1960s, the United States suffered from unemployment combined with an external deficit (zone I). Some economists urged, on the basis of these theoretical considerations, that fiscal policy should be eased and monetary policy tightened. Indeed, taxes were cut by the Kennedy administration to pull the country out of recession, and for some time an attempt was made to allow short-term interest rates to rise to attract capital from abroad. Yet for the most part, U.S. fiscal and monetary policy moved in the same direction—either relaxed together or tightened together—in the 1950s, 1960s, and 1970s. The first time fiscal and monetary policy went strongly in opposite directions was the 1980s. We will elaborate on this episode in the next chapter.

The Assignment Problem

Governments sometimes deal with the diversity of information and goals within the policy-making arena by decentralizing, parceling out responsibility for various policy targets to different agencies. One agency might be put in charge of trade policy, for example. The danger is that agencies might find themselves working at cross-purposes. In such a situation each views the other as representing the sort of political obstacles to successful policy-making noted toward the end of the chapter.

We now examine a very stylized (simplified) version of decentralization. The two agencies to be examined, the central bank and the treasury, possess the tools of monetary policy (either the interest rate or the money supply) and fiscal policy (either government spending or tax rates), respectively. This analysis will show that internal and external balance (point E in Figure 22.A.1) can be reached if policy makers act independently and without direct coordination. However, just which responsibility goes to which authority turns out to be important. That is, one policy goal can be assigned to each authority, as long as the assignments are made correctly. This is the same problem examined in Chapter 18, only now the two instruments are fiscal and monetary policy, whereas there they were fiscal policy and the exchange rate.

Suppose, arbitrarily, that government policy makers tell the central bank to pursue external balance. It follows the rule: Lower the interest rate when there is an external surplus; raise it when there is a deficit. To the treasury, responsible for fiscal policy, goes the instruction: Raise government spending when there is unemployment; cut it when there is inflationary pressure. Suppose that the country finds itself with the combination of deficit and potential inflation indicated by A. The central bank acts first, leaping into action by raising the interest rate so as to attain external balance at C'. That step mitigates inflationary pressure but does not eliminate it. The treasury therefore cuts government spending, bringing the economy to point F in Figure 22.A.1. The central bank now finds it must back off, as a surplus emerges, and lower the interest rate a bit at point I. Because inflation is revived by the interest rate cut, the treasury keeps cutting government spending. Their separate actions are pulling the economy toward internal and external balance at E. This policy assignment appears to work.

Suppose the policy makers had made the opposite assignment, telling the central bank to look after internal balance and the treasury to mind external balance. Start again from A, indicating inflation and an external deficit. The central bank girds itself to fight inflation, raising the interest rate and bringing the system to C on the YY schedule. What the treasury now observes, however, is not the initial deficit, but an external surplus, which it attacks by *raising* government expenditure. Here is the problem. If the treasury seeks external balance, the system reaches a point on BB directly east of C. Inflation is again unleashed, and the central bank hastens to raise the interest rate further. The point indicating the economy's actual state, rather than approaching E, proceeds northeast in zone III. Thus it moves away from equilibrium, until some higher authority realizes that something is amiss and changes the policy assignments. What this example indicates is a quite general conclusion: Assigning each target to a single policy instrument can work, but the assignment must be right. The right assignment is determined by a rule of comparative advantage: *Give each target to the authority whose instrument has the relatively greater influence on it.* Figure 22.A.1 shows that monetary policy's comparative advantage under a fixed exchange rate lies in pursuing external balance. That is the whole reason why BB is flatter than YY. Chapter 19's Appendix B referred to the general rule as Mundell's principle of effective market classification.[7]

---

[7]As we see in Chapter 23, monetary and fiscal policy have very different effects under floating exchange rates than under fixed rates. One implication is that the correct answer to the assignment problem is probably reversed. When exchange rate effects are taken into account, fiscal policy has a greater effect on the trade balance and monetary policy a smaller effect, so that fiscal policy should be assigned to external balance and monetary policy to internal balance. James Boughton, "Policy Assignment Strategies with Somewhat Flexible Exchange Rates," in B. Eichengreen, M. Miller, and R. Portes, eds., *Exchange Rate Regimes and Macroeconomic Policy* (London: Academic Press, 1989).

CHAPTER 23

Fiscal and Monetary Policy Under Modern Financial Market Conditions

Two key macroeconomic aspects of modern international financial markets are the market determination of exchange rates among the major countries and high capital mobility. The first half of this chapter traces the implications of progressively higher degrees of capital mobility for a regime of freely floating exchange rates. The second half considers the extreme case of perfect capital mobility, thus reaching the logical extreme of the progression of cases considered earlier.

Equilibrium at a given exchange rate often entails a balance-of-payments surplus or deficit, but such disequilibria will eventually have to be corrected, if not by a deliberate change in government policy, then by an automatic mechanism of adjustment. In particular, if a country is running a balance-of-payments deficit, the central bank is losing reserves and will eventually have to allow the money supply to fall if it wishes to remain on a fixed exchange rate. We explored in Chapter 22 the implications of allowing money to flow out through the balance of payments. The alternative possibility is that instead of abandoning the money supply that it had previously set, the central bank abandons the exchange rate. In other words, the central bank can allow the currency to depreciate until the balance-of-payments deficit is eliminated. This will happen automatically if the country is on a floating exchange rate regime to begin with, as are the United States and most large industrialized countries.[1]

What makes this analysis different from that in Section 18.1, where we first examined floating rates? We have now introduced capital mobility. In Chapter 22 we saw how capital mobility means that changes in the interest rate have implications for the capital account and therefore for the balance of payments. If the central bank follows a regime of sterilized intervention to keep both the exchange rate and money supply constant, then there are no further immediate implications for the level of income. However, the change in the balance of payments will itself have implications for the level of income, when either the money supply is allowed to change (as in the monetary approach to the balance of payments, previously considered) or when the exchange

---

[1] A majority of continental European countries irrevocably fixed their exchange rates vis-à-vis each other in the European monetary union of 1999. As a unit they float against the dollar, yen, and Canadian dollar. Nonetheless, the floating rate model can be used to study changes in monetary or fiscal policy that the European countries all enact *jointly*. Other floating currencies include the Swiss franc, the pound, the Australian dollar, the Mexican peso, the Brazilian real, and the Chilean peso.

rate is allowed to change (as under floating exchange rates, to be considered now). In each case, the effect on the balance of payments derived at a given exchange rate holds the key to the effect on income under floating rates.

When the exchange rate is floating and the central bank does not intervene, the overall balance of payments, BP, is always zero. In algebraic terms, Equation 22.4 must hold continuously. In terms of the graphical apparatus derived previously, the economy must always be on the BP schedule. If a shock threatens to cause a move off it, the exchange rate will adjust automatically to shift the curve. As we have already seen, a devaluation, because it stimulates net exports, shifts the BP curve to the right, and a revaluation of the currency shifts it to the left. Under floating rates, whenever the economy is at a position that threatens to lie off the BP curve, the currency will instantly depreciate or appreciate to the degree necessary to eliminate the gap.

Recall that, although the balance of payments is always zero, this does not mean that the trade balance is necessarily zero. At any point in the upper part of the BP curve, the interest rate is attracting a capital inflow that is financing a trade deficit. In the lower part of the curve, there is a capital outflow offsetting a trade surplus.

23.1   Fiscal Policy Under Floating: An Effect Mitigated by Capital Mobility

We now consider a fiscal expansion, such as an increase in government expenditures or a cut in taxes. We begin with the case of no capital movements and then progress to higher degrees of capital mobility, just as in the case of fixed exchange rates.

We saw in Figure 22.2(a) that the fiscal expansion shifts the IS curve out and raises income.[2] The higher level of imports produces a balance-of-payments deficit. This is point A in Figure 23.1(a). A situation that under fixed exchange rates produces a balance-of-payments deficit, under floating exchange rates automatically produces a depreciation of the currency. The depreciation stimulates the $\overline{X} - \overline{M}$ component of the trade balance, which we know causes both the BP curve (Equation 22.5) and the IS curve (Equation 22.2) to shift to the right. We also know that depreciation shifts the BP curve to the right faster than the IS curve. This is fortunate because, on the one hand, the economy is always at the intersection of the IS and LM curves and, on the other hand, the balance of payments will remain in deficit and the currency will have to keep depreciating as long as the economy is to the right of the BP curve. Eventually the depreciation will have shifted the BP curve sufficiently far to the right that it will catch up with the IS-LM intersection. Then all three curves will intersect at the same place, point B in Figure 23.1(a). Only there will the balance of payments be zero, as it must be under floating.

Because of the additional stimulus from depreciation, the fiscal expansion raises income by a greater amount under floating than under fixed exchange rates (B lies to the right of A). This is the same result obtained in Section 18.1 before the effect of the

---

[2]Recall from Chapter 18 that the increase in income at A is equal to the simple open economy multiplier, $\Delta \overline{G}/(s + m)$, minus an allowance for crowding-out of investment by the higher interest rate.

FIGURE 23.1

Fiscal Expansion Under Floating Exchange Rates

A fiscal expansion shifts the *IS* curve to *IS'*, raising *Y* and *i* to *A*. (a) Without capital mobility, the trade deficit at *A* requires a depreciation, which stimulates net exports and thus further raises *Y* to *B*. (b) With low capital mobility, the balance-of-payments deficit is smaller at *A*, so the required depreciation and the further stimulus to *Y* at *B* are smaller. (c) With high capital mobility, the balance-of-payments is in surplus at *A*, so a small appreciation is required, which discourages net exports; thus the increase in *Y* at *B* is smaller than in the earlier cases.

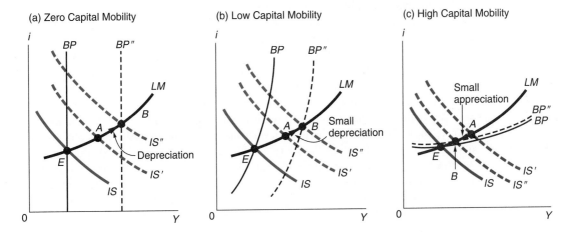

interest rate on expenditure was introduced. It was described then as the result of floating exchange rates "bottling up" disturbances so that their full effect is felt in the country of origin.[3]

What changes with the introduction of capital mobility? As Figure 23.1(b) shows, the higher interest rate now attracts a capital inflow. There is an improvement in the capital account that partially offsets the deterioration in the trade balance. If the degree of capital mobility is relatively low, the net effect is still to worsen the overall balance of payments at a given exchange rate. Thus the effect under floating rates is again to depreciate the currency. The resulting stimulus to net exports again shifts both the *BP* and *IS* curves rightward until the *BP* curve catches up and all three curves intersect at the same point. Figure 23.1(b) shows this as a movement from *A* to *B*. As in Figure 23.1(a), the stimulus to income is greater under floating than under fixed rates. Introducing capital mobility, however, has made a difference. The capital inflow means that the potential balance-of-payments deficit that would exist if the exchange rate were to remain unchanged is smaller, and so the size of the needed depreciation is

---

[3]The effect on income is given by $\Delta \overline{G}/s$, minus an allowance for crowding-out by the higher interest rate, the same as it would be in a closed economy. A comparison with the preceding footnote shows that the effect is greater under floating rates. In the event of a liquidity trap, so that the *LM* curve is flat, income increases by the full amount of the rightward shift of the *IS* curve: $\Delta \overline{G}/(s + m)$ in the case of fixed rates, and $\Delta \overline{G}/s$ in the case of floating rates. The same would be true if the central bank were to follow a monetary policy of automatically accommodating changes in fiscal policy in such a way as to keep the interest rate unchanged.

smaller. Thus the rightward shift and the additional stimulus to output are not as great in Figure 23.1(b) as in 23.1(a).

With higher degrees of capital mobility comes the loss of *all* additional stimulus from floating rates. To see why, recall that under conditions of high capital mobility, the improvement of the capital account was more than enough to offset the deterioration of the trade balance. This lesson from Figure 22.2(c) is represented by point *A* in Figure 23.1(c). Under fixed exchange rates, the overall balance of payments actually went into surplus. This means that under floating exchange rates, the currency will *appreciate* to clear the balance of payments, not depreciate. The effect is to discourage net exports rather than to encourage them. The *BP* and *IS* curves shift left rather than right. The curves keep shifting until the *BP* schedule catches up with the *IS-LM* intersection and all three curves meet at a point, such as *B*, in Figure 23.1(c). The fiscal expansion has still increased income. However, the increase in income is not only less than it was under floating rates with no capital mobility, it is also less than it was under fixed exchange rates—because the foreign sector now enters negatively rather than positively.[4]

The finding is thus that under a regime of floating exchange rates capital mobility reduces the effectiveness of fiscal policy. This is exactly the opposite to that of the case under a regime of fixed exchange rates. We saw in our discussion of the monetary approach to the balance of payments that the higher the degree of capital mobility, the faster money comes into the country through the balance of payments to augment the effect of the fiscal expansion on income. Although capital mobility undermines fiscal policy under floating, it augments fiscal policy under fixed rates.

At *B* the economy is running a continuing trade deficit, financed by the capital inflow attracted by the higher interest rate. This is an equilibrium situation. There is no automatic monetary mechanism of adjustment because under floating exchange rates there are no changes in reserves, and so the question of whether the central bank sterilizes never even arises. (As much money flows in through the capital-account surplus as flows out through the current-account deficit.)

Effects of U.S. Budget Deficits in Recent Decades

The perfect illustration of this model is the great U.S. fiscal expansion undertaken by the Reagan administration in the form of its 1981–1983 tax cuts and simultaneous increases in defense spending. Between 1980 and 1985 there was an increase in the structural budget deficit equal to 3 percent of GDP. (Structural means that the increase in the deficit was not due to lower tax receipts arising from a fall in income, as happened in the 1981–1982, 1990–1991, and 2001 recessions.) As mentioned previously, this fiscal expansion was unusual not only in its magnitude but also in that it was not at all

---

[4]How do we know that under conditions of floating rates and high capital mobility the fiscal expansion still has a positive effect on income despite the loss in net exports? That is, how do we know that the three-curve intersection at *B* takes place to the right of starting point *E*? If the currency appreciation were so great that the *IS* curve shifted as far back to the left as *E*, then the balance of payments would pass into deficit because *i* and *Y* would be unchanged, leaving only the negative effect of the appreciation. For the overall balance of payments to be in equilibrium, the appreciation has to stop while there is still some surplus left on the capital account, that is, with *i* higher than at the starting point.

accommodated by monetary policy. The Federal Reserve, having undertaken a commitment in 1979 to restrict monetary growth in order to fight inflation, allowed interest rates to rise sharply. From 1979 to mid-1982, the short-term interest rate rose by 2 percent and the long-term interest rate by 5 percent. Just as the model predicts, the higher interest rates attracted a large capital inflow from abroad and caused a large appreciation of the dollar.

International investors care not only about nominal interest rates in various currencies but also about expectations as to how much the currency is going to be worth in the future. Chapter 27 will add expectations to the model. For now, it is important to realize that a domestic firm's decision whether or not to undertake investment in plant and equipment depends not on the nominal interest rate, but on the *real* interest rate, that is, the interest rate adjusted for expected inflation. Nominal interest rates began to decline in mid-1982 when the Federal Reserve began to ease up slightly on monetary growth. Yet expected inflation was declining more rapidly. In other words, real interest rates remained high after 1982.[5]

Between 1980 and 1984 the dollar appreciated by 58 percent against a weighted average of other currencies.[6] As we saw in the discussion of the J-curve in Chapter 16, a change in the exchange rate actually takes several years to have its effect on net exports. The U.S. trade deficit hit a then-record level in 1983, and it continued to mount steadily thereafter, peaking in 1987. Imports, in particular, increased rapidly. Part of the increase in imports could be explained by the growth in income in those years, but much of it was related to the high value of the dollar making other countries' goods cheaper than U.S. goods. Both the income effect and the exchange rate effect are precisely what is predicted from a fiscal expansion in Figure 23.1(c).

There is a neat way of summing up the effects of a fiscal expansion under modern conditions: In addition to crowding out investment (and other components of expenditure coming from the domestic sector) via higher real interest rates, the fiscal expansion also crowds out net exports (expenditure coming from the international sector) via a higher value of the currency.

The general principle can be seen from the national saving identity derived in Chapter 17:

$$S + T - G \equiv I + CA$$

Private saving, S, plus public saving, $T - G$, is equal to investment in the stock of physical capital, I, plus the accumulation of claims against foreigners through the current-account balance, CA. As a matter of accounting this equation must hold at all times, regardless of how its components are determined and what happens to interest and

---

[5]Real interest rates among other major industrialized countries rose also, but not by as much, on average, as in the United States. Various measures of the long-term real interest *differential* show a peak in 1984 of about 4 percent, as compared to approximately zero in 1980.

[6]This is the appreciation in nominal terms. The appreciation in real terms was 52 percent. (The source is the Federal Reserve Board's index with multilateral trade weights. Consumer price indices (CPIs) are used for the real exchange rate.) The small difference between these numbers means that very little of the change in the exchange rate was offset by changes in the countries' price levels. In other words, the Keynesian assumption appears justified: To analyze the effects of changes in policy, prices can be taken as given in the relatively short run.

exchange rates. Table 17.1 presents the relevant numbers for recent U.S. history. The federal budget, shown in column 4, ran a deficit of about 3 percent of GDP during the 1980s and early 1990s; government saving was negative. The private saving rate (column 1) did not rise. Thus, much of private saving, S, went to finance the budget deficit. Total net national saving (shown in column 5) fell from 9 percent of GDP in the 1970s, to 4 or 5 percent of GDP in the late 1980s and early 1990s.[7] This low level of domestically available funds was not enough to finance investment in plant and equipment, let alone to undertake any net lending overseas.

The national saving identity says that as a simple matter of arithmetic, when there is a fall in national saving, there must be a fall in investment, I, a fall in the current-account balance CA (which is also an increase in borrowing from abroad), or some combination of the two. In a closed economy, all the burden of the crowding-out caused by a fiscal expansion must fall on investment. This principle had some relevance for the United States in earlier decades and has some relevance for some other countries even today. However, as a consequence of the high degree of capital mobility in the United States today, much of the burden of the crowding-out instead falls on net exports. Investment in the late 1980s and early 1990s as a share of GDP was down about 3 percentage points from the level of the 1970s. This means that the 5-point fall in national saving was reflected partly as a fall in investment, but partly as a net capital inflow, as seen in Table 17.1. and Figure 23.2.[8]

A current-account deficit, when viewed from its more flattering profile, is the same thing as a capital inflow. It makes sense that a decision by the government to run a deficit, that is, to borrow—if it is not offset by the actions of domestic residents—is reflected in a deficit for the country as a whole, that is, national borrowing from the rest of the world. In an economic sense, it is as if foreign investors were financing the U.S. budget deficit. This is the famous problem of the *twin deficits*—budget deficit and trade deficit.

In the 1990s the federal government got its finances under control. Tax increases and caps on real expenditure were enacted toward the beginning of the decade and gradually paid off. By 1998 the budget deficit had been eliminated, and rising surpluses followed, as column (3) in Table 17.1 shows. The idea of the twin deficits would lead us to expect that the elimination of the budget deficit was matched by the elimination of the trade deficit. Instead, the trade deficit reached new highs. Why?

At the same time that the public sector was moving toward record surpluses, the private sector was moving toward record deficits. The U.S. economic expansion that began in 1992 and continued strong to 2000—the longest lasting on record—was led by a boom in private domestic demand. (In terms of the Mundell-Fleming models, the *IS* curve in the 1990s shifted out because of an expansion of private demand, not an expansion of public demand as in the expansions of the 1960s, 1970s, and 1980s.) The boom took the form of rapid increases in consumer expenditures and business invest-

---

[7]When the term *net* is applied to national saving, investment, or output, it means net of the depreciation of the capital stock. The country must devote a certain amount of saving and investment each year to replace worn-out old machines and buildings before it can start increasing the size of the capital stock.

[8]The last section of the appendix to Chapter 21 discusses the saving-retention coefficient, which answers the following question: For a given exogenous change in national saving, how much is retained domestically, that is, is reflected as a change in investment, and how much is reflected as a change in borrowing from abroad?

FIGURE 23.2

National Saving, Investment, and Current Account as Shares of GDP

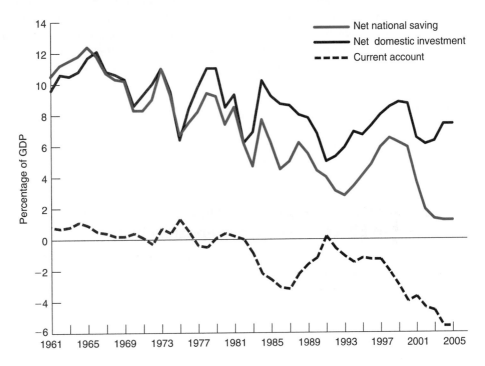

ment in equipment and software. These increases, in turn, were probably attributable to soaring wealth in the stock market and to new opportunities in information technology, both being components of what was called the "new economy." Whatever the origins, it is clear that U.S. investment increased more rapidly than national saving. The difference was the widening current account deficit. The United States continued to borrow from abroad, but now to finance private sector deficits rather than public sector deficits.

The years 2001 to 2005 saw a return to the 1980s pattern of large budget deficits arising from both large tax cuts and rapid increases in spending, together with low private saving. Thus net national saving as a share of GDP fell even below the earlier record lows, as Figure 23.2 shows. The result was the return of the twin deficits: the U.S. current account reached record levels—over 6 percent of GDP in 2005.[9]

---

[9]In some other respects, the policy mix launched under the Bush administration in 2001 differed strikingly from the Reaganomics mix. Monetary policy was accommodating, interest rates were low, and the dollar, if anything, depreciated. In terms of the Mundell-Fleming model, when Reagan shifted out the *IS* curve in the early 1980s, Fed chairman Paul Volcker kept the *LM* curve firmly in place whereas when President George W. Bush shifted out the *IS* curve in the early 2000s, Chairman Alan Greenspan shifted the *LM* curve out as well. In this respect, the 2002–2003 period was more reminiscent of the Vietnam expansion of the late 1960s, under Presidents Johnson and Nixon, than of the Reagan period. In 2005–2006, however, the Fed raised U.S. interest rates back above European interest rates, thus returning toward the mix of tight money and loose fiscal policy.

Imagine that the capital inflow of the 1980s, 1990s, and 2000s had somehow been prevented. Imagine, for example, that the government had been willing and able to impose effective capital controls (which is unlikely). Then the trade deficit would not have deteriorated so much. This sounds like a favorable effect; but investment would have been at a lower level because interest rates would have been forced up. The burden of crowding-out simply would have been redistributed from net exports to investment. Producers who rely on foreign customers would have been helped, but sectors sensitive to interest rates would have been hurt. Examples of industries sensitive to net foreign demand include agriculture, semiconductors, textiles, and scientific instruments. An example of an industry that is sensitive to interest rates is construction. Many industries, such as autos, aircraft, earth-moving equipment, and other capital goods, are sensitive to both, and so lose either way. (For them, the desired policy is a strong budget surplus and national saving.)

23.2   Monetary Policy Under Floating: An Effect Enhanced by Capital Mobility

We now consider the effects of a monetary expansion, for progressively greater degrees of capital mobility. We have already seen what happens with a given exchange rate when an increase in the money supply shifts the LM curve to the right: The higher level of income leads to a trade deficit and also to a deficit in the overall balance of payments. The equilibrium was represented by point M in Figure 23.3(a), which becomes point A in Figure 23.3(a). When the experiment is translated to the case of floating rates, the currency must depreciate to eliminate the deficit. The depreciation stimulates net exports (relative to what they would be at point A, not relative to what they were at point E before the expansion raised income and therefore imports). It thus shifts the BP and IS curves to the right, until all three curves intersect at the same point. With no capital mobility, this is point B in Figure 23.3(a). The monetary expansion stimulates income by more under floating exchange rates than under fixed exchange rates. (Point B lies to the right of A.)

What difference does the introduction of capital mobility make in this context? Figure 23.3(b) illustrates the case of partial capital mobility. Again there is a deficit at a given exchange rate, point A, implying a depreciation, a rightward shift of the BP and IS curves, and further stimulus to income. The only difference arises from the capital outflow in response to the fall of the domestic interest rate below the foreign level. The overall balance of payments at point B in Figure 23.3(b) is larger than in Figure 23.3(a), where there was only a deficit on the *trade* account to contend with. This implies that the depreciation of the currency must be even greater if it is to equilibrate the balance of payments. Thus the stimulus to net exports, and therefore to income, is even greater. Indeed, the depreciation is sufficiently great that the trade balance is in surplus at B despite the increase in income. The surplus on the current account is just offset by the deficit on the capital account resulting because the interest rate at B is still lower than it was at starting point E. The bottom line is that capital mobility enhances the effec-

FIGURE 23.3

Monetary Expansion Under Floating Rates

A monetary expansion shifts the *LM* curve out to *LM'*, lowering *i* and raising *Y*. (a) Even without capital mobility, the trade deficit at *A* requires a depreciation, which further raises *Y* at *B*. (b) With some capital mobility, the balance of payments deficit is larger at *A*; this requires a larger depreciation, which raises *Y* even further at *B*. (c) With high capital mobility, the deficit at *A*, depreciation, and stimulus at *B* are all larger still.

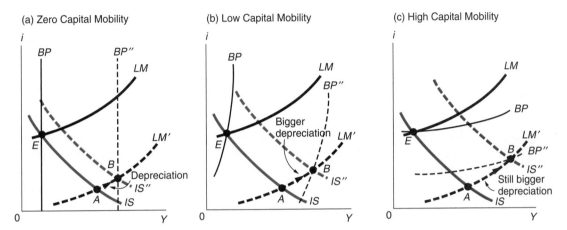

tiveness of monetary policy. In addition to the usual route of stimulating investment and other components of domestic demand via lower interest rates, the expansion also stimulates foreign demand via a lower value for the currency.[10]

Now we progress to the case of high capital mobility in Figure 23.3(c). The story is similar. However, there is an even greater capital outflow in response to the same decline in the interest rate. Thus the depreciation of the currency and the further stimulus to net exports, and therefore to income at *B*, are even greater than in the case of lower capital mobility. Notice that as a consequence of the high degree of capital mobility, the interest rate does not fall as far below the foreign interest rate as before. This means that the stimulus to investment is not as large as before. When capital mobility is sufficiently high, more of the stimulus comes from net exports than from domestic demand.[11]

---

[10]This Mundell-Fleming result that a monetary expansion gives rise to a capital outflow (and corresponding current-account surplus) is based on the assumption that capital flows depend only on interest rate differentials. When capital flows are allowed to depend also on exchange rate expectations, as in Chapter 27, this result need not hold.

[11]The rightward shifts of the *BP* and *IS* curves in Figure 23.3(c) are so great that one might wonder whether the interest rate, *i*, at *B* is still lower than at *E*. The answer is that it is. To see this, imagine what would happen if *i* returned to its original level. Then the capital account, *KA*, would still be at its original level, which implies that the trade balance, *TB*, would still be at its original level ($TB = -KA$). So would investment, *I*. Yet total output, *Y*, has increased, which cannot happen if there is no reason for any of its components, $C + I + G + TB$, to increase. To stimulate *I* and *TB*, *i* must be lower.

The main result is that the effectiveness of monetary policy at changing output is enhanced the greater the degree of capital mobility. Notice that this is just the opposite of the result obtained from the monetary approach to the balance of payments under fixed exchange rates. When the central bank chooses to keep the exchange rate fixed, high capital mobility means that any given expansion in domestic credit simply flows out through the balance of payments that much faster. When the country chooses to keep the money supply fixed and instead let the exchange rate adjust, high capital mobility means that any given expansion has an extra impact via depreciation. This is one reason why a country where the financial markets have become more developed and more integrated into world markets may opt to switch from a fixed exchange rate regime to a floating rate, assuming that it wishes to be able to pursue an independent monetary policy.

The results for monetary policy are also just the opposite of the results for fiscal policy. The key to the differences is the reaction of the interest rate. A monetary expansion operates by *lowering* the interest rate, causing capital to *flow out* of the country. This effect subtracts from the income expansion in the case of fixed rates, but enhances it when the exchange rate is allowed to change. A fiscal expansion, in contrast, operates by *raising* the interest rate and attracting a capital *inflow*. Thus the effects are the opposite of those achieved with monetary policy: They add to the income expansion in the case of fixed rates and subtract from it in the case of floating rates.

Three Examples of Powerful Monetary Contractions

The way that changes in monetary policy operate in a modern, floating rate, mobile-capital economy is illustrated by developments at the end of the 1970s in the United States. By 1979 public exasperation with inflation had become sufficiently great that there was something of a consensus that the top priority should be bringing inflation down, even if the cost might be a recession. The Federal Reserve Board under Chairman Paul Volcker tightened monetary policy. Interest rates shot up in 1980, and the contractionary effects in investment and other components of spending were soon felt in the 1980 and 1981–1982 recessions. The unemployment rate reached a postwar high in 1982. One reason why the recession was more severe than many expected and why the inflation rate came down more rapidly than many expected was the strong appreciation of the dollar that began in 1980. This chapter has already discussed the role of the fiscal expansion in driving up interest rates and the value of the dollar in the early 1980s. Many observers think that the monetary contraction was the origin of the 1980–1982 phase of this process. As in the model just developed, a leftward shift of the *LM* curve raises interest rates, attracts capital from abroad, appreciates the currency, and worsens the trade balance. Thus the brunt of the recession is borne by exchange-rate-sensitive industries in addition to interest-rate-sensitive industries.

The expansion that began in 1983 eventually returned the economy to the same position in the business cycle as before the recession. Because its origin was a fiscal expansion, real interest rates remained high. Comparing 1985 to 1980, the net policy change was neither contraction nor expansion, but rather a shift in the *mix* of monetary and fiscal policy. The mid-1980s mix implied high real interest rates and a high real value for the dollar. As a consequence, the composition of GDP featured higher shares for C and G at the expense of lower shares for I and $X - M$.[12]

A similar sequence of events occurred in the United Kingdom. When Margaret Thatcher became prime minister in 1979, she imposed tight monetary targets. The pound appreciated sharply (although this may have been related as much to an increase in North Sea oil wealth as to the tight money policy). British firms that had been dependent on export demand or that competed directly with imports, particularly in manufacturing, were hit very hard as a consequence of their loss in international competitiveness. The resulting decline in this sector was labeled "deindustrialization." Unemployment rose steadily (from 5 percent in 1979 to 12 percent in 1982), although, as in the United States, the benefit of lower inflation did eventually arrive. The point again is that exchange rate effects enhance the impact of changes in monetary policy, for better or for worse.[13]

Yet another example is Japan. In 1988–1989, the Bank of Japan followed an expansionary monetary policy, buying dollars to support the value of the U.S. currency against the yen and keeping real interest rates low in Japan. The result was what has become known as the bubble economy: strong growth coupled with soaring prices in the equity and real estate markets. During the 1990–1992 period, the Bank of Japan reversed policy and raised interest rates sharply. This move succeeded in its intended purpose, which was to burst the financial bubble. It also had the effect, however, of setting in motion a new upsurge in the value of the yen and a serious recession in Japan. As a result of *endaka* (the strong yen), previously invincible exporters found themselves in 1995 with prices that were no longer competitive on world markets. Monetary policy still has strong effects on the economy.

23.3 Policy Under Perfect Capital Mobility

Chapter 21 showed that transaction costs, capital controls, and other barriers that can separate international investors from the portfolios they wish to hold are close to negligible among most of the large industrialized countries. Thus the degree of capital mobility is not just high, but close to infinite. The parameter k in Equation 22.1, the responsiveness of capital flows to rates of return, is close to infinite. This case is the natural limit of the logical progression—zero, low, and high capital mobility—that we have

---

[12]Given total GDP, what would be the point in altering its composition through such a monetary/fiscal policy mix? An advantage is that the strong dollar, by lowering import prices, helped bring inflation down faster than would otherwise have been the case. But there are a number of disadvantages, especially in terms of longer-run consequences. In the first place, when investment is crowded out today, it means that the capital stock will be lower in the future, and so real growth is lower in the long run. Second, net exports are crowded out. This gives rise to strong protectionist pressures from the adversely affected sectors, which can have damaging effects on the efficiency of the economy. Furthermore, when the country runs a current-account deficit, it means that it is borrowing from abroad. As a result, the country will be poorer in the future and at the mercy of foreign creditors.

[13]British macroeconomic policy from 1979 to 1981 is described by Willem Buiter and Marcus Miller in "Changing the Rules: Economic Consequences of the Thatcher Regime," *Brookings Papers on Economic Activity*, no. 2 (1983): 305–379.

been considering. One advantage of studying the polar case of perfect capital mobility is that the relative effects of monetary policy and fiscal policy are sharpened; the results stand out quite clearly, whereas in the case of partial capital mobility the graphs can be messy, as the reader no doubt noticed.

Recall that the slope of the BP curve is m/k. As k goes to infinity, the slope goes to zero. In other words, the BP curve becomes flat. The flat line is drawn at the level of the home interest rate, i, that is equal to the world rate, i^*. If i were to rise above i^*, even for just an instant, the differential would immediately attract a very large capital inflow. All foreign investors would want to acquire the better-paying assets in the home country rather than those in their own country; domestic residents would seek to borrow at the cheaper rate abroad. Such capital flows will arbitrage away the interest differential, that is, will keep it from opening up to begin with. Thus, another way of saying that k is infinite is to say that $i - i^*$ is always zero, as is clear from Equation 22.5.

Fixed Exchange Rates and Perfect Capital Mobility

We return briefly to the case of fixed rates, beginning with a fiscal expansion. In Figure 23.4(a) the IS curve once again shifts right. The increase in the demand for money drives up the interest rate to point A as usual, attracting a large capital inflow. More precisely, *if* the economy could remain at A, then the higher interest rate *would* attract a capital inflow, and the central bank would have to make the usual decision under fixed rates as to whether to sterilize it. The potential inflow, however, is so large that the central bank has no option. There is no limit to the quantity of foreign exchange it would have to buy up in return for domestic currency until it exhausted its holdings of domestic assets. (In the case of a fiscal contraction that lowers the interest rate, there is no limit to the quantity of foreign exchange the central bank would have to supply in exchange for domestic currency until it exhausted its holdings of foreign assets.) If the central bank does not wish to abandon the exchange rate peg, it will have to abandon its money supply target: It must allow the inflow of reserves through the capital account to swell the domestic money supply. The increase in the money supply will shift the LM curve to the right, to LM'' in Figure 23.4(a). The shift must be great enough that the intersection with the new IS' curve, at point B, is on the BP line. Only then will the interest rate, i, be back at level i^*, as it must be if the capital inflow is not to be infinite.

Income is much higher at point B than at A.[14] The case of perfect capital mobility is the limit of the progression of cases illustrated in Figures 22.2(a), 22.2(b), and 22.2(c). With high capital mobility, the effect of the fiscal expansion on income is supplemented by an increase in the money supply in the long run. With infinite capital

---

[14]Indeed, the increase in income is the full Keynesian multiplier effect, without any of the usual crowding-out from a higher interest rate. An increase in government spending, $\Delta \overline{G}$, always shifts the IS curve to the right by $\Delta \overline{G}/(s + m)$. Usually the final effect on income is less because the economy is at a point like A. However, when capital mobility is so high that it prevents the interest rate from rising, income increases by the full amount of the rightward shift. In this case, international capital flows have the same effect as an automatically accommodating monetary policy.

FIGURE 23.4

Perfect Capital Mobility

When capital mobility ties i to the world interest rate $i*$, the BP schedule is flat. The potentially infinite capital inflow that would result from a fiscal expansion to A means that (a) under fixed rates, the reserve inflow must be large enough to shift the LM curve instantaneously all the way out to B, or (b) under floating rates, the appreciation must be large enough to return the IS curve all the way back to E. The potentially infinite capital outflow that would result from a monetary expansion means that (c) under fixed rates, the reserve outflow must be large enough to return the LM curve all the way back to E, or (d) under floating rates, the depreciation must be large enough to shift the IS curve all the way out to B.

(a) Fiscal Expansion, Fixed Rates

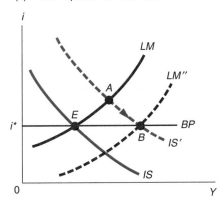

(c) Monetary Expansion, Fixed Rates

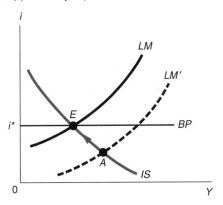

(b) Fiscal Expansion, Floating Rates

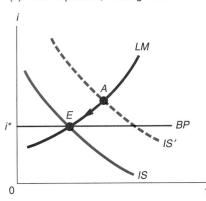

(d) Monetary Expansion, Floating Rates

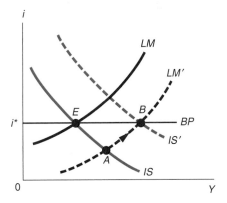

mobility, the effect is even stronger in that (1) the money flows in instantaneously, whether the central bank attempts to sterilize it or not, and (2) the increase in the money supply is greater.

We now consider a monetary expansion. In Figure 23.4(c), the increase in the money supply shifts the LM curve rightward to LM' and drives down the interest rate.

The lower interest rate at point A gives rise to a capital outflow. More precisely, the interest rate *would* fall if the economy could remain at point A. Yet there is no limit to the potential magnitude of the capital outflow. If the central bank tries to maintain both its exchange rate target and its new money supply target, it will rapidly exhaust its entire stock of foreign exchange reserves. If it chooses to stay with the fixed exchange rate, it will be forced to give up its money supply target and allow the outflow of reserves through the capital account to reduce the money supply. The reduction in the money supply immediately shifts the LM curve back to the left until it returns to the original LM curve. Only when the money supply is back to its preexpansion level at point E will the interest rate have returned to the world level; only then will domestic investors stop pumping capital out of the country. At point E there is no effect on income at all.

Again, this case is the limit in the progression illustrated in Figure 22.3(a), 22.3(b), and 22.3(c). Under the monetary approach to the balance of payments, any increase in the money supply eventually flows back out through the balance of payments when the central bank decides to give up the attempt to sterilize the outflow, with the process proceeding more rapidly the higher the degree of capital mobility. In the case of perfect capital mobility, the central bank could not sterilize the outflow even if it wanted to and even in the short run. Thus, the expansion in income does not actually take place even in the short run. Point A is purely a hypothetical location.

Even though Figure 23.4(c) looks precisely the same after the monetary expansion as before, one detail has changed. Recall that the total money supply is given by international reserves plus domestic credit. When the central bank increased the money supply, it did so by increasing the supply of domestic credit, that is, its holdings of net domestic assets. (In the United States, this would normally mean purchasing Treasury securities.) When the money flowed back out, it was international reserves that were lost. Thus the *composition* of the monetary base has been permanently altered, as between net domestic assets and international reserves.

Notice incidentally that besides being flat, the BP schedule has a subtly different interpretation under perfect capital mobility, as does its algebraic representation, Equation 22.5. When capital mobility is less than complete, the BP schedule is the set of points for which the balance of payments is zero. When capital mobility is infinite, however, the BP schedule is the set of points for which the balance of payments is neither plus infinity nor minus infinity. This is just another way of saying that the economy must always be on the BP schedule: i is tied to i^*. It also means that, given that the economy is on the schedule, neither the net capital flow nor the overall balance of payments can be determined. They will not necessarily be zero.

Our conclusions are quite striking. In a regime of fixed exchange rates, fiscal policy reaches its peak effectiveness under perfect capital mobility, but monetary policy *loses* all effectiveness under perfect capital mobility. In both cases, the key to the conclusion is that potentially infinite capital flows prevent the interest rate from deviating from the world level. In both cases, the IS curve alone determines the level of income. Attempts to shift the LM curve by increasing domestic credit have no effect because the money simply flows out of the country as fast as it is created.

The Impossible Trinity, and the Example of European Monetary Integration

There follows from our results a simple rule applicable to programs of economic integration like that undertaken by the countries of Europe. *Of the Impossible Trinity— fixed exchange rates, financial openness, and monetary independence—a country can choose to have any two attributes, but it cannot choose all three.*

The European Monetary System was formed in 1979 by Germany, France, Italy, and other members of the European Economic Community seeking to stabilize their exchange rates. Initially, France and Italy retained a degree of ability to use monetary policy independently. This independence was not entirely inconsistent with exchange rate stability because they retained capital controls.

However, in the late 1980s France and Italy removed those controls, as we have seen. Simultaneously, they sought to achieve greater exchange rate stability. Spain joined the Exchange Rate Mechanism in 1989, and Britain in 1990. Spain joined the others in freeing capital controls in 1991.

This combination of fixed exchange rates and financial integration put European countries in the category of economy described by Figure 23.4(c). We have seen that under these conditions, with both the exchange rate and the interest rate tied down, monetary policy is powerless to affect the level of economic activity within the country. The lesson is that France, Italy, and the other individual countries of Europe had to be prepared politically for the loss of their monetary independence, or the plan for exchange rate fixity with full financial integration would not be successful.

European politicians find the principle of economic integration very attractive. In December 1991 an EC summit meeting at Maastricht in the Netherlands affirmed the members' political commitment to the European Economic and Monetary Union (EMU). They agreed on plans for renouncing exchange rate realignments (the discrete changes in the midpoint of the range that had occurred periodically from 1979 to 1987), narrowing the margins (which had been at plus or minus 2¼ percent for most members), and eventually adopting a single currency (now called the euro) by 1999.

The commitment was soon tested by increases in German interest rates. As we saw in Section 22.2, the Germans had recently increased government spending and investment in connection with unification with East Germany. At the same time, the Bundesbank had its own reasons for maintaining monetary discipline. It wished to head off inflation. At a time of slowdown in worldwide economic growth, however, Germany's partners in the EMS would not have chosen of their own volition the higher interest rates that were produced by the German monetary/fiscal policy mix.

The Maastricht Treaty was to be ratified in 1992 by the individual member countries. At first, the political leaders assumed that their populations and parliaments would readily approve the plans for the EMU. But as dates for the referenda drew near, popular opposition began to mobilize. Those opposed feared a loss of economic sovereignty under the treaty in general, and they particularly disliked the high interest rates that Germany was forcing on them at the time.

The trigger for the subsequent crisis was a (narrow) rejection of the treaty by Danish voters, followed by polls indicating that the same outcome was possible in France. Meanwhile, the Bundesbank turned down requests, particularly from the British, for lower interest rates. It began to look like the political leaders had made commitments that implied a greater loss of monetary sovereignty than their populations were willing to accept. Speculators in the foreign exchange market, anticipating an imminent unraveling of the European Monetary System, began to sell the currencies of those countries where popular opposition to high interest rates seemed to be greatest, and to buy deutschemarks. The massive selling pressure was too intense for the central banks who were trying to defend the parities. In September 1992 the speculators won out. Italy and the United Kingdom were forced to drop out of the Exchange Rate Mechanism (ERM) altogether, that is, to allow their currencies to float. Spain and Portugal chose to remain in, but they had to devalue. After a similar crisis in August 1993, France was forced to widen its bands to 15 percent. These developments were precisely the opposite from what had been anticipated under the plans for the EMU.

The ERM crises of 1992–1993 illustrate the principle of the Impossible Trinity. Faced with a hard choice among sacrifice of monetary sovereignty, sacrifice of fixed exchange rates, or sacrifice of open capital markets, only a few countries like the Netherlands ultimately turned out to be truly prepared to give up all monetary sovereignty at that time. Italy and the United Kingdom gave up fixed exchange rates instead. Spain gave up open capital markets, temporarily reimposing control on capital outflows.

Later in the decade, commitment to the Maastricht Treaty grew beyond question. The EMU successfully took effect among eleven qualifying countries in 1999. (A twelfth, Greece, joined in 2000.) Exchange rates among the members are now "irrevocably fixed." Indeed, the central banks of participating European countries have no ability to undertake independent monetary policy. Rather, they function merely as branches of the European System of Central Banks, much as do the district banks of the Federal Reserve System in the United States. This abandonment of monetary independence and even of national currencies is historically unprecedented among major sovereign countries. Strains are already evident. The interest rate appropriate for Italy does not suit Ireland and vice versa. Some Italian politicians have expressed second thoughts. Those members of the European Union that have not yet joined the EMU will have a hard time deciding whether to take the plunge (the United Kingdom, Sweden, and Denmark, plus ten countries, mostly in Central Europe, that joined the EU in 2005).

Floating Exchange Rates and Perfect Capital Mobility

So far the conclusion has been that when capital is perfectly mobile, the central bank has to abandon its money supply target *if* it does not wish to abandon its exchange rate target. What if the monetary authorities respond to the potentially limitless inflow of reserves (which comes, for example, with an increase in interest rates) by allowing the currency to appreciate? What if they respond to the potentially limitless outflow of reserves (which comes, for example, with a decrease in interest rates) by allowing the currency to depreciate? This is the case of floating exchange rates, with which we now conclude the taxonomy of cases. Floating rates allow the country to recapture its monetary independence despite perfect capital mobility. The *LM* curve will shift when the domestic central bank deliberately decides to change monetary policy and *only* when it decides to do so.

Figure 23.4(b) illustrates the fiscal expansion. Again, the capital inflow that would be attracted by the higher interest rate at point *A* is infinite, but under floating rates the currency instantly appreciates, reducing net exports and shifting the *IS* curve back to the left.[15] This is the same thing that happened with less-than-perfect capital mobility in Figure 23.1(c), but now the potential capital inflow and the appreciation of the currency are so large that the *IS* curve shifts all the way back to the starting point at *E*. This must be the case if the domestic interest rate is not to exceed the world rate. It also means that there is no effect on income at all; fiscal policy loses all power under floating exchange rates. This is the ultimate extrapolation of the argument that under floating rates, the higher the capital mobility, the lower the effectiveness of fiscal policy.

Even though Figure 23.4(b) looks the same after the fiscal expansion as before, it is not true that nothing at all has changed. The currency has appreciated in the meantime, which means that if the trade account was originally in balance, it is now in deficit. The trade deficit must be financed by a capital inflow for the overall balance of payments to be zero. Recall that when k is infinite, $i = i^*$ no longer implies that the capital account is necessarily zero. Rather, foreigners lend the amount necessary to finance the current-account deficit. They are happy to do so, as long as the home country pays the going rate of return.

Even though total GDP has not changed, the *composition* of GDP has. The share going to net exports is smaller. The share going to government expenditure is larger. Or, if the fiscal expansion took the form of a tax cut that increased households' disposable income, rather than an increase in government expenditure, then it is the share of GDP going to consumption that is larger. There is no crowding-out of investment because the interest rate has not risen. Even though crowding-out caused by the fiscal expansion is 100 percent (i.e., there is no effect on total GDP), all the crowding-out is now borne by the international sector.[16]

Finally, consider a monetary expansion under floating rates. When the *LM* curve shifts to *LM'*, the capital outflow that would take place at point *A* is infinite. Yet the currency instantly depreciates, stimulating net exports, shifting the *IS* curve to the right, and adding to the expansion of income. This is also what happened with less-than-perfect capital mobility, but now the shift continues until the economy moves all

---

[15]As in the case of imperfect capital mobility, the appreciation causes the *BP* schedule, as well as the *IS* curve, to shift to the left. However, because the *BP* curve is flat, horizontal shifts make no difference.

[16]In practice, there are a number of reasons why even under modern conditions of highly integrated financial markets, most countries cannot borrow an unlimited amount at a given interest rate: (1) If the country is large, it will drive up the world interest rate, as we will see in Chapter 25. (2) If the currency is expected to depreciate in the future (perhaps because of a large accumulation of indebtedness to foreigners), foreign investors will demand a higher interest rate on domestic assets in compensation, as we will see in Chapter 27. (3) If foreigners are highly risk averse and wish to diversify their portfolios, they may become reluctant to put an ever-increasing share of their wealth into domestic assets, as we will see in Chapter 28.

the way to the original interest rate at point *B*. The effect of the monetary expansion on income is not only greater than it was under fixed exchange rates, it is also greater than it was under lesser degrees of capital mobility. Monetary policy reaches its peak effectiveness under floating rates and perfect capital mobility. One way of describing the result is in terms of the money market equilibrium condition, Equation 22.4. Normally, when there is an increase in the real money supply, the interest rate falls, so as to help increase the demand for money and restore equilibrium. Here, however, the interest rate is tied to the foreign interest rate. As a result, the increase in income must be so great that the increase in the transaction demand for money alone equals the increase in the money supply.

An implication is that the change in the exchange rate must be very large to generate the necessary increase in income, especially in the short run when the elasticities of export and import demand are low. This property of the model with perfect capital mobility helps explain the observed fact that floating exchange rates are highly variable.

In addition to the magnitude of the increase in income, a further striking result of perfect capital mobility is that the monetary expansion operates *entirely* via the international sector, that is, by depreciating the currency and stimulating net exports. *None* of the expansion comes from the usual domestic route, that is, by reducing the interest rate and stimulating investment.

To summarize the conclusions regarding perfect capital mobility, there is a neat symmetry in the results. Under fixed exchange rates, fiscal policy reaches its peak effectiveness and monetary policy becomes completely powerless. Under floating exchange rates, by contrast, fiscal policy loses all power and it is monetary policy that reaches its peak effectiveness. Some of the results seem too strong to be taken literally. For example, it is hard to believe that a monetary expansion under floating rates has none of its effect via domestic demand. More generally, there is an obvious problem with the proposition that international capital flows force the domestic interest rate into continuous equality with the foreign interest rate. Interest rates are in fact observed to differ across countries. For example, the U.S. interest rate has exceeded the Japanese interest rate for years. How can such differentials exist if transaction costs, capital controls, and other barriers to the movement of capital across national boundaries are as low as was argued in Chapter 20? Why doesn't all the capital flow to the country paying the higher interest rate?

The answer is that one country's interest rate is measured in dollars and the other's in yen. Investors will not treat the two interest rates as the same because of the likelihood of future changes in the exchange rate. If investors think there is a danger that the dollar will depreciate in the future, then they will only be willing to hold dollar assets if the dollar interest rate is higher than that on yen assets, thus compensating them for their threatened loss. Chapter 27 will introduce exchange rate expectations as a factor that enters investors' calculations in addition to interest rates. As a result, some of our conclusions regarding the operation of monetary and fiscal policy will be modified.

Consider point *B* in Figure 23.3, where a monetary expansion has driven down both the interest rate and the value of domestic currency. We have argued that in the absence of barriers to capital flows, this point is not an equilibrium because the domestic interest rate is lower than the foreign interest rate. This argument changes when allowance is made for investors' expectations of possible changes in the exchange rate. If investors have an expectation that domestic currency will appreciate in the future, then they may be happy at *B* holding domestic assets, despite the lower interest rate.

Why should they have an expectation of future appreciation? At *B* the currency has depreciated, perhaps considerably. If investors' expectation of the long-run or future exchange rate has not changed much, then they will expect the currency to appreciate in the future because it is below that value now. This is called *overshooting*. Today's depreciation of the currency generates the expectation of a future appreciation back in the direction from which it came. If expectations are formed in this manner, then *B* can be an equilibrium after all. This makes the model developed here more realistic. The first implication of introducing expectations is that the domestic interest rate can lie below the world interest rate despite perfect capital mobility. The second is that some of the stimulus to output can come from domestic demand such as investment; it need not all come from net foreign demand such as exports. The third is that the exchange rate doesn't have to move quite as far as was previously thought, when higher output had to bear the entire burden of higher money demand.

An analogous point applies in the case of a fiscal expansion. Point *B* in Figure 23.1(c) could be an equilibrium, despite the fact that the interest rate is higher at home than abroad, provided investors hold the expectation that the domestic currency will depreciate in the future. Investors will indeed hold such an expectation after the currency has appreciated to get to *B*, provided their expectation of the future level of the exchange rate does not change much. If there is an expectation of future depreciation that is enough to compensate, then the domestic interest rate can lie above the world rate despite perfect capital mobility. A second realistic consequence is that there is now some crowding-out of investment; net exports do not bear the entire burden of the crowding-out, as they appeared to in Figure 23.4. A third is that total crowding-out of other sectors by the fiscal expansion is less than 100 percent: There is some expansionary effect on aggregate GDP after all. A fourth implication is that the movement in the exchange rate need not be quite as large as when it had to shift the *IS* curve all the way back to *E*.

Chapter 27 will explore at greater length the determination of expectations and the role that this additional factor has in the determination of the exchange rate. The chapter will concentrate on the effects of changes in monetary policy, including not just the short-run effects on the exchange rate at a point like *B* in Figure 23.3, but also the effects expected with the passage of time.[17]

---

[17]We will see the effects of the monetary expansion as the price level adjusts over time. It will turn out that at point *B* in Figure 23.4(d), the expectation of future appreciation of the currency is precisely the correct one for investors to have. The situation is a little different for a fiscal expansion. Expected future adjustment of the price level is not sufficient for investors at point *B* in Figure 23.4(c) to hold an expectation of future depreciation. For that we would need to introduce expected future adjustment of the level of foreign indebtedness. Jacob Frenkel and Assaf Razin, "The Mundell-Fleming Model a Quarter Century Later: A Unified Exposition," *IMF Staff Papers,* 34, no. 4 (December 1987): 567–620.

23.4 Summary

This chapter showed the difference that international capital mobility makes under floating exchange rates in the modern world economy, particularly regarding the effects of monetary and fiscal policy. It turns out to make quite a difference. As in the preceding chapters, a country's capital account depends on the difference between its interest rate and foreign interest rates. The implications are quite different under floating exchange rates, however, than they are when the exchange rate is held fixed.

A monetary expansion causes depreciation of the currency, which tends to stimulate the trade balance. The effect is greater, the higher the degree of capital mobility, and thus the greater the capital outflow in response to the decline in the interest rate. When capital mobility is very high, a monetary expansion has a major effect on output, but the effect comes primarily through currency depreciation stimulating net foreign demand rather than through the traditional channel of a lower interest rate stimulating domestic demand.

Although capital mobility changes the results in one direction for the case of monetary policy (giving it a greater effect on total GDP), it changes it in the opposite direction in the case of fiscal policy (giving it a smaller effect). If capital mobility is high, the capital inflow attracted by a fiscal expansion causes the currency to appreciate, which in turn discourages net exports. The higher the degree of capital mobility, the higher the crowding-out of the trade balance via a higher valued currency—as opposed to the traditional crowding-out of investment via a higher interest rate—and the smaller the effect of the fiscal expansion on total GDP.

The switch in macroeconomic policy undertaken in the United States in the 1980s offers a good illustration of these principles. The government enacted a large fiscal expansion in the early 1980s, with the Federal Reserve keeping a firm rein on monetary policy. The result of this unprecedented shift in the monetary/fiscal policy mix was an increase in U.S. interest rates, a large capital inflow, an appreciation of the dollar, and an unprecedented U.S. trade deficit. Germany in 1990–92 and the United States in 2005 offer more recent examples.

CHAPTER PROBLEMS

1. A country imports wine, exports steel, and has a floating exchange rate. If it raises government spending on health care, increasing the budget deficit, how are the following four domestic interest groups affected: hospital workers, steel mills, wineries, and construction workers? How does your answer depend on the degree of international capital mobility?

2. This question refers to ten possible Keynesian small-country models:

    Interest rate fixed (e.g., accommodating monetary policy)
    a. closed economy
    b. open economy; fixed exchange rates
    c. open economy; floating exchange rates

Open economy: interest rate determined by IS-LM

d. no capital mobility; fixed exchange rates; reserve flows sterilized

e. no capital mobility; fixed exchange rates; reserve flows not sterilized

f. no capital mobility; floating exchange rates

g. low capital mobility; floating exchange rates

h. high capital mobility; floating exchange rates

i. perfect capital mobility; floating exchange rates

j. perfect capital mobility; fixed exchange rates

The government increases expenditure. In each case, indicate under which of the two models there is a larger effect on income, and explain why (in a few words, or with a graph labeled with letters).

1. a vs. b	5. d vs. f	9. h vs. i
2. b vs. c	6. d vs. g	10. d vs. j
3. b vs. d	7. f vs. g	11. b vs. j
4. d vs. e	8. d vs. h	

3. You are the finance minister of the country of Fuji, which still has some capital controls in place. A large trading partner has undertaken a fiscal expansion, pushing its interest rate above yours and causing capital to flow from Fuji to the other country. (The interest rates are not equalized because of the capital controls.) The authorities in the other country are unhappy with the fact that their currency has appreciated against yours and with the consequent trade deficit. They ask you to remove your capital controls, with the aim of helping their currency depreciate against yours and improving their trade balance. How do you respond?

Extra Credit

4. For this question, it will help to use linearized versions of Equations 22.2 and 22.3:

$$Y = (\overline{A} - bi + \overline{X} - \overline{M})/(s + m)$$

$$M/P = KY - hi$$

A fiscal expansion is known to cause the currency to appreciate if the degree of capital mobility, k, is sufficiently high. What exactly is the necessary condition on k (in Equation 22.4) in terms of the other parameters?

SUGGESTIONS FOR FURTHER READING

Cooper, Richard. "The U.S. Payments Deficit and the Strong Dollar: Policy Options," *The U.S. Dollar—Recent Developments, Outlook, and Policy Options* (Federal Reserve Bank of Kansas City, 1985), p. 157. Discusses alternative explanations for the strength of the dollar in the early 1980s and the resulting trade deficit (most importantly the shift in the monetary/fiscal mix).

Eichengreen, Barry, and Charles Wyplosz. "The Unstable EMS," *Brookings Papers on Economic Activity* (1993): 51–143. European central banks in 1992 found they could not defend their declared exchange rate targets in the face of huge capital movements.

Fleming, J. M. "Domestic Financial Policies Under Fixed and Under Floating Exchange Rates," *IMF Staff Papers,* 9, no. 3 (1962): 369–379. The complete Mundell-Fleming model succinctly developed.

Frankel, Jeffrey. "Could the Twin Deficits Jeopardize U.S. Hegemony?" *Journal of Policy Modeling* (forthcoming in 2006). Is 2001–2006 a replay of 1981–1985? Or rather, of 1966–1971?

Mundell, Robert. "Capital Mobility and Stabilization Policy Under Fixed and Flexible Rates," *Canadian Journal of Economics and Political Science* (November 1963): 475–485. The original model with perfect capital mobility.

CHAPTER 24

Crises in Emerging Markets

The globalization of financial markets, a trend that Chapter 21 examined at length, has come increasingly to encompass not only industrialized countries, but developing countries as well. The term *emerging market* attained popularity in the early 1990s, to describe middle-income countries where financial markets had begun to develop and to open up to global investors.

Modern financial markets have many advantages. As the analysis of Section 21.5 showed, a capital-poor country can finance investment more cheaply by borrowing from abroad than if it had to do it entirely out of domestic saving. Nevertheless, financial markets have disadvantages as well. Financial crises hit many borrowing countries in Latin America in 1982, Mexico in 1994, East Asia in 1997, Russia in 1998, Turkey in 2001, and Argentina in 2002. As currency values and securities prices plummeted, the adverse effects went far beyond losses to international investors. Most of these countries suffered severe recessions. Living standards fell, particularly for many who had only managed to lift themselves out of poverty relatively recently. Such trials and tribulations have motivated the emerging market governments, along with the international financial community, to think hard about what can be done to reduce the frequency and severity of crises.

24.1 Inflows to Emerging Markets

We can view recent history in cycles. There was a boom in loans to developing countries in the late 1970s and early 1980s; it turned to bust with the debt crisis that began in Mexico in 1982 and soon spread to other debtors. A new boom began after 1990 as the dark line in Figure 24.1 shows. Capital flooded back into Latin America after the seven-year hiatus, reached record levels in East Asia, and found its way also to countries in Central Europe and other corners of the globe. A new bust phase followed in the latter half of the 1990s. The years 2001 to 2005 saw the beginning of a new phase of inflows. We consider the origins of 1990s-type inflows in this section, and the bust phase in subsequent sections.

Origins

In the early 1990s, or again in the years 2001 to 2005, a typical emerging market country found itself in the situation of point B in Figure 24.1: above the $BP = 0$ line. In other words, it ran a surplus on the overall balance of payments, generally consisting of

FIGURE 24.1

Flows to Developing Countries (Low and Middle Income)
Capital Account Surplus, Current Account, and Change in Reserves
(as a percentage of total GDP)

Capital flows fell off after the crises of 1982 and 1998, in each case requiring countries to reverse
the trade deficits they had been financing up to that point. A new capital account boom started in
the years 2002 to 2005, but this time the borrowers were more cautious: They used the inflows to
build up reserves sharply, rather than to run current account deficits as in the previous two cycles.

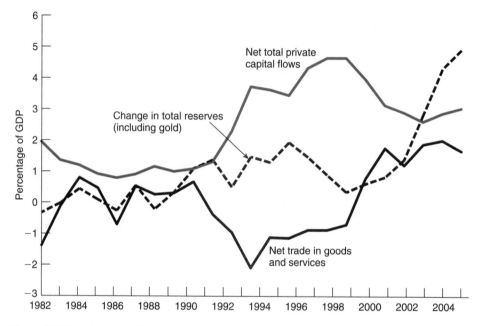

Source: World Development Indicators.

large capital inflows that were more than enough to finance any current account
deficit. How had it gotten there?

Although the situation of course varied from country to country, the causal factors
generally fell into two broad categories: internal and external. Each factor can be considered in terms of Figure 24.1.

The first set of causes consisted of internal policy reforms and other domestic
factors.

1. *Monetary stabilization.* Countries that had experienced high rates of inflation in
the 1970s and 1980s—in some cases even hyperinflation—had succeeded in bringing
their inflation rates down sharply by the early 1990s. Examples include Bolivia, Israel,
Mexico, Argentina, and Brazil. Contraction of the real money supply was often a component of the stabilization plan, which would be a leftward shift of the *LM* curve.
Where expectations were successfully stabilized, there was also an increase in money

demand, which again shifts the *LM* curve leftward. Either way, the economy would end up at a point like *B*, where the monetary stabilization attracts a capital inflow.

2. *Spending boom.* Economic liberalization can lead to a boom in investment, as firms respond to a better environment for business. It can also lead to a boom in consumption as households respond to newly available consumer goods and newly available consumer credit. Mexico after NAFTA went into effect in January 1994 was a good example. Either way, the *IS* curve shifts out, which is again a way to get to a point like *B*. The payments surplus is analogous to the Dutch disease discussed in Section 20.2.

3. *Capital account liberalization.* Many countries removed previously existing controls on the inflow of capital.[1] A financial opening of this sort is an increase in the degree of capital mobility, k, and an increase in $\overline{KA}$ as well. It rotates the $BP = 0$ curve downward. A country may be initially sitting at point *B* with a $BP = 0$ line running right through it, and then find after capital-account liberalization that the same point now corresponds to a balance of payments surplus.

Other reforms accompanying liberalization helped promote the capital inflow. Liberalization with respect to trade and finance created a market-oriented environment in which foreigners felt more welcome than in the past. Privatization of state-owned enterprises (airlines, power utilities, telephone companies) offered new assets for investors to buy. Policies to peg or target the exchange rate reduced fears of devaluation.

The other set of factors consisted of external developments.

1. *Low rates of return in industrialized countries.* U.S. interest rates fell in the years 1990 to 1993, as the result of a U.S. recession. Investors accustomed to high interest rates in the 1980s looked around for new places to put their money. High rates of return in the emerging markets caught their attention. In terms of the graph, a fall in i^* is a vertical downward shift of the $BP = 0$ curve. Even if there has been no increase in the domestic interest rate at point *B*, the country now finds itself in the surplus zone.[2] The same thing happened again in the 2001–2003 period: The Federal Reserve under Chairman Alan Greenspan responded to a U.S. recession by cutting interest rates to the lowest levels in half a century, encouraging money to flow to emerging markets. Borrowing at low U.S. interest rates and lending elsewhere is called the "carry trade."

2. *The Brady Plan.* In the late 1980s some economists had argued that the existence of a large debt overhang constituted a disincentive to the debtor countries. The overhang discouraged them from investing in projects that would generate earnings of foreign exchange because they feared that the payoff would just go to the foreign creditors. The argument was that outright forgiveness or writing-down of the debt would encourage investment and growth, and result in a larger economic pie for all parties to

---

[1]Some countries also removed existing controls on capital outflows. Investors may be reluctant to put their funds into a country if they are unsure of being able to get them out again. Thus liberalization of outflows can sometimes encourage inflows.
[2]Guillermo Calvo, Leo Leiderman, and Carmen Reinhart, "Capital Inflows and Real Exchange Rate Appreciation in Latin America: The Role of External Factors," *IMF Staff Papers* 40, no. 1 (1993): 108–150.

share.[3] The Brady Plan, put forth by the U.S. Treasury in 1989, was a step in the direction of debt reduction, with the remaining loans securitized as so-called *Brady bonds.* The timing of subsequent capital inflows into countries that underwent Brady restructuring is very suggestive: There had been a cleaning of the slate that, at a minimum, provided a psychological boost for new lending.

3. *Financial innovations* to enhance the availability of funds. Innovations such as *country funds, American Depository Receipts* (ADRs), and Global Depositary Receipts (GDRs) have made it easier than previously for investors in rich countries to buy securities in emerging markets. Country funds offer foreign investors a selected basket of securities in a particular country, even when the local stock market in general has not been opened up to them directly. ADRs can be bought conveniently in New York but are certificates of ownership of equities in another country. Even more conveniently for rich-country investors, some companies in middle-income countries such as Mexico and Israel have decided to list their shares directly on the New York Stock Exchange or Nasdaq. Others, however, have recently been deterred by higher standards for corporate reporting.

The share of saving in rich countries invested by institutional investors, rather than by individuals, has been steadily increasing. Institutional investors include pension funds, mutual funds, and hedge funds. Hedge funds are speculative funds catering to wealthy individuals.[4] Institutional investor managers are better able to acquire the information needed to invest in foreign securities than are most individual investors. They often find emerging markets attractive for two reasons. First, they expect the returns to be high. A country with a high marginal product of investment will experience a capital inflow if it opens up to international investors (as illustrated formally in Figure 21.4). Second, these markets offer fund managers an opportunity to diversify their portfolios, and thus reduce their overall risk (as explained in Chapter 28).

4. *Moral hazard.* When some form of insurance protects people against the worst consequences of disaster, they may no longer have the incentive to take actions that could help prevent the damage from arising in the first place. This principle is called moral hazard. Some critics argue that capital flows to emerging markets in the 1990s were encouraged by moral hazard: Borrowers and lenders believed that the IMF or G7 would "bail them out" in the event of a crisis, and thus they lacked the incentive to be sufficiently careful. Some, for example, believe that the enlarged amount of money used to save Mexico in January 1995 encouraged reckless capital flows to East Asia and Russia thereafter. When the G7 and IMF finally "pulled the plug" on Russia in August 1998, they usefully served notice that such debtors would not be bailed out indefinitely.

---

[3]Paul Krugman, "Financing versus Forgiving a Debt Overhang," *Journal of Development Economics,* 1989.
[4]The name "hedge funds" sounds puzzling because they are famous for exposure to risk. The explanation is that, at least according to the original theory, hedge funds place bets where prices are out of line with fundamentals—for example, arbitraging a difference in interest rates—and then use derivatives to hedge any risks that are not logically connected to the particular bet they are making. But a more accurate description is they are funds that are exempt from regulatory constraints because each is held by a small number of wealthy investors who are presumed to be able to look out for themselves.

Management of Capital Inflows

Although most countries want to attract investment from abroad, there can be too much of a good thing. Anyone who runs up a large debt runs the danger that there will be trouble in the future if creditors suddenly demand repayment, or even if they merely lose willingness to continue lending new money. Figure 24.1 shows that in the early 1990s, developed countries used their rising private capital inflows to finance trade deficits, which they were then forced to reverse abruptly when capital inflows fell after the Asia/Russia crises of 1998. The same thing had happened after the international debt crisis of 1982. This can be a reason to try to limit the magnitude of indebtedness. In any case, capital inflows pose questions of macroeconomic management that must be answered one way or another.

Figure 24.2 illustrates four major possible macroeconomic strategies for dealing with a capital inflow.

(A) *Allow inflow of money.* First, as the level of reserves increases through the balance-of-payments surplus, the central bank could passively allow it to feed through as an increase in the money supply. In this case the *LM* curve shifts outward over time, as we saw in our discussion of the monetary approach to the balance of payments. The advantage of this path is that the surplus is automatically self-correcting.

The disadvantage is that the increase in the money supply can be inflationary. In terms of the Mundell-Fleming model, one could imagine that output is already at the level of potential output $\overline{Y}$ at point *B*, and that any movement further to the right will overheat the economy and eventually put upward pressure on prices. More generally, increases in the money supply tend to lead to inflation in the long run. For a country that has in the past suffered chronically from inflation, and recently defeated it with great difficulty, this path is worrisome. (We consider inflation in more detail in Chapter 26.)

Hong Kong is an example of an economy that allowed surpluses in the early 1990s to increase the money supply. Indeed, under its currency board arrangement, it had no choice. Prices, especially for real estate, boomed as a result.

FIGURE 24.2

Alternative Ways of Managing Capital Inflows

At point *B*, the country is experiencing a surplus in the balance of payments. It can allow the money to flow in, moving over time in the direction indicated by point *A*; sterilize the inflow, remaining at point *B*; allow the currency to appreciate, moving in the direction of *C*; or impose capital controls, swinging the $BP = 0$ line toward *D*.

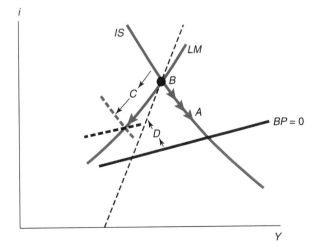

(B) *Sterilize inflow*. When reserves are flowing in through the balance of payments, the alternative to allowing them to increase the money supply is to sterilize them. Under the sterilization option, the economy for the time being simply remains at point *B*. Because the upward pressure on the money supply and aggregate demand has been shut off, inflation need not be a concern.

One disadvantage of sterilization is that it can be difficult. In the United States, with its deep, liquid securities markets, sterilizing an increase in reserves is a simple matter of open market sales of securities by the central bank, to take money out of the hands of the public. This is often more difficult in a country where domestic financial markets are less well developed. A central bank can require commercial banks to hold extra domestic reserves, and thereby try to eliminate any positive effect on M1. But this places a burden on the banks that may be inconsistent with plans to make them competitive. Alternatively, the central bank can create a new security, a "sterilization bond," that it sells to the public at large thereby taking domestic money out of circulation. But it may have to pay a high interest rate to induce the public to take these new assets voluntarily. Thereafter—because the interest rate that the central bank pays out on these sterilization bonds exceeds the interest rate it is earning on its holdings of U.S. Treasury bills or other international reserves—the central bank incurs what is called a *quasi-fiscal deficit*.

A related disadvantage to sterilization of a capital inflow is that it cannot be sustained indefinitely. By keeping the domestic interest rate high at point *B*, the central bank prolongs the capital inflow and forestalls adjustment. This is especially true if capital mobility is high. In the limiting perfect-capital mobility case of Section 23.3, sterilization quickly becomes impossible.

In the early 1990s Colombia, Korea, Indonesia, and some other countries attempted to sterilize large capital inflows. Although the central banks were able to "buy time" by this strategy, they eventually gave it up because there was no end in sight to the pattern of high interest rates and accumulating debt. The case of China's sterilized inflows after 2001 is discussed in the next subsection.

(C) *Allow appreciation*. The alternative to allowing the money supply to adjust automatically is to allow the exchange rate to adjust automatically. In response to a balance of payments surplus, this means allowing the currency to appreciate. The loss of price competitiveness has a negative effect on net exports, which can eventually return the overall balance of payments to zero. In terms of Figure 24.2, the *IS* curve shifts left to point *C*.

The advantage of appreciation is that weak demand and direct downward pressure on import prices both put a strong lid on inflation. One disadvantage is the danger of recession, especially in the tradable goods sectors that lose competitiveness from the currency appreciation. A second reason why some governments are reluctant to let their currencies float arises if they are strongly attached to a long-term strategy of pegging the exchange rate, for example, because it was instrumental in an earlier program of monetary stabilization. The arguments for fixed versus floating exchange rates are summarized in Chapter 26.

Korea allowed its currency to appreciate in the late 1980s, in response to large balance of payments surpluses.

(D) *Impose controls*. The fourth choice is to impose—or reimpose—controls on capital inflows. If the controls are effective, they will tilt the $BP = 0$ line upward. If the shift goes far enough, the new $BP = 0$ line may run through point B, which means that the balance of payments surplus has been eliminated. At times in the early 1990s, Chile, Colombia, and Malaysia imposed controls to discourage capital inflows. China and India delayed removing the controls that they had long maintained. The clearest disadvantage to controls on capital inflows is that the country passes up an opportunity to finance its development by borrowing abroad at a relatively lower interest rate. Instead, it has to finance investment out of higher-cost domestic funds.

A fifth possible option is a fiscal contraction, to shift the *IS* curve leftward. Many of these countries had already made substantial progress at eliminating large budget deficits, however, despite political difficulties. Indeed, to the extent that budget deficits lack long-run sustainability and undermine confidence in monetary stability, their elimination can sometimes be a cause of capital inflows rather than the reverse.

The Case of China's Balance-of-Payments Surplus

The large balance-of-payments surplus in China in the years following 2001 offers a good case study for these questions. It also had much in common with contemporaneous events in India and many other developing countries that found themselves at a point like B in Figure 24.2.

The Chinese surpluses had three components:

1. *Large inflows of foreign direct investment*. China encouraged inward FDI as a deliberate part of its successful development strategy because it lacked domestically technical and managerial know-how and high-quality systems of corporate governance and finance to go with its cheap manufacturing labor force.

2. *Large inflows of short-term portfolio capital*. These flows were motivated by speculation that the local currency—called the yuan or renminbi ("People's Currency")—would be revalued upward against the dollar. They circumvented capital controls and largely escaped official measurement, showing up only as the statistical discrepancy.

3. *A growing trade surplus*, including a large bilateral trade surplus with the United States. The importance of the latter was mainly political, as American manufacturers and members of Congress increasingly blamed China for the overall U.S. trade deficit and for slow growth in employment and real wages, even though the economic connection was small and tenuous. (Most of the goods that the United States has started buying from China in recent years would otherwise be bought from other Asian countries, not from domestic producers.)

China's exchange rate policy from 1997 to 2005 was in effect to peg the yuan to the U.S. dollar. China from 2002 to 2005 was like many other developing countries in that it decided to use the private capital inflows to build up strong holdings of foreign exchange reserves. Some expansion of the money supply was easily accepted as the counterpart to the very rapid growth of the overall economy. (It is appropriate for the money supply to increase if money demand is increasing.) But the primary response beginning in 2003 was to sterilize the monetary inflow. In other words, to manage the inflows the Chinese authorities mainly chose option (B). As a result, fears of overheating and inflation were not borne out. The sterilization largely took the form of raising the reserve requirements on domestic commercial banks, and also inducing them to absorb large quantities of sterilization bonds issued by the central bank at low interest rates. This policy was successful from the standpoint of the central bank but may have exacerbated the already-weak balance sheets of the commercial banks.

The government was under a lot of pressure to consider alternative (C), that is, to move to a more flexible exchange rate system, which, under the conditions of the period, would likely lead to strong appreciation of the yuan. The United States urged this option on China, under the reasoning that the dollar needed to depreciate to reduce the record U.S. trade deficits and the yuan was the last of the major currencies to cling to the dollar rather than allowing appreciation against it. Many economists found the appreciation alternative to be in China's interest as well, for a variety of reasons. China's balance-of-payments surplus was so large that it was piling up levels of foreign exchange reserves far higher than it was likely ever to need, surpassing Japan in 2006 and thereby becoming the world's largest holder of reserves. Much of these reserves is U.S. Treasury bills that pay much lower rates of return than the return China must pay for the capital that is flowing in. Appreciation would slow down the reserve accumulation and alleviate the choice between overheating and sterilization. Another argument is the Balassa-Samuelson effect (see Section 19.2), which implies that a country with productivity growth as rapid as China's must experience a real appreciation of the currency. More generally, there is the argument that a country as large as China needs to have its own independent currency (see Section 26.5)—to achieve expenditure switching through changes in the nominal exchange rate rather than the price level. Finally, experience shows that the best *exit strategy* from a peg is for the authorities to choose increased flexibility in good times (when the balance of payments is strong), rather than waiting until some future crisis forces the currency off its peg.

In 2005 the People's Bank of China finally announced it was moving to a more flexible, less dollar-oriented exchange rate policy. But the political leaders in Beijing did not get where they are today by doing anything suddenly. The move toward greater flexibility in the yuan/dollar exchange rate looked to be very gradual.

Warning Indicators and the Composition of Capital Inflows

Everyone would like to be able to predict ahead of time when a crisis will happen. This is not easy to do. Even private "rating services" professionals, who make their living by evaluating the risk of bonds from various issuers, have a poor track record. Indeed, if it were easy to predict the date of a crisis, according to the theory of efficient markets, investors would not have their money in the country at that date in the first place. But there are certain warning indicators that may signal that a country is at increased risk.[5]

---

[5]Graciela Kaminsky, Saul Lizondo, and Carmen Reinhart, "Leading Indicators of Currency Crises," *IMF Staff Papers* 5, no. 1 (1998): 1–48; and Jeffrey Frankel and Andrew Rose, "Currency Crashes in Emerging Markets," *Journal of International Economics,* 41, no. 3/4 (1996): 351–366.

Traditional indicators are measures of aggregate indebtedness, such as the ratio of debt to GDP,[6] the ratio of debt service to exports, or the ratio of the current account to GDP. One long-standing rule of thumb, for example, is that current account deficits in excess of 4 percent of GDP enter a danger zone. Such predictors are of limited use, however, and not just because they have little basis in theory. Many countries are observed to run large current account deficits for years, and yet are able to finance them without getting into trouble. It depends how the funds are used.

Borrowing to finance large budget deficits is clearly problematic. For this reason, periodically someone will assert that a given country need not worry about a current account deficit because the government budget is in balance, and thus it is only the private sector that is borrowing from abroad. There is a certain logic to the argument that decisions made freely by consenting adults who face explicit price signals (interest rates, in this case) are less likely to get into trouble than governments spending somebody else's money. Nevertheless, this principle has gone wrong frequently enough to earn the name "Lawson fallacy" (after the British finance minister who downplayed fears regarding his country's current account deficit in the late 1980s). Examples of countries that borrowed to finance private deficits rather than public deficits and yet experienced crises include Chile in 1981 and Mexico in 1994.

Out of those experiences, a new guideline emerged: A country is more likely to get into trouble if an inflow goes to finance consumption, whether public or private, instead of investment. After all, the key to sustainable borrowing is to use the funds to build up a productive capital stock, so that the country will be able tomorrow to produce, export, and earn the foreign exchange that it will need to pay back the debt incurred today. East Asian countries in the 1990s, with their high rates of saving and investment, seemed by this criterion to be unimpeachable, despite their large current account deficits. Only when they too were hit by crises in 1997–1998 did the flaw in this logic become clear. Much of the finance had gone to investment in unprofitable heavy manufacturing and real estate. A Korean firm that borrows heavily in order to invest in auto or steel factories may have trouble paying the money back if those sectors already have excess capacity.

Indicators that concern the composition of capital inflow, rather than the total amount, appear to be statistically useful at predicting the probability of currency crashes. Countries that borrow funds short term are more likely to get into trouble, especially if those funds are intermediated through the banking system and denominated in dollars or other foreign currencies. Countries that borrow long term are less likely to get into trouble especially if the inflow takes the form of foreign direct investment rather than bank loans. One theory is that bank flows in particular are more vulnerable to moral hazard problems than are other modes of finance. A mismatch of short-term bank liabilities with longer-term bank assets (e.g., real estate) leaves a country vulnerable. FDI is thought to be relatively more stable than banking inflows. Likewise, flows of longer-term securities have the advantage that the price of a stock or bond adjusts automatically in the event of adverse developments ("risk sharing"), with

---

[6]A high debt/GDP ratio is problematic, not so much in itself, but because of the danger that the country will find itself on an explosive path of *rising* debt/GDP. See the chapter supplement on debt dynamics.

fewer sticky issues of bankers' negotiating over terms of rollovers or restructuring. An alternative theory is that a run-up of short-term bank credit is a symptom of coming problems, rather than a cause, much as an individual who tries to charge his mortgage payments on his credit card reveals that he is overextended.

Countries that accumulate a high level of international reserves are less likely to have problems. The lesson drawn from past crises persuaded many developing countries to build up their reserves sharply in the period after 2001, as Figure 24.1 shows. One of the most useful summary indicators of danger is the ratio of short-term debt to reserves. As this ratio rises above 1, the danger of a crisis rises with it.[7]

24.2   Managing Outflows

There comes a day when capital flows are no longer sufficient to finance the current-account deficit. Perhaps the country has suffered a fall in world demand for its main exports. Examples include the fall in the price of oil and other basic commodities that hurt Mexico in the early 1980s or the overcapacity in the world market for semiconductors and other electronics goods that hit East Asia in 1996. Perhaps an increase in U.S. interest rates has slowed down capital flows, as it did to Latin American countries in the years 1980 to 1982 and again in 1994. Or perhaps local political instability has scared off investors, as did the assassination of the leading Mexican presidential candidate in January 1994 or the uncertainties over presidential succession in Indonesia in 1997–1998.

Figure 24.3 illustrates the plight of such a country. Point B now lies below the $BP = 0$ schedule, signaling that it is running a balance-of-payments deficit. How should the government manage these outflows? Once again, it has several macroeconomic policy options from which to choose.

(A) *Allow outflow of money.* If the central bank does not sterilize the reserve outflow, then the declining money supply will gradually shift the LM curve, moving the economy up and to the left. Higher interest rates will work to contract spending. The result will be slowing growth, perhaps exacerbated by domestic banking failures. Argentina is an example of an economy that allowed deficits in 1995 and 1999–2000 to impose a contractionary monetary policy. Under its quasi-currency board arrangement (which it called the convertibility plan), it had no choice. The result was sharp recessions both times.

(B) *Sterilize outflow.* Sterilizing the reserve outflow is an alternative to letting the money supply fall. The economy remains at point B in Figure 24.3, at least for the time being. This is a case of financing a deficit rather than adjusting. Sterilization can be a sensible strategy if there are grounds for hope that the deficit is temporary. Faced with a balance-of-payments deficit in 1994, the Bank of Mexico chose to sterilize, by expand-

---

[7]How much reserves is enough? The traditional rule of thumb was phrased in terms of trade: A country needs a minimum level of reserves that is enough to pay for three months of imports. As the source of a balance-of-payments crisis has shifted from the trade account to the capital account, a new rule of thumb has been proposed, the "Guidotti rule": A country should try to have enough reserves so that it could cover all debt coming due over the next year, in the event that creditors suddenly lost willingness to roll it over or extend new loans.

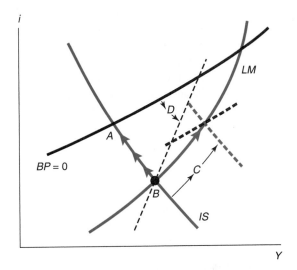

FIGURE 24.3

Alternative Ways of
Managing Capital Outflows

At point *B*, the country is
experiencing a deficit in the
balance of payments. It can allow
the money to flow out, moving
over time in the direction indicated
by point *A*; sterilize the outflow,
remaining at point B; allow the
currency to depreciate, moving
in the direction of *C*; or impose
capital controls, swinging the
$BP = 0$ line toward *D*.

ing domestic credit. Policy makers were optimistic that inflows would return when the political situation stabilized. The ruling political party also did not want to risk contraction in an election year. As a result, reserves had been run down by the time the new government took office in December.

(C) *Allow depreciation.* The alternative to automatic adjustment by allowing the money supply to fall is automatic adjustment by allowing the currency to depreciate. The positive effect on net exports can eventually return the overall balance of payments to zero. In terms of Figure 24.3, the *IS* and $BP = 0$ curves shift right to point *C*.

(D) *Reimpose controls on capital outflow.* The fourth option is to impose, or reimpose, controls on capital outflows. The goal is usually to shift the $BP = 0$ line downward, thereby allowing a low domestic interest, to sustain growth, without accelerating a capital outflow that would threaten the currency. One disadvantage is that the controls may not be very effective. Malaysia adopted controls to prevent investors from taking money offshore in 1998. Tight administrative control made this strategy more effective than it might have been in a more open society. Even when such controls are enforceable, a second disadvantage is that they are likely to scare investors away from the country in the future.

Countries that postpone adjustment may find that it becomes more costly later on. Their options will be sharply limited if they fall victim to a speculative attack.

24.3   Speculative Attacks

When speculators fear that a devaluation may be coming, to protect themselves against the expected loss in the value of the domestic currency they will seek to trade it in for foreign currency. The central bank may very quickly lose large amounts of its foreign exchange reserves in such an episode, which is known as a *speculative attack*. Absent a successful defense, the authorities are forced to abandon their previous exchange rate target—to devalue or depreciate the currency. To resist is to face the loss of all their reserves, after which they have to depreciate anyway. Hemorrhaging of reserves was the proximate cause, for example, of the Bretton Woods system's final demise in 1973, Britain's departure from the European Exchange Rate Mechanism in 1992, Mexico's ill-fated devaluation in December 1994, the East Asian currency crises of 1997, the Russian crisis of 1998, the Brazilian devaluation of 1999, the Turkish devaluation of 2001, and many others.

Economists' theories of speculative attacks have organized themselves into three "generations." Each generation of models was launched by a seminal article or articles, of which a key feature was an attempt to answer the question, "Why do crises occur when they do?" Each relied on the assumption that speculators think ahead and form their expectations rationally. But before we consider the question of timing, it may be useful to explain the three categories in terms of their attempts to answer a less technical and more inflammatory question: Whose fault is the crisis? Generation I says domestic macroeconomic policy, Generation II says volatile international financial markets, and Generation III says domestic financial structure. In neutral language, the explanations are, respectively, excessive monetary and fiscal expansion, "multiple equilibria," and moral hazard. In finger-pointing language, the respective culprits are irresponsible domestic policy makers, crazy international investors, and crony capitalists.

First Generation: Overly Expansionary Macroeconomic Policy

The first generation of speculative attack models attributes speculative attacks ultimately to overly expansionary macroeconomic policies. Most textbook analysis falls into this category. Budget deficits must be financed by borrowing or monetary expansion. Either way, the result is a current account deficit. If nothing is done to adjust, eventually the country will run out of reserves. Macroeconomic overexpansion and overvaluation were the standard diagnoses of balance of payments crises in developing countries before 1995, and were the basis of most adjustment programs administered by the International Monetary Fund. The international debt crisis of the 1980s is an important example.

What determines the timing of the attack? The seminal article in the first generation approach was by Paul Krugman.[8] Consider a country in which, because of ongoing monetary or fiscal expansion, the balance-of-payments deficit is a steady $1 billion a year. If it has reserves of $5 billion, then apparently it can hold out for five years. Absent some change, it will run out of reserves at the end of that time and be forced to devalue or depreciate, by enough to eliminate the deficit.

Krugman's contribution was to identify, in a country that will eventually run out of reserves, the time at which the attack will come. It will be sooner than five years. If

---

[8]"A Model of Balance of Payments Crises," *Journal of Money, Credit and Banking*, 11 (1979): 311–325; reprinted in Krugman's *Currencies and Crises* (Cambridge, MA: MIT Press, 1992), pp. 61–76. Robert Flood and Peter Garber produced a more accessible version of the model: "Collapsing Exchange Rate Regimes: Some Linear Examples," *Journal of International Economics*, 17 (1984): 1–14.

speculators are rational, they will not wait until then. To do so would mean holding an asset—domestic currency—while knowing that it will suffer a discrete loss in value in the immediate future. Any self-respecting speculator would instead shift his or her money out of the country at an earlier date. When they all do this, they move the date of the crisis forward. One might then try to take this logic to the other limit, reasoning that the attack must take place much earlier, the moment when the pattern of over-expansion and eventual devaluation first become clear. But this also is not the right solution. As long as the central bank has plenty of reserves to defend the exchange rate, speculators will be happy to wait. There is an intermediate date, when the remaining stock of reserves has been run down to just the right level: still high enough that the speculators can get their money out, but no higher than that. That is when the attack occurs. The remainder of the reserves are then suddenly depleted in a single day. This theory helps explain why the level of reserves is statistically a useful predictor, a low level of reserves signaling danger of crisis.

Second Generation: Multiple Equilibria

The second generation of models argue that more than one possible outcome—crisis and no-crisis—can be consistent with equilibrium, even if there has been no change in true fundamentals.[9] The multiple equilibrium approach took its inspiration from the crises in the European Exchange Rate Mechanism (ERM) of 1992–1993.

There had always been some who claimed that financial markets were excessively volatile, that they alternated waves of optimism and pessimism. But the usual view among academic economists as well as the international financial establishment had been that markets are based in economic fundamentals; so declining market prices or flows are merely the messenger or symptom of underlying problems. This view became harder to maintain as a sequence of currencies succumbed to attack. The attack on France in 1993 was particularly puzzling because the government had over the preceding years succeeded in attaining a level of macroeconomic discipline that by most indicators looked as great as that of Germany, its partner in the ERM. Moreover, after the bands were widened, the crisis passed without a substantial further depreciation of the franc, even though there had been no tightening of macroeconomic policy in the meantime. How then could the fundamentals have been responsible for the earlier speculative pressure? Also puzzling was that Sweden and the United Kingdom had shown a willingness to raise interest rates to extremely high levels to defend the krona and the pound in 1992, yet speculators were unimpressed and persisted in those attacks nonetheless. Such a response, known as the *interest rate defense,* is apparently no longer guaranteed to work.

The point is most easily understood as a game played among speculators, along the lines of the classic "prisoners' dilemma." Consider two large speculators. Each realizes that if the other sells, the resulting depreciation will reduce the value of his or her holdings of domestic currency. Neither wants to stand pat if the other might sell. Thus an

---

[9]Maurice Obstfeld, "The Logic of Currency Crises," *Cahiers Economiques et Monetaires,* 43 (1994): 189–213.

equilibrium might entail both selling, even though everyone may be worse off after the devaluation.

Can one say anything about what conditions will make a country vulnerable to such an attack? If the fundamentals are particularly weak, both speculators will sell. For example, if the central bank holds a sufficiently low level of reserves, then each speculator knows that if he chooses to sell his domestic currency, he will deplete the central banks' holdings of foreign reserves, and thereby force a devaluation. Each knows this, and so will sell to avoid being the one left "holding the bag." If the fundamentals are particularly strong, there will be no attack. For example, if the level of reserves is sufficiently high that both speculators know they can't break the bank even acting together, they have no reason to attack. The interesting case comes in the intermediate range. If the fundamentals are bad but not terrible, then the country is vulnerable to an attack. But the game theory cannot predict what the outcome will be in this case. The attack and no-attack outcomes are equally valid equilibria. This is what we mean by multiple equilibria.

One variant is an international version of a standard model of domestic *bank runs*. Each bank depositor is motivated to take her money out of the bank only if she thinks others might do the same, so that there might not be enough cash to go around. The recommended solution is deposit insurance and adequate reserve holdings by the banks.[10]

Another variant treats monetary policy as endogenous. After all, why should governments decide to embark on a dangerous path of excessive money growth that they stubbornly maintain regardless of adverse developments? The ultimate fundamentals are not macroeconomic policies, but rather the political conditions that might make the benefits of devaluation and monetary expansion more likely to outweigh the costs, from the viewpoint of the monetary authorities. Some suggest that a key fundamental variable, determining whether a country is in the intermediate range where speculative attacks are a danger, is the level of unemployment; some say it is the level of debt.[11] If these indicators are at particularly high levels, then the tight monetary policy necessary to fight a speculative attack will involve particularly high costs relative to benefits. This is because the high interest rates may spark banking failures or social unrest. Speculators know that the high interest rates are not politically sustainable, which makes an attack more likely even if the policy makers sincerely do their best to hold the line.

Third Generation: "Crony Capitalism" and Moral Hazard

If crises of the 1970s and 1980s were represented by the first-generation approach, and if the 1992–1993 ERM crises inspired the second-generation models, then the East Asian crises of 1997–1998 provided motivation for the third-generation models.

Unlike Latin America and other parts of the world with a history of large budget deficits, high-inflation monetary policies, and overvalued currencies, East Asia in the

---

[10]Douglas Diamond and Philip Dybvig, "Bank Runs, Deposit Insurance, and Liquidity," *Journal of Political Economy*, 91 (June 1983): 401–419. An international version is Roberto Chang and Andres Velasco, "Liquidity Crises in Emerging Markets: Theory and Policy," in *NBER Macroeconomics Annual* (Cambridge, MA: MIT Press, 2000).

[11]Maurice Obstfeld, "Models of Currency Crises with Self-Fulfilling Features," *European Economic Review*, 90 (April 1996): 1037–1047.

latter third of the twentieth century earned a reputation for fiscal discipline and monetary stability. This record was largely maintained right up until the crisis. True, Thailand and Korea clung to overvalued currencies in the sense that they depleted their net reserves in futile attempts to defend the exchange rate, before trying something else. But there had been little evidence of profligate monetary and fiscal policy on the part of these governments or of currencies that were overvalued in real terms. Indeed, westerners had argued earlier that such high-growth countries should experience real appreciations, under Balassa-Samuelson reasoning (Section 19.2, especially footnote 11).

The third-generation approach instead interprets recent crises as illustrations of the perils of moral hazard. Borrowers and lenders are less likely to be careful evaluating the true profitability of investment opportunities if they believe they will be bailed out in the event that the project goes badly. As already noted, some believe that international bailouts by the IMF and G-7 create the moral hazard problem. But in the third-generation models, the root-cause locus of moral hazard is at the national level rather than the international level. If moral hazard at the international level were the original and only root of the problem, then it would follow that the amount of capital flowing from rich to poor countries overall would be greater than socially optimal. But instead, the amount of capital flowing, on average, is *less* than predicted by neoclassical optimizing economic models of the type illustrated in Section 21.5. In other words, the large existing differences across countries in capital/labor ratios and therefore in the rate of return to capital predict that capital flow should be larger than what we observe, not smaller.

The phrase "crony capitalism" became suddenly popular in 1997 to describe newly evident flaws in the structure of Asian financial systems. In fairness, some of these same characteristics had been seen as strengths of Asian economies a short time earlier. Business deals are said to be dominated by personal connections (*guan xi* in China), large family-run conglomerates (*chaebol* in Korea), comprehensive clusters of allied firms (*keiretsu* in Japan), or insider links to the government (charges of corruption, collusion, and nepotism—which protesters sloganized as "KKN"—regarding President Suharto in Indonesia). Firms fund investments by borrowing from bankers with whom they have close personal or political ties. The loans may come from a bank to which the firm is affiliated, in which case they are called connected or related lending, or they may come under guidance by the government, in which case they are called directed lending. Corporations often pursue "empire building," seeking to maximize their size, without regard to profitability or shareholder value.

An idealized version of American capitalism is held up as a contrasting example: Transactions among corporations are said to be made at "arm's length," based on explicit contracts enforced under a transparent legal system. Corporations rely heavily on securities markets to fund investment, where rules require accounting by recognized standards, public disclosure of information, and pursuit by managers of maximization of returns to shareholders. The Asian system is termed "relationship based," and the American system "market based."[12]

---

[12]Beginning in 2001, U.S. corporations suffered accounting and management scandals of their own, suggesting that Americans needed to listen to some of the lectures they had been giving others.

The third-generation model starts from the assumption that government officials have a pot of resources that can potentially be used to bail out political cronies if they get into financial difficulty.[13] This pot is mainly identified with the central banks' holdings of foreign exchange reserves, but it could also include funds that the country can borrow from the IMF, the government's claim on revenue from export taxes, or any profitable state-owned enterprises or other holdings that the government could sell off—whatever sources of hard currency the government can lay its hands on in the event of a crisis. Well-connected banks and businesspeople are able to borrow from abroad to finance risky projects—such as real estate development or a new factory in the already glutted steel industry. They are aware of the risk. But they believe that they will be bailed out by the government if things go badly. In the worst countries, they have been explicitly promised that they will be bailed out. In other cases, the government may have tried to declare in advance that it will not be responsible for private debts, but this disclaimer is not believed.[14]

Why does the crisis occur when it does? Asian countries did not suddenly develop critical structural flaws in their financial systems for the first time in 1997. The timing of the attack again comes out of the calculations of speculators who worry that if they wait too long, there will not be enough foreign exchange reserves to go around. But there is a key difference from the first-generation models, which watched reserves decline steadily over time and identified the timing of the attack as the point at which reserves sank to a particular critical level. The third-generation models watch liabilities rise steadily over time, artificially encouraged by moral hazard. They identify the timing of the attack with the point at which the liabilities have climbed to the critical level given by the level of reserves. At that point, speculators suddenly cash in their investments. If they waited any longer they might not be able to get their money out. The speculative attack, as usual, then forces the central bank to abandon the exchange rate.

24.4 Contagion

One distinctive feature of recent crises is that turmoil has spread beyond the country where it first surfaced. The tendency to spill over to other countries is called contagion.

Contagion is not a precisely defined financial term. It means something more than the evident fact that prices of stocks, bonds, and foreign exchange are correlated across countries. Such correlation could readily be explained by common shocks. A global fall

---

[13]The key references are Michael Dooley, "A Model of Crises in Emerging Markets," *Economic Journal,* 110, no. 460 (January 2000): 256–272, and Paul Krugman, "Balance Sheets Effects, the Transfer Problem and Financial Crises," in P. Isard, A. Razin, and A. Rose, eds., *International Finance and Financial Crises: Essays in Honour of Robert P. Flood, Jr.* (New York: Kluwer Academic Publishers, 1999): 31–34. Also Giancarlo Corsetti, Paolo Pesenti, and Nouriel Roubini, "What Caused the Asian Currency and Financial Crisis?" *Japan and the World Economy,* 11 (1999): 305–373.

[14]Carlos Diaz-Alejandro, "Good-bye Financial Repression; Hello Financial Crash," *Journal of Development Economics,* 19 (September 1985). A "no bailout" declaration lacks credibility particularly in the case of domestic banks. When the crisis comes, the pressure for the government to rescue insolvent banks will be irresistible for two reasons. (1) Most depositors are small savers, not sophisticated investors; and (2) bank failures can have a devastating effect on the rest of the economy, particularly because banks constitute the payments system.

in commodity prices will hurt all commodity exporters. Contagion carries the connotation that a shock may spread from one country to another for reasons other than economic fundamentals. The international debt crisis of the 1980s spread from Mexico to Argentina, Brazil, and other highly indebted countries around the world. But it was not generally called contagion, perhaps because it seemed explainable by adverse fundamentals.

Even a country with strong fundamentals may find, when a neighbor suffers a speculative attack, that it is attacked in turn. In 1995 the repercussions of the Mexican peso crisis soon hit Argentina and others in the hemisphere. They were labeled the "tequila effect," implying that even though it was Mexico who had had too much to drink, others shared the hangover.

The spillover need not reflect irrationality on the part of investors. If two countries are major trading partners, or if they compete in third-country export markets, the second country may find when the first devalues that the loss in export competitiveness forces it to devalue in turn. Because there is a heavy geographic pattern in trade, it is natural to suspect such competitiveness effects when the contagion runs along regional lines. For example, in July 1997, it had already been clear that Thailand was in trouble; but after the Thai devaluation, the crisis spread throughout the region, including to Taiwan, Hong Kong, Indonesia, and Malaysia. Some of these economies had been thought to have good macroeconomic fundamentals. The explanation is in part that they produce goods that compete with Thai exports. When Thailand devalued, Taiwan felt obliged to follow suit, to remain competitive. Another explanation for contagion involves financial linkages. Bankruptcies in Indonesia, for example, exacerbated pressures on firms in Hong Kong, Korea, and Singapore because they lost money that had been invested in Indonesian firms. Less directly, when one country gets into trouble a second may be impacted if Japanese or American banks that lent to both countries, or mutual funds that invested in both, are forced by losses in the first to sell assets in the second.

Figure 24.4 shows "sovereign spreads," that is, the premia that global investors demand to hold countries' bonds (relative to U.S. Treasury bills). It also shows an aggregate measure called the Emerging Market Bond Index (EMBI). The Mexican peso crisis was reflected in a sharp rise in spreads in Latin America and, to a lesser extent, emerging markets worldwide. Similarly, the Thai crisis of 1997 showed up as an increase in the interest rates that other Asian emerging market borrowers had to pay.

In the past, currency crises seemed to cluster largely along regional lines. But contagion more recently has jumped oceans. August 1998 brought a new round of trouble when attempts to stabilize Russia ended with default on its debt and devaluation of the ruble. Speculative pressure immediately turned to Brazil, even though the two countries share little in the way of trade links or other common characteristics. The Russian shock had a severe impact in Latin American. It also affected Asia, and the global EMBI index. The point is that crises are often now global.

A crash in one country can induce speculators to reevaluate their perceptions regarding others. The 1997 Thai crisis caused investors to switch from the previous interpretation of the tigers' growth records as an "Asian miracle," to the new "crony capitalist" view. The 1998 Russian crisis caused some to switch from the belief that the

FIGURE 24.4

Emerging Market Bond Index (EMBI) and Spreads for Some Individual Countries

During the emerging market crises of the 1990s, sovereign spreads (the interest rates that debtor countries must pay on their bonds, above and beyond U.S. Treasury bill rates) were highly correlated. This is evidence of contagion.

IMF would rescue major debtors, to the logic that if a country as important as Russia could be allowed to default, anybody could. Other explanations for contagion involve herd behavior, increased risk aversion, an international drying up of liquidity, and even financial panic.

24.5 IMF Country Programs

What happens when a country's reserves run out, so that remaining at point *B* in Figure 24.3 is no longer an option? The choices can be stark.

Most countries in this position call in the International Monetary Fund, even if they were reluctant to do so earlier. If the victim is a relatively important country, then the G-7 powers may receive calls at the same time. "Important" here can mean either that it is large enough to have "systemic implications" (i.e., its default would threaten others with contagion) or that it has friends in high places because of geopolitical considerations (e.g., Russia's nuclear weapons make it difficult to ignore).

The first thing that the international financial community tries to do is ascertain if the problem is one of *liquidity* or of *solvency*. In a liquidity crisis, the economy is seen to be sound in terms of economic fundamentals and to need only short-term loans to tide it over. In such cases, the IMF operates as the international version of a *lender of last resort*. This refers to the classic role played at the national level by the central bank, when it lends freely to domestic banks that, although fundamentally sound, are caught short of liquidity. If the country is thought to be insolvent, this means its problems run deeper, requiring fundamental policy reforms and perhaps a restructuring of its international obligations. In practice, many crises are an uncomfortable mixture of liquidity and solvency problems.

IMF rescue programs have two big components. First, the international financial community tries to meet the financing gap in the country's balance of payments. Second, the country agrees to adjust or reform its policies. These promises are embodied in a *letter of intent* from the local government to the IMF.

Each of the two components is necessary. Financing is made conditional or contingent on policy reform, under the practice of *conditionality*. On the one hand, financing without policy reform would probably do little to restore investor confidence and, even if it did, might lead to another crisis down the road. On the other hand, plans for policy reform without financing would typically be insufficient to satisfy the immediate balance of payments constraint. Furthermore, conditionality provides an incentive for countries to agree to initiate painful but needed reforms and then to follow through on the plans under subsequent monitoring by IMF teams. Often these are policy changes such as cuts in public spending that the country's finance minister knew all along were desirable but that the government found politically difficult. Historically, one role of the IMF and World Bank has been to take the blame politically for unpopular policy measures. Recently, however, these two international financial institutions have lost enthusiasm for this role. The new wisdom is that countries must "take ownership" of their policy reforms, or else their promises may never in the end be genuinely fulfilled. This principle holds even more clearly for the sort of longer term reforms that are associated with World Bank programs.

Filling the Financing Gap

Even after accounting for the projected effect of improvements in macroeconomic policy on the trade balance and capital account of the crisis country, there is still likely to be a gap in the balance of payments that needs to be financed. The first source of financing in an IMF program is an IMF loan. Indeed, any member country is entitled, just for asking, to a first "tranche," which is commensurate with the amount of hard currency it put into the kitty when it originally joined the institution. Then, even if a country needs to go beyond a traditional "stand-by arrangement," further funds are available through a number of facilities at the IMF.

Sometimes the IMF loans are not enough, however. In a few major crises, the package has included additional funds from several sources. One is the G-7, especially in some rescue programs where the magnitude of the loans needed to restore confidence has dwarfed the resources available from the IMF. In the so-called Paris Club, the major rich countries often agree to reschedule their government loans (many of which were originally made to encourage their countries' exports). Another source to help fill the financing gap is the General Arrangements to Borrow (GAB) and New Arrangements to Borrow (NAB), which include wider sets of countries that can afford to lend funds. A third source is the World Bank, even though its job is supposed to be longer-term development loans, rather than short-term balance-of-payments loans. All these loans pay interest, notwithstanding skepticism on this score from taxpayers in the creditor countries.

The goal of the country program is always to restore confidence and thereby restore the flow of private capital. The IMF's "seal of good housekeeping" signals private investors that it is okay to resume lending. When this works, the new private capital flows are much greater than the money actually put in by the IMF. In some major crises, it requires some twisting of the arms of individual investors, as we will see later in the discussion of private sector involvement.

Policy Conditionality

Traditional IMF programs typically involve some mixture of two sorts of macroeconomic policy adjustment: contractionary monetary (and fiscal) policy and devaluation. In Section 18.2, we called them expenditure-reducing policies and expenditure-switching policies. It is not hard to see why these same medicines are prescribed over and over again: They are designed to cure excessive current account deficits. An increase in interest rates has the additional goal of improving the capital account. Nevertheless, the appropriateness of these remedies has been increasingly questioned.

That IMF-inflicted austerity is wildly unpopular with internal political constituents is nothing new. A typical way for a desperate government to respond to the need to cut expenditure is to reduce existing subsidies on basic foodstuffs or fuel, for example. (The government is typically less willing to cut the Army's pay.) Sometimes the population reacts in riots, which can turn violent and in some cases have led to the overthrow of the head of state. No easy solution is likely to exist, however, if a government has been living beyond its means, and nobody is willing to put up the money to pay the bills.

The traditional macroeconomic prescription has been increasingly widely questioned on two grounds. First, the origins of the East Asia crisis did not seem to fit the traditional diagnosis—overexpansion and overvaluation—as closely as, for example, was true in earlier crises in Latin America. Second, the IMF programs were accompanied immediately by severe recessions.

That the origins of a crisis may lie in multiple equilibria or moral hazard rather than the usual macroeconomic excesses, is not necessarily a reason to abandon conditionality. Rather, it is a reason to make the program conditional on specific reforms tailored to the conditions in the country in question, perhaps deep reforms in the structure of the economy. Recent IMF programs have tended to emphasize *structural conditionality*. This trend began with the need for thorough market reforms in Russia and the other transition economies that emerged from the breakup of the former Soviet bloc in 1990. The trend grew in 1997–1998, in an attempt to address the flaws in

East Asian economic structures popularly known as crony capitalism. Common elements of the reforms include improvements in corporate governance, prudential banking regulation, bankruptcy laws, and government treatment of protected monopolies. Critics charge that the IMF's lists of structural reforms are excessively long and detailed and represent an intrusion into local sovereignty. A famous example is the IMF's insistence that President Suharto agree to dismantle the monopoly that controlled Indonesia's clove industry. The IMF is accused of "mission creep," that is, attempting to expand its bureaucratic turf beyond its original mandate. It must be noted, however, that the criticism regarding excessively detailed conditionality tends to cut against another, equally common, criticism of the same programs—namely that they apply a "cookie-cutter" approach not individually tailored to the circumstances of each country.

The reforms, although never easy politically, are not necessarily imposed by the IMF on a reluctant government. In each of the three major East Asian programs, Thailand, Korea, and Indonesia, the reforms were not enacted until there was a change in government. Populations, angered by the crises, threw out the incumbents and gave the new governments enough political support to begin reforms. Admittedly, the IMF itself was a target of popular anger even more than the incumbent governments.

The other grounds that have led to widespread questioning of the traditional macroeconomic approach are the observation that the IMF programs seem to be followed by sharp recessions. Recall our framework of internal and external balance (illustrated by the Swan diagram of Figures 18.5 or 20.5). Why can't the external financing objective be met while simultaneously preserving internal balance? In the effort to restore external balance, the economy often overshoots internal balance and moves sharply into the zone of excess supply. One reason for the contractions is that macroeconomic austerity is still as important a part of IMF conditionality as are structural reforms. The initial programs in Thailand and Korea, for example, called for fiscal contractions and sharp increases in interest rates. Structural conditionality can also contribute to a contraction of the real economy, as when insolvent banks were closed down in Indonesia despite the absence of deposit insurance to protect depositors.

A key question is the desirable mix of monetary contraction and devaluation—alternative ways of addressing a balance-of-payments deficit. Critics have charged that the IMF forced the East Asian countries to raise interest rates too much. Banks and corporate borrowers that were not already insolvent were rendered insolvent by the high interest rates. The critics point out that an increase in interest rates may not even accomplish the desired aim of attracting a new capital inflow if investors know that the risk of default goes up when the interest rate goes up.[15]

We must ask what is the alternative to contraction, because something must be done to satisfy the external financing problem created when foreign investors pull out. Identifying the alternative—what would have happened in the absence of the IMF program—is always the difficulty in evaluating its success. We would not want to condemn

---

[15]For example, Jason Furman and Joseph Stiglitz, "Economic Crises: Evidence and Insights from East Asia," *Brookings Papers on Economic Activity,* 2 (1998): 115–135.

hospitals on the grounds that their occupants die more often than residents of apartment buildings.

Some critics argue that an alternative combination, lower interest rates and more devaluation, could have achieved the same external balance while simultaneously maintaining internal balance. But by the time the country is in crisis, it may be too late. As we see in the next section—and contrary to the models of earlier chapters—devaluation can pose dangers of bankruptcy and recession similar to the dangers posed by monetary contraction. If a country has depleted its reserves and lost the confidence of its investors, there may no longer exist any combination of interest rate and exchange rate that can restore both external and internal balance.[16] There may be no way of avoiding a recession. The most important lesson is that countries should not postpone balance-of-payments adjustment until they have run out of reserves and investor confidence because at that point crisis may be inevitable.

24.6   Contractionary Effects of Devaluation

In the models of earlier chapters, a devaluation had a clearly expansionary effect on output and employment. As long as the Marshall-Lerner condition was satisfied, net foreign demand for domestic products—that is, the trade balance—increased, working to raise output and employment. However, countries forced to devalue, usually because they are running out of foreign exchange reserves, often express the view that devaluation has a contractionary effect on output and employment rather than an expansionary one.[17] There are a number of channels through which such effects could possibly occur. Although some are also very relevant for large industrialized countries, many are peculiar to small countries and developing countries. We will consider eight possible contractionary effects that can arise in various contexts, the first six operating through the demand for domestic goods and the last two operating through supply. Many of these concern structural characteristics of typical developing countries that are of interest in their own right.

Negative Effects on Aggregate Demand

The first problem arose in Chapter 16: If the country begins with a high initial volume of imports—and countries usually devalue only when they have a trade deficit—then, because the devaluation raises the cost of imports in domestic terms, the trade balance may worsen in domestic terms, even if the demand elasticities are high enough to satisfy the simple Marshall-Lerner condition. If domestic demand does not rise at the same time, then the total effect on the demand for domestic goods will be contractionary. Of course, sufficiently large elasticities will solve this problem. Developing countries often argue, however, that their elasticities are low. This is particularly true of

---

[16]See the problems at the end of the chapter.
[17]There are other drawbacks to devaluation, particularly the exacerbation of inflation, regardless of the effect on output. This aspect is considered further in Chapter 26.

their elasticity of demand for imports they cannot produce domestically, such as oil, luxury consumer goods, or capital goods. Also, it can be argued that the world demand for the exports of even a small country may fall far short of the infinite elasticity that was assumed in Chapter 20. Textiles produced in Guatemala are not quite perfect substitutes for textiles produced in China.

Many of the products exported by developing countries face import barriers from the industrialized world (not to mention from other developing countries). If the devaluing country is constrained from increasing its exports, and its import bill increases with the devaluation, then domestic output will suffer from a loss in demand.

The second contractionary effect of devaluation is the real balance effect, first developed as part of the monetary approach in Chapter 19, then extended in Section 20.3. A devaluation raises the price of traded goods proportionately, thereby raising the general price level and reducing the real money supply to the extent that traded goods are important in the basket. The lower real money supply then reduces expenditure. In the flexible-price model, markets clear, by assumption, and so total output and employment do not fall. The contractionary effect on domestic spending is offset one for one by the stimulus to net exports, so the total is unchanged. However, if we allow for slowly adjusting prices of nontraded goods, the contractionary effect on domestic expenditure can translate into an excess supply of goods. Total output and employment in the economy may fall if the demand for nontraded goods falls by more than the net foreign demand for traded goods rises. To take an example, a feature of Poland's "shock therapy" reform program of January 1990 was a devaluation of almost 50 percent. The real balance effect, although helping to produce a trade surplus, also helped produce a sharp fall in output and employment.[18]

The third effect of a devaluation, attributed to Carlos Diaz-Alejandro, enters when we introduce distinctions between different classes of consumers.[19] When wages, W, are sticky, a devaluation reduces real wages by increasing prices. Indeed, the only way it stimulates the production of tradable goods is by reducing W/P_t, the real wage in terms of traded goods. It is easy to see why workers might object to a devaluation. However, if workers' share of national income falls, then firm owners' share of national income rises. Thus it is more difficult to see why there should be a contractionary effect on total demand, as is often claimed, rather than simply a negative effect on the equality of the distribution of income.

Diaz-Alejandro's argument is that different sectors have different marginal propensities to consume. Owners of firms might have a lower propensity to consume than workers. The specific example he had in mind was Argentina, where the most important tradable goods were traditionally wheat and cattle, which are raised by large landowners. A devaluation raises the prices of these commodities and causes a redistribution of real income away from urban workers (who consume wheat and meat and import other goods that are also now more expensive), and toward the landowners. If

---

[18]John Williamson, *The Economic Opening of Eastern Europe* (Washington, DC: Institute for International Economics, 1991).

[19]Carlos Diaz-Alejandro, "A Note on the Impact of Devaluation and the Redistribution Effect," *Journal of Political Economy* (December 1963): 577–580.

the landowners have a lower propensity to consume than the urban workers do, the net effect on aggregate demand will be negative. Such distributional effects of a devaluation are likely to be more important for developing countries than for industrialized countries.[20]

The fourth potential contractionary effect of a devaluation, the *balance sheet* effect, has perhaps been the most important in recent emerging market crises. It concerns debt rather than money. Small countries that find they must devalue often have already accumulated sizable debts to the rest of the world, in the form of bonds they have sold to foreign residents or loans they have received from foreign banks. Such debts are usually denominated in dollars or other foreign currencies; foreign investors are reluctant to hold assets denominated in local currency precisely because they fear that the country will devalue the local currency and thereby reduce the value of those assets to foreigners. Because the inability to borrow in local currency often seems beyond the control of the developing country governments, it has been called the problem of *original sin*. Residents of the home country lose if their debt is denominated in a foreign currency, such as the dollar, and the country is forced to devalue. Because it now costs more units of local currency to buy one dollar, servicing the debt—that is, making the interest payments and paying off the principal in installments—is more expensive in terms of the local currency, the problem of *currency mismatch*. Households and firms may respond to the deterioration in their net wealth position (the increase in the valuation of their liabilities) and in their cash flow (the increase in their debt service requirements) by cutting back expenditures. This is the balance sheet effect.[21] After the sudden devaluation of the Mexican peso in December 1994, to take one example, the resulting increase in the cost of the large outstanding dollar debts bankrupted some businesses and contributed to a recession in Mexico. The same thing happened on a larger scale in 1997 and 1998 in Thailand, Indonesia, and Korea.

A fifth potential effect of a devaluation concerns the speculative buying of goods. Speculative buying of goods may be the only way that people can protect the real value of their wealth against high expected inflation rates, particularly in countries where a full range of bonds and stocks are not available because financial markets are not fully developed. If people think that a devaluation and consequent price increases are com-

---

[20]In developing countries, differences in income, and especially in wealth, are often greater than in industrialized countries. An increase in firms' profits is likely to be distributed less widely through the population. Furthermore, access to consumer credit is more limited. Those living closer to the margin of subsistence are likely to have little saving and even less scope for borrowing, so their marginal propensity to consume is likely to be very close to 1. This is why redistributional effects are likely to be larger in developing countries.

[21]The net wealth of the citizens of a country in the aggregate is a determinant of private spending, along with such variables as income. There is an interesting question as to what sort of bonds should be counted as part of net wealth. We usually do not count citizens' holdings of corporate debt because the corporations are owned by other citizens, so in total the assets and liabilities cancel out, much as with an IOU between two individuals. (This is called *piercing the corporate veil*.) Some economists argue analogously that citizens' holdings of bonds issued by their government should not be counted as net wealth. The argument is that an increase in the national debt means that the government will have to raise taxes at some point in the future, and far-sighted citizens will weigh those implicit future tax liabilities negatively when figuring their net wealth, and thus fully cancel out the positive effect of the bonds held. This doctrine is called *Ricardian equivalence*. The subject is addressed in the appendix to Chapter 21. In any case, it is clear that holdings of foreign bonds (or indebtedness to foreigners) count positively (or negatively) in net national wealth, as do holdings of physical capital.

ing in the future, they may buy consumer durables and other such goods in anticipation. In Chile in the mid-1970s, for example, many residents believed that the government would be unable to maintain the peso at its high value; in anticipation of future devaluation, they bought consumer appliances and other durable goods.[22] Although such purchases can have an expansionary effect at the time of the purchases, the devaluation itself may remove this speculative motive for spending and result in a contraction.[23]

The sixth contractionary effect that has been identified arises when there are important tariffs on tradable goods. A devaluation will raise the price of the traded good proportionately and therefore the amount of tariff revenue that must be paid to the government. As with any tax increase, this will have a negative effect on the private sector's disposable income and therefore on its expenditures. This effect is likely to be more important in developing countries than in industrialized countries because only the former tend to rely on tariffs for a significant fraction of government revenue.[24]

Negative Effects on Aggregate Supply

The two remaining effects of devaluation arise in relation to aggregate supply rather than aggregate demand. They work to raise the price level for any given quantity of output supplied or, equivalently, to reduce the quantity of output supplied for any given price level. Thus they can be more troublesome than the six contractionary demand effects, which can in theory be offset by expansionary monetary or fiscal policy if desired.

Effect number seven, one of the most important for industrialized countries and developing countries alike, relates to the prices of raw materials and other imported inputs. (These are the intermediate goods or fragmented production of Chapter 9.) In Mexico in 1982–1983, for example, foreign exchange became very scarce, mostly because of successive devaluations of the peso in response to the international debt crisis. As a result, companies were forced to cut output severely—even of products for which there was adequate demand—for lack of necessary industrial materials, mechanical parts, and other inputs that had previously been imported. The same thing happened in Korea and some other East Asian countries after the currency crises of 1997.

For oil-importing countries, the most important input is usually oil. Energy is a factor of production like labor and capital. Most countries take the price of oil and other fossil fuels as determined completely on world markets. Thus a devaluation translates directly into a proportionate increase in the price that firms have to pay for fuel

---

[22]Rudiger Dornbusch, reprinted as "Overborrowing: Three Case Studies," in R. Dornbusch, *Dollars, Debts and Deficits* (Cambridge, MA: MIT Press, 1986).

[23]Another potential explanation for observed coincidence of devaluation and recession arises if contractionary monetary and fiscal policies are imposed at the same time as a devaluation. Although the policy changes are distinct and have distinct effects, it can be difficult to disentangle them empirically. The tendency for such policy changes to occur at the same time may account for some claims that devaluations are observed to have a negative association with output. Richard Cooper, "Currency Devaluation in Developing Countries," *Essays in International Finance*, 86 (Princeton: Princeton University Press, 1971), offers a classic account of devaluation that presents the six contractionary effects discussed so far.

[24]Paul Krugman and Lance Taylor, in "Contractionary Effects of Devaluation," *Journal of International Economics*, 8, no. 3 (1978): 445–456.

expressed in domestic currency. The increase in marginal cost relative to the price of the good the firm is producing will induce it to reduce output. The outcome can be analogous to the recession suffered by most countries in 1974 following the quadrupling of the world price of oil. The negative effect on a country's aggregate supply is the same, whether the reason for an increase in the price paid for imported oil is a worldwide price increase or an increase in the individual country's exchange rate.[25]

Eighth on the list, a parallel supply effect, again as important for many industrialized countries as for developing countries, concerns wages. When workers see increases in the prices of tradable goods that they consume, they may ask for increases in their nominal wages to make up for the loss in purchasing power. In some countries, particularly those with a recent history of high rates of inflation, wage contracts may be indexed. That is, they may be written so that increases in the consumer price index that occur during the period of the contract are automatically reflected in the wage rate. Thus a subsequent devaluation will, in part, be passed through to higher wages. The increase in labor costs means that firms again face higher marginal costs relative to the product price and may respond by reducing supply.[26]

Examples are not hard to find. When Chile devalued its currency in 1981 to speed up the adjustment of the relative price of nontraded goods, it found that its existing wage-indexation arrangements were an obstacle to adjustment.[27] Israel and Brazil are two countries that carried indexation of wages (and indeed of most prices and other nominal magnitudes) the furthest in the 1970s and early 1980s. As the inflation rate accelerated, the Brazilians began to adjust wages automatically for inflation with greater frequency. Also note that in some developing countries, the process whereby urban workers fight for increases in nominal wages to make up for the loss of purchasing power caused by higher prices for the tradable goods that they consume involves strikes and other forms of social conflict. This is costly to the entire country in terms of lost output, not to mention the noneconomic costs.

Thus there are many possible routes through which a devaluation might have contractionary effects on output. For any given country, however, only some of the effects will be important. Furthermore, some effects could lead to increased output. Most important, remember the original and primary reason for believing that a devaluation will have an expansionary effect: It stimulates exports and discourages imports. What is the net effect of all these factors likely to be on output? Sebastian Edwards studied the effect of devaluation on output for twelve developing countries during the period 1965 to 1980. He found that devaluations generate a small contractionary effect in the first

---

[25]Such "supply shocks" are analyzed in Chapter 26.

[26]Wage indexation in industrialized countries is another topic covered in Chapter 26.

[27]It has been argued that this is one reason why Chilean unemployment rose sharply thereafter. Vittorio Corbo, "Reforms and Macroeconomic Adjustments in Chile During 1974–1984," in *World Development,* 13, no. 8 (1985): 893–916. He uses precisely the model developed in Chapter 20 to argue that an increase in spending (related in part to a swelling of the money supply in 1980) and an overvalued currency moved Chile in 1981 to a point of balance-of-payments deterioration like *G* in our Figure 20.4. He further argues that the government at first relied on the monetary approach to the balance of payments to restore equilibrium but failed to realize that an immediate fall in the relative price of nontraded goods was necessary to reverse the deterioration in the trade balance.

year, but the effect is completely reversed in the second year and becomes expansionary. In the long run, there is no effect, presumably because price levels and other nominal magnitudes adjust, so the nominal devaluation ceases to be a real devaluation.[28]

24.7 Capital Controls

One policy option for coping with a crisis—an alternative to monetary contraction or devaluation, but one that the IMF has not sanctioned—is imposing capital controls. This alternative is often suggested by those who observe that modern financial markets do not seem to work as smoothly as the theory predicts.

Review of Arguments on Efficiency of Financial Markets

As already noted, financial integration between an emerging-market country and the rest of the world has many advantages. First, for a successfully developing country, the rate of return to domestic capital is high and investment can be financed more cheaply by borrowing from abroad than out of domestic saving alone. At the same time, investors in richer countries can earn a higher rate of return on their saving by investing in the emerging market than they could domestically. Second, everyone benefits from the opportunity to diversify away risks and smooth disturbances. Third, letting foreign financial institutions into the country improves the efficiency of domestic financial markets. Overregulated and potentially inefficient domestic institutions are subject to the harsh discipline of competition and the demonstration effect of having examples to emulate. At the same time, the governments face the discipline of the international capital markets in the event they make policy mistakes (e.g., in their domestic regulatory duties).

Recent crises, however, suggest that financial markets do not always work quite as perfectly as the happy view of the economic theorist suggests. It is difficult to argue that investors have punished countries when and only when the governments are following bad policies. First, large inflows often give way suddenly to large outflows, with little news appearing in between that might explain the change in sentiment. Second, contagion sometimes spreads to countries where fundamentals appear strong. Third, the recessions that have hit emerging market countries have been of such magnitude that it is difficult to argue that the system is working well. More generally, capital flows appear to be procyclical, whereas theory says they should be *counter*cyclical.

Modern financial markets do not work perfectly. But we are better off with them than without them. As countries industrialize, open markets should be the goal—eventually, if not right away. The interesting question in the meantime is whether or not there exists some possible tinkering with the freedom of capital movement that might potentially reduce the frequency or severity of the crises that occur.

---

[28]Sebastian Edwards, "Are Devaluations Contractionary?" *Review of Economics and Statistics*, 68, no. 3 (1986): 501–508.

Four Possible Aims of Controls

It is important to distinguish among different kinds of capital controls. In particular, it is important to ask: What would be the precise aim of capital controls? We consider four possible aims.[29]

- to discourage **capital outflows** in the event of a balance-of-payments crisis.
- to discourage **capital inflows in the aggregate,** before a crisis.
- to modify the *composition* **of capital inflows,** in particular to discourage short-term banking inflows, relative to other inflows.
- to decouple **domestic interest rates** from foreign, with the aim of restoring some monetary independence.

We consider each of these categories in turn.

(1) *Discouraging capital outflows.* Controls on capital outflows have been very common among developing countries. If a speculative attack occurs, they can help slow down or minimize the loss of reserves or the required increase in interest rates. Controls are generally leaky, however. Even if successfully enforced, controls on outflows can weaken the discipline that international financial markets place on the quality of macroeconomic policy. Governments have all too often used controls to shield themselves temporarily from the implications of bad policies.

(2) *Discouraging capital inflows.* The usual motivation for controls on inflows is to prevent overvaluation and overindebtedness, and thereby prevent a crisis from occurring in the first place. It is probably easier to keep capital out than to keep it in. Some countries appear to have had some success discouraging inflow, so as to limit real appreciation and aggregate debt. Controls may have a role to play as a temporary measure when a country faces a large upsurge of inflows. They might help a government "play for time" until it can determine whether the funds are going to useful investments, which will generate the foreign exchange earnings needed in the future to service the debt, or whether they are instead going, for example, to consumption. After several years, policy makers may have a better idea whether their country is the next tiger, justifying the inflows, or merely the subject of a speculative bubble.

(3) *Modifying the* **composition** *of capital inflows.* We have noted that the composition of inflow is statistically a leading indicator of the probability of severe currency crashes occurring. The higher the reliance on foreign-currency borrowing that is short-term or intermediated through banks, the higher the probability of crisis. Although statistical correlation need not imply causality, this conclusion is consistent with claims that short-term flows are prone to moral hazard and asset mismatch, proposals for controls that would seek to change the composition of capital inflows, as opposed to the total magnitude. Taxes or restrictions on short-term inflows may shift the composition toward longer maturities.

Chile imposed a famous tax on inflows in 1991. It took the form of a requirement that a percentage of any foreign borrowing be left in a non-interest-bearing deposit

---

[29]The Tobin tax has a fifth aim: to reduce the volatility of floating exchange rates. It is discussed in Chapter 27.

maintained at the central bank for up to one year. In addition, there was a long-standing requirement that all FDI stay in the country for at least one year. These controls apparently succeeded in changing the composition of the capital inflow to Chile in the 1990s, in the direction of longer-term maturities, while having little effect on the total magnitude.[30]

Some countries aim their restrictions specifically at banks. High reserve requirements on banks' foreign borrowing fall well within the kind of enhanced prudential banking regulation that is widely recommended for emerging markets.

(4) **Decoupling interest rates.** The fourth possible motivation applies to controls on all capital account transactions: to decouple domestic interest rates from foreign interest rates, and thereby retain some independence for monetary policy, while simultaneously pursuing an exchange rate objective. Recall the Impossible Trinity: monetary independence, fixed exchange rates, and open capital markets. By relinquishing the third objective, a country can attain the other two.

The Highway Analogy

A popular analogy is used to illustrate the proper role of government intervention and the moral hazard problem in the context of efficient capital markets, and it can be extended to illustrate the proper sequencing of financial liberalization as well. The analogy is that today's financial markets are like superhighways. They get you where you want to go fast. By this is meant that they are useful: They help countries finance investment and therefore growth. But accidents occur, and they tend to be bigger than they used to be when people were not able to drive so fast. The lesson is not that superhighways are bad. But drivers need to drive carefully, society needs speed limits, and cars need airbags.

When international investors suddenly lose their enthusiasm for lending to a country, requiring the rapid elimination of the previous current account deficit, it is called a "sudden stop."[31] Contagion that hits many countries at once is analogous to multicar pileups.

Some say country policies cannot be to blame if emerging markets are observed to get into trouble all at the same time. But even when a particular dangerous stretch of roadway is observed to produce more than its share of accidents, the quality of the cars and drivers still helps determine who will be the victims and who will escape. This includes not just precautions taken ahead of time, but also how the driver reacts in the short period of time between the point when the hazard is identified (sudden stop)

---

[30]Sebastian Edwards, "Capital Flows, Real Exchange Rates, and Capital Controls: Some Latin American Experiences," in S. Edwards, ed., *Capital Flows and the Emerging Economies* (Chicago: University of Chicago Press, 2000).

[31]For example, Guillermo Calvo and Carmen Reinhart, "When Capital Inflows Come to a Sudden Stop: Consequences and Policy Options," in Peter Kenen and Alexander Swoboda, eds., *Key Issues in Reform of the International Monetary System* (Washington, DC: International Monetary Fund, 2001).

and the time of potential impact (crash). If the authorities use this interval to postpone adjustment, by running down reserves and shifting their balance sheets toward short-term dollar-denominated debt, then the magnitude of the economic impact is likely to be larger when it comes.

The moral hazard problem is that IMF/G-7 bailout programs to reduce the impact of a crisis reduce the incentive of borrowers and lenders to be more careful in the future. The bailout programs are represented in the analogy by the seat belts and airbags, which cushion the driver in the event of an accident. It is a standard principle of economics that actions in one area can generate partly offsetting reactions in another. That is not in itself a reason not to take action. In our highway example, drivers may react to airbags by driving faster and less safely than they used to. But that is not a reason to dispense with airbags.

The capital controls are represented by speed bumps or posted speed limits, which are necessary when coming into a town, even if not on an open highway. Drivers sometimes have the illusion that in the event of a sudden obstacle, they can respond quickly enough to avoid a crash. In part because crashes involve others, the public has an interest in keeping speeds safe.

A country with a primitive domestic financial system should not necessarily be opened up to the full force of international capital flows before the appropriate domestic market reforms and prudential financial regulations have been put into place. If the planned route for a superhighway draws near to a primitive village, it is not a good idea to design an off-ramp that dumps high-speed traffic into the center of town before its streets are paved, intersections are regulated, and pedestrians learn the dangers of walking in the street. But neither is it practical or desirable to try to insulate the village from the modern world indefinitely. The lesson is that emerging-market countries should not let financial opening get out ahead of domestic reforms. That may mean slowing down the former or accelerating the latter.

24.8 Reform of International Financial Architecture

The international community has looked for ways to modify the international financial system so as to reduce the frequency and severity of crises. Who is the "international community"? All shareholders of the International Monetary Fund (i.e., all 184 member governments) are represented by the executive directors, in proportion to country quotas, which in turn are roughly proportionate to economic size. But important decisions have often been made in the G-7 and G-10, in which only the largest industrialized countries are allowed.

After the East Asia crisis of 1997, the major emerging-market governments gained a bit more of a voice. In 1999 three new bodies were established. A Group of 20 was created to foster dialogue among key countries. The International Monetary and Financial Committee (formerly the Interim Committee) of the IMF considers major issues on the agenda of the IMF's semiannual meetings. And a Financial Stability Forum was inaugurated to coordinate among financial supervisory authorities. The latter, for example, produced a "blacklist" of twenty-five offshore financial centers that had been havens for money laundering or had generally abided insufficiently by international standards of supervision and information sharing, and it put pressure on them to be more cooperative.

What reforms to minimize the danger of future crises did all these meetings produce? Reforms have been classified into three categories: transparency, strengthening financial institutions, and private sector involvement.

Transparency means making information publicly available, to allow accountability for decisions. At the level of domestic borrowers, for example, firms are told to upgrade their corporate accounting, to enable investors to judge their profitability and creditworthiness. At the national level, governments are now encouraged through the IMF's Special Data Dissemination Standard (SDDS) to put their macroeconomic statistics online, including the sort of figures on foreign exchange reserves that have in the past been incomplete during the critical run-ups to some major crises. At the international level, the IMF has admitted that even that institution itself needs to become more transparent. To the extent its shareholders agree, it now publishes country reports, and even Letters of Intent, that previously would have been confidential. The affected member countries do not always agree to this. One danger is that if the IMF announces it sees serious problems in a country, it may instigate a loss of confidence and crisis that would otherwise not occur. A second danger is that the national officials may become reluctant to discuss their problems freely with the IMF staff in the first place if they fear public disclosure.

Strengthening financial institutions includes a variety of ideas for trying to make banks and other financial institutions less vulnerable. Improved banking supervision within each borrowing country is at the top of the list. On the investing side, the Basel Accord, which sets minimum guidelines for capital to be maintained by banks, is undergoing a reform with respect to the weights placed on various kinds of loans in the formula. Hedge funds and other highly leveraged institutions have also come in for careful scrutiny, especially in light of the collapse of Long Term Capital Management, an American hedge fund, after the Russian crisis of August 1998.

Private sector involvement in rescue packages refers to the widely agreed need to make sure that any funds coming from the IMF or other public agencies are used, not to "bail out" private investors, but to "bail them in." Bailing out refers to allowing banks or securities investors to take their money out of the crisis country without accepting their fair share of the losses. Bailing in means requiring investors to roll over loans or to agree to a "standstill," as their share of the burden of filling the financing gap. In the international debt crisis of 1982, the creditor banks were told that they must get together and share in "involuntary lending," or else the G-7 and IMF would let the debtors default. Similarly, in the Korean rescue package of December 1997, banks were asked to stretch out maturities, relative to the terms originally agreed, as the price of a successful program.[32] Without private sector involvement, the moral hazard problem is exacerbated. If investors can earn the high rates of return that emerging markets pay

---

[32]Renegotiating lending terms in the event of a crisis can be more difficult when there are thousands of bondholders. One recent reform is the use of Collective Action Clauses in bond contracts, so that a minority of bondholders cannot obstruct a proposed restructuring that a large majority agrees to be beneficial.

during booms, and avoid the losses when things go badly, then they truly have an incentive to lend recklessly.

The G-7 and IMF came in for much harsh criticism for their handling of the crises that took place between 1994 and 2002.[33] The critics are far from united in specifying what they want done differently. One of the most common recommendations is that the IMF and the World Bank should go back to their "core competencies," each specializing in the separate jobs they were originally assigned. This means the IMF should concentrate on short-term problems of balance-of-payments financing and leave long-term development loans and poverty reduction for the World Bank. Concretely, it has been suggested that the Fund should transfer its Poverty Reduction and Growth Facility (which was previously called the Structural Adjustment Facility) to the Bank. Another proposal that has commanded sufficiently widespread support to become a political reality is forgiveness of government loans to a number of highly indebted poor countries. These are countries that (1) have not developed sufficiently to be able to attract private capital, (2) have such high public debts relative to their economic prospects that they are unlikely to be able ever to repay them, and (3) have agreed to reforms, particularly to use the funds freed up by forgiveness for socially useful programs like education and health.

24.9 Summary

Emerging markets received heavy capital inflows in the early 1990s, in part because of internal reforms that made them attractive places to invest, and in part related to external developments. The receiving countries responded to the inflows with some combination of sterilization, money growth, and currency appreciation. In the latter part of the 1990s, however, boom turned to bust, in a pattern reminiscent of the 1982 debt crisis. Many countries failed to adjust to their new balance of payments deficits. They ran their reserves low and became vulnerable to speculative attack. Speculative attacks have variously been attributed to bad macroeconomic policies, to multiple equilibria in international financial markets, and to structural flaws in the financial system that give rise to moral hazard. When a crisis hits one country, contagion can spill over to bystander countries, including to those that may have had stronger fundamentals than the original offender.

Countries hit by currency and financial crises often seek help from the International Monetary Fund. An IMF program consists of two parts: (1) funds to fill the financing gap in the country's balance of payments, of which an IMF loan is often a relatively small part, and (2) policy conditions, such as devaluation, macroeconomic austerity, or structural reforms, that the country must carry out to receive the money. An alternative strategy, not approved by the IMF, is a policy of prohibiting capital outflows.

---

[33]The most important of the critiques was the "Report of the International Financial Institution Advisory Commission," chaired by Allan Meltzer, submitted to the U.S. Congress and U.S. Department of the Treasury, in March 2000. It recommended replacing ex-post conditionality with ex-ante preconditions for IMF loans. The result would be less resources flowing to emerging market countries, but the authors may consider that desirable on moral hazard grounds.

The programs have often been accompanied by sharp recessions, in part because devaluation can be contractionary, through a variety of effects that were left out of the models in earlier chapters. Some of the factors concern demand: If a devaluation makes people poorer, they will spend less. Some concern supply: If a devaluation raises the prices of inputs, firms will cut back production.

After the East Asia crisis of 1997–1998, many critics argued there must be a better way. It is unlikely that any sweeping reform could be made that would eliminate the danger of crises in emerging markets. But there have been calls for increased transparency, stronger banking regulation, reduced moral hazard, and clearer differentiation of responsibility between the IMF and World Bank, among other proposals. Meanwhile, the years 2001 to 2005 saw a new wave of capital inflows to emerging markets.

CHAPTER PROBLEMS

Extra Credit (Calculus Required)

Some critics of the IMF response to the East Asia crises of 1997–1998 charge that national governments were forced to adopt excessively high interest rates, resulting in needless recessions. We now use the framework of internal and external balance to examine this question. We will work in terms of the exchange rate E and interest rate i because these are the policy instruments under direct control of the central bank.

The trade balance is given by $TB = xE - mY$. The capital account of the balance of payments is given by $KA = \overline{KA}$. (The reason that a higher interest rate does not attract a capital inflow may be that the higher probability of default counteracts higher i, so that global investors don't perceive a higher expected return overall. This is the view of Joe Stiglitz.)

1. Assume income is given by $Y = A(i) + TB$ where absorption, A, is a function of the interest rate, and $\dfrac{dA}{di} < 0$.

   a. Solve for Y as a function of i and E.

   b. Solve for TB as a function of i and E.

   c. Draw the relationship between i and E that gives internal balance (output equal to potential), putting i on the horizontal axis. What is the slope, $\left.\dfrac{dE}{di}\right|_{Y=\overline{Y}}$? What is the intuition?

   d. Draw the relationship between i and E that gives external balance (balance of payments equal to zero). What is the slope, $\left.\dfrac{dE}{di}\right|_{BP=0}$? What is the intuition?

   e. Assume an exogenous adverse balance of payments shock, a downward shift in $\overline{KA}$ (a "sudden stop"). Illustrate graphically. Can we be confident in what direction i and E should be moved, so as to preserve external balance without causing a recession?

   f. What do you think the IMF critics have in mind when they say that interest rates were raised too high in the 1997–1998 crises?

2. Now assume that devaluation has a contractionary effect on domestic demand because of a balance sheet effect from dollar debts:

$$Y = A(i, E) + TB \quad \frac{\partial A}{\partial i} < 0, \frac{\partial A}{\partial E} < 0.$$

   a. Now what is the slope, $\left.\dfrac{dE}{di}\right|_{Y=\bar{Y}}$? Draw the relationship between i and E that gives internal balance (output equal to potential). Assume that the stimulus to net exports is small in the short run because the elasticities are small. What is the intuition?

   b. Again, if there is an exogenous adverse balance of payments shock, can we be confident in what direction i and E should be moved, so as to preserve external balance without causing a recession? Explain.

SUGGESTIONS FOR FURTHER READING

Calvo, Guillermo, Leo Leiderman, and Carmen Reinhart. "Inflows of Capital to Developing Countries in the 1990s," *Journal of Economic Perspectives*, 10, no. 2 (1996): 123–139. How can inflows be managed?

Cline, William. *International Debt Re-examined* (Washington, DC: Institute of International Economics, 1995). Retrospective on the developing countries' debt crisis of the 1980s, from the author of an influential early diagnosis.

Edwards, Sebastian. "How Effective Are Capital Controls?" *Journal of Economic Perspectives*, 13, no. 4 (September 1999): 65–84. Are controls like those imposed on inflows by Chile in the 1990s a solution?

Eichengreen, Barry. *Toward a New Financial Architecture: A Practical Post-Asia Agenda* (Washington, DC: Institute for International Economics, 1999). A review of proposals for reform, including both those under way within the international financial establishment and those from critics.

Eichengreen, Barry, and Brad deLong. "Between Meltdown and Moral Hazard: The International Monetary and Financial Policies of the Clinton Administration," in Jeff Frankel and Peter Orszag, eds., *American Economic Policy in the 1990s* (Cambridge, MA: MIT Press, 2002). The role played by the U.S. government in managing the emerging market crises of the 1990s.

Feldstein, Martin, ed. *Economic and Financial Crises in Emerging Market Economies* (Chicago: University of Chicago Press, 2003). Economists and policy makers come together to decide what we have we learned from recent crises.

Frankel, Jeffrey. "Contractionary Currency Crashes in Developing Countries," *IMF Staff Papers*, 52, no. 2 (2005): 149–192. Finance ministers are almost twice as likely to lose their jobs in the year following a big devaluation as otherwise. Why are currency crashes so costly, economically and politically?

Goldstein, Morris. *The Asian Financial Crisis* (Washington, DC: Institute of International Economics, 1998). Explains origins of the crisis and outlines corrective policy measures and reforms.

Lizondo, Saul, and Peter Montiel. "Contractionary Devaluation in Developing Countries: An Analytical Survey," *IMF Staff Papers* (March 1989). A review of possible effects.

Radelet, Steven, and Jeffrey Sachs. "The East Asian Financial Crisis: Diagnosis, Remedies, Prospects," *Brookings Papers on Economic Activity*, 1 (1998): 1–74, 88–90. Here is the view that IMF austerity in 1997 needlessly worsened the crisis.

CHAPTER 25

Interdependence and Policy Coordination

Chapter 18 showed how floating exchange rates could help insulate countries from each other's policy changes or from other disturbances. This complete insulation or independence held only under certain very special conditions, however—most importantly the absence of capital flows. This chapter will show that even with freely floating exchange rates, countries are in fact interdependent. What happens in the United States has important effects in Europe or Japan and vice versa.

The fact that the world is so interdependent leads to a new topic: international macroeconomic policy coordination. National policy makers may be able to do better by setting their policies cooperatively than they can when each acts independently.

25.1 International Transmission of Disturbances Under Floating Exchange Rates

Recall that under floating exchange rates, the overall balance of payments must sum to zero. We last considered the effect of one country's expansion on another country's economy in Chapter 18. At that point we were assuming that the net capital flow was zero. It followed that the exchange rate always adjusted automatically so as to ensure that the trade balance was zero. In a model in which the trade balance was the only channel through which one country's disturbances affected another's, floating exchange rates provided complete insulation. It was almost as if each country were a closed economy with no trade. In practice, substantial international synchronization of business cycles has continued since 1973: worldwide recession in 1974–1975, 1980 to 1982, 1991, and 2001, and worldwide recovery after each. The extent of synchronization seems, if anything, to have exceeded that during the fixed exchange rate era. This may be related in part to supply shocks or other commonly shared disturbances.

This section examines the two major routes via which disturbances can penetrate through the insulation provided by floating exchange rates. The first is the presence of capital flows, introduced in Chapters 22 and 23, which allow international transmission via the trade balance. The second consists of various effects that exchange rate changes can have on national economies *other* than the effect through the trade balance.

Transmission via Capital Flows

Even when the exchange rate adjusts so that the overall sum of the trade balance plus the capital account is zero, the existence of any kind of net capital flow implies that the trade balance is not zero. If one country goes into trade deficit, the change will be transmitted to the rest of the world as a trade surplus. The trade imbalance is financed by a flow of capital from the surplus country to the deficit country.

We now examine the two-country version of the Mundell-Fleming model of floating exchange rates introduced in Chapter 23 to show how monetary or fiscal expansion in one country is transmitted to the other. *Any* degree of capital mobility would be sufficient to establish transmission. Perfect capital mobility will be assumed here, in part because it gives a simpler model than partial capital mobility and in part because this assumption has accurately described the major industrialized countries in recent years. There will be no more modeling of the capital account as a finite flow responding to a given interest rate differential.

The foreign country is modeled analogously to the home country. Call the home country the United States and the foreign country, Europe. Figure 25.1 shows the two side by side. Recall that under perfect capital mobility, arbitrage equates the U.S. and European interest rates (omitting for now any expectation of future changes in the exchange rate): $i = i^*$. This means that the two points representing the two countries' equilibrium positions must lie on the same horizontal line. Otherwise, if one country had a higher interest rate, there would be a potentially infinite demand for its assets, with potentially infinite borrowing in the low-interest country. E and E^* represent the initial equilibrium points.

Fiscal Expansion in a Large Country

A U.S. fiscal expansion would shift the *IS* curve out to *IS'* if there were no other change in the exchange rate. However, as in Chapter 23, the large capital inflow that would be attracted by the higher interest rate at point *A* causes the dollar to appreciate, worsening the U.S. trade balance and shifting the *IS* curve back to the left. Under perfect capital mobility, the appreciation of the dollar and the backward shift of the *IS* curve continue until the parity condition, $i = i^*$, is restored. Previous chapters have all taken i^* as exogenously fixed, with the implication that the equilibrium is back at the starting point, *E*. But i^* need not be exogenous, as we will now see.

Saying that the dollar appreciates is the same as saying that the European currency, the euro, depreciates. Saying that the U.S. trade balance worsens is the same as saying that the European trade balance improves. Therefore, as the U.S. *IS* curve shifts left, the European *IS** curve shifts right. Intuitively, expenditure has been switched from U.S. goods to European goods. The two curves will shift until their intersections with their respective *LM* curves occur at the same horizontal level—at points *B* and *B**, respectively. Only then are interest rates equalized. Both intersections lie on the country's *BP* curve, as floating rates imply they must; but the curve has shifted to a higher level.

Figure 25.1 shows how two of the (overly strong) results derived earlier must now be modified. First, the insulation property of floating rates is undone by international

FIGURE 25.1

Fiscal Expansion in a Two-Country, Mundell-Fleming Model

Despite perfect capital mobility, the United States can drive up the interest rate because of its large presence in world capital markets. After a U.S. fiscal expansion (to A) causes the dollar to appreciate, the European IS^* curve shifts right as the IS curve in the United States shifts left. Equilibrium entails expansion both for the United States at B and Europe at B^*.

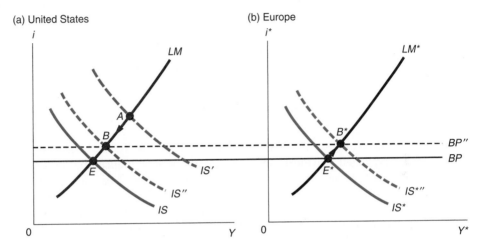

capital mobility. Through the channel of the trade balance, the fiscal expansion is transmitted positively to Europe as an increase in the demand for European output.

Furthermore, a property of fiscal expansion established in Chapter 23, that it is ineffective at raising domestic output under perfect capital mobility, is now also undone. Previously it was assumed the home country was sufficiently small in world capital markets that it could take the foreign interest rate, i^*, as given. If the country is as large as the United States, however, then it is large enough to drive up interest rates everywhere in the world simultaneously. The fiscal expansion succeeds in raising i to the extent that it also raises i^*. Thus it succeeds in raising Y to the extent that it also raises Y^*, without violating equilibrium in the financial markets. The large-country assumption restores effectiveness to fiscal policy despite perfect capital mobility.[1]

The U.S. fiscal expansion that generated U.S. recovery in 1983–1984 is a perfect illustration of international transmission. As already noted, U.S. interest rates rose, attracting a capital inflow from abroad, and the dollar continued to appreciate against the European currencies and the yen. The U.S. trade deficit rose sharply, resulting in a

---

[1]It is the assumption of capital mobility, however, that restores transmission between countries, regardless of their size. Even if the home country is small, its fiscal expansion will have a positive dollar effect on the rest of the world that, although small as a proportion of foreign GDP, is significant relative to domestic GDP. Similarly, a fiscal expansion abroad will have a positive effect on the home country that is significant relative to home GDP. The original reference is Robert Mundell, "A Reply, Capital Mobility and Size," *Canadian Journal of Economics and Political Science*, 30 (1964): 421–431.

corresponding improvement in trade balances in Europe, Japan, and almost everywhere else. The U.S. expansion thus did much to pull the rest of the world out of recession at the same time as it did so domestically.

Another example is Germany's 1990–1992 increase in spending in association with its absorption of the former East Germany. The higher spending drove up German interest rates, attracted a capital inflow, appreciated the mark, and in a short time changed a large German current-account surplus into a deficit. Germany's trade balance loss was its trading partners' gain.

The U.S. fiscal expansion that contributed to U.S. recovery after the recession of 2001 did not fit the pattern of higher interest rates and a stronger dollar. Why not? It was accompanied by a strong monetary expansion.[2]

Monetary Expansion in a Large Country

We next consider, in Figure 25.2, a U.S. monetary expansion. It would shift the *LM* curve out to *LM'* if there were no change in the exchange rate. However, as was explained previously, the large capital outflow induced by the lower interest rate at point *A* causes the dollar to depreciate. This improves the U.S. trade balance (relative to what it would be at point *A*) and shifts the *IS* curve out to the right. Under perfect capital mobility, the dollar depreciation and the outward shift of the *IS* curve must continue until $i = i^*$ is restored. Previously i^* was taken as exogenously fixed, with the implication that the equilibrium was all the way out to point *B* in Figure 23.4(d). There was very strong stimulus to output, all coming from net foreign demand. This need no longer be the case, however. Saying that the dollar depreciates is the same as saying that the euro appreciates. Saying that the U.S. trade balance improves is the same as saying the European trade balance worsens. Therefore, as the U.S. *IS* curve shifts right, the European *IS** curve shifts left. The two curves will shift until their intersections with their respective *LM* curves occur at the same horizontal level: at points *B* and *B**, respectively, in Figure 25.2.

As with the fiscal expansion, two of the strong results derived earlier are overturned. First, the monetary expansion is transmitted abroad. However, the transmission is now negative, or inverse: European income *falls* because of the lost net exports. As a result of lower transactions demand for money in Europe, i^* falls as well.

Because the U.S. monetary expansion succeeds in lowering i^*, it lowers i as well: The United States is large in world financial markets, so it can drive down interest rates everywhere simultaneously. This allows the second new finding. The monetary expansion does not cause as big a depreciation as in the small-country case of Chapter 23, so there is not as large a stimulus to net foreign demand. The lower interest rate means that some of the expansion will come from domestic demand. This is a more realistic result than when it appeared that all of the expansion had to come from a large increase in net foreign demand. The British monetary contraction that began in 1979,

---

[2]The monetized fiscal expansion of 2001 thus had more in common with the Vietnam-related expansion of the late 1960s than with Reaganomics.

FIGURE 25.2

Monetary Expansion in a Two-Country, Mundell-Fleming Model

After a U.S. monetary expansion (to A) causes the dollar to depreciate, the European IS* curve shifts left as the IS curve in the United States shifts right. Equilibrium entails expansion for the United States at B but contraction for Europe at B*.

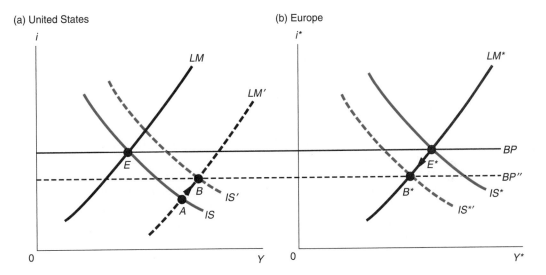

for example, resulted in a subsequent loss of net exports as a result of the higher value of the pound, and it also resulted in a loss of domestic demand in construction and other sectors, as a result of the higher interest rates. The same was true of the U.S. monetary contraction of 1980 to 1982.

Transmission via (Nontrade) Exchange Rate Effects

Whether or not there are international capital flows, and therefore nonzero trade balances, developments in one country can be transmitted to the other country's economy if the exchange rate has effects in addition to its effect on the trade balance. To begin with, an increase in the euro/dollar exchange rate will certainly be felt in Europe as an increase in the euro prices that Europeans have to pay for imports. For there also to be an impact on European output requires some additional effect. Four possibilities are effects on saving, money demand, prices of imported inputs, and wages. All four can result from higher import prices in Europe.

The effect on European saving is the Laursen-Metzler-Harberger effect, developed in the appendix to Chapter 18. A rise in the euro/dollar rate is an adverse shift in the terms of trade for European households: It is a fall in the purchasing power of a unit of European output over a basket of consumer goods that includes imports. Europeans react as they would to any loss in real income, by reducing saving (for any given level of real income measured in *domestic* units) so as to smooth consumption over time.

The higher level of expenditure raises real output and employment in Europe. If the increase in the euro/dollar rate originated in the U.S. fiscal expansion, then the rise in European output means that transmission is positive. If it originated in a U.S. monetary contraction, then the rise in European output means that transmission is inverse. In both cases, the Laursen-Metzler-Harberger effect reinforces the same pattern of transmission that we have just seen brought about by high capital mobility.

The next three possible exchange rate effects, however, go the other way. They are each reasons why an increase in the euro/dollar rate might lower output in Europe.

First is a possible effect via the demand for money. Previous chapters have viewed P, the price level for domestically produced goods, as the appropriate variable for determining money demand. In the Mundell-Fleming model, P is fixed in the short run. Thus the exchange rate does not enter into the money-demand equation. However, the CPI could be considered the appropriate variable for determining money demand as easily as P. If imports have a weight of α in the European CPI, then a 1 percent increase in the euro/dollar rate that raises European import prices by 1 percent will raise the CPI and reduce the real money supply by α percent. Thus it will shift the LM curve to the left and have a contractionary effect on European output. If the dollar appreciation originated in a U.S. fiscal expansion, then the potential decrease in European output represents inverse transmission. If it originated in a U.S. monetary contraction, then it represents positive transmission. In either case, the effect via money demand is the opposite of the effect via the trade balance that appears in the standard Mundell-Fleming model. The contractionary effects in Europe was one of the arguments open to those Europeans who claimed that the U.S. policy mix of the early 1980s—tight money and a loose budget, resulting in a strong dollar—had adverse effects on European growth.

The effects just mentioned come via aggregate demand. There are two remaining effects, both of which come via aggregate supply rather than aggregate demand. If the price of oil or other imported inputs is set in dollars, then the increase in the euro/dollar rate will raise the price of the input for European firms. Finally, if European wages are tied or *indexed* to the European CPI, then the increase in the euro/dollar rate will raise European wages relative to the price of goods produced in Europe. Either way, European firms find that their input costs have gone up relative to the price of the goods they produce, which will cause them to cut back on output. The contractionary supply effects, like the contractionary demand effects, can reverse the transmission results of the Mundell-Fleming model. To understand aggregate supply effects fully requires a more detailed examination of the supply relationship than we have previously carried out. The next chapter is a convenient place to do it.

25.2 Econometric Models of the Interdependent World Economy

Having looked at a bewildering variety of possible routes for transmission of monetary and fiscal policy, some affecting other countries' levels of economic activity positively, some affecting them negatively, we naturally might wonder which effects are likely to dominate in practice.

Economists have built a number of econometric models of the world macroeconomy, each including the major countries or blocs of countries. Often these models are quite large in terms of the number of equations or the amount of work they require. Some of the models are built and maintained in private consulting firms that make economic forecasts for corporate clients. Some are at agencies of national governments or at multinational public institutions. Some are at universities.

The models also differ in their economic philosophies. Some are extremely Keynesian, showing little or no effect of a monetary expansion on prices. Others represent the New Classical school of thought, featuring rational expectations and frictionless determination of wages and prices. Most adopt the intermediate synthesis view taken in this text. This still allows for tremendous divergence among the models, however. Even within the same overall model specification, different estimates of parameter values can have very different implications concerning issues such as whether international transmission is positive or negative.

The models are often used in simulations to predict the effect of a given policy change, relative to some baseline predicted path for the world economy. It can be difficult to compare the results of any two models because the policy experiment being conducted may differ between the two. The simulation results from one model say that a Japanese fiscal expansion would appreciate the yen, and those from another say it would depreciate the yen. One possibility is that the models truly differ; the first, for example, incorporating a high degree of capital mobility for Japan and the second a low degree. However, another possibility is that the first simulation is considering the experiment with the M1 money supply held constant, so that the fiscal expansion pushes the interest rate far up, whereas the second is holding something else constant (the monetary base, or even the interest rate itself), with the result that a fiscal expansion automatically leads to an accompanying increase in M1.

A project undertaken under the auspices of the Brookings Institution asked twelve leading international econometric models to perform simulations for some carefully specified macroeconomic policy experiments.[3] Tables 25.1 and 25.2 show the results in the second year after a fiscal expansion and a monetary expansion, respectively. The twelve models with their abbreviations are as follow: MCM—the Federal Reserve Board's Multi-Country Model; COMPACT—the European Community Commission's model; EPA—the Japanese Economic Planning Agency's model; LINK—Project Link, which puts together the various models of national economies that had already been built in the respective countries; LIV—the Liverpool model of Patrick Minford, a new classical British economist who advised Prime Minister Margaret Thatcher; MSG—the McKibbin-Sachs Global model, which assumes rational expectation, but is otherwise somewhat Keynesian, built by Jeffrey Sachs of Columbia University and Warwick McKibbin of Australia National University; MINIMOD—a smaller approximation of the MCM, built by staff of the International Monetary Fund; VAR—estimates by

---

[3]The model simulations were presented and evaluated in Ralph Bryant, Dale Henderson, Gerald Holtham, Peter Hooper, and Steven Symansky, eds., *Empirical Macroeconomics for Interdependent Economies* (Washington, DC: Brookings Institution, 1988).

TABLE 25.1

Fiscal Policy: Simulation Effect in Second Year
of Increase in Government Expenditure (1 Percent of Output)

	Y	CPI	i	Currency Value	CA	$CA*$	$i*$	$CPI*$	$Y*$
Fiscal Expansion in United States	**Effect in United States**					**Effect in Rest of OECD**			
	(in percentage)		(Pts.)	(in percentage)	($B)	($B)	(Pts.)	(in percentage)	
MCM	+1.8	+0.4	+1.7	+2.8	−16.5	+8.9	+0.4	+0.4	+0.7
COMPACT[a]	+1.2	+0.6	+1.5	+0.6	−11.6	+6.6	+0.3	+0.2	+0.3
EPA[b]	+1.7	+0.9	+2.2	+1.9	−20.5	+9.3	+0.5	+0.3	+0.9
LINK	+1.2	+0.5	+0.2	−0.1	−6.4	+1.9	NA	−0.0	+0.1
LIV	+0.6	+0.2	+0.4	+1.0	−7.0	+3.4	+0.1	+0.6	−0.0
MSG	+0.9	−0.1	+0.9	+3.2	−21.6	+22.7	+1.0	+0.5	+0.3
MINIMOD	+1.0	+0.3	+1.1	+1.0	−8.5	+5.5	+0.2	+0.1	+0.3
OECD	+1.1	+0.6	+1.7	+0.4	−14.2	+11.4	+0.7	+0.3	+0.4
TAYLOR[c]	+0.6	+0.5	+0.3	+4.0	NA	NA	+0.2	+0.4	+0.4
WHARTON	+1.4	+0.3	+1.1	−2.1	−15.4	+5.3	+0.6	−0.1	+0.2
DRI	+2.1	+0.4	+1.6	+3.2	−22.0	+0.8	+0.4	+0.3	+0.7

	Y	CPI	i	Currency Value	CA	$CA*$	$i*$	$CPI*$	$Y*$
Fiscal Expansion in Rest of OECD	**Effect in Rest of OECD**					**Effect in United States**			
	(in percentage)		(Pts.)	(in percentage)	($B)	($B)	(Pts.)	(in percentage)	
MCM	+1.4	+0.3	+0.6	+0.3	−7.2	+7.9	+0.5	+0.2	+0.5
COMPACT[a]	+1.3	+0.8	+0.4	−0.6	−9.3	+3.0	+0.0	+0.1	+0.2
EPA[b]	+2.3	+0.7	+0.3	−0.7	−13.1	+4.7	+0.6	+0.3	+0.3
LINK	+1.2	+0.1	NA	−0.1	−6.1	+6.3	+0.0	+0.0	+0.2
LIV	+0.3	+0.8	+0.0	+3.3	−17.2	+11.9	+0.8	+3.1	−0.5
MSG	+1.1	+0.1	+1.4	+2.9	−5.3	+10.5	+1.3	+0.6	+0.4
MINIMOD	+1.6	+0.2	+0.9	+0.6	−2.2	+3.2	+0.3	+0.2	+0.1
OECD	+1.5	+0.7	+1.9	+0.9	−6.9	+3.3	+0.3	+0.2	+0.1
TAYLOR[c]	+1.6	+1.2	+0.6	+2.7	NA	NA	+0.4	+0.9	+0.6
WHARTON	+3.2	−0.8	+0.8	−2.4	−5.5	+4.7	+0.1	−0.0	+0.0

[a]Non-U.S. short-term interest rate NA; long-term rate reported instead.
[b]Non-U.S. current account refers to Japan, Germany, United Kingdom, and Canada.
[c]CPI NA; GNP deflator reported instead.
Source: Frankel and Rockett (1988).

Christopher Sims and Robert Litterman obtained by Vector AutoRegression (a technique that uses no economic theory, but merely looks for regular patterns in the data); OECD—the Interlink model built by staff members at the Organization of Economic Cooperation and Development (an agency with a membership of thirty industrialized countries and a Secretariat in Paris); TAYLOR—a rational expectations model by John Taylor of Stanford University, an official in both the first and second Bush administrations; WHARTON—a generally Keynesian model, originally built by Nobel laureate Lawrence Klein of the University of Pennsylvania; and DRI—the model of Data Resources, Inc., Lexington, Massachusetts, a firm that sells economic forecasts to corporations and government agencies.

The Results for Fiscal Policy

Table 25.1 summarizes the effects of a fiscal expansion, an increase in government spending equal to 1 percent of income, according to eleven models in the simulations. The variables shown are output, the consumer price index, the short-term interest rate, the exchange rate, and the current account. The first five columns show the variables in the region originating the fiscal expansion, the last four columns the foreign region.

As expected, the models all show a positive effect on output. The numbers in the first column can be read as fiscal multipliers.[4] They are mostly in the range of 1 to 2. Almost all the models show increases in the price level and the interest rate, from which follows some crowding-out of interest-sensitive sectors such as construction.

The main ambiguity in theory, as we saw in Section 23.1, is whether the fiscal expansion causes the currency to appreciate: whether capital mobility is sufficiently high that the capital inflow attracted by higher interest rates is more than enough to finance the increased imports resulting from higher income. However, the eleven models in Table 25.1 show relatively little disagreement in practice. All but two show an appreciation of the dollar when the United States is the country initiating the fiscal expansion. This would not have been the case in the 1960s; it reflects the high degree of capital mobility that has evolved.[5]

In almost all the models, the simulations show that fiscal expansion is transmitted positively to the foreign region. This is not surprising because the current account worsens in the originating region and thus improves in the foreign region. The positive transmission does indicate, however, that the three possible contractionary effects of a currency depreciation (the ones studied in Section 25.1, via money demand, wages, or imported-input prices) either are not operating, or at least are not operating strongly enough to outweigh the increase in net export demand falling on the goods of the foreign region.

The Results of Monetary Policy

Table 25.2 summarizes the effects of a monetary expansion equal to 4 percent of the money supply (phased in over the first year). The simulations show more conflict among the models than do the results of a fiscal expansion. They all agree that the monetary expansion drives down the interest rate and thereby stimulates domestic income, and they generally agree that it depreciates the currency. Yet they divide almost evenly on the question of whether the domestic trade balance improves, causing the foreign trade balance to worsen and foreign income to decrease. That is, they disagree on whether international transmission is inverse.[6]

---

[4]Because $(\Delta Y/Y)/(\Delta G/Y)$ is the same as $\Delta Y/\Delta G$.

[5]When the fiscal expansion originates in other countries, the appreciation of their currency is not as great as when the fiscal expansion originates in the United States. Indeed, there are four models that indicate a depreciation of the foreign currencies against the dollar. This largely reflects a belief that Japan and Europe are not as open financially as the United States (and perhaps also that the LM curve is steeper in the United States, so that interest rates tend to rise more easily than in the rest of the world).

[6]The Mundell-Fleming model says that this inverse transmission should occur. As we saw in the preceding chapter, the lower interest rate that results from a monetary expansion leads to a net capital outflow, which corresponds to a current-account deficit abroad. However, the introduction of expectations into investors' asset preferences, as in Chapter 27, can reverse this effect.

TABLE 25.2

Monetary Policy: Simulation Effect in Second Year of Increase in Money Supply (4 percent)[a]

	Y	CPI	i	Currency Value	CA	CA*	i*	CPI*	Y*
Monetary Expansion in United States	Effect in United States					Effect in Rest of OECD			
	(in percentage)		(Pts.)	(in percentage)	($B)	($B)	(Pts.)	(in percentage)	
MCM	+1.5	+0.4	−2.2	−6.0	−3.1	−3.5	−0.5	−0.6	−0.7
COMPACT[b]	+1.0	+0.8	−2.4	−4.0	−2.8	+1.2	−0.5	−0.4	+0.2
EPA[c]	+1.2	+1.0	−2.2	−6.4	−1.6	−10.1	−0.6	−0.5	−0.4
LINK	+1.0	−0.4	−1.4	−2.3	−5.9	+1.5	NA	−0.1	+0.1
LIV	+0.1	+3.7	−0.3	−3.9	−13.0	+0.1	−0.1	−0.0	−0.0
MSG	+0.3	+1.5	−0.8	−2.0	+2.6	−4.4	−1.2	−0.7	+0.4
MINIMOD	+1.0	+0.8	−1.8	−5.7	+2.8	−4.7	−0.1	−0.2	−0.2
VAR[d]	+3.0	+0.4	−1.9	−22.9	+4.9	+5.1	+0.3	+0.1	+0.4
OECD	+1.6	+0.7	−0.8	−2.6	−8.4	+3.1	−0.1	−0.1	+0.3
TAYLOR[d]	+0.6	+1.2	−0.4	−4.9	NA	NA	−0.1	−0.2	−0.2
WHARTON	+0.7	+0.0	−2.1	−1.0	−5.1	+5.3	−1.3	−0.1	+0.4
DRI	+1.8	+0.4	−2.3	−14.6	−1.4	+14.5	−1.1	−1.3	−0.6

	Y	CPI	i	Currency Value	CA	CA*	i*	CPI*	Y*
Monetary Expansion in Rest of OECD	Effect in Rest of OECD					Effect in United States			
	(in percentage)		(Pts.)	(in percentage)	($B)	($B)	(Pts.)	(in percentage)	
MCM	+1.5	+0.6	−2.1	−5.4	+3.5	+0.1	−0.2	−0.2	−0.0
COMPACT[b]	+0.8	+1.0	−1.0	−2.3	−5.2	+1.9	+0.0	+0.1	+0.1
EPA[c]	+0.0	+0.0	−0.1	−0.1	−0.1	+0.1	−0.0	−0.0	+0.0
LINK[e]	+0.8	−0.6	NA	−2.3	−1.4	+3.5	+0.0	−0.0	+0.1
LIV	+0.4	+2.8	−0.9	−8.4	+7.1	−8.2	−1.1	−3.4	+1.6
MSG	+0.2	+1.5	−0.7	−1.4	−15.9	+12.0	−1.2	−0.6	+0.3
MINIMOD	+0.8	+0.2	−1.8	−4.8	+3.6	−1.4	−0.6	−0.5	−0.3
VAR[b]	+0.7	−0.5	−3.0	−5.5	+5.2	−10.0	+0.6	−0.7	+1.2
OECD	+0.8	+0.3	−1.3	−2.1	−1.6	+2.3	−0.2	+0.1	+0.1
TAYLOR[b]	+0.8	+0.7	−0.3	−3.5	NA	NA	−0.2	−0.5	−0.1
WHARTON	+0.2	−0.1	−0.8	+0.2	+2.6	+0.5	+0.0	+0.0	+0.0

[a] The increase in the money supply is phased in over four quarters.
[b] Non-U.S. short-term interest rate NA; long-term rate reported instead.
[c] Non-U.S. current account is Japan, Germany, United Kingdom, and Canada.
[d] CPI NA; GNP deflator reported instead.
[e] Appreciation of non-U.S. currency NA; depreciation of dollar reported instead.
Source: Frankel and Rockett (1988).

Many of the models say that the higher imports drawn in by higher income are more than enough to offset the effect of the exchange rate on the trade balance, with the result that the expansion is transmitted positively, rather than negatively, to the foreign region. In large part this comes from observing the effect in the second year after the change in policy. The full effect of the exchange rate on the trade balance is not felt until the third year or later. However, it is possible to sum up the results of all the models by saying that under floating exchange rates, one country's monetary expansion appears to have only small effects on other countries' incomes because the income and exchange rate effects on the trade balance roughly cancel each other out.

25.3 International Macroeconomic Policy Coordination

We have examined a wide variety of channels whereby policy changes in one country have effects in other countries. Policy makers have become increasingly aware of this interdependence of their national economies.

The Institutions of International Cooperation

A number of institutions have been established to facilitate discussion of economic issues that concern all countries and to facilitate coordination of their policies. The IMF conducts "surveillance" of the policies of the major industrialized countries, although its influence on them is inevitably far less than on the poorer, indebted countries who have little choice but to listen to the fund's advice. Each year the OECD sponsors meetings of cabinet ministers from its member countries, supported by regular meetings of the Economic Policy Committee and Working Party 3, in addition to a plethora of other meetings of specialists from the member countries dealing with particular economic sectors. Central bankers from the Group of Ten industrialized countries meet regularly, often in association with the Bank for International Settlements.[7]

In 1975, at the suggestion of French president Valéry Giscard d'Estaing, the heads of states of large industrialized economies met at Rambouillet, France. The purpose on that occasion was to ratify politically the movement from fixed exchange rates to floating exchange rates, which market forces had imposed on the world monetary system a few years earlier. The summit meetings have continued each year since then, bringing together leaders from the group of seven largest industrialized countries, known as the G-7: the United States, Japan, Germany, France, the United Kingdom, Italy, and Canada. The most substantive G-7 summit meeting took place in Bonn, Germany, in 1978. There Japan and Germany agreed to the U.S. plan for joint expansion, according to which the three countries would be the "locomotives" pulling the world economy out of the stagnation that had followed the 1974 oil shock. The U.S. motive behind the locomotive theory was the fear that if the United States continued to expand on its own, it would suffer an enlarged trade deficit.

In recent years, the earlier spirit of informal discussion has been lost and the summit meetings have become mammoth media events. (The group was expanded to include Russia in 1997, so it is now the G-8.) Beginning in September 1985, the focus shifted—for the purpose of serious economic policy-making—to the regular meetings

---

[7]The BIS was originally set up after World War I to facilitate the reparations payments that appeared in the discussion of the transfer problem in Chapter 17. From its headquarters in Basel, Switzerland, the BIS continues to function as the central bankers' exclusive club.

of the finance ministers. The occasion then was a meeting that took place at the Plaza Hotel in New York and produced the Plaza Accord, under which the United States agreed to cooperate in bringing down the value of the dollar. The finance ministers meet regularly to discuss the macroeconomic and financial interactions of their economies.

The Theory of Gains from International Policy Coordination

How should all these meetings and institutions be viewed? Are the meetings just media events, opportunities for the heads of state to escape domestic political difficulties and be seen on television looking statesmanlike? Are the institutions simply overpaid bureaucracies whose principal mission is the sampling of continental cuisine? Although sometimes it might seem that way, there are some good arguments in favor of international cooperation.

There is an elegant theory of the economic gains from international macroeconomic policy coordination: Two or more countries will in general be better able to attain their economic objectives if they set their policies jointly than if they set them independently. The alternative, in which each country independently sets its own policies, taking the policies of the others as given, is called the noncooperative equilibrium, also termed the Nash equilibrium.

There are a number of ways in which spillover effects among countries can render the noncooperative equilibrium unsatisfactory. Each defines a "game" between national policy makers.

The game that comes up most often, particularly when the world is in recession because of inadequate demand, could be called "exporting unemployment." Consider the United States and Europe. Each must decide whether or not to follow expansionary demand policies. Table 25.3 shows the four possible outcomes. If Europe has a trade balance objective, it will be reluctant to expand, for fear that the United States will be less expansionary and leave Europe with a trade deficit. Similarly, the United States will be reluctant to expand, for fear that Europe will be less expansionary and leave the United States with a trade deficit. The result is that each country will hold back its level of demand in an effort to improve its trade balance at its neighbor's expense. This policy is self-defeating when the countries try it simultaneously, plunging the world into a recession where everyone loses. This noncooperative equilibrium occurs in the first cell of the table.

The solution to the exporting unemployment problem is the "locomotive strategy": Both countries should agree to expand simultaneously, whether by means of fis-

TABLE 25.3

The Game of "Exporting Unemployment"

	United States Contracts	United States Expands
Europe Contracts	Recession in both countries; $TB = 0$	TB favors Europe
Europe Expands	TB favors United States	Boom in both countries; $TB = 0$

cal policy or by some combination of fiscal and monetary policy, so that output is higher everywhere with no change in the trade balance.[8] This is the logic behind the policy package adopted at the Bonn summit of 1978.

A particular variety of the exporting unemployment game, called "competitive depreciation," arises when fiscal policy is the tool used and exchange rates are floating. Then each country has an especially strong temptation to contract because a fiscal contraction will lower interest rates, cause its currency to depreciate, and provide further improvement in its trade balance at its neighbor's expense. In the 1930s each country devalued in a (vain) attempt to gain a trade advantage against the other. (Recall "beggar-thy-neighbor" policies.)

Other games are possible as well. Under a system of floating exchange rates, one possibility is the game of "competitive appreciation" (the opposite of the competitive depreciation game). It is illustrated in Table 25.4. This game depends on the assumption that each country has as its ultimate objective, in addition to high output, low inflation as measured by the CPI. It can, of course, be difficult to attain both of these objectives simultaneously. There is a trick, however, whereby a country can attain both objectives. It can keep the overall CPI stable, even if output is growing rapidly and thereby putting upward pressure on the prices of domestically produced goods. The trick is to appreciate the currency—for example, through a combination of tight monetary policy and loose fiscal policy that drives up interest rates and makes the country's assets attractive to international investors. The point is that the strong currency will reduce the price of *imports*, when expressed in domestic currency. To the extent that imports have a share in the CPI, the overall inflation rate can be kept down, even if the prices of *domestic* goods are rising. Some economists have attributed such a motive to the U.S. government's adoption of its 1980s policy mix of tight money and loose fiscal policy.[9]

Notice, however, that this trick can only be brought about at the expense of the country's neighbors—by exporting inflation. If the first country experiences an appreciation and downward pressure on its CPI, then its neighbors are experiencing depreciation and upward pressure on their CPIs. The noncooperative equilibrium appears again in the first cell of Table 25.4. Both countries are keeping interest rates high in unsuccessful attempts to appreciate their currency. The result is worldwide recession. The cooperative solution is that both agree simultaneously to lower interest rates. Then they can attain stronger economies with no adverse effect on their exchange rates or CPIs.

A more permanent solution to problems of competitive appreciation or depreciation would be for the countries to agree to a system of fixed exchange rates. Then the leaders do not have to get together to negotiate over specific macroeconomic policies. Perceptions that competitive devaluation had helped prolong the Great Depression of the 1930s were a major reason why the delegates to the Bretton Woods conference of 1944 chose a system of fixed exchange rates for the postwar international monetary

---

[8]The supplement to this chapter presents the more complete analysis of the exporting unemployment game that is relevant when each country has a continuous range of macroeconomic expansion or contraction options from which to choose, as opposed to the simple choice presented in Table 25.3 (expand vs. contract).
[9]Jeffrey Sachs, "The Dollar and Policy Mix: 1985," *Brookings Papers on Economic Activity*, 1 (1985): 117–186.

TABLE 25.4

The Game of "Competitive Appreciation"

	United States Raises Interest Rate, i	United States Lowers Interest Rate, i
Europe Raises i^*	Recession in both: no change in exchange rate or CPI	Dollar depreciates: U.S. import prices and CPI go up; European CPI goes down
Europe Lowers i^*	Dollar appreciates: U.S. CPI goes down; European CPI goes up	Boom in both countries: no change in exchange rate or CPI

system. In the language of the Articles of Agreement of the International Monetary Fund, the members agreed to refrain from manipulating their exchange rates to seek "unfair advantage."

Obstacles to Successful Coordination

If international policy coordination was really as easy as Tables 25.3 and 25.4 make it appear, it might seem odd that agreements do not take place more often than they do. A number of obstacles make coordination difficult in practice. Even if the setting is as simple as we have laid out, there is first of all the problem of dividing the gains from cooperation between the two countries. In any game there is the possibility that both parties will bargain "tough," with the result that the potential gains are lost to both. Then there is the issue of enforcement of the agreement. The United States, knowing that Europe has set its money supply at the level agreed on, may be tempted to reduce its own money supply because that will move it to higher levels of economic welfare. Of course, if the bargain were explicit, this deviation from the agreement would constitute cheating. The gains would be at most short run; when Europe realizes that America has broken the agreement, it too will change its policy settings, causing a return to the non-cooperative state. Even if no automatic penalty is built in for cheating, America will be discouraged from breaking the agreement if it is concerned that it would acquire an undesirable reputation as an untrustworthy party in potential future agreements.

A different difficulty arises from the fact that in the games described so far, policy makers are maximizing their objectives only period by period. If coordination constitutes joint expansion, as in the locomotive game, then this will raise inflation in the current period. If the current period is the only one that matters, then the policy makers will already have factored in the inflation correctly when mapping out their policy preferences. However, the expansion will also raise expected inflation in the next period, so workers will demand higher wages and there will be a higher level of actual inflation in the future for any given level of output, as we see in Chapter 26. In such circumstances, coordinating period by period may actually be harmful in the long run.[10]

---

[10]The damage to inflation-fighting credibility is offered as an argument why countries might be better off renouncing coordination altogether, in Kenneth Rogoff, "International Macroeconomic Policy Coordination May Be Counterproductive," *Journal of International Economics,* 18 (May 1985): 199–217.

A final obstacle to successful macroeconomic policy coordination arises from uncertainty. So far we have assumed that policy makers know precisely (1) what their proper objectives are (for example, what weight should be placed on full employment versus inflation); (2) where their economies are relative to the target optimums (the baseline forecast); and (3) what effect given changes in the policy instruments will have on the economy (the size of the multipliers in the correct model of the world macroeconomy). In reality, however, policy makers are uncertain about each of the three. The third kind of uncertainty is illustrated in Table 25.2 by the disagreement among the major econometric models as to the effects of monetary policy. All three kinds of uncertainty make it difficult for each country in the bargaining process to know even what policy changes it should *want* its partners to make. A number of pessimistic conclusions emerge. Given differing perceptions, the policy makers may not be able to agree on a coordination package. Even if they do agree, the effects may be different from those anticipated.[11]

The standard German view of the joint expansion agreed on at the 1978 Bonn summit is that it turned out to have been undesirable because by the end of the decade the priority had shifted back to fighting inflation. One possible way to understand this view is to see it as an example of uncertainty about the baseline position of the economy relative to the optimum: The 1979 oil price increase associated with the fall of the shah of Iran moved the world economy to a more inflationary position than had been anticipated at the time of the summit meeting. Another way to understand it is to see it as an example of disagreement over the correct model. In the model that the United States has in mind, a monetary expansion can raise output and employment, whereas in the Germans' model, monetary expansion simply goes into prices. Conflicting perceptions as to how the economy works make international coordination difficult, as much today as in 1978.

Thus the gains from international coordination are not as automatic as is suggested by the simple model illustrated here. The potential gains are still there, however. There are also other, more broadly defined arguments in favor of cooperation that include, for example, the exchange of information among countries. Sometimes the international meetings help give the individual countries the clarity of vision, sense of purpose, and political momentum needed to accomplish tasks (like cutting budget deficits) that some leaders in the individual governments considered to be in their individual national interests all along but were unable to accomplish in isolation.

It is inevitable that national leaders will, to an increasing extent, have to work together, particularly in time of crisis. It is good that policy makers maintain steady contact and do not wait for a crisis to become acquainted.

---

[11]Jeffrey Frankel and Katharine Rockett, "International Macroeconomic Policy Coordination. When Policy-Makers Do Not Agree on the True Model," *American Economic Review* (June 1988): 318–340. Furthermore, even if the effects of coordination are as anticipated, the gains are generally estimated to be small, as was first shown in Gilles Oudiz and Jeffrey Sachs, "Macroeconomic Policy Coordination Among the Industrial Economies," *Brookings Papers on Economic Activity,* 1 (1984): 1–64. The reason is that the magnitude of international transmission effects is estimated to be relatively small.

25.4   Summary

This chapter showed that even with freely floating exchange rates, countries are interdependent. Only a small country can afford to ignore the effects its policy changes have on its trading partner because for a large country some of the effects bounce back. This chapter extended the Mundell-Fleming model of Chapter 23 to large countries and considered other extensions as well. The most important channel of transmission between countries is the trade balance. Wherever there are net capital flows, there are nonzero trade balances. There are also other possible channels of transmission. Econometric models suggest that the overall effect of a fiscal expansion in one country is the obvious one: There is an increase in demand for the net exports of the other country. Thus the expansion is transmitted positively. The overall transmission effect of a monetary expansion appears to be small, however, because the income and exchange rate effects on the trade balance tend to cancel each other out.

The fact that the world is interdependent leads to the topic of international macroeconomic policy coordination. National policy makers may be able to do better by setting their policies cooperatively than they can in the (Nash) noncooperative equilibrium, where each acts independently. For example, in a worldwide recession, with each country afraid to expand its economy on its own for fear of a deterioration of its trade balance, there can be gains from a general agreement to expand cooperatively.

CHAPTER PROBLEMS

1. The country of Bretagne holds its real money supply, M/P, constant, but the rest of the world undertakes a monetary expansion that drives down interest rates in Bretagne as well. Which is greater: the stimulus to its economy from lower interest rates or the loss of demand (net exports) when its currency appreciates against the rest of the world? I.e., does Y rise or fall? (*Hint:* Consider the money market equilibrium condition.)
2. When the country of Euphoria adopts a combination of easy fiscal and tight monetary policy, and exchange rates are flexible, is a foreign country suffering from unemployment likely to be pleased with the consequences? A foreign country suffering from inflation? A foreign country with a large external debt denominated in the currency of Euphoria?

Extra Credit

3. This problem concerns interdependence and the coordination of fiscal policy between two countries: Melanzane and Rigatoni. The country of Melanzane has two target variables: the domestic price level, p, and the exchange rate, s, valued in Melanzane-per-Rigatoni currency units (because the country wants to stabilize the two components of the CPI: domestic prices and import prices), both in log form. These target variables are affected both by the government spending of Melanzane, g_M as a percentage of

GDP, and the government spending of its trading partner, Rigatoni, g_R as a percentage of GDP.

$$p = A + Cg_M + Fg_R$$
$$s = B + D(g_R - g_M)$$

a. In a standard Mundell-Fleming model, on what would the sign of D depend? What do most multicountry econometric models say about the signs of $C, D,$ and F?

b. Assume that Melanzane wishes to reduce both s and p to zero. This could be the aftermath of an increase in oil prices that has raised A and B above zero. Solve for the optimal combination of g_M and g_R that would be preferred by Melanzane if it had its first choice. Assume that the signs of $C, F,$ and D are as in (a). What is the sign of $(g_M - g_R)$, that is, would Melanzane prefer that it cut spending more or that Rigatoni cut spending more? Why? Show the optimal point for Melanzane on a graph analogous to that in the chapter supplement.

c. If Melanzane seeks to minimize a quadratic loss function

$$L = p^2 + \omega s^2$$

where ω is the weight placed on the exchange rate objective, derive its reaction function, giving g_M as a function of g_R. How will Melanzane react to a fiscal contraction by Rigatoni, if exchange rate effects are not very important (i.e., if D and ω are low), and why? If they (D and ω) are high?

d. Assume that Rigatoni has a similar objective function, with its prices determined analogously. Indicate on a graph what optimal combination of g_M and g_R would be preferred by Rigatoni, and its reaction function. Describe the Nash noncooperative equilibrium. What sort of cooperative bargain would raise economic welfare and why?

SUGGESTIONS FOR FURTHER READING

Fischer, Stanley. "International Macroeconomic Policy Coordination." In Martin Feldstein, ed., *International Policy Coordination* (Chicago: University of Chicago Press, 1988). A relatively comprehensive yet concise survey of the literature, including some of the skeptics.

International Monetary Fund, *World Economic Outlook* (Washington, DC: IMF, April 2006). Twice a year the IMF Research Department presents forecasts of the major economies and reviews current policy issues such as current account imbalances.

Oudiz, Gilles, and Jeffrey Sachs. "Macroeconomic Policy Coordination among the Industrial Economies," *Brookings Papers on Economic Activity,* 1 (1984): 1–76. A readable introduction to international policy coordination and the first serious attempt to quantify the gains.

Swoboda, Alexander, and Rudiger Dornbusch. "Adjustment Policy and Monetary Equilibrium in a Two-Country Model." In M. Connolly and A. Swoboda, eds., *International Trade and Money* (London: George Allen and Unwin, 1973). A clear exposition of the two-country Mundell-Fleming model, using a graph with Y and Y^* on the axes, as in our Figure 17.6.

Willett, Thomas. "Developments in the Political Economy of Policy Coordination," *Open Economies Review,* 86, no. 2 (1999): 221–253. A review of twenty-nine conclusions from the literature.

CHAPTER 26

Supply and Inflation

Chapters 19 and 20 made the extreme classical assumption that output is fixed at potential output. Other chapters have made the opposite extreme assumption, that supply is infinitely elastic at a given price level. The latter assumption is relatively realistic in the very short run. The former assumption is realistic in the long run. But for many policy-making questions, we are interested in an intermediate time span. What happens over the first year, for example?

In this chapter we explore the supply side of the economy. Relative to earlier chapters we introduce two new variables: the wage rate, and expectations regarding future inflation. We use the model to examine such questions as the advisability of wage indexation, central bank independence, and monetary unions. The last section of the chapter considers how countries should choose their exchange rate regime. These choices influence whether a country will be prone to inflation.

26.1 The Aggregate Supply Relationship

If all wages and prices are perfectly flexible, a 10 percent monetary expansion is reflected in a 10 percent increase in prices, with no effect on real output. If wages and prices are fixed, an expansion of demand instead goes into higher output. This section and the next consider a more complete range of possible aggregate supply relationships, showing how changes in monetary policy are reflected in *both* output and prices.

To begin, we review the aggregate demand relationship familiar from introductory macroeconomics. Imagine that the price level rises for some reason (such as an oil price increase or other adverse supply shock). Then, for any given nominal money supply, M, the real money supply falls and the LM curve shifts left. The reduction in demand reduces output. This inverse relationship between P and Y is the downward-sloping AD curve drawn in Figure 26.1.

Now consider an exogenous increase in aggregate demand—for example, a monetary expansion. The AD curve shifts to the right. Equivalently, the curve shifts up. In fact, it can be determined precisely how much a 10 percent increase in the money supply shifts the curve vertically upward: 10 percent. Only if the increase in P were proportionate to the increase in M would Y be unchanged because only then would M/P and the LM curve be unchanged. Therefore, for any given level of output on the aggregate supply curve, the corresponding price level is now found at a point 10 percent higher than before. That does not mean that a 10 percent monetary expansion will

FIGURE 26.1

The Aggregate Demand Curve and an Upward Shift

The *AD* curve slopes down because a higher *P* implies a lower real money supply, *M/P*, and therefore lower income, *Y*. A 10 percent increase in the money supply, *M*, shifts the *AD* curve up by 10 percent.

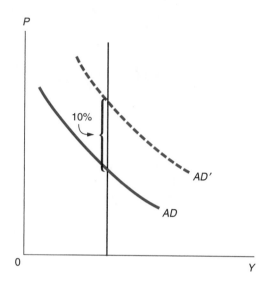

in fact result in an immediate 10 percent increase in the price level. This depends on aggregate supply.

The aggregate supply relationship is less straightforward than the aggregate demand relationship. At least five alternative supply relationships have been proposed by various economists: (1) frictionless neoclassical, (2) Keynesian, (3) Friedman-Phelps "expectations augmented," (4) Lucas-Sargent-Barro "New Classical," and (5) indexed wages. Five may seem like a large number of alternative relationships to consider, but the following survey will place them all into a common overall framework.

The framework for these supply relationships is the following equation, which gives the level of output, *Y*, relative to potential output, $\overline{Y}$.

$$(Y/\overline{Y}) = (wP/W)^{\sigma} \tag{26.1}$$

The exponent σ is the elasticity of supply with respect to the price level, given the wage rate, *W*. In other words, it is the percentage increase in output that firms choose to supply when the price level goes up by 1 percent.

Equation 26.1 can be derived from the assumption that competitive firms choose employment so as to maximize profits. Figure 26.2(a) shows the firm's production function, giving output as a function of *N*, the number of workers employed. It begins steep and then becomes less so. The slope, which is the marginal product of labor, is graphed in Figure 26.2(b). With the real wage on the vertical axis, this curve also represents the firm's demand for labor. It slopes downward because when the real wage falls, it pays firms to hire more workers.[1] The additional workers produce more output, as we see returning to the upper graph.

---

[1]The marginal product of labor falls until it equals the lower real wage. The relationship among *Y*, *N*, and *W/P* is explored more formally in Problem 2 at the end of this chapter.

FIGURE 26.2

The Demand for Labor

Firms' demand for labor, N, is a downward-sloping function of the real wage, W/P, because a profit-maximizing firm produces where the marginal product of labor, the slope of the firm's production function, is equal to the real wage.

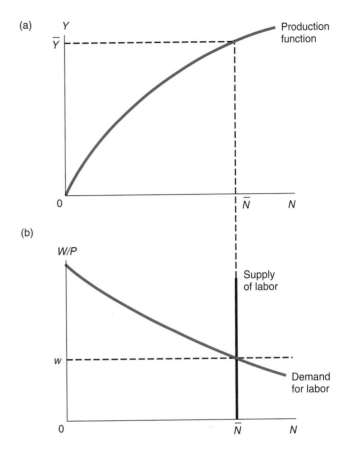

We thus have a very intuitive way to interpret Equation 26.1. When firms receive higher prices, relative to the cost of their variable input, the incentive provided by higher profits encourages them to produce more.

Frictionless Neoclassical Supply Relationship

In the absence of frictions in either prices or wages, labor will be fully employed and output will be fixed at potential output, $\overline{Y}$. This implies an inelastic aggregate supply relationship. It could be interpreted as the vertical line in Figure 26.1, if it is drawn at $Y = \overline{Y}$.

In terms of the general supply relationship, Equation 26.1, the level of real wages, W/P, adjusts frictionlessly to equal w. As a result the available labor force is fully employed (or at least is employed up to the natural rate of employment):

$$N = \overline{N}$$

It then follows from the production function in Figure 26.2(a) that output, Y, is at the corresponding full-capacity level. If in Figure 26.2(b), $W/P > w$ and there is danger of an excess supply of labor, then the wage rate is driven down instantly to increase the demand for labor. If $W/P < w$ and there is danger of excess demand for labor, then the wage rate rises instantly to choke off the demand for labor and restore equilibrium. In short, the real wage adjusts so that labor demand equals labor supply. This is why output is at the full-employment level irrespective of aggregate demand.

In the frictionless neoclassical model, any increase in aggregate demand goes entirely into prices and wages rather than output or employment. A 10 percent monetary expansion, for example, simply raises W and P by 10 percent, as in Figure 26.1.

Those subscribing to the frictionless model—and thus believing that Y is always equal to $\overline{Y}$—recognize that output does change over time. However, they interpret all changes in Y as changes in $\overline{Y}$. The aggregate supply curve is still vertical, but its location often shifts. Growth theory shows us how potential output changes gradually, over the course of decades. Growth proceeds in line with the accumulation of the capital stock (through investment), the labor force (through population growth and migration), and human capital (through education and training), and in line with improvements in productivity (through technological and managerial innovation) and the efficiency with which the economy is organized (through competitive markets, with government intervention only where appropriate, and good institutions, such as the clear property rights and absence of corruption).

Economists who subscribe to *real business cycle theory* view even short-run fluctuations as changes in $\overline{Y}$ attributed to changes in tastes and technology: supply shifts such as changes in productivity and increases in the labor force (or in the natural rate of employment of a given labor force, $\overline{N}$, due, for example, to "changes in workers' preference for leisure").[2]

Modified Keynesian Supply Relationship

The Keynesian view, of course, emphasizes wage and price rigidity, so that the aggregate supply curve is not vertical. Until now, we have been representing this view by the extreme opposite assumption, that the curve is horizontal: Firms simply set prices, $P = \overline{P}$, and then supply whatever output is demanded at that price. This may, in fact, be an adequate assumption to describe the very short run. To consider what happens in the slightly longer run (for example, in the course of a year) means allowing the supply relationship to have some upward slope.

One convenient way of allowing the supply curve to have some upward slope is to allow goods prices to be flexible, but to assume that wages, W, are predetermined. Wages may be set in contracts—for example, the outcome of bargaining between individual labor unions and firms, or between a national labor federation and the government in some more centralized economies. Such contracts often last for longer than one year; they may build in future step increases in the wage rate. The important point for present purposes is that the path of W is preset and exogenous for the life of the

---

[2]International versions of the real business cycle approach include David Backus, Patrick Kehoe, and Finn Kydland, "International Business Cycles vs. Evidence," *Federal Reserve Bank of Minneapolis Quarterly Review*, 17, no. 4 (Fall 1993): 14–29.

contract. The contracts may even be implicit: Some employers, especially larger firms, establish a reputation for not trying to take advantage of their workers when the labor market is slack (i.e., by threatening to hire other workers at lower wages when there is a lot of unemployment) and the workers reciprocate by not taking advantage of the employer when the labor market is tight (i.e., by threatening to leave in order to get higher wages when there are a lot of unfilled vacancies).

Whatever the rationale, consider the wage set at some exogenous level, $W = \overline{W}$. Then the all-purpose supply relationship, Equation 26.1, becomes:

$$Y/\overline{Y} = (wP/\overline{W})^{\sigma} \tag{26.2}$$

The curve is graphed in Figure 26.3. Say we start at the full employment point, A, where $P = \overline{W}/w$, so that $Y = \overline{Y}$. A monetary expansion or other increase in demand equal to 1 percent now goes partly into output and partly into prices, as at point B. Think of the expansion as raising the level of output chosen by firms *because* their product price, P, rises relative to the cost of their variable input, W. They choose to expand in response to the incentive of more lucrative profit margins. Equivalently, output and employment rise because the real wage has fallen.[3]

An adverse supply shock can be viewed as a fall in productivity, causing a fall in the potential output term in Equations 26.1 and 26.2 from $\overline{Y}$ to $\overline{Y}'$. A prime example is the 1973–1974 increase in world oil prices, which caused the 1974–1975 world recession. Another example, mentioned in Section 25.1, might be the increase in oil prices faced by a country whose currency has depreciated sharply against the dollar. Other examples of supply shocks include technological booms, hurricanes, and good or bad harvests.

An adverse supply shock shifts the aggregate supply curve left. What happens then depends on the aggregate demand policy the country chooses, which in turn depends on the country's priorities. If it wishes to avoid inflation even at the cost of a loss in output, it can restrict demand to keep the country at point C. This is essentially what Switzerland did in 1974. After a blip of inflation related to the oil price increase, price stability was immediately restored. The cost was a large recession, although most of the reduction in employment was suffered by guest workers from southern European countries. The opposite extreme is to follow an expansionary demand policy to maintain the level of output and employment at point D, even at the cost of a large increase in the price level. This was essentially the choice that Sweden made in 1974. The intermediate possibility is to keep aggregate demand policy approximately unchanged, as at point F, suffering the adverse supply shift partly in the form of inflation and partly in the form of recession. This was the U.S. choice in 1974.

The wage rate stays fixed only for the life of the contract. Notice that an increase in the wage rate will shift the aggregate supply curve up: It will take a proportionately

---

[3]One possible problem with this model of supply is shared with the other models discussed here, which assume firms to be always on their (short-run) neoclassical production functions. The problem is that it implies real wages and productivity are countercyclical, that is, they fall in economic booms and rise in recessions. The empirical evidence tends not to support this proposition for big countries. An alternative modeling approach to get an upward-sloping supply curve assumes that prices are sticky in the very short run but adjust partway within any given period in response to excess demand for goods. This approach is adopted in Section 27.4.

FIGURE 26.3

Short-Run Supply Curve

If the nominal wage is fixed at $\overline{W}$, then the aggregate supply curve slopes upward: An increase in the price level P in response to higher demand (e.g., at point B) reduces W/P and so encourages firms to raise Y. An adverse supply shift causes the curve to shift up to AS'.

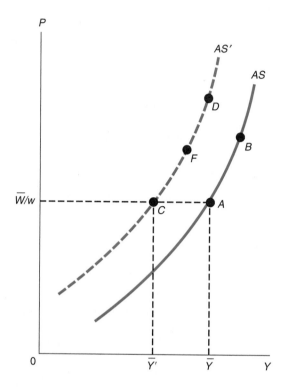

higher P to call forth any given level of Y. If the increase in W is exogenous because of increased militancy by labor unions, for example, then it is another example of a supply shock. W will also tend to rise endogenously—over time—if there has been an increase in demand leading to a tight labor market. A tight labor market means that unemployment is low, the number of job vacancies is unusually high, and many workers are working overtime; in other terms, $N > \overline{N}$. As W rises in response to the high demand for labor, the gradually shifting aggregate supply curve will cause P to rise as well.[4] Thus an expansion of demand that raises prices only fractionally during the life of the contract will have a greater effect on prices thereafter. This point was neglected by Keynesians in the 1960s and leads to the next model.

Friedman-Phelps Supply Relationship

Milton Friedman and Edmund Phelps added expected inflation to the supply relationship. They pointed out that the wage rate $\overline{W}$ set by workers and employers should reflect any inflation expected to take place during the life of the contract. They set

---

[4]In an open economy under floating exchange rates, the rise in P may be more rapid. A monetary expansion will cause the currency to depreciate and import prices to rise. Firms may pass on to consumers the higher prices they have to pay for oil and other imported inputs, in the same way that they pass on higher labor costs. Staff of the Federal Reserve Board estimate that a 10 percent depreciation of the dollar raises the U.S. price level by 1.5 percent over the next few years. The effect is certainly greater in smaller, more open countries.

$\overline{W} = wP^e$, where P^e represents the expected price level at the time the contract was signed. Substituting into Equation 26.2, the aggregate supply relationship becomes:

$$Y/\overline{Y} = (P/P^e)^\sigma \qquad (26.3)$$

The short-run AS curve always passes through the reference point ($P = P^e$ and $Y = \overline{Y}$), as is illustrated at point A in Figure 26.4. In other words, if the price level in a given period turns out to be what was expected, $P = P^e$, then the real wage will be at the correct level, w, to clear the labor market ($N = \overline{N}$), and the economy will be at full capacity ($Y = \overline{Y}$). If the price level turns out to be higher than expected, however, then Y will turn out higher than $\overline{Y}$. That is, the economy will turn out to be at some point along the upper portion of the AS curve. The reason firms decide to step up their level of activity is the same as seen earlier: ex post, the real wage has fallen. If a surprise monetary expansion raises the price level unexpectedly ($P_1 > P_0^e$), then output will rise ($Y_1 > \overline{Y}$), again shown at point B. If the unexpected rise in the price level is 1 percent, then by Equation 26.3 the rise in output is σ percent.

Along with the introduction of price expectations, the other half of the Friedman-Phelps relationship is the proposition that expected inflation adjusts to actual inflation, with the passage of time. The expected future price level is heavily influenced by whatever price level is observed most recently. In the second period the AS curve still passes through the reference point ($P = P^e$, $Y = \overline{Y}$), but because workers have raised their P^e in response to the higher P observed in the previous period (P_1), this reference

FIGURE 26.4

Friedman-Phelps Supply Curve, in the Short and Long Run

If the nominal wage is proportional to the expect price level, P^e, then AS again slopes up, so an outward shift of demand to AD' raises output Y to B—but only in the short run. Over time, workers update P^e to reflect the actual P; as a result W and P rise and Y falls back toward the level of potential output.

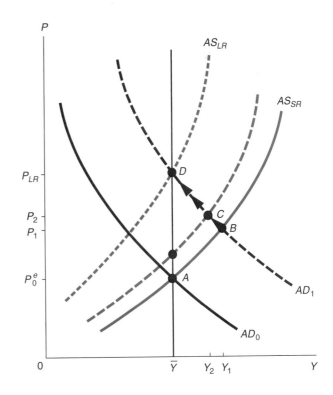

point is now higher than it was before. It follows that the short-run curve has shifted up in the second period. If demand remains at AD_1, there is a move to a point like C. More of the higher level of aggregate demand takes the form of higher wages and prices (P_2), and less takes the form of higher output (Y_2). It is again true in the second period that the price level is higher than the expected level, P^e, which has two implications: (1) Y is still above $\overline{Y}$, and (2) P^e will then have to rise still further, shifting the AS curve up again in the third period. The logic is repeated in subsequent periods. As long as the economy is operating beyond normal full capacity, the price level keeps rising. The reason is that for Y to be greater than $\overline{Y}$, it must be true (by Equation 26.3) that the price level is higher than was expected in that period, from which it follows that workers will adjust their expected price level further, and higher wages will be passed through to higher actual prices. This process of adjustment will continue until Y is restored to $\overline{Y}$, because Equation 26.3 shows that only then will $P^e = P$. In other words, in the long run the aggregate supply curve is vertical at $Y = \overline{Y}$. P, P^e, and W have all gone up by the same percentage as the money supply, so all real variables have returned to their original levels: M/P, P/P^e, W/P, and Y. This is the neutrality proposition again.

Lucas-Sargent-Barro Supply Relationship

Members of the "New Classical" macroeconomic school, such as Robert Lucas, Thomas Sargent, and Robert Barro, adopted the Friedman-Phelps assumption that only unanticipated increases in the price level could raise Y above $\overline{Y}$. However, they carried further the idea that people are smart enough to adjust their expectations in an intelligent way. They objected to the idea that people could be so foolish as persistently to underestimate (or overestimate) the price level for many consecutive periods. This reasoning led them to the conclusion that output could not exceed (or fall short of) potential output for many consecutive periods.

To understand the new classical model, consider first what would happen if people magically had perfect foresight, that is, if they could anticipate any increase in aggregate demand with precise accuracy. Then P^e would always equal P. Thus Y would always equal $\overline{Y}$. In the period that the AD curve shifts up, the short-run AS curve shifts up by precisely the same distance, so that all intersections occur on the same vertical line (the same as point D in Figure 26.4, only it holds not just in the long run but also in the short run).

Now we follow Lucas, Sargent, and Barro in making the assumption of rational expectations, the phrase most often associated with this school of thought.[5] Expectations are said to be rational if the variable in question, in this case P, can differ from what was expected only by a random error in term, ε:

$$P/P^e = 1 + \varepsilon \tag{26.4}$$

When we say that the expectational error, ε, is random, we mean that it is uncorrelated with all information available at the time the expectation was formed. The argument is

---

[5] The name "New Classical" is sometimes preferred because the assumption of rational expectations means little in this context without the prior assumption that only unanticipated increases in the price level raise output.

that a rational worker will already have made use of such information in making his or her optimum forecast of the future price level. Sometimes ε will be positive and sometimes negative, but on average it will equal zero, in which case $P^e = P$.

Substituting Equation 26.4 into 26.3,

$$Y/\overline{Y} = (1 + \varepsilon)^\sigma \tag{26.5}$$

We see that Y can sometimes deviate from $\overline{Y}$, for example, when an unexpected monetary expansion raises P. But this can only happen randomly, implying that the government cannot vary policy in any useful way. If monetary policy cannot have systematic effects, then it is of little use to the policy maker. The government wants to be able to expand at certain times, such as when a recession threatens or prior to an election. Yet, if it follows systematic practices, the public will anticipate such expansions. If a recession threatens or an election approaches, P^e will go up just at the moment when the government expands. The result will be no change in P/P^e, and therefore no change in Y. Only random changes in policy can effect P/P^e, and therefore output, and they are not useful from the standpoint of policy-making.

In each of the four aggregate supply cases we have considered so far, no special significance attaches to whether the economy is open or closed. An increase in demand for domestic goods, whether from the domestic side or the foreign side, simply goes into output or prices depending on what is assumed about the supply behavior of domestic firms. In the following case, however, more depends on whether the economy is open or closed.

26.2 Supply Relationship with Indexed Wages

Some economies, particularly those with a record of price instability, have adopted an arrangement whereby wages are automatically indexed to the price level. Whatever the increase in the price level during the life of the labor contract, the wage rate would automatically increase by a corresponding amount, whether the increase in the price level was accurately foreseen or not. If the wage indexation was complete, then wages would go up by the same percentage as the price level; in other words, a given real wage was assured. In the United States the indexation feature of a wage contract was known as COLA or "cost of living adjustment" clause, but the indexation to the CPI was usually less than 100 percent, and such contracts are no longer in widespread use. Italy for years had its *scala mobile* (moving stairway), which automatically compensated much of the industrialized work force for any increases in the CPI. Chapter 21 noted that two middle-income countries, Brazil and Israel, went the furthest toward fully indexing their economies in the 1970s and early 1980s.

Wages Indexed to Prices of Domestic Goods

An important issue is the selection of the good or goods used in determining the price index to which the wage is tied. Consider what happens when wages are indexed only to the price of domestically produced goods, either because trade is not important to the economy or because the producers do not wish to accept the risk of having their wage bill fluctuate with import prices. The wage indexation equation is $W = \overline{w}P$, where $\overline{w}$ is the target real wage negotiated by workers and employers. Then Equation 26.1 becomes

$$(Y/\overline{Y}) = (w/\overline{w})^\sigma \tag{26.6}$$

Assuming that the target real wage is indeed the one appropriate to clear the labor market, $\overline{w} = w$, then the economy always operates at full employment: $N = \overline{N}$ and $Y = \overline{Y}$. When there is an increase in the monetary supply, it does not matter whether the increase was anticipated beforehand or not. The increase in the price level is automatically incorporated into wages by the indexation mechanism, so that there is no effect on real wages. Although protecting real wages is the usual motivation behind wage indexation, it also ensures there is no effect on the demand for labor and other real magnitudes. Equation 26.6 states that output is the same regardless of the price level. In other words, indexation duplicates the vertical aggregate supply curve, although here it derives its verticality through a route quite different from the frictionless neoclassical model.

Is it a good idea for a country to adopt wage-indexation arrangements? Two advantages are apparent. First, they protect workers' incomes. Second, they help stabilize output and employment in the face of monetary disturbances and other disturbances to aggregate demand. Indexation automatically insulates the real economy from such fluctuations.

There are also two good arguments against indexation, however. First, precisely because it makes any given level of inflation easier to live with, indexation can undermine the will to fight inflation.[6] For this reason, some high-inflation countries that undertook monetary stabilization plans in the mid-1980s reduced their degree of indexation, such as Israel in 1985. Brazil tried to end indexation as part of its Cruzado plan in 1986, and it succeeded in its more successful *real* stabilization of 1994. Argentina legally abolished indexation in 1991, and Italy decided to abolish the *scala mobile* in 1993.

Second, indexation can be harmful in the face of supply disturbances. This possibility arises because the real wage frozen into the system, $\overline{w}$, may be the wrong one. Imagine that $\overline{w}$ is originally set at the level thought to guarantee employment at the natural rate, $N = \overline{N}$, but that there is subsequently an adverse shift in productivity—caused, for example, by an increase in the price of oil. Then the new real wage consistent with the natural rate of unemployment, called the "warranted" real wage, w, may turn out to be lower than $\overline{w}$. Because wage indexation prevents unemployment from lowering the real wage, there will now be unemployment above the natural rate. Furthermore, monetary or fiscal expansion won't help because the problem is that the real wage is frozen at the wrong level. In terms of Equation 26.6, as long as $\overline{w}$ remains above the current w, then Y will be less than $\overline{Y}$. Such a disequilibrium in the labor market is termed *classical unemployment*, as opposed to *Keynesian unemployment*, which results from inadequate aggregate demand.

---

[6]Stanley Fischer and Lawrence Summers, "Should Governments Learn to Live with Inflation?" *American Economic Review,* 79, no. 2 (May 1989): 382–387.

Many continental European countries are characterized by wage indexation and other forms of real wage rigidity to a greater extent than the United States. Often, such as in Germany, there is little in the way of formal indexation, but there is rather what might be called "implicit" indexation: a tacit understanding or social compact not to reduce real wages. American labor markets in general operate more freely. Furthermore, to the extent that U.S. wages *are* rigid, they are more likely to be rigid in *nominal* terms than in real terms.[7] It has been suggested that in the late 1970s the warranted real wage, w, fell behind the real wage embodied in European labor contracts, $\overline{w}$, and that this explains why European unemployment remained so high even long after the 1970s oil shocks and recessions. In the 1970s the six core members of the European Union employed almost the same number of workers combined as did the United States. By 2005 employment among the six had increased only 28 percent, cumulatively. During the same twenty-five years, U.S. employment increased 80 percent.

Wages Indexed to the CPI Basket

In practice, when wages are indexed, they are usually indexed to the CPI, which represents the basket of goods consumed by the workers, rather than to the prices of the products being produced. Thus imports can affect indexation if they constitute a significant part of consumption. Assume that the CPI gives a weight of α to imports and a weight of $(1 - \alpha)$ to domestically produced goods, and that the price of imports, P_M, exhibits full pass-through of changes in the exchange rate. Then a 1 percent increase in the euro/dollar rate raises the German CPI by α percent, even without any change in the price level, P, of goods produced in Germany. If wages are even partially indexed to the CPI, the nominal wage, W, will rise relative to P. Even though workers care about the CPI, firm managers care only about the product they are producing. They raise or lower their demand for labor depending on its marginal product relative to W/P, *the real wage expressed in terms of the product price.* If indexation to the CPI is complete, then even with no change in P, there will be an increase of α percent in W, and therefore in W/P. Figure 26.2(b) shows that the increase in the real wage in terms of the product price, P, lowers firms' demand for labor because their profit margins are reduced. Figure 26.2(a) shows how the lower demand for labor translates into lower output. The aggregate supply curve shifts backward and output falls. Thus a depreciation of the euro is contractionary for Europe.

If a German fiscal contraction is the original source of the increase in the euro/dollar rate, then the fall in German output provides an interesting result: Fiscal policy is an effective tool despite perfect capital mobility.[8]

---

[7]Japan traditionally represents yet a third arrangement. At large Japanese corporations, a substantial proportion of an employee's annual compensation takes the form of a semiannual bonus, whose size varies depending in part on how profitable the year has been. Some observers believe that this form of "profit sharing" keeps real wages in Japan close to the productivity of labor, and thus may account for stability in employment in that country.

[8]Chapter 25 began by pointing out that in a large country, a fiscal expansion affects output even if capital is perfectly mobile. The new result, however, is that if wages are indexed to the CPI, fiscal expansion also works even in a small country.

Thus changes in fiscal policy have real effects on an *open* indexed economy, even though they have no real effects on a *closed* indexed economy: When a change in fiscal policy changes the real exchange rate, the change in import prices opens up a gap between the CPI and the domestic-produced price level, *P*. That is why, even when the wages are fully indexed to the CPI, a change in fiscal policy changes the real wage and has real effects.[9]

26.3 Inflation

The conclusion that emerges from our consideration of aggregate supply relationships is rather pessimistic with regard to the prospects for discretionary monetary policy, that is, monetary policy as a tool to be applied by the government as seems best year by year. Although the government can succeed in raising output and employment in a given year, the cost is higher inflation that gets built into expectations. A period of growth in excess of potential will have to be "paid back" in the future, with a period when growth is *less* than potential, to get the expected inflation rate back down. In the long run, there is no stable usable trade-off between output and inflation. Years when inflation is unexpectedly high must be offset by years when it is unexpectedly low.

Most countries have positive inflation rates most of the time. Some suffer from chronic high inflation rates, although far fewer today than was true in the 1970s and 1980s. Why is inflation so common? What are the costs? And what can be done about it?

Why Is There Inflation?

Let us begin with the question: Why do central banks inflate, given that gains in output have to be repaid by losses later? There are three possible reasons.

1. *The government has a low discount rate,* meaning it puts little weight on the future relative to the present. It believes it has to deliver strong growth in output and employment today, to satisfy voters. Even if it is aware of the eventual cost posed by rising inflation, it figures that it must first win the upcoming election, or it won't be around tomorrow.

2. *The government can't credibly commit not to inflate.* The public knows that a government with discretionary monetary policy will always be tempted to expand. After all, most people most of the time would like growth and employment to be higher than they are, if this were possible. The public's fears that the government will give in to temptation become incorporated into expectations of inflation, and thereby into actual wages and prices. As a result, the government has to engage in a certain monetary casing just to accommodate these expectations—just to bring output up to potential. The outcome is the worst of both worlds: chronic inflation with no gain in real output. The government should proclaim that it is giving up on trying to affect out-

---

[9]Jeffrey Sachs, "Wages, Flexible Exchange Rates, and Macroeconomic Policy," *Quarterly Journal of Economics* (1980): 731–747.

put and will concentrate on trying to achieve zero inflation. If this proclamation is believed, then it will lower expectations of inflation, and shift the *AS* curve down, as desired. But such proclamations are not in themselves generally credible. This is known as the problem of *time inconsistency*.

3. *Seignorage.* The government gets to spend the money it prints. Imagine a government that feels it must maintain a certain level of spending but cannot finance it by either taxation or borrowing. Then the only alternative is printing money. But there are drawbacks, and they become increasingly severe as the central bank abuses its ability to print money. It is not just that the resulting high inflation may be bad for the economy. At high inflation rates, the population will lose its willingness to hold the money that is being printed. Even a government that cares only about its own revenue needs must worry about "killing the goose that lays the golden egg" when the goose is given only worthless paper to eat.

Costs of Inflation

At low rates of inflation, inflation is not very harmful. An economy can live with it, especially if the price increases are spread uniformly around the economy and the inflation has been fully built into expectations. But low inflation can lead to higher inflation. At high rates of inflation, the costs can be substantial. Severe monetary instability can have very negative consequences for the economy. One estimate is that the costs begin to show up as a negative effect on long-term real growth when inflation exceeds a threshold of around 40 percent.

What are these costs? We know that the demand for real money balances depends negatively on the opportunity cost of holding money. This opportunity cost goes up when inflation goes up. Households and firms find that they have to devote a higher fraction of their time and energy managing the finances ("trips to the bank")—time and energy that could otherwise be spent engaged in more productive activities. We also know that the advantage of having money in the first place, as opposed to barter, is that it facilitates exchanges of goods and services. This breaks down at high inflation rates. Prices can no longer do their job of signaling demand and supply in individual markets because consumers and producers have trouble distinguishing changes in relative prices from the general increase in the price level.

How to Achieve Credibility

The trick is for the central bank to establish credibility, to create expectations that it will not inflate. Such expectations should allow low actual inflation, without loss of output. There are three ways of seeking credibility.

1. *Central bank independence.* The government can *delegate* monetary policy to an independent central banker who believes in fighting inflation and do so inside an institutional structure where he or she is shielded from political pressures. This recommendation from monetary theory has been put into practice by many countries in recent years. The central bank is given independence by setting it up as an agency outside of the finance ministry and the rest of the government, letting it determine its own budget, setting long terms for the governors, and making it impossible to remove them for political reasons.

2. *Reputation.* A central bank can establish a reputation for monetary rectitude. Usually it must earn the reputation via a track record, which may mean proving a willingness to have the country suffer high interest rates and recession. The German central bank, the Bundesbank, had a good "hard money" reputation throughout the postwar period because its explicit mandate was to fight inflation, and everyone considered this credible because Germans were known historically to have developed a strong aversion to inflation.

3. *Rules.* A third way to enhance credibility is to commit publicly to a fixed rate of growth in some nominal magnitude—such as the money supply, price level, or exchange rate. We consider such rules in the next section.

26.4 Alternative Anchors for a Country's Money

For policy makers to achieve credibility may require tying their hands in some way so that in the future they cannot follow expansionary policies even if they want to. Otherwise, they may be tempted in a particular period (such as an election year) to reap the short-run output and employment gains from expansion, knowing that the major inflationary costs will not be borne until the future. It may seem surprising that policy makers can raise economic welfare by *giving up* the ability to use monetary policy freely. Yet Equation 26.3 shows that if the authorities make a credible commitment that convinces the public they will not be inflating the future, the downward shift in P^e will mean the country can enjoy a lower level of P for any given level of Y. A central bank that would like to constrain itself, so that in the future it can resist the political pressures and economic temptations of expansion, is like Odysseus in the Greek myth. As his ship was approaching the rocks from where the seductive Sirens lured weak-willed sailors to their doom, Odysseus had his sailors tie him to the mast. But how can a central bank make such a binding commitment?

Monetarists and Gold Bugs

A government can tie its hands, committing to a near-zero inflation rate, by means of what is called a *nominal anchor*. This is a commitment to base monetary policy on some fixed nominal magnitude, thus eliminating the danger of runaway money growth and inflation.

Two examples of nominal anchors are the money supply and the price of gold. The monetarists argue for a system under which the central bank rigidly commits to a fixed (low) rate of growth of the money supply. The advantage of such a commitment is a reduction in the average inflation rate. The disadvantage is that this prevents the monetary authorities from responding to future disturbances. For example, if there is an exogenous upward shift in the demand for money (shifting the *LM* curve to the left) and the central bank is constrained from accommodating it with an increase in the money supply, then it will cause an undesired deflation, perhaps a recession. Such velocity shocks are often severe. For this reason, the Federal Reserve Board abandoned its policy of pursuing targets for the M1 money supply a few years after adopting it in 1979.

The appendix to Chapter 19 explored the gold standard of the nineteenth century. "Gold bugs" have argued for a return to a system under which the central bank rigidly commits to a fixed price of gold, standing ready to buy gold if its price threatens to fall and to sell gold if its price threatens to rise. The problem with such a system is that a shift in the demand for gold will be needlessly transmitted to the general economy, much like shifts in the demand for money. Shifts in the demand for gold have been large in recent years. In both cases, committing monetary policy either to a fixed money growth rule or to a fixed price of gold, the disadvantage of allowing needless disturbances in the economy seems large.

The Exchange Rate as a Nominal Anchor

A solution for some countries is to choose a fixed exchange rate as the nominal anchor. Many smaller countries peg their currencies to a major country's currency they believe to be stable, partly as a way of resisting future temptations to expand.

Let us make this point concrete. Imagine that purchasing power parity (PPP) held well enough that, even if the domestic price level, P, were not tied to the exchange rate in the very short run, the public at the beginning of a given year anticipated that the price level would obey PPP during the coming year: $P^e = (SP^*)^e$. Then a pre-announced commitment to fixing the exchange rate ($S = \bar{S}$) would effectively induce the public to expect an inflation rate during the coming year no higher domestically than abroad: $P^e = \bar{S}P^{*e}$. Assuming the foreign country is expected to have a low inflation rate, the expected inflation rate would be low at home as well.[10] Then domestic workers would moderate their wage demands, and prices would follow suit. In terms of Equation 26.3, P^e would shift downward, with the result that a lower P could be achieved even without a loss in Y.

As we have seen, there is a cost to committing to a fixed exchange rate: A small country that opts to peg its currency to that of a larger country will lose the ability to conduct a monetary policy that is independent from its partner's. What sort of country would be willing to pay that cost? One answer to this question is a country that has a history of chronic monetary instability, in the form of high and variable inflation rates. There the priority on a credible anti-inflationary policy may be high enough to justify giving up monetary independence.

When the major currencies began to float against each other in 1973, the initial reaction among most smaller and developing countries was to continue to peg toward

---

[10]The qualification can be important. After the breakup of the Soviet Union in 1991, many of the newly independent republics at first thought they might remain in the ruble zone, anchoring their new currencies to the Russian currency. As Russian money creation and inflation accelerated, however, it quickly became apparent to the republics that attempting to use the ruble as an anchor would be like a rowboat attempting to anchor itself to a moving ship.

one of the major currencies, such as the former colonial power in the case of many African countries or the dollar in the case of most Latin American countries. Devaluations followed, however, and most of these links have long since been broken. Even the French-speaking countries of West and Central Africa, which had been the most steadfast in keeping their currencies pegged to a major currency, the French franc (largely because France granted them large subsidies to do so), devalued in 1994.

After some unpleasant experiences with high inflation rates in the 1970s, a number of countries sought to reestablish credible exchange rate targets as cornerstones of anti-inflation programs. They included Italy and other previously inflation-prone European countries that in effect tied their currencies to the deutschemark in the 1980s, either as formal members of the European Monetary System (Italy, France, Ireland, Spain, and Portugal) or through unilaterally declared pegs (Sweden).[11]

They also included a number of Latin American countries that have tried to reestablish a link with the dollar as the basis of monetary stabilization programs. Argentina's austral plan and Brazil's cruzado plan were both introduced in 1985. In both cases, the governments failed to back up the plans with adequate monetary restraint, with the result that inflation and balance-of-payments deficits soon returned and the pegs to the dollar had to be abandoned.

An Israeli plan, also instituted in 1985, met with more success. Argentina introduced its convertibility plan in 1991, and Brazil its "real" plan in 1994. Both can be judged successes in light of the many previous disinflation attempts that had failed in those countries. Why do some exchange-rate-based plans succeed while others fail? The first key to success is supplementing the exchange rate target with budget and monetary discipline (a strategy that is known as an *orthodox* stabilization plan), rather than relying on direct wage and price controls to do all the work (a strategy known as the *heterodox* plan).

Even when the government sincerely intends to adopt sufficiently strict fiscal and monetary policies, workers may ask for higher wages nonetheless. They are particularly likely to do so if inflation has been high in the past, or if they are skeptical that the government's disinflation plan will be sustained in the future. Higher wages will in turn lead to higher prices. The fixed exchange rate in fact does not prevent this. (PPP does not in fact hold at a one-year horizon.) As the currency becomes progressively overvalued in real terms, the trade deficit will widen. A balance-of-payments deficit may result, depleting the central bank's reserves over time. If speculators are skeptical that the plan will be sustained, capital will leave the country, thereby accelerating the balance-of-payments problem. In this case the loss of reserves will eventually force a devaluation, and therefore the end of the plan. This was exactly the sort of crisis that hit the Mexican peso in December 1994. Russia was forced to abandon its exchange rate target in 1998 and Brazil in 1999. Turkey's exchange-rate-based stabilization came to a similar end in 2001.

---

[11]Francesco Giavazzi and Marco Pagano, "The Advantage of Tying One's Hands: EMS Discipline and Central Bank Credibility," *European Economic Review*, 32 (June 1988): 105–182. Some authors, however, see from the evidence no sign that the costs (lost output) to a small European country of a program to reduce inflation were any lower when joining the EMS was part of the program. Susan Collins, "Inflation and the European Monetary System," in F. Giavazzi, S. Micossi, and M. Miller, eds., *The European Monetary System* (Cambridge, UK: Cambridge University Press, 1988).

That so many exchange rate targets ultimately have had to be abandoned does not mean that the strategy of using them as part of the original disinflation plan was a mistake. Economists often recommend as an *exit strategy* that the central bank abandon a fixed exchange rate, in favor of a more flexible arrangement, at a time when demand for the currency is strong. This advice makes sense if the alternative might in the future be that it is forced to abandon the peg at a more difficult time, when confidence is under attack.

Inflation Targeting

When a country moves toward more flexible exchange rates, something else should take the place of the exchange rate target as the nominal anchor of monetary policy, so as to keep expectations aligned with a low-inflation monetary path. Recall the goal of keeping expected inflation low and stable in Equation 26.3, so as to deliver lower actual inflation for any given level of output. With monetarism and the gold standard largely discredited as nominal anchors, what does that leave?

The new popular choice is inflation targeting.[12] The central bank publicly commits to announced targets for the yearly increase in the CPI itself. If the central bank misses the target that has been announced, the governor is required to give the government an official explanation. Early adopters of inflation targeting included New Zealand, Canada, the United Kingdom, and Sweden. Many emerging market countries began to follow suit in the years 1998 to 2000: Israel, the Czech Republic, Poland, Brazil, Chile, and South Africa.

One problem with setting a rigid target for the CPI is that abiding by it would prove onerous in the face of a supply shock such as the increase in the price of oil that hit many oil-importing countries in 2005. In practice, central banks allow a temporary deviation from their target range in such cases, giving an explanation for the cause. Some explicitly target "core inflation," which leaves out the more volatile prices of food and energy (but does not specifically accomplish the goal of distinguishing import shocks from export shocks). There are other reasons as well that a government may wish ex post to deviate from the inflation target that was announced ex ante. In practice, many central banks follow a very flexible form of inflation targeting called the Taylor rule: The interest rate instrument is used so as to try to correct, not just deviations of inflation from the announced target, but also deviations of output from its desired level.

26.5 The Choice of Exchange Rate Regime

The question of what exchange rate regime to choose—fixed, floating, or something else—is an old one. But it has been faced anew by many countries in recent years, from emerging market countries responding to currency crises to European countries deciding whether to join the EMU.

---

[12]For example, Lars Svensson, "Inflation Targeting as a Monetary Policy Rule," *Journal of Monetary Economics,* 43 (1999): 607–654.

We have seen a variety of arguments in this text in favor of fixed exchange rates and a variety of arguments against them. To summarize the arguments in favor of fixed exchange rates: (1) They reduce the transactions costs and uncertainty facing importers, exporters, and international borrowers and lenders;[13] and (2) they can provide a nominal anchor for monetary policy. The argument against fixed exchange rates is that they reduce the ability of the government to pursue independent monetary policy (especially if capital market integration is high) and to accommodate terms of trade shocks. Which side of the debate should dominate?

Intermediate Exchange Rate Regimes

There is in reality a continuum of exchange rate regimes. In between fixed and floating are four intermediate regimes:

1. *Target zone, or band.* The central bank announces a central parity and margins around it. It is prepared to intervene to keep the exchange rate within that range. A target zone with narrow bands is almost the same as a fixed exchange rate; wide bands approach floating. There are two versions of target zone. In one, the central parity is adjusted in line with inflation or other economic fundamentals. In the other, the central parity is fixed, to preserve a nominal anchor. (Section 27.3 explores the theory of target zones.)

2. *Crawling peg.* The central bank follows a policy of devaluing the currency a small amount each week. The goal is to offset inflation, to avoid becoming overvalued in real terms. In one version, full *indexation of the exchange rate,* the aim is specifically to hold the real exchange rate constant. In another version, the *tablita,* the preannounced rate of crawl is less than the inflation rate. The aim of the latter arrangement, popularized by Argentina in the late 1970s, is to use the exchange rate to continue putting some downward pressure on inflation.

3. *Basket peg.* In some cases, countries decide not to peg to a major currency because, in a world where the major currencies are floating against each other, fixing the exchange rate vis-à-vis one currency means incurring variability against the others. This may not be an issue for a country that trades mostly with the United States or mostly with Europe. But for a country that trades with many partners, a simple policy of pegging to one of them will result in a variable effective (i.e., trade-weighted) exchange rate. An alternative is pegging to a weighted basket of currencies. Such *basket pegs* have been popular with some East Asian and Middle Eastern countries. Despite the theoretical advantage of this exchange rate arrangement, governments in practice may find it a strong temptation to devalue a bit under a basket peg, especially when the weights in the basket have been kept secret.

---

[13]Some empirical studies have found a negative effect of exchange rate uncertainty on the volume of trade. If a country goes beyond fixing its exchange rate and actually adopts the currency of a neighbor, then it not only eliminates exchange rate uncertainty vis-à-vis that neighbor but eliminates transaction costs as well. Andrew Rose found a surprisingly large effect of currency unions in his influential paper, "One Money, One Market: Estimating the Effect of Common Currencies on Trade," *Economic Policy*, 15 (April 2000): 7–45.

4. *Adjustable peg.* Many fixed exchange rates do not last for long. In some cases, as under the Bretton Woods system, the official policy is that the peg will be adjusted in the event of a fundamental disequilibrium. In theory, an *escape clause* could specify that the currency will be devalued if there is a sufficiently large adverse shift in the terms of trade or a sufficiently large loss of reserves. In practice, the circumstances that will trigger the realignment are seldom made explicit.

The Corners Hypothesis

Each of the countries in East Asia and elsewhere that underwent currency crises in the late 1990s had been following an exchange rate target at the time. Most of the targets were combinations of the intermediate regimes just listed. Most of the countries, under intense speculative attack, abandoned their targets and moved to a regime of increased flexibility—full-fledged floating in the case of Mexico, Brazil, and Chile. Ecuador in 1999 moved in the opposite direction, to full-fledged dollarization. A new conventional wisdom was born: Intermediate exchange rate regimes are no longer viable. Countries under speculative pressure must move to one corner or the other.

At one polar extreme is free floating. Managed floating is also considered in the flexible corner, provided no specific target is set for the exchange rate.

The other corner is an institutionally fixed exchange rate. This is a legal or institutional commitment, something beyond the simple declaration of a fixed exchange rate, which after all can always be abandoned in the future. What is needed for full credibility is a commitment that is seen by the public to be so binding that it would be difficult or impossible to undo in the future even if desired. The firm-fix corner includes three cases.

1. *Currency union* is the polar extreme. Member countries share a common currency and a common central bank. The EMU is the important example.

2. *Dollarization* is when a country officially adopts the dollar as its legal tender. The country does not get a vote on the Federal Reserve Board. Official dollarization is more extreme than private dollarization. Official dollarization is certainly easier if the private economy is already heavily dollarized, however, which is the case in much of Latin America. (This regime could as easily be applied with respect to the euro or some other currency.)

3. *Currency board* was defined in Section 19.1. Argentina, Hong Kong, and some Eastern European countries already had versions of currency boards in place when speculative pressures hit emerging markets in the late 1990s. Hong Kong and others managed successful defenses, preserving their fixed exchange rate arrangements. Of course any country that adopts a confining straightjacket may live to regret it. The cost of maintaining such a commitment in the event of reserve loss can be a severe recession.

Both corners—floating and fixing—offer the central bank a sort of immunity from speculative attack against its reserves. Under floating the central bank is under no obligation to pay out foreign exchange reserves—or even to hold any. Under monetary union the central bank and its reserves go out of existence. Speculators cannot attack something that does not exist. Only time can test the prediction that countries will increasingly move toward the corners of either floating or institutionally fixed exchange rates. In practice, most self-declared floaters exhibit a "fear of floating" in that they continue to intervene regularly in the foreign exchange market to dampen big movement. In the opposite corner, ardor for the currency board option began to cool when Argentina was forced to abandon its convertibility plan in 2001. Intermediate regimes, it seems, are still very much with us. But it is clear that the high capital mobility of the modern system does sharpen the trade-off between the advantages of exchange rate stability and those of monetary independence.

Optimum Currency Areas

No single exchange rate arrangement is right for all countries. The desirable arrangement depends on specific characteristics of the country in question. The characteristic most important for this choice is the country's degree of openness. The advantages of a fixed exchange rate tend to be greater for a small open country; the advantages of a flexible exchange rate tend to be smaller.

Consider the two advantages of a fixed exchange rate stated earlier, regarding uncertainty and the nominal anchor. If traded goods constitute a large proportion of the economy, then exchange rate uncertainty is a more serious issue for the country in the aggregate. Such an economy may be too small and too open to have an independently floating currency. At the same time, because fixing the exchange rate in such a country goes further toward fixing the entire price level, the credibility of benefits discussed in the preceding section are likely to be larger. In terms of Equation 26.3, an exchange rate anchor is more likely to tie down P^e in an open country than in a relatively closed one, and thus more likely to reduce actual P without a loss in Y.[14]

Furthermore, the chief advantage of a floating exchange rate, the ability to pursue an independent monetary policy, is in many ways weaker for an economy that is highly integrated with its neighbors. This is because there are ways that such a country or region can cope with an adverse shock even in the absence of discretionary changes in macroeconomic policy. Consider first, as the criterion for openness, the marginal propensity to import. In terms of the model of Chapter 17, variability in output under a fixed exchange rate is low when the marginal propensity to import is high. In other words, openness acts as an automatic stabilizer.[15]

Consider next, as the criterion of openness, the ease of movement of labor between the country or region in question and neighboring regions. If the economy is highly integrated with its neighbors by this criterion, then workers may be able to respond to a local recession by moving across the border to get jobs, so the need for a local monetary expansion or devaluation is less extreme. Of course the neighboring region may be in

---

[14]David Romer, "Openness and Inflation: Theory and Evidence," *Quarterly Journal of Economics,* 108, no. 4 (1993): 869–903.

[15]You were asked to figure out the relative stabilizing properties of fixed versus floating exchange rates in Problem 2 in Chapter 18.

recession too. To the extent that shocks to the two economies are correlated, however, monetary independence is not needed in any case: The two can share a monetary expansion in tandem. There is no need for a flexible exchange rate between them to accommodate differences.

In the case of a very small region or other economic unit, the argument is clear. Consider an American state (or a Canadian province, British county, etc.). In the limiting case think of a city or square block. Such an economic unit is clearly too small to have its own currency. Its residents would have to consult the day's exchange rate postings and go to the bank to convert currency every time they wanted to buy something in the next city or the next block. A unit this small should adopt the currency of a neighboring region with which it is highly integrated, thus forming a larger currency area. In other words, the smaller unit does not constitute an *optimum currency area.*

An optimum currency area can be defined as a region for which it is optimal to have its own currency and its own monetary policy: *A region that is neither so small and open that it would be better off pegging its currency to a neighbor, nor so large that it would be better off splitting into subregions with different currencies.*[16]

Geographical regions within a country go beyond pegging their exchange rates to each other and literally use the same currency. The dollar bills issued by the Dallas Federal Reserve Bank are perfect substitutes for the dollar bills issued by the Boston Fed. Occasionally, sovereign nations also use other nations' currencies. Panama, for example, allows the U.S. dollar to circulate as legal tender. Lesotho, Nambia, and Swaziland allow the South African rand to circulate similarly. There are also currency unions in Western and Central Africa and in the eastern Caribbean. The European Economic and Monetary Union is by far the most important example. But these cases are exceptions. Most countries want to retain their own currencies—either for reasons of political pride or to get the economic seignorage that comes with the right to print money—even if they choose to fix the exchange rate.

The Case of German Monetary Union

Some economists consider the German monetary union of 1990, in which the *länder* of the former East Germany were joined to those of the former West Germany, to be an example of how *not* to go about forming a monetary union. It is not that the reunited Germany does not meet the criterion for an optimum currency area. As a result of the close cultural links within what used to be a single country, the extent of trade and labor mobility has rapidly returned to a high level—high enough to justify the adoption of a common currency. Especially important in the decision to undertake monetary union, as in other currency areas, was a political willingness for the more fortunate Western *länder* to help out the less fortunate Eastern ones with large fiscal transfers.

---

[16]The phrase *optimum currency area* was coined by Robert Mundell, "A Theory of Optimum Currency Areas," *American Economic Review* (November 1961): 509–517. He was thinking of openness in terms of labor (the degree of labor mobility across the region's borders versus within the region), rather than in terms of openness of trade. The idea of using the proportion of the economy composed of traded goods as the criterion for whether a region is large enough to have its own currency was suggested by Ronald McKinnon, "Optimum Currency Areas," *American Economic Review,* 53 (September 1963): 717–724.

The major mistake that the German government appears to have made was to miss its one and only chance to get the exchange rate right, between östmarks and deutschemarks, before the monetary union. Productivity among workers in the East was only a fraction of productivity in the West, and it would take time before the former acquire the physical and human capital to close the gap. Wages must accurately reflect the differential in productivity if firms are to have adequate incentive to establish factories in the East and hire workers. The relatively easy way to accomplish this would have been to peg the exchange rate at a multiple, such as two östmarks per deutschemark. For political reasons the German government pegged the exchange rate at one to one in 1990. Unemployment in the East soared dramatically in the years following the union. The cost of paying the unemployment benefits created problems for even the powerhouse German economy. If wages were perfectly flexible, then it would be immaterial at what rate the two currencies had been unified, but this is clearly not the case (or wages in the East would have responded to the high unemployment rates by falling, which they did not do). The period of adjustment has been predictably prolonged.[17]

Is Europe an Optimum Currency Area?

There is little point in even trying to impose exchange rate stability if a country is not politically ready to accept the loss of sovereignty in economic policy-making. An attempt to peg the exchange rate under such circumstances would fail as soon as a future disturbance forced the government to choose politically between the fixed exchange rate policy and an alternative such as counteracting an increase in unemployment.

We saw in Section 23.3 that plans for the eventual European Monetary Union, agreed on at Maastricht in 1991, ran into difficulty in the crises of 1992 and 1993. Since then, the membership of the European Community has expanded into an even larger European Union, with the accession of Austria, Finland, and Sweden, and then with the addition of ten new members in 2005, most of them in Central Europe. Is this too large or diverse a collection of countries to constitute an optimum currency area?

Our discussion of optimum currency areas indicated several economic criteria, generally falling under the rubric of the degree of economic integration. We saw that regional units are more likely to benefit, on net, from joining together to form a monetary union if (1) they trade a lot with each other, (2) there is high degree of labor mobility among them, (3) the economic shocks they face are highly correlated (so-called symmetric shocks), or (4) there exists a federal fiscal system to transfer funds to regions that suffer adverse shocks.

Each of these criteria can be quantified, but it is very difficult to know what is the critical level of integration at which the advantages of belonging to a currency area outweigh the disadvantages. The states of the United States constitute a possible standard of comparison. It seems clear that the degree of openness of the states, and the degree of economic integration among them, are sufficiently high to justify their use of

---

[17]Hans-Werner Sinn, "Germany's Economic Unification: An Assessment After Ten Years," *Review of International Economics,* 10, no. 1 (2002): 113–128.

a common currency. How do the members of the European Union compare to the states in this regard? U.S. states are more open than European countries, by both the trade and labor mobility criteria. It appears that when an adverse shock hits a region of the United States such as New England or the oil states of the South, outmigration of workers is the most important mechanism whereby unemployment rates and wages are eventually reequilibrated across regions.[18] Labor mobility among European countries is much lower than in the United States. Americans are six times as likely to move between states as Europeans are to move across national boundaries within the European Union. Workers are slow to move from Italy to Ireland, even when the unemployment rate is high in the former and job vacancies are going unfilled in the latter. Thus, by the labor mobility criterion, European countries are less well-suited to a common currency than are American states.[19]

The other two criteria are also better satisfied within the United States than within Europe. Disturbances across U.S. regions have a relatively high correlation, compared to members of the European Union.[20] When disparities in income do arise in the United States, federal fiscal policy helps narrow them. Estimates suggest that when a region's per capita income falls by one dollar, the final reduction in its disposable income is only 70 cents. The difference, a 30 percent cushioning effect, consists of an automatic decrease in federal tax receipts plus an automatic increase in unemployment compensation and other transfers. Neither the fiscal transfer mechanisms that were already in place within the European Union nor those under the EMU (so-called structural funds) are as large as those in the U.S. federal fiscal system.[21]

By these optimum currency area criteria, the European Union is not as good a candidate for a monetary union as is the United States. This helps account for the deep ambivalence over the euro that remains among the population of many European countries. An interest rate that suits Ireland, when growing rapidly and in danger of overheating, may be considered intolerably high in Italy, when stagnating.

All is not lost, however. In the first place, some northern European countries probably do meet the criteria. These relatively small and open economies are linked to the German economy sufficiently closely that they are willing in essence to subordinate their monetary policies to Frankfurt: the Netherlands, Luxembourg, Austria, and Belgium.

---

[18]Oliver Blanchard and Lawrence Katz, "Regional Evolutions," *Brookings Paper on Economic Activity,* 1 (1992): 1–61.

[19]Barry Eichengreen, "European Monetary Unification," *Journal of Economic Literature,* 31, no. 3 (1993); and Jorg Decressin and Antonio Fatas, "Regional Labor Market Dynamics in Europe," *European Economic Review,* 39 (1995): 1627–1655.

[20]Tamin Bayoumi and Barry Eichengreen, "Shocking Aspects of European Monetary Unification," in F. Giavazzi and F. Torres, eds., *The Transition to Economic and Monetary Union in Europe* (New York: Cambridge University Press, 1993). An analysis of which countries stood to gain or lose the most from subordinating their economies to a single European monetary policy was offered by Alberto Alesina and Vittorio Grilli, "The European Central Bank: Reshaping Monetary Policies in Europe," in M. Canzoneri, V. Grilli, and P. Masson, eds., *Establishing a Central Bank: Issues in Europe and Lessons from the US* (Cambridge, UK: Cambridge University Press, 1992), pp. 49–77.

[21]Xavier Sala-i-martin and Jeffrey Sachs, "Fiscal Federalism and Optimum Currency Areas," in Canzoneri, et al., 195–219; Tamin Bayoumi and Paul Masson, "Fiscal Flows in the United States and Canada: Lessons for Monetary Union in Europe," *European Economic Review,* 39 (1995): 253–275.

Under the terms of Maastricht, the countries admitted to the EMU effective in 1999 were only those that met four tests. The candidate's currency must have succeeded in remaining within the EMS band for two years; its inflation rate must be close to that of the three best performing EU countries; the same must hold for its interest rates; and its budget deficit and debt should not exceed specified fractions of GDP. The signers of the agreement hoped in this way to assure convergence of macroeconomic policies. The four Maastricht tests do not coincide completely with the optimum currency area criteria. This is particularly true of the fiscal tests, which were adopted, not as optimum currency criteria, but rather because large budget deficits and debts are bad in their own right, and because they might in practice someday force the European Central Bank to bail a country out.[22] Nevertheless, European leaders judged the northern European countries named earlier as meriting admission, as well as six other countries that undertook strong efforts to reduce their budget deficits and interest rates in time to qualify: France, Italy, Spain, Portugal, Ireland, and Finland. The transition among the eleven to a common currency, the euro, went smoothly in 1999. The United Kingdom, Sweden, and Denmark opted out voluntarily, for the time being. Greece joined in 2001. Some Central European countries are planning to join soon as well.

The second point is that European countries are gradually becoming more highly integrated with each other economically and more willing to think of themselves as Europeans, so they are a bit more likely to meet the optimum currency area criteria with each decade that passes. A case in point is France. The predecessor to the EMS in the 1970s was the Snake.[23] Each time the French franc bumped up sharply against the limit in the Snake band, the French government would drop out of the agreement, rather than alter its policies. The EMS, founded in 1979, constituted a more serious attempt at stabilization of European exchange rates and was more successful in the 1980s than the Snake had been. Its first important test arose when the socialist François Mitterrand first came to power in France in 1981 and tried to expand the French economy at a time when other European countries were not expanding theirs. The consequent balance of payments deficit and downward pressure on the French franc forced Mitterrand to choose between abandoning the expansionary policies and abandoning the exchange rate constraint. Partly for the sake of the EMS and the cause of European integration, he chose the former. Thereafter the French monetary authorities were determined to maintain sufficiently anti-inflationary policies to keep the franc as strong in value as the mark.[24]

---

[22]Candidates are required to get their budget deficits below 3 percent of GDP. Under the Stability and Growth Pact (SGP), the same limit is supposed to apply even after a country is admitted to EMU. In practice, however, members are able to violate this limit with impunity, at least the larger ones. Yet the SGP has proven difficult to reform. On the one hand, countries need to be able to run deficits during temporary downturns in economic demand, if for no other reason than because tax receipts slow. On the other hand, governments allowed to run cyclical deficits will claim that every downturn is temporary. One promising model is an institution that Chile uses to enforce fiscal rules: An independent panel of experts is delegated the task of deciding whether each year's output fluctuations are temporary and demand driven versus permanent and supply driven.

[23]Why "Snake"? The system established in 1971 had the world's major currencies fluctuating within certain margins of each other and the European currencies fluctuating within a narrower band. The pattern that the movement of the European exchange rates made over time looked like a "snake within a tunnel."

[24]Jeffrey Sachs and Charles Wyplosz, "The Economic Consequences of François Mitterrand," *Economic Policy,* 2 (1986): 261–313.

European integration continues to increase, partly as a result of such measures as the removal of barriers to trade and labor mobility. Even if some EU members do not satisfy the criteria for joining the optimum currency area today, perhaps they will in the future.[25]

26.6 Summary

This chapter explored the aggregate supply side of the economy in some detail. It considered a number of possible alternative supply relationships that had different implications for the ability of monetary policy to affect domestic output. In the frictionless neoclassical model, an increase in the money supply has no effect on output and employment but rather goes proportionately into prices and wages. In the modified Keynesian model, the wage is fixed. It follows that an expansion succeeds in raising output to a degree (as in the simple Keynesian model of earlier chapters) but also raises the price level to a degree. Indeed, from the viewpoint of firms, the level of output they choose to supply increases *because* the price at which they can sell their goods rises relative to the wage. In the Friedman-Phelps model, workers raise their wage demands as they adjust their price expectations upward. In the long run, the aggregate supply curve becomes vertical, as in the frictionless neoclassical model, and the money supply increase has no effect on output. In the Lucas-Sargent-Barro model, the only effect that the government can have on output is the useless one of randomly changing the money supply in unexpected directions. For practical policy-making purposes, the aggregate supply curve is vertical even in the short run. Finally, with indexed wages, monetary policy again has no effect and the aggregate supply curve is vertical even in the short run. The fixed level of output can be the wrong one, however, if real wages fail to fall in the aftermath of a fall in productivity.

The chapter concluded by considering the formation of monetary unions and other ways that a country can commit itself to monetary discipline. A commitment to monetary discipline via a nominal anchor offers a country the advantage that, by reducing workers' expectations of monetary expansion, it reduces wages and prices. For a country too small and too open to constitute an independent optimum currency area, the gains from pegging its currency to a neighbor's (acquiring a stable anchor for monetary policy as well as reducing exchange rate uncertainty) outweigh the loss of monetary independence. For large countries, the option of a fixed exchange rate is generally less practical. Alternative nominal anchors have been proposed, although some of these— fixing the rate of growth of the money supply and fixing the price of gold—are largely obsolete because they have the major drawback that disturbances such as shifts in the demand for money or in the demand for gold can have large undesired impacts on the economy. Inflation targeting, under which the nominal anchor is the CPI itself, has become the most popular nominal rule.

---

[25]Jeffrey Frankel and Andrew Rose, "The Endogeneity of the Optimum Currency Area Criterion," *Economic Journal*, 104 (449) (July 1998): 1009–1025.

CHAPTER PROBLEMS

1. Equation 26.2 says that when there is an expansion of aggregate demand, the percentage increase in output equals σ times the percentage increase in P. If nominal GDP $(= PY)$ goes up by 1 percent, what fraction of this takes the form of an increase in Y? What fraction in P? If wages adjust over time, how do these fractions change?

Extra Credit

2. **a.** Let the production function be $Y = \phi N^\beta$, where N is the number of workers employed. What factors determine ϕ? If you know calculus, show that the marginal product of labor, dY/dN, can be expressed as

$$\beta \phi^{1/\beta} Y^{-(1-\beta)/\beta}$$

Why is the marginal product low when Y is high?

   b. If firms maximize profits competitively, so that they choose the level of employment and output where the marginal product of labor is equal to the real wage, show how employment, N, can be expressed as a function of the real wage. I.e., derive an equation to describe Figure 26.2(b). Then show how output, Y, can be expressed as a function of the real wage. You have now derived Equation 26.1 from the text, $(Y/\overline{Y}) = (wP/W)^\sigma$. What must σ equal? If $\overline{Y} \equiv \phi \overline{N}^\beta$, what must w equal?

   c. If an oil shock causes ϕ to fall, what must happen to W/P if full employment is to be maintained?

3. Assuming complete indexation, $\delta = 1$, it is shown in the supplement that the supply curve is given by Equation 26.S.5.

$$(Y/\overline{Y}) = (P/SP^*)^{\alpha\sigma}$$

Try to figure out whether a monetary expansion raises Y. If it does, what must happen to the real exchange rate? What would you expect to happen to the trade balance $X - M$? To the net capital inflow? To total demand for domestic goods, $C + I + G + X - M$? What do you conclude about the effect on Y?

SUGGESTIONS FOR FURTHER READING

Bernanke, Ben, Thomas Laubach, Frederic Mishkin, and Adam Posen. *Inflation Targeting: Lessons from the International Experience* (Princeton: Princeton University Press, 1999). The new conventional wisdom says that an inflation target is the best nominal anchor for monetary policy. Perhaps Bernanke, who became chairman of the Federal Reserve in 2006, will bring inflation targeting to the United States.

Calvo, Guillermo, and Carlos Vegh. "Inflation Stabilization and Nominal Anchors," *Contemporary Economic Policy,* 12 (April 1994): 35–45. The experiences of Latin American countries with stabilization plans based on exchange rate targets, versus money supply targets.

Edwards, Sebastian. "Exchange Rates as Nominal Anchors," *Weltwirtschaftliches Archiv,* 129 (1993). A review.

Eichengreen, Barry. *International Monetary Arrangements for the 21st Century* (Washington, DC: Brookings Institution, 1994). A review of exchange rate regimes in place, and alternative options for the future.

Frankel, Jeffrey. "Experience of and Lessons from Exchange Rate Regimes in Emerging Economies." In Asian Development Bank, ed., *Monetary and Financial Integration in East Asia: The Way Ahead,* vol. 2 (New York: Palgrave Macmillan Press, 2004), pp. 91–138. A survey.

Posen, Adam, ed. *The Euro at Five: Ready for a Global Role?* (Washington, DC: Institute for International Economics, 2005). How successful has the euro been so far?

Rogoff, Kenneth. "Globalization and Disinflation," *Economic Review, Federal Reserve Bank of Kansas City,* 88, no. 4 (2003): 45–78. Why has inflation come down almost everywhere in the world over the last twenty-five years? Perhaps a shift of parameters reflecting increased global competition can explain it, within the time consistency framework.

Willett, Thomas, and Fahim Al Marhubi. "Currency Policies in the Formerly Centrally Planned Economies," *The World Economy,* 17, no. 6 (November 1994): 795–817. Countries in Eastern Europe and the former Soviet Union face a choice regarding exchange rate arrangements. This is a good review of the issues in the optimum currency area framework.

PART VI

The Determination of Exchange Rates in International Asset Markets

Chapter 27 ▪ Expectations, Money, and the Determination of the Exchange Rate
PAGE 573

Chapter 28 ▪ Exchange Rate Forecasting and Risk
PAGE 607

Expectations, Money, and the Determination of the Exchange Rate

We now turn our attention explicitly to the determination of exchange rates in international financial markets. In Chapter 23 we adopted the assumption of perfect capital mobility, or perfect international integration of financial markets: There are no transaction costs, capital controls, or other barriers separating international investors from the portfolios they would like to hold. We will maintain this assumption. Large quantities of capital are ready to move back and forth across national boundaries at will. Because investors adjust their portfolios instantaneously in response to changes in rates of return, exchange rates are volatile. The exchange rate is now the relative price of foreign versus domestic *assets,* rather than the relative price of foreign versus domestic *goods.* Thus it is not surprising that exchange rates turn out to be as volatile as the prices of bonds, equities, gold, and other assets, in contrast to the much more stable national price levels. Refer back to Figure 19.4 for an illustration of this volatility.

In Chapters 21 and 22, the international portfolio investor's decision concerning what country's asset to hold depended only on interest rates. This chapter introduces an additional factor that enters investors' decision making: expectations about future changes in exchange rates. It was reasonable to omit this factor when we were studying a fixed exchange rate and assuming the rate had little likelihood of being changed. Under the modern floating rate system, however, investors are forced to wager on exchange rate movements every time they invest internationally. We begin by focusing on a key building block of models of exchange rate determination: international interest rate parity conditions.

27.1 Interest Rate Parity Conditions

If the dollar is expected to lose value in the future against the yen, then Japanese investors will subtract the expected rate of dollar depreciation from the dollar interest rate when contemplating the purchase of U.S. assets. Similarly, U.S. investors will add the expected rate of yen appreciation to the yen interest rate when contemplating the purchase of Japanese assets. If investors do not care about any factors other than the expected rates of return on the two countries' assets, then they will buy the asset with the higher expected return and sell the other, a process that continues until expected returns are equalized across countries. This means that the expected rate of depreciation of the domestic currency, Δs^e, will be equal to the nominal interest differential.

$$i - i^* = \Delta s^e \tag{27.1}$$

This condition is known as *uncovered interest parity*.

Uncovered interest parity is somewhat similar to *covered* interest parity, the arbitrage condition, Equation 21.2, introduced in Chapter 21:

$$i - i^* = fd \tag{27.2}$$

where *fd* is the forward discount. There is an important difference, however. In the absence of transaction costs, capital controls, and so on, any deviations from Equation 27.2 would mean that investors could risklessly make as much money as they wanted, simply by borrowing in the low-interest-rate country and lending in the other, covering on the forward exchange market. There would be no risk of capital losses (or gains) because the exchange risk is hedged on the forward exchange market. It is very unlikely that such golden profit opportunities exist; indeed, Chapter 21 showed that covered interest parity holds for most industrialized countries.

Uncovered interest parity is another matter. Here investors buying a foreign asset with an apparently high rate of return expose themselves to the risk that whatever is earned in interest will be outweighed by unexpected adverse movements in the exchange rate. Thus uncovered interest parity is a stronger hypothesis than covered interest parity. It will hold only if investors treat domestic currency and foreign currency assets as *perfect substitutes* in their portfolios. In particular, uncovered interest parity will hold only if exchange risk is not important to investors. (This would be the case if investors are relatively certain as to the future exchange rate or, alternatively, if they are risk neutral, i.e., they are unconcerned about risk.)

Expected depreciation and exchange risk are the two factors that can separate domestic and foreign interest rates, even in the absence of barriers to international capital movement. This chapter considers only expected depreciation. We consider exchange risk in Chapter 28.[1]

We will be using Equation 27.1 throughout this chapter. It is important to clarify from the outset that the uncovered interest parity condition is not necessarily a statement about causality; it is not a model specifying the determination of interest rates. Equation 27.1 is an equilibrium condition. It is entirely consistent with the idea that the interest rate is determined to give equilibrium in the money market, as assumed in previous chapters. This chapter simply adds Equation 27.1 as one of the equations that will have to be satisfied simultaneously if investors are to be happy with the portfolios they are holding.

---

[1]Note that if Equations 27.1 and 27.2 both hold, then we have $fd = \Delta s^e$. This is another way of saying there is no exchange risk premium in the foreign exchange market. (Equation 21.A.3 defined the exchange risk premium. Chapter 28 will discuss it further.)

27.2   The Monetary Model of Exchange Rates with Flexible Prices

Under the assumptions (1) that no transaction costs, government controls, or other barriers are discouraging international trade in bonds, and (2) that investors treat different countries' assets as perfect substitutes in their portfolios, it is as if there is only one type of bond in the world. Different countries' bonds can be aggregated together, as long as they all pay the same expected rate of return; investors will be indifferent to which country's bonds they hold. This is what is meant by assuming uncovered interest parity.

The first half of the chapter will also make some analogous assumptions about goods markets: (1) there are no transportation costs, government controls, or other barriers discouraging international trade in goods, and (2) consumers' tastes are such that they treat different countries' goods as perfect substitutes. Thus it is as if there is only one type of good in the world. Countries' goods can be aggregated together so long as their relative prices are fixed. This is what is meant by purchasing power parity, the condition covered extensively in Chapter 19. That chapter distinguished between the *monetary* approach to the balance of payments, so named because it devotes special attention to international flows of money, and the *monetarist* and *new classical* models, which add the assumption that prices are perfectly flexible so that goods markets always clear. This chapter can be thought of as the monetary approach to the *exchange rate,* the floating rate version of the model studied in Chapter 19 for the case of fixed rates. Only in the first half of this chapter do we add the assumption that goods prices are perfectly flexible, to get what might be called the monetarist or new classical model of the exchange rate.

Why return to the assumption of price flexibility, given all the evidence against it reported earlier? First, the model in which there is only one good as well as one bond in the world is a conveniently simple starting point from which to begin the exploration of the complexities of modern exchange rate theory. Second, purchasing power parity (PPP) is not a bad approximation for considering the very long run (or for considering other cases where there are large changes in money supplies, price levels, and exchange rates, as in hyperinflation). Section 27.3 will reintroduce short-run deviations from PPP: variation in the real exchange rate related to monetary disturbances in the presence of sticky goods prices.

We first brought up the importance of exchange rate expectations at the end of the presentation of the Mundell-Fleming model in Chapter 23, which assumed that prices were fixed in the short run. The discussion there noted that investors might expect the exchange rate in the future to move, from wherever it happened to be at the moment, in the direction of long-run equilibrium. This is how we will model expectations in this chapter. First, however, it will be helpful to have an idea of the long-run equilibrium toward which the exchange rate is expected to move. This is another reason for beginning here by studying the long-run equilibrium in which PPP holds.

We repeat the PPP assumption:

$$\bar{S} = \frac{P}{P*} \tag{27.3}$$

Here $\overline{S}$ denotes the level of the exchange rate (the "spot" price of foreign exchange), P the domestic price level, and P^* the foreign price level. Placing a bar over the exchange rate indicates that—ultimately—the equation is taken seriously only in long-run equilibrium. $\overline{S}$ is on the left side here because the focus is on how exchange rates are determined. This is in contrast to Chapter 19, which dealt with fixed exchange rates. There the domestic price level was determined by the exchange rate set by the government, so P was on the left side.

Equation 27.3 is incomplete as a theory of what determines the exchange rate because it simply pushes the question back one step. It says that the exchange rate moves in proportion to the price level. What determines the price level?

The Exchange Rate as the Price of Money

The other essential equation in the monetary model of the exchange rate is the one that sets the real supply of money, M/P, equal to the real demand for money, L.

$$M/P = L(i, Y) \tag{27.4}$$

As in the derivation of the LM curve (Equation 22.4), this equation assumes that the demand for money is a decreasing function of the interest rate, i, because people wish to hold less money when other assets pay a higher rate of return compared to money, but an increasing function of income, Y, because people have a greater need for money with which to undertake transactions when income is higher.[2] To treat the relationship as a theory of how the price level is determined, solve for P.

$$P = M/L(i, Y) \tag{27.5}$$

It makes sense to think of the price level as being determined to set money demand equal to money supply because prices are assumed perfectly flexible. Notice that a 10 percent increase in the money supply causes the price level to increase by 10 percent.

The supply and demand for money in the foreign country is modeled in precisely the same way.

$$P^* = M^*/L^*(i^*, Y^*) \tag{27.6}$$

Now take the ratio of the two price level equations, and substitute it into Equation 27.3.

$$\overline{S} = \frac{M/L\,(i, Y)}{M^*/L^*(i^*, Y^*)} = \frac{M/M^*}{L(i, Y)/L^*(i^*, Y^*)} \tag{27.7}$$

Equation 27.7 has a simple intuitive interpretation. The exchange rate is defined as the price of foreign currency in terms of domestic currency. Thus we are now modeling it as the relative price of foreign money rather than the relative price of foreign goods. As such, it should be determined by the relative supply and demand for money. Notice that the foreign money supply, M^*, appears in the denominator. An increase in M^* will

---

[2]It is possible to derive a money demand function from principles of optimization. Robert Lucas, "Interest Rates and Currency Prices in a Two-Country World," *Journal of Monetary Economics*, 10 (1982): 335–360.

cause a decline in the price of foreign money—the exchange rate, $\overline{S}$—just as an increase in the supply of bananas causes a fall in the price of bananas. An increase in the demand for foreign money, L^*, will have the opposite effect: an increase in the price of foreign money, just as an increase in the demand for bananas causes an increase in the price of bananas. What about the effect of domestic factors? The domestic money supply, M, is in the numerator. An increase in the domestic money supply causes an increase in the exchange rate, a depreciation of the currency. (This is the same result seen in previous chapters.) Finally, an increase in the domestic demand for money causes a decrease in the exchange rate.

The nature of the exchange rate's dependence on the money supplies is very simple: It is directly proportionate to M and inversely proportionate to M^*. When the domestic money supply increases by 10 percent relative to the foreign money supply, the exchange rate goes up by 10 percent because the price level goes up by 10 percent. This is the property of *homogeneity* of nominal variables. See Figure 27.1(a) later in this chapter.

The money demand variables do not necessarily enter in as simply as the money supply variables. For convenience, however, we will adopt a simple functional form for the money demand function, in which the demand for money is proportional to real income in the same way as it is proportional to the price level.[3] Then Y and Y^* will determine the exchange rate in simple ratio form. We also adopt the simplifying assumption that the interest rates enter in simple difference form, represented by the function λ ( ):

$$\overline{S} = \frac{M/M^*}{Y/Y^*} \lambda (i - i^*) \tag{27.8}$$

The simpler functional form chosen for Equation 27.8 clarifies how the exchange rate depends on Y, Y^*, i, and i^*.[4] An increase in domestic real income, Y, has a negative effect on $\overline{S}$—that is, it causes the domestic currency to appreciate—and an increase in foreign income has the opposite effect. An increase in the interest differential, $i - i^*$, has a positive association with $\overline{S}$—that is, it causes the domestic currency to depreciate.[5]

These effects are precisely the reverse of the effects that income and the interest rate appeared to have on the exchange rate in the Mundell-Fleming model in preceding chapters. The apparent contradictions merit some explanation.

First consider the effect of income. Recall exchange rate determination in the Mundell-Fleming model. There an increase in income, Y, because it meant higher demand for imports and a deteriorated trade balance, required a depreciation of the

[3]In other words, the demand for nominal money balances is proportional to nominal GDP, which is PY. This assumption holds, for example, in the quantity theory of money, in which velocity, PY/M, is constant. In that model, however, money demand does not depend on the interest rate.

[4]There is a particular functional form for $L(i, Y)$ that allows the interest rates to enter in simple difference form, as in Equation 27.8: the exponential function. The chapter supplement offers a formal presentation of the model in logs.

[5]Equation 27.8 could be applied to a context of fixed exchange rates as easily as to floating rates, or to a context in which the central bank intervenes in the foreign exchange market to some intermediate degree. Lance Girton and Don Roper, "A Monetary Model of Exchange Market Pressure Applied to the Postwar Canadian Experience," *American Economic Review*, 67, no. 4 (1977): 537–548.

currency.[6] Equation 27.8 implies the reverse relationship with Y. The difference is that this section assumes that prices are perfectly flexible and that Y is therefore always at the level of potential output, where all resources in the economy are fully employed. Think of Y as having a bar over it (like $\overline{S}$) to indicate that it refers to potential output. In this context, if income increases, it is not because of expansionary monetary policy or any other kind of increase in demand, but because of supply-side factors such as a higher level of national resources or an improvement in economic efficiency. In other words, when prices are perfectly flexible, all changes in output are changes in potential output. When income increases because of such reasons, it is a sign of strength in the economy and tends to appreciate the currency because it raises the demand for money. For example, appreciation of the yen in the 1970s and 1980s was attributed to rapid growth in the Japanese economy. Appreciation of the dollar in the latter half of the 1990s was attributed to rapid growth in the U.S. economy.

Now consider the effect of interest rates. In the Mundell-Fleming model (with partial capital mobility), an increase in the interest differential, because it improved the capital account, required an appreciation of the currency. In Equation 27.8, in contrast, an increase in the interest differential is associated with a depreciation of the currency. It is important to see the reason for this difference as well.

From the covered interest parity condition, Equation 27.2, the forward discount can be substituted in place of the interest differential. Furthermore, the uncovered interest parity condition, Equation 27.1, shows that the expected depreciation variable can be substituted in place of the interest differential. We can rewrite Equation 27.8 as follows:

$$\overline{S} = \frac{M/M^*}{Y/Y^*} \lambda \left(\Delta s^e \right) \tag{27.9}$$

An increase in the expected rate of depreciation of the currency, Δs^e, has a positive effect on today's exchange rate (it causes the currency to depreciate today). It is clear why: If investors expect the domestic currency to lose value over the coming period, they will choose to shift their portfolios out of that currency and into other assets to protect themselves against the expected future losses. When they seek to shift out of the domestic currency, they drive down its value today ($\overline{S}$ rises). There is an important principle here. If expectations regarding what will happen in the future change, even if no other variables change today, then today's exchange rate will change. In this context, a high interest rate is not a sign of strength for a currency. Rather, it reflects expected future depreciation and is thus a sign of weakness.[7] This is why a high (nomi-

---

[6]In Problem 5 at the end of the chapter, you are asked to solve the balance-of-payments equilibrium condition (Equation 22.4) for S.

[7]When investors shift their portfolios out of domestic money in response to expectations of depreciation, what do they shift into? They shift into either domestic or foreign bonds. It makes no difference which, because under the assumption of perfect substitutability, or uncovered interest parity, domestic and foreign bonds are essentially the same thing. In a different version of the model, the *currency substitution* model, people are thought to shift directly from domestic money to foreign money. However, unless they are planning on actually traveling to the foreign country to buy goods, there is in reality little reason for them to hold foreign money. To do so would be to voluntarily give up the interest that could be earned on foreign bonds.

nal) interest rate is not necessarily associated with a strong currency, as it is in the Mundell-Fleming model.

So far, we have represented the rate of return variable (the opportunity cost of holding domestic money) of Equation 27.8 in three ways: as the interest rate differential, the forward discount, and the expected rate of depreciation. There is yet a fourth way to express the rate of return variable, and it will help clarify the first three expressions.

Equation 27.3 expressed purchasing power parity in terms of *levels;* but it can also be expressed in terms of *rates of change:*

$$\Delta \bar{s} = \Delta p - \Delta p^* \tag{27.10}$$

where $\Delta \bar{s}$ is the annualized percentage rate of change of the exchange rate in long-run equilibrium, Δp is the domestic inflation rate, and Δp^* is the foreign inflation rate. Equation 27.10 says that if the domestic inflation rate exceeds the foreign inflation rate, then the domestic currency depreciates at the rate of the inflation differential, to prevent the country's goods from becoming overpriced in world markets.[8]

If the exchange rate acts according to Equation 27.10, investors are presumably aware of this and form their expectations accordingly. Then expected depreciation is equal to the expected inflation differential.

$$\Delta s^e = \Delta p^e - \Delta p^{*e} \tag{27.11}$$

In other words, investors expect the domestic currency to lose value to the extent that they expect its purchasing power over goods to deteriorate at a faster rate than for the foreign currency.

Observe that if the interest differential is equal to the expected rate of depreciation (Equation 27.1, the uncovered interest parity condition) and the expected rate of depreciation is in turn equal to the expected inflation differential (Equation 27.11, PPP in rate of change form), then it follows that the interest differential is equal to the expected inflation differential.

$$i - i^* = \Delta p^e - \Delta p^{*e}$$

This can also be represented as the domestic *real* (that is, expected-inflation adjusted) interest rate equal to the foreign real interest rate.

$$i - \Delta p^e = i^* - \Delta p^{*e}$$

This condition is called *real interest parity.*[9]

---

[8]Again, the empirical evidence in Chapter 19 showed that PPP is unlikely to hold in the short run. Remember, however, that the model in this section properly applies only to long-run exchange rate determination. The short-run deviations from the equation will be developed soon enough.

[9]Real interest parity could also be obtained through an alternative route—if the real interest rate in each country were tied to a technological constant, the marginal product of capital. In practice, however, real interest rates are observed to be neither constant over time nor equal across countries at a point in time. (Again, only as a description of the long run is the flexible-price view of the world that provides real interest parity meant to be taken literally.)

Using Equation 27.11, we can substitute the expected inflation differential into Equation 27.9.

$$\overline{S} = \frac{M/M^*}{Y/Y^*} \lambda \left(\Delta p^e - \Delta p^{*e}\right) \qquad (27.12)$$

Now we see that investors will seek to shift out of a currency, thus causing it to depreciate, when it is expected to lose future value in the sense of a high expected rate of inflation.

Venezuela is an example of a country with a high rate of inflation, as compared to the United States. The Venezuelan inflation differential has held consistently enough in the past that by now it is built into expectations and the interest differential. Japan is an example of a country that has long had a low inflation rate, which has become similarly built into its economy. Thus PPP states that the Venezuelan bolivar will depreciate over time while the yen will appreciate over time. The monetary theory also states something stronger, however. It states that when there is a sudden increase in expected future inflation—for example, because a new, more expansionary head of the central bank is appointed—the currency depreciates immediately.

Expectations of Money Growth

What determines the expected inflation rate? Many factors affect the inflation rate, especially in the short run. In the simple monetary model, however, the rate of money creation, exogenously set by the central bank, drives everything. This can be seen from the money market equilibrium condition, Equation 27.4. Remember that, because prices are perfectly flexible, income in the equation is tied to the exogenous level of potential output. Imagine that the inflation rate, although not zero, is in a steady state, that is, it is constant and has been fully incorporated into expectations and interest rates. It follows from Equation 27.4 that the given rate of increase of the price level presupposes a money growth rate of the same magnitude. If the money growth rate is exogenously set by the central bank, the inflation rate necessarily adjusts accordingly. The point can be made in terms of the *LM* curve used so extensively in the preceding chapters: If the money growth rate were *not* fully reflected in the inflation rate, that is, if the real money supply were increasing, then the *LM* curve would be shifting to the right and real income would be increasing. For there to be a steady state, the ratio of the money supply to the price level must be constant.

What is the effect on the exchange rate of a permanent increase in the money growth rate of, say, 1 percent per annum? The inflation rate goes up permanently by 1 percent per annum. As soon as the change is recognized by the public, expected depreciation and the interest rate go up by the same 1 percent. As a result, the demand for the currency falls. If the change is recognized at the same moment that it actually takes effect, as it will be if the central bank announces the change in policy, then the price of the currency falls instantaneously. Figure 27.1(a) shows this as a discrete upward jump in the exchange rate (and in the price level). This jump occurs even though the level of the money supply does not jump discretely, only its rate of growth does. Thus the per-

FIGURE 27.1

The Effect of Changes in the Money Supply on the Equilibrium Exchange Rate

When the money supply, M, jumps to a higher level, the equilibrium price level, P, and spot rate, $\bar{S}$, jump in proportion, as in (a). When the money supply grows at a faster rate, the equilibrium price level and spot rate grow at the same faster rate. In addition, there is a sudden drop in demand for the currency when investors discover the change, as in (b).

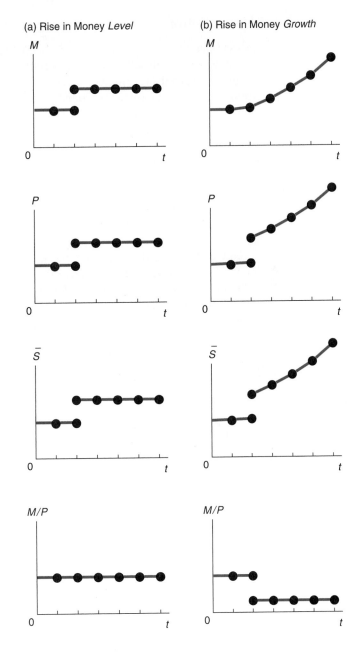

(a) Rise in Money *Level*

(b) Rise in Money *Growth*

centage change in the exchange rate in any given interval of time can be greater than the percentage change in the money supply observed during that interval (particularly if the interval is short). This will happen if the change in the money supply is thought to signal a permanent change in the per annum money growth rate.

Hyperinflation

An example where this framework, the monetary approach to the exchange rate, is thought to apply well is the case of hyperinflation. As we noted in Section 19.3, hyperinflations occurred in a number of central European countries in the aftermath of World War I. The German experience, from February 1920 to November 1923, has been extensively studied. In October 1923 the rate of money growth reached 1,300 percent *per month.* The inflation rate reached 29,586 percent per month. That is just over 20 percent per day; at that rate, the price level doubles in less than four days! Fascinating stories abound of what life was like under such conditions. Wages were paid twice a day so workers could shop at lunchtime before prices rose again. So much paper currency was needed to make simple purchases that a wheelbarrow might be needed to carry it to the store. It is said that one shopper left a wheelbarrow full of cash briefly, and found on returning that the wheelbarrow had been stolen, but the currency had been left.

In October 1923 the rate of depreciation of the mark reached 29,957 percent per month. The price level and exchange rate were going up at roughly the same rate—that is, the real exchange rate had reached a steady state. However, in the transition to this steady state, the price level (and exchange rate) had gone up more than the money supply: *Real* money balances fell to a fraction (0.15) of their original level, as in the bottom panel of Figure 27.1(b).

Figure 27.2 illustrates the change in real money balances for thirteen hyperinflations of the past century. The worse the hyperinflation, the more extreme the fall in real money holdings. This reflects the fact that the real demand for the currency depends negatively on the rate at which it is expected to lose value. Thus it is not quite true in the new classical model that no change in a monetary variable can have an effect on any real variable. (We are classifying the level of real money balances as a real variable.) A change in the money growth *rate* has an effect on the level of real money balances.[10] Nevertheless, whether the change occurs in the level of the money supply or in its rate of change, there is still no effect on the real interest rate or real exchange rate.[11]

When the Money Supply Follows a Random Walk

The case already considered, where people expect a constant growth rate of domestic money indefinitely into the future, is relatively easy to understand. In this case, the various versions of the rate of return on alternative assets—the expected inflation differential, nominal interest differential, forward discount, and expected rate of depre-

---

[10]This property is called a lack of "superneutrality."
[11]See Rudiger Dornbusch, "Lessons from the German Inflation Experience of the 1920s," in R. Dornbusch, S. Fischer, and J. Bossons, eds., *Macroeconomics and Finance: Essays in Honor of Franco Modigliani* (Cambridge, MA: MIT Press, 1987), pp. 337–366. The seminal statement of the flexible-price version of the monetary approach to the exchange rate was made in the context of the German hyperinflation: Jacob Frenkel, "A Monetary Approach to the Exchange Rate: Doctrinal Aspects and Empirical Evidence," *Scandinavian Journal of Economics* (1976): 200–224. The classic study of money demand in interwar hyperinflation is Philip Cagan, "The Monetary Dynamics of Hyperinflation," in Milton Friedman, ed., *Studies in the Quantity Theory of Money* (Chicago: University of Chicago Press, 1956).

FIGURE 27.2

Real Money Holdings in Great Hyperinflations of the Twentieth Century

Real money holdings fall in hyperinflations because the demand for money depends on expected rates of return. The larger the increase in the inflation rate, the bigger the fall in real money.

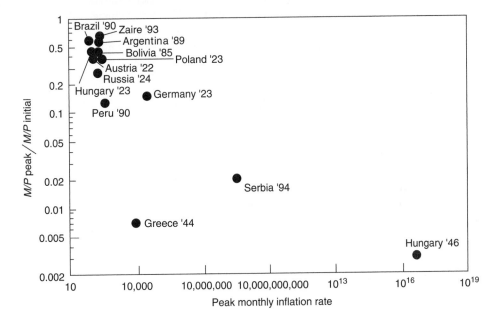

ciation—are all equal to the expected money growth rate differential. The public's expectations as to the future path of the money supply in the long run, however, may not be accurately described by a single constant growth rate. Consider two alternatives.

First, what happens if the money supply is thought to follow a random walk? That is, although people know the money supply will probably change, they think it could as easily go down as up. At any point in time, the best forecast of the change in money supply is zero. As a matter of fact, there is indeed a great deal of "noise" in the monthly money supply numbers that are reported, for example, by the Federal Reserve. This means that when the central bank reports an increase in the money growth rate in a given month, the chances are good that the increase is purely transitory and does not signal a new, permanently higher money growth rate.

If the expected values of the future money supply changes are zero, then the expected inflation differential, expected depreciation rate, and interest rate differential are also zero.[12] The middle term disappears from the equations for $\overline{S}$ derived earlier. A

---

[12]Any increase in money demand coming from growth in potential output is omitted here. If money demand increases, the currency can appreciate even without a change in the money supply. There also has long been a gradual downward trend in real money demand arising from innovation in banking. For example, since the invention of automatic teller machines, there has been less need to carry cash around.

1 percent increase in the money supply, although it has a 1 percent effect on the price level and exchange rate, has no further effects. This case is illustrated in Figure 27.1(a) for a single change in the money supply. The exchange rate simply follows a random walk in lockstep with the domestic money supply (relative to the foreign money supply). Note that these are the only circumstances—random-walk money supplies in a flexible-price monetary model—under which the exchange rate should theoretically be expected to follow a random walk. Most of the time there will be some reason to expect future depreciation (or appreciation) over a long horizon, as in a high- (or low-) inflation country.

When the Money Supply Is Expected to Jump in the Future

What happens if the public suddenly raises its estimate of the probability that the money supply will be increased in four years because the more expansionary of two political parties will come to power in the next presidential election? Four years from now, assuming the anticipated increase in the money supply indeed materializes, the exchange rate will increase proportionately. It might seem that an event so far off in the future would have no effect on *today's* exchange rate. This supposition turns out to be incorrect, however, assuming that investors' expectations are *forward looking,* or rational. Under rational expectations, investors know the true model that determines the exchange rate. They form their expectations of the future exchange rate by taking the mathematical expectation, using all available information including their knowledge of the true model. In other words, *expectations,* meaning what investors anticipate, are now the same as *mathematical expectation,* meaning the average realized value given all available information.[13]

Rational investors, in estimating how much the currency will be worth next period, will think further ahead in the future than just one period. They will make the following calculation. They will realize that if it is known that the money supply and the exchange rate will increase in year 4, then in year 3 investors will shift their portfolios out of the domestic currency to protect themselves from the capital loss expected over the subsequent period. They will realize that, as a result, some of the depreciation will take place in year 3. However, if it can be foreseen that the currency will depreciate in year 3, then it can be foreseen that investors in year 2 will shift out of the domestic currency to protect themselves from the expected loss; some of the depreciation thus takes place in year 2. If the currency is expected to depreciate in year 2, by the same logic it will depreciate in year 1. Finally, if the domestic currency is expected to depreciate in year 1, then rational investors living in the present will shift their portfolios out of it immediately. If *all* today's investors make this calculation, they will cause the currency to depreciate today, even if the money supply is not expected to increase for four years.

---

[13]Chapter 26 explained that workers who have rational expectations forecast the price level optimally and determine their wage demands accordingly. Here investors who have rational expectations forecast the exchange rate optimally and determine their asset demands accordingly. In both cases, the individuals are assumed to have as much knowledge of the correct model of the economy, and as much up-to-date information on the economic variables, as the economists building the model.

In theory, if investors suddenly decided for some reason that the money supply was going to increase in the year 2100, by the same logic there would be an effect on today's exchange rate. The effect on today's exchange rate is smaller, the further into the future is the expected increase in the money supply. Future changes in the money supply are *discounted* back to the present. So, reassuringly, the anticipation of an increase in the money supply in the year 2100 would have a negligibly small effect on the exchange rate today.

27.3   Two Examples of the Importance of Expectations

The expectation regarding future changes in the exchange rate plays a key role, as we have seen. We further offer two specific illustrations of this point, while staying within the framework of the same model.

Speculative Bubbles

Exchange rates are often alleged to fluctuate excessively, in the sense that "unnecessary" movement in the exchange rate takes place even in the absence of any movement in fundamental macroeconomic variables such as the money supply. We have just seen in the preceding section that today's exchange rate can move in a given period without any movement in the money supply taking place in that period. This is not a valid example of excess variability, however, because such movements are caused by expectations of actual movements in the money supply, even if the latter do not take place in the same period. The question arises whether changes in expectations that shift demand for the currency and thus cause the exchange rate to move can occur with no basis in fundamentals at all.

Financial commentators have discussed the possibility of *speculative bubbles* ever since such classic historical episodes as the Dutch tulip bulb mania of the seventeenth century and the South Seas Company stock market bubble of the early eighteenth century, which even took in Sir Isaac Newton. In recent years, large puzzling movements in exchange rates have been identified as speculative bubbles by some. The final 20 percent appreciation of the dollar in the eight months preceding its peak in 1985, for example, seems difficult to explain otherwise. (Refer ahead to Figure 27.4(b).) The same is true of the appreciation of the yen up to 1995.

When the exchange rate is on a speculative bubble path, it wanders away from the equilibrium value dictated by macroeconomic fundamentals because of self-confirming expectations. Such a bubble would arise as follows. In period 0, speculators suddenly decide for some reason that the currency is going to depreciate in period 1. (For example, even without any good reason to expect a future change in fundamentals, speculators may form their expectations by simplistically extrapolating a recent blip in the exchange rate.) To protect themselves against the feared depreciation, they sell the currency and drive down its price in period 0. Is such behavior irrational? Not necessarily. The currency might actually depreciate in period 1, justifying their fears; it will do so if there is a fall in demand for it in period 1, which will happen if there is an expectation of further depreciation in period 2. Is it irrational to expect a depreciation in period 2? Not if there is a fall in demand for it in period 2 because of an expectation of depreciation in period 3. Similarly, it will be rational to expect depreciation in period 3 if depreciation is also expected in period 4, and so forth. If there is an ultimate day of reckoning on which the value of the currency is known to be tied down to some specific value, this will prevent the speculative bubble from getting started. But without such a day of reckoning, there is nothing in the expectations logic that prevents the exchange rate from soaring indefinitely high, regardless of the economic fundamentals. Although society in the aggregate will probably be harmed by such unnecessary movements, each individual speculator will feel constrained to follow the herd because, given that everyone else is pushing the exchange rate up, the individual would lose money by trying to buck the trend alone.

In practice, the exchange rate does not shoot off to infinity, that is, diverge indefinitely far from the long-run value implied by fundamentals. At most, it wanders away from fundamentals equilibrium for a short time before the bubble bursts. It is possible, however, that such bubbles regularly form and subsequently burst, thus adding to the variability of floating exchange rates. Some of those who believe this phenomenon is important argue that a more interventionist policy on the part of the government might be able to reduce unnecessary volatility in the economy even without a change in monetary policy.

Target Zones and the Honeymoon Effect

Some economists who dislike the high variability of floating exchange rates, but who recognize that fixed exchange rates are not a practical alternative for large industrialized countries, propose the adoption of a system of *target zones* for the dollar, yen, and European currencies. Under this system the countries involved would (1) agree on the fundamental equilibrium value of each exchange rate (subject to periodic review), (2) agree on fairly wide bands within which exchange rates would be free to fluctuate, and (3) commit to altering monetary policies when exchange rates threaten to violate those bands.[14] Critics of such schemes object on the basis that governments are not very good at choosing the correct fundamental equilibrium rates.

The theory of target zones shows—when the authorities are credibly committed to using monetary policy to stabilize the exchange rate within the announced bands—that speculation can help in this effort. The theory was developed in the 1980s to describe the Exchange Rate Mechanism of the EMS.[15] Let us assume that France and Germany announce that the franc/mark rate will be subject to specified margins around the central rate, say plus or minus 2¼ percent. (This was the actual width of the band from 1979 to 1993. Denmark still maintains such a band.) What happens if, subsequently, French

---

[14]John Williamson, "Target Zones and the Management of the Dollar," *Brookings Papers on Economic Activity,* 1 (Washington, DC: Brookings Institution, 1986): 165–174.
[15]Paul Krugman, "Target Zones and Exchange Rate Dynamics," *Quarterly Journal of Economics,* 106 (1991): 669–682.

FIGURE 27.3

The Target Zone

If expectations played no role, then the monetary authorities would have to intervene as soon as fundamentals had drifted as far as $\pm 2\frac{1}{4}$ percent, at D_1. But speculation helps reduce the range of variation of S.

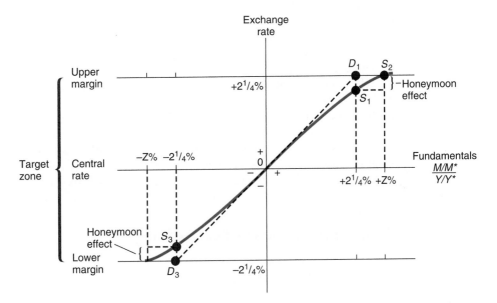

or German economic fundamentals drift in a particular direction and the exchange rate draws near to one of the proclaimed margins of the target zone?

The horizontal axis of Figure 27.3 measures economic fundamentals. Assume the franc/mark rate is determined by the monetary model, as represented by Equation 27.9, so that fundamentals are represented simply by $(M/M^*)/(Y/Y^*)$. The vertical axis measures the franc/mark exchange rate, S. Let us say that the exchange rate nears the upper margin because real growth in Germany exceeds real growth in France. If the monetary authorities do not have a genuine commitment to the target zone arrangement, then there is nothing to stop the exchange rate from going right through the boundary. But let us assume the authorities are in fact prepared to adjust monetary policy to keep the exchange rate inside the band. This means that the Bank of France is prepared to reduce French money growth to offset the decrease in the relative demand for francs.

It might appear that as soon as the macroeconomic fundamentals, $(M/M^*)/(Y/Y^*)$, reach the level of 2¼ percent above the central rate, where the diagonal line crosses the upper margin for S at point D_1, the Bank of France must step in to prevent the rate from breaching the limit. But we must remember that the exchange rate is determined not just by the current fundamentals but also by investor expectations, Δs^e. When the exchange rate nears the upper margin, speculators are aware that it is much more likely in the future to move down rather than up because the central bank will intervene against an upward movement. In other words, Δs^e is negative. Investors respond with a reduced demand for marks. The result is that when fundamentals are at D_1, the equilibrium value of the exchange rate is at S_1. Thus speculation works to narrow the range of variation of the exchange rate, even before the authorities roll up their sleeves. The difference between the two points has been called the *honeymoon effect*. Not until the fundamentals reach some more extreme limiting point, indicated in Figure 27.3 by $+Z\%$, will the exchange rate draw so close to the boundary of the target zone that the Bank of France is forced to intervene by taking francs out of circulation. This is point S_2.

The same honeymoon effect holds at the lower margin. If the fundamentals drift to 2¼ percent below the central rate, speculators know that a future increase is more likely than a future decrease. They respond by increasing their demand for marks. They push the exchange rate up from point D_3 to point S_3. The honeymoon effect pushes other points off the diagonal line as well, into a curve with a flattened S shape. The key point is that speculation helps narrow the range of variation. The catch, once again, is that the authorities' commitment to intervene when necessary must be credible.

27.4 Overshooting and the Real Exchange Rate

The equation developed in Section 27.2 has a number of problems if it is intended as a complete theory. Chief among them is that it at best explains only movement in the *nominal* exchange rate. As a consequence of the flexible-price, or PPP, assumption, it cannot account for movement in the *real* exchange rate. Chapter 19 showed that the evidence is strongly against PPP—in other words, against a constant real exchange rate—in the short run. It appears that goods prices are in fact sticky, whether as a result of imperfect information, contracts, costs incurred in changing prices, or inertia in consumer habits. As a result, disturbances in the nominal exchange rate are reflected as disturbances in the real exchange rate, which die out only very slowly over time. This was the justification for the constant-price assumption made in the Keynesian and Mundell-Fleming models (Chapters 17–18 and 22–23, respectively). Assuming that goods prices are literally constant is too extreme, however. In the presence of excess demand for goods, prices do eventually adjust upward. The flexible-price monetary model went to the opposite extreme and assumed there are no barriers to prevent goods prices from adjusting instantaneously. This section develops the sticky price version of the monetary model. It is a realistic synthesis of the two extremes. It turns out to be equivalent to the Mundell-Fleming model in the short run and the monetarist model in the long run. The model is from a classic article by Rudiger Dornbusch.[16]

The effort to derive the long-run equilibrium exchange rate, $\overline{S}$, in the first half of the chapter has not been wasted. This section merely adds in $S - \overline{S}$, short-run deviations of the exchange rate from that equilibrium.

---

[16]"Expectations and Exchange Rate Dynamics," *Journal of Political Economy* (1976): 1161–1174.

International Differences in Real Interest Rates

Related to the problem that real exchange rates are not constant is the problem that real interest rates also are not constant. National differences in nominal interest rates do not fully reflect differences in expected inflation rates. In the 1970s there was a rough correspondence between interest rates in the major industrialized countries and their inflation rates. Those countries that experienced substantial increases in inflation also experienced substantial increases in nominal interest rates. Thus the pattern of the 1970s was loosely consistent with the idea that nominal interest rate differentials reflect expected inflation differentials. In other words, the pattern was consistent with the real interest parity condition used to derive Equation 27.12.

This pattern broke down after 1980. Nominal interest rates rose in all countries and came down only slowly after 1984, even though inflation began declining steadily in 1981. The U.S. interest rate rose the furthest, even though inflation in the United States fell more rapidly than in Japan and Germany. In the early 1990s the situation reversed: The real interest rate in Germany rose above the U.S. real interest rate. In short, real interest differentials became large and highly variable in the 1980s and 1990s.[17] For this reason, the models cannot remain in the simple form that assumes real interest parity. Variation in the real interest rate differential must be included as an additional factor in the model of variation in the real exchange rate.

We retain the assumption that expected returns are equalized across countries when expressed in common currency units: Not only are there no barriers that slow down portfolio adjustment, but investors treat domestic and foreign bonds as perfect substitutes in their portfolios.[18] Thus uncovered interest parity holds as before.

$$i - i^* = \Delta s^e$$

Subtracting the expected inflation differential, $\Delta p^e - \Delta p^{*e}$, from both sides yields an analogous parity condition in real terms:

$$(i - \Delta p^e) - (i^* - \Delta p^{*e}) = \Delta s^e - \Delta p^e + \Delta p^{*e}$$

or

$$r - r^* = (\Delta s_{\text{real}})^e \tag{27.13}$$

---

[17]One can sometimes come to different conclusions regarding real interest rates, depending on the precise measure one uses for expected inflation. The apparent variation in real interest rates in the 1970s was small enough that some economists attributed it entirely to the problem of measurement, believing that, ex ante, real interest rates were, in truth, constant. But movements in the 1980s were so large, regardless of what measure one uses for expected inflation, that it was no longer possible to argue that real interest rates were constant. Real interest rates for the United States and an average of ten trading partners are shown in Figure 27.4(a).
[18]Saying that expected rates of returns are equalized across countries when expressed in common units is not the same as saying that real interest rates are equalized across countries. A country's real interest rate is the return on its bonds, expressed in terms of purchasing power *over that country's goods*. An international investor has an incentive to arbitrage away any differentials in interest rates when expressed in a common currency, but there is no incentive to arbitrage away a differential between the U.S. rate of return expressed in terms of U.S. goods and the German rate of return expressed in terms of German goods. If PPP held, then the two calculations would be the same. However, this section allows for the fact that PPP does not hold.

where r and r^* are the domestic and foreign real interest rates, and $(\Delta s_{\text{real}})^e$ is the expected rate of change of the real exchange rate, SP^*/P, algebraically equal to the expected rate of change of the nominal exchange rate minus the expected inflation differential. Equation 27.13 shows that the differential in real interest rates is equal to the expected rate of real depreciation of the currency. Intuitively, if investors expect a country's currency to be depreciating in real terms, they will not be willing to hold its assets unless they are compensated by a higher real interest rate.

To take an example, we have noted that in 1984–1985 the U.S. real interest rate was above its major trading partners' real interest rates. We now see that this differential was signaling that investors expected the dollar to depreciate in real terms in the future. (They turned out to be right.) To take a different example, Chile had very high real interest rates in the late 1970s, signaling in part that investors considered the government's attempt to peg the value of the currency at a high level to be unsustainable. (They too turned out to be right.)

Regressive Expectations

The next question is what determines expectations. It is always difficult to model expectations because it is difficult to know what goes on inside people's minds. Yet it is natural to suppose that, when the exchange rate is observed to deviate from the long-run equilibrium level, investors will expect it to move back in the direction of that equilibrium over time. For this purpose we need to know what we mean by the long-run equilibrium. PPP is a good candidate for the long-run equilibrium. In fact, we used the assumption of PPP in the monetary model at the beginning of the chapter to represent the long-run equilibrium level of the exchange rate, $\overline{S}$.

Section 19.2 showed that after a disturbance there is a slow but positive tendency for the real exchange rate to return toward PPP until the next disturbance comes along. The tendency to return to equilibrium is so slow—and new disturbances come along so often—that it is difficult to detect. When a large enough data sample is examined, however, it is possible to detect a tendency for the exchange rate to eliminate 15 percent or more of the existing gap per year. If this tendency to *regress* toward equilibrium exists in the real exchange rate, then investors are presumably aware of it. (This is another application of the idea that investors are rational.) Thus investors are said to have *regressive expectations:*

$$\Delta s^e_{\text{real}} = -\theta(S - \overline{S})/\overline{S} \qquad (27.14)$$

The equation says that when the currency is thought to be overvalued, that is, to have a higher current value than is given by long-run equilibrium, $\overline{S}$, investors will expect it to depreciate in the future. When the currency is thought to be undervalued, that is, to have a lower current value than in long-run equilibrium, investors expect it to appreciate in the future. The parameter θ is the rate at which the real exchange rate is expected to regress toward equilibrium.

Before proceeding with Equation 27.14, it would be reassuring to have some evidence that this is, in fact, how expectations are formed. A number of surveys periodically ask bankers, foreign exchange traders, economists, and other market participants their expectations regarding the exchange rate. Although different survey respondents form their expectations in different ways, some systematic patterns are evident. After the dollar appreciated sharply above its PPP level in the early 1980s, for example, the survey respondents reported an expectation that it would depreciate in the future. According to two surveys, the median investor in 1984 expected the dollar to depreciate at a rate of 8.5 percent to 10.0 percent over the following year, against an average of the mark, yen, pound, French franc, and Swiss franc.[19] Equation 27.14 turns out to fit these data well; the parameter θ is estimated at 0.2. It is often dangerous to put too much faith in responses to surveys. In this case, however, it is reassuring that the speed at which people seem to expect the exchange rate to regress to PPP is in the general range of estimates of the speed at which it does in fact regress to PPP.

The Effect of Monetary Policy on the Real Interest Rate and Real Exchange Rate

We now combine Equations 27.13 and 27.14

$$r - r^* = -\theta(S - \overline{S})/\overline{S}$$

and solve for the exchange rate as a function of the real interest differential.

$$(S - \overline{S})/\overline{S} = -(1/\theta)(r - r^*) \tag{27.15}$$

Equation 27.15 says that when the domestic real interest rate exceeds the foreign rate, the value of the domestic currency exceeds its long-run equilibrium value. Why?

Consider an increase in the Canadian real interest rate, as for example occurred in the 1988–1990 monetary contraction. It quickly leads to an increase in international investors' demand for Canadian assets, causing the Canadian dollar to appreciate. When the currency appreciates above its long-run equilibrium value, investors expect that in the future it will have to come back down because it is overvalued. How much does the currency appreciate? Until it has gone far enough that the expectation of future depreciation back toward equilibrium is large enough to offset the interest differential. Only then will investors be willing to hold other assets despite the fact that they do not pay as high an interest rate as Canadian assets. In other words, the overvaluation must be sufficiently large to offset the interest differential in the minds of investors. Loosely speaking, capital comes into the country and the currency appreciates until this condition is met. More precisely, the appreciation should be simultaneous with the increase in the interest rate and the resulting increase in demand for domestic assets. No measurable net capital inflow need actually take place. Recall that the exchange rate adjusts instantaneously so as to equate supply and demand.

Notice in Equation 27.15 that if θ is large, the coefficient $(1/\theta)$ is small. A given increase in the real interest differential will be associated with only a small appreciation of the currency because this is sufficient to generate the necessary expectation of future depreciation. If the expected speed of adjustment is low, however, then the effect on the

---

[19]This is as contrasted with the average for the period 1976 to 1979, before the dollar appreciation had begun, when expected depreciation was −0.2 percent. Jeffrey Frankel and Kenneth Froot, "Using Survey Data to Test Standard Propositions Regarding Exchange Rate Expectations," *American Economic Review,* 77, no. 1 (1987): 133–153.

exchange rate can be large. For example, if θ is 0.2, then a .01 increase in the real interest rate causes a 5 percent (.01/0.2) appreciation of the currency.

Let us return to the example of the shift in U.S. monetary policy that took place in 1979. In the late 1970s monetary policy had been loose in the United States and the inflation rate was high. As a result, real interest rates became low, even below zero. (Although nominal interest rates were relatively high by historic standards, the inflation rate was just as high.) Figure 27.4(a) shows how low U.S. real interest rates were in the late 1970s. In this period the dollar depreciated to what was then its lowest level of the floating rate era. Then, in October 1979 the Federal Reserve Board under Chairman Paul Volcker dramatically shifted monetary policy to a tighter stance to fight inflation. Interest rates rose sharply in early 1980, and the dollar appreciated in response to the increased attractiveness of U.S. assets. The nominal interest rate differential between the United States and its trading partners, approximately zero in the period 1976 to 1979, rose to about .03 in the period 1981 to 1982.

The real interest rate differential continued to rise through mid-1984, mostly in the form of declining expectations of U.S. inflation. The rise was clear for long-term interest rates, shown in Figure 27.4(a). The increase in real rates of return made U.S. assets more attractive and caused the dollar to appreciate. Figure 27.4(b) shows how the real value of the dollar increased with the real interest rate differential. As of mid-1984, a real interest rate differential as large as 3 or 4 percent on ten-year bonds implied that investors expected the dollar to depreciate in real terms at a rate of at least 3 percent per year on average over the next ten years, or 30 percent altogether. If ten years is considered the appropriate length of time needed for the real exchange rate to return virtually all the way to its long-term equilibrium level, then this simple calculation suggests that investors considered the dollar to be about 30 percent above its long-run equilibrium.[20]

In terms of the Mundell-Fleming graph, the U.S. economy in the mid-1980s could be represented as an *IS-LM* intersection at a real interest rate in excess of that prevailing in the rest of the world. The reason has been discussed before: an imbalanced mix of monetary and fiscal policy. Chapter 23 raised the question of how a positive real interest differential like this could be consistent with perfect capital mobility. Now we know the answer: Because the dollar had appreciated so far above its long-run equilibrium, there was an expectation of future dollar depreciation that was sufficient to offset the interest differential in investors' minds.

Long-Run Equilibrium

We have shown that the level of the exchange rate, S, relative to its long-run equilibrium, $\overline{S}$, is determined by the real interest rate differential, itself determined by such factors as monetary policy. If $\overline{S}$ is constant, for example, movement in S is entirely

---

[20]The argument for looking at long-term real interest rate differentials to see how overvalued the market considers the currency to be was developed by Peter Isard, "An Accounting Framework and Some Issues for Modeling How Exchange Rates Respond to the News," in Jacob Frenkel, ed., *Exchange Rates and International Macroeconomics* (Chicago: University of Chicago Press, 1983).

FIGURE 27.4

U.S. and Foreign Real Interest Rates and the Exchange Rate

(a) The U.S. real interest rate was low in the late 1970s and high in the early 1980s, both absolutely and relative to Group of 10 trading partners. (b) The big swings in the real interest differential usually coincide with swings in the value of the dollar.

(a) Nominal and Real Long-Term Interest Rates

(b) The Dollar and Real Interest Rates

explained by movement in the real interest rate differential. In general, however, it is unlikely that the long-run equilibrium rate is constant. Even assuming that the long-run equilibrium *real* exchange rate is constant,[21] it cannot be assumed that the equilibrium *nominal* exchange rate, $\overline{S}$, is constant. Because it is a nominal magnitude, like the price levels, it will follow a rising path over time in an economy with a high rate of money growth and inflation.

Section 27.2 used PPP to derive a model of the exchange rate. At that point we were operating under the assumption that prices were perfectly flexible, whereas we have recognized since then that they are in fact sticky. In the long run, prices *are* flexible, however. Thus PPP can be used to characterize long-run equilibrium. So, although Equation 27.12 no longer serves as a model of the moment-to-moment exchange rate, S, it now serves nicely as a model of the long-run equilibrium exchange rate, $\overline{S}$.

The next task is to see how the exchange rate moves from the short-run equilibrium to the long run. The transition from short run to long run is illustrated in Figure 27.5, which shows the exchange rate on the horizontal axis and the price level on the vertical axis. The proportionality between $\overline{S}$ and P that holds in PPP equilibrium is graphed as an upward-sloping 45° line. It is necessary to be on the PPP line only in the long run. This means that when the money supply goes up permanently by 10 percent and the price level eventually rises proportionately, the exchange rate too will eventually rise by the same 10 percent. This is a movement up along the PPP line, from point A to point B.

Equation 27.15 indicates that in the long run, with the exchange rate at its equilibrium level ($S = \overline{S}$), the real interest rate differential is zero ($r = r^*$). The explanation is that if there is no reason for investors to expect future depreciation of the currency (in real terms), then they have no reason to require a (real) interest rate differential to be willing to hold the currency. This international equalization of real interest rates is similar to the real interest parity condition that followed from Equation 27.11 in Section 27.2, but now we see that it holds only in long-run equilibrium.

The Path from Short-Run Overshooting to Long-Run Equilibrium

The central question addressed by the overshooting model is: What happens in the immediate aftermath of an increase in the money supply? It would clearly be wrong to assume that the economy will stay on the PPP line; goods markets do not adjust fast enough to guarantee this in the short run. The assumption that goods prices are sticky means that when the nominal money supply, M, increases by 10 percent, the real money supply, M/P, on impact, also increases by 10 percent, because prices do not move at all in the short run. Money market equilibrium then requires that the monetary expansion will drive down the interest rate. (In terms of the Mundell-Fleming

---

[21]The possibility that the long-run equilibrium real exchange rate might itself change cannot be ruled out. Japan long had an upward trend in the long-run equilibrium real value of its currency. To take another example, it has been suggested that the long-run equilibrium real value of the dollar is lower than it was in the 1980s because the United States has run up $3 trillion in international debt, which requires a permanent improvement in the trade balance to earn the foreign exchange to service the debt.

FIGURE 27.5

The Dornbusch Overshooting Diagram

An increase in the money supply, *M*, raises the price level, *P*, and spot rate, *S*, proportionately in the long run by PPP (at *B*). In the short run, however, *P* is tied down. As a result, *S* increases more than proportionately in the short run at *C*; that is, it overshoots its long-run equilibrium.

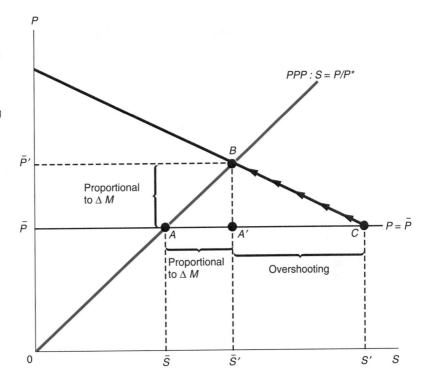

model, the *LM* curve shifts to the right.) The lower interest rate in the home country, in turn, causes international investors to head for the exits. The decline in demand for domestic assets causes the currency to depreciate.

We can figure the size of the depreciation. $\bar{S}$ alone increases by the same 10 percent as the money supply. But the total change in *S* is greater: Equation 27.15 says that $S/\bar{S}$ increases by $(1/\theta)$ times the fall in the interest rate.[22] Only when the currency has depreciated that far do investors have the necessary expectation of appreciation back toward long-run equilibrium that they must have if they are to hold domestic assets willingly, despite the fact that these assets pay a lower rate of interest than foreign assets. We have just derived the now-classic *overshooting* result of Rudiger Dornbusch: Even though the long-run equilibrium exchange rate increases by the same proportion as the money supply, the short-term equilibrium exchange rate increases more than proportionately.

---

[22] The fall in the nominal rate is in turn $1/\mu$ times the increase in the money supply, where μ is the semielasticity of money demand with respect to the interest rate. (See the chapter supplement.)

If the monetary expansion raises the level of output, then the interest rate will not fall by as much as it would if the level of output were constant. As a result, the currency will not overshoot its long-run equilibrium by as much. Conversely, if the monetary expansion raises the expected inflation rate, then the real interest rate will fall by more than the nominal interest rate, and as a result the currency will overshoot its long-run equilibrium by more. But this does not qualitatively change the results described in the text. The algebra for these cases, and indeed for this entire section, can be found in Rudiger Dornbusch, "Expectations and Exchange Rate Dynamics," *Journal of Political Economy*, 84, no. 6 (1976), 1161–1176.

Where is the economy now in Figure 27.5? In the short run it cannot leave the horizontal latitude of the starting point, A, because P is tied down. S increases, which means a move to the right in the graph. How far? The economy moves further than point A' because if it stopped there, S would have increased only by the same percentage as $\overline{S}$. S must increase by more than $\overline{S}$. Thus the economy moves, on impact, to a point like C.[23]

Establishing the short-run equilibrium, C, and the long-run equilibrium, B, prompts the next question: How do we get from here to there? At point C several factors are stimulating the demand for goods. First, the real interest rate has fallen, which should stimulate the domestic demand for capital goods, construction, and consumer durables. Second, the real value of the currency has fallen. Indeed, any point below or to the right of the PPP line is a point where domestic goods are cheaper than foreign goods. This should stimulate the demand for domestically produced tradable goods, such as the foreign demand for exports. The increased demand for goods will put upward pressure on prices. The price level will be somewhat higher after a little time has passed.

As the price level, P, slowly rises to higher levels, the real money supply, M/P, slowly declines to lower levels, although it is still higher than it was before the increase in M. (The LM curve slowly shifts back to the left.) As a result, the interest rate slowly rises, although it is still lower than the foreign interest rate. Equation 27.15 shows that as the interest rate rises, the currency appreciates back toward its long-run equilibrium; international investors no longer find domestic assets quite so unattractive. Thus, as we move up in Figure 27.5 (higher P), we also move back to the left (lower S).[24]

The process continues as long as the real money supply is greater than it was before the monetary expansion—that is, as long as the real interest rate and real currency values are low—because the excess demand for goods continues to cause prices to rise. When the price level has risen by the same proportion as the money supply, then the real money supply, real interest rate, and real exchange rate are all back to their original levels. Only then is there no excess demand for goods and no need for prices to continue rising. This long-run equilibrium is none other than point B, the PPP point at which all nominal magnitudes have increased by the same percentage. This illustrates a general principle that has recurred over several previous chapters: In the long run in which all real magnitudes have had time to return to their equilibrium values, all nominal magnitudes must change proportionately. Figure 27.6(a) shows how, after the initial overshooting caused by the increase in the level of the money supply, the real money supply and real interest rate return over time to their original levels, and as a consequence the exchange rate gradually approaches its new equilibrium level.

Notice the correspondence between what investors at point C thought would happen in the future and what actually did happen. In the short-run overshooting equilibrium at C (when the price level had not yet had time to adjust to the increase in the

---

[23]Point C corresponds to point B in the Mundell-Fleming diagram, Figure 23.3. The interest differential is now attributed to the expectation of future appreciation (rather than to imperfect capital mobility).

[24]The downward-sloping line connecting points B and C represents equilibrium in the asset markets, the relationship that must hold between P and S (via the interest rate, i) for the given money supply, M, to be willingly held.

FIGURE 27.6

Overshooting Effects of Changes in the Money Supply

(a) After a jump in the *level* of the money supply, P can only increase slowly. As a result, the real money supply M/P, real interest differential, $r - r^*$, and spot rate, S, temporarily deviate from their long-run equilibriums. (b) An increase in the *rate of change* of the money supply causes similar deviations from long-run equilibrium, but now equilibrium is itself a moving target.

(a) Rise in Money *Level*

(b) Rise in Money *Growth*

money supply), investors thought the currency would appreciate in the future because they had regressive expectations. We have just established that this is, in fact, what happens as the price level adjusts: S does indeed move in the direction of $\bar{S}$. If investors have rational expectations, then they know the complete model, and the rate at which they expect S to move toward $\bar{S}$ is precisely the rate at which it does so.

The model studied at the beginning of this chapter, where goods prices were perfectly flexible, can be viewed as a special case of the complete model. It is the case where adjustment in the goods markets is instantaneous. If the rate of change of prices is highly responsive to the excess demand for goods, then the system will move to point B very quickly. In the limit, the system will jump from A to B instantaneously. In that case, PPP always holds, $S = \overline{S}$, and Equation 27.12 constitutes a complete analysis of exchange rate determination. The Mundell-Fleming model can be viewed as the opposite extreme, where the speed of adjustment in goods markets is very slow.[25]

Exchange Rate Volatility

We have seen what happens in the aftermath of a single monetary disturbance. However, in practice, if one looks for the nominal exchange rate to follow the path of Figure 27.5 in the aftermath of an overshooting episode—a smooth return to long-run equilibrium—one is likely to be disappointed. In the real world, new disturbances come along all the time, so that before the exchange rate has had time to return much of the way toward its equilibrium, a new policy change in one direction or the other is likely to occur.[26] The effect on the exchange rate of any given monetary disturbance is as we have just seen it to be, notwithstanding the possibility of future disturbances. When each new change in the money supply hits, the exchange rate changes more than proportionally; it then begins to move gradually back toward its long-run equilibrium, until the next monetary disturbance comes along.

Empirically, changes in the exchange rate are more variable than changes in the money supply or the price level. It is an attractive property of the overshooting model that it can explain this variability in exchange rates without having to appeal to speculative bubbles or irrationality on the part of investors. The volatility of exchange rates in the model is a consequence of the fact that asset markets adjust instantaneously while good markets adjust slowly. If goods prices adjusted instantaneously, there would be no overshooting of the exchange rate. Exchange rate changes would be no more variable than changes in the money supply.

There is an analogy with a law of chemistry called Le Châtelier's principle. When one variable in a physical system (such as the pressure or temperature of a gas) is constrained from changing in response to a disturbance (such as a change in its volume), one or more of the other variables in the system must change by more than it otherwise would, to compensate. Paul Samuelson first pointed out the possible application to economics: When one price is constrained from changing in response to a change in supply of a commodity, some other price must change by more to compensate. William Branson has pointed out the relevance for overshooting of the exchange rate: When the general price level is constrained from changing in response to a change in the money supply, the exchange rate changes more than proportionally to compensate.

---

[25] This discussion of overshooting has considered only changes in the level of the money supply. Changes in the expected growth rate of the money supply also cause overshooting, as illustrated in Figure 27.6(b).
[26] Refer back to Figure 19.3 for an idea of the frequency of disturbances to the real exchange rate in 200 years of U.S.–U.K. history.

Furthermore, the slower is the speed of adjustment (expected by investors), θ in Equation 27.14, the greater is the degree of overshooting.[27] This happens because if the speed of exchange rate adjustment, θ, is low, then for any given fall in the interest differential, it takes a large undervaluation of the exchange rate to generate the necessary expectation of future appreciation equal to the interest differential. In terms of Figure 27.5, if θ is low, the asset market equilibrium line is flat and the exchange rate has to increase even further than C before investors are willing to hold domestic assets. If the expected speed of adjustment is very high, however, then a movement just slightly beyond A', an increase in S just a little more than proportionate to the increase in the money supply, will be sufficient to satisfy investors.

Without knowing precisely the size of θ (or the other parameters in the monetary model), we cannot say the observation that exchange rates are much more variable than money supplies necessarily means that exchange rates are excessively variable. The variability may simply be the overshooting phenomenon in operation.

27.5   Two More Examples of the Importance of Expectations

We have emphasized throughout this chapter the important role that expectations play in determining exchange rates in modern asset markets. We illustrate the point with two more examples.

The Example of Official Announcements of Economic Statistics

Government announcements illustrate the importance of changes in expectations. Consider the case of the weekly money announcements. Every week, the Federal Reserve Board announces what the money stock was in the preceding week. In the early 1980s the announcements were made at 4:10 p.m. on Friday afternoons and referred to the money stock nine days earlier. The financial markets looked forward to each week's announcement with both eagerness and trepidation. When the time drew near, trading slowed down and even stopped as traders gathered around the newswire or computer terminal. When the announcement came out, prices in the various financial markets would jump in reaction, and trading would take off again. The most widely remarked reaction took place in the credit markets. When the Fed announced a money supply that was greater than observers had previously been expecting, interest rates would immediately jump up in reaction (or bond prices would jump down, which is another way of saying the same thing).[28] When the Fed announced a money supply that was smaller than had been expected, interest rates would fall in reaction.

---

[27]The expected speed of the rate of exchange rate adjustment, θ, in turn depends on the actual speed of adjustment of goods prices, assuming that expectations are rational.

[28]Bond prices move inversely with the interest rate. If the interest rate is 5 percent, then a one-year Treasury bill with a face value of $10,000 will have a price of about $9,500, so that investors who buy the Treasury bill have the same rate of return as if they put their money into the bank and earned the interest. If the interest rate goes up, then the price investors will be willing to pay for the $10,000 Treasury bill necessarily goes down.

What was the reason for these reactions? They might seem puzzling, considering the theory that an increase in the money supply works to lower the interest rate rather than to raise it. The first thing to realize is that the interest rate movements on Friday afternoons were not directly caused by the changes in the money supply itself—which had taken place a week earlier—but rather by the effect of the new information on *expectations* as to future monetary policy.

According to the theory of efficient markets, it is only the *unanticipated* component of the announced change in the money supply that matters. If the announcement reports an increase no larger than had been previously expected, then there should be no effect on prices in the bond market, foreign exchange market, or any other financial markets. Economists often refer to the importance of "news," to signify that it is only new information that matters.

There are two possible different explanations for a rise in the nominal interest rate in response to a money announcement: a rise in the expected inflation rate or a rise in the real interest rate. The rise in the nominal interest rate could be related to a rise in the expected inflation rate, if investors concluded from the announcement of an increase in the money supply that the Fed planned a faster rate of money growth in the future than had previously been expected. This is the case where investors do not put much credence in the money growth target that the Fed has announced for the year and interpret deviations of the money supply from the previously expected path as evidence that the Fed has changed its target. Conversely, the rise in the nominal interest rate would be related to a rise in the real interest rate if investors interpret the announcement as a sign that the Fed will tighten monetary policy in the near future. This is a reasonable thing to expect the Fed to do if the increase in the money stock occurred for reasons beyond its control (e.g., banks can expand credit to a certain degree, without there necessarily having been a change in Fed policy), and if it is seriously committed to keeping the money supply within its previously set target range. In other words, this is the case where the Fed's commitment to the preannounced target is credible to the financial markets.

How is it possible to tell, at any particular time, which is the real cause of an increase in the nominal interest rate? The foreign exchange market provides the answer to this question. If there is an expectation of looser monetary policy and higher expected inflation, the exchange rate models predict that the dollar will fall on the news. Conversely, if there is an expectation of tighter monetary policy and a higher real interest rate, the dollar should rise on the news.

The evidence suggests that in the late 1970s, the Fed's money growth targets were not very credible. The dollar often fell in value immediately following announcements of money supplies that were greater than had been expected. Investors worried about excessive money growth and the inflationary consequences.

After October 1979, however, the Fed switched to a new set of operating procedures designed to set a firm course for the money supply, with the aim of fighting inflation. The pattern of reaction to the weekly money announcements switched as well. In the early 1980s there was a clear pattern in which both the interest rate and the dollar rose immediately in response to announced money figures that were greater than expected. This suggests (1) that investors during this period expected the Fed to correct deviations from the target, (2) that investors believe that monetary contraction raises real interest rates, and (3) that higher real interest rates make U.S. assets more attractive and cause the dollar to appreciate, as in the overshooting model.[29]

The importance of the weekly money announcements diminished after 1982, when the Federal Reserve started paying less attention to the money supply because innovations in the banking sector and other shifts in the demand for money had taken much of the meaning from M1 and the other traditional measures of monetary policy. The Federal Reserve Board then stopped all pretense of setting M1 targets. As a result, interest rates and exchange rates no longer respond strongly to the money announcements. However, there are still macroeconomic variables that provoke major reactions when announced. After news suggesting strong economic growth, such as a decline in the unemployment rate or an increase in retail sales or durable goods orders, the dollar tends to appreciate. Investors figure, as in the monetary models, that higher domestic output raises the demand for domestic money.[30] Similarly, when there is an announcement of a better trade balance than had been expected, the dollar tends to appreciate.[31]

Is Speculation Stabilizing?

It might seem that overshooting is an example of what is called *destabilizing speculation*—that investors, by freely buying and selling foreign exchange based on their expectations of changes in the exchange rate, make the exchange rate more variable than it would otherwise be. This is not the case, however. The overshooting model just developed illustrates the general principle that expectations are stabilizing rather than destabilizing, as long as an increase in the level of the current exchange rate causes investors to reduce their expectations as to its future rate of change. (This is the case in regressive expectations, represented by Equation 27.14: S enters with a negative sign.) The reason is that if investors act on the basis of such expectations, they will buy the currency when its value is low and sell when its value is high. This will raise the currency's price when it would otherwise be low and lower the price when it would otherwise be high. This type of speculation works to moderate the fluctuations that would otherwise occur in the exchange rate.

Investors, or speculators, who buy low and sell high will also make a profit. This is why Milton Friedman argued that stabilizing speculators would prosper. Any speculators who were destabilizing would be buying high and selling low. They would lose money and thus soon be driven out of business.

---

[29]Charles Engel and Jeffrey Frankel, "Why Interest Rates React to Money Announcements: An Explanation from the Foreign Exchange Market," *Journal of Monetary Economics*, 13 (1984): 31–39.

[30]Gikas Hardouvelis, "Economic News, Exchange Rates and Interest Rates," *Journal of International Money and Finance*, 7 (1988): 23–25.

[31]The trade balance has no effect on the exchange rate in the model developed in this chapter (beyond the effect of any of the other components of GDP $\equiv C + I + G + X - M$). This is a consequence of the assumption that when a country runs a trade deficit, the rest of the world is willing to lend it however much money it needs to finance its deficits—regardless of how much debt it has already incurred in the past—so long as it pays the world rate of interest. The next chapter introduces a role for the debt, so that the trade balance again matters for exchange rate determination.

It has sometimes been suggested that the government should try to discourage speculation—for example, by enacting capital controls or a tax on foreign exchange transactions, thereby returning the economy to a lower degree of international capital mobility. James Tobin wrote that "we need to throw some sand in the well-greased wheels" of international financial markets through a small tax on all foreign exchange transactions.[32] If investors act on the basis of the type of stabilizing expectations studied here, Tobin's proposal to discourage speculation would increase overshooting rather than reduce it, assuming the new barrier to international capital flows was effective. If investors had to overcome a significant transaction cost to buy a foreign currency, then the exchange rate would have to drift even further from its long-run equilibrium before the expectation of future appreciation was sufficiently great to inspire investors to buy it.

What, then, do proponents of such antispeculator taxes have in mind? They have in mind that speculators do not form expectations in a stabilizing manner, such as is given by Equation 27.14. Rather, they believe that speculators form their expectations by simply extrapolating past trends. Such forecasting rules are called *bandwagon expectations:* If investors actually act on the basis of them, they jump on the bandwagon whenever the currency starts to move in one direction or the other. In such case, they can create the sort of speculative bubbles described in Section 27.3. Investors buy when the currency is already high, thereby pushing it higher (until the bubble bursts); they sell the currency when it is already low, thereby pushing it lower. In such an environment, speculation would indeed increase exchange rate volatility.

Which expectations, stabilizing or destabilizing, prevail in practice? Under normal circumstances, when markets are functioning properly, economists believe that expectations are formed predominantly in a stabilizing manner. For example, during the period 1982 to 1984, because the dollar had risen above its PPP equilibrium, many forecasters expected it to depreciate in the future. Any investors who acted on the basis of such expectations, far from being the cause of the appreciation of the dollar, were selling dollars and thus dampening the price below what it would be otherwise.

There are times, however, when most market participants seem to lose sight of economic fundamentals and to extrapolate trends instead. As noted earlier, some observers have argued that July 1984 to February 1985 was such a period, with the final appreciation of the dollar up to its peak attributable to a speculative bubble rather than to fundamentals. Figure 27.4 does make it appear this way: The 1985 spike in the dollar is a major movement in the exchange rate that does not correspond to a movement in the real interest rate differential. In this view, the dollar did more than overshoot its long-run equilibrium; it overshot its short-run equilibrium as well.[33] A similar overvaluation appeared in the years 2001 to 2002, particularly against the euro.

---

[32]James Tobin, "A Proposal for International Monetary Reform," *Eastern Economic Journal,* 4, nos. 3–4 (1978): 153–159.
[33]Paul Krugman, "Is the Strong Dollar Sustainable?" *The U.S. Dollar—Recent Developments, Outlook, and Policy Options* (Kansas City: Federal Reserve Bank of Kansas City, 1985), pp. 103–133.

The view that the dollar was following a speculative bubble path by the end of 1984 would be sympathetic to the switch at the U.S. Treasury from a noninterventionist policy of benign neglect of the dollar under Secretary Donald Regan from 1981 to 1984, to a more activist policy under Secretary James Baker beginning in 1985. The switch was symbolized in September 1985 by the Plaza Accord, in which the finance ministers of the G-5 countries agreed to try to bring the dollar down. The Plaza is widely regarded as a case of successful management of the exchange rate by policy makers. Unfortunately, government officials are not always more skilled at identifying when the exchange rate has departed from fundamentals than are private investors.

Keep in mind that the existence of a speculative bubble does not mean it is easy for an investor to profit from it. The knowledge that the bubble must eventually burst does not mean investors can confidently expect to make money by moving into another currency (or "selling short") because there is no telling how long the bubble will continue, and the investor who does not go along with the trend will lose money as long as it continues.

27.6 Summary

This chapter examined how monetary forces determine the exchange rate under a floating rate system. This required introducing exchange rate expectations, in addition to interest rates, as a factor in determining investors' decisions regarding what assets to hold. Modern models of exchange rate determination share the property of perfect international capital mobility. If there is also perfect substitutability between domestic and foreign bonds, then uncovered interest parity holds: The interest differential must be just large enough to offset investors' expected depreciation of the domestic currency.

The chapter introduced a flexible-price version of the monetary model, in which purchasing power parity holds, which is relevant for long-run equilibrium. The resulting equation shows how the exchange rate, as the relative price of two currencies, is determined by the supply and demand for two currencies. It is useful for seeing how (1) an exogenous increase in real income raises the demand for money and thus causes the currency to appreciate, (2) an increase in the current level of the money supply causes an immediate proportionate depreciation of the currency in equilibrium, and (3) an increase in the expected future rate of growth of money and inflation causes an immediate fall in the equilibrium value of the currency.

These results pertain to long-run equilibrium. The rest of the chapter explained that the short-run equilibrium is characterized by overshooting. When the money supply increases, the currency immediately depreciates *more* than proportionately; that is, it depreciates by more than it will in the long run. This is a consequence of goods prices being sticky in the short run. The increase in the nominal money supply is an increase in the real money supply. It reduces the interest rate, causing investors to shift their demand to foreign assets and causing the domestic currency to depreciate. This much is similar to the effects of monetary expansion in the Mundell-Fleming model of Chapters 22 and 23. The new effect is that today's depreciation generates the expectation among investors that the currency will in the future have to appreciate back toward long-run equilibrium. This expectation of appreciation must be just sufficient to offset the interest differential, for investors to be willing to hold domestic assets. Thus when a loose monetary policy pushes the domestic real interest rate below the foreign real interest rate, it will also push the real value of the currency below its usual level.

Modern models of exchange rate determination share another property: They are designed to fit the empirically observed high variability of floating exchange rates. These models explain such variability in three respects. First, because the exchange rate is seen to be determined in financial markets, it can be as volatile as the prices of stocks, bonds, precious metals, and other assets. The expectation of a future loss in the value of the currency is enough to cause a large shift in demand and thus a large fall in the equilibrium value of the currency today. Second, when goods prices adjust slowly but asset markets adjust instantly, the exchange rate in the short run overshoots its long-run equilibrium. Third, when a speculative bubble gets started, the exchange rate can deviate even from the short-run equilibrium that is determined by the monetary fundamentals.

CHAPTER PROBLEMS

1. If there is a downward shift in the demand for dollars because of increased use of credit cards, what is the effect on the exchange rate?
2. Assume in the monetary model with flexible prices that the public decides today the money supply is expected to jump in the future. Draw the versions of the graphs of the four variables that correspond to Figure 27.1.
3. **a.** If an investor were able to predict that a country's currency will appreciate in the future because of a slower inflation rate in that country than in others, does this mean that the investor can necessarily earn a higher return by holding that currency?
   b. What if the investor were able to predict that a currency will appreciate in the future because it has already overshot (downward) its long-run equilibrium?
4. Are the following three statements true or false?
   i.   If a country has a high interest rate, then its assets will be attractive to hold, and so the value of the currency will be high.
   ii. If a country has a high interest rate, investors must expect that its currency will lose value in the future.
   iii. If investors expect that a currency will lose value in the future, then they will have a low demand for it and it will have a low value today.
   How do statements ii and iii together appear to contradict statement i? Can you reconcile the three statements with each other? (*Hint:* It might help to distinguish *why* the interest rate is high.)
5. The following is the balance-of-payments equilibrium condition from the Mundell-Fleming model, Equation 23.4, with exports depending on the exchange rate, *S*, and

foreign income, Y^*, and imports depending on Y. (All relationships here are assumed to be linear, and m and m^* are the marginal propensities to import.)

$$\chi S + m^*Y^* - mY + \overline{KA} + k(i - i^*) = 0$$

a. Turn this equation into a model of exchange rate determination by solving for S.
b. What policies determine i?
c. Explain why the signs on Y, Y^*, i, and i^* here differ from those in Equation 27.8.

SUGGESTIONS FOR FURTHER READING

Dornbusch, Rudiger. "Expectations and Exchange Rate Dynamics," *Journal of Political Economy* (December 1976): 1161–1176. The classic paper on the overshooting of the exchange rate in response to a change in the money supply.

Frankel, Jeffrey, and Andrew Rose. "Empirical Research on Nominal Exchange Rates." In G. Grossman and K. Rogoff, eds., *Handbook of International Economics* (Amsterdam: Elsevier, 1995). A survey of studies, including the new "microstructure" of the foreign exchange market.

Friedman, Milton. "The Case for Flexible Exchange Rates," *Essays in Positive Economics* (Chicago: University of Chicago Press, 1953). The arguments for floating, twenty years ahead of their time.

Taylor, Mark. "The Economics of Exchange Rates," *Journal of Economic Literature*, 83, no. 1 (1995): 13–47. A survey of the literature on exchange rate determination, including the monetarist model, overshooting, target zones, and the news.

CHAPTER 28

Exchange Rate Forecasting and Risk

Chapter 27 considered the macroeconomic determination of the exchange rate and explored the effects of monetary policy, particularly from the viewpoint of the monetary policy maker. This chapter begins by looking at this issue from the viewpoint of the individual market participant, who must take the movements in the exchange rate as given.

28.1 Forecasting the Spot Exchange Rate

Those who forecast the exchange rate for a living quickly discover that the real world is less straightforward than the theory of exchange rate determination might make it appear. Chapter 27 assumed that everyone knew with confidence what the correct model was, except perhaps for a disagreement between the flexible-price version of the monetary model and the sticky-price version. The fact is, there are many conflicting approaches to forecasting. One consequence is that investors can disagree widely on their exchange rate forecasts.[1]

Forecasting Methods in Actual Use and Their Performance

As distressing as it is for economists to admit, many professional exchange rate forecasters do not base their forecasts on any model of monetary policy or other fundamental economic variables, even simple ones. So-called technical analysts instead forecast by using computer techniques, or hand-drawn graphs in the case of more old-fashioned chartists, to try to uncover trends in the exchange rate. One of the most popular rules calls for buying a currency whenever the short-term moving average (the average over the preceding week, for example) rises above the longer term moving average (over the preceding month), and selling whenever the reverse happens. The *momentum* models call for buying when the current price exceeds the average price, for example, over the

---

[1]In one survey, market participants' forecasts of the exchange rate at a 6-month horizon vary over a high-low range that averages 15 percent. Jeffrey Frankel and Kenneth Froot, "Chartists, Fundamentalists, and Trading in the Foreign Exchange Market," *American Economic Review,* 80, no. 2 (1990): 181–185.

preceding six weeks. Such techniques, in effect, forecast by extrapolating past trends and thus generally fall into the category of expectations that are destabilizing if acted on by investors.[2]

The same can be true of an econometric forecasting approach called ARIMA (AutoRegressive Integrated Moving Average). A simple example of an ARIMA model is a prediction that if the spot rate went up 1 percent last week, then it will go up AR percent this week, where AR is the autoregressive coefficient.

How well do all these techniques forecast the spot rate? The answer is not well, if the criterion is to forecast with small errors. The generalization applies not just to economic fundamentals models, technical analysis, and ARIMA techniques, but to virtually any forecasting approach imaginable. This is because exchange rates are so volatile. Even spot traders who claim to be highly successful will admit that they lose money on many of their trades.[3]

We should not be surprised that a large proportion of the movement in the exchange rate cannot be forecast by any technique. Even if the spot rate behaved precisely as predicted by a model, such as the monetary equation of exchange rate determination developed earlier, one could not accurately forecast the future exchange rate without knowing the future values of the money supplies, income levels, and so on. If the exchange rate departs from the economic fundamentals because of a speculative bubble, then the forecast errors will be that much larger.

Professional forecasters intending to earn a return on their investment of time and expertise can, at best, hope to predict the direction of movement correctly slightly more than half the time. Thus, when testing the performance of the various techniques, we should keep in mind that we cannot hope to forecast a large proportion of the movement in the spot rate. A useful benchmark for comparison is the random walk. Forecasters would hope to be able to predict the future spot rate better than the current spot rate does.[4] In other words, although they should not be so ambitious as to hope to predict all or most of the movement in the exchange rate, neither should they be so unambitious as to expect to be able to predict *none* of the movement.

When Chapter 19 first introduced the concept of the random walk, we noted that the real exchange rate has a tendency to return over time to the long-run equilibrium dictated by purchasing power parity. In other words, the principle of regression to PPP

---

[2]There are probably as many methods of technical analysis as there are technical analysts, but most fit this description. They tend to be used to forecast at short horizons of one month or less. Fundamentals are used at longer horizons. Mark Taylor and Helen Allen, "The Use of Technical Analysis in the Foreign Exchange Market," *Journal of International Money and Finance,* 11, no. 3 (1992): 304–314.

[3]The percentage of traders who can truthfully expect to make money is not as high as it sounds when listening to them talk. For every winner there must be a loser. There is a sample selection problem, however. If each month half the traders win and half lose, at random, and each month some of the ones who lose badly decide to abandon this line of work, then more than half the traders remaining in the sample at any time will truthfully be able to claim that they made money over the preceding month.

[4]Recall from Chapter 27 that there is no theoretical reason to expect the exchange rate to follow a random walk. This point is often misunderstood. As Section 28.2 will show, if some component of changes in the spot rate—such as that reflected in the forward discount—were predictable, it would not violate the rational expectations hypothesis. The hypothesis says only that the economist should not be able to forecast easily a greater percentage of movement in the spot rate than the market can.

might be used to obtain a better predictor than the random walk. This information is of some benefit in predicting the spot rate over the long term. Thus it might be used by a portfolio fund manager in deciding whether to buy (and hold) foreign securities or by a corporate executive in deciding whether to build a factory in a foreign country. The rule would be to invest in the country where the value of the currency is below its long-run PPP equilibrium because the currency can be expected to rise again in the future. However, because the speed of regression to PPP is so slow and large new disturbances come along so frequently, the information is not of much use in predicting the spot rate a few months or less into the future.

Richard Meese and Kenneth Rogoff studied the ability of a number of models to predict the exchange rate at horizons of several months. Included were the monetary model (both the flexible-price or monetarist version of Section 27.2 and the sticky-price version of Section 27.4) as well as the ARIMA model. Their finding was that at horizons of one, six, or twelve months into the future, all models are outperformed by the simple random walk. That is, a forecaster would be more successful using the current spot rate.[5] This was a discouraging discovery for exchange rate modelers. In view of how frequently one hears of an econometric finding that the exchange rate follows a random-walk model, it is important to note that such outcomes are failures to find anything that explains movement in the exchange rate. Random walk results are useful because they remind economists of the extent of their ignorance. But they are not evidence *in favor* of a model, in any meaningful sense.

Others have found somewhat greater success by including the lagged value of the exchange rate in addition to the other variables on the right-hand side of the equation.[6] For a forecaster who must predict the future exchange rate, the conclusion seems to be as follows: It would be difficult to make any prediction using *only* information on macroeconomic variables such as the money supplies, income levels, interest rates, and inflation rates. There is more useful information in today's spot rate than in everything else combined. However, given that today's spot rate is known, the monetary model seems to contain additional information that is of some help in predicting the direction of future movement, especially at longer horizons. In short, the optimal predictor would use *both* the information contained in today's spot rate and the information contained in the monetary model. Evidently there must be important elements missing from the monetary equation of exchange rate determination, unobserved elements that behave much like a random walk and thus are picked up by the lagged spot rate. Possible missing elements include speculative bubbles and permanent shifts in the real exchange rate.

---

[5]"Empirical Exchange Rate Models of the Seventies: Do They Fit Out of Sample?" *Journal of International Economics,* 14 (February 1983): 3–24; and "The Out-of-Sample Failure of Empirical Exchange Rate Models: Sampling Error or Misspecification?" in Jacob Frenkel, ed., *Exchange Rates and International Macroeconomics* (Chicago: University of Chicago Press, 1983), pp. 67–105. The monetary model does begin to perform slightly better when forecasting more than 12 months into the future.

[6]Ronald MacDonald and Mark Taylor, "The Monetary Model of the Exchange Rate: Long-Run Relationships, Short Run Dynamics, and How to Beat a Random Walk," *Journal of International Money and Finance,* 13, no. 3 (1994): 276–290; Nelson Mark, "Exchange Rates and Fundamentals: Evidence of Long-Horizon Predictability," *American Economic Review,* 85 (1995): 201–218.

Does the Forward Exchange Market Give an Unbiased Predictor?

Consider the owner of a small company involved in international trade who must guess what the exchange rate will be in three months to decide what currency a payment should be made in or what price to set for a product. The owner is bewildered by the proliferation of different exchange rate models and by the knowledge that no single model performs particularly well. The owner also suspects that much relevant information comes out every day (for example, a speech by the chairman of the Federal Reserve Board) that is not captured in any of the statistical models, and he or she does not have the time or resources to monitor such news each day.

An easy strategy is to use the three-month forward rate as the forecast of the future spot rate. (Chapter 21 introduced the forward exchange market.) What makes this strategy so easy is that it simply means looking up the forward rate in the newspaper or on the computer.

Furthermore, this owner would not necessarily do any better than the forward rate by subscribing to a forecasting service or hiring a staff forecaster. All the useful information contained in the various models, along with the latest bits of news, may already be reflected in the forward rate if the *efficient markets hypothesis* holds. The efficient markets hypothesis is closely related to the rational expectations hypothesis.[7] It states that any excess profit opportunities in the financial markets based on publicly available information will be quickly eliminated. Imagine, for example, that it were possible to use an ARIMA model to forecast better than the forward rate. In such a circumstance many speculators would rush to take advantage of the profit opportunity. They would buy forward currency whenever the ARIMA model predicted a price higher than the forward rate, and vice versa; before long they would drive the forward rate into equality with the forecast of the model. Thus whatever useful information there is in the ARIMA model should already be contained in the forward rate. The same applies to whatever useful information there is in technical analysis, in the monetary models, and in the day's news.

There have been a great many studies testing whether the forward market offers an unbiased predictor of the future spot rate.[8] Unbiased means there is no obvious alternative predictor that performs better on average. Consider the following equation, which relates the observed change in the spot rate to the change the forward discount would have predicted ahead of time.

$$\Delta s_{t+1} = \alpha + \beta \, fd_t + \varepsilon_{t+1} \tag{28.1}$$

---

[7]The efficient markets hypothesis not only requires that investors form their expectations rationally, but it requires a second condition as well: that there be few transaction costs or other market imperfections that prevent investors from buying and selling freely on the basis of these expectations. This allows investors' expectations to be fully reflected in the marketplace. Under normal circumstances, this second condition is easily met in well-developed financial markets. The small size of transactions costs can be shown directly, as it was in Chapter 21.

[8]Surveys of this literature include Robert Hodrick, *The Empirical Evidence on the Efficiency of Forward and Futures Foreign Exchange Markets* (Chur, Switzerland: Harwood Academic Publishers, 1988); and Charles Engel, "The Forward Discount Anomaly and the Risk Premium: A Survey of Recent Evidence," *Journal of Empirical Finance*, 3 (1996): 123–191.

The subscripts denote time: fd_t is the one-month percentage forward discount (on the domestic currency) observed at the present time, and Δs_{t+1} is the percentage change in the exchange rate (the percentage depreciation of the domestic currency) that takes place over the coming month.

As is usual in econometrics, we proceed by specifying a hypothesis and then seeing whether the data are favorable or unfavorable to it. In the present case, we are interested in the hypothesis that the forward discount is an unbiased predictor of the change in the exchange rate. This hypothesis, if true, implies in Equation 28.1 the condition $\beta = 1$. It might also include the condition $\alpha = 0$. Thus the hypothesis becomes:

$$\Delta s_{t+1} = fd_t + \varepsilon_{t+1} \qquad (28.2)$$

The term ε is the error that investors make at predicting Δs. Under the efficient markets hypothesis, ε must be random, uncorrelated with any information available to investors at time t.[9]

The unbiasedness hypothesis actually consists of two hypotheses that are tested at the same time.

1. The *rational expectations hypothesis* is stated as

$$\Delta s_{t+1} = \Delta s_t^e + \varepsilon_{t+1} \qquad (28.3)$$

In other words, the proposition is that investors predict the change in the exchange rate with an error term that is purely random. Notice that the hypothesis does not claim that the prediction error is necessarily small, only that it is unbiased—equal to zero on average.

2. The *zero exchange risk premium hypothesis* is stated as

$$fd_t - \Delta s_t^e = 0 \qquad (28.4)$$

The exchange risk premium has been defined as the expression that appears on the left side of Equation 28.4 (in the appendix to Chapter 21, Equation 21.A.3). It will be zero if risk is not important to investors. That is, if investors care only about expected rates of return and nothing else, they will drive them into equality across currencies.

Check for yourself that Equations 28.3 and 28.4 together imply unbiasedness of the forward discount, Equation 28.2. It would be preferable to test the rational expectations hypothesis by itself. This is difficult, however, because it is difficult to observe investors' expectations. Instead, the two hypotheses are tested at the same time, by testing whether $\beta = 1$ in Equation 28.1. The major disadvantage of this strategy is that if it is decided that the data do not support $\beta = 1$, it is impossible to determine which of the two hypotheses fails to hold.

Of the many econometric studies performed on Equation 28.1 and others like it, most find that the data in fact do not support the unbiasedness hypothesis. Typically,

---

[9]The logic is the same as for the ε term in Equation 26.5, which represented the error that workers make at predicting inflation.

the estimate of β is not 1 but is significantly less. This indicates that the forward discount is a biased forecast of the future change in the spot rate. Some estimates put β in the vicinity of 0.5. This would mean that when the dollar sells at a forward discount of 4 percent per annum, the best guess is that it will depreciate at 2 percent per annum. Similarly, if the dollar sells at a forward *premium* of 4 percent per annum, the best guess is that it will *appreciate* at 2 percent per annum.

Many estimates put the coefficient even further from 1, in the vicinity of 0. If β were 0, this would mean that, regardless of the forward market, the best guess for the future spot rate is today's spot rate—in other words, no change. This is another random-walk finding, and it is much in line with the findings of Meese and Rogoff described previously.

How should economists interpret such findings? One possibility is that speculators are simply bad forecasters, that the rational expectations hypothesis 1 does not hold. One researcher, for example, interprets such findings as evidence that speculators are "overly excitable," that they have a false confidence in their ability to predict changes in the exchange rate. They would do better on average if they calmed down a bit, instead of always predicting that the exchange rate is about to shoot off in one direction or the other.[10]

Most economists, however, are extremely reluctant to accept this interpretation. They believe in hypothesis 1 on a priori grounds. The logic, once again, is that if it were so easy to make excess profits (on average), speculators would have already taken advantage of the opportunity. For this reason, most economists consider it more likely that the findings of bias are evidence against hypothesis 2—in other words, that the findings are evidence in favor of the existence of an exchange risk premium that separates the forward discount from investors' expectations of depreciation.[11]

28.2   The Role of Exchange Risk

Under the risk premium interpretation of the finding of bias (the finding of $\beta < 1$ in Equation 28.1), some positive part of the forward discount is a risk premium. Risk-averse investors will take a large position in a currency that they perceive as risky only if they are offered as compensation a higher expected rate of return than on other currencies. This can explain the difference between the forward discount and expected depreciation; it is the premium that the risk-averse investors demand to hold a risky currency.

The Exchange Risk Premium

The risk premium interpretation says that when the pound is selling at a forward discount, it must be because investors consider the pound riskier to hold than other currencies, and they therefore demand extra compensation for holding it. This is perhaps

---

[10]John Bilson, "The Speculative Efficiency Hypothesis," *Journal of Business,* 54 (1981): 435–451. Some direct evidence is offered by Kenneth Froot and Jeffrey Frankel, "Forward Discount Bias: Is it an Exchange Risk Premium?" *Quarterly Journal of Economics,* 104, no.1 (February 1989): 139–161.

[11]For example, Eugene Fama, "Forward and Spot Exchange Rates," *Journal of Monetary Economics,* 14 (1984): 319–338.

most clearly shown by using the covered interest parity condition to substitute the nominal interest differential, $i - i*$, in place of the forward discount, *fd,* obtaining the alternate (but equivalent) definition of the exchange risk premium:

$$rp_t \equiv i_t - i_t^* - \Delta s_t^e$$

Now it is readily apparent that if the risk premium on a particular currency is positive, then that means investors are receiving a higher expected return to compensate for holding assets in that currency. Consider the case of random-walk expectations ($\Delta s^e = 0$), for example. A British interest differential of 4 percent signifies that speculators demand an expected return 4 percent higher than the expected return on other currencies before they are willing to take an open position in pounds. It is analogous to the premium that the stock market pays relative to bonds: The rate of return on stocks is, on average, significantly higher than the interest rate, with the difference being interpreted as the premium that investors require to bear the greater risk that attaches to stocks.[12]

It might seem that investors would find holding foreign currency in general to be risky, that foreign currency must pay a positive risk premium to compensate domestic investors for holding it. No such general rule can hold for all currencies, however. If one currency pays a positive risk premium, then the other pays a negative risk premium. Viewed from the vantage point of the global investor, the dollar could be the riskier currency as easily as the pound.

What Makes a Currency Risky?

The dollar generally sells at a forward discount against the yen. As we would expect to follow, by covered interest parity, dollar assets generally pay a higher interest rate than yen assets. If the findings of bias are to be interpreted as evidence of a risk premium, it would follow that international investors must perceive the U.S. dollar as riskier than the yen. That would explain why they demand a higher interest rate to hold dollar assets.

What makes an investor perceive some currencies as more risky and others as less risky? Essentially three factors contribute to exchange risk. We are not including default risk and the risk of capital controls, which pertain to the identity of the issuer of a security, rather than to its currency of denomination.

First is the *variability* of the value of that currency, in terms of other currencies and in terms of purchasing power over goods (i.e., the variability of the price level).[13] The currency of a country with an unstable monetary policy, which leads to a highly variable price level and exchange rate, is viewed as risky.

---

[12]It is easy to test Equation 28.1, with the interest differential, $i - i*$, substituted for the forward discount, *fd.* Just as before, the results show biased predictions of the future exchange rate. Just as before, the finding of bias could be interpreted either as a bias in expectations or as a risk premium.

[13]By *variability* we mean the degree of uncertainty regarding the value of the currency next period. If an exchange rate were highly variable, but the movements were mostly predictable, then uncertainty would be low. In practice, however, exchange rate movements are mostly unpredictable. Therefore, uncertainty is almost the same as the measured variability in exchange rate changes.

It is easy, but wrong, to slip into the habit of viewing dollars as completely safe. It is wrong because investors ultimately care about the *real* value of their wealth, its purchasing power over the goods they consume, not about the dollar value per se. It follows immediately that a foreign citizen will consider the dollar risky if its exchange rate vis-à-vis the foreign currency is uncertain. (We are assuming here that the foreign investor cares about purchasing power over goods produced in the foreign country. To the extent that the investor also consumes some American goods, the real risk of holding dollars will be somewhat reduced.)

The fact that the investor cares about purchasing power over goods also implies that even an American who consumes only American goods should consider the dollar a bit risky to the extent that dollar prices of goods are uncertain. This is inflation uncertainty. As we have seen, the price level is actually much less variable than the exchange rate. For this reason, Americans would not go too far wrong by viewing their own currency as safe. However, exceptions arise in small, very open economies (such as those studied in Chapter 19) and in economies with a high degree of monetary instability. Residents of Russia, for example, should view foreign currency as less risky than their own.

We have been thinking of the potential holder of a foreign currency asset as an individual consumer or household. What if it is a corporation? In theory, this should not make any difference. Corporations are owned by people (the shareholders), who consume goods just like everybody else. If the manager of the corporation operates in the shareholders' interest, then the outcome should be the same as if the shareholders were making the investment decisions themselves.

In practice, however, corporate behavior can and does deviate from this theoretical ideal. If corporate managers do not have confidence that stock market investors can see through all the complexities of modern finance and accounting, they may be reluctant to make an investment that does not "look good on the books" even if they believe it is in the true interest of the company. To take one example, every March, Japanese banks rush to convert their foreign holdings into yen, to achieve mandated currency balances in time for the end-of-fiscal-year "book closing." To take a U.S. example, in 1976 when the Financial Accounting Standards Board adopted a rule (FASB 8) requiring companies to translate their overseas earnings into dollars at the current exchange rate, many companies suddenly altered their behavior so as to reduce exposure in foreign currency. They knew that such exposure would show up on their annual reports as earnings that were highly variable in terms of dollars. They sought to hedge their foreign earnings—for example, by selling foreign exchange on the forward market.[14] Although some hedging might always be prudent for a company with large overseas operations, in this case the change in corporate behavior in response to FASB

---

[14]Patricia Revey, "Evolution and Growth of the United States Foreign Exchange Market," *Federal Reserve Bank of New York Quarterly Review,* 6 (Autumn 1981): 32–44. Incidentally, the rule has since been abolished; the earnings reports of a multinational corporation need no longer show an overseas subsidiary's gains or losses from exchange rate changes.

8 was a sign that managers did not think that their shareholders would see through the accounting rule change. Such managers may err in the direction of the simple rule that the domestic currency is safe and the foreign currency is risky.

The second factor that makes a currency appear risky from the viewpoint of an individual investor is related to the quantity of assets the investor already holds denominated in that currency. The principle of *portfolio diversification* states that investors can reduce the risk in their overall wealth by diversifying their portfolio among many different assets. Even if each of several currencies has the same degree of variability, investors will be less vulnerable if they hold some of each than if they put all their eggs in one basket. This assumes the movements of the various currencies are at least partly independent, and thus it is very unlikely that all of them will sharply lose value at the same time. Usually some will go up and some down, and the overall return on the diversified portfolio will be much more stable than if the entire portfolio were allocated to just one of the assets.[15]

Thus, if investors already hold a large amount of Australian dollar bonds in their portfolio, they will consider it risky to acquire additional Australian dollar assets. It would be safer to add to their holdings of other assets, to remain well diversified. They will be willing to accept additional Australian dollar assets only if the return is sufficiently high as to compensate for the risk of going further out on a limb, of being further exposed in Australian dollar.[16]

The third factor is the extent to which movement in the currency value is *correlated* with movement in the values of other assets that investors hold. Correlation refers to the tendency for both assets to go up at the same time and go down at the same time. If the currency is highly correlated with other assets that the investors already hold, then it should be viewed as risky. The Swiss franc, for example, is highly correlated with the euro. If investors already hold many euros, then even if they hold no Swiss francs, they should realize that the prospect of acquiring some Swiss currency would add to their overall risk as much as would the acquisition of more euros. In this case the Swiss franc offers little opportunity for diversification: When the euro falls, the Swiss franc will fall right along with it.[17] Conversely, if the currency has a low correlation with other assets

---

[15]The optimal degree of portfolio diversification is derived in the supplement to this chapter.
[16]Consider another example, like the FASB 8 story, of how a corporation's behavior in practice can deviate from the theoretical ideal of diversification. Imagine that the New York office is highly exposed in yen and the London office is highly exposed in euros. The company in the aggregate may in fact be well diversified. Yet if each office does not know what the other is doing—or if each manager is more worried about the variability of his own performance and the risk of being terminated if he suffers large losses than he is about the big picture—then each may anxiously hedge or unload his or her holdings, even at a loss. As communications and computer technology and risk management techniques become more and more sophisticated, however, corporations get better and better at keeping track of changes in their global currency exposure and at responding appropriately. In this sense, actual corporate financial practices are becoming more like the theoretical ideal.
[17]Similarly, although a well-diversified portfolio would hold both stocks and bonds, the return on Swiss bonds is correlated with the return on Swiss stocks; thus an investor who already holds a lot of one should regard the other as risky. The return on a country's bonds is correlated with the return on its stocks and other assets, not just because of the exchange rate factor, but for another reason as well. If the country's economy turns out to do poorly, it may be reflected not only in its stock market but also in increased probability of default on bonds.

that investors already hold, they should view it as subtracting from their overall risk because it offers a valuable opportunity for diversification.[18]

This is especially true if the correlation happens to be negative. The returns on gold and the dollar, for example, are negatively correlated with each other. In those months when the value of the dollar goes up, the price of gold goes down, and vice versa. Thus, even if the dollar and gold are each highly variable when considered alone, a portfolio that holds some of each will be less variable. In the limit, imagine that the two were perfectly negatively correlated: For every 1 percent that the dollar moved, the price of gold could be relied on to move 1 percent in the opposite direction. In this special case, a portfolio allocated half to dollars and half to gold would be completely safe. The return on the overall portfolio would be guaranteed beforehand, regardless of price fluctuations, because the returns on the two halves would cancel each other out.

We have now seen that, from the viewpoint of the individual investor, it is important to look at more than just the expected return when deciding whether to acquire a country's currency. It is also important to look at the risk of the asset, where the risk that a given asset would bring to the portfolio is determined not only by (1) uncertainty regarding its future value, but also by (2) the assets that the investor already holds, and (3) the correlation of the return on the currency in question with the return on the other assets.

We have also seen that the existence of risk causes investors to view domestic and foreign bonds as imperfect substitutes, with the result that expected returns need not be equalized internationally. If we return to the issue of the determination of the exchange rate by aggregate behavior in the marketplace, it is now apparent that a condition assumed by the monetary models in Chapter 27, uncovered interest parity, need not hold. Thus we must go back and modify the model of exchange rate determination.

28.3 Portfolio Balance Effects on the Exchange Rate

In the monetary models of Chapter 27, the stock of government debt had no effect on the exchange rate. Only the stock of money did. In this section we examine possible effects of the stocks of debt and other non–money assets. To do so, it is necessary to introduce the portfolio balance model.[19] To gain the insights provided by this new model, it is not necessary to jettison what you learned in Chapter 27. Rather, we are adding some possible effects in the foreign exchange market to what we have previously studied.

---

[18]Financial analysts speak of the *beta* of a stock or other security, which reflects the correlation of its return with the return on the overall portfolio of securities that the market holds. A security with a high beta is risky for investors; it should pay a high expected return to compensate them for holding it. This is the lesson of what finance theorists call the capital asset pricing model.

[19]Important early applications of the portfolio balance model to the subject of floating exchange rates include William Branson, "Asset Markets and Relative Prices in Exchange Rate Determination," *Sozialwissenschaftliche Annalen*, 1 (1977): 69–89; Stanley Black, "International Money Markets and Flexible Exchange Rates," *Studies in International Finance*, 32 (Princeton, NJ: Princeton University Press, 1973); Pentti Kouri, "The Exchange Rate and the Balance of Payments in the Short Run and in the Long Run: A Monetary Approach," *Scandinavian Journal of Economics*, 78, no. 2 (1976): 280–304.

Previous chapters assumed that investors were willing to absorb indefinitely large quantities of a country's bonds as long as the country was willing to pay the world interest rate. The quantity of bonds issued did not in itself necessarily have any effects on the financial markets. Now, however, we recognize that investors care, not just about expected return, but about risk as well. Investors will not willingly hold increasing quantities of a country's bonds at an unchanged interest rate. Individual investors can, of course, simply decide not to hold an asset denominated in a currency viewed as risky. (They could also decide to hold it but to sell the currency risk to somebody else on the forward exchange market.) In the aggregate, however, assets exist, and someone has to hold them. When the Australian government issues bonds, for example, even if the original buyer resells them or hedges the currency risk on the forward market, someone somewhere must end up with increased exposure in Australian dollars. Risk aversion on the part of investors thus implies that when governments change the supplies of bonds denominated in various currencies, it does have an effect in the financial markets. It has an effect on the equilibrium prices at which investors are willing to hold these assets.[20]

In the portfolio balance approach, the exchange rate is viewed not simply as the relative price of domestic and foreign money supplies but as the relative price of bonds and other assets as well. The model allows us to study two new effects on the exchange rate: *sterilized foreign exchange intervention* by central banks and what we might call *satiation* of investor holdings of a country's assets.

Sterilized Foreign Exchange Intervention

Part IV introduced intervention in the foreign exchange market—central bank purchases or sales of foreign currency in exchange for domestic currency. At that point the discussion focused on the system of fixed exchange rates, under which central banks are obligated to intervene as often as necessary to maintain the parity. The larger countries, of course, operate under flexible exchange rates, except within the EMU. Nevertheless, all central banks do intervene from time to time. Often they *lean against the wind:* Central banks sell a currency when it is appreciating and buy when it is depreciating, to try to dampen the fluctuations.

Chapter 19 discussed in particular the option of sterilizing intervention: offsetting it by central bank operations in the domestic open market so as to leave the overall money supply unchanged. Assume that the intervention consists of buying up dollar currency that private agents want to get rid of (and giving them yen in exchange), as it will if the aim is to increase the value of the dollar. In this case, sterilization involves following this up by buying dollar bonds from private agents (and giving them dollar currency in exchange), so as to restore the amount of dollar currency in the hands of

---

[20]Two qualifications are needed. First, for simplicity we have made the assumption here that governments denominate their bonds in their own currency. In practice, governments sometimes denominate their bonds in other currencies. Second, we are also ruling out Robert Barro's "Ricardian equivalence" (discussed in the appendix to Chapter 22). This is the proposition that for every dollar of bonds Australia's government sells to the public, Australian taxpayers feel an offsetting liability in the form of future taxes, with the result that behavior is unaffected. If this proposition held, then it is possible that no investor would need to incur exposure to the exchange risk of holding Australian dollars because such risk is fully diversifiable.

the public to its original level. On those occasions when the Federal Reserve intervenes, it routinely and immediately sterilizes its intervention in this way.[21] The other central banks do not sterilize quite as completely as the Fed does.

Chapter 23 showed that when perfect capital mobility ties the domestic interest rate to the foreign interest rate, successful sterilized intervention is impossible. If the Bank of Sweden were to try to support the krona in the foreign exchange market without allowing the domestic money supply to fall, it would quickly find that for every krona it created through the purchase of domestic bonds, it lost another krona of foreign exchange reserves: This is called complete offset of domestic credit creation. The Swedish central bank would have to abandon the attempt to determine simultaneously the exchange rate and the money supply or face rapid depletion of its foreign exchange reserves.

If investors treat domestic and foreign bonds as imperfect substitutes because of exchange risk (or for any other reason), then the possibility of successful sterilized intervention is resurrected. The reason is as follows. When the central bank has completed its sterilization, the supply of domestic money in the hands of the public has not changed (by the definition of sterilization), but the supply of domestic bonds in the hands of the public has decreased. In the monetary model, the supply of bonds had no effect. As noted, only the supply of money had an effect. In the portfolio balance model, however, the change in the supply of bonds does have an effect. The exchange rate is the relative price of dollar bonds as much as it is the relative price of dollar currency; it is determined by the supply of and demand for all assets (domestic versus foreign). Thus a decrease in the supply of dollar assets can cause an increase in the price of dollar assets, that is, an appreciation of the dollar, even if the currency component has not changed.[22]

At the Versailles Summit of 1982, the United States agreed to study the effectiveness of intervention, as a concession to the French. The report released the following year concluded that intervention that is sterilized does not have significant effects on exchange rates, except perhaps very briefly. It is believed that domestic and foreign bonds, although not literally perfect substitutes, are close enough that relatively little effect results from changes in their relative supply, especially on the scale that is relevant.

In 1985 the U.S. Treasury, in response to an ever-worsening trade deficit and resultant protectionist fever in Congress, made an abrupt about-face. The Treasury's newfound support for coordinated foreign exchange intervention to bring the value of the

---

[21]Even though the Federal Reserve trading desk in New York sterilizes any foreign exchange intervention on the same day it occurs, the Federal Reserve Open Market Committee that meets every six weeks or so in Washington may sometimes take the exchange rate into account when setting monetary policy (for example, when giving the open market trading desk in New York its instructions for the subsequent six weeks).

[22]The decrease in the supply of domestic bonds should also cause the domestic interest rate to fall, to induce investors to hold a smaller share of their portfolio in the form of domestic bonds. As a consequence of imperfect substitutability, the domestic expected rate of return is no longer perfectly tied down to the world interest rate. Dale Henderson, "Exchange Market Intervention Operations: Their Effects and Their Role in Finance Policy," in J. Bilson and R. Marston, eds., *Exchange Rate Theory and Policy* (Chicago: University of Chicago Press, 1984).

dollar down produced the Plaza Accord. The day after the agreement was announced (September 22), the dollar fell more than 4 percent. As already noted, the dollar depreciation continued over the next few years. Many observers consider this to have been a successful initiative on the part of the U.S. Treasury. Others believe there were good reasons why the dollar would have come down anyway. However, even those who believe that intervention efforts, like the one agreed under the Plaza Accord, are effective do not believe that the primary effect comes from the changed asset supplies that investors must absorb in their portfolios. These *portfolio effects* are still considered relatively small.

The major effect must come instead via investors' expectations regarding the future exchange rate. The 1985 announcement by the U.S. government that it now considered the dollar to be too high and wanted it to fall, for example, may have caused investors to expect a more expansionary monetary policy in the future.[23] As we saw in Chapter 27, even a small change in expectations can cause a relatively large change in demand for a currency and therefore in the exchange rate. This is why a major announcement by central bank governors or treasury secretaries can have a major effect even on a day when no intervention actually takes place, whereas intervention with no public announcement is likely to have little effect. Central banks continue periodically to intervene, sometimes with success and sometimes without it. In mid-1995, when the yen/dollar rate had reached a record low of 80, G-7 intervention succeeded in reversing the depreciation of the dollar.

Satiation in Holdings of a Country's Debt and the Hard Landing

The only way that the public's holdings of bonds (or money, for that matter) can change suddenly is through operations in the financial markets on the part of the central bank, such as the intervention operations just discussed. However, the public's holdings of bonds change steadily over time whenever a country borrows to finance deficits. The budget deficit is the yearly change in the government debt outstanding. In Chapter 22 we examined the effects of a fiscal expansion. One effect was a current-account deficit financed by a capital inflow from abroad. However, we ignored any further effects of the stock of government debt that builds up over time via a budget deficit, or the stock of national indebtedness to foreigners that builds up over time via a current-account deficit. The country illustrated in Figure 23.1 apparently could go on running a budget deficit and current-account deficit forever.

In reality, a country that borrows must eventually pay back. What mechanism forces this result if a profligate country is inclined to go on borrowing indefinitely? The portfolio balance model says that investors will become increasingly reluctant to hold larger and larger quantities of a given country's bonds. The problem may be small under normal conditions, but if the magnitude of the debt becomes large enough, investors will eventually become *satiated* with their holdings. If investors are forced to

---

[23]This has been called the signaling effect of foreign exchange intervention. Michael Mussa, *The Role of Official Intervention*, Occasional Paper No. 6 (New York: Group of Thirty, 1981).

absorb ever-greater quantities in their portfolios despite their reluctance, one of several outcomes must occur. First, the exchange value of the currency may fall. Recall the assumption that the debt is denominated in the currency of the issuing country. If the nominal quantity of the debt is increasing at 10 percent per year, then the exchange rate must also change 10 percent per year, if international investors do not wish to allow that country's debt to grow as a share of their portfolios. This relationship between the supply of bonds and the exchange rate is the portfolio effect or *valuation effect*. Second, the interest rate may be driven up, to make the assets more attractive to investors.[24]

Until recently, there was some reason to believe the portfolio balance model might have only limited relevance for large industrialized countries. The United States, Japan, Germany, and the United Kingdom were all creditor countries that held foreign assets more than they issued liabilities to foreigners. It seemed that they could borrow large amounts at the world interest rate if they so chose. Smaller countries were more likely to find that their cost of borrowing rose with the amount borrowed. (This is especially true of developing countries.) However, because smaller countries usually borrow in foreign currency rather than in their own currency, the portfolio balance model in its simple form does not apply.[25]

The massive increase in U.S. borrowing from abroad since 1980, however, has raised the question whether the world's investors might not become satiated with their holdings of dollars. The United States continues to run current-account deficits. It follows that the country must continue to borrow from abroad, one way or another. This leaves unresolved the issue of the terms under which this borrowing takes place. If international investors at some point become reluctant to accept ever-larger quantities of dollars into their portfolios, one of the following will result: (1) an increase in U.S. interest rates to induce them to increase the share of their portfolios allocated to U.S. assets, or (2) a further depreciation of the dollar to keep that share from rising, or (3) both could happen, which would be an unpleasant "hard landing" for the dollar.

28.4 Summary

This chapter covered three topics regarding international finance under floating exchange rates: exchange rate forecasting, the exchange risk premium, and portfolio balance.

---

[24]The portfolio-balance model has recently been resurrected to consider the valuation effect in the context of the need to finance the U.S. current-account deficit. U.S. net international indebtedness has not risen as much as one might expect because rising debt has been partly offset by a rise in the value of U.S. assets held abroad when measured in dollars, which in turn is partly attributable to a depreciation of the dollar. Pierre-Olivier Gourinchas and Helene Rey, "From World Banker to World Venture Capitalist: The U.S. External Adjustment and the Exorbitant Privilege," and Philip Lane and Gian Maria Milesi-Ferretti, "A Global Perspective on External Positions," both published in Richard Clarida, ed., *G7 Account Imbalances: Sustainability and Adjustment* (Chicago: University of Chicago Press, 2006).

[25]If a country's international borrowings are denominated in the same currency as other assets held by investors, then the exchange rate is not the relative price of foreign and domestic assets and, therefore, cannot be determined by the valuation effect. However, it can still be determined by the need to pay back debt in the long run. An increase in foreign indebtedness will still cause the country's currency to depreciate. Investors realize that a depreciation will be needed sooner or later to improve the trade balance and service the debt.

In practice, forecasters do not all use monetary models, such as the one developed in Chapter 27. Many use other approaches, including technical analysis.

Even within the theory presented in Chapter 27, a large fraction of exchange rate changes should be unpredictable. However, the forecasting performance of exchange rate models is worse than it should be. Often it seems that the fraction of exchange rate changes that can be predicted is zero, that is, the exchange rate follows a random walk. At longer horizons, however, the exchange rate does tend to move in the direction of the equilibrium dictated by monetary fundamentals.

A popular way of forecasting the future spot rate is by using the forward rate. However, "the random-walk spot rate" characterization of other forecasting methods applies to the forward rate as well: Tests show that the forward discount is a biased forecaster, that the forward rate is a worse forecaster than could be achieved by placing more weight on the spot rate alone. One possible interpretation of this finding is a failure of rational expectations and of the efficient markets hypothesis. Most economists, however, interpret the finding of bias in the forward discount as evidence of an exchange risk premium.

An exchange risk premium arises when risk-averse investors look not only at the expected return in deciding whether to acquire a country's currency, but also at risk. The theory of portfolio diversification says that the risk a given asset would bring to the investor's portfolio is determined not only by uncertainty regarding its future value, but also by the asset quantities that the investor already holds and by the correlation of the return on the currency in question with the return on the other assets.

If investors treat domestic and foreign bonds as imperfect substitutes in their portfolios because of risk, then the portfolio balance model applies. This framework makes it possible to talk about two effects on the exchange rate that have previously been omitted. First is the effect of sterilized foreign exchange intervention. Second is the effect of investor satiation with holdings of a given country's bonds. Even though both effects probably exist, the degree of substitutability among countries' bonds is generally thought to be high enough that the effects are small.

CHAPTER PROBLEMS

1. You are the treasurer of a U.S. company that holds open positions (working balances or accounts payable) in foreign currencies. Your bank levies a small but appreciable charge for hedging these positions in the forward market. If you believe the foreign exchange market is efficient, and your company is neutral about risks, will you hedge? What if your company is risk averse? What if your company also has obligations in foreign currencies (bills for imported inputs or employees' wages at foreign subsidiaries)? What if you think that the market sometimes is a poor forecaster of future exchange rates?

2. If the dollar is selling at a forward discount of 4 percent per annum and you think the dollar is going to depreciate at 2 percent over the next year, should you "go long" in dollars, or "sell the dollar short"? (Assume you are risk neutral.)

3. The chapter supplement shows that when two assets each have the same variance, V, the variance of the overall portfolio is given by $V(r) = x^2V + (1 - x)^2V$, where x and $(1 - x)$ are the shares of the portfolios allocated to the two assets, and the returns on the two are assumed to be independent.
    a. Calculate $V(r)$ for $x = 0, .4, .5, .6$ and 1.0. Draw a graph of $V(r)$.
    b. If you know calculus, differentiate $V(r)$ with respect to x, to find the allocation of the portfolio that minimizes risk.

Extra Credit

4. If you know how to use the mathematical expectation, show how to go from Equation 28.S.1 for the return on the portfolio (in the supplement)

$$r = xr^€ + (1 - x)r^\$$$

    to Equation 28.S.3

$$V(r) = x^2 V(r^€) + (1 - x)^2 V(r^\$) + x(1 - x)2\text{Cov}(r^€, r^\$)$$

    You will need to use the definition of the variance of r,

$$V(r) = E(r - Er)^2$$

    and the covariance,

$$\text{Cov}(r^€, r^\$) = E[(r^€ - Er^€)(r^\$ - Er^\$)]$$

5. a. If you know calculus, show how to use Equation 28.S.3 and 28.S.4 in the derivative of the welfare function, Equation 28.S.6, to obtain the expression for the optimally diversified portfolio, x. (This derivation is carried out in the supplement for the special case where the dollar is viewed as completely safe, but now we want to see it applied to the more general case.)
    b. What is the optimal x if the real value of the dollar is completely certain? Why?
    c. What is x if the real value of the euro is completely certain? Why?
    d. Assuming that both the real values of the euro and yen are uncertain, what is x if the investor is infinitely risk averse? (This is called the minimum variance portfolio.) How do you think it might be affected by the share of European goods in the consumption basket of the investor in question? How might it be affected by uncertainty regarding the European inflation rate?

SUGGESTIONS FOR FURTHER READING

Dominguez, Kathryn, and Jeffrey Frankel. *Does Foreign Exchange Intervention Work?* (Washington, DC: Institute for International Economics, 1993). Includes an empirical analysis of the effects after the Plaza Agreement.

Froot, Kenneth, and Richard Thaler. "Anomalies: Foreign Exchange," *Journal of Economic Perspectives,* 4, no. 3 (1990): 179–192. How should we interpret findings that the forward rate is a biased predictor of future spot rates?

Lewis, Karen. "Puzzles in International Financial Markets." In G. Grossman and K. Rogoff, eds., *Handbook of International Economics* (Amsterdam: North-Holland, 1995). Why is the forward rate a biased predictor? And why do many investors hold less foreign securities than called for in a well-diversified basket (a tendency known as the "home-country bias")?

MacDonald, Ronald, and Mark Taylor. "Exchange Rate Economics," *International Monetary Fund Staff Papers,* 39, no. 1 (1992): 1–57. A survey of the literature on exchange rate determination, including the portfolio-balance model.

MacDonald, Ronald, and Mark Taylor, eds. *Exchange Rate Economics,* International Library of Critical Writings in Economics (U.K.: Edward Elgar Publishing, 1992). A collection of papers by various authors on the determination of exchange rates.

Sarno, Lucio, and Mark Taylor. "Official Intervention in the Foreign Exchange Market: Is It Effective and, If So, How Does It Work?" *Journal of Economic Literature,* XXXIX (September 2001): 839–868.

PART VII

Supplements for Selected Chapters

SUPPLEMENT TO CHAPTER 2: The Equations of Exchange Equilibrium

This supplement introduces the notation and structure of the formal models that we develop in subsequent supplements.

For notation, D refers to demands and x to production. Thus D_F signifies the home country's demand for food, and x_C^* the foreign country's production of clothing. The asterisk symbolizes foreign variables, as in the text. The price of commodity j is denoted by p_j if a monetary unit of account is used for the home country or p_j^* if the foreign country uses a different unit of account or if the foreign price differs. In the two-commodity food and clothing example, the home country's prices are p_F and p_C. The relative price of food is p_F/p_C. Because the phrase "terms of trade" is so prominent in the real models of trade, the simple p (in the home country) and p^* (in the foreign country, if prices are different) denote the terms of trade, the relative price of food.

The use of equations is not completely forsaken in the text. For this reason a different numbering scheme is required for the supplements. Thus Equation 2.S.4 refers to the fourth equation in the supplement to Chapter 2.

This account of the basic model begins by stating prices in monetary units. The budget constraint for this model posits that for each country the value of aggregate demand must be restricted to, and equal to, the value of production. Thus:

$$p_C D_C + p_F D_F = p_C x_C + p_F x_F \qquad (2.S.1)$$

$$p_C^* D_C^* + p_F^* D_F^* = p_C^* x_C^* + p_F^* x_F^* \qquad (2.S.2)$$

Assume that in a trading context the home country will import food. Then rewrite these two equations to highlight, on the left side, the country's demand for imports and, on the right side, the corresponding supply of exports.

$$p_F(D_F - x_F) = p_C(x_C - D_C) \qquad (2.S.3)$$

$$p_C^*(D_C^* - x_C^*) = p_F^*(x_F^* - D_F^*) \qquad (2.S.4)$$

The importance of *relative* prices is brought out by dividing Equation 2.S.3 by p_C and Equation 2.S.4 by p_C^*. Furthermore, in a free-trade equilibrium with no barriers to costless movement of commodities between countries, relative prices in the two countries are brought into line so that

$$p(D_F - x_F) = (x_C - D_C) \qquad (2.S.5)$$

$$(D_C^* - x_C^*) = p(x_F^* - D_F^*) \qquad (2.S.6)$$

The symbol p represents the relative price of food.

Suppose the terms of trade, p, clear the world market for food. That is, the home country's excess demand, $(D_F - x_F)$, equals the foreign country's excess supply, $(x_F^* - D_F^*)$. In such a case it is obvious from Equations 2.S.5 and 2.S.6 that the world's clothing market must be cleared as well: $(D_C^* - x_C^*)$ will equal $(x_C - D_C)$.

One consequence of this phenomenon is that free-trade market equilibrium can be expressed by the statement that *either* world demand and supply are equal for food (as in Equation 2.S.7) *or* they are equal for clothing (as in Equation 2.S.8):

$$D_F + D_F^* = x_F + x_F^* \tag{2.S.7}$$

$$D_C + D_C^* = x_C + x_C^* \tag{2.S.8}$$

If the budget constraints in Equations 2.S.5 and 2.S.6 are always satisfied, Equation 2.S.7 implies Equation 2.S.8, or vice versa. Oddly enough, neither market-clearing equation is typically used in the literature of the pure theory of trade. Rather, they are replaced by the equivalent statement that in free-trade equilibrium, the value of the home country's imports equals the value of the foreign country's imports. This balance of payments equilibrium condition, in Equation 2.S.9, follows from the two budget constraints, Equations 2.S.5 and 2.S.6, and either Equation 2.S.7 or 2.S.8.

$$p(D_F - x_F) = (D_C^* - x_C^*) \tag{2.S.9}$$

This redundancy in stating equilibrium conditions is two-sided. On the one hand, it reveals that the model is more simple than a mere scanning of equations might reveal: There is only one market, and if world demand for clothing balances world production at specified terms of trade, then the food market must be cleared as well. Furthermore, the value of each country's demand for imports would, at those market-clearing terms of trade, equal the other country's demand for imports. On the other hand, it implies there are several ways to describe the same equilibrium: The food market is cleared, the clothing market is cleared, or the home country's demand for imports equals, in value, the foreign country's demand for imports. Saying the same thing in three different ways can be confusing.

Changes in Real Incomes

Throughout, assume that a community's level of satisfaction or real income depends only on the bundle of commodities it consumes. For the two-commodity example this can be stated formally as

$$u = u(D_C, D_F)$$

The symbol u represents some arbitrary index used to measure utility or the level of welfare. Differentiate this expression to obtain

$$du = \frac{\partial u}{\partial D_C} dD_C + \frac{\partial u}{\partial D_F} dD_F$$

which states that when the amounts consumed are altered, utility changes by an amount that depends on the marginal utility of a commodity (e.g., $\partial u / \partial D_F$ for food) multiplied by the change in the quantity of it consumed. The arbitrariness of the utility index can be removed by dividing both sides of this equation by the marginal utility of clothing.

$$\frac{du}{\partial u / \partial D_C} = dD_C + \frac{\partial u / \partial D_F}{\partial u / \partial D_C} dD_F$$

The left-hand term is positive only if utility has increased. Furthermore, it is a measure of the change in utility expressed in units of clothing (the *utils* cancel out). Call this change in real income in clothing units dy. The right-hand side can be simplified by noticing that the coefficient of dD_F is the *marginal rate of substitution,* the amount of clothing that must be added to compensate for a loss of one unit of food along an indifference curve. In a market equilibrium, however, this amount corresponds to the relative price of food, p. Thus, Equation 2.S.10 can be derived as the basic expression for a change of real income.

$$dy = dD_C + pdD_F \qquad (2.S.10)$$

It could almost be taken as a *definition* of real income changes—the sum of consumption changes with each such change weighted by the relative price of that commodity.

The budget constraint,

$$D_C + pD_F = x_C + px_F \qquad (2.S.11)$$

reveals that the *source* of any change in real income must reside in either a change in the endowment bundle or a change in the terms of trade. To see this, differentiate to obtain

$$dD_C + pdD_F + D_Fdp = dx_C + pdx_F + x_Fdp$$

Subtract D_Fdp from both sides, and use Equation 2.S.10 for dy to obtain

$$dy = -(D_F - x_F)dp + (dx_C + pdx_F) \qquad (2.S.12)$$

This basic expression for the change of real income in the home country provides the following breakdown.

1. The term $-(D_F - x_F)dp$ is the *terms-of-trade effect.* Assume the home country is a net importer of food, and let M denote $(D_F - x_F)$. If the terms of trade deteriorate for the home country, dp is positive and real income at home falls by Mdp, an amount proportional to the volume of imports.

2. The term $dx_C + pdx_F$, the price-weighted sum of any change in the home country's production bundle, enters directly into the measure of a change in real income.

A Basic Production Relationship

If production possibilities are shown by a bowed-out transformation schedule (as in Figure 2.3), a rise in food's relative price, p, would encourage food production and discourage clothing output. Nonetheless, for output movements along the transformation schedule,

$$dx_C + pdx_F = 0 \qquad (2.S.13)$$

The reason is simple: At a competitive equilibrium (e.g., point B in Figure 2.3) the absolute value of the slope of the transformation schedule, $-(dx_F/dx_C)$, must equal clothing's relative price, $1/p$. Of course in the special case of rigid production [Figure 2.4(a)], both dx_C and dx_F are separately zero.

Substitution and Income Effects

Appendix B to Chapter 2 suggested that any change in price has both a substitution and an income effect on quantity demanded. The decomposition into these two effects can be expressed algebraically for small price changes, making use of Equation 2.S.12's expression for the change in real income, which is simplified by Equation 2.S.13's relationship among outputs.

The demand for any commodity depends on all prices and income. Alternatively, in a two-commodity model it depends on relative price, p, and real income, y.[1] For example, consider the home country's demand for food, written as in Equation 2.S.14.

$$D_F = D_F(p, y) \qquad (2.S.14)$$

Differentiate this with respect to food's relative price, p, to obtain

$$\frac{dD_F}{dp} = \frac{\partial D_F}{\partial p} + \frac{\partial D_F}{\partial y} \cdot \frac{dy}{dp}$$

The first term is the substitution effect of a price rise—as p rises, food demand falls along an indifference curve. The second composite term shows the two aspects of the income effect described in the text. The term dy/dp shows how real income at home has been affected by the rise in food's relative price. Equation 2.S.12 reveals that dy/dp is just $-(D_F - x_F)$ because any output response along the transformation curve has negligible impact on real incomes (by Equation 2.S.13). If food is imported, dy/dp is negative. The other term, $\partial D_F/\partial y$, expresses the change in demand for food as a consequence of a unit rise in incomes with prices constant. This is not a pure number because D_F is measured in food units and y in clothing units. Therefore define α_F as p times $(\partial D_F/\partial y)$, so that α_F is the home country's marginal propensity to consume food. This is a pure number, between 0 and 1 if neither commodity is "inferior." Therefore Equation 2.S.15 depicts the breakdown of dD_F/dp into substitution and income effects.

$$\frac{dD_F}{dp} = \frac{\partial D_F}{\partial p} - \frac{(D_F - x_F)}{p} \cdot \alpha_F \qquad (2.S.15)$$

This breakdown of demand shows the importance of the direction of trade. If food is imported at home, both income and substitution terms combine to reduce food demand as the relative price of food rises. However, if food were exported, the income

---

[1]The change in real income, dy, has been defined by Equation 2.S.10. Mathematical liberties are taken here in using the symbol y for real income itself. However, this supplement requires only the expression for dy because it considers only "small" changes in prices and demands.

effect of a rise in food's price would be positive, running counter to the substitution effect and, in some cases, resulting in more food being demanded locally.

The Hat Notation

It will often prove convenient to express the change in a variable, dx, as a fraction of the original value of that variable, x. A hat symbol, $\wedge$, denotes this relative change. Thus, for any variable, x,

$$\hat{x} \equiv \frac{dx}{x}$$

The Elasticity of Demand for Imports

This discussion of the components of demand behavior can be added to a consideration of production changes to investigate the *elasticity of demand for imports, ε,* defined as

$$\varepsilon \equiv -\frac{\hat{M}}{\hat{p}} \tag{2.S.16}$$

where the minus sign is used to make ε a positive number. M, of course, refers to home imports of food,

$$M = D_F - x_F$$

We argued in the text that three ingredients are involved in the expression for ε, the elasticity of demand for imports. As we now show, ε can be expressed as the simple sum of (1) $\bar{\eta}$, the pure substitution elasticity of demand, (2) m, the marginal propensity to import, and (3) e, the elasticity of supply for import-competing production:

$$\varepsilon = \bar{\eta} + m + e \tag{2.S.17}$$

To see this, differentiate the expression for M and use hat notation:

$$-\frac{\hat{M}}{\hat{p}} = -\frac{D_F}{M} \cdot \frac{\hat{D}_F}{\hat{p}} + \frac{x_F}{M} \cdot \frac{\hat{x}_F}{\hat{p}}$$

The expression for

$$-\frac{D_F \hat{D}_F}{M \hat{p}}$$

follows readily from Equation 2.S.15. Let $\bar{\eta}$ represent the (negative of the) pure substitution term in demand,

$$\bar{\eta} \equiv \frac{p}{-M} \cdot \frac{\partial D_F}{\partial p}$$

and m the marginal propensity to import, which is the marginal propensity to consume the imported good (food) at home, α_F. Finally, define the elasticity of import-competing production, e, as[2]

$$e \equiv -\frac{p}{M} \cdot \frac{dx_F}{dp}$$

Combining yields the final breakdown for the elasticity of demand for imports, ε.

Comparative Advantage and the Gains from Trade

A basic line of argument reveals how competitive behavior leads to gains from international trade when countries take advantage of world markets to import commodities that are relatively inexpensive compared to autarky. In striving for generality, this discussion removes the two-commodity (food and clothing) limitation and considers a country originally consuming and producing many commodities before international trade. Let autarky market-clearing prices and quantities be indicated by the ^{0} superscript, so that before trade, item by item

$$D_i^0 = x_i^0 \tag{2.S.18}$$

International trade frees a country from the necessity of providing all its own requirements; imposed instead is a balance-of-payments constraint that the overall value of consumption match that of national production. Letting the superscript ^{1} denote free-trade variables,

$$\Sigma p_i^1 D_i^1 = \Sigma p_i^1 x_i^1 \tag{2.S.19}$$

A country is considered to gain from international trade if, in a trade equilibrium, it chooses a consumption bundle, D^1, that (at free-trade prices, p^1) costs at least as much to purchase as does the autarky bundle, D^0. Such a choice is taken to *reveal* a preference for the consumption choice available with trade because it is selected either (1) despite the higher price tag, or (2) if the price tag is the same but the bundle chosen, D^1, is different from D^0.[3]

$$\text{Gains if} \quad \Sigma p_i^1 D_i^1 \geqq \Sigma p_i^1 D_i^0 \tag{2.S.20}$$

This criterion provides one of the two fundamental building blocks for the general argument. The other compares the aggregate value of production at a given set of prices with any alternative production pattern along a given production-possibilities

---

[2]An equivalent expression for e is

$$\frac{\hat{X}}{(\widehat{1/p})}$$

with demands constant, which could be termed the elasticity of export supply. (X represents $x_C - D_C$ for the home country.)

[3]In Figure 2.6 consumption point F is preferred to E even though they cost the same. We are assuming strictly bowed-in indifference curves.

schedule. The basic production relationship states that a price line is tangent to the transformation curve at the point chosen. The bowed-out shape of the transformation curve implies that should any other production combination have been chosen at the same prices, it would have a lower aggregate value. This statement holds for any number of commodities and any set of prices. In particular, at free-trade prices, p^1, the value of production bundle x^1 is greater than that of autarky bundle x^0 at those same prices. That is,

$$\Sigma p_i^1 x_i^1 > \Sigma p_i^1 x_i^0 \qquad (2.S.21)$$

if the transformation schedule is smoothly bowed out.

These results provide the basis for two propositions. First, the production relationship shown in Inequality 2.S.21 is used to prove that Inequality 2.S.20 is indeed satisfied. Adding up the value (at free-trade prices) of autarky consumption and production from Equation 2.S.18,

$$\Sigma p_i^1 D_i^0 = \Sigma p_i^1 x_i^0$$

Now substitute this and Equation 2.S.19 into Inequality 2.S.21 to establish Inequality 2.S.20. Free trade leads to gains.

The second proposition concerns the *pattern of trade* according to comparative advantage that leads to these gains from trade. It generalizes the notion that to obtain gains when trading, a country should export commodities produced relatively cheaply at home and import commodities that are relatively inexpensive on world markets. Because it is established that free trade leads to gains, at autarky prices the consumption bundle purchased with free trade must have been out of consumers' reach. They could not afford to purchase the superior bundle, D^1, or they would have done so. This implies that

$$\Sigma p_i^0 D_i^1 > \Sigma p_i^0 D_i^0 \qquad (2.S.22)$$

As for production comparisons at autarky prices, the notion that at *any* given prices production responds to maximize the aggregate value of produced income leads to the following:

$$\Sigma p_i^0 x_i^1 < \Sigma p_i^0 x_i^0 \qquad (2.S.23)$$

The logic is the same as that leading to Inequality 2.S.21, except that at autarky prices, p^0, the production bundle x^0 has greater value than x^1. Let E_i^1 be defined as imports of commodity i in the trade situation, $D_i^1 - x_i^1$. Because the right sides of Inequalities 2.S.22 and 2.S.23 are the same, subtraction reveals that

$$\Sigma p_i^0 E_i^1 > 0 \qquad (2.S.24)$$

That is, if evaluated at autarky prices, imports in the aggregate exceed exports. At free-trade prices, of course, they must have the same value if trade is balanced.

$$\Sigma p_i^1 E_i^1 = 0 \qquad (2.S.25)$$

(This restates Equation 2.S.19.)

The final step involves subtracting Inequality 2.S.24 from Equation 2.S.25 to obtain

$$\Sigma(p_i^1 - p_i^0)E_i^1 < 0 \qquad (2.S.26)$$

This states that *on average* any commodity, i, imported with free trade has an autarky price, p_i^0, higher than its trade price, p_i^1. It is not possible to establish such a relationship item by item, but Inequality 2.S.26 shows that in the aggregate with trade, a country imports goods that are relatively cheaper and exports goods that are relatively expensive.[4]

The line of argument developed here is pursued in the supplement to Chapter 12, where we consider situations in which tariffs or export taxes distort home prices from world prices.

SUPPLEMENT TO CHAPTER 3: Stability and Comparative Statics in the Basic Trade Model

Stability in the two-commodity world trade model requires that an increase in the relative price of food reduces world excess demand for food. Conditions sufficient to guarantee stability can be derived and presented in two alternative, but equivalent, ways.

The Marshall-Lerner Stability Condition

This form of the condition concentrates on the elasticity of each country's demand for imports. World excess demand for food is the difference between the home country's excess demand, M, and the foreign country's intended exports of food. Assuming a budget balance, these intended food exports have a value equivalent to foreign import demand (for clothing). This value is M^*/p. (The division by p is to change from clothing units to food units.) Therefore, stability requires an increase in p to lower $(M - M^*/p)$. That is, the condition for stability is

$$\frac{dM}{dp} < \frac{d(M^*/p)}{dp}$$

This inequality can be slightly modified (1) by dividing the denominators of both sides by p to highlight the *relative* price change, dp/p. (A circumflex—hat—denotes relative changes: dp/p is written as $\hat{p}$). Then, (2) divide the numerator on the left side by M and the numerator on the right side by M^*/p (which equals M at the initial equilibrium). Making use of the hat notation for relative changes, the inequality becomes

$$\frac{\hat{M}}{\hat{p}} < \frac{(\widehat{M^*/p})}{\hat{p}} \qquad (3.S.1)$$

---

[4] To see why you should not expect an item-by-item correspondence, suppose that commodity *17* is slightly more expensive with trade than it is at home in autarky. Some major items of consumption that are good substitutes for commodity *17* might become even more expensive with trade, thus deflecting demand onto commodity *17*. Additionally, or alternatively, resources could be drained away from commodity *17* toward other commodities that have risen in price with trade. The net result? Commodity *17* might end up as an import instead of an export.

By definition, the elasticity of home demand for imports along the offer curve is $\varepsilon \equiv -\hat{M}/\hat{p}$; foreign ε^* is $-\hat{M}^*/(\widehat{1/p})$, which is equivalent to $\hat{M}^*/\hat{p}$.[1] Because Inequality 3.S.1 can be written as

$$\frac{\hat{M}}{\hat{p}} < \frac{\hat{M}^* - \hat{p}}{\hat{p}}$$

substituting for ε and ε^* yields

$$\varepsilon + \varepsilon^* > 1 \qquad (3.S.2)$$

This is known as the *Marshall-Lerner condition for stability*. It suggests that for the market to be stable, offer curves cannot be too inelastic. The offer curves in Figure 2.A.3 intersect at stable equilibrium point Q. Note that at that point ε is less than 1 but ε^* exceeds unity, so the Marshall-Lerner condition is obviously satisfied. To illustrate an unstable equilibrium, both offer curves must be inelastic. Instability requires the offer curves to cut each other in the direction opposite to that shown in Figure 2.A.3, as at point Q in Figure 3.B.1(b).

An Alternative Form for the Stability Condition

Concentrate on the excess world demand curve for food, but generalize by assuming many countries in the trading world. Some will be food importers, others exporters. The condition for market stability is that the slope of the excess world demand curve for food be negative, or

$$\Sigma \frac{dD_F^i}{dp} - \Sigma \frac{dx_F^i}{dp} < 0$$

Multiply each term by $-p$, which also changes the direction of the inequality sign. Next, divide and multiply each term in the first sum by D_F^i, country i's demand for food, and each term in the second sum by x_F^i. Finally, divide all terms by total world demand, ΣD_F^i, or by the equivalent (in the neighborhood of equilibrium) total world supply, Σx_F^i. At this stage the condition for stability is

$$\Sigma \lambda_F^i \left\{ -\frac{p}{D_F^i} \cdot \frac{dD_F^i}{dp} \right\} + \Sigma \rho_F^i \left\{ \frac{p}{x_F^i} \cdot \frac{dx_F^i}{dp} \right\} > 0 \qquad (3.S.3)$$

In Inequality 3.S.3 two sets of weights appear in the summations. λ_F^i is the fraction of total world food consumption represented by country i's demand, $D_F^i/\Sigma D_F^i$. Similarly, the ρ_F^i are production weights; ρ_F^i equals $x_F^i/\Sigma x_F^i$. The λ and the ρ sums each add to unity.

The final step involves breaking down the demand elasticities into income and substitution terms and defining the appropriate supply elasticities. The breakdown of

---

[1]The relative change in a ratio, such as $(\widehat{x/y})$, is the difference between the relative change in the numerator and denominator: $\hat{x} - \hat{y}$. Because 1 is a constant, $(\widehat{1/p})$ equals $-\hat{p}$.

home food demand in response to price was shown in Equation 2.S.15, and is repeated here for country i as Equation 3.S.4.

$$\frac{dD_F^i}{dp} = \frac{\partial D_F^i}{\partial p} - \frac{(D_F^i - x_F^i)}{p} \alpha_F^i \tag{3.S.4}$$

Multiply Equation 3.S.4 by $-p/D_F^i$ and define the pure substitution term, $-\frac{p}{D_F^i} \cdot \frac{\partial D_F^i}{\partial p}$, as $\overline{\omega}_F^i$, which must be positive.[2] This yields

$$-\frac{p}{D_F^i} \cdot \frac{dD_F^i}{dp} = \overline{\omega}_F^i + \frac{(D_F^i - x_F^i)}{D_F^i} \alpha_F^i \tag{3.S.5}$$

Similarly, define

$$\frac{p}{x_F^i} \cdot \frac{dx_F^i}{dp}$$

as e_F^i. This own-supply response to price must be positive.

Sweeping countries together, let S be defined as

$$S \equiv \Sigma \lambda_F^i \overline{\omega}_F^i + \Sigma \rho_F^i e_F^i$$

That is, S is the sum of two terms: The first is the positive-weighted average of each nation's substitution elasticity of demand, and the second is the weighted average of own-production elasticities. In similar fashion for income effects, let γ be defined as

$$\gamma \equiv \Sigma(\lambda_F^i - \rho_F^i)\alpha_F^i$$

Each country's marginal propensity to consume food, α_F^i, has as a weight in γ the fraction of total world food production represented by that country's net *imports* of food. If country i exports food, $\lambda_F^i - \rho_F^i$ would be a negative fraction. Substituting these terms into Inequality 3.S.3 yields Inequality 3.S.6 as an alternative basic stability condition.

$$S + \gamma > 0 \tag{3.S.6}$$

This form of the stability condition is in some ways more revealing than the equivalent Marshall-Lerner expression, Inequality 3.S.2. Substitution effects both in consumption and production are contained in the term S and must be positive. Thus high values help ensure stability. As the price of food rises, in every country consumers substitute away from demanding food and resources are attracted to food production. γ captures the effect of a rise in food's price in redistributing real incomes toward countries exporting food and away from food importers. If all countries share identical marginal propensities to consume food, α_F^i, γ must vanish and the market will be

---

[2] Note that for the home country importing F, $\overline{\omega}_F$ is smaller than the trade substitution elasticity, $\overline{\eta}$, defined in the supplement to Chapter 2. Indeed, $\overline{\omega}_F$ is (M/D_F) times $\overline{\eta}$. They would be equal only if no food were produced at home.

stable. If, on average, food importers have a higher marginal propensity to consume food, γ would be positive and market stability would be guaranteed. Returning to the two-country case in which the home country imports food (denoted by M), we have

$$\gamma = \frac{M}{D_F + D_F^*}(\alpha_F - \alpha_F^*)$$

Thus stability would be endangered if foreign food exporters had a higher α_F^* than home food importers. Note, however, that γ's absolute size tends to be small if the volume of trade is small relative to total world consumption. In such a case the market is apt to be stable regardless of taste differences.

Comparative Statics

This chapter discussed several comparative statics exercises involving changes in tastes, the composition of outputs, growth, and international transfers. The basic equilibrium relationship for all these exercises (except transfers) is the balance-of-payments condition (see also Equation 2.S.9)

$$pM = M^* \qquad (3.S.7)$$

The method of comparative statics involves seeing how a disturbance to the market causes prices to change so as to restore the equilibrium relationship shown by Equation 3.S.7. That is, anything that causes imports in either country to change must bring about an equilibrating price response.

Proceed formally by differentiating Equation 3.S.7, making use of the hat notation for relative changes.

$$\hat{p} + \hat{M} = \hat{M}^* \qquad (3.S.8)$$

Imports in either country respond to a change in the terms of trade—this is what the offer curves describe. In addition, a disturbance may *shift* one or more offer curves. Let the relative change in imports at home that would take place at *constant terms of trade* be denoted by $\hat{M}|_{\bar{p}}$. This is the shift in the home offer curve. Similarly, $\hat{M}^*|_{\bar{p}}$ denotes the relative shift in the foreign offer curve. Putting these two sources of import change together,

$$\hat{M} = -\varepsilon\hat{p} + \hat{M}|_{\bar{p}} \qquad (3.S.9)$$

$$\hat{M}^* = \varepsilon^*\hat{p} + \hat{M}^*|_{\bar{p}}$$

Substitute these into Equation 3.S.8 and solve for the relative change in the terms of trade that serves to clear markets to get

$$\hat{p} = \frac{(\hat{M}|_{\bar{p}} - \hat{M}^*|_{\bar{p}})}{\Delta} \qquad \text{where } \Delta \equiv \varepsilon + \varepsilon^* - 1 \qquad (3.S.10)$$

This is a basic, and readily understandable, result. From the Marshall-Lerner stability expression, Inequality 3.S.2, the denominator, Δ, must be positive. This shows that the less sensitive imports are to price changes (small Δ), the more the relative price must adjust to clear markets. Furthermore, the numerator of Equation 3.S.10 has a ready interpretation. It shows the relative increase in world excess demand for the home country's import commodity (food) at the initial prices. In other words, Equation 3.S.10 shows that the equilibrium relative price of food rises if the excess world demand curve for food shifts to the right and the market is stable.

In many applications of the basic trade model, the aim is to analyze how real incomes at home and abroad are affected. The expression for real income changes at home was developed in the supplement to Chapter 2. A slight rewriting of Equation 2.S.12 yields

$$dy = -pM \cdot \hat{p} + (dx_c + pdx_F) \tag{3.S.11}$$

There is a terms-of-trade effect and a direct effect from production changes. Recall that for movements along the transformation curve, $dx_c + pdx_F$ equals zero. Therefore, the second part of dy in Equation 3.S.11 picks up the value of *shifts* in the transformation curve.

Now consider the following scenarios, in each of which there is a shock or disturbance to a preexisting world trade equilibrium balancing home and foreign import demands. The first involves only a change in the *composition* of outputs at home, the next two applications involve *growth*, and the final scenario deals with the *transfer* problem. In each case focus on the change in the terms of trade and on the consequent effects on real incomes:

1. *A change in the composition of home outputs.* In this case assume that at constant prices food output increases ($dx_F > 0$), and clothing output falls ($dx_C < 0$), but at initial prices there is no change in the value of aggregate production ($dx_C + pdx_F = 0$). This means that at the initial price there is no alteration in home *demand* for food importables (both price and income are constant at the initial price). Yet *production* rises, and this causes demand for imports to fall ($dM = -dx_F$). Abroad no changes take place at the initial prices. Substitution into Equation 3.S.10 reveals that

$$\hat{p} = -\frac{1}{M \cdot \Delta} dx_F \tag{3.S.12}$$

With the terms of trade improving, so must real income at home. Equation 3.S.11 thus gives

$$dy = \frac{pdx_F}{\Delta} \tag{3.S.13}$$

The more inelastic are world demand and supply, the more successful would be a policy of substituting import-competing production, x_F, for exportables, x_C. This is a theme picked up by the tariff literature.

2. *Export-led growth.* Suppose growth is biased, so that at initial prices only the output of exportables at home expands ($dx_C > 0$), but at constant prices $dx_F = 0$. No *shifts* in demand or supply take place abroad. At initial prices there is no change in production of food (importables), but because incomes expand at *initial* prices, so does demand. That is, $dM = dD_F$, and $dD_F = (m/p)(dx_C)$. Demand for food rises by an amount determined by the marginal propensity to import food, m, and the increase in initial incomes in food units, dx_C/p. Substituting into Equation 3.S.10 yields

$$\hat{p} = \frac{m}{pM \cdot \Delta} dx_C \qquad (3.S.14)$$

The terms of trade have deteriorated and, by Equation 3.S.11, this deterioration offsets at least a part of the initial growth effect on real incomes.

$$dy = \left(\frac{\Delta - m}{\Delta}\right) dx_C \qquad (3.S.15)$$

The expression in parentheses provides the condition for immiserizing growth. Stability ensures that Δ is positive, but if elasticities are nonetheless low, Δ may not exceed the home marginal propensity to import. In such a case, real incomes at home would fall despite output growth.

3. *Balanced growth.* The kind of growth just discussed was quite biased—at initial prices only the home country's export good expanded, which ensures a deterioration in its terms of trade. Yet what about balanced growth? Suppose the home country's transformation schedule shifts outward uniformly at rate μ—both dx_C/x_C and dx_F/x_F equal μ at initial prices. Assume also that demand for both goods expands in a balanced fashion at initial prices. Then imports (at initial prices) must also expand at rate μ. Substitute into Equation 3.S.10 to show that neutral growth must cause a deterioration in the terms of trade (assuming no growth abroad).

$$\hat{p} = \frac{\mu}{\Delta} \qquad (3.S.16)$$

It proves convenient to express the change in real income (given in Equation 3.S.11) in relative terms. $\hat{y}$ is dy divided by initial income, $(x_C + px_F)$. That is,

$$\hat{y} = -\theta_M \hat{p} + \mu$$

where θ_M represents the share of imports in the national income and μ, of course, is the growth rate at initial prices. This expression is perfectly general. Substituting the terms-of-trade change shown by Equation 3.S.16 for the case of balanced growth yields

$$\hat{y} = \left(\frac{\Delta - \theta_M}{\Delta}\right)\mu \qquad (3.S.17)$$

This result shows that even balanced growth can be immiserizing, for it does worsen the terms of trade. If elasticities are sufficiently low, their sum may not exceed unity by more than the share of imports in the national income. Equation 3.S.17 should be compared with Equation 3.S.15. Retaining the assumption that at constant prices growth in demand is proportional, the marginal propensity to import, m, is the same as the fraction of total income spent on importables (including domestic production as well as imports). Unless production of importables is nonexistent, this must exceed the share of income represented by total imports, θ_M. Export-led growth is more apt to worsen real incomes than is balanced growth.

4. *The transfer problem.* Discussion of the transfer problem requires a bit more preparation. The basic equilibrium relationship set out in Equation 3.S.7 rests on the classical form of the budget constraint: In each country all earned income is spent. The transfer process has the home country spending less than its produced income by the amount of transfer (call it T in units of clothing), matched by an equal amount of excess spending (over earned income) abroad. This implies that the value of spending on imports at home must also be cut below the value of foreign imports by the amount of the transfer.[3] This is the following basic relationship.

$$pM = M^* - T \tag{3.S.18}$$

Assume that initially there is no transfer ($T = 0$). Differentiation of Equation 3.S.18 yields

$$\hat{p} + \hat{M} = \hat{M}^* - \frac{dT}{pM} \tag{3.S.19}$$

Proceeding as before (in the development of Equation 3.S.10), the result is

$$\hat{p} = \left(\hat{M}\big|_{\bar{p}} - \hat{M}^*\big|_{\bar{p}} + \frac{dT}{pM} \right)/\Delta \tag{3.S.20}$$

With a transfer of purchasing power there are no production changes at the initial terms of trade.[4] Demand for imports falls at home and rises abroad, however. That is, $\hat{M}\big|_{\bar{p}} = -mdT/pM$, and $\hat{M}^*\big|_{\bar{p}} = m^*dT/pM$. In other words, the impact of the direct redistribution of income on the terms of trade is shown by

$$\hat{p} = \frac{-(m + m^* - 1)}{\Delta} \cdot \frac{dT}{pM} \tag{3.S.21}$$

This expression confirms Chapter 3's statement that with transfer the terms of trade might go in either direction. Note that the numerator can also be written as $[(1 - m^*) - m]$ or, to use the earlier terminology, as $\alpha_F^* - \alpha_F$. Whether the real income transfer is a consequence of a change in the terms of trade (as in the stability expression, Inequality 3.S.6) or of a direct transfer of purchasing power (as in Equation 3.S.21), the same comparison between foreign α_F^* and home α_F, the marginal propensities to consume a particular commodity in the two countries, is required.

---

[3]The home budget constraint becomes $D_C + pD_F = x_C + px_F - T$. Rewriting, $p(D_F - x_F) = (x_C - D_C) - T$. When markets clear, home-intended exports equal foreign imports, M^*.
[4]Ignored here is the chapter's discussion of a possible transfer of real resources. A general treatment of the transfer problem, which includes possible supply reactions, is R. W. Jones, "Presumption and the Transfer Problem," *Journal of International Economics* (August 1975): 263–274, reprinted in his *International Trade: Essays in Theory* (Amsterdam: North Holland, 1979), Chapter 10.

This supplement concludes by confirming Chapter 3's argument that even if the terms of trade move in favor of the transferor, real income for the transferor cannot improve. The equivalent of Equation 3.S.11 for the transfer problem is[5]

$$dy = -pM\hat{p} - dT$$

Direct substitution of $\hat{p}$ into this expression yields

$$dy = -\left\{ \frac{\varepsilon + \varepsilon^* - (m + m^*)}{\Delta} \right\} dT$$

However, the supplement to Chapter 2 decomposed the elasticity of import demand (ε, and, by analogy, ε^*) into a substitution term in consumption ($\bar{\eta}$ and $\bar{\eta}^*$), a positive elasticity in production (e and e^*), and the import propensity (m and m^*). Therefore, with transfer, the expression for dy can finally be given as follows:

$$dy = -\frac{\{\bar{\eta} + \bar{\eta}^* + e + e^*\}}{\Delta} dT \qquad (3.S.22)$$

Real income for the transferor must decline, as is demonstrated in Figure 3.4.

SUPPLEMENT TO CHAPTER 5: The Specific-Factors Model of Production

This supplement provides a formal analytic treatment of the model of production described in Chapter 5. The community produces two commodities, clothing and food. Labor (L) and capital (K) are combined to produce clothing. The input requirements *per unit* output of clothing are denoted by a_{LC} and a_{KC}. Labor is also used to produce food, in cooperation with land (T). Thus, the per-unit output requirements in the food sector are a_{LF} and a_{TF}. Capital and land are each used specifically only in one sector, whereas labor is mobile between sectors.

The Distribution of Income

Pure competition is assumed to prevail, assuring that commodity prices (p_C and p_F) reflect units costs of production. These costs, in turn, depend in part on the input mix used in production (the a_{ij}'s) and in part on factor prices. The wage rate is denoted by w, and the amount that must be paid per unit rental on capital is given by r_K and the rental on land by r_T. The competitive profit conditions are thus summarized as follows.

$$a_{LC}w + a_{KC}r_K = p_C \qquad (5.S.1)$$

$$a_{LF}w + a_{TF}r_T = p_F \qquad (5.S.2)$$

---

[5]Here dy is interpreted as the change in current real consumption. Left out of this account is the possibility that the transfer represents a loan, which will be repaid in the future. Presumably this does not by itself lower real income for the transferor. Also left out of this account in the expression that follows is the possibility that trade involves other countries in addition to the transferor and transferee. In such a case a transfer welfare paradox is possible, wherein real income may improve for the transferor. For a general discussion of this issue, with references to the literature, see R. W. Jones, "Income Effects and Paradoxes in the Theory of International Trade," *Economic Journal* (June 1985): 330–334.

Techniques of production are chosen so as to minimize the costs of producing a unit of output in the face of prevailing factor prices. To see what this entails, consider the clothing sector. The assumption of constant returns to scale implies that the *unit isoquant* captures all there is to know about techniques of production. At the point of cost minimization, the isocost line—with slope given by (minus) the ratio of factor prices, $-(w/r_K)$—is tangent to the unit isoquant, with slope da_{KC}/da_{LC}. That is, cost minimization entails that

$$w\,da_{LC} + r_K\,da_{KC} = 0$$

Once again it proves convenient to write these changes in *relative* terms (denoted by ^). Thus $\hat{a}_{LC}$ is da_{LC}/a_{LC}. Also, write the factor *distributive shares* as θ_{LC} and θ_{KC}, respectively, where, for example, θ_{LC} is wa_{LC}/p_C. Therefore, in the clothing sector, cost minimization entails

$$\theta_{LC}\hat{a}_{LC} + \theta_{KC}\hat{a}_{KC} = 0 \tag{5.S.3}$$

Similarly, in the food sector,

$$\theta_{LF}\hat{a}_{LF} + \theta_{TF}\hat{a}_{TF} = 0 \tag{5.S.4}$$

Each of these expressions states that if labor is used more intensively, less of the specific factor need be used along the unit isoquant. The left side in Equations 5.S.3 and 5.S.4 shows, for each industry, the relative change in unit costs involved in substituting one input for another. At a point of cost minimization this change must be zero: All cost reductions have already been taken at the minimum cost point.

It is now possible to confirm Chapter 5's argument that each commodity price change is flanked by the changes in the returns to productive factors used in that industry. Differentiate Equations 5.S.1 and 5.S.2, put into relative terms, and simplify by using Equations 5.S.3 and 5.S.4 to obtain

$$\theta_{LC}\hat{w} + \theta_{KC}\hat{r}_K = \hat{p}_C \tag{5.S.5}$$

$$\theta_{LF}\hat{w} + \theta_{TF}\hat{r}_T = \hat{p}_F \tag{5.S.6}$$

Thus each commodity price change must be a weighted average of factor price changes, with the weights given by distributive shares—reflections of the importance of each factor in unit costs. Suppose now that commodity prices are disturbed—that clothing's price rises while the price of food remains unchanged. Equations 5.S.5 and 5.S.6 then suggest that some factor's return will rise relatively by more than p_C has while some other factor's return will fall absolutely (because $\hat{p}_F = 0$). As is easily shown, capitalists are the clear gainers and landlords the losers. This is established by first showing that the wage rate must rise, but not as much, relatively, as the price of clothing.

The wage rate is determined by the condition that the labor force be fully employed. The clothing sector's demand for labor is written as $a_{LC}x_C$, where x_C shows the scale of output. Output is restricted by the availability of capital, however. If a_{KC} denotes the quantity of capital used per unit and if K units of capital are all the economy possesses, clothing output must be given by

$$x_C = \frac{K}{a_{KC}}$$

Therefore, the clothing sector's labor demand can be written as $(a_{LC}/a_{KC}) \cdot K$. In similar fashion the food sector's demand for labor must be $(a_{LF}/a_{TF}) \cdot T$. Thus the following is the statement that all the economy's labor force is fully employed:

$$\frac{a_{LC}}{a_{KC}} \cdot K + \frac{a_{LF}}{a_{TF}} \cdot T = L \qquad (5.S.7)$$

Differentiate this, assuming now that K and T remain constant but L may change, to obtain

$$\lambda_{LC}(\hat{a}_{LC} - \hat{a}_{KC}) + \lambda_{LF}(\hat{a}_{LF} - \hat{a}_{TF}) = \hat{L} \qquad (5.S.8)$$

where the λ's correspond to the fraction of the economy's labor force used in each sector.

To proceed, reconsider the relationship between the wage rate and the value of labor's marginal product in each sector. These must be equal. Figure 5.S.1 illustrates how the quantity of labor used per unit of capital (a_{LC}/a_{KC}) depends inversely on the real wage in the clothing sector (w/p_C). (For a given clothing price this curve is the same as that drawn in Figure 5.3, reading from right to left.) The curve shows the marginal physical product of labor in clothing. Define the *elasticity* of labor's marginal product curve, γ_{LC}, as

$$\gamma_{LC} \equiv \frac{-(\hat{a}_{LC} - \hat{a}_{KC})}{(\hat{w} - \hat{p}_C)} \qquad (5.S.9)$$

Similarly, in the food industry,

$$\gamma_{LF} \equiv \frac{-(\hat{a}_{LF} - \hat{a}_{TF})}{(\hat{w} - \hat{p}_F)} \qquad (5.S.10)$$

FIGURE 5.S.1

The Elasticity of Labor's Marginal Product

A drop in the real wage from $0A$ to $0B$ would encourage labor to be used more intensively—an increase in the labor/capital ratio from $0A'$ to $0B'$. The elasticity of labor's marginal product in clothing, γ_{LC}, is defined as $-(\hat{a}_{LC} - \hat{a}_{KC})$ divided by $(\hat{w} - \hat{p}_C)$.

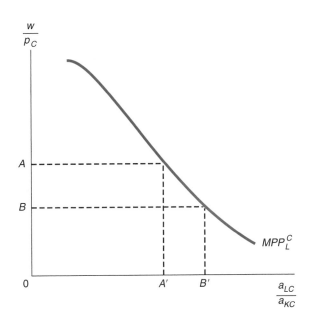

These concepts are crucial. Substitute the expressions for the elasticities γ_{LC} and γ_{LF} into Equation 5.S.8 to obtain

$$\lambda_{LC}\gamma_{LC}(\hat{w} - \hat{p}_C) + \lambda_{LF}\gamma_{LF}(\hat{w} - \hat{p}_F) = -\hat{L} \qquad (5.S.11)$$

Solving explicitly for the change in the wage rate in terms of the commodity price changes and any change in the labor force,

$$\hat{w} = \beta_C\hat{p}_C + \beta_F\hat{p}_F - \frac{1}{\gamma}\hat{L} \qquad (5.S.12)$$

where

$$\beta_C \equiv \lambda_{LC}\frac{\gamma_{LC}}{\gamma}$$

$$\beta_F \equiv \lambda_{LF}\frac{\gamma_{LF}}{\gamma}$$

and

$$\gamma \equiv \lambda_{LC}\gamma_{LC} + \lambda_{LF}\gamma_{LF}$$

γ_{LC} and γ_{LF} are the elasticities of labor's marginal product curve in each sector, and γ is the economywide weighted average of these two elasticities. γ directly provides the answer to the following question: If commodity prices are constant and the wage rate rises by 1 percent, by what percentage will the entire economy's demand for labor fall? If γ is large, the answer is that the economy's demand for labor would be reduced by a relatively large amount. Conversely, Equation 5.S.12 shows that a given increase in the labor force would, at constant commodity prices, reduce the wage rate, but not by very much if γ is large. The β coefficients, which add to unity, reveal the power of each separate commodity price to influence the wage rate. At constant overall factor endowments, the wage rate change is trapped between (i.e., is a positive weighted average of) the commodity price changes. Therefore, if clothing's relative price increases ($\hat{p}_C > \hat{p}_F$), this relationship, coupled with Equations 5.S.5 and 5.S.6, establishes that

$$\hat{r}_K > \hat{p}_C > \hat{w} > \hat{p}_F > \hat{r}_T$$

The specific factors are most radically affected by price changes. The mobile factor (labor) finds its return rising in terms of one sector and falling in terms of the other. The algebraic demonstration supplements the diagrammatic illustration of a price change in Figure 5.2.

The expression for each β coefficient in Equation 5.S.12 allows a further refinement. Consider only β_C, the relative effect of an increase in clothing's price on the wage rate. This coefficient was explicitly defined in Equation 5.S.12, but rewrite it as

$$\beta_C = \theta_C \cdot \frac{\lambda_{LC}}{\theta_C} \cdot \frac{\gamma_{LC}}{\gamma}$$

Reading from right to left, the term γ_{LC}/γ can be considered the *relative* degree of substitutability of the demand for labor in the clothing sector—a comparison of γ_{LC} with the economywide average, γ. Call this term s_C. Next is the expression λ_{LC}/θ_C, where θ_C denotes the share of clothing production in the national income, $p_Cx_C/(p_Cx_C + p_Fx_F)$.

This expression also reflects a "relative" for the clothing industry; it is a measure of *relative labor intensity* for clothing. The concept of relative factor intensity in a two-factor setting comes into its own in Chapter 6 and the supplement to Chapter 6. Here it is used to compare λ_{LC}, the fraction of the labor force used in clothing, with θ_C, the fraction of the economy's entire input base used in clothing. (Thus, if λ_{LC}/θ_C were unity, clothing would be neither labor intensive nor labor unintensive.) Call this term i_C. Then β_C is the product of three terms:

$$\beta_C = \theta_C \cdot i_C \cdot s_C$$

That is, a price rise in clothing has a more severe impact on the wage rate (1) the more elastic is the demand for labor in clothing compared with the economywide average (i.e., the higher is s_C), (2) the more labor intensive is the clothing sector (i.e., the higher is i_C), and (3) the more important is production of clothing as a fraction of national income produced (i.e., the higher is θ_C).[1]

Outputs, Prices, and Factor Endowments

Outputs respond to changes in relative prices along the transformation schedule. Outputs also respond to changes in factor endowments (at constant commodity prices). Chapter 5 showed how an ample supply of capital lends a presumption that relatively much clothing is produced. By contrast, plentiful land encourages food production. Now endowments of capital and land are kept constant, but the implication for outputs (and thus for positions of comparative advantage) of changes in labor abundance are explored.

If, as assumed, the total capital stock is kept fixed, clothing output can expand only by using capital less intensively. Similarly, because x_F equals T/a_{TF}, food output can change only if a_{TF} is altered, given that overall land is fixed in supply. Combining shows that

$$\hat{x}_C - \hat{x}_F = \hat{a}_{TF} - \hat{a}_{KC} \tag{5.S.13}$$

The ingredients are at hand to solve separately for $\hat{a}_{TF}$ and $\hat{a}_{KC}$. From Equations 5.S.4 and 5.S.10,

$$\hat{a}_{TF} = \theta_{LF}\gamma_{LF}(\hat{w} - \hat{p}_F)$$

Similarly, Equations 5.S.3 and 5.S.9 can be solved for $\hat{a}_{KC}$:

$$\hat{a}_{KC} = \theta_{LC}\gamma_{LC}(\hat{w} - \hat{p}_C)$$

The change in the wage rate is provided by Equation 5.S.12, so that Equation 5.S.13 can be written as

$$\hat{x}_C - \hat{x}_F = \sigma_s(\hat{p}_C - \hat{p}_F) + \frac{1}{\gamma}(\theta_{LC}\gamma_{LC} - \theta_{LF}\gamma_{LF})\hat{L} \tag{5.S.14}$$

---

[1]This decomposition is discussed and applied in R. W. Jones, *Globalization and the Theory of Input Trade* (Cambridge, MA: MIT Press, 2000). An application to the question of the effect of tariffs on real wages in the specific-factors model is found in R. Ruffin and R. Jones, "Protection and Real Wages: The Neoclassical Ambiguity," *Journal of Economic Theory* (April 1977): 337–348.

where

$$\sigma_s \equiv \beta_C[\theta_{LF}\gamma_{LF}] + \beta_F[\theta_{LC}\gamma_{LC}] > 0$$

The effect of a change in relative commodity prices on relative outputs along the transformation schedule (i.e., for given factor endowments) is captured by the positive term σ_s, the elasticity of supply of relative outputs. Because the β's add to unity this is generally larger the greater are the elasticities of labor's marginal product curves in the two sectors.[2] The coefficient of $\hat{L}$ reveals that two distinct features of the technology determine the composition of output. As the labor supply expands (at given terms of trade), clothing output will tend to expand more than does the food sector if the elasticity of labor's marginal product is higher in clothing (i.e., if $\gamma_{LC} > \gamma > \gamma_{LF}$). This is one feature. However, the comparison of labor's distributive shares, θ_{LC} and θ_{LF}, is also important. The clothing sector tends to expand relative to food if θ_{LC} exceeds θ_{LF}. As the supplement to Chapter 6 reveals, this comparison of distributive shares is a comparison of *relative labor intensity* in the two sectors.[3] In the Heckscher-Ohlin model in Chapter 6, these factor intensity comparisons assume critical importance.

SUPPLEMENT TO CHAPTER 6: The Two-Sector Heckscher-Ohlin Model

The two-sector Heckscher-Ohlin model of production assumes each of two outputs (clothing, food) is produced in a constant returns to scale competitive setting with the use of two primary inputs (labor, capital). The productive factors are each homogeneous and mobile between sectors. Prices are flexible and both inputs are fully employed.

$$a_{LC}x_C + a_{LF}x_F = L \tag{6.S.1}$$

$$a_{KC}x_C + a_{KF}x_F = K \tag{6.S.2}$$

Furthermore, unit costs in each sector are equated to the prevailing commodity price (if output is positive):

$$a_{LC}w + a_{KC}r = p_C \tag{6.S.3}$$

$$a_{LF}w + a_{KF}r = p_F \tag{6.S.4}$$

Again, w refers to the wage rate, and now the common return to capital in the economy is denoted by r.

---

[2] The supplement to Chapter 6 compares this expression for σ_s with the comparable elasticity in the Heckscher-Ohlin model by making further simplifying assumptions.

[3] With reference to the definition of the relative degree of substitutability, s_c (and s_F for the food sector), on the one hand, and i_C (and i_F) for relative labor intensities, on the other hand, the coefficient of $\hat{L}$ in Equation 5.S.14 can also be written as $\theta_L [i_C s_C - i_F s_F]$, where θ_L is labor's distributive share in the national income. Thus, as the labor force expands at constant commodity prices, clothing output is apt to rise relatively more than food output to the extent that clothing is relatively labor intensive and has a relatively high elasticity of demand for labor.

Equations of Change: Prices

As in the specific-factors model of Chapter 5, techniques of production are chosen so as to minimize unit costs. This condition implies Equations 6.S.5 and 6.S.6: The distributive-share weighted average of changes in input-output coefficients along the unit isoquant in each industry must vanish near the cost-minimization point.[1]

$$\theta_{LC}\hat{a}_{LC} + \theta_{KC}\hat{a}_{KC} = 0 \tag{6.S.5}$$

$$\theta_{LF}\hat{a}_{LF} + \theta_{KF}\hat{a}_{KF} = 0 \tag{6.S.6}$$

These relationships are crucial, for they suggest that differentiating Equations 6.S.3 and 6.S.4 totally yields

$$\theta_{LC}\hat{w} + \theta_{KC}\hat{r} = \hat{p}_C \tag{6.S.7}$$

$$\theta_{LF}\hat{w} + \theta_{KF}\hat{r} = \hat{p}_F \tag{6.S.8}$$

These conditions state that in each industry the distributive-share weighted average of factor-price changes equals the relative commodity-price change. They correspond to Equations 5.S.5 and 5.S.6 for the specific-factor models. Yet now more can be said: This pair of equations links the commodity-price changes ($\hat{p}_C, \hat{p}_F$) to the pair of factor-price changes ($\hat{w}, \hat{r}$). Factor prices are determined *uniquely* by commodity prices, as long as both commodities are produced, and assuming the techniques used in clothing and food differ.

This qualification about techniques refers to the capital/labor ratio employed in the two sectors. As in the text, assume that food always is produced with a higher capital/labor ratio than clothing. This comparison must then be revealed in a ranking of distributive shares. Specifically, labor's distributive share in labor-intensive clothing, θ_{LC}, must exceed that in capital-intensive food, θ_{LF}. To see this, compute the determinant of coefficients in Equations 6.S.7 and 6.S.8. Call this determinant $|\theta|$. By definition,

$$|\theta| \equiv \theta_{LC}\theta_{KF} - \theta_{LF}\theta_{KC}$$

Substitute the formal definition of each distributive share (e.g., θ_{LC} is wa_{LC}/p_C) to obtain

$$|\theta| = \frac{wr}{p_C p_F}(a_{LC}a_{KF} - a_{LF}a_{KC})$$

Therefore, $|\theta|$ is positive if clothing is labor intensive. However, because distributive shares in any industry add to unity, θ_{KF} is $1 - \theta_{LF}$, and θ_{KC} is $1 - \theta_{LC}$. Therefore, $|\theta|$ can be written as

$$|\theta| = \theta_{LC} - \theta_{LF}$$

---

[1]This states that an isocost line is tangent to the unit isoquant. Details are provided in the supplement to Chapter 5.

The relationships shown by Equations 6.S.7 and 6.S.8 underlie the shape of the curve in Figure 6.4. Subtract Equation 6.S.8 from Equation 6.S.7 to obtain

$$|\theta| \cdot (\hat{w} - \hat{r}) = (\hat{p}_C - \hat{p}_F) \tag{6.S.9}$$

Thus an increase in labor-intensive clothing's relative price must raise the wage/rent ratio by a magnified amount. Even more can be said: If $\hat{p}_C$ is greater than $\hat{p}_F$ and clothing is labor intensive,

$$\hat{w} > \hat{p}_C > \hat{p}_F > \hat{r}$$

The factor-price changes are magnified reflections of the commodity-price changes. The *Stolper-Samuelson theorem* asserts that an increase in labor-intensive clothing's price (with food prices constant) must unambiguously raise the *real wage*. This follows directly from this chain of inequalities.

If two countries share the same technology and produce both goods in common, free trade in commodities will not only equate commodity prices, it will also result in *factor-price equalization*. Simply treat the variables in Equations 6.S.7 and 6.S.8 as relative differences between countries. Thus, if $\hat{p}_C = \hat{p}_F = 0$ with free trade, then $\hat{w}$ and $\hat{r}$ must be zero.

Equations of Change: Outputs

The pair of full-employment equations suggests that outputs respond both to factor endowment changes and to changes in intensity of techniques. Differentiate Equations 6.S.1 and 6.S.2 totally, and let λ_{ij} refer to the fraction of the total supply of factor i that is employed in commodity j.

$$\lambda_{LC}\hat{x}_C + \lambda_{LF}\hat{x}_F = \hat{L} - (\lambda_{LC}\hat{a}_{LC} + \lambda_{LF}\hat{a}_{LF}) \tag{6.S.10}$$

$$\lambda_{KC}\hat{x}_C + \lambda_{KF}\hat{x}_F = \hat{K} - (\lambda_{KC}\hat{a}_{KC} + \lambda_{KF}\hat{a}_{KF}) \tag{6.S.11}$$

Each equation points out the limitation on outputs provided by the overall endowment of the factor, as well as the intensity with which that factor is used. Consider the changed techniques in clothing: $\hat{a}_{LC}$ and $\hat{a}_{KC}$. Equation 6.S.5 provided one relationship between these two changes. Another follows from the definition of the *elasticity of substitution* between labor and capital in the clothing sector.[2]

$$\sigma_C \equiv \frac{\hat{a}_{KC} - \hat{a}_{LC}}{\hat{w} - \hat{r}} \tag{6.S.12}$$

Solve Equations 6.S.5 and 6.S.12 to obtain

$$\hat{a}_{LC} = -\theta_{KC}\sigma_C(\hat{w} - \hat{r})$$

$$\hat{a}_{KC} = \theta_{LC}\sigma_C(\hat{w} - \hat{r}) \tag{6.S.13}$$

---

[2]You may wonder how the elasticity of substitution, σ_C, is related to the elasticity of labor's marginal product in clothing, γ_{LC}, defined in Equation 5.S.9. Because $\hat{w} - \hat{p}_C$ is equal to $\theta_{KC}(\hat{w} - \hat{r})$, from Equation 6.S.7 or 5.S.5, γ_{LC} equals σ_C divided by θ_{KC}.

Comparable solutions are obtained for changes in the labor and capital coefficients in the food sector—merely replace C with F in the subscripts of Equation 6.S.13.

With these solutions now in hand, reconsider expressions such as $\lambda_{LC}\hat{a}_{LC} + \lambda_{LF}\hat{a}_{LF}$, which shows for the economy as a whole how much of an increase or reduction in labor is required at unchanged outputs. Suppose the wage/rent ratio rises. Both industries will economize on labor. Thus Equations 6.S.10 and 6.S.11 can be rewritten as

$$\lambda_{LC}\hat{x}_C + \lambda_{LF}\hat{x}_F = \hat{L} + \delta_L(\hat{w} - \hat{r}) \qquad (6.S.14)$$

$$\lambda_{KC}\hat{x}_C + \lambda_{KF}\hat{x}_F = \hat{K} - \delta_K(\hat{w} - \hat{r}) \qquad (6.S.15)$$

where

$$\delta_L \equiv \lambda_{LC}\theta_{KC}\sigma_C + \lambda_{LF}\theta_{KF}\sigma_F$$

$$\delta_K \equiv \lambda_{KC}\theta_{LC}\sigma_C + \lambda_{KF}\theta_{LF}\sigma_F$$

Subtract Equation 6.S.15 from Equation 6.S.14 and let

$$|\lambda| \equiv \lambda_{LC} - \lambda_{KC}$$

Then

$$(\hat{x}_C - \hat{x}_F) = \frac{1}{|\lambda|}(\hat{L} - \hat{K}) + \frac{(\delta_L + \delta_K)}{|\lambda|}(\hat{w} - \hat{r}) \qquad (6.S.16)$$

If clothing is labor intensive, $|\lambda|$ is a positive fraction.[3] Finally, substitute the link between factor and commodity prices provided by Equation 6.S.9 to obtain

$$(\hat{x}_C - \hat{x}_F) = \frac{1}{|\lambda|}(\hat{L} - \hat{K}) + \sigma_S(\hat{p}_C - \hat{p}_F) \qquad (6.S.17)$$

where

$$\sigma_S \equiv \frac{\delta_L + \delta_K}{|\lambda||\theta|} > 0$$

Several features of the two-sector production model are revealed by Equation 6.S.17. First, note that σ_S must be positive because δ_L and δ_K are each positive and $|\lambda|$ and $|\theta|$ must have the same sign. If, as is assumed, clothing is labor intensive, both $|\lambda|$ and $|\theta|$ are positive. If clothing were capital intensive, each would be negative, making the product $|\lambda||\theta|$ positive once again. σ_S denotes the elasticity of supply along the bowed-out transformation curve. Second, note that at constant prices the coefficient of $\hat{L} - \hat{K}$ in Equation 6.S.17 reveals how the transformation schedule shifts as factor

---

[3] $|\lambda|$ is clearly the determinant of coefficients in Equations 6.S.14 and 6.S.15. The argument is similar to the one used in discussing $|\theta|$.

endowments change. It confirms the magnification effect of uneven growth of factor endowments on outputs if the terms of trade are constant. If $\hat{L}$ exceeds $\hat{K}$,

$$\hat{x}_C > \hat{L} > \hat{K} > \hat{x}_F$$

If only labor expands, one output must actually fall—the Rybczynski result.[4]

Output Responses to Price Changes: Sector-Specific and Heckscher-Ohlin Models

Outputs are more responsive to price signals in the Heckscher-Ohlin model than in the specific-factor model because all factors are mobile between sectors. The following discussion probes more deeply into each model's expression for the elasticity of supply along the transformation curve, σ_S, to point out the basic similarity and the basic difference between models.[5]

In the Heckscher-Ohlin model, the elasticity of supply with respect to prices was shown by σ_S in Equation 6.S.17. δ_L and δ_K each contain a blend of information on the degree of factor substitutability in the two sectors, σ_C and σ_F. Thus σ_S can be rewritten as

$$\sigma_S = \frac{Q_C \sigma_C + Q_F \sigma_F}{|\lambda||\theta|} \tag{6.S.18}$$

where

$$Q_C \equiv \theta_{LC}\lambda_{KC} + \theta_{KC}\lambda_{LC}$$

$$Q_F \equiv \theta_{LF}\lambda_{KF} + \theta_{KF}\lambda_{LF}$$

Clearly, σ_S is larger the greater is the elasticity of factor substitution for either sector. To simplify, suppose $\sigma_C = \sigma_F = \sigma$. Furthermore, note that

$$Q_C + Q_F + |\lambda||\theta| = 1$$

Therefore in the Heckscher-Ohlin model the assumption of a common degree of factor substitutability in each sector leads to the following as the expression for σ_S:

$$\sigma_S = \frac{1 - |\lambda||\theta|}{|\lambda||\theta|}\sigma \tag{6.S.19}$$

Two features of the model lead to elastic responses of outputs along the transformation schedule: first, a high degree of factor substitutability in each sector (σ), and second, fairly similar factor proportions, as shown by low values for $|\lambda||\theta|$. If factor

---

[4]See the reference in footnote 2 of Chapter 6. This supplement is based on R. W. Jones, "The Structure of Simple General Equilibrium Models," *Journal of Political Economy*, 73 (December 1965): 557–572, reprinted in his *International Trade: Essays in Theory* (Amsterdam: North-Holland, 1979).

[5]More details of this comparison are provided in R. W. Jones, *International Trade: Essays in Theory* (Amsterdam: North-Holland, 1979), Chapter 7.

proportions were identical, $|\lambda||\theta|$ would equal zero. By contrast, if labor were used only in one sector and capital in the other, $|\lambda||\theta|$ would equal 1 and σ_S would be zero.

In the sector-specific model, the expression for σ_S was given in Equation 5.S.14. The elasticities of labor's marginal product curves, γ_{Lj}, are related to the elasticity of factor substitution.[6] Thus γ_{LC} equals σ_C/θ_{KC}, and γ_{LF} equals σ_F/θ_{TF}. As in the Heckscher-Ohlin case, simplify by assuming a common value for $\sigma = \sigma_C = \sigma_F$ because intersectoral differences between σ_C and σ_F do little to change the value of σ_S (in either model). Furthermore, simplify by equating labor shares between sectors. The rationale here is that the Heckscher-Ohlin model focuses on the difference between factor intensities in the two sectors and assumes the *same* degree of factor mobility between sectors. (It assumes that labor and capital are each perfectly mobile between sectors.) By contrast, the sector-specific model focuses on the different degree of factor mobility between factors (labor perfectly mobile, capital—or land—completely immobile). It seems fair, therefore, to allow the same degree of labor intensity between the two sectors as captured by θ_{LC} and θ_{LF}. Thus the share of the specific factor in each industry is the same. Let θ_S denote the common value of θ_{KC} and θ_{TF}.

These simplifications allow σ_S for the sector-specific model in Equation 5.S.14 to be rewritten as

$$\sigma_S = \frac{1 - \theta_S}{\theta_S} \sigma \tag{6.S.20}$$

A comparison with Equation 6.S.19 for the Heckscher-Ohlin model reveals (1) the common role in the two models played by the elasticity of factor substitution, σ, and (2) the focus in the sector-specific model on the importance of sector specificity as captured by θ_S, the share in the national income of specific factors. A greater degree of factor specificity implies a lower value for σ_S, precisely as (in the Heckscher-Ohlin model) a greater disparity in factor proportions implies a low σ_S. Each model is designed to focus on a different feature of the technology, with somewhat analogous results in terms of the response of outputs to prices.

SUPPLEMENT TO CHAPTER 10: Real Incomes, Prices, and the Tariff

Real Incomes and the Optimum Tariff

Recall from the supplement to Chapter 2 the basic expression for the change in the home country's level of real income, dy, in terms of the domestic price-weighted sum of consumption changes. This was Equation 2.S.10, reproduced here.

$$dy = dD_C + pdD_F \tag{10.S.1}$$

This expression needs no modification in the case of tariffs, for it rests on the simple notion that real income depends only on the quantities of each commodity consumed

---

[6]See footnote 2.

and the relative valuation at the margin of one commodity in terms of another, as reflected in the *domestic* relative price of food, p.

The home country's budget constraint indicates the source of a change in real incomes. With a tariff, however, the budget constraint can be written either in terms of domestic or world prices. It is instructive to look at each in turn.

In terms of domestic prices, aggregate spending at home, $D_C + pD_F$, is limited to the value of income, which is derived both from income earned in producing commodities, $x_C + px_F$, and from the proceeds of the tariff revenue. In the case of ad valorem tariffs, revenue depends on the home country's quantity of food imports, M, the foreign relative price of imports, p^*, and the tariff rate, t, and is the product of these three terms:

$$D_C + pD_F = x_C + px_F + tp^*M \qquad (10.S.2)$$

Figure 10.4 illustrates this form of the budget constraint with all items measured in food units instead of clothing units. With post-tariff consumption at J, the aggregate value of incomes at domestic prices is $0E$, the value of incomes earned in production is shown by $0C$, and CE is the tariff revenue.

Consider, now, a small change in the tariff rate. This change leads to changes in prices, the consumption bundle, and production so that

$$dD_C + pdD_F + D_Fdp = dx_C + pdx_F + x_Fdp + d(tp^*M)$$

Shift D_Fdp to the right-hand side to obtain

$$dD_C + pdD_F = -Mdp + (dx_C + pdx_F) + d(tp^*M) \qquad (10.S.3)$$

Note that the left-hand side is, by the definition given in Equation 10.S.1, the increase in the home country's real income, dy. Furthermore, the expression $dx_C + pdx_F$ on the right-hand side must vanish, because the slope of the transformation schedule, dx_F/dx_C, must equal the negative of clothing's relative *domestic* price, $1/p$.[1] Thus Equation 10.S.3 can be simplified as

$$dy = -Mdp + d(tp^*M) \qquad (10.S.4)$$

That is, the sources of any real income gain to the home country are to be found in (1) a change in the domestic relative price of imports, dp, where any decrease in this price will raise real incomes at home by a factor given by the volume of imports, M; and (2) any increase in the tariff revenue, $d(tp^*M)$.

This provides one decomposition of real income changes, highlighting *domestic* prices and tariff revenue. An alternative, but equivalent expression, one emphasizing *world* prices (the terms of trade), is more frequently used in the literature. Expenditure and income are related by world prices. The domestic relative price of food, p, is given by $(1 + t)p^*$; substituting this quantity into Equation 10.S.2, and noticing that M is given by excess food demand, $D_F - x_F$, results in

$$D_C + p^*D_F = x_C + p^*x_F \qquad (10.S.5)$$

---

[1]See the supplement to Chapter 2 for a more complete account.

This equation states that at *world* prices the value of the home country's consumption bundle exactly equals the value of its production bundle. This equality is illustrated in Figure 10.4 by the fact that the post-tariff consumption bundle, J, and production bundle, B, both lie on line 4, whose slope, $-(1/p^*)$, indicates the world terms of trade. Differentiate 10.S.5 to obtain

$$dD_C + p^*dD_F = -Mdp^* + (dx_C + p^*dx_F)$$

Add and subtract pdD_F on the left-hand side and pdx_F on the right-hand side. This yields

$$(dD_C + pdD_F) + (p^* - p)dD_F = -Mdp^* + (dx_C + pdx_F) + (p^* - p)dx_F$$

As already explained, $dD_C + pdD_F$ is the definition of the increase in real income at home, and $dx_C + pdx_F$ vanishes if resources are allocated at the optimal point along the transformation schedule. Because the change in imports, dM, is equal to $dD_F - dx_F$, the entire expression reduces to

$$dy = -Mdp^* + (p - p^*)dM \qquad (10.S.6)$$

It is difficult to overestimate the importance of the breakdown represented by Equation 10.S.6 in understanding the welfare significance of tariffs. The first term, $-Mdp^*$, is the terms-of-trade effect, now stated in terms of world prices. Any policy that depresses the relative price at which the home country can purchase its imports in the world market will favorably affect welfare at home by an amount proportional to the volume of imports. If trade is impeded, however, as it will be if a tariff exists, the second term, $(p - p^*)dM$, must also be taken into account. $(p - p^*)$ is the tariff wedge—it is the discrepancy (tp^*) between the relative domestic price of imports and the world price of imports. This second term indicates that any increase in the home country's level of imports must increase real income if the cost of obtaining imports in the world market (as shown by p^*) falls short of the relative value of imports in the local market (as shown by p). Any policy pursued by the home country that restricts imports entails a welfare loss if a tariff wedge has raised the domestic (relative) price of imports over the world level. This loss is directly proportional to the extent of the tariff rate.

We are now in a position to develop a formula for the *optimum tariff rate*. In Equation 10.S.6 the expression for dy can be set equal to zero if we are considering small variations in the tariff rate around the optimal rate that maximizes real income. (In Figure 10.6, $dy = 0$ at the optimal tariff rate t_0.) Replace $p - p^*$ by the equivalent expression, tp^*:

$$Mdp^* = tp^*dM$$

Dividing both sides by p^*M, and recalling the use of the hat notation to express relative changes (e.g., $\hat{M}$ is defined as dM/M), the optimal tariff can be expressed as

$$t = \frac{1}{\hat{M}/\hat{p}^*} \qquad (10.S.7)$$

The foreign offer curve remains stationary, but the home offer curve does not. Therefore, if $\hat{M}$, the relative change in the home country's import demand, could be linked to $\hat{M}^*$, the relative change in foreign import demand, the expression for the optimal tariff given by Equation 10.S.7 could be translated into an expression involving ε^*, the elasticity of import demand along the foreign offer curve.

The relationship between M and M^* is simple—it is given by the equilibrium condition of Equation 10.S.8, which states that at world prices the value of the home country's imports is equated to the value of foreign imports (or home country exports).

$$p^*M = M^* \tag{10.S.8}$$

Taking relative changes in Equation 10.S.8 yields

$$\hat{p}^* + \hat{M} = \hat{M}^* \tag{10.S.9}$$

Therefore $\hat{M}/\hat{p}^*$ equals $(\hat{M}^*/\hat{p}^*) - 1$. But $\hat{M}^*/\hat{p}^*$ is merely the definition of ε^*, the elasticity of the foreign country's demand for imports along its offer curve.[2] This shows that the formula for the optimum tariff given in Equation 10.S.7 can be rewritten as

$$t = \frac{1}{\varepsilon^* - 1} \tag{10.S.10}$$

This formula needs to be interpreted carefully. It seems to state that if the foreign offer curve is inelastic ($\varepsilon^* < 1$) the tariff should be negative. This interpretation of the relationships underlying the formula would be incorrect. Reconsider Equation 10.S.6. If the foreign offer curve is inelastic, an increase in the tariff would cause home imports to increase. The terms of trade improve for the home country, and with ε^* less than 1, foreigners offer more food for export. (See the discussion in the appendix to Chapter 10.) On both counts dy in Equation 10.S.6 must be positive. The home country should raise its tariff until it reaches the elastic stretch of the foreign offer curve. Only then will a favorable movement in the terms of trade be countered by an unfavorable cutback in the volume of imports.

The Impact of Tariffs on World and Domestic Prices

Tariffs create wedges between domestic import prices and world prices. A natural presumption is that the imposition of a tariff drives up the price of imports at home relative to other goods while it depresses the world price. As we shall see, this may not always follow. What is required is an explicit solution for each of these price changes, and a sharp distinction must be drawn between shifts of demand curves and movements along demand curves.

---

[2]This elasticity formulation was introduced in Chapter 2. Because $1/p^*$ is the relative price of the foreign country's import (clothing), ε^* is defined as *minus* $\hat{M}^*$ divided by $(\widehat{1/p^*})$, which is equivalent to *plus* $\hat{M}^*/\hat{p}^*$.

Equation 10.S.9 revealed the equations of change that can be used to solve for the change in world prices, $\hat{p}^*$. The change in foreign imports, $\hat{M}^*$, is captured by movements along the foreign offer curve because our tariff does not cause their demand curve to shift. Thus

$$\hat{M}^* = \varepsilon^* \hat{p}^* \tag{10.S.11}$$

The expression for $\hat{M}$ is more complicated. A change in the tariff rate shifts the home country's offer curve. Therefore $\hat{M}$ will exhibit a mixture of such a shift and a move along the home country's offer curve. Specifically, the home offer curve is shown as $M = M(p^*, t)$ and the rate of change can be decomposed as follows:

$$\hat{M} = -\varepsilon\, \hat{p}^* + \beta dt \tag{10.S.12}$$

where β, defined literally as $(1/M)(\partial M/\partial t)$, is the shift in the home country's offer curve at given world terms of trade. One of the primary objectives is to develop an explicit expression for β to guarantee that it is negative. Figure 10.5 showed that an increase in t would reduce imports at given world terms of trade.

Substituting Equation 10.S.11 for $\hat{M}^*$ and Equation 10.S.12 for $\hat{M}$ into Equation 10.S.9 yields the following solution for the effect of a tariff on world terms of trade.

$$\hat{p}^* = \frac{1}{\Delta} \beta dt \tag{10.S.13}$$

where

$$\Delta = \varepsilon + \varepsilon^* - 1$$

The expression Δ captures the Marshall-Lerner condition for market stability discussed in the supplement to Chapter 3. Assuming the market to be stable, the sum of import-demand elasticities must exceed unity, and Δ must therefore be positive. Thus, if the home country's offer curve shifts inward (β will be shown to be negative), the world relative price of our import falls.

Home prices are linked to foreign prices by the tariff rate: $p = (1 + t)p^*$. Assuming that trade is initially free, taking relative changes in these terms yields

$$\hat{p} = \hat{p}^* + dt \tag{10.S.14}$$

With the solution for the terms-of-trade change, $\hat{p}^*$, given by Equation 10.S.13, the next step is to substitute to obtain the solution for the change in the relative domestic price of imports, $\hat{p}$:

$$\hat{p} = \frac{1}{\Delta}(\Delta + \beta)dt \tag{10.S.15}$$

Although Δ is positive, this discussion has maintained (and will subsequently prove) that β is negative. This argument underscores the doubts expressed in the text concerning whether an increase in t must protect the import-competing industry.

Elasticity and Shift of the Home Offer Curve

To simplify matters at this stage, continue to assume that initially there is free trade so the initial value of t is zero.[3] The forces at work along the home country's offer curve were displayed in Equation 2.S.17 for the home elasticity of import demand:

$$\varepsilon = \bar{\eta} + e + m$$

An improvement in the terms of trade encourages imports by (1) causing consumers to *substitute* toward the now-cheaper imports ($\bar{\eta}$); (2) causing resources to be allocated away from now-cheaper import-competing goods toward exports (e); and (3) raising real incomes, with part of the gain spilling over to importables (m).

The *shift* in the home offer curve reveals the forces encouraging a reduced volume of imports *at the initial terms of trade* as the tariff is raised. The hike in t at initial p^* raises domestic p and thus reduces imports via a substitution effect in consumption, $\bar{\eta}$, and a substitution effect in production, e. However, because the terms of trade are unchanged, so is real income; thus the (m) term in ε is missing from the shift. The reason: Because trade is initially free ($p^* = p$ initially), the expression for real income changes reduces to the terms-of-trade effect,

$$dy = -Mdp^*$$

which is zero if the terms of trade are held constant. That is, the *shift* in the offer curve is shown by

$$\beta = -(\bar{\eta} + e) \tag{10.S.16}$$

The Metzler Tariff Paradox

It is now possible to develop an explicit criterion for the paradoxical case in which a tariff so depresses the terms of trade that the relative domestic price of imports falls as well. Substitute the expression for β in Equation 10.S.16 into the expression for $\hat{p}$ in Equation 10.S.15 to obtain

$$\hat{p} = \frac{1}{\Delta}(\varepsilon + \varepsilon^* - 1 - \bar{\eta} - e)dt$$

Given the breakdown of home ε, the solution for $\hat{p}$ is

$$\hat{p} = \frac{1}{\Delta}(\varepsilon^* + m - 1)dt \tag{10.S.17}$$

The argument in Chapter 10 suggested that a tariff could fail to protect if the foreign import demand elasticity, ε^*, were sufficiently small. Equation 10.S.17 reveals that the critical value for this elasticity is $(1 - m)$ or, more simply, the country's propensity to consume its export commodity.

---

[3]A more general treatment is provided in R. W. Jones, "Tariffs and Trade in General Equilibrium: Comment," *American Economic Review*, 59 (June 1969): 418–424.

The appendix to Chapter 10 shows, in Figure 10.A.2, an offer curve diagram in which the Metzler tariff paradox may hold. The razor's-edge case in which the income-consumption curve is tangent at Q to the foreign offer curve, $0_T R^*$, corresponds to ε^* being equal to $1 - m$ in Equation 10.S.17.

SUPPLEMENT TO CHAPTER 11: Tariffs, Growth, and Welfare

This supplement continues the algebraic analysis of tariffs initiated in the supplement to Chapter 10. It provides a formal proof of the fact that the maximum-revenue tariff rate exceeds the optimal rate. For a given degree of protection, a criterion is developed relating growth to welfare changes. Finally, a broader analysis of the tariff, making use of matrix algebra, allows an easy overview of the question of gains from trade and commercial policy.

The Maximum-Revenue Tariff

The supplement to Chapter 10 expressed the home country's budget constraint in terms of domestic prices (see Equation 10.S.2). When differentiated, this expression led to an expression for the change in real income in terms of the change in the domestic price ratio and the tariff revenue. This was Equation 10.S.4, reproduced here.

$$dy = -Mdp + d(tp^*M) \tag{11.S.1}$$

Consider this expression in conjunction with Figure 11.1. The optimal tariff rate is t_0, and the optimal tariff formula (Equation 10.S.10) showed that near t_0, the foreign offer curve must be elastic. This means that the tariff must be protective in the sense of raising p with a small further increase in t. Thus the $-Mdp$ term in Equation 11.S.1 is negative in the neighborhood of the optimum tariff, where dy equals zero. As a consequence, $d(tp^*M)$ must be positive. That is, at rate t_0 in Figure 11.1, the curve plotting the tariff revenue against the tariff rate must be positively sloped. Tariff revenue reaches a maximum at the higher rate, t_2.

Growth with Protection

The supplement to Chapter 3 analyzed the possibility of *immiserizing growth*—a situation in which expansion of a country's production of exportables during the growth process causes such a deterioration in the terms of trade that the community's welfare actually falls.

Examine here the case of a country with fixed tariff rates and *given world prices*. For some reason (growth of resources, improvement in technology) the country's transformation schedule shifts outward, so that at the fixed domestic prices (given world prices adjusted for fixed tariff rates) aggregate output expands. The budget constraint is shown by

$$D_C + p^* D_F = x_C + p^* x_F \tag{11.S.2}$$

(This repeats Equation 10.S.5.) Differentiation leads to

$$dD_C + p^*dD_F = dx_C + p^*dx_F \tag{11.S.3}$$

Note there is no terms-of-trade effect because p^* is assumed constant. Add and subtract pdD_F on the left-hand side.

$$(dD_C + pdD_F) + (p^* - p)dD_F = dx_C + p^*dx_F$$

The first expression in parentheses is, of course, the change in home real income, dy. The change in home consumption of food, dD_F, can only be explained by income effects because domestic prices are constant. That is, with the home country's marginal propensity to import food denoted by m,

$$dD_F = \frac{m}{p}dy$$

The fraction $(p^* - p)/p$ is minus $t/(1 + t)$ so that

$$\left(1 - m\frac{t}{1 + t}\right)dy = dx_C + p^*dx_F \tag{11.S.4}$$

This expression provides the criterion with which to judge growth in a protected economy. Real income gains are registered only if growth results in a greater aggregate production *evaluated at world prices.* This may seem paradoxical. The criterion for judging an increase in welfare is to measure consumption changes at *domestic prices,* yet production changes should be evaluated at world prices because world prices measure the trade-off between production and consumption (see Equation 11.S.2). Figure 11.4 illustrated how various possibilities of output expansion from point A—points D, B, C, or E, all showing a 25 percent gain in output at domestic prices—resulted in different real income gains. For point E the value of output actually fell at world prices.

Tariffs, Gains from Trade, and Welfare: A General Analysis

Turn, now, to a different question: How can welfare or real income of an economy be compared in two situations in which prices, quantities traded, and trade restrictions may differ by more than a small amount? There is no restriction on the number of commodities produced or consumed at home or abroad. For notation, x is the vector of quantities produced at home, D is the vector of quantities demanded or consumed, p is the vector of prices ruling in the home country, and p^* is the vector of prices ruling abroad.[1] Not all commodities need be produced at home, so that in the vector $x = (x_1, x_2, \ldots, x_n)$ some entries may be zero. Similarly, not all commodities produced need be demanded locally, so that in the vector $D = (D_1, D_2, \ldots, D_n)$ some entries may also be zero. The two situations to be compared are denoted by a single prime and a double prime. Thus, in the initial situation, home prices are given by the vector $p' = (p_1', p_2', \ldots, p_n')$. This vector may or may not represent a situation in which some international trade takes

[1] The analysis in this section rests heavily on Michihiro Ohyama, "Trade and Welfare in General Equilibrium," *Keio Economic Studies,* 9 (1972): 37–73.

place. In the second situation prices have altered at home to $p'' = (p_1''\ p_2'', \ldots, p_n'')$. Let the vector E represent the home country's set of *excess demands:*

$$E \equiv D - x$$

An element E_i in the vector E is positive if commodity i is imported at home, negative if i is exported, and zero if high transport costs or tariffs result in no international exchange of the ith commodity.

The basic criterion by which welfare in the double-prime situation is contrasted to welfare in the single-prime situation involves a comparison of the value of aggregate demand in each, when the prices used for the evaluation are in both instances those of the double-prime situation. Thus welfare is deemed to have risen if

$$p''D'' - p''D' > 0 \qquad (11.S.5)$$

This inequality states that if the initial bundle of goods consumed, D', could have been purchased in the double-prime situation, the community is assumed to have increased its real income.

This assumption is illustrated for the two-commodity case in Figure 11.S.1. The fact that the consumption bundle in the single-prime situation, D', lies below the line showing prices in the double-prime situation (and supporting demand, D'') is taken as a sufficient criterion for establishing that point D'' represents a higher level of welfare. Clearly, if indifference curves do not intersect, point D' must lie on a lower indifference curve than point D''.

The vector of excess demands equals the vector of total demands minus the vector of production. Turn this equation around to state that demand equals excess demand *plus* production. Making this substitution for both the single-prime and the double-prime situations in the improvement in welfare criterion, Inequality 11.S.5, yields the following inequality as an equivalent expression.

$$p''(E'' - E') + p''(x'' - x') > 0 \qquad (11.S.6)$$

FIGURE 11.S.1

The Welfare Criterion for Two Commodities

Two alternative consumption bundles are illustrated: D' and D''. The prices ruling when D'' is consumed are shown by line p''. The welfare criterion whereby situation double-prime is superior to situation single-prime is shown by the fact that D' lies below line p'', which means $p''D'' - p''D' > 0$.

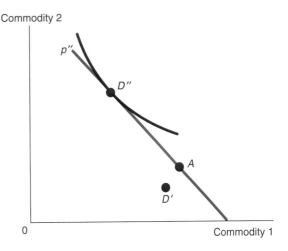

Prices at home in the double-prime situation will differ from prices abroad for any traded commodity that is subject to a tariff, an export tax, or a subsidy in the home country. Let the matrix T'' represent these taxes and/or trade subsidies. T'' is a *diagonal matrix*, all of whose elements are zero except the diagonal terms. What does the entry t_i'' represent? This depends on whether commodity i is imported (E_i positive), in which case a positive t_i'' represents a tariff and a negative t_i'' an import subsidy, or exported (E_i negative), in which case an export tax is a negative t_i'' and an export subsidy a positive t_i''. In short, $t_i'' p_i^{*''} E_i''$ is positive if the government collects tax revenue and negative if the government is subsidizing a trade flow. For any commodity i

$$p_i'' = (1 + t_i'')p_i^{*''}$$

where $p_i^{*''}$ is the world price of commodity i. This can be summarized in matrix notation by making use of the identity matrix, I, whose off-diagonal elements are all zero, and with 1's all along the diagonal.

$$p'' = (I + T'')p^{*''} \tag{11.S.7}$$

The home country's budget constraint states that the value at world prices of aggregate excess demand is zero, both for the double-prime and single-prime situations.

$$p^{*''}E'' = 0 \tag{11.S.8}$$

$$p^{*'}E' = 0 \tag{11.S.9}$$

Furthermore, if the single-prime situation refers to the pretrade situation at home, each element of the vector E' would have to equal zero because in equilibrium, local demand would have to be balanced by local sources of supply.

All the ingredients are now at hand to transform the welfare criterion, Inequality 11.S.6, into an explicit listing of the sources of an improvement in real incomes. To proceed, merely substitute the relationship shown in Equation 11.S.7 between domestic and world prices into the first term in Inequality 11.S.6.

$$p''(E'' - E') = (I + T'')p^{*''}(E'' - E')$$

This expression, in turn, equals

$$p^{*''}E'' - p^{*''}E' + T''p^{*''}(E'' - E')$$

Notice, however, that by Equation 11.S.8, $p^{*''}E''$ vanishes. This statement of the budget constraint at world prices applies as well to the single-prime situation (shown by Equation 11.S.9), and thus allows $p^{*'}E'$ (equal to zero) to be added to the expression. Thus rewritten, the expression becomes

$$-(p^{*''} - p^{*'})E' + T''p^{*''}(E'' - E')$$

Substitute this expression for $p''(E'' - E')$ back into Inequality 11.S.6 to obtain the basic welfare criterion.

$$-(p^{*''} - p^{*'})E' + T''p^{*''}(E'' - E') + p''(x'' - x') > 0 \tag{11.S.10}$$

Each of the three terms in this inequality should be familiar from the preceding discussion.

1. The term $-(p^{*\prime\prime} - p^{*\prime})E'$ is the terms-of-trade effect. If the two primed situations represent different trading equilibria that are very close to each other, and if only one relative price (because only two commodities) exists, it is shown by the $-M dp^*$ term in Equation 10.S.6. The general expression states that the community's welfare improves to the extent that the world price falls for any commodity imported ($E_i' > 0$), or rises for any commodity exported ($E_i' < 0$).

2. The term $T'' p^{*\prime\prime}(E'' - E')$ measures the change in the volume of trade for all commodities for which domestic prices, p'', differ from world prices, $p^{*\prime\prime}$. The term $T'' p^{*\prime\prime}$ is the tariff wedge. Returning again to the case in which only two commodities are traded (and the two situations are very close to each other), we see that this term reduces to the $(p - p^*)dM$ term in Equation 10.S.6. It states in general that real income is improved if the level of imports increases for any commodity worth more at home (as indicated by p'') than it costs to obtain in world markets (as indicated by $p^{*\prime\prime}$).

3. The term $p''(x'' - x')$ must in any case be greater than or equal to zero. It shows the change in real income attributable to the change in production. In the absence of distortions, x'' is the point on the transformation schedule that maximizes the value of output at domestic prices when these are given by p''. Therefore, the value of any other production possibility, say x', at these prices (p''), must be less. If the single-prime and double-prime situations are very close together in the two-commodity model, this term reduces to $dx_C + p dx_F$. As was argued in Chapter 2 and subsequently, this reduction approaches zero as an expression of the equality between the domestic price ratio and the slope of the transformation schedule.

This line of reasoning has been useful in comparing two states of trade, differing from each other in prices—perhaps as a result of changes in tariffs. It is also useful in comparing a state of trade (in the double-prime situation) with the pretrade situation. In such a case each element in the vector E' goes to zero. The welfare criterion, Inequality 11.S.10, then assumes the special form

$$T'' p^{*\prime\prime} E'' + p''(x'' - x') > 0 \qquad (11.S.11)$$

Because the production term, $p''(x'' - x')$, must be nonnegative, as was just argued, this criterion yields a powerful result. Suppose that a complex mixture of tariffs and trade subsidies exists. Is the community better off than with no trade? The question needs to be raised because an export subsidy by itself can reduce welfare at home—this is akin to giving something away. The term $T'' p^{*\prime\prime} E''$ represents the *net* tariff and subsidy revenue to the home government. The criterion reveals that regardless of the pattern of subsidies, if this net revenue is positive, trade must be superior to no trade.[2] Note that it

---

[2]This result is derived in M. Ohyama, "Trade and Welfare in General Equilibrium."

is *sufficient* that the net revenue be positive for the double-prime situation to represent an improvement. However, even if net revenue is negative, it is possible for D'' to be preferred to D'.

This result, that trade distorted by the presence of trade taxes and subsidies is nonetheless superior to autarky as long as the net tariff revenue is positive, is illustrated in Figure 11.S.2. The tax-distorted consumption equilibrium at point G is similar to that illustrated in Figure 10.4's standard depiction of the effect of a tariff on real incomes. Price lines labeled P show a higher relative domestic price for importables than does price line P^*, which reflects world prices. Behind the tax barriers, producers select point A and consumers choose G; these points have equal value at world prices, but the value of the consumption bundle at domestic prices exceeds the value of production by the amount of the net tariff revenue. Key to the argument that distorted trade with positive net tariff revenue is superior to autarky is the comparison between consumption point N, which would be selected if domestic price line P indicated world prices (i.e., tariff revenues were zero), and autarky bundle H. If the country were offered terms-of-trade P, differing from autarky prices (the slope at H), the country would gain. If, in addition, consumers were provided a boost to their disposable incomes in the form of a positive net tariff revenue, real incomes (at G) would rise even further. Indeed, even if, on net, the budget line were reduced slightly below line NA, reflecting a small negative tax revenue (subsidies exceeding taxes), trade might be preferable to autarky, but a sufficient condition for distorted trade to lead to gains over autarky is a positive value for net tariff revenue.

FIGURE 11.S.2

Positive Tax Revenue
Leads to Gains

Domestic prices, represented
by the *P* lines, are distorted
from world prices, shown
by the *P** line. Production
is at *A*, consumption at *G*.
N is superior to autarky
bundle *H*, as is *G*, as long
as net tariff revenue is
positive.

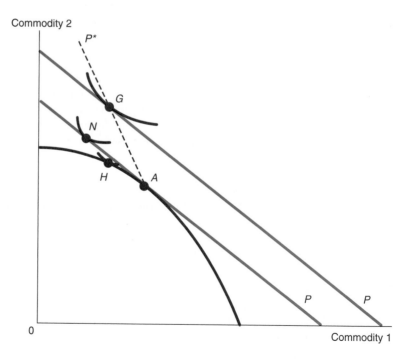

SUPPLEMENT TO CHAPTER 12: Imperfect Competition, Trade Restrictions, and Welfare

The supplement to Chapter 10 developed an expression for the way in which a country's aggregate real income is affected by changes in levels of protection when markets are perfectly competitive. The basic statement was contained in Equation 10.S.6, which showed how an increase in the rate of protection might aid by improving a country's *terms of trade* (lowering p^*, the relative world price of imports), but most likely at the expense of lowering the *volume of trade* (a negative dM), in a situation in which protection has raised the domestic price of imports, p, above the world price, p^*. The domestic price reflects the value to the home country of obtaining another unit of imports, whereas the foreign price indicates the real cost of obtaining another unit of imports. When elements of imperfect competition characterize home markets for importables or exportables, the breakdown of real income changes for competitive markets shown in Equation 10.S.6 needs to be supplemented to take into account the fact that any change in the economy's composition of outputs also affects aggregate welfare.

A useful starting point is the statement that, when evaluated at world prices, the economy's aggregate consumption bundle must match the value of aggregate production. (The rationale: At world prices the value of exports equals the value of imports under the assumption that trade is balanced.) Returning to the standard two-commodity model, this is the relationship shown in Equation 10.S.5, reproduced here:

$$D_C + p^*D_F = x_C + p^*x_F \tag{12.S.1}$$

Proceeding as in the supplement to Chapter 10, total differentiation of both sides and a subsequent addition and subtraction of pdD_F on the left-hand side and pdx_F on the right-hand side yields

$$(dD_C + pdD_F) + (p^* - p)dD_F = -Mdp^* + (dx_C + pdx_F) + (p^* - p)dx_F$$

As in previous discussions, the country is assumed to import food (M). The expression can be simplified, as the change in the economy's level of real income, dy, is the first expression, $(dD_C + pdD_F)$, and the wedge separating foreign and home food prices, $(p^* - p)$, multiplied by the changes in consumption, dD_F, and local production, dx_F, can be combined to yield

$$dy = -Mdp^* + (p - p^*)dM + (dx_C + pdx_F) \tag{12.S.2}$$

The first two terms of Equation 12.S.2 are familiar from the tariff analysis in the supplement to Chapter 10, corresponding to the terms-of-trade effect and the volume-of-trade effect, respectively. Of course, a tariff that improves the terms of trade usually does so at the expense of a cutback in imports. The optimal rate of tariff in the absence of monopoly pricing involves a trade-off between the terms-of-trade effect and the volume-of-trade effect. In a competitive market setting, the final term, $(dx_C + pdx_F)$, vanishes. However, if competition locally is less than perfect, the relative price does not reflect the ratio of marginal costs. Let c denote the ratio of the marginal cost of producing food to the marginal cost of producing clothing, that is, the marginal opportunity cost of producing food (much as p denotes the relative domestic price of food). The term $(dx_C + cdx_F)$ equals zero because the slope of the transformation schedule indicates, in general, marginal opportunity costs. Therefore, Equation 12.S.2 can be written as

$$dy = -Mdp^* + (p - p^*)dM + (p - c)dx_F \qquad (12.S.3)$$

The last term in this equation reveals that if markets are imperfectly competitive at home, even small changes in the composition of output have welfare consequences. This exposes the basis for *industrial policy* in managing a nation's commercial policy instruments. Suppose, for example, that a local monopoly in producing food has caused its price to exceed marginal costs. Consider a tariff initially set at a rate that would be optimal for a *competitive* economy—that is, a rate for which any further increase in the tariff would cause a volume-of-trade loss just balancing the terms-of-trade gain. Equation 12.S.3 suggests that if competition is less than perfect in the import-competing food sector, a further increase in the tariff rate would still contribute positively to national welfare because it would encourage a reallocation of resources toward producing more of the importable (food)—the value of food locally, p, exceeds its marginal cost of production, c. Tariff policy thus may have a further dimension—it provides a second-best means of encouraging output in a sector in which the existence of monopoly power has curtailed output below the competitively optimal level.

Figure 12.1 showed an initial equilibrium at point B or B' on the transformation curve when food production is characterized by local monopolistic behavior. (The clothing sector is competitive, with price equal to marginal cost.) With the domestic price of food exceeding marginal cost, the budget line showing domestic prices at B or B' is flatter than the transformation schedule, so any policy encouraging a reallocation of resources in favor of food production tends to raise national income.

Suppose, instead, that some element of local monopoly control exists in the export sector (clothing), so that at an initial free-trade equilibrium the relative domestic price of food falls short of its relative marginal cost. If the country can improve its terms of trade with a tariff, Equation 12.S.3 reveals that the temptation to pursue a protectionist policy is limited both by the volume-of-trade effect once the tariff is sufficiently high and by the deleterious effect on welfare of an expansion in the competitive import-competing sector (food). If the volume of trade is somewhat limited (small value of M), and if the discrepancy between relative food price, p, and cost, c, is relatively large in absolute value (p lies below c if clothing is the monopolistic sector), the country may find free trade a better policy than any tariff level despite the forgone terms-of-trade improvement.

Expressions such as Equation 12.S.3 are useful in appraising the welfare consequences of the use of various instruments of commercial policy. In some cases, simplifications of the expression are allowed or modifications required. For example, suppose a small country has no influence on its terms of trade—then the first term in Equation 12.S.3 vanishes. If an import quota has been imposed and is binding, a loosening up of quota restrictions directly raises welfare as the volume of allowed imports increases. In such a setting the domestic price of food will fall as foreign sources supply a larger share of the home market, and this encourages local demand (a welfare gain). Because the change in imports equals the change in demand less the change in local supply, the last two terms in Equation 12.S.3 can be rewritten as

$$(p - p^*)dD_F + (p^* - c)dx_F$$

Thus a loosening of quota restrictions encourages demand, which raises welfare but cuts back on local production. Of crucial relevance in appraising the consequences of such a cut is the relationship between the *world* price of food and local marginal costs. Even if domestic price exceeds marginal cost (with a local imperfectly competitive food industry), if world price is lower than marginal cost, the cutback in food production further improves welfare.

Finally, note the modifications required if the country has restricted imports with VERs (voluntary export restrictions urged on foreign suppliers) instead of quotas. In such a case the home country receives none of the revenue represented by the gap between home and foreign prices. This implies that the first term in Equation 12.S.3 should be replaced by $-Mdp$ because p represents the price the country must pay to foreigners when VERs are imposed, and the second term, $(p - p^*)dM$, is deleted because the spread between home and foreign prices no longer accrues to the home government. One immediate consequence for a small open economy in a competitive setting (so that p^* remains constant and the last term in Equation 12.S.3 can be ignored): Reductions in levels of protection must raise real incomes whether imports have been restricted by quotas or VERs. Reductions in import quotas lead to positive values for $(p - p^*)dM$; reductions in VERs lower the domestic price of importables and thus lead to positive values of $-Mdp$.

Subsidies with International Duopoly

The appendix to Chapter 12 described the potential for a strategic use of a subsidy on exports in a global market characterized by duopoly.[1] Here we provide some of the algebraic underpinning for the result that an export subsidy may be used to raise the real income in the home country.

The setting: Home and foreign country each have a single firm producing a commodity not consumed in either country. In each case the commodity is exported to a third market in which there are no competing producers. Each firm is assumed to have constant marginal costs—c at home and c^* in the foreign country. The home country's government, however, supports its home firm by granting an export subsidy of amount s

---

[1]The pioneering work in this area is by James Brander and Barbara Spencer. In particular see their "International R&D Rivalry and Industrial Strategy," *Review of Economic Studies*, 50 (October, 1983): 707–722, and "Export Subsidies and International Market Share Rivalry," *Journal of International Economics*, 18 (1985): 83–100.

per unit of output, so that *net* marginal costs at home are $c - s$. Demand for the commodity in the third market is given by

$$p = p(q + q*)$$

That is, price depends on total home and foreign output. Each firm is attempting to maximize its profits by picking the appropriate output level, assuming its rival's output remains unchanged (this is the so-called Cournot assumption). Thus marginal revenue for the home firm is $(p + qp')$ and for the foreign firm is $(p + q*p')$, where p' denotes the slope of the market demand curve and is negative. Profit maximization for each firm under the Cournot assumption involves setting marginal revenue equal to marginal cost. The reaction function shown for the home firm in Figure 12.A.1 illustrates how home output rises (for a given subsidy rate) for each unit fall in $q*$. In the case of linear demand (p' is a constant), each unit fall in $q*$ leads to a one-half unit rise in home output, q. The Cournot market equilibrium position is at the point of intersection of these two reaction functions.

An increase in the home government's rate of subsidy, s, to the home firm serves to shift outward the home reaction function in Figure 12.A.1. For a small change in s, ds, this process can be depicted algebraically by differentiating each firm's first-order condition for profit maximization (i.e., an equation matching marginal revenue with (net) marginal cost). Assuming linear demand (i.e., $p'' = 0$), this leads to

$$2p'dq + p'dq* = -ds$$

$$p'dq + 2p'dq* = 0$$

Solving for the change in each firm's output shows dq equal to $\{\frac{2}{3p'}\}ds$ and $dq*$ equal to $\{\frac{1}{3p'}\}ds$. Thus an increase in the subsidy rate raises home output by twice as much as it lowers the foreign firm's output. The subsidy clearly is of benefit to consumers in the third market.

Subsidizing the home firm obviously benefits the home firm as well. But how about real incomes at home, where the increase in the home firm's profits must be offset by the increased export subsidy? The profits of the home firm are given by $[p - (c - s)]q$, and the change in these profits as a consequence of the raised subsidy rate is shown by

$$[p + qp' - (c - s)]dq + qp'dq* + qds$$

The coefficient of dq vanishes by the first-order condition for profit maximization. Because both p' and $dq*$ are negative, the next term, sometimes called the *strategic effect,* must be positive, whereas the last term is clearly positive because it shows the raised subsidy rate on the firm's initial output. Against this expression must be set $(qds + sdq)$, the increase in the government's outlay on export subsidies. The first term, qds, just cancels the last term in the expansion in firm profits. If the subsidy rate were initially zero, the net welfare change for the home country would be just the positive term, $qp'dq*$, the strategic effect. Thus some subsidy is beneficial to the country as a whole. But all good things come in moderation, and too high a rate of subsidy would not be optimal. In Figure 12.A.1 the optimal point for the home country is where one of its isoprofit curves is tangent to the foreign reaction function. The appendix discusses possible counterarguments to the logic that a country can advance its cause by subsidizing the export activities of one of its firms; certainly one such warning would be the possibility that the foreign government retaliates.

SUPPLEMENT TO CHAPTER 16: Import and Export Elasticities

Under what conditions does a devaluation improve the trade balance? The answer when producers are assumed to supply exports and imports with infinite elasticity is the Marshall-Lerner condition. First we prove this. Then we relax the assumption of infinite elasticities.

Proof of the Marshall-Lerner Condition

For notational simplicity, we adopt the normalization $\overline{P} = 1$ and $\overline{P}* = 1$ in the proof of this proposition. Then the trade balance expressed in foreign currency is

$$TB* = (1/E)X_D(E) - M_D(E)$$

Differentiate with respect to E.

$$dTB*/dE = -(1/E^2)X + (1/E)(dX_D/dE) - dM_D/dE$$

Multiply by E^2/X. The derivative is positive if

$$-1 + (E/X)(dX_D/dE) - (E^2/X)(dM_D/dE) > 0$$

Using the definitions of the elasticities,

$$\varepsilon_X \equiv (dX_D/dE)E/X \qquad \varepsilon_M \equiv -(dM_D/dE)E/M,$$

the condition becomes

$$-1 + \varepsilon_X + (EM/X)\varepsilon_M > 0$$

Starting from a position of balanced trade, $EM = X$, the equation reduces to the Marshall-Lerner condition asserted in Chapter 16.

When Supply Elasticities Are Finite

Consider the case where supply of X and M is not infinitely elastic. Figure 16.S.1 illustrates this general case. True, a devaluation still shifts the import demand curve and the export supply curve (which was a horizontal line in Figure 16.2) down. In addition, it remains true that import spending falls and that the effect on export revenue is ambiguous because any given quantity of exports translates into a smaller value when expressed in foreign currency. Thus the basic conclusions are similar, but the relevant condition necessary for the trade balance to improve includes supply as well as demand elasticities. (See Problem 6 at the end of Chapter 16.)

FIGURE 16.S.1

Effect of a Devaluation with Less Than Infinitely Elastic Supply

The devaluation can lower prices when expressed in foreign currency. Panel (a) shows the effect on imports, and (b) shows the effects on exports.

(a) Imports

Price in foreign currency, P^*

$M_S(P^*)$

$M_D(EP^*)$

$M_D(E'P^*)$

0

M

(b) Exports

Price in foreign currency, P/E

$X_S(P)$

$X_S(P)$

$X_D(P/E)$

0

X

SUPPLEMENT TO CHAPTER 19: The Monetarist Two-Country Model of the Balance of Payments

Chapter 19 assumed that the home country's money supply is too small to affect substantially the world money supply or world price level. To be sure, when international reserves are flowing out through a balance-of-payments deficit, the rest of the world is running a balance-of-payments surplus. However, it was assumed that the reserve flow is just a drop in the ocean so far as the rest of the world is concerned. This supplement relaxes the small-country assumption and moves to a two-country world. A domestic monetary expansion will succeed in raising the price level in the world to the extent that it raises the world money supply. As Appendix B mentioned, the two-country model is useful for understanding the gold standard, as well as for understanding the Bretton Woods system, with the United States in the 1960s increasingly playing the role of the country with a balance-of-payments deficit, and Europe the role of the surplus country.[1]

---

[1]The model in this supplement is drawn from the first half of Rudiger Dornbusch, "Devaluation, Money, and Nontraded Goods," *The American Economic Review*, 65, no. 5 (1973): 871–880.

Determination of the Balance of Payments in the Two Countries

We model the foreign country just as we modeled the domestic country in the chapter. The rate of increase of the foreign money supply, H^*, is related to the foreign excess demand for money. The foreign excess demand for money is, in turn, an increasing function of foreign nominal income, or of the foreign price level, with foreign real income determined at $\overline{Y}^*$ by exogenous supply factors, and a decreasing function of the foreign money supply, M^*.

$$H^* \equiv M^* = \delta K \overline{Y}^* P^* - \delta M^* \tag{19.S.1}$$

We multiply through by the exchange rate to work in terms of domestic currency.

$$EH^* = \delta K \overline{Y}^* P^* - \delta E M^* \tag{19.S.2}$$

Here we have applied PPP ($P = EP^*$). Equation 19.S.2 represents the foreign payments surplus measured in domestic currency. Its negative is the domestic payments surplus measured in domestic currency:

$$BP = -EH^* = -\delta K \overline{Y}^* P + \delta E M^* \tag{19.S.3}$$

This is a second equation describing the balance of payments, in addition to Equation 19.5. It represents, for a given foreign money supply, M^*, a negative dependence of the domestic balance of payments on the price level. An increase in the domestic price level under fixed exchange rates is an increase in the world price level. As far as the foreign country is concerned, it raises the foreign demand for money and leads to a foreign payments surplus, which is a domestic payments deficit.

The downward-sloping $BP = -EH^*$ schedule, Equation 19.S.3, is shown in Figure 19.S.1 on the same axes as the upward-sloping $BP = H$ schedule, Equation 19.5. Because both equations must hold, short-run equilibrium is given by the intersection of the two schedules, at point A initially.

Determination of the World Price Level

It is possible to solve the two simultaneous equations for the world price level expressed in domestic currency.

$$\delta K \overline{Y} P - \delta M = \delta K \overline{Y}^* P + \delta E M^*$$

$$P = \frac{M + EM^*}{K(\overline{Y} + \overline{Y}^*)} \tag{19.S.4}$$

The numerator is the total world money supply measured in domestic currency. Considered in the aggregate, Planet Earth is, after all, a closed economy, so it makes sense that the world price level should be proportionate to the world money supply. Equation 19.S.4 is shown in Figure 19.S.1 as a vertical line at the price level P.

The Effect of an Increase in One Country's Money Supply

An increase in the domestic money supply shifts the country's H schedule down by $\delta \Delta M$, precisely the same as in the small-country model of Figure 19.16: An excess supply of money leads to "dishoarding." The H schedule also can be viewed as shifting

FIGURE 19.S.1

Monetary Expansion in the Monetarist, Two-Country Model

A monetary expansion of 1 percent will raise the world price level by ψ percent, where ψ is the domestic country's fraction of the world's money supply. As with a small country (where $\psi = 0$), the expansion shifts the H schedule downward leading to a temporary excess supply of money and balance-of-payments deficit.

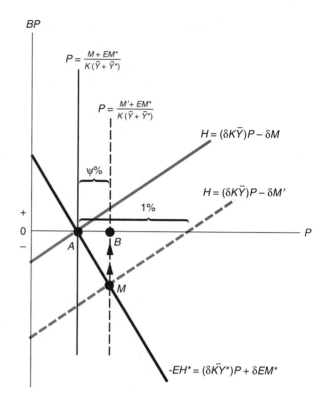

horizontally to the right by the same proportion as the increase in the money supply: If the price level were for some reason to increase by the same proportion as the money supply, the excess supply of money would remain at zero.

When the country was small, the world price level was unchanged; but now it is recognized that the monetary expansion will raise the world price level to the extent that the domestic country is large. Define the domestic country's share in the world money supply.

$$\psi \equiv M/(M + EM^*)$$

A 1 percent increase in the domestic money supply is a ψ percent increase in the world money supply. As shown in Equation 19.S.4, it raises the world price level by ψ percent, whether that is measured in terms of domestic currency, P, or foreign, P^*. In Figure 19.S.1, the monetary expansion shifts to the right not only the domestic H line but the price level line as well. This means that the money demand function must be evaluated at a higher price level, at point M. Under the previous small-country case, ψ was negligible, and so the price level rose negligibly. There was an increase in the money supply of, say, 1 percent, with no increase in money demand. Now there is a 1 percent increase in the money supply with a ψ percent increase in money demand. There is still an excess supply of money (equal to $1 - \psi$ percent of the original money supply), and therefore a balance-of-payments deficit, but they are not as large as in the small-country case.

What is happening in the foreign country? Its money supply has not changed, but it is faced with a ψ percent increase in the price level. Therefore, its demand for money goes up by ψ percent. It has an excess demand for money (equal to ψ percent of its money supply) that is the counterpart of the domestic country's excess supply of money, causing a foreign balance-of-payments surplus that is the counterpart of the domestic country's balance-of-payments deficit.

Over time, the domestic country loses gold to the foreign country. Under the non-sterilization assumption, the domestic money supply falls and the foreign money supply rises. The domestic H schedule shifts upward and the *negative* foreign schedule, $-EH^*$, shifts upward as well. The economy follows a sequence of intersections, moving upward from M along the new price level line. The transfer of money from the home country to the foreign country gradually alleviates the excess demand in the foreign country. Long-run equilibrium is reached when both countries return to a zero balance of payments, at point B. There the supply of money equals the demand for money in both countries. Because the price level has risen by ψ percent in both countries and the demand for money is proportional to the price level, this can only mean that the supply of money has increased by ψ percent in both countries. The world money supply has increased by ψ percent. In the short run the expansion took place entirely in the domestic country, but in the long run it is distributed equiproportionately across both countries.

SUPPLEMENT TO CHAPTER 24: Debt Dynamics

An explosive or unsustainable path for debt is defined as one where the expected ratio of debt to GDP rises without limit. The general framework is known as debt dynamics. We will apply it here to domestic government debt, but it could as easily be applied to foreign debt. For simplicity, assume no inflation.

Define $b \equiv \frac{Debt}{Y}$. We are concerned with the rate of change of this ratio:

$$\frac{db}{dt} = \frac{dDebt/dt}{Y} - \frac{Debt}{Y^2} \, dY/dt$$

$$= \frac{TotalFiscalDeficit}{Y} - \frac{Debt}{Y} \frac{dY/dt}{Y}$$

$$= \frac{primarydeficit + rDebt}{Y} - bn$$

where $n \equiv$ *growth rate*, and the primary deficit is the name for the budget deficit exclusive of interest payments. Therefore,

$$\frac{db}{dt} = d + rb - bn$$

$$= d + (r - n)\, b,$$

where $d \equiv$ *primary deficit*$/Y$. The equation says that to keep the debt ratio from exploding (to avoid $\frac{db}{dt} > 0$), we need either $d < 0$ or $r < n$.

Consider the implications. A country may have a sustainable budget balance one day, and yet if it is hit by a sudden rise in interest rates or fall in the growth rate, through no fault of its own, it can find itself on an unsustainable path. To get back on a sustainable path, it will have to respond by raising the primary budget balance. This means adopting a contractionary fiscal policy at precisely the time when the economy has already slowed down anyway. But the government may have no choice because of the exigencies of international capital markets. This may help explain why so many developing countries exhibit procyclical fiscal policies, rather than the countercyclical policies that would be desired to stabilize the growth rate. The ultimate conclusion is that countries are better off if they do not make themselves vulnerable by high debt ratios in the first place.

SUPPLEMENT TO CHAPTER 25: The Locomotive Theory

This supplement explores the theory of international macroeconomic policy coordination. Table 25.3 illustrated the game of exporting unemployment for the simple case where each country faces a binary choice of expand or contract. Here we present the complete analysis with a continuous range of policy options.

Assume that the United States and Europe seek to attain two objectives, internal balance, $Y = \overline{Y}$, and external balance, $TB = 0$, and that each has only one policy instrument, the money supply, M.[1] Figure 25.S.1 shows how the two countries set their monetary policies, with Europe's money supply, M_E, on the horizontal axis and America's, M_A, on the vertical axis.

First consider the problem from the U.S. point of view. There is some combination of the two money supplies that is optimal from the American viewpoint, represented by point A. A is in the lower right area, indicating that the United States would prefer that the other country do the expanding, enabling the United States to run a trade surplus while maintaining high output.[2] Of course, the other country will not generally set its money supply at the level desired. How should the United States set M_A, if it has to take M_E as given? Radiating out from A are a series of concentric indifference curves representing successive levels of American economic welfare further and further from the optimum. For any given level of M_E, the United States should choose the level of

---

[1]We do the theory with two targets and one instrument, to keep it simple. We could introduce additional policy targets for each country, such as the exchange rate or the CPI. We could also introduce additional policy instruments for each country, such as fiscal policy. But one point to keep in mind is that if each country has as many independent policy instruments as policy targets, then it can obtain its optimum regardless of what the other country does. (Think back to our analysis of internal and external balance in section 22.6.) In this case, a change in American policy has an effect in Europe if European policy makers do not change their policy settings, but it is an effect that they can fully offset if they choose, without cooperation from the United States. Issues of conflict and coordination arise if each country has more targets than it has independent instruments, the usual case.

[2]We will assume for purposes of discussing Figure 25.S.1 that a monetary expansion in one country has a positive effect on the other country's trade balance and income, even though this is true only in some of the models shown in Table 25.2. Otherwise, the curves might look different.

FIGURE 25.S.1

The Gains from International Monetary Coordination

Each country's reaction function indicates how it would set its money supply if it took the other's as given. The Nash noncooperative equilibrium occurs at N. In this case, cooperation would take the form of both countries agreeing to joint monetary expansion. Higher welfare is attained at a cooperative point such as B.

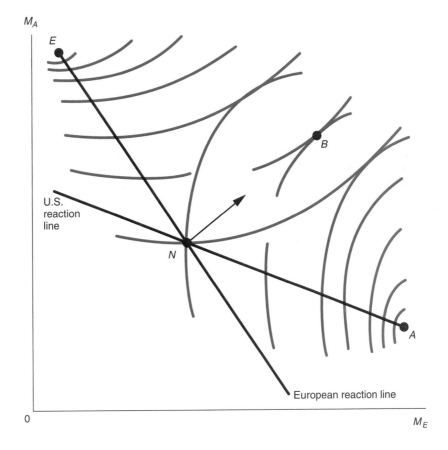

M_A that brings it to the highest indifference curve possible. This will be the point where the vertical line corresponding to M_E is tangent to an indifference curve. Thus, tracing out the set of points where the U.S. indifference curves run vertically will trace out its *reaction line*, which shows how it will set its money supply as a function of Europe's. Notice that, in this diagram, the reaction line is downward sloping: the more Europe withholds monetary expansion, the more America expands to compensate. This is half the story.

Now consider the problem from Europe's viewpoint. Europe's optimum is the point E, located in the upper left area, indicating that Europe, too, would prefer that its trading partner be the one to expand. Successive indifference curves radiate out from

E. How should Europe set M_E, if it takes M_A as given? To get as close to the optimum as possible, it should choose the point where the horizontal line corresponding to M_A is tangent to one of its indifference curves. Thus tracing out the set of points where Europe's indifference curves run horizontally will trace out Europe's reaction line, which shows how it will set its money supply as a function of that of the United States.

The situation without coordination is the Nash noncooperative equilibrium, defined as the point at which each country is setting its money supply at the optimal level, given what the other country is doing. This is represented by point *N* in Figure 25.S.1, where the two reaction lines intersect. It is now clear why the noncooperative point is suboptimal. There is a package of policy changes that will leave both countries better off. As the diagram is drawn, the Pareto-superior package consists of joint expansion by the two countries, moving in the northeastward direction. This illustrates the locomotive theory—that is, each country is afraid to expand on its own for fear of adverse trade balance consequences. (The figure could also have been drawn so that coordination dictated some other combination of policy changes, for example, cooperative discipline in the competitive depreciation game.) This package raises welfare in both countries because it moves both to higher indifference curves. Ideally they will agree to a bargain that is Pareto-optimal—such as point *B* where the indifference curves are tangent—that is, a bargain that maximizes some weighted sum of the two countries' welfares as an omniscient world social planner would do. Any point in the lens-shaped area (the area bounded by the two indifference curves that run through point *N*) will entail gains from cooperation for both countries.

SUPPLEMENT TO CHAPTER 26: Real Wage Indexation

This supplement considers what happens when wages are indexed (either partially or completely) to the CPI:

$$W = \overline{w}\mathrm{CPI}^\delta \tag{26.S.1}$$

where δ is the degree of indexation. If $\delta = 1$, then indexation is complete and the real wage—expressed in terms of the CPI—is fixed at the target level, $W/\mathrm{CPI} = \overline{w}$.

From Equation 26.1, the supply relationship is now

$$(Y/\overline{Y}) = (wP/\overline{w}\mathrm{CPI}^\delta)^\sigma \tag{26.S.2}$$

Assume that the target real wage, $\overline{w}$, is appropriately set to the warranted real wage, w, the one consistent with full employment. Also assume an open economy in which imports have a weight of α in the CPI.

$$\mathrm{CPI} = (SP^*)^\alpha P^{1-\alpha} \tag{26.S.3}$$

where the price of imports is given by the exchange rate, *S*, times the foreign price level, P^*. Substituting Equation 26.S.3 in Equation 26.S.2, the general supply relationship is

$$(Y/\overline{Y}) = [P/(SP^*)^{\alpha\delta}P^{(1-\alpha)\delta}]^\sigma \tag{26.S.4}$$

For simplicity, consider the case where indexation is complete: $\delta = 1$. Then

$$(Y/\overline{Y}) = (P/SP^*)^{\alpha\sigma} \tag{26.S.5}$$

We readily see that real depreciation is contractionary, not expansionary as in a nonindexed economy. A 1 percent decrease in P/SP^* reduces output by $\alpha\sigma$ percent. The reason, as explained in the text, is that a real depreciation that leaves W/CPI unchanged necessarily raises W/P when it raises W. The result is that changes in fiscal policy have real effects. A domestic fiscal expansion that causes a real appreciation because of high capital mobility raises domestic output, Y. Notice that if imports are not important ($\alpha = 0$), there is little effect on Y.

Now consider international transmission in a two-country model. We model the foreign country just like the domestic country.

$$(Y^*/\overline{Y}^*) = (SP^*/P)^{\alpha^*\sigma^*} \tag{26.S.6}$$

Looking at Equations 26.S.5 and 26.S.6 together reveals a remarkable property. The only circumstance that allows an increase in domestic output—a decrease in the real exchange rate SP^*/P—is also the only circumstance that allows a decrease in foreign output. Y and Y^* can vary from their potential output levels, but to the extent that output goes up in one country, it must go down in the other! A fiscal expansion in the foreign country, which raises foreign output to the extent it raises SP^*/P, reduces domestic output to the same extent. The only scope for variation in the real wage comes from real variation in the real exchange rate. This is why what goes up in one country, goes down in the other. This is an extreme case of inverse transmission of policy.

What about monetary policy? Although it remains true that any policy that changes the real exchange rate changes output, a monetary expansion in a completely indexed economy does not succeed in changing the real exchange rate. Rather, a 10 percent increase in the money supply raises S and P proportionately, with no real effects in either country, assuming indexation is complete ($\delta = 1$).[†]

SUPPLEMENT TO CHAPTER 27: The Monetary Model of the Exchange Rate

Flexible-Price Version

This first part of the supplement presents formally the complete model described in Section 27.2: the monetary approach to exchange rate determination with perfectly flexible goods prices.[1] Logarithms are used so that equations that would otherwise be multiplicative come out linear (additive). The PPP equation (Equation 27.3) thus becomes

$$s_t = p_t - p_t^* \tag{27.S.1}$$

[†]This point is explored in Problem 3 in the chapter problems.

[1]See Michael Mussa, "The Exchange Rate, the Balance of Payments, and Monetary and Fiscal Policy Under a Regime of Controlled Floating," and other papers, in Jacob Frenkel and Harry Johnson, eds., *The Economics of Exchange Rates* (Reading, MA: Addison-Wesley, 1978).

where s_t is the log of the exchange rate, p_t is the log of the domestic price level, and p_t^* is the log of the foreign price level. (The equation implies that the percentage change of the exchange rate is equal to the percentage change of the domestic price level minus the percentage change of the foreign price level.) The money demand equations (Equations 27.4 and 27.6) become

$$m_t - p_t = y_t - \mu i_t \tag{27.S.2}$$

$$m_t^* - p_t^* = y_t^* - \mu i_t^* \tag{27.S.3}$$

where m_t and m_t^* are the logs of the countries' money supplies, y_t and y_t^* are the logs of their income levels, and μ is the semielasticity of money demand with respect to the interest rate. (For simplicity, this parameter is assumed to be the same in both countries. Also, the elasticity of money demand with respect to income has been assumed equal to 1, as in the text.) Combining the three equations gives the equation of exchange rate determination:

$$s_t = (m_t - m_t^*) - (y_t - y_t^*) + \mu(i_t - i_t^*) \tag{27.S.4}$$

This is just the logarithmic version of Equation 27.8; indeed, it furnishes the justification for entering the interest rates in difference form in the text. It is easy to see how a 1 percent increase in the domestic money supply causes a 1 percent depreciation of the domestic currency and how anything that causes an increase in the demand for domestic money (a rise in income or fall in the interest rate) has the opposite effect.

The uncovered interest parity condition is

$$i_t - i_t^* = \Delta s_t^e$$

Substitute into Equation 27.S.4 to get the logarithmic version of Equation 27.9.

$$s_t = (m_t - m_t^*) - (y_t - y_t^*) + \mu(\Delta s_t^e) \tag{27.S.5}$$

If the currency is expected to depreciate over the coming period ($\Delta s_t^e > 0$), the result is a low demand for the currency today and a high exchange rate. Under rational expectations it is possible to substitute the rationally expected future exchange rate, $E_t s_{t+1}$ (conditional on information available at time t), in place of the investors' expected rate, s_t^e.

$$s_t = \tilde{m}_t + \mu(E_t s_{t+1} - s_t) \tag{27.S.6}$$

where for ease of notation $\tilde{m} \equiv (m_t - m_t^*) - (y_t - y_t^*)$. The equation can be solved for the current exchange rate, which in Equation 27.S.6 appears on both sides.

$$s_t = \frac{1}{1 + \mu} \tilde{m}_t + \frac{\mu}{1 + \mu} E_t s_{t+1} \tag{27.S.7}$$

This equation shows clearly how a change in expectations can cause today's exchange rate to change, even in the absence of any change in today's macroeconomic fundamentals.

What determines the expected value of next period's exchange rate? Equation 27.S.7 itself. Move it one period into the future and then take the expectation

$$s_{t+1} = \frac{1}{1+\mu}\tilde{m}_{t+1} + \frac{\mu}{1+\mu}E_{t+1}s_{t+2}$$

$$E_t s_{t+1} = \frac{1}{1+\mu}E_t\tilde{m}_{t+1} + \frac{\mu}{1+\mu}E_t s_{t+2} \tag{27.S.8}$$

Equation 27.S.8 can be substituted into Equation 27.S.7 to get today's exchange rate as a function of two-period-ahead expectations.

$$s_t = \frac{1}{1+\mu}\tilde{m}_t + \frac{\mu}{1+\mu}\frac{1}{1+\mu}E_t\tilde{m}_{t+1} + \left(\frac{\mu}{1+\mu}\right)^2 E_t s_{t+2} \tag{27.S.9}$$

Pushing the expectation one step further into the future may not seem very helpful, except that the process can be repeated.

$$E_t s_{t+2} = \frac{1}{1+\mu}E_t\tilde{m}_{t+2} + \frac{\mu}{1+\mu}E_t s_{t+3} \tag{27.S.10}$$

Substitute Equation 27.S.10 into Equation 27.S.9 and continue iteratively to get the following infinite series:

$$s_t = \frac{1}{1+\mu}\left[\tilde{m}_t + \frac{\mu}{1+\mu}E_t\tilde{m}_{t+1} + \left(\frac{\mu}{1+\mu}\right)^2 E_t\tilde{m}_{t+2}\right.$$

$$\left. + \left(\frac{\mu}{1+\mu}\right)^3 E_t\tilde{m}_{t+3} + \cdots\right] \tag{27.S.11}$$

It is now clear that the entire expected future path of the relative money supply matters for determining today's exchange rate. The sum of the series is not infinite (assuming the money process itself is not explosive) because each stage multiplies by a factor $\mu/(1+\mu)$, which is less than 1. Today's exchange rate can be considered as a present discounted sum of future money supplies.

We will use Equation 27.S.11 for three experiments that were also considered in the text. First, what happens if people suddenly decide today that the money supply will be increased by 1 percent at some point T periods into the future? It is immediately clear from Equation 27.S.11 that today's exchange rate will increase by $[1/(1+\mu)]$ $[\mu/(1+\mu)]^T$ percent. The chapter explained why: Forward-looking investors realize that the currency will lose value in the future, so they seek to shift out of it today. This is the case illustrated in Figure 27.1(c).

Second, what happens if the current money supply goes up by 1 percent? It depends how the expectations of future money supplies are affected. If the change in the current money supply is purely transitory (i.e., if the level is expected to go back down next period), then the current exchange rate goes up by $1/(1+\mu)$ percent. The current depreciation is less than proportionate because speculators increase their demand for the currency in the knowledge that it will be gaining value over the *coming* period, thus partly offsetting the effect of the increase in supply.

What if all the future money supplies are expected to be higher by the same 1 percent as the current money supply? This will be the case if the money supply is thought to follow a random walk. (The increase in the level of the expected money supply is permanent, but the increase in the growth rate is transitory.) When $\Delta \tilde{m}_t = \Delta E_t \tilde{m}_{t+1} = \Delta E_t \tilde{m}_{t+2} = \cdots$, then Equation 27.S.11 becomes the sum of a geometric series.[2]

$$\Delta s_t = \frac{1}{1 + \mu}\left[1 + \frac{\mu}{1 + \mu} + \left(\frac{\mu}{1 + \mu}\right)^2 + \cdots\right]\Delta \tilde{m}_t$$

$$= \frac{1}{1 + \mu}\left[\frac{1}{1 - (\mu/1 + \mu)}\right]\Delta \tilde{m}_t = \Delta \tilde{m}_t \quad (27.S.12)$$

In other words, the exchange rate goes up by the same 1 percent as the relative money supply. This is the case illustrated in Figure 27.1(a). When the money supplies follow random walks, the exchange rate moves in proportionate lockstep.

Finally, consider the case where the money supply is expected to rise at a new steady-state growth rate of 1 percent per annum (relative to the foreign money supply and to the countries' real incomes). Then for any period T years in the future, the money supply is expected to be T percent higher. The answer, although we omit its derivation from Equation 27.S.11, is that the effect on today's exchange rate is a depreciation of μ percent. The depreciation occurs at the moment that investors revise their expectation of the money growth rate, as illustrated in Figure 27.1(b). Subsequently, if the money supply does indeed grow at a 1 percent faster rate, as expected, then the exchange rate increases at a 1 percent faster rate from then on. Equation 27.S.5 shows that a 1 percent increase in the rate of expected depreciation causes a μ percent depreciation today.

Recall that μ is the semielasticity of money demand with respect to the rate of return on alternative assets. John Bilson, for example, obtained an estimate of 2.3, for the long-run semielasticity of the mark/pound exchange rate.[3] This estimate implies that when news about faster money growth raises the expected inflation rate by 1.0 percent per annum, the immediate impact on the equilibrium exchange rate is a depreciation of 2.3 percent (even before taking into account any overshooting, of the type discussed in Section 27.4 and the chapter appendix).

The Overshooting Model of the Exchange Rate

We can continue to use logs to represent the monetary model when goods prices are sticky. The assumption that expected real depreciation is formed regressively is written as,

---

[2]Recall that the sum of a geometric series is 1 over the quantity 1 minus the factor that multiplies each term to get the next.

[3]John Bilson, "Rational Expectations and the Exchange Rate," in Jacob Frenkel and Harry Johnson, eds., *The Economics of Exchange Rates*, p. 92.

$$\Delta s^e_{real} = -\theta(s - \bar{s}) \tag{27.S.13}$$

Expected real depreciation is set equal to the real interest differential by international equalization of expected rates of return. Then, solving for the exchange rate shows how the percentage "undervaluation" is related to the real interest differential:

$$s - \bar{s} = -(1/\theta)(r - r^*) \tag{27.S.14}$$

Equation 27.S.14 describes the magnitude of overshooting relative to long-run equilibrium. An increase in the real interest rate makes domestic assets more attractive and causes the currency to appreciate.

An increase in the level of the money supply causes a proportionate increase in the long-run equilibrium exchange rate, as we know from the earlier flexible-price model, and in addition causes the exchange rate to overshoot. The magnitude of the overshooting is $1/\theta$ times the decrease in the interest rate (by Equation 27.S.14), which in turn is $1/\mu$ times the percentage increase in the money supply (by Equation 27.S.2), assuming that y_t as well as p_t is slow to respond. Thus a 1 percent increase in the money supply has a total initial impact on the exchange rate of $[1 + (1/\mu\theta)]$ percent.

SUPPLEMENT TO CHAPTER 28: The Optimally Diversified Portfolio

This supplement develops the theory of optimal portfolio diversification described in Chapter 28.[1] To simplify, assume there are only two assets, euros and dollars. The problem is how investors should allocate their portfolios between these two assets.

Use x to denote the share of the portfolio that investors decide to allocate to euros and $(1 - x)$ to dollars. The ex post real rate of return on the investors' total portfolio, r, is given by

$$r = xr^{€} + (1 - x)r^{\$} \tag{28.S.1}$$

where $r^{€}$ is the ex post real return on euros and $r^{\$}$ is the ex post real return on dollars. The investors care about two things: the mean or average return on their overall portfolio (they want it to be high) and the risk or uncertainty in their overall portfolio (they want it to be low). The average return is measured by the statistical concept of the *expected value,* represented by E; the expected return on the portfolio is given by

$$E(r^{€}) = xE(r^{€}) + (1 - x)E(r^{\$}) \tag{28.S.2}$$

(The E passes right through the x and $1 - x$: The expected value of half of the Dow Jones index is equal to half the expected value of the Dow Jones index.) The risk is measured by the statistical concept of the *variance,* represented by V. Basic properties

---

[1] Two of the papers that spell out optimal diversification of the international portfolio in more detail are Michael Adler and Bernard Dumas, "International Portfolio Choice and Corporation Finance: A Survey," *Journal of Finance,* 38 (1983): 925–984; and Jeffrey Frankel, "In Search of the Exchange Risk Premium: A Six-Currency Test Assuming Mean-Variance Optimization," *Journal of International Money and Finance,* 1 (December 1982): 255–274.

of the variance can be used to show how the variance of the overall portfolio depends on the allocation share, x, and on the individual variances.[2]

$$V(r) = x^2V(r^{\text{€}}) + (1 - x)^2V(r^{\$}) + x(1 - x)2\text{Cov}(r^{\text{€}}, r^{\$}) \qquad (28.\text{S}.3)$$

The last term represents the covariance, which reflects the correlation between the return on euros and the return on dollars. One lesson to be drawn from Equation 28.S.3 is that overall risk, $V(r)$, will be greater if the two returns are highly correlated. Chapter 28 mentioned that investors should be happy if they can hold a pair of assets that have a low correlation.

Consider first the case where the two currencies happen to have the same variances: $V(r^{\text{€}}) = V(r^{\$})$, which will be represented by $\overline{V}$. Is the overall risk in the portfolio the same regardless of the allocation x because each asset has the same variance? The answer is no. Diversification among assets allows investors to reduce their risk.[3] If $x = 1$ (the portfolio is allocated entirely to euros), then $V(r) = V(r^{\text{€}}) = \overline{V}$; and if $x = 0$ (the portfolio is allocated entirely to dollars), then $V(r) = V(r^{\$}) = \overline{V}$; but if x is anything in between, $V(r)$ is lower than $\overline{V}$. This is an example of the gains from diversification.[4] Risk-averse investors will not put all their portfolio into euros, even if the expected return on euros is greater than the expected return on dollars.

Now take the case where the dollar is considered completely safe. This will be the case if the investors are American residents seeking to minimize the risk of their position expressed in terms of dollars. (Perhaps they consume only U.S. goods with prices predetermined in dollars, or perhaps they represent a corporation seeking to minimize variability in terms of dollars for accounting reasons.) The returns expressed in dollars are given by $r^{\$} = i^{\$}$ (the U.S. interest rate) and $r^{\text{€}} = i^{\text{€}} + \Delta s$ (the European nominal interest rate plus the rate of appreciation of the euro against the dollar), respectively. The interest rates are already determined at the time the investors make their decision; this means that their variances are zero. Only the change in the spot exchange rate is uncertain. Equation 28.S.2 for the mean becomes

$$E(r) = x(i^{\text{€}} + E\Delta s) + (1 - x)(i^{\$}) \qquad (28.\text{S}.4)$$

Equation 28.S.3 for the variance reduces to

$$V(r) = x^2V(\Delta s) \qquad (28.\text{S}.5)$$

The expressions for the mean and variance can be used to see how investors will choose x. If they are extremely risk averse, caring little for expected returns and seeking only to minimize variance, then they will choose $x = 0$ because that way they can

---

[2] The variance of r is defined as $E(r - Er)^2$. If this concept is unfamiliar, notice that it indicates how far away (by the square of the distance) r is from Er, on average. Two properties are needed to derive Equation 28.S.3: The variance of x times a random variable is equal to x^2 times the variance of the variable; and the variance of the sum of two variables is equal to the sum of the variances of the two variables, plus 2 times the covariance.
[3] The one exception arises where the returns on the two securities are perfectly correlated. In that case, it is not possible to reduce risk at all by diversification because holding one is just like holding the other. [Exercise: Find $V(r)$ in Equation 28.S.3 when $\text{Cov}(r^{\text{€}}, r^{\$}) = V(r^{\text{€}}) = V(r^{\$})$. Does it depend on x?]
[4] Assume for simplicity that the covariance is zero. Then $V(r) = x^2\overline{V} + (1 - x)^2\overline{V}$. The variance of the overall portfolio is minimized by setting $x = \frac{1}{2}$. You are asked to show this in Problem 3 at the end of Chapter 28.

attain $V(r) = 0$. In other words, they will hold no euros at all, only dollars. This makes sense because of the assumption that they view the dollar as entirely safe.

In general, however, investors care about both the mean and variance. Assume that they seek to maximize a function, Φ, of the mean and variance $\Phi[E(r), V(r)]$. To choose the value of x that maximizes welfare, differentiate Φ with respect to x,

$$d\Phi/dx = [d\Phi/dE(r)][dE(r)/dx] + [d\Phi/dV(r)][dV(r)/dx] \qquad (28.S.6)$$

and substitute derivatives of the mean from Equation 28.S.4 and the variance from Equation 28.S.5.

$$d\Phi/dx = [d\Phi/dE(r)][i^\euro + E\Delta s - i^\$] + [d\Phi/dV(r)][2xV(\Delta s)]$$

Finally, set the derivative equal to zero, and solve for x to find the investor's optimal portfolio allocation.

$$x = \frac{[i^\euro + E\Delta s - i^\$]}{\{[-d\Phi/dV(r)]/[2d\Phi/dE(r)]\}V(\Delta s)} \qquad (28.S.7)$$

The expression inside the curly brackets measures how much the investors dislike risk relative to how much they like expected gains. It is often known as the coefficient of relative risk aversion, and so is denoted here by RRA $\equiv \{[-d\Phi/dV(r)]/[2d\Phi/dE(r)]\}$. Recall also the definition of the risk premium on euros.

$$rp \equiv [i^\euro + E\Delta s - i^\$] \qquad (28.S.8)$$

Thus the expression for the optimal portfolio can be written more compactly as:

$$x = \frac{rp}{\text{RRA } V(\Delta s)} \qquad (28.S.9)$$

This equation states that the share of the portfolio allocated to euros (x) depends (1) positively on the expected rate of return relative to dollars (rp); (2) inversely on the coefficient of relative risk aversion (RRA); and (3) inversely on the variance of the change in the exchange rate. Notice again that if the investors are highly risk averse (RRA is large), then they will hold few euros. What happens if the investors do not mind risk at all? They are said to be risk neutral. When RRA $= 0$, the denominator is zero. Of course, x cannot be infinite, but the investors are infinitely responsive to expected rates of return. This is the case when euros and dollars are perfect substitutes.

The consequences are seen more clearly by inverting Equation 28.S.8.

$$rp = [\text{RRA } V(\Delta s)]x \qquad (28.S.10)$$

Now it is clear that if investors have zero risk aversion, then their infinite sensitivity to expected returns ensures that the risk premium is zero. This is the case of uncovered interest parity. The same holds if there is no uncertainty regarding the future exchange rate, $V(\Delta s) = 0$. In general, however, with nonzero uncertainty and nonzero risk aversion, the risk premium should also be nonzero. Consider, finally, what happens if x, the share of the portfolio consisting of euros, increases (e.g., because European governments issue more bonds, which someone in the market must hold). Then rp increases: Euros have to pay a higher expected return to induce investors to hold them.

Index

Absolute advantage
  footloose inputs, 137–139
  tax effects, 140–141
Abowd, J. M., 154n
Accommodating transactions, 285–286
Adelman, M. A., 208n
Adjustable peg, 561
Advance deposits on imports, 332
Agriculture
  trade pattern, 8
  trade restrictions, 228–229, 231
Aircraft market, 216–218
Allen, H., 608n
Al Marhubi, F., 569
American Depository Receipts, 492
Announcements, economic statistics, 599–601
Antidumping policies
  consequences, 237–238
  procedure, 236–237
Appreciation, emerging-market currencies, 494, 496
Arbitrage, 22, 360, 415, 442
Argentina, 435, 490, 561
ARIMA forecasting model, 608–609
Artis, M., 252n, 269, 421n
ASEAN group, 137, 261
Assignment problem, 350–352, 465–466
Auquier, A. A., 211n
Australia, 86, 155, 391, 392

Backus, D., 546n
Balance sheet effect, 512
Balassa, B., 364
Baldwin, R., 215n
Baldwin, R. E., 113n, 195n, 196n
Bananas, trade in, 232
Barro, R., 441, 550, 617n

Basel Agreement, 433, 519
Basket peg, 560
Bates, R. H., 209n
Baumol, W. J., 110n, 148
Bayoumi, T., 565n
"Beggar thy neighbor" policies, 331, 537
Beladi, H., 131n
Bergsten, C. F., 269, 303
Bergstrand, J., 364n
Bernanke, B., 568
Bhagwati, J., 53, 70n, 193n, 201, 222, 244, 265n
Bilson, J., 612n
Black, B., 616n
Blackman, S. A. B., 148
Blanchard, O., 565n
Blonigen, B. A., 238n
Bogetik, Z., 370n
Bolivia, 403, 490
Borjas, G. J., 166
Boughton, J., 466n
Bovard, J., 197n
Bown, C. P., 238n
Box diagram
  consumption, 31–32, 185
  production, 118–119
Bradford, C. I., 262n, 264n
Brady Plan, 491
Brainard, S. L., 161n
Brander, J. M., 214n, 225n
Branson, W., 598, 616n
Brazil, 209, 219, 435, 490, 551, 558
Brock, W. A., 191n, 201
Bryant, R., 531n
Buchanan, J., 193n
Budget constraint, 14–16
Buffer stocks, 209
Buiter, W., 477n

Bulgaria, 355
Burmeister, M. E., 256n

Cagan, P., 369, 582n
Cain, G. G., 113n
Cairncross, A. K., 155n
Calvo, G., 491n, 517n, 522, 569
Canada
    capital mobility, 155, 451
    export tax, 175
    floating exchange rate, 368
    gains from Free Trade Agreement, 255
    inflation targeting, 559
    intellectual property rights, 209
    pollution, 265
    real interest rate, 591
Canada-U.S. Free Trade Agreement, 255
Canzoneri, M., 565n
Capital controls,
    developing country crises, 515–518
    liberalization, 419
    operation, 419–420
    possible legitimate aims, 515–516
Capital mobility,
    fixed exchange rates, 450–452, 478–480
    monetary policy, 452–454
Capital stock, international, 156–157
Caribbean Basin Initiative, 256
Caves, R. E., 158n, 166, 211n
Ceglowski, J., 68
Central American Free Trade Agreement, 256
Chang, K., 261n
Chang, R., 502n
Chile, 403, 497, 513, 590
China
    access to entrepreneurial resources, 260–261
    balance of payments, 495–496
    counterfeit goods, 219–220
    exports, 4–5, 239
    foreign direct investment, 434, 495
    growth, 109
    regionalized development, 260–261
    trade disputes, 240
    wages, 68, 110
Clausing, K., 256n

Cline, W. R., 113n, 117, 522
Collins, S., 558n
Colombia, 494
Commodity agreements, international, 208–209
Common Fund, 209
Common market, defined, 247
Comparative advantage
    financial assets, 445
    Heckscher-Ohlin model, 102–103
    longevity of, 109
    pollution abatement, 265
    production model, 25–27
    specific factors model, 86–87
Compensation, 28
Composite traded commodity, 73–74
Conditionality (IMF), 507–510
Contagion, 504–506
Cooper, R. N., 380n, 487, 513
Corbo, V., 391n, 514n
Corden, W. M., 90n, 190n, 201, 336n, 408
Corn Laws, 86
Corsetti, G., 504n
Counterfeit goods, 219–220
Countervailing duties, 236
Covered interest arbitrage, 428–431, 574
Crawling peg, 560
Crony capitalism, 503–504
Crowding out, 445, 471–474
Currency boards, 356, 561
Currency mismatch, 512
Currency union, 561
Customs union, defined, 247

Davutyan, N., 372n
Deardorff, A. V., 191n, 232n, 242n
Debt neutrality, 441–442
De Gregorio, G., 364n
DeLong, B., 522
De Melo, J., 391n
Denmark, 482, 586
Derivatives, 432
Destler, I. M., 244
Devaluation
    contractionary effect, 510–513
    effect over time, 382–384

monetary contraction alternative, 509–510
nontraded goods, 405–406
real balance effect, 387–389
de Vanssay, 191n
Developing countries
export-led growth, 260–262
import substitution, 261–263
international borrowing, 156–157
technology adaptation, 162
trade agreements, 231
trade structure, 5–6
Diamond, D., 502n
Diaz-Alejandro, C., 504n, 511
Diminishing returns, 79–80
Disintermediation, 434n
Doha Round, 231
Dollar, D., 110n, 264n
Dollarization, 561
Dominguez, K., 622
Dooley, M., 504n
Dornbusch, R., 37, 399n, 400n, 404n, 408, 513n,
    542, 582n, 588, 595, 605
Dragutinovic, D., 370n
Dumping
policy toward, 236–238
steel industry, 205–206
theory of, 215–216
Durability, specific factors, 109
Dutch disease, 88–90, 141, 196, 402–404
Dybvig, P., 502n

East Germany, absorption, 528
Econometric models, 530–538
Economic union, defined, 247
Economies in transition
central planning's legacy, 257–258
comparative advantage, 258–259
International Monetary Fund programs, 508
trade with centrally planned economies,
    257–258
trade with Western Europe, 5–6, 258
Edelstein, M., 155n
Edwards, S., 426n, 440, 514, 517n, 522, 569
Effective exchange rate, 291
Eichengreen, B., 377, 380n, 488, 522, 565n, 569

Elasticity pessimism, 297–298
Engel, C., 368n, 601n, 610n
Enright, M. J., 261n
Environmental quality. See Pollution
Escape clause, 236
Estonia, 355
Estrin, S., 260n
Euro, 417
Euromarkets, 412–414
European Economic and Monetary Union,
    308, 417, 481
European Exchange Rate Mechanism, 368,
    482, 500, 501, 586
European Monetary System, 421–423, 452,
    481, 558
European Union
accession, transition economies, 258
income distribution, 28
industrial policy, 217–218
nontariff barriers, 238, 254
optimum currency area, 564–567
trade creation, diversion, 252
trade disputes, 232, 240
Exchange rates
demand supply determinants, 291–293
disturbance transmission, 529–530
expectations, 580–582
monetary determinants, 576–577
nominal anchor, 557–559
portfolio balance effects on, 616–617
Exchange risk premium, 612–613
Export tax, 175
External balance
capital mobility, 459–461
devaluation, 333–337, 339–340
fiscal policy, 455
monetary policy, 339, 452–453
nontraded goods, 401–404
zones of imbalance, 461–464

Factor-Price Equalization Theorem, 99,
    104, 151
Fair price, 191
Falvey, R., 130n
Fama, E., 612n

Feenstra, R. C., 5n, 244
Feldstein, M. S., 442, 522
Fieleke, N., 432n
Financial Accounting Standards Board, 614
Financial crises, 433, 435–436
Financial integration, 435–536
Financial repression, 424
Financial Stability Forum, 518
Fiscal policy
    capital mobility, 450–452
    econometric estimates, 531–539
    external balance, 333–335, 338–340, 455,
        457–459, 468–470, 478–480
    internal balance, 333–334, 335–336, 338–340,
        455, 468–470, 478, 484
    multiplier effect, 327–329
    wage indexation, 553
Fischer, S., 541, 552
Flan, H., 215n
Fleming, J. M., 488
Floating exchange rates
    capital mobility, 482–485
    countries' experience, 367–368
    1930s experience, 29
    transmission of disturbances, 328–330
Flood, R., 500n
Footloose activities
    absolute and comparative advantage,
        137–139
    Newly Industrializing Countries, 136–137
Foreign currency options, 432
Foreign exchange futures, 431
Forward exchange market, 427–428, 610–612
Foreign exchange market
    bid-ask spreads, 415
    size, 413
    two-tier, 332–333
    vehicle currencies, 416–417
Forward rate bias, 610–612
Foreign Sales Corporations, 232
France, 43, 156, 421, 452, 481, 482, 501, 558
Frankel, J. A., 246n, 252n, 269, 431n, 488, 496n,
        522, 539n, 567n, 569, 591n, 601n, 605, 607n,
        612n, 622
Freeman, R. B., 113n, 154n
Free trade areas

defined, 247
    U.S.-Canada-Mexico, 255–256
Frenkel, J., 371n, 377n, 440, 485n, 582n
Friedman, M., 427n, 605
Froot, K., 591n, 607n, 612n, 623
Funabashi, Y., 541
Furman, J., 509n

Gains from trade
    domestic monopoly, 203–205
    exchange model, 20–21
    factor mobility, 151, 153
    production model, 22–24
    Ricardian model, 61–62
Garber, P., 500n
General Agreement on Tariffs and Trade,
        231–232
Geography, economic, 112
Germany, 43–44, 67, 156, 389, 445, 481, 501
Giavazzi, F., 558n
Giddy, I., 432n
Gilbert, C. L., 209n, 222
Giovannini, A., 364n
Girton, L., 457n, 577n
Global Depository Receipts, 492
Globalization, 4, 6, 69, 242
Gold standard, 355, 378–382, 556–557
Goldstein, A. E., 223, 523
Goldstein, M., 324, 440
Golub, S., 68
Gould, D. M., 166
Goodhart, C., 419n
Gourinchas, P. O., 620n
Graham, E. M., 158n, 166
Graham, F., 77
Gravity model, 246–247
Greenspan, A., 473n, 491
Gresser, E., 196n
Grieco, P. L. E., 264n
Griffin, J. M., 208n, 223
Grilli, E. R., 136n
Grilli, V., 565n
Grossman, G. M., 194n
Group of Seven (G-7), 503, 506, 507,
        520, 535
Group of 20, 518

Growth, economic
   comparative advantage changes, 109–110
   immiserizing, 42–43
   openness, linked to, 263–264
   specific factors model, 84–85
   tariff protection and welfare, 197–199
   terms of trade, 42–43
Guidotti rule, 498n

Hamilton, C., 233
Harberger, A. C., 348n
Harduvelis, G., 601n
Harris, R. G., 255n
Heckscher, E., 95, 117
Heckscher-Ohlin Theorem, 110–112, 137, 156
Hedge funds, 492, 519
Henderson, D., 457n, 618n
Helpman, E., 117, 132, 194n
Hodrick, R., 610n
Holzman, F. D., 257n
Honeymoon effect, 586
Hong Kong, 109, 137, 140, 261, 320, 355, 493,
      505, 561
Hooper, P., 324
Horioka, C., 442n
Houthakker, H. S., 320n
Hufbauer, G. C., 264n, 269
Hughes, K., 260n
Hungary, 370
Hume, D., 356
Hyperinflation, 369–372, 582

Immiserizing growth, 42–43
Impossible trinity, 481–482
Income distribution
   Heckscher-Ohlin model, 99, 103–104
   production model, 27–28
   specific factors model, 80–83
Income-consumption curve, 183–184
Income effect, 33–34, 45–46
Increasing Cost, Law of, 18–19
Indexation, wages, 551–554
India, 109
Indifference curves, 16–17
Indonesia, 109, 261, 391, 426, 494, 505, 512
Infant industry protection, 262

Inflation
   cost of, 555
   policy coordination, 554–558
   reasons for, 554–555
   targeting, 559
   United States, 459–460
Innovation, financial, 426–427
Intellectual property rights, 218–220, 231
Interest equalization tax, 412
Interest rate defense, 501
Internal balance
   devaluation, 335–336
   fiscal policy, 334–335, 455, 478–480
   monetary policy, 478–480
   nontraded goods, 461–466
   zones of imbalance, 461–464
International Monetary and Financial
      Committee, 518
International Monetary Fund, 500, 503,
      506–509, 518, 520
Intertemporal optimization, 273, 436–439, 441
Intertemporal trade
   goods, 48–50
   capital, 436–439
Intra-industry trade
   defined, 47
   prevalence, 122–123
Investment income, 276
Ireland, 368, 558
Irwin, D., 201, 244
Isard, P., 592n
Israel, 490, 551
Italy, 421, 481, 482, 551, 558
Ito, T., 270

Japan
   capital controls, 420
   exchange rate and foreign investment, 299
   exchange rate variability, 365
   finished goods imports, 135
   food import restrictions, 86
   liquidity trap, 341
   monetary policy, 377
   real balance effect, 389
   saving rate, 157, 438
J-curve, 298–300, 471

Johnson, H. G., 153, 199, 202, 346, 357, 377
Jones, R. W., 53, 89n, 93, 114n, 117, 118, 131n,
    142, 148, 149, 152n, 214n

Kaminsky, G., 496n
Katrak, H., 214n
Katz, L., 565n
Kehoe, P., 546n
Kennedy Round, 230
Keynes, J. M., 44–45, 380n
Khan, M., 324
Kierzkowski, H., 130n, 142, 149
Klein, L., 532
Konnings, J., 238n
Korea, 67, 109, 137, 140, 261, 494, 503,
    505, 512
Kose, M. A., 440
Kouri, P., 616n
Kravis, I., 361n
Kreinen, M. E., 230n, 252, 320
Krueger, A. O., 8n, 193n, 202, 232n, 244, 256n,
    267n, 270
Krugman, P., 77, 112n, 132, 158n, 166, 202,
    213n, 223, 346, 418n, 492n, 500, 504n,
    513n, 586n, 602n
Kuhn, P., 154n
Kuwait, 135
Kydlund, F., 546n

Labor theory of value, 60
Lal, A. K., 259n
Laursen, S., 348n
Laursen-Metzler-Harberger effect, 347,
    529–530
Lavergne, R. P., 195n
Law of one price, 360
Lawrence, R. Z., 223
Leamer, E. E., 111, 117
Lee, H.-H., 132
Lee, J. W., 242n
Lee, N., 252n, 269
Leiderman, L., 491n, 522
Lender of last resort, 507
Leontief, W. W., 111
Lewes, K., 623

Liberalization
    domestic financial markets, 424
    international capital flows, 419–420
    optimal order, 423–424
    trade in financial services, 424–425
Licensing, technology, 162
Lincoln, E. J., 135n
Lipsey, R. E., 361n
Liquidity trap, 341
Liquidity versus solvency, 507
Lithuania, 355
Litterman, R., 532
Lizondo, S., 496n, 523
Lloyd, P., 132
Locomotive theory, 316–317
London Interbank Offered Rate, 413
Lothian, J., 366n
Lowinger, T. C., 259n
Lucas, R., 550, 576n
Lyons, R., 416n

Maastrict Treaty, 254, 481
MacDonald, R., 609n, 623
Magee, S. P., 191n, 201, 320n
Malaysia, 109, 261, 505
Managed floating, 285–286
Marginal propensity to import, 44,
    307, 343
Marin, D., 280n
Marjit, S., 131n
Mark, N., 609n
Markusen, J. R., 152
Marquez, J., 324
Marshall-Lerner condition, 296–297, 299
Marshall Plan, 44, 293
Maskus, K. E., 111n, 219n, 223
Mayer, W., 93, 109n, 191n
McCallum, J., 227n
McGuire, S. M., 223
McKibbin, W., 531
McKinnon, R., 424n, 425n, 563n
Meade, J., 316n, 333n
Meese, R., 609
Metzler, L., 348n
Meadows, D. H., 136n

Mexico, 239, 255–256, 265, 490, 497, 498, 500, 512, 513, 558
Migration
    gains from, 153
    guest workers, 153
    income distribution, 153–154
    U.S. inflow, 153–154
Miller, M., 477n
Minford, P., 531
Monetary base, 354
Monetary policy
    anchor, nominal, 556–559
    econometric estimates, 531–535
    external balance, 339–340, 474–475, 478, 484
    internal balance, 474–475, 478, 484
    internal balance, 347–349
    optimum currency areas, 562–563
    real exchange rate, 590–592
    trade balance, 384–387
Money demand, 384–386, 530
Money supply. See also Monetary policy
    announcements, 599–601
    balance of payments, 354–355, 357–358
    expectation patterns, 585–588
    international reserves, 382–384
    nominal anchor, 556–559
Monopolistic competition
    conditions for, 125
    firm's equilibrium, 126
    market equilibrium, 127
    welfare significance, 128–129
Monopoly, domestic
    curbed by trade exposure, 203–205
    international dumping, 205–206
Monopoly, international
    exploitation of, 210–213, 223–225
    resistance to, 213–215, 218
Montiel, P., 523
Moral hazard, 492, 503, 518
Moran, T. H., 166
Multicommodity trade
    Heckscher-Ohlin model, 106–108
    production model, 47
Multicountry trade
    production model, 47–48

Ricardian model, 68–69
Multifiber Arrangement
    proliferation, 238–239
    welfare consequences, 239–240
Multinational enterprise
    affinity for R&D, 160
    bases for, 158–160
    developing countries, 160–161
    exchange rates' influence, 161
    international distribution, 159
    intra-industry foreign direct investment, 160
    merchandise trade, 161–162
    spillover benefits, 163
    tariff inducement, 161, 199
    technology transfer, 162
    welfare effects, 162–163
Multiplier, open economy, 312–314
Mundell, R., 333n, 357, 377, 389n, 458n, 461, 488, 527n, 563n
Murrell, P., 259n
Mussa, M., 109n, 303, 368n, 440, 619n
Mutti, J., 223

Natural resources
    terms of trade, 135–136
    U.S. trade structure, 134–135
Nam, C. H., 263n
National Savings Identity, 310
Neary, J. P., 90n
Netherlands, 402
Newly Industrialized Countries, 261–262, 320
Ng, F., 143
Noland, M., 261n
Nontariff trade barriers, incidence, 233
Nontraded goods
    devaluation, 396–398, 405–406
    Dutch disease, 402–404
    expenditure disturbances, 393–395
    internal balance, 398–400
    money supply, 401–402, 404–405
    Ricardian model, 72–73
    specific factors model, 90

North American Free Trade Agreement
  confounding events, 255
  environment issues, 176
  evidence on performance, 256
  Mexico's spending boom, 491
  public choice, 196–197
Nugent, J. B., 250n
Nziramasanga, M., 259n

Obstfeld, M., 350n, 501n
Offer curve, 34–35, 182–185
Official reserve transactions, 275, 277, 279
Ohlin, B., 45, 117
Oil prices. *See also* Organization of Petroleum
    Exporting Countries
  cartel determined, 207–208
  income distribution, 29–30
  supply shock, 547
Optimal tariff, 177–178, 182–183, 251
Optimum currency area
  criteria, 562–563
  European Union, 564–567
  German monetary union, 560–561
Organization of Petroleum Exporting
    Countries
  cartel operation, 207–208
  international lending, 44, 157, 413
  unilateral transfers, 314
Original sin, 512
O'Rourke, K. H., 166
Ostry, S., 244
Oudiz, G., 539n, 541
Outsourcing
  advanced-country wages, 144–146
  defined, 133
  determinants, 142–144
  production model, 48
Outward-looking growth, 110
Overseas outsourcing, 276, 425
Overshooting, 588–590

Pagano, M., 558n
Park, J. H., 238n
Parsons, D. O., 206n
Patrick, H. T., 222, 244

Pesetti, P., 504n
Petith, H. C., 251n
Petrovic, P., 370n
Pippinger, J., 372n
Philippines, 261
Policy coordination
  international practice, 535–536
  obstacles, 538–539
  theoretical gains, 536–538
Pollution
  international spillovers, 176, 265–266
  tradable rights, 176–177
  trade policy, 176–177, 242
Pomfret, R., 270
Porter, M. E., 112n
Portfolio capital
  nineteenth century, 155–156
  recent patterns, 157
Portugal, 482, 558
Posen, A., 346, 569
Prasad, E., 440
Preferential trading arrangements
  distribution of gains, 250–251
  reorganization of industries, 253–254
  understated gains, 253–254
  versus multilateral, 266–267
  welfare gain or loss, 250
Price-specie-flow mechanism, 356
Primary product prices
  trends, 136
  variability, 135, 155
Product differentiation, 123–124, 246
Production-possibilities schedule. *See*
    Transformation curve
Productivity shocks, 69–70
Profit conditions, competitive, 65
Prusa, T. J., 238
Public choice
  conservative social welfare function, 194
  lobbying model, 193
  pollution controls, 265–266
  special groups' rivalry, 196–197
  special protection, 241–242
  voting model, 193
Pugel, T. A., 206n

Purchasing power parity
  defined, 359
  deviations, extent of, 360–361, 365–369
  deviations, reasons for, 361–365
  hyperinflation, 369–372
  monetary model exchange rate, 575–576
  nontraded goods, 362–364

Quantitative restrictions, 234, 332
Quasi-fiscal deficit, 494

Radelet, S., 523
Radford, R. A., 22
Ray, E. J., 196n, 206n
Razin, A., 350n, 485n
Real balance effect, 373–374, 387–389, 511
Real Business Cycle models, 359, 546
Real interest parity, 579n
Regional agglomeration, 112
Regressive expectations, 590
Reinhart, C., 491n, 496n, 517n, 522
Remittances, emigrants', 276, 278
Reserves, international
  money supply, 382–384
Revey, P., 614n
Rey, H., 620n
Ricardo, D., 59, 77
Rigid technology, 96–99
Robinson, S., 256n
Rockett, K., 539n
Rogoff, K., 440, 538n, 569, 609
Romalis, J., 256n
Romer, D., 562n
Roper, D., 577n
Rose, A., 496n, 560n, 567n
Roubini, N., 504n
Ruffin, R., 114n
Russia, 39, 46, 403, 435, 505–506, 508, 558

Sachs, J., 263, 531, 537n, 539n, 541, 554,
  565n, 566n
Sala-i-martin, X., 565n
Salter, W. E. G., 395n
Samuelson, P., 35, 70n, 77, 104, 118, 202,
  364n, 598

Sargent, T., 550
Sarno, L., 623
Satiation, debt holdings, 619–620
Saudi Arabia, 134
Savings retention coefficient, 442
Scale economies
  multinational enterprises, 161
  outsourcing, 142–143
Schott, J. J., 232n, 244, 269
Schulze, C., 223
Scott, E. E., 261n
Securitization, 433–435
Seigniorage, 418, 555
Shaw, E. S., 424n
Sims, C., 532
Singapore, 109, 137, 261, 320
Singh, J., 163n
Sinn, Hans-Werner, 564n
Smoot-Hawley Act, 227, 229, 331
Sovereign spreads, 505–506
Spain, 481, 558
Special Drawing Rights, 277, 381, 417
Speculation
  bubbles, 585–586
  devaluation, 512
  foreign exchange market, 418
  prisoner's dilemma game, 501–502
  stabilizing, 601–603
Speculative attacks
  conditions for, 499–504
  contagion, 504–506
Spencer, B. J., 214n, 225n
Srinavasan, T. N., 265n
Stability
  barter exchange, 53–55
  financial crises, 501–502
  foreign exchange market, 295–297,
    303–305
Stability and Growth Pact, 566n
Steel industry, 205–206
Stein, E., 246n
Sterilization, 354–356, 494, 498–499, 617
Stern, R. M., 111n
Stiglitz, J., 509n
Stockman, A., 366n

Stolper, W. F., 104n, 118, 202
Stolper-Samuelson Theorem, 104–105, 191
Subsidies, industrial, 217–218
Substitution effect, 32–34, 45–46
Sudden stops, 517
Sugar trade, 240–241
Summers, L., 552n
Supply relationships
    aggregate, 549–551
    Friedman-Phelps, 548–550
    Lucas-Sargent-Barro, 550–551
    modified Keynesian, 546–648
    frictionless neoclassical, 545–546
Sveikauskas, L., 111n
Svensson, L., 350n, 559n
Swagel, P., 242n
Swan, T., 336n, 400n
Sweden, 40, 156, 482, 501, 547
Switzerland, 547
Swoboda, A., 461, 542

Taiwan, 109, 110, 137, 261, 320, 505
Target zone, exchange rate, 560, 586n
Tariffs
    demand effect, 172–174
    foreign direct investment, 199
    growth and welfare, 197–199
    imports effect, 174
    income distribution, 40–41
    multilateral reduction, 229–231
    production effect, 171–172
    reciprocal liberalization, 229–231,
        232–233
    revenue effect, 187–188
    second-best instrument, 189–192
    terms of trade, 40–42
    unemployment, 200
Taxes
    capital flows, 423–424
    turnover taxes, 423–424
Taylor, A., 368n
Taylor, J., 532
Taylor, L., 513n
Taylor, M., 366n, 421n, 605, 608n, 609n, 623

Technical change
    commodity trade pattern, 71–72
    single traded good, 74
Teece, D. J., 223
Terms of trade
    economic growth, 42–43
    exchange model, 14–16
    tariff effect, 40–42
    temporary shifts, 348–349
    transfer process, 44–46
Thailand, 140, 261, 505, 512
Thaler, R., 623
Thierfelder, K., 256n
Tobin, J., 602n
Todd, S., 260n
Tokyo Round, 230
Tollison, R., 193n
Tourism, 7
Trade creation, 247–248
Trade diversion, 248–249
Transfer process, capital
    real resources, 46–47
    nineteenth century pattern, 155–156
    unilateral transfers, 43–45, 314–315
Transformation curve
    Heckscher-Ohlin model, 102
    production model, 16–20
    Ricardian model, 60–61
    rigid technology, 97–98
    specific factors model, 80–81, 93–94
Transition economies. *See* Economies in
    transition
Transportation costs, 5, 108, 246–247,
    278, 361
Trefler, D. C., 111, 112, 113
Triffin, R., 381
Tullock, G., 193n
Turkey, 193a, 435

Unemployment
    tariffs, 200
    transitional, 77–78
Unilateral transfers, 276–277,
    314–315

United Kingdom
  capital controls, 421
  capital exports, 154–156, 452
  emigration, 154–156
  inflation targeting, 559
  liberalization, 411
  monetary policy, 477, 501, 528
  North Sea Oil, 90
United States
  agriculture exports, 86
  balance of payments accounts, 286
  capital controls, 412–413
  capital mobility, 451–452
  current account balance, 319–332, 381
  dollar's currency-market status, 417–418
  exchange rate, 298
  financial regulation, 424
  foreign debt, 620
  government deficits, 441–442, 470–471
  monetary policy, 476–477
  natural resources, 134–135
  real balance effect, 389
  real interest rates, 592
  saving, 310
  sugar policy, 240–241
  tariff structure, 195–196
  trade structure, 5–7
  wages, 67
Unit-value isoquants, 105–106
Unskilled labor. *See also* Wage determination
  causes of wage decline, 112–114
  migration, 154
  specific factors model, 88
  tariff protection, 196
Uruguay Round, 230–231, 234, 236, 332

Valuation effect, 283n, 620
Vandenbussche, H., 238n
Vanek, J., 134n
Variety, taste for, 133–135
Vegh, C., 569
Velasco, A., 502n
Verdier, D., 194n
Vertical differentiation, 130–131

Viner, J., 247
Volcker, P., 473n
Voluntary export restrictions, 234–236

Wage determinants
  indexation, 514, 551–554
  international differences, 66–67
  Ricardian model, 65–66
  specific factors model, 81–82
Wang, Z. K., 258n, 270
Wanniski, J., 378
Warner, A., 263
Wei, S.-J., 246n, 440
Wells, L. T., 161n
Wheat, durum, 197
Willett, T., 542, 569
Williamson, J., 356n, 511n, 586n
Williamson, J. G., 166
Winters, L. A., 258n, 270
Wolf, H., 364n
Wolff, E. J., 110n, 148
Wooton, I., 154n
World Bank, 520
World Trade Organization, 188, 218, 231
Wright, G., 134, 166
Wriston, W., 146n
Wyplosz, C., 488, 566n

Xiong, W., 208n

Yanchus, 191n
Yang, M. C., 136n
Yeats, A., 143
Yeung, B., 223
Yotopoulos, P. A., 250n
Young, A., 141
Yugoslavia, 370

Zecker, J. R., 379n